DISCARDED

S0-AEC-058

FOOTNOTES TO WORLD HISTORY

A Bibliographic Source Book

by

HAROLD S. SHARP

The Scarecrow Press, Inc.

Metuchen, N.J. & London

1979

Ref
D
20
S52

Library of Congress Cataloging in Publication Data

Sharp, Harold S
    Footnotes to world history.

    Bibliography: p.
    Includes index.
    1. World history--Bibliography. 2. Chronology, Historical.
I. Title.
Z6201. S52   [D20]   016. 909   78-23417
ISBN 0-8108-1185-5

Copyright © 1979 by Harold S. Sharp

Manufactured in the United States of America

Lovingly dedicated to Marjorie,

who would have helped had she been here.

TABLE OF CONTENTS

FOREWORD

The gratifyingly enthusiastic acceptance of Footnotes to American History* by reference librarians, students, reviewers and the general public has inspired the author to complete this companion book. Like its predecessor it seeks to describe in capsule form various historical events and provide a list of published sources of additional information on each one. It deals with world history, excluding America, and ranges in time from the legendary inundation of the continent of Atlantis about the 10th millennium B.C. to the Arab Oil Embargo of 1973-74. In all, 304 events are described in short narrative form. Some of these are of major historical importance; others, while comparatively minor, are significant in terms of human interest. An index at the back of the book guides the user to the names of specific persons, to places and to subjects.

For those persons who wish only a quick identification of a particular event the descriptive paragraphs should be sufficient. The lists of "suggested readings" following each narrative indicate sources of additional information about that entry, should these be desired.

These lists (bibliographies) are by no means all-inclusive. Many other sources of information exist. Standard history textbooks, biographies of persons involved and in-depth accounts of particular historical events in books, periodicals, newspapers and dissertations can supply additional detailed information. These may be located in the public library by means of the card catalog which lists the books and other source materials to be found there.

In addition to these specific sources there are many general reference books which may be consulted for guidance to information concerning the historical events covered. Assistance in using these tools may be had from the reference department of the public library where such publications constitute a part of the permanent reference collection. Some of these, which suggest information sources, are described below.

Cumulative Book Index: a World List of Books in the English Language. New York: H. W. Wilson, 1898-- This index lists

---

*Sharp, Harold S. Footnotes to American History: A Bibliographic Source Book. Metuchen, N.J.: Scarecrow Press, Inc., 1977.

all books included by author, title, subject and editor and gives a complete bibliographic citation for each book covered in the author entry.

Subject Guide to Books in Print: an Index to the Publisher's Trade List Annual. New York: R. R. Bowker, 1957--. This annual publication indexes books in print by subject heading.

Paperbound Books in Print. New York: R. R. Bowker, 1955--. This monthly publication lists new titles in paperback as well as titles still in print by author, title and subject.

Poole's Index to Periodical Literature, 1802-1881. Rev. ed. Boston: Houghton Mifflin, 1891. 2 vols.

_____. _____, Supplements, January, 1882-January, 1907. Boston: Houghton Mifflin, 1887-1908. 5 vols. This is a subject index to 590,100 articles in 12,241 volumes of 470 American and English periodicals.

Nineteenth Century Readers' Guide to Periodical Literature, 1890-1899. With supplementary indexing, 1900-1922. New York: H. W. Wilson, 1944. 2 vols. This author, subject and illustrator index to 51 periodicals (1003 volumes) covers the period from 1890 through 1899.

Readers' Guide to Periodical Literature, 1900--. New York: H. W. Wilson, 1905--. Indexes more than 130 well-known general American and Canadian magazines. Each article is entered by author, as many subjects as needed, and by title.

Biography Index. New York: H. W. Wilson, 1956--. This quarterly, cumulated in annual and three-year volumes, gives birth date and, where applicable, death date of each person listed, together with his nationality and profession or occupation. It also cites sources of biographical information concerning each person.

Book Review Digest. New York: H. W. Wilson, 1905--. This monthly, except February and July, indexes reviews of current books which appear in more than 70 periodicals, showing these reviews in digest form. It has a title and subject index in each issue. A cumulated subject and title index is published every five years.

New York Times Index. New York: New York Times, 1851--. (Semi-monthly, annual cumulation.) This newspaper index gives the exact references to date, page and column. Summaries of articles may answer questions making it unnecessary to refer to the paper itself.

Times (London). Index to the Times. London: London Times, 1907--. (Bimonthly since 1957.) This indexes the final edition of the London Times.

Book Review Index. Detroit: Gale Research Company, 1965--.
(Bimonthly, quarterly cumulations, annual index.) This publica-
tion indexes reviews appearing in more than 200 periodicals.
Excerpts are not given.

Choice: Books for College Libraries. Chicago: American Library
Association, 1964--. (Monthly except August.) This publication is designed to meet the needs of college, junior college and
other libraries concerned with acquiring academic materials.
It makes evaluative comparisons.

Webster's Biographical Dictionary. Springfield, Mass.: G. & C.
Merriam Co., 1971. This pronouncing biographical dictionary
is not restricted by period, nationality, race, religion, or occupation. It gives brief, condensed biographical sketches of
prominent persons living and dead.

Essay and General Literature Index. New York: H. W. Wilson,
1900--. This is a cumulative author and subject index to
articles which are published as parts of books.

Dictionary of National Biography. London: Smith, Elder, 1885-
1901. 63 vol. plus 5 supplements. Additional supplements to
1950. Reissued in 22 vol. by Oxford University Press. The
first major biographical tool of the English-speaking world. Includes biographies of all noteworthy deceased inhabitants of
Great Britain, Ireland and the Colonies from the earliest historical period to the time of publication, depending on volume.
Listed are important legendary figures, such as Robin Hood,
the "very famous, the famous and the infamous." Includes bibliographies.

United States Catalog. New York: H. W. Wilson, 1928. 4th edition. Lists books in print January 1, 1928. Earlier editions:
1st: Books in print, 1899. Minneapolis: H. W. Wilson, 1900.
2nd: Books in print, 1902. Minneapolis: H. W. Wilson, 1903.
3rd: Books in print, 1912. New York: H. W. Wilson, 1912.
This publication was designed to provide a consolidated publishers' catalog showing all books available for purchase. The first
edition was an author catalog with a title index. Subsequent editions contain author, title and subject entries in one alphabet,
with author entries the most complete. It was replaced by the
Cumulative Book Index following the publication of the 4th edition
in 1928.

Some users of this book may wish to locate stories or novels
concerning events in world history. Two guides to fiction of this
type are:

Logasa, Hannah. Historical Fiction: Guide for Junior and Senior
High Schools and Colleges, Also for General Reader. Philadelphia: McKinley Publishing Co., 1964.

McGarry, Daniel D., and Sarah Harriman White. World Historical
Fiction Guide: An Annotated Chronological, Geographical, and
Topical List of Selected Historical Novels. 2d ed. Metuchen,
N.J.: Scarecrow Press, 1973.

In addition to the above information sources, the reader may
often profit by consulting a standard encyclopedia for information
concerning an historical event. It is important to realize that many
of the larger encyclopedias have cross-references or indexes which
guide the user to information contained in articles of larger scope.
For example, details on the EMS Telegram (1870) might be given
in an article on Otto von Bismarck. The index would indicate this.

Three standard multi-volume encyclopedias which are found
in most public library reference collections are:

Encyclopaedia Britannica: A New Survey of Universal Knowledge.
Chicago: Encyclopaedia Britannica, Inc., © 1977. 30 vols.
This is the oldest and most famous encyclopedia in the English
language.

Encyclopedia Americana. New York: Americana Corporation, ©
1977. 30 vols. This is the oldest major American encyclopedia
still in print.

Collier's Encyclopedia. New York: Crowell-Collier Educational
Corporation, © 1976. 24 vols. This is the newest of the general encyclopedias.

All these encyclopedias contain bibliographies directing the
user to additional information on most subjects covered. They also
publish annual yearbooks which consider happenings during the previous calendar year.

There are, needless to say, many other encyclopedias and
sources of historical information. These are treated in several
publications, two of the best of which are:

Winchell, Constance M. Guide to Reference Books. 9th edition.
Chicago: American Library Association, 1976 (plus supplements).
This annotated list of reference books is well indexed, brings
books together by subject, and indicates their comparative
value.

Murphey, Robert W. How and Where to Look It Up. New York:
McGraw-Hill, 1958. This source book contains much information on using a library reference collection and also cites specific publications containing information on many subjects.

While this book was being prepared many persons gave willing assistance. Particularly helpful were Delia Bourne, Linda Chapman, Helen Colchin, Geri Cubbal, Janet Gerber, Mary Grigsby,
John Hall, Helen Mustin, Susan Pallone, Martha Rogers, Peter

Scott, Richard Seagly, Earlene Shoemaker, Theodore Thieme and Susan Wever--all members of the staff under Fred Reynolds, librarian of the Fort Wayne and Allen County Library, Fort Wayne, Indiana. Also helpful were my parents, Mary and Harold Sharp, who located much information for me in the Oakland, California, Public Library, as did my niece, Miss Ann Sharp. Reference librarians at the Indiana University Library, Bloomington, and the staff of the Indianapolis Public Library gave willing and helpful assistance. I wish to express my deep appreciation to all these persons at this time.

Harold S. Sharp

Fort Wayne, Indiana
January, 1978

THE INUNDATION OF ATLANTIS
(c. 10th millennium B.C.)

Over the centuries many cities have been built, have prospered for a time and then have vanished. In some cases these
cities were conquered and destroyed by enemies. In others a seat
of government was moved to a new location, a tidal wave, fire or
an earthquake destroyed them or perhaps a trade route shifted. A
natural resource, such as gold in the case of modern Western American mining towns, may have become exhausted.

Archaeologists and historians have confirmed the existence of
such ancient cities as Nineveh, Angkor, Petra, Knossos and Crus-
timius. However, the lost continent of Atlantis which, according
to legend, sank beneath the waters of the Atlantic Ocean almost
12,000 years ago, presents a mystery about which people still speculate. The Atlantis legend has inspired over 2,000 books, articles,
short stories, motion pictures and even an epic poem. It has been
considered by scientists who have consulted old manuscripts, excavated in search of civilizations long gone and explored the ocean
floor with searchlights, diving suits, cameras and sophisticated
electronic equipment. The question, however, is still unanswered:
Did such a continent as Atlantis exist and, if so, did it sink beneath the waters as legend says? A vanished city is one thing; a
continent is something altogether different.

The first reference to Atlantis is found in the writings of
the Greek philosopher Plato who published two dialogues, Timaios
and Kritias (Critias), around 355 B.C. In these Socrates talks with
his friends, one of whom tells the story of Atlantis. These two
dialogues contain the only direct mention of the lost continent which
has come down to us in the ancient literature.

In Timaios Plato's great-grandfather, Kritias, states that
he heard the story of Atlantis from his grandfather, who heard it
from his father, who, in turn, heard it from Solon, the Athenian
statesman. Solon was said to have heard it from a priest in the
Egyptian city of Saïs, about 590 B.C., while on a visit.

The priest's story related that approximately 9,000 years be-
fore an island larger than Asia Minor and Libya combined, called
"Atlantis," had existed in the Atlantic Ocean, east of the Straits of
Gibraltar. It was wealthy, prosperous, rich in natural resources
and was ruled by a communist military caste. When, after the
Creation, the gods divided up the world, the island was given to

1

Poseidon, the sea god, who married Kleito, a mortal. Atlas, one of their sons, together with his brothers, all ruling as kings, built the city of Atlantis on the island and founded a flourishing civilization. The city was circular, fifteen miles across, with a canal through the middle, connecting the sea with an irrigated plain about 230 miles wide and 340 miles long. Palaces and temples occupied the center of the city, which consisted of concentric rings of land and water, connected by bridges and tunnels.

For hundreds of years following the Creation the Atlanteans prospered and eventually conquered all the Mediterranean peoples except the Athenians. Then Athens was demolished by a gigantic earthquake which destroyed her army and also sank the island of Atlantis beneath the sea.

In Kritias, a later work, Plato records the history of Atlantis, depicting it as a Utopian commonwealth. The Atlanteans "had remained virtuous, like the Athenians of that later day." However, because of the infusion of an excessive human strain into the original combination of human and divine bloodlines, they eventually suffered a moral decline, becoming "greedy, corrupt and ambitious." Zeus decided to punish them and called a meeting of the gods to discuss the matter. Here Plato's Kritias ends and the promised details of the Atheno-Atlantean war are not disclosed.

Several ancient writers after Plato refer to his Atlantis story but none of them seem to have taken it factually, considering it merely allegorical fiction in which the Greek philosopher put forth his theories concerning the perfect state. However, the legend remained, though more or less dormant, until the fifteenth century when it was revived following the explorations of such navigators as Christopher Columbus and Vasco da Gama. America was identified with it by some scholars of the day, even though Atlantis was supposed to have sunk into the ocean. Many maps showed non-existent islands, miraculously raised above sea level. Sir Francis Bacon, the English philosopher and statesman, in his The New Atlantis, speaks of a South Sea island inhabited by Atlanteans. These people, said Bacon, had migrated from the original Atlantis when a great flood devastated it. Voltaire has given credence to the legend. Ignatius Donnelly, an American writer, scholar and politician in the late 19th century, wrote concerning the legend and attempted to show that it had a basis of fact. Dr. Paul Schliemann, grandson of Heinrich Schliemann who excavated the site of ancient Troy, asserted that his grandfather had left him certain evidence proving the Atlantis legend to be factual, but this evidence was never produced.

Other scientists and pseudo-scientists have written books and articles on the subject. Their theories are generally discredited by archaeologists and geologists as unsound and unsubstantiated. It is largely held today that Plato wrote a type of pioneer allegorical science-fiction in which he set forth his own political doctrines. While based on certain historical facts such as floods, wars and the fall of ancient cities, his Timaios and Kritias seem to have been taken far more literally than he ever intended.

Suggested Readings

Babcock, William H. Legendary Islands of the Atlantic: A Study in Medieval Geography. New York: American Geographical Society, 1922.

Bacon, Edward, ed. Vanished Civilizations of the Ancient World. London: McGraw-Hill, 1963.

Bessmertny, Alexandre. L'Atlantide (Exposé des hypothèses à l'énigme de l'Atlantide). Paris: Payot, 1935.

Björkman, Edwin. The Search for Atlantis. New York: Knopf, 1927.

Braghine, A. The Shadow of Atlantis. New York: Dutton, 1940.

Bramwell, James. Lost Atlantis. New York: Harper, 1938.

Chapin, Henry. The Search for Atlantis. New York: Crowell-Collier, 1968.

Churchward, James. The Children of Mu. New York: Ives Washburn, 1931-1945.

_____. The Lost Continent of Mu. New York: Ives Washburn, 1933-1963.

_____. The Sacred Symbols of Mu. New York: Ives Washburn, 1933-1945.

De Camp, L. Sprague. Lost Continents (The Atlantis Theme in History, Science and Literature). New York: Gnome Press, 1954.

_____, and Catherine C. De Camp. "Atlantis and the City of Silver" in their Ancient Ruins and Archaeology. Garden City, N.Y.: Doubleday, 1964.

Donnelly, Ignatius. Atlantis: The Antediluvian World. New York: n.p., 1882.

Doyle, Arthur Conan. Maracot Deep (science fiction). Garden City, N.Y.: Doubleday, 1929.

Marx, Robert F. Pirate Port: The Story of the Sunken City of Port Royal. Cleveland: World, 1967.

Plato. "Timaeus and Critias" in his The Works of Plato. New York: Tudor Publishing Co., n.d.

Plutarch. Parallel Lives of the Noble Greeks and Romans. Translated with an introduction by Bernadotte Perrin. New York: Crowell, 1914-1928.

Schreiber, Hermann, and George Schreiber. Vanished Cities. New York: Knopf, 1957.

Scott-Elliot, W. The Story of Atlantis and the Lost Lemuria. London: Theosophical Publishing House, 1896-1930.

Silverberg, Robert. Lost Cities and Vanished Civilizations. Philadelphia: Chilton, 1962.

Spence, Lewis. Atlantis in America. New York: Brentano's, 1925.

_____. The History of Atlantis. London: Rider & Co., 1926.

_____. The Problem of Atlantis. New York: Brentano's, 1924-1925.

_____. The Problem of Lemuria (The Sunken Continent of the Pacific). Philadelphia: David McKay, 1933.

Spencer, J. W. "Submarine Valleys off the American Coast and in the North Atlantic," Bulletin of the Geological Society of America, Vol. XIV, 1903.

Steiner, Rudolf. Atlantis and Lemuria. London: Anthroposophical
    Publishing Co., 1923
"Submarine Valleys," Geographical Review, Vol. XXIII, 1933.

THE ORIGIN AND DEVELOPMENT OF
THE WRITTEN WORD (c. 3500 B. C.)

Writing is defined as "the art of recording ideas on a material substance by means of symbols that can be understood without oral interpretation." James Henry Breasted, the American
Orientalist, archaeologist and historian, regarded writing as "the
greatest influence in uplifting the human race." Its value is in-
calculable. It spans the entire history of visual communication
from early pictorial symbols, such as the cave paintings of the
Paleolithic era, to alphabetical writing which came into being sometime between 1800 and 1000 B. C.

True writing was preceded by memory-jogging systems, for
example the notched sticks used by the Australian aborigines and
the knots in strings as exemplified by the Peruvian quipus. These
devices had to be supplemented by oral explanations and consequently fell short of being true writing.

In its most primitive form writing was pictographic. Objects
were represented by pictures of those objects. Pictographic writing was used by the natives of Egypt, Mesopotamia and by the American Indians, among others.

The next ("ideographic") stage in the advance of writing satisfied the need for expressing simple abstract ideas. The ideograph was a composite character which was formed by combining
pictures. A two days' journey could be represented by a picture
consisting of a sign for the sun inscribed twice over the sign representing a canoe. The ideograph thus became a simplified symbol
rather than a picture of an object. Eventually the ideograph became simpler, less pictorial and more symbolic, as in the Egyptian
picture writing where sorrow, originally depicted by a person weep-
ing, was later represented by an eye shedding tears.

The representing of ideas by pictures was cumbersome because there is virtually no limit to the number of ideas or objects.
It was realized that sounds, on the other hand, are comparatively
few in number, so the ancient Egyptians and others devised symbols, called phonograms, to represent combinations of sounds. In
Egyptian phonetic writing certain signs came to represent the basic
sounds corresponding to the individual letters of the alphabet. This
led to alphabetic writing, in which it is possible to represent all
possible words with a comparatively few symbols (letters) for the
sound elements. Some peoples, such as the Egyptians, combined
pictograms and ideographs with phonograms. Their writing remained

transitional between the ideographic and alphabetical systems.

About the year 1000 B. C. the Semitic people living in Palestine and the Sinai Peninsula achieved complete alphabetical writing systems, deleting all pictorial elements from their script and using symbols only to indicate the elements of sound. The Semitic alphabet was adopted by the Greeks and this, in turn, spread throughout the Mediterranean world, giving rise to many modified forms, including the Etruscan, Oscan, Umbrian and Roman.

Alphabetic writing is the most efficient method of relating spoken to written languages and there have been no major improvements in this type of communication since the days of the Phoenicians. Shorthand and the symbols used in mathematics, chemistry and statistics are comparatively modern inventions, used for specialized purposes.

Suggested Readings

Breasted, James Henry. Development of Religion and Thought in Ancient Egypt. New York: Harper Torchbooks, 1955 (Originally published 1912).

Chiera, W. They Wrote on Clay. Chicago: University of Chicago Press, 1938

Cleator, P. E. Lost Languages. New York: John Day, 1961.

Davies, Nina M. Picture Writing in Ancient Egypt. New York: Oxford University Press, 1958.

Diringer, David. The Alphabet: A Key to the History of Mankind. New York: Funk & Wagnalls, 1968.

———. Writing. New York: Frederick A. Praeger, 1962.

Doblhofer, Ernst. Voices in Stone: The Decipherment of Ancient Scripts and Writings. Translated by Mervyn Savill. New York: Viking Press, 1961.

Driver, Godfrey R. Semitic Writing. Oxford: The University Press, 1954.

Friedrich, J. Extinct Languages. New York: Philosophical Library, 1957.

Gardiner, Alan H. Egyptian Grammar: Being an Introduction to the Study of Hieroglyphics. New York: Oxford University Press, 1957.

———. The Kadesh Inscriptions of Ramses II. Oxford: The University Press, 1960.

Gelb, I. J. A Study of Writing. Chicago: University of Chicago Press, 1952.

Gleason, H. A. An Introduction to Descriptive Linguistics. New York: Holt, Rinehart and Winston, 1965,

Irwin, K. G. The Romance of Writing. New York: Viking Press, 1967.

McMurtrie, Douglas C. The Book. New York: Covici-Friede, 1937.

Mason, W. A. A History of the Art of Writing. New York: Macmillan, 1928.

Mertz, Barbara. Temples, Tombs and Hieroglyphs: The Story of Egyptology. New York: Coward-McCann, 1964.

Moorhouse, A. C. The Triumph of the Alphabet. New York: Henry Schuman, 1953.
Moran, H. A. , and D. H. Kelley. The Alphabet and the Ancient Calandar Signs. Palo Alto, Calif.: Daily Press, 1969.
Ogg, Oscar. The 26 Letters. New York: Crowell, 1961.
Palmer, Geoffrey. The Quest for the Dead Sea Scrolls. New York: John Day, 1964.
Pei, Mario. Language for Everybody. New York: Devin-Adair, 1956.
Rappaport, Uriel. The Story of the Dead Sea Scrolls. Irvington-on-Hudson, N. Y.: Harvey House, 1967.
Ullman, B. L. Ancient Writing and Its Influence. New York: Cooper Square Publishers, 1963.

THE INVENTION OF THE WHEEL (c. 3500 B. C.)

The word "wheel" is defined as "a circular frame or solid disk arranged to turn on a central axis, as in vehicles, machinery, etc. " It is considered the most significant mechanical principle ever discovered and applied by man. According to some authorities the wheel was invented by an unknown genius in Mesopotamia shortly before the Bronze Age. It was prerequisite to the development of the wheeled cart and represented a major milestone in the advance of civilization.

In its original primitive form the wheel was a wooden disk mounted on a round axle to which it was fastened with wooden pins. Later the solid disk was replaced by a lighter one from which sections had been carved. This led to the development of a circular frame consisting of several sections and to the invention of radial spokes.

In due course the wheel became known and used throughout the world, although it was never adopted by the simpler Asiatic peoples, the African Negroes or the natives of Oceania. It was essentially unknown in pre-Columbian America.

The rotary motion principle of the wheel was applied in countless ways. One early development was the potter's wheel which some archaeologists believe preceded the wheeled vehicle. The Chinese developed a single-wheeled wheelbarrow in the first century A. D. This was in use in Europe by the twelfth century. Ox-drawn two-wheeled and four-wheeled carts and wagons were developed. These were first used as hearses for noblemen but eventually also came to be employed as carriers of goods.

Once the basic principle of the wheel and axle had been discovered it was applied to such devices as pulleys, water mills and windmills, the last appearing in Persia in the seventh century A. D. Archimedes (c. 287-212 B. C), the Greek mathematician and inventor,

described gears and cogwheels in his writings.   Leonardo da Vinci
(1452-1519) and Galileo Galilei (1564-1642) applied the wheel to other more sophisticated inventions which, in turn, helped bring on
the Industrial Revolution.

One invention led to another.   The steam engine of James
Watt (1736-1819) made possible the steamboat, locomotive and large
stationary engines.   Watt's steam engine could not have been built
had not the wheel been discovered.   It is extremely difficult to
name a modern mechanical device which does not use the wheel
principle.   Though simple in concept, the wheel is vital to the development of modern machines and without it present-day technology
would be impossible.

Suggested Readings

Burlingame, Roger.   Inventors Behind the Inventor.   New York:
    Harcourt, Brace, 1947.
Childe, V. Gordon.   "Rotary Motion" in A History of Technology,
    Vol. I.   Oxford: The University Press, 1954.
_____. "Wheeled Vehicles" in A History of Technology, Vol. I.
    Oxford: The University Press, 1954.
Ekholm, Gordon F.   "Transpacific Contacts" in Prehistoric Man in
    the New World.   Chicago: University of Chicago Press, 1964.
Forbes, Robert J.   "Hydraulic Engineering and Sanitation" and "Pow-
    er" in A History of Technology, Vol. II.   Oxford: The Univer-
    sity Press, 1956.
Heath, Sir Thomas L.   Archimedes.   New York: Macmillan, 1920.
Jope, E. M.   "Vehicles and Harness" in A History of Technology,
    Vol. II.   Oxford: The University Press, 1956.
Kirby, Richard S. , et al.   Engineering in History.   New York:
    McGraw-Hill, 1956.
Krober, A. L.   Anthropology.   New York: Harcourt, Brace, 1948.
Rolt, L. T. C.   The Mechanicals: Progress of a Profession.   Lon-
    don: William Heinemann, 1967.
Usher, Abbott P.   A History of Mechanical Inventions.   New York:
    McGraw-Hill, 1929.
Wailes, Rex.   "Windmills" in A History of Technology, Vol. III.
    Oxford: The University Press, 1957.

THE INVENTION OF BRONZE AND THE
DISCOVERY OF IRON (c. 3300 B. C. and c. 1500 B. C.)

Bronze is a durable brown alloy consisting of approximately
nine parts of copper to one part of tin.   Iron, like copper and tin,
is a metallic element.   It is ductile, malleable and silver-white in
color.   Both bronze and iron played an important part in man's
transition from the stone (Neolithic) age to the age of metals.

About 5000 B. C. man learned to mine and smelt copper and work it by heating and casting; he was then able to fashion tools which could not be made from wood, bone or stone. Somewhere around 3300 B. C. the art of alloying two or more metals was discovered, as were annealing and tempering. Copper and tin ores were both available in Northeast Persia and archaeologists believe that rudimentary metallurgy was first discovered there. The knowledge diffused slowly to other areas of the ancient world and the Bronze Age thus began at a later date in each successive region.

Copper was alloyed with tin and cast into arrowheads, spearheads and tools. The cutting edges were hardened by hammering and by quenching--plunging the heated metal into cold water. Bronze proved superior to the comparatively soft copper which, when fashioned into various objects, had a tendency to twist out of shape. For this reason no true Copper Age existed, except in Egypt where tin ore was not available. Various methods for fashioning the metal into finished products were discovered. This led to the invention of such implements as daggers, swords and tools which could not be made of stone.

The Bronze Age was succeeded by the Iron Age (about 1500 B. C.) which, as the former had, started in one region--Asia Minor--and spread slowly to other areas.

Wrought iron was originally used for decorative purposes. It was made by hammering the small particles of iron left when copper was smelted. About 1500 B. C. it was learned that iron, after being repeatedly heated and hammered, became harder than bronze and would keep its hardness for an extended period of time. Quenching, which was used in the fashioning of copper, was found to be equally effective for treating iron. Iron was more abundant than were copper and tin, the components of bronze. Consequently it was comparatively cheap and its use became more widespread than bronze. Axes, scissors, hoes, scythes and other tools were fashioned from it. It was also used for ornamental purposes and in the manufacture of swords, daggers and other weapons.

The Hittites of Asia Minor enjoyed a monopoly in iron manufacturing around 1500 B. C. They guarded their technological secrets jealously but when their empire broke up after 1200 B. C. information concerning the working of iron spread through Palestine, the Nile Valley, continental Europe, Africa, and elsewhere.

In modern days steel, which is iron in modified form, is used in hundreds of ways. Steel is essentially iron alloyed with carbon and other constituents. Such inventions as the Bessemer converter and the open hearth furnace have made it possible to produce various kinds of steel in quantity and to melt and re-use steel scrap.

Suggested Readings

Aitchison, Leslie. A History of Metals. New York: Interscience
    Publishers, 1960.
Aldred, Cyril. Egypt to the End of the Old Kingdom. New York:
    McGraw-Hill, 1965.
Asimov, Isaac. The Egyptians. Boston: Houghton Mifflin, 1967.
Bromhead, C. N., et al. "From Early Times to the Fall of the
    Ancient Empires" in Singer, Charles, et al., eds. A History
    of Technology. Vol. I. Oxford: Clarendon Press, 1955.
Childe, V. Gordon. What Happened in History. Baltimore: Pen-
    guin Books, 1954.
Derry, T. K., and Trevor I. Williams. A Short History of Tech-
    nology from the Earliest Times to A. D. 1900. New York: Ox-
    ford University Press, 1960.
Falls, C. B. The First 3,000 Years: Ancient Civilizations of the
    Tigris, Euphrates, and Nile River Valleys and the Mediterran-
    ean Sea. New York: Viking Press, 1960.
Forbes, Robert J. Man the Maker: A History of Technology and
    Engineering. New York: Henry Schuman, 1950.
_____. Metallurgy in Antiquity. Leiden: E. J. Brill, 1964.
_____. Studies in Ancient Technology. Leiden: E. J. Brill,
    1964.
Gurney, Oliver R. The Hittites. Baltimore: Penguin Books, 1961.
Lucas, A. Ancient Egyptian Materials and Industries. London:
    E. J. Arnold, 1962.
Schaeffer, C. F. A. "The Appearance and Spread of Metal" in La-
    rousse Encyclopedia of Prehistoric and Ancient Art. New York:
    Prometheus Press, 1966.
Singer, Charles, et al., eds. A History of Technology. Oxford:
    Clarendon Press, 1954-1958.
Warren, Ruth. The Nile: The Story of Pharaohs, Farmers, and
    Explorers. New York: McGraw-Hill, 1968.

THE BUILDING OF THE PYRAMID OF CHEOPS
(c. 2900-2877 B. C.)

Giza, Egypt, is the site of three great pyramids. These
are generally considered the most celebrated group of monuments
of the ancient world. Altogether about eighty pyramids were erected. These were designed as tombs for the Egyptian pharaohs and
the greatest of them all was that of Cheops (Khufu) who ruled from
about 2900 to 2877 B. C. in the fourth dynasty. The other two great
pyramids were built by Chephren and Mycer, pharaohs of the same
dynasty.

Cheops' pyramid is the largest stone structure in the world.
Herodotus, the Greek historian, writing about 449 B. C. , stated that
100,000 men worked for twenty years to build it. These figures are
now considered excessive. It is currently thought that not more than

4,000 men did the actual construction work while perhaps 16,000
others quarried and transported blocks of stone from Aswan and
the Mukattam Hills.

It is estimated that some 2,300,000 separate blocks of limestone and granite, weighing from 2 to fifteen tons each, were used
in the pyramid. The base covers 13.1 acres. Each of the four
sides of the base measures 755 feet and the structure is calculated
to weigh more than 5 million tons. It was originally 481 feet high.
The top 31 feet have worn away over the centuries as has the original limestone facing.

The Cheops pyramid contains interior passageways, the upper levels of which are open to visitors today. The entrance is
on the north side, 49 feet above ground level. A corridor, once
blocked with granite to foil tomb robbers, leads to the Great Chamber which measures 153 feet long, 30 feet high and only seven feet
wide. An antechamber leads to the royal funerary room where the
sarcophagus of Cheops stands.

Copper saws and chisels were used to cut the comparatively
soft limestone and dolomite hammers were employed on the harder
granite. Gangs of workmen dragged the stones to the construction
site on sledges and to the Nile River where they were floated from
Aswan to Giza on heavy barges.

The technique by which the heavy stones were moved to the
higher courses of the pyramid is open to conjecture. It is generally supposed that they were dragged on sledges to their final positions on mud-brick ramps constructed on each corner against the
outer surface, although other methods may have been employed.

Suggested Readings

Aldred, Cyril. Egypt to the End of the Old Kingdom. New York:
    McGraw-Hill, 1965.
Asimov, Isaac. The Egyptians. Boston: Houghton Mifflin, 1967.
Barker, Felix, in collaboration with Anthea Barker. "Into the Un-
    known" in their The First Explorers: Encyclopedia of Discov-
    ery and Exploration, Vol. I. London: Aldus Books, 1971.
Barnard, F. A. P. The Imaginary Meterological System of the Great
    Pyramid of Gizeh. New York: Wiley, 1884.
Baumann, Hans. The World of the Pharaohs. New York: Pan-
    theon Books, 1960.
Bonwick, James. Pyramid Facts and Fancies. London: Kegan
    Paul, 1877.
Borchardt, Ludwig. Gegen die Zahlenmystic an der grossen Pyra-
    mide bei Gize. Berlin: Verlag von Behrend & Co., 1922.
Casson, Lionel, and the editors of Time-Life Books. Ancient Egypt.
    New York: Time, Inc., 1965.
Cohen, Daniel. Secrets from Ancient Graves: Rulers and Heroes of
    the Past Whose Lives Have Been Revealed Through Archaeology.
    New York: Dodd, Mead, 1968.

Corbin, Bruce. The Great Pyramid: God's Witness in Stone. Guth-
    rie, Okla. : Truth Publishing Co. , 1935.
Cottrell, Leonard. Land of the Pharaohs. Cleveland: World, 1960.
_____. Warrior Pharaohs. New York: Putnam, 1969.
Davidson, David, and Herbert Aldersmith. The Great Pyramid:
    Its Divine Message. London: Williams and Norgate, 1924.
DeCamp, L. Sprague, and Catherine C. DeCamp. "Pyramid Hill
    and the Claustrophobic King" in their Ancient Ruins and Arch-
    aeology. Garden City, N. Y. : Doubleday, 1964.
Edgar, Morton. The Great Pyramid: Its Time Features. Glas-
    gow: Bone & Hulley, 1924.
Eduards, I. E. S. The Pyramids of Egypt. Baltimore: Penguin
    Books, 1961.
Edwards, Amelia B. Egypt and Its Monuments. New York: Har-
    per, 1891.
Fakhry, Ahmed. The Pyramids. Chicago: University of Chicago
    Press, 1961.
Falls, C. B. The First 3,000 Years: Ancient Civilizations of the
    Tigris, Euphrates, and Nile River Valleys and the Mediter-
    ranean Sea. New York: Viking Press, 1960.
Hawkes, Jacquetta, and the editors of Horizon Magazine. Pharaohs
    of Egypt. New York: American Heritage, 1965.
Knight, Charles S. The Mystery and Prophecy of the Great Pyra-
    mid. San Jose, Calif. : Rosicrucian Press, 1928-1933.
Lange, K. , and M. Hirmer. Egypt: Architecture, Sculpture,
    Painting in Three Thousand Years. London: Phaidon Press,
    1961.
Lewis, H. Spencer. The Symbolic Prophecy of the Great Pyramid.
    San Jose, Calif. : Rosicrucian Press, 1936.
Mertz, Barbara. Temples, Tombs and Hieroglyphs: The Story of
    Egyptology. New York: Coward-McCann, 1964.
Murray, Margaret A. "The Great Pyramid" in Hamerton, J. A. ,
    ed. Wonders of the Past: The Romance of Antiquity and Its
    Splendours, Vol. III. New York: William H. Wise, 1933.
Peet, T. Eric. "The Pyramids of Egypt" in Hamerton, J. A. , ed.
    Wonders of the Past: The Romance of Antiquity and Its Splen-
    dours, Vol. II. New York: William H. Wise, 1933.
Sewell, Barbara. Egypt Under the Pharaohs. New York: Putnam,
    1968.
Smith, W. Stevenson. The Art and Architecture of Ancient Egypt.
    Baltimore: Penguin Books, 1958.
Smyth, C. Piazzi. Life and Work at the Great Pyramid. Edin-
    burgh: Edmonston & Douglas, 1867.
_____. Our Inheritance in the Great Pyramid. London: Daldy
    & Isbiter, 1877.
Warren, Ruth. The Nile: The Story of Pharaohs, Farmers, and
    Explorers. New York: McGraw-Hill, 1968.
Woldering, Irmgard. The Art of Egypt: The Time of the Pharaohs.
    New York: Greystone Press, 1963.

THE BOOK OF THE DEAD (c. 2500 B. C.)

The best known book of the ancient Egyptians is The Book
of the Dead, a more exact title for which is The Book of Coming
Forth by Day. It is chiefly instruction in right living, i. e. , ethical, moral and religious guidelines. A number of copies exist, some
extremely old and others of comparatively later dates, produced
mostly after 1550 B. C. These copies vary in some particulars but
all contain guidance and instructions to the soul (the "Ka") after the
death of the body and during the Ka's journey to Anenti, the region
of the dead.

The Book was inscribed on the sarcophagi in the pyramids of Egyptian kings about 2500 B. C.   Later it was written
on sheets of papyrus and placed in or near the coffins of the
dead.   Thus, the deceased could refer to the texts in case of
necessity.

It was believed that knowledge of the formulas, prayers
and hymns given in the Book would enable the Ka to ward off
demons attempting to impede its progress to Anenti. It was also believed that the Book would help the Ka pass the tests imposed by the judges in the hall of Osiris, the Egyptian god of
the underworld.

Chapter 125 of the Book is representative of the whole.
This chapter, which dates from about 1550 B. C. , includes a picture of the god Osiris seated in his hall in the hereafter. Also
shown are a set of scales on which the heart of a dead man
is balanced against the symbol of Maat, the goddess of justice.
Anubis, the soul leader, conducts the weighing and records the
result of the interrogation upon which depends the ultimate fate
of the Ka.

The subject matter of the examination consists of a formal-
ized greeting to Osiris followed by a series of declarations by the
dead man, called "negative confessions. " Here the deceased denies
committing acts which were considered by the ancient Egyptians as
immoral.   These included such things as inflicting pain, murder,
theft, oppression of one's family and dishonesty in business transactions.   The mere recital of the negative confession assured the
Ka a place in paradise and it was not necessary that the statements
made be truthful.

Instructions for living a good life were laid down in an earlier book, known as "The Precepts of Ptah-Hotep. " This, a papyrus
manuscript written by Ptah-Hotep, a high court official about 2500
B. C. , is the oldest Egyptian manuscript so far discovered.   It was
directed to the writer's son and orders him to be considerate of
others, listen to "those of experience, " treat his wife kindly and
obey his master cheerfully and willingly.

Suggested Readings

Aldred, Cyril. Egypt to the End of the Old Kingdom. New York: McGraw-Hill, 1965.

————. The Egyptians. London: Thames and Hudson, 1961.

Asimov, Isaac. The Egyptians. Boston: Houghton Mifflin, 1967.

Bacon, Edward, ed. Vanished Civilizations of the Ancient World. London: McGraw-Hill, 1963.

Baumann, Hans. The World of the Pharaohs. New York: Pantheon Books, 1960.

Breasted, James Henry. Development of Religion and Thought in Ancient Egypt. New York: Harper Torchbooks, 1955 (Originally published 1912).

Casson, Lionel, and the editors of Time-Life Books. Ancient Egypt. New York: Time, Inc., 1965.

Cottrell, Leonard. Land of the Pharaohs. Cleveland: World, 1960.

Cross, E. A. "The Book of the Dead" and "The Precepts of Ptah-Hotep" in his World Literature. New York: American Book Co., 1935.

Falls, C. B. The First 3,000 Years: Ancient Civilizations of the Tigris, Euphrates, and Nile River Valleys and the Mediterranean Sea. New York: Viking Press, 1960.

Frankfort, Henri. Egyptian Religion: An Interpretation. New York: Harper & Row, 1948.

————, et al. The Intellectual Adventures of Ancient Man. Chicago: University of Chicago Press, 1946.

Hawkes, Jacquetta, and the editors of Horizon Magazine. Pharaohs of Egypt. New York: American Heritage, 1965.

Mercer, Samuel A. B. The Religion of Ancient Egypt. London: Luzac and Company, 1949.

Mertz, Barbara. Red Land, Black Land: The World of the Ancient Egyptians. London: Hodder and Stoughton, 1967.

————. Temples, Tombs and Hieroglyphs: The Story of Egyptology. New York: Coward-McCann, 1964.

Sewell, Barbara. Egypt Under the Pharaohs. New York: Putnam, 1968.

Warren, Ruth. The Nile: The Story of Pharaohs, Farmers, and Explorers. New York: McGraw-Hill, 1968.

Wilson, John A. The Culture of Ancient Egypt. Chicago: University of Chicago Press, 1951.

Woldering, Irmgard. The Art of Egypt: The Time of the Pharaohs. New York: Greystone Press, 1963.

Zandee, J. Death as an Enemy According to Ancient Egyptian Conceptions. Leiden: E. J. Brill, 1960.

THE PROMULGATION OF THE CODE
OF HAMMURABI (c. 1750 B.C.)

Hammurabi, King of Mesopotamia from about 1790 to 1750 B.C., is considered one of the greatest kings of Babylonia. During

his reign he promulgated his famous Code, a set of amendments of
existing laws.   These were carved on a stele of black dolomite
some seven feet high which was found in Susa, Iran, by a group
of French excavators during the winter of 1901-1902.   At the top
of the text is a carved relief showing Hammurabi standing before
the sun god Shamash, patron of justice.   Shamash is depicted hand-
ing the king the official symbols of authority.   The stele, which
was taken to Susa by an ancient ruler as a trophy of war, is now
on exhibition at the Louvre in Paris.

The laws appearing on the stele were of great interest to
archaeologists because they were the first collection of laws known
to antedate those in the Bible.   While this Code of Hammurabi is
not the earliest such document it is the best preserved and most
extensive of its kind known from the ancient Middle East.

The stele contains three sections: a poetic prologue, the
laws themselves, and an epilogue.   The prologue proclaims the
justice of the king and the epilogue reiterates his praise of his
own righteousness, commends his enactments to posterity and calls
down curses on "whoever shall alter his laws or deface his stele. "

The laws, 282 in number, are grouped by subject, such as
offenses against the administration of justice, offenses against property, regulations pertaining to trade and commerce, property
rights, wage and fee rates, laws concerning agriculture, family relationships and the sale of slaves.

A three-layered division of society is indicated.   The highest class includes the king, military officials, wealthy merchants
and land owners.   A lower class, consisting of laborers and farmers, is indicated and at the bottom are placed the slaves, prisoners of war and those who had lost their freedom through debt.

According to the Code, women had property and other rights,
which were spelled out.   They could divorce, transact business and
inherit and bequeath property.   The criminal laws seem extremely
harsh by today's standards, following the principle of an eye for
an eye.   "If a man destroy the eye of another man, they shall destroy his eye.   If he break a man's bone, they shall break his
bone. "

The main principle of the Code was that "the strong shall
not injure the weak, " and was backed by the authority of the Babylonian gods and the state.

The laws of Babylonia, as set forth in the Code, are significant in that they furnish information about an ancient civilization.
Further, in Hammurabi's redaction a relationship is shown to those
of the Old Testament and from there to modern legal concepts.   Because of the parallels between the Code and the Old Testament some
scholars feel that the Hebrew laws were adapted from Babylonian
sources.

Suggested Readings

Bacon, Edward, ed.   Vanished Civilizations of the Ancient World.
    London: McGraw-Hill, 1963.
Cohen, Daniel.   Secrets from Ancient Graves: Rulers and Heroes
    of the Past Whose Lives Have Been Revealed Through Archae-
    ology.   New York: Dodd, Mead, 1968.
Driver, Godfrey R. , and John C. Mills, eds.   The Babylonian Laws.
    Oxford: Clarendon Press, 1952.
Falls, C. B.   The First 3,000 Years: Civilizations of the Tigris,
    Euphrates, and Nile River Valleys and the Mediterranean Sea.
    New York: Viking Press, 1960.
Frankfort, Henri, et al.   The Intellectual Adventures of Ancient
    Man.   Chicago: University of Chicago Press, 1946.
Gadd, Cyril J.   Hammurabi and the End of His Dynasty.   Cam-
    bridge: The University Press, 1965.
Gordon, Cyrus.   Hammurabi's Code: Quaint or Forward Looking?
    New York: Holt, Rinehart, 1957.
Kramer, Samuel Noah.   The Sumerians: Their History, Culture
    and Character.   Chicago: University of Chicago Press, 1963.
Petrie, Sir W. M. Flinders.   Seventy Years in Archaeology.   Lon-
    don: Sampson, Low, Marston & Co. , 1931.
Pritchard, James B. , ed.   Ancient Near Eastern Texts Relating to
    the Old Testament.   Princeton, N. J. : Princeton University
    Press, 1950-1955.
Speiser, E. A.   "Authority and Law in Mesopotamia, " Journal of
    the American Oriental Society, Supplement 17, 1954.
Woolley, C. Leonard.   Digging Up the Past.   New York: Scribner's,
    1931.

THE BATTLE OF KADESH (1296 B. C.)

     James Henry Breasted, the American Orientalist, archaeol-
ogist and historian, has called the Battle of Kadesh, fought by the
Egyptians and the Hittites in Southern Syria in 1296 B. C. , "the
earliest battle in history in which strategy can be studied in detail. "
C. W. Ceram regards it as one of antiquity's most important military engagements because it "decided the fate of Syria and Palestine. " Information concerning it has been derived from pictorial
and hieroglyphic reports carved on the walls of Egyptian temples
along the Nile River and from Hittite cuneiform inscriptions which
have come down to the present day.

     Since the days of the Egyptian pharaoh Thutmose III, who
reigned in the early fifteenth century B. C. , Egypt had been inter-
mittently at war with the Hittites, an ancient people who flourished
in Asia Minor and adjoining regions.   Ramses II ascended the Egyptian throne about 1304 B. C. and took steps to reassert Egyptian
dominance in Syria.   In the early years of his reign he engaged in
an important military campaign against the Hittites.   He sent an

army north to secure harbors and a year later took personal command of a large force in Palestine. This force was composed of
four divisions: Amen, Ptah, Ra and Set. Many of his soldiers
were charioteers armed with bows and spears.

Ramses' divisions were opposed by a Hittite army led by
their ruler Muwatalli (Muwatallish). It consisted of between 16,000
and 20,000 men, a force approximately equal in number to the
Egyptian army. At least half the Hittite army was composed of
charioteers.

Muwatalli concealed his army from the Egyptians and sent
scouts with instructions to permit themselves to be captured and
give Ramses and his generals false information concerning the location of the Hittite troops. This maneuver was successful. Ramses, believing the enemy to be far to the north, permitted his soldiers to straggle, with gaps between the four divisions.

Ramses led Amen, his advance division, across the Orontes
River, west of Kadesh, and then learned that the Hittite forces
were dangerously near. He sent a messenger to bring the Ra division forward. Muwatalli's chariots attacked the Ra division on
the flank, overwhelming it. The Hittites then fell upon Ramses
and his Amen division, encircling it. At least half of Ramses'
army had been killed or its members scattered and the Ptah and
Set divisions were too far in the rear to help him.

According to the hieroglyphics carved on the Egyptian temple
walls, Ramses then charged into the Hittites in his chariot and
drove them back. Reinforcements arrived from the Ptah division
and Muwatalli's men were repulsed.

The Hittite king brought up reinforcements and made a series of six charges against the Egyptians. These were unsuccessful,
Ramses' rearmost division having arrived at the scene of battle.

The outcome of the Battle of Kadesh was indecisive. The
Set division had taken no part in the fighting and eight thousand of
Muwatalli's foot soldiers had not been used. The Egyptian hieroglyphics claim a victory for Ramses and the Hittite inscriptions report the battle as an overwhelming victory for their forces.

After several more years of war in Palestine and Syria a
treaty of permanent peace was negotiated in 1272 B.C. Ramses
married a Hittite princess and the remainder of his long reign was
peaceful.

Suggested Readings

Aldred, Cyril. Egypt to the End of the Old Kingdom. New York:
    McGraw-Hill, 1965.

_____. The Egyptians. London: Thames and Hudson, 1961.
Asimov, Isaac. The Egyptians. Boston: Houghton Mifflin, 1967.
Baumann, Hans. The World of the Pharaohs. New York: Pan-
    theon Books, 1960.
Breasted, James Henry. Ancient Records of Egypt. New York:
    Russell and Russell, 1962 (Originally published 1906).
_____. The Battle of Kadesh. Chicago: University of Chicago
    Press, 1904.
Ceram, C. W. "The Battle of Kadesh" in The Secret of the Hittites.
    New York: Knopf, 1963.
Cottrell, Leonard. Land of the Pharaohs. Cleveland: World, 1960.
_____. Warrior Pharaohs. New York: Putnam, 1969.
Creasy, Edward S. Fifteen Decisive Battles of the World. Har-
    risburg, Pa.: Stackpole Books, 1957.
Falls, C. B. The First 3,000 Years: Ancient Civilizations of the
    Tigris, Euphrates, and Nile River Valleys and the Mediterran-
    ean Sea. New York: Viking Press, 1960.
Falls, Cyril, ed. Great Military Battles. New York: Macmillan,
    1964.
Gardiner, Alan H. Egypt of the Pharaohs. New York: Oxford
    University Press, 1966.
_____. The Kadesh Inscriptions of Ramses II. Oxford: The
    University Press, 1960.
Hawkes, Jacquetta, and the editors of Horizon Magazine. Pharaohs
    of Egypt. New York: American Heritage Publishing Co., 1965.
Lehmann, Johannes. The Hittites: People of a Thousand Gods.
    New York: Viking Press, 1977.
Mitchell, Lieut.-Col. Joseph B., and Sir Edward S. Creasy. Twen-
    ty Decisive Battles of the World. New York: Macmillan, 1964.
Pritchard, James B., ed. The Ancient Near East: An Anthology
    of Texts and Pictures. Princeton, N.J.: Princeton University
    Press, 1958.
_____. Ancient Near Eastern Texts Relating to the Old Testa-
    ment. Princeton, N.J.: Princeton University Press, 1955.
Sewell, Barbara. Egypt Under the Pharaohs. New York: Putnam,
    1968.

THE HEBREW EXODUS FROM EGYPT (c. 1275 B.C.-1250 B.C.)

The ancestors of the Hebrews, according to the Biblical account in Genesis and Exodus, had settled in the delta area of Egypt
some 430 years prior to the Exodus. They came to be looked upon
with hostility by the pharaoh Ramses II and other Egyptians because
of their growing numbers and for other reasons. The Pharaoh enslaved them, putting them to work on projects of his own, particularly the construction of the cities Pithom and Ramses.

Somewhere around 1275-1250 B.C. Moses, a Levite who had
been educated in the household of an Egyptian king, identified himself with his own oppressed people and, after killing an Egyptian

taskmaster, fled to the Sinai Peninsula where he became acquaint-
ed with the Midianite nomads.   In Sinai he was instructed by Yahweh (God) to lead the people out of Egypt to freedom in the Promised Land.

He talked with the Egyptian pharaoh, who refused to give
the Hebrews permission to leave in spite of the divine signs and
omens sent by God to persuade him to consent.   The pharaoh finally agreed to permit Moses and his people to depart after a plague
killed the first-born male child of every household in Egypt but the
first-born males of the Israelites were spared.

Moses led the Israelites into the wilderness.   They had been
gone a day when the pharaoh sent soldiers after them.   The Red
Sea miraculously opened up, permitting the Israelites to pass.   The
soldiers, following them, were drowned when the waters closed back
in.

For forty years Moses and his followers wandered in the
desert.   The Israelites became dissatisfied with their leader and
began to "murmur against God. "   Yahweh's response was to send
"manna and quail" to satisfy hunger and to cause water to flow
from a rock to quench thirst.

Moses retired to Mount Sinai where he was given the Ten
Commandments.   While he was gone the Israelites persuaded his
brother Aaron to fashion a golden calf for them to worship.   Upon
his return from the mountain Moses destroyed the calf as he felt
that the people were worshiping in an unacceptable manner.

Moses did not reach the Promised Land as did his followers.
He died in the territory of Moab on Mount Nebo.

As time went by the Exodus became a symbol of departure
from conditions unworthy of humanity to a promised land representing freedom and justice.

Suggested Readings

Bright, John.   A History of Israel.   Philadelphia: Westminster
     Press, 1959.
Buber, Martin.   Moses: The Revelation and the Covenant.   Lon-
     don: Horovitz Publishing Co. , 1946.
Daube, David.   The Exodus Pattern in the Bible.   London: Faber
     & Faber, 1963.
Driver, Samuel R.   "Exodus" in Cambridge Bible Commentary.
     Cambridge: The University Press, 1911.
Eissfeldt, Otto.   The Old Testament: An Introduction.   Translated
     by Peter R. Ackroyd.   New York: Harper, 1965.
Gray, John.   Archaeology and the Old Testament World.   London:
     Nelson, 1962.

Hagedorn, Hermann. "Moses" in his The Book of Courage. Phil-
    adelphia: Winston, 1920.
McNeile, Alan H. "The Book of Exodus" in Westminster Commen-
    taries. London: Methuen, 1908.
Meek, James Theophile. Hebrew Origins. New York: Harper &
    Row, 1960.
Noth, Martin. Exodus: A Commentary. Translated by J. S. Bow-
    den. Philadelphia: Westminster Press, 1962.
Pritchard, James B. , ed. The Ancient Near East: An Anthology
    of Texts and Pictures. Princeton, N. J. : Princeton University
    Press, 1958.
    _____ . Ancient Near Eastern Texts Relating to the Old Testa-
    ment. Princeton, N. J. : Princeton University Press, 1950-1955.
Rad, Gerhard von. The Problem of the Hexateuch and Other Essays.
    Translated by E. W. T. Dicken. New York: McGraw-Hill, 1966.
Renan, E. History of the People of Israel. Boston: Houghton
    Mifflin, 1886-1896.
Rowley, H. H. From Joseph to Joshua: Biblical Translations in
    the Light of Archaeology. London: Oxford University Press,
    1950.
Rylaarsdam, J. Coert. "The Book of Exodus" in The Interpreter's
    Bible. Abingdon: Cokesbury, 1952.
Sellin, Ernst. Introduction to the Old Testament. Revised and
    rewritten by George Fohrer; translated by David E. Green.
    Abingdon: Cokesbury, 1968.

THE WRITING OF THE GREAT EPIC POEMS
(c. 1200-800 B. C. to 1674 A. D.)

Epic poetry, as distinguished from lyric poetry and dramatic poetry, is usually in the form of a long narrative poem known
as an epic.   "It deals with action of broad sweep and grandeur,
and of traditional or historic interest. " Lyric poetry is sung.   It
expresses more personal emotion than does epic poetry and "has
the form and musical quality of a song and especially the character
of a songlike outpouring of the poet's own thoughts and feelings. "
Dramatic poetry is acted, as in the plays of Shakespeare and his
contemporaries.   Epic poems are traditionally recited, not sung
or acted.

There have been a number of great epic poems written over
the centuries, ranging from the Iliad and Odyssey of Homer who,
according to authorities, lived sometime between 1200 B. C. and
850 B. C. , to John Milton's Paradise Lost.   The latter was completed by 1663 or 1665, published in 1667 in ten books and enlarged
to twelve books in 1674.   These epic poems are far more than entertaining stories.   They "serve often to sum up and express the
ideals or nature of an entire nation at a significant or crucial period of its existence. "

Epic poems often recount the heroic deeds of a national hero, as in the case of the Cid (c. 1040-1099), as described in Poema de mio Cid (c. 1140). They may also deal with a legendary or semi-legendary person whose accomplishments gratify a sense of national pride, as exemplified by Beowulf which appeared in the latter part of the 8th century. Some were developed from folk poetry orally transmitted by tribal bards, as in the case of the Nibelun-genlied (c. 1200), which inspired several of the operas of Richard Wagner. Others were composed by known authors, as was Milton's Paradise Lost. The Song of Roland (c. 1100) is attributed to Tu-roldus, an unidentified minstrel poet or scribe who combined history and fiction and based his poem on a legend concerning Roland, nephew of Charlemagne, King of the Franks and Emperor of the West.

The subject matter of the folk epic usually was created over an extensive period of time antedating the epic. Shorter folk songs, composed before the creation of the epic, were combined in the latter poem. Such consolidation is exemplified by the French Chan-sons de Geste (10th and 11th centuries) which evolved into the Song of Roland, mentioned above.

While epic material abounds in the histories of many nations, in some instances it has not been brought together in the form of an epic poem. The Eastern European Russians and Siberian Tar-tars have no great epic poem glorifying a great national leader, al-though many epic and epic-lyric songs are found in their literature. The Celts have produced cycles of epic poems as, for example, the Ossianic, the Arthurian and the Robin Hood legends, but these have not been welded into a single poem of epic proportions. Some authorities feel that Poema de mio Cid and its successor, Crónica del Cid (c. 1284) do not qualify as true epic poems. They have, however, been used in Pierre Corneille's play Le Cid (1636) and in Jules Massenet's opera Le Cid (1885).

Epic poetry is not confined to the Greek, Anglo-Saxon or Germanic nations. The Indian (Asiatic) Mahabharata and Ramayana are well known and highly regarded as examples of Sanskrit epics. The former is ascribed to the poet Valmiki who flourished in the 3rd century B.C. The Aeneid of Vergil (70-19 B.C.), built around the legend of the wanderings of Aeneas after the fall of Troy and his settlement in Latium, is considered one of the world's greatest epics. The Persian poet Firdausi spent almost 35 years writing his great epic Shah-Namah (Book of Kings), the first edition of which was published in 1010. In 60,000 rhyming couplets it re-counted the story of Persian kings, both legendary and historical, down to the Moslem conquest of 641 A.D.

Other great literary epics include the Portuguese Luisads of Luiz Vaz de Camoëns, published in 1572; the Italian Orlando Furioso of Lodovico Ariosto, published in 40 cantos in 1516 and 46 cantos in 1532; and Rinaldo and Gerusalemme Líberata (Jer-usalem Delivered), composed by Torquato Tasso and published in

1562 and 1575, respectively. Tasso's Il Mondo Creato, a religious
poem completed about 1590, is also considered a poem of epic
proportions. Edmund Spenser's Faerie Queene, three books of
which were published in 1590 and three more in 1596, is also considered great epic poetry.

Mock epics appeared in the 17th and 18th centuries, including Samuel Butler's Hudibras (Part I, 1663; Part II, 1664; Part III,
1678) and Alexander Pope's The Rape of the Lock (1712). These
and others satirize contemporary ideas and customs in a form and
style which burlesque those of the serious epic.

Suggested Readings

Alden, Raymond MacDonald. Poems of the English Race. New
    York: Scribner's, 1921.
Auslander, Joseph, and Frank Ernest Hill. The Winged Horse:
    The Story of the Poets and Their Poetry. Garden City, N.Y.:
    Doubleday, 1927.
Bekker, Hugo. The Nibelungenlied: A Literary Analysis. Toron-
    to: University of Toronto Press, 1971.
Bury, J. B. The Cambridge Medieval History, Vol. VI. Cam-
    bridge: The University Press, 1957.
Committee on College Reading: Atwood H. Townsend, chairman
    and general editor. Good Reading. New York: New American
    Library, 1954.
Cross, E. A. World Literature. New York: American Book Co.,
    1935.
Eliot, Charles W., ed. The Harvard Classics. New York: Col-
    lier, 1909.
Godolphin, Francis Richard Borroum, ed. The Latin Poets. New
    York: Modern Library, 1949.
Holland, Rupert Sargent. Historic Poems and Ballads. Philadelphia:
    G. W. Jacobs & Co., 1912.
Homer. The Iliad of Homer. Done into English Prose by Andrew
    Lang, Walter Leaf and Ernest Myers. London: Macmillan,
    1935.
    _____. The Odyssey of Homer. Translated into English Verse
    by Herbert Bates. New York: Harper, 1929.
Jones, G. F. The Ethos of the Song of Roland. Baltimore: Johns
    Hopkins University Press, 1963.
Le Gentil, Pierre. The Chanson de Roland. Translated by Fran-
    ces F. Beer. Cambridge, Mass.: Harvard University Press,
    1969.
Macy, John. The Story of the World's Literature. New York:
    Boni & Liveright, 1925.
Masson, David. The Life of John Milton. New York: Peter Smith,
    1946.
Otis, Brooks. Ovid as an Epic Poet. Cambridge: The University
    Press, 1966.
Saillens, Emile. John Milton: Man, Poet and Polemicist. Oxford:
    Basil Blackwell, 1964.

Stefferud, Alfred, ed.   The Wonderful World of Books.   New York:
    New American Library, 1954.
Thoy, Macy.   The Study of the Nibelungenlied.   Oxford: Clarendon
    Press, 1940.
Vance, E.   Reading the Song of Roland.   Englewood Cliffs, N. J.:
    Prentice-Hall, 1970.
Walshe, Maurice O'Connell.   Medieval German Literature: A Sur-
    vey.   Cambridge, Mass.: Harvard University Press, 1962.

THE INAUGURATION OF THE
OLYMPIC GAMES (776 B. C.)

Modern Olympic Games have been held every four years
since 1896, with the exception of those originally scheduled for
1916, 1940 and 1944, when World Wars I and II interfered.   They
were revived by Pierre de Coubertin, a Frenchman, in imitation
of the Games of ancient Greece.

The first Olympics on record took place in 776 B. C., honoring the god Zeus.   The series was ended in 393 A. D. with the
decline of ancient Greek civilization when they were abolished by
the Roman emperor Theodosius.

According to tradition, the Games began at Olympia, in the
northwest corner of the Peloponnesus peninsula, when Coroebus
emerged the victor in a foot race against competitors whose names
are lost to history.   The Games in which he participated had been
preceded by others which were local in nature.   In 776 B. C. the
Games became international and attracted athletes from distant cities.

At first the agenda included only foot racing and wrestling,
with the Spartans generally the winners.   In the seventh century
B. C. such events as chariot racing and single horse feats were
added.   The Spartans later withdrew from competition, probably because the control of the Games had passed to Pheidon, tyrant of
Argos, who was a sworn enemy of Sparta.

The program was expanded further in 472 B. C.   The length
of time assigned to the Games was increased to five days, with
the first being devoted to the religious aspects of the festival.   Following this such events as the pentathlon, chariot and horse races
were featured.   On the third day the younger boys entered into competition with each other, and on the fourth day grown men boxed,
wrestled, ran, jumped and engaged in a foot race while wearing arm-
or.   The fifth and last day was given over to sacrifices to the gods
in the morning and an evening feast at which the winners were presented with wreaths of wild olive leaves.

Competition was open to all persons who cared to enter and

who spoke the Greek language.   Consequently, contestants and spectators came from all parts of the ancient world.   During the season of the Games a general truce was proclaimed and travelers
were guaranteed safe passage from and to their homes.

The Olympic Games served as a model for other festivals,
such as the Pythian Games (582 B. C.), inaugurated at Delphi; the
Isthmian Games (581 B. C.), established at Corinth; and the Nemean
Games (573 B. C.), held at Nemea.   These were, like the Olympic
Games, a combination of religious festival and athletics.

Suggested Readings

Bushnell, A. S., ed.   United States Olympic Book.   New York:
    United States Olympic Committee, 1964.
Gardiner, E. Norman.   Greek Athletic Sports and Festival.   Lon-
    don: Macmillan, 1910.
_____.   History and Remains of Olympia.   Oxford: Clarendon
    Press, 1925.
Hamerton, J. A., ed.   "Olympia and Its Sacred Games" in his Won-
    ders of the Past: The Romance of Antiquity and Its Splendours,
    Vol. IV.   New York: William H. Wise, 1933.
Harris, H. A.   Greek Athletes and Athletics.   London: Hutchinson,
    1964.
Jaeger, Werner.   "The Aristocracy: Conflict and Transformation"
    in Paideia, the Ideals of Greek Culture.   Oxford: Basil Black-
    well, 1947.
Kaneko, Akitomo.   Olympic Gymnastics.   New York: Sterling Pub-
    lishing Co., 1976.
Kieran, John, and Arthur Daley.   The Story of the Olympic Games,
    776 B. C to 1968.   Revised edition.   Philadelphia: Lippincott,
    1969.
Lattimore, Richard.   The Odes of Pindar.   Chicago: University of
    Chicago Press, 1947.
McKay, Jim.   My Wide World.   New York: Macmillan, 1973.
Mandell, Richard D.   Nazi Olympics.   New York: Macmillan, 1971.
Robinson, R. S.   Sources for the History of Greek Athletics.   Ur-
    bana, Ill. :   University of Illinois Press, 1955.

THE ORIGINATION OF COINAGE (c. 650 B. C.)

With the invention of coinage somewhere in Lydia, Asia Minor, about 650 B. C., man overcame one of the greatest obstacles
to the development of commerce and industry.   Coins, issued by
the authority of government for use as money, made it possible to
avoid the cumbersome and inconvenient barter system.

Prior to the coinage of money, trading had been accomplished
by the exchange of goods in bulk or by the use of gold and silver,

in bar or granular form, in the settling of accounts.   Transactions
of these types were often unsatisfactory.   For example, a man who
had grain to dispose of might be offered clay pottery in trade.   He
had the choice of accepting the pottery without knowing where he
might sell it or else keeping his grain.   If he were offered gold
or silver he had no way of ascertaining the purity of the metal and
hence its value.   Governments experienced difficulties when paying
soldiers and civil employees.   Roman legionnaires were paid for
their services in salt which the legionnaire had to trade for other
goods he needed as best he could.

    The invention of coinage, or minting, offered a solution to
these problems.   Coins were identical pieces of precious metal
whose weight and purity were guaranteed by the authority which issued them.

    For several centuries Greece and other city-states issued a
great variety of coins.   This lack of standardization made it difficult for merchants and others to carry on commercial dealings
without the aid of money changers.   These men depended on their
knowledge of the metallic purity of the various coins in which they
trafficked and weighed them carefully to forestall the acceptance of
clipped and counterfeit money.   Under the Roman empire this multiplicity was ended and the standardization of sizes, weights and
values of coins was established through the forbidding of unauthorized private minting.

    Coins were struck rather than cast.   A pair of dies were
made from metal harder than that from which the coins were to be
produced.   The obverse die was placed in a hole in a heavy iron
block in which it fit tightly.   The blank, a piece of metal, heated
and carefully weighed, was placed on top of the obverse die
and the reverse die was then inserted in the hole.   The three
layers of metal were then struck with a hammer, producing a
coin which was stamped on both sides with the appropriate inscriptions.

    The first metals used for minting coins were silver and elec-
trum, the latter an amber colored alloy of gold and silver.   At
first gold alone was seldom used for coinage, except to compensate
for a shortage of silver.   Later it was used more frequently, especially in Persia and Rome.   Bronze became a coin metal about
the fourth century B. C., being used in place of silver for minor
coins of lesser value.

    Today it would be impossible to conduct business without
coins, "paper money" and the various negotiable instruments which
evolved from them.   Money today as well as in ancient times represents three things: a medium of exchange, a store of purchasing
power and a measure of value.   By the end of the third century
B. C. coins were being minted and circulated throughout the ancient
world.

Suggested Readings

Angell, N. The Story of Money. New York: Stokes, 1929.
Bolkenstein, H. Economic Life in Greece's Golden Age. Leiden:
    E. J. Brill, 1958.
Capen, Louise I. Across the Ages. New York: American Book
    Co. , 1940.
Coulborn, W. A. L. An Introduction to Money. London: Longmans,
    Green, 1938.
Halm, G. N. Monetary Theory. Philadelphia: Blakiston, 1946.
Head, Barclay V. Historia Numorum. Oxford: Clarendon Press,
    1911.
Jevons, W. Stanley. Money and the Mechanism of Exchange. New
    York: Appleton, 1883.
Kraay, Colin M. , and Max Hirmer. Greek Coins. London: Thames
    and Hudson, 1967.
_____, and Vera M. Emeleus. The Composition of Greek Silver
    Coins. Oxford: Ashmolean Museum, 1962.
Mattingly, Harold B. Roman Coins. London: Methuen, 1960.
Michell, Humfrey. The Economics of Ancient Greece. Cambridge:
    The University Press, 1940.
Reed, H. L. Money, Currency, and Banking. New York: McGraw-
    Hill, 1942.
Robertson, D. H. Money. New York: Harcourt, Brace, 1929.
Seltman, Charles. Greek Coins. London: Methuen, 1955.

THE DRACONIAN CODE (621-620 B. C.)

Draco was a semi-mythical Athenian lawgiver of the 7th century B. C. According to Greek tradition he drew up the first code of law for the Athenians in 621 or 620 B. C. Much conflicting evidence concerning him and the laws he codified and wrote down exists, although both are mentioned in a number of sources.

Prior to Draco the laws had been interpreted and administered arbitrarily by aristocratic magistrates. Draco's code became famous for its harshness, with death the penalty for almost all crimes. Aristotle, in his Rhetoric, said that "they are not the laws of a man but of a 'snake,' so severe are they. "

According to some sources, Draco's legislation appeared to cover, in addition to homicide, such crimes as adultery, theft, vagrancy, neglect of the gods, the corruption of youth and violation of the oath taken by jurors. Draco's laws regarding homicide recognized the responsibility of the state, not the victim's family, in punishing the murderer. Thus, blood feuds were to be avoided.

Draco did not change the constitution or initiate new legislation. Rather, he reduced customary law to an orderly and usable form in writing.

The severity of Draco's laws became legendary in terms of the "greatness and severity of their penalties. " Plutarch, in his life of Solon, reports that the latter repealed these laws (in the 6th century B. C.) because, with the exception of homicide, they prescribed punishments regarded as too severe. "Idleness or stealing a cabbage or an apple were capital offenses as serious as sacrilege or murder, " and it was contended that Draco's laws "were written, not in ink, but in blood. " When asked why he assigned the death penalty for most crimes, Draco replied, "Small ones deserve that, and I have no higher for the greater crimes. "

Suggested Readings

Adcock, F. E. "Draco" in Cambridge Ancient History. New York: Macmillan, 1930.

Bohannan, Paul, ed. Law and Warfare: Studies in the Anthropology of Conflict. Garden City, N. Y. : Natural History Press, 1967.

Bonner, Robert J. , and Gertrude Smith. The Administration of Justice from Homer to Aristotle. Chicago: University of Chicago Press, 1930-1938.

Bromberg, Walter, M. D. "The Graeco-Roman Codes" in his Crime and the Mind. New York: Macmillan, 1965.

Davis, William Stearns. A Day in Old Athens: A Picture of Athenian Life. Boston: Allyn and Bacon, 1914.

Greenidge, A. H. J. A Handbook of Greek Constitutional History. New York: Macmillan, 1896.

Hignett, C. H. History of the Athenian Constitution to the End of the Fifth Century B. C. Oxford: Clarendon Press, 1952.

Jones, J. Walter. The Law and Legal Theory of the Greeks: An Introduction. Oxford: Clarendon Press, 1956.

Linforth, Ivan M. Solon the Athenian. Berkeley, Calif. : University of California Press, 1949.

Plutarch. Parallel Lives of the Noble Greeks and Romans. Translated with an introduction by Bernadotte Perrin. New York: Crowell, 1914-1928 (Originally written c. 105-115 A. D.).

Stroud, Ronald Sidney. The Law of Drakon on Homicide (Ph. D. dissertation, University of California, 1965).

Tod, Marcus N. A Selection of Greek Historical Inscriptions to the End of the Fifth Century B. C. Oxford: Clarendon Press, 1946.

Webster, Thomas Bertram Lonsdale. Everyday Life in Classical Athens. New York: Putnam, 1969.

Woodhouse, William J. Solon the Liberator. New York: Octagon Books, 1965.

THE FALL OF BABYLON TO THE PERSIANS (539 B. C.)

Babylon was a city in ancient Mesopotamia located beside the

Euphrates River just north of modern Hilla and about 55 miles
south of modern Baghdad in Central Iraq.   It probably came into
existence around 3000 B. C. , reaching its zenith under Hammurabi
about 1750 B. C.   It became the most important commercial center
of the Tigris-Euphrates Valley.

After the fall of Nineveh (612 B. C.) Babylon became the capital of a new dynasty of Chaldean rulers, beginning with Nabopolas-
sar who was followed by Nebuchadrezzar (or ... nezzar).   The latter enlarged and beautified Babylon and other cities as his part in
a religious revival.   He created the famous Hanging Gardens for
a Median princess who became his wife.   He also designed and installed an effective system of military defenses.

In 556 B. C. Nabonidus, an official "not directly of royal
descent, " was crowned king.   He was more interested in archaeology and religion than in affairs of state and was absent from Babylon on expeditions to Syria and Arabia much of the time.   During
his absences his son Belshazzar ruled in his place.

When Nabonidus sought to rebuild a temple to the god Sin in
Harran, Northern Mesopotamia, he sought military aid from Cyrus,
the ruler of Persia, Harran then being held by the Medes.   With
Babylonian support Cyrus conquered the Medes and then marched
westward, there to capture territory formerly ruled by Nebuchadrezzar.   Other military expeditions were equally successful, and
by 540 B. C. only Babylon remained unconquered.

Nabonidus returned to Babylon to defend his kingdom.   He
lacked sufficient soldiers to man all the fortifications built by Nebuchadrezzar and so concentrated on a smaller area, putting Belshazzar in command of part of his army.

Cyrus had gained the admiration and respect of some of the
residents of Babylon.   In October, 539 B. C. , with the aid of a
fifth column composed of his Babylonian admirers, he breached the
Chaldean defenses.   A battle was fought in which Belshazzar was
killed.   Within a few days the forces of Nabonidus were defeated
and he, the last independent King of Babylon, fled.

Legend has it that Cyrus diverted the Euphrates River into
an old floodway, allowing his army to enter the city through a dry
river bed.   Another source states that "the army of Cyrus entered
Babylon without a battle" and was greeted with cheers by many of
the citizens.

The Chaldean dynasty was defeated but Babylon remained a
cultural and economic center until the time of Alexander the Great,
who planned to make it the capital of his eastern empire.   After
Alexander's death in 323 B. C. it gradually lost importance.

Suggested Readings

Albright, William F. From the Stone Age to Christianity. Balti-
   more: Johns Hopkins University Press, 1957.
Betten, Francis S. The Ancient World, from the Earliest Times
   to 800 A. D. Boston: Allyn and Bacon, 1916.
Daugherty, Raymond P. Nabonidus and Belshazzar. New Haven,
   Conn. : Yale University Press, 1929.
Finegan, Jack. Light from the Ancient Past. Princeton, N. J. :
   Princeton University Press, 1949.
Frankfort, Henri. The Birth of Civilization in the Near East.
   Bloomington, Ind. : Indiana University Press, 1951.
Gadd, Cyril J. Hammurabi and the End of His Dynasty. Cam-
   bridge: The University Press, 1965.
_____. The History and Monuments of Ur. Cambridge: The
   University Press, 1929.
Herodotus. The Histories. Translated by A. de Setincourt. Bal-
   timore: Penguin Books, 1954.
_____. The Persian Wars. Translated by G. Rawlinson. New
   York: Random House, 1942.
Lamb, Harold. Cyrus the Great. New York: Ramdom House,
   1960.
Olmstead, Albert T. History of the Persian Empire. Chicago:
   University of Chicago Press, 1948.
Oppenheim, Adolph Leo. Ancient Mesopotamia. Chicago: Univer-
   sity of Chicago Press, 1964.
Pritchard, James B. , ed. The Ancient Near East: An Anthology
   of Texts and Pictures. Princeton, N. J. : Princeton University
   Press, 1958.
_____. Ancient Near Eastern Texts Relating to the Old Testa-
   ment. Princeton, N. J. : Princeton University Press, 1950-
   1955.
Renault, Mary. Lion in the Gateway: The Heroic Battles of the
   Greeks and Persians at Marathon, Salamis and Thermopylae.
   Edited by Walter Lord. New York: Harper, 1964.
Rogers, Robert W. A History of Babylonia and Assyria. New
   York: Abingdon Press, 1915.
Roux, Georges. Ancient Iraq. Cleveland: World, 1964-1965.
Saggs, Henry W. F. The Greatness That Was Babylon. New York:
   Hawthorn Books, 1962.
Wohil, Howard. "A Note on the Fall of Babylon, " Journal of the
   Ancient Near Eastern Society of Columbia University, Spring,
   1969.

THE PERSIAN INVASION OF GREECE (480-479 B. C.)

   The information we have concerning the invasion of Greece
by the Persian king Xerxes I in 480-479 B. C. comes down to us
from History of the Persian Wars, written by the Greek historian
Herodotus who flourished in the 5th century B. C. This writing is

divided into nine books. The first five tell the story of Cyrus
(560-529 B. C.) and the founding of the Persian Empire. Books
six to nine give the history of the repeated Persian attacks upon
Greece proper, led by Darius I and his son, Xerxes. They describe the defeats of the Persians at Marathon, the battles of Thermopylae and Salamis and the final Persian defeats at Plataea and
Mycale.

The Persian Empire was founded by Cyrus, surnamed The
Great. Before his death in battle in 529 B. C. he had succeeded
in bringing the Greek Ionian states under Persian control. He was
succeeded as King of Persia by Darius I and the Greeks, resenting
the loss of their sovereighty, rebelled. This attempt was unsuccessful and by 493 B. C. Darius had reimposed Persian authority
on the Greeks. He then decided to punish the Ionian cities and
their allies in the revolt but his first and second attempts failed,
his fleet being destroyed in a storm in 492 B. C. and his army suffering a stinging defeat at Marathon, in Attica, two years later.

Darius planned a third attack but died in 486 B. C. before
this could be inaugurated. His son Xerxes, who succeeded him on
the Persian throne, set about carrying out his father's plans. In
480 B. C. a Persian force of more than 100,000 soldiers and a
fleet of 600 war galleys was assembled. The Greeks and their allies, in turn, brought a defending army together and it was decided
to fight under the leadership of Spartan officers. In August the
Persians met the Greeks at Thermopylae where the Greeks held a
narrow pass with a comparatively small detachment of infantry led
by the Spartan king Leonidas. According to Herodotus' account,
Leonidas and his men were able to hold the Persian horde at bay
for three days. Then the Persians marched around the pass through
the hills and attacked the Greeks from the rear. Leonidas and his
men were cut off and all died fighting.

The Greek fleet of about 600 vessels then retreated and
anchored off the island of Salamis. The Persian naval force attacked and by the end of the day the Greeks overwhelmed their enemies. Losing the Battle of Salamis caused Xerxes to withdraw a
portion of his men to Attica, leaving the rest to spend the winter
in Boeotia. The Battle of Plataea, a land engagement fought in
the spring of 479 B. C. , ended in another victory for the Greeks,
led by the Spartan regent Pausanias. Simultaneously the Greek
navy sought out and defeated the Persian ships off the island of
Mycale. This victory ended the Persian attempts to invade Greece,
although it did not end the wars between the two. By 477 B. C.
most of Ionia was freed of Persian rule and Athens rose to a position of great military importance.

Suggested Readings

Albright, William F. From the Stone Age to Christianity. Balti-
     more: Johns Hopkins University Press, 1957.

Betten, Francis S. The Ancient World, from the Earliest Times
    to 800 A.D. Boston: Allyn and Bacon, 1916.
Burn, A.R. Persia and the Greeks. New York: St. Martin's
    Press, 1962.
Cross, E.A. "Herodotus: History of the Persian Wars; Leonidas
    at Thermopylae" in his World Literature. New York: Amer-
    ican Book Company, 1935.
Elson, Henry W. Modern Times and the Living Past. New York:
    American Book Company, 1935
Frankfort, Henri. The Birth of Civilization in the Near East.
    Bloomington, Ind.: Indiana University Press, 1951.
Herodotus. The Histories. Translated by A. de Setincourt. Bal-
    timore: Penguin Books, 1954.
_____. The Persian Wars. Translated by G. Rawlinson. New
    York: Random House, 1942.
Hignett, C.H. Xerxes' Invasion of Greece. Oxford: Clarendon
    Press, 1963.
How, W.W., and J.A. Wells. A Commentary on Herodotus. Ox-
    ford: Clarendon Press, 1912.
Lamb, Harold. Cyrus the Great. New York: Random House, 1960.
Olmstead, Albert T. History of the Persian Empire. Chicago:
    University of Chicago Press, 1948.
Renault, Mary. Lion in the Gateway: The Heroic Battles of the
    Greeks and Persians at Marathon, Salamis and Thermopylae.
    Edited by Walter Lord. New York: Harper, 1964.
Thucydides. The Peloponnesian Wars. Translated by Benjamin
    Jowett; revised and abridged with an introduction by P.A. Brunt.
    New York: Twayne, 1963.

THE ANALECTS OF CONFUCIUS (c. 470 B.C.)

        Confucius (c. 551-479 B.C.), a Chinese philosopher, devel-
oped a major system of thought which is still taught today, particularly in the Orient. He may not have put all the principles of
his philosophy into writing and the Analects of Confucius, a collection of maxims which form the basis of his moral and political
philosophy, were possibly written in part by him in his old age and
published by his disciples following his death. These constitute one
of the most important of the Chinese classics.

        The principles of Confucianism are found in nine ancient
Chinese works handed down by Confucius and his followers. These
are divided into two groups: the Five Classics and the Four Books,
the Analects being one of the latter.

        The Five Classics originated long before the time of Confu-
cius and include the following titles. (1) The Classic of Changes
is a manual of divination, which was probably compiled prior to the
11th century B.C. and to which supplements were added by Confucius and his disciples. (2) The Classic of History comprises a col-

lection of ancient historical documents.   (3) The Classic of Poetry
is an anthology of ancient poems.   (4) The Classic of Rites, which
was destroyed in the 3rd century B. C. , was concerned with principles of conduct to be observed at public and private ceremonies.
The Record of Rites, assembled after the loss of the Classic of
Rites, contains much of the information which originally appeared
in its predecessor.   (5) The last of the Five Classics is the Spring
and Summer Annals, reputedly compiled and edited by Confucius
himself.   It is a history of events in the Chinese state of Lu beginning about 700 B. C. and continuing into the reign of Confucius'
contemporary, Duke Ai.

The Four Books are compilations of the sayings of Confucius
and commentaries by his disciples.   These consist of the Analects,
the Great Learning, the Doctrine of the Mean and the Book of Men-
cius.   This last contains the teachings of one of Confucius' followers who carried the latter's work on after his death.

Confucius regarded himself as "a transmitter, not an orig-
inator. "   His works consist primarily of comments on the Chinese
classics and many disciples have added much to the Confucian literature.   He is especially remembered for his apothegms.   His
teachings were practical and ethical rather than religious.   He advocated reverence for parents and held that "proper outward acts
based on the five virtues of kindness, uprightness, decorum, wisdom and faithfulness comprise the whole duty of man. "   He regarded government as paternalistic and he advised each individual
to observe his duties toward the state.

In the centuries following his death the influence of his teachings was so great that "they practically molded the Chinese nation. "

Suggested Readings

Chang, Chi-yun.   A Life of Confucius.   Translated by Shib Chao-
      yin.   Taipei: China Culture Publishing Foundation, 1954.
Creel, H. G.   Chinese Thought from Confucius to Mao Tse-tung.
      New York: New American Library, 1951.
_____.   Confucius, the Man and the Myth.   New York: John
      Day, 1949.
Dawson, M. M.   The Conduct of Life: The Basic Thoughts of Con-
      fucius.   New York: Garden City Publishing Co. , 1942.
Doeblin, Alfred.   The Living Thoughts of Confucius.   New York:
      Longmans, Green, 1940.
Kaizuka, Shigeki.   Confucius.   Translated by Geoffrey Bownas.
      London: George Allen & Unwin, 1956.
Kelen, Betty.   Confucius in Life and Legend.   New York: Thomas
      Nelson, 1971.
Waley, Arthur.   Three Ways of Thought in Ancient China.   Garden
      City, N. Y. :   Doubleday, n. d.
Ware, James R.   The Sayings of Confucius.   New York: New Amer-
      ican Library, 1955.

Wilhelm, Richard. <u>Confucius and Confucianism.</u> Translated by
    George H. Danton and Annina Periam Danton. New York:
    Harcourt, Brace, 1931.

THE DEATH OF SOCRATES (399 B. C.)

    Socrates, a Greek philosopher and teacher, was born in Ath-
ens, the son of a sculptor. As a young man he received the regular elementary education in literature, music and gymnastics, and
later rhetoric and dialectics of the Sophists. He may have followed
his father's profession for a time, although there is no proof of it.
He did serve with distinction as an infantryman in the Athenian
army, but is remembered as a man who spent his time "walking
in the Agora or sitting in some quiet place talking to those who
came to him to learn." He was not a writer and what is known
of him today comes from the reports of two of his pupils and admirers, Plato and Xenophon.

    His disciples, largely wealthy young Athenians, were en-
couraged to discover the truth. He questioned them, insisting on
accurate definitions of terms, clear thinking and exact analysis.
He precipitated dialogues by means of questions and answers. He
did not believe in the form of democratic government then existing
in Athens and made fun of its pretenses. Because he did not lead
his pupils to the temples of the gods he was charged with impiety
and misleading the young men of the city. Brought before an Athenian popular jury of 500, chosen alphabetically, he was found
guilty by a small majority and condemned to drink the poisonous
hemlock. Although he could have appealed and won over a majority to set him free he did not do so. His friends contrived a way
for him to escape from prison but he declined to go.

    On his last day of life Socrates' friends gathered at the
prison to await the end. He said, "Be of good cheer, and say that
you are burying my body only." He then bathed. At sunset the
jailer appeared and apologized for what he had to do: require the
prisoner to drink the cup of hemlock.

    Crito, one of the friends who had come to bid Socrates good-
bye, urged him to delay the drinking of the poison. Socrates replied that he had nothing to gain by extending a life already gone,
and asked that the hemlock be brought to him. The jailer handed
him the cup and, in reply to Socrates' question as to the best way
to proceed, suggested that he drink the poison and then walk "until
your legs are heavy. Then lie down and the poison will act." After a short, silent prayer to his god, Socrates drained the cup.

    Although his friends Crito and Apollodorus broke into tears,
Socrates remained calm and counseled patience and forebearance.
His legs became heavy and he lay down. Gradually paralysis

set in, starting at the feet and extending gradually to the heart.
The dying man requested Crito to discharge a debt for him: a cock
he owed to Asclepius.   Crito said, "The debt shall be paid.   Is
there anything else?"

Socrates did not answer.   He was dead.

Suggested Readings

Anderson, Maxwell. Barefoot in Athens (play). New York: Sloane,
    1951.
_____. "Barefoot in Athens" (play condensation) in Mantle,
    Burns, ed. The Best Plays of 1951-1952. New York: Dodd,
    Mead, 1952.
Aymer, Brandt, and Edward Sagarin.   "Socrates" in their A Pic-
    torial History of the World's Great Trials. New York: Crown
    Publishers, 1967.
Church, F. J. The Trial and Death of Socrates: Being the Euthy-
    phron, Apology, Crito and Phaedo of Plato. London: Mac-
    millan, 1880.
Cornford, Francis Macdonald. Before and After Socrates. Cam-
    bridge: The University Press, 1932.
Cross, E. A. "Plato" and "Socrates" in his World Literature.
    New York: American Book Co. , 1935.
Grote, George. Life, Teachings and Death of Socrates. New York:
    Stanford & Delisser, 1858.
Hagedorn, Hermann. "Socrates" in his The Book of Courage. Phil-
    adelphia: Winston, 1920.
Hammond, Nicholas Geoffrey Lemprière. A History of Greece to
    322 B. C. Oxford: Clarendon Press, 1959.
Hopkinson, Leslie White. "Socrates" in his Greek Leaders. Bos-
    ton: Houghton Mifflin, 1918.
Jaeger, Werner. "The Memory of Socrates" in his Paideia, the
    Ideals of Greek Culture. Oxford: Basil Blackwell, 1947.
Levin, Richard, ed. The Question of Socrates. New York: Har-
    court, Brace, 1961.
McKown, Robin. "Socrates" in his Seven Famous Trials in History.
    New York: Vanguard Press, 1963.
Phillipson, Coleman. The Trial of Socrates. London: Stevens &
    Sons, 1928.
Plato. Collected Works: The Apology of Socrates, Phaedo, Crito.
    A Version by Henry Cary. London: George Bell & Sons, 1890.
_____. "Crito: Socrates in Prison"; "Phaedo: The Last Day
    of Socrates' Life"; and "The Symposium: The Character of
    Socrates" in his The Works of Plato. Translated into English
    with Analysis and Introduction by B. Jowett, M. A. New York:
    Dial Press, 1936.
_____. Socrates: A Translation of the Apology, Crito and Parts
    of the Phaedo. Edited by W. W. Godwin. New York: Scrib-
    ner's, 1878.
Robinson, C. E. The Days of Alkibiades. New York: Longmans,
    Green, 1916.

Spiegelberg, Herbert, and B. Q. Moran, eds. The Socratic Enigma.
    Indianapolis: Bobbs-Merrill, 1964.
Tappan, Eva March.   "Two Philosophers, Socrates and Plato"
    in her Old World Hero Stories.   Boston: Houghton Mifflin,
    1937.
Taylor, A. E. Socrates.   London: Davies, 1932.
Versenyi, Laszlo. Socratic Humanism.   New Haven, Conn. : Yale
    University Press, 1963.
Winspear, Alan D. , and Tom Silverberg.   Who Was Socrates? New
    York: Russell & Russell, 1960.

ARISTOTLE AND THE SYLLOGISM (335-323 B. C.)

        The syllogism is Aristotle's greatest, but by no means his
only, contribution to logic.   It is his technical formulation of the
procedure which, he felt, is always followed in demonstrative, as
distinct from intuitive, reasoning.   It is a set of three propositions.
Two of these are called premises because they contain a common
term, and the third proposition, the conclusion, constructs a new
proposition out of the two terms not common to the premises.   An
example follows:

        All men are mortal.   (Major premise)
        John is a man.   (Minor premise)
        John is mortal   (Conclusion)

        Aristotle, a Greek philosopher and teacher, wrote copiously,
many of his treatises consisting of lectures delivered to his disciples in the school (the Lyceum) at Athens.   He was concerned
with logic, metaphysics, natural science, ethics and politics.   His
writings on logic, edited by Theophrastus, one of his pupils, were
given the title Organon.   This consisted of the Categories, Topics,
Sophistical Refutations, On Interpretation, Prior Analytics and Pos-
terior Analytics.   The theory of the syllogism is developed in Pri-
or Analytics, where the term is defined in Aristotle's own words.
It is mentioned in Topics as well.

        After defining the term, Aristotle proceeds to analyze in de-
tail the forms that the terms and premises must have in order to
yield a conclusion that is valid.   As set down by Aristotle, the
laws of reasoning are threefold: the law of identity, the law of con-
tradiction and the law of excluded middle.   In the first, A is always the same as A.   In the second, A cannot be both A and not-B.
In the third A must be either B or not-B.

        Aristotle was concerned almost entirely with deductive logic,
which progresses from the general to the particular and the establishment of this form of syllogistic reasoning was applied to Euclidean geometry.   Inductive reasoning, developed largely by Sir Francis Bacon and later by John Stuart Mill, is the reverse of deduc-

tive reasoning in that it involves progressing from the particular
to the general. Although furnishing a high degree of probability
inductive reasoning lacks the certitude of the deductive process.

Some authorities question Aristotle's claim to complete orig-
inality in the field of forms of argument. They contend that at
least a portion of his ideas was based on the teachings of the Greek
philosopher Plato, whose student he was. However, it is generally
agreed that Aristotle was the first man to study the forms of argument systematically and analyze such forms in terms of their rules
and structure.

Suggested Readings

Bochenski, Innocenty M.   A History of Formal Logic.   Notre Dame,
    Ind. : Notre Dame University Press, 1961.
Boole, George.   An Investigation of the Laws of Thought.   Glou-
    cester, Mass. : Peter Smith, 1966 (Originally published 1854).
Carnap, Rudolph.   Introduction to Symbolic Logic and Its Applica-
    tions.   New York: Dover, 1958.
Chase, Stuart.   Guides to Straight Thinking: With Thirteen Falla-
    cies.   New York: Harper, 1956.
Church, Alonzo.   Introduction to Mathematical Logic.   Princeton,
    N. J. : Princeton University Press, 1956.
Cohen, Morris R. , and Ernest Nagel.   Logic and the Scientific
    Method.   New York: Harcourt, Brace, 1934.
Copi, Irving.   Introduction to Logic.   New York: Macmillan, 1968.
Eaton, Ralph.   General Logic.   New York: Scribner, 1931.
Ehlers, Henry J.   Logic: Modern and Traditional.   Columbus,
    Ohio: Merrill, 1976.
Enriques, F.   The Historic Development of Logic.   Translated by
    J. Rosenthal.   New York: Holt, 1929.
Ferguson, John.   Aristotle.   New York: Twayne, 1972.
James, William.   The Meaning of Truth: A Sequel to Pragmatism.
    Ann Arbor, Mich. : University of Michigan Press, 1970.   (Or-
    iginally published 1909).
_____ .   Pragmatism: A New Name for Some Old Ways of Think-
    ing.   Edited by Frederick Burkhardt, et al.   Cambridge, Mass. :
    Harvard University Press, 1976 (Originally published 1907).
Kneale, William, and Martha Kneale.   The Development of Logic.
    Oxford: The University Press, 1962.
Kyburg, Henry.   Probability and Inductive Logic.   New York: Mac-
    millan, 1970.
Lloyd, G. E. R.   Aristotle: The Growth and Structure of His Thought.
    Cambridge: The University Press, 1968.
Lukasiewicz, Jan.   Aristotle's Syllogistic from the Standpoint of
    Modern Formal Logic.   2nd edition.   Oxford: The University
    Press, 1957.
Mates, Benson.   Stoic Logic.   Berkeley, Calif. : University of
    California Press, 1961.
Patzig, Gunther.   Aristotle's Theory of the Syllogism.   New York:
    Humanities Press, 1968.

Quine, Willard Van Orman. Mathematical Logic. Cambridge,
    Mass.: Harvard University Press, 1947.
Randall, John R.   Aristotle.   New York: Columbia University
    Press, 1960.
Robinson, Daniel Sommer.   The Principles of Reasoning.   New
    York: Appleton-Century-Crofts, 1947.
Robinson, James Harvey.   The Mind in the Making.   Revised edi-
    tion. New York: Harper, 1950.
Rose, Lynn C.   Aristotle's Syllogistic.   Springfield, Ill.: Thomas,
    1968.
Ross, David.   Aristotle.   New York: Barnes & Noble, 1966.
Salmon, Wesley C.   Logic.   Englewood Cliffs, N. J.: Prentice-
    Hall, 1963.
Schiller, F. C. S.   Formal Logic.   London: Macmillan, 1931.
Solmsen, Friedrich.   "Dialectic Without the Forms" in Owen, G. E.
    L., ed. Aristotle on Dialectic.   London: Oxford University
    Press, 1968.
Tarski, Alfred.   Introduction to Logic and to the Methodology of
    Deductive Science.   Oxford: Oxford University Press, 1965.

THE FOUNDING OF ALEXANDRIA (331 B. C.)

Alexander the Great (356-323 B. C.), King of Macedon and
considered one of the greatest generals of ancient times, took
Egypt from the Persians in 332 B. C. He planned to make it a province of his own and, with this in mind, set about establishing a
new Hellenic city which would become its capital. This was to be
named Alexandria, in honor of himself.

A site was chosen on the coast, on the western edge of the
Nile delta where Racondah had existed as a fishing village as early
as 1500 B. C.   Dinocrates, a famous architect, prepared the original plans.   The work began in 331 B. C. and construction took several years to complete, still proceeding during the reigns of Ptolemy I and Ptolemy II, Alexander's successors.   By 80 B. C., when
Alexandria passed officially under Roman jurisdiction, it had become the largest provincial capital of the Roman empire, with a
population of over 300,000.

As originally laid out, the city followed the grid pattern
developed in the fifth century B. C.   Two broad avenues divided it
into four quarters, with Canopus Street, a processional boulevard,
running east and west and bisected by a lesser street running north
and south.   The civic center was located at the intersection of the
two streets and included the court of justice, the gymnasium, a series of sacred groves and an artificial hill dedicated to the god Pan.

One quarter of the city was inhabited mostly by Egyptians
and half-caste Greeks and another quarter was occupied by Jews.

A third quarter near the waterfront constituted the Greco-Macedonian area and there warehouses and wharves were located. The royal quarter contained the monumental tomb of Alexander, the Serapeum, an imposing temple and the palace complex, Alexandrian Library, and museum. A stone lighthouse, designed by Sostratus of Cnidus, over 400 feet high, stood on the nearby island of Pharos. One of the seven wonders of the ancient world, it was connected with the city by a mole nearly three quarters of a mile long. In the third century B. C. the culture of Alexandria Surpassed that of Athens and such ancient scholars and poets as Aristophanes, Callimachus, Erasistratus and Philo lived and worked there.

Alexandria was occupied by Julius Caesar in 47 B. C. and was ruled by Mark Antony and Octavian. It was comparatively prosperous when, after a siege lasting fourteen months, it fell to the Arabs in 646 A. D. , following which it declined to little more than a relic of a glorious past.

Suggested Readings

Barker, Felix, in collaboration with Anthea Barker. "Alexander the Great" in their The First Explorers: Encyclopedia of Discovery and Exploration, Vol. 1. London: Aldus Books, 1971.
Cadoux, C. J. Ancient Smyrna: A History from the Earliest Times to 324 A. D. Oxford: Basil Blackwell, 1938.
Davis, Simon. Race Relations in Ancient Egypt. London: Methuen, 1951.
Downey, Glanville. A History of Antioch in Syria. Princeton, N. J.: Princeton University Press, 1961.
Hopkinson, Leslie White. "Alexander the Great" in his Greek Leaders. Boston: Houghton Mifflin, 1918.
Jones, A. H. M. The Greek City from Alexander to Justinian. Oxford: Clarendon Press, 1940.
Kenton, Frederic G. Books and Readers in Ancient Greece and Rome. Oxford: Clarendon Press, 1951.
Marrou, Henri I. A History of Education in Antiquity. Translated by G. Lamb. New York: Sheed & Ward, 1956.
Mercer, Charles E. , and the editors of Horizon Magazine. Alexander the Great. New York: American Heritage, 1963.
Myers, Philip van Ness. Ancient History. Boston: Ginn, 1904.
Parsons, Edward A. The Alexandrian Library. New York: Elsevier Press, 1952.
Sandys, Sir John Edwin. A History of Classical Scholarship, Vol. I. Cambridge: The University Press, 1903.
Tarn, W. W. Alexander the Great. Cambridge: The University Press, 1948.
_____. Hellenistic Military and Naval Developments. Cambridge: The University Press, 1930.
Wilcken, Ulrich. Alexander the Great. Translated by G. C. Richards. London: Chatto and Windus, 1932.

THE DEVELOPMENT OF GEOMETRY (c. 300 B. C.)

Geometry is the branch of mathematics which deals with the properties of space. Since earliest times men have found it necessary to solve problems involving such things as the measurement of land and the laying out of accurate right angles for the corners of buildings. Solutions to these problems were, of necessity, sought on an individual basis as no general laws of computation then existed.

In time it became obvious to certain mathematically-minded men that these complex problems could be solved by the application of general principles common to all of them. The type of empirical geometry which first flourished in ancient Egypt was systematized by the Greeks. Thales of Miletus, a Greek scientist and philosopher (c. 640-546 B. C.), is generally recognized as the founder of Greek geometry. Better known is Pythagoras (c. 582-c. 500 B. C.), the Greek mathematician and philosopher whose Pythagorean theorem is remembered by every school-child. Pythagoras pioneered in the systematization of geometry as did Hippocrates of Chios, Plato, Euxodus and, above all, Euclid.

Euclid, a Greek mathematician, flourished about 300 B. C. He made geometry a deductive science. His Elements, a comprehensive treatise on mathematics in thirteen volumes, was used as a textbook for over a thousand years and a modified version is used today in high school classes where plane geometry is taught. It is believed that Euclid, while making several original discoveries in the theory of numbers, consolidated and rearranged the work of earlier mathematicians.

Elements contains 465 propositions, each of which is proved by logical deductions. All geometrical laws are general statements, postulated absolutely rather than in terms of approximations. All terms are defined and all conclusions are logically established. Examples of the theorems proved by Euclid's deductive method are "the sum of the interior angles of any triangle is equal to the sum of two right angles, " and "the square of the hypotenuse of a right angle triangle equals the sum of the squares of the other two sides" (the Pythagorean theorem).

The first printed version of Euclid's works was a translation from the Arabic into Latin, made by Erhard Patdolt in 1482. Translations were also made by Bartolomeo Zamberti (1505), Commandinus (1572) and others.

Modern mathematicians have proven that certain general problems posed by the mathematicians of ancient Greece cannot be solved with the use of ruler and compass alone. Other unsolvable problems are the squaring of the circle, the duplication of the cube and the trisecting of the angle.

Suggested Readings

Barker, Stephen F. Philosophy of Mathematics. Englewood Cliffs, N. J. : Prentice-Hall, 1964.

Bell, E. T. The Development of Mathematics. New York: Mc-Graw-Hill, 1940.

_____. Men of Mathematics. New York: Simon & Schuster, 1937.

Cajori, Florian. A History of Mathematics. New York: Macmillan, 1922.

Coolidge, J. L. A History of Geometrical Methods. Oxford: Clarendon Press, 1940.

Courant, Richard, and Herbert Robbins. What Is Mathematics? London: Oxford University Press, 1941.

De Morgan, A. A Budget of Paradoxes. Chicago: Open Court, 1915.

Dickson, L. E. New First Course in the Theory of Equations. New York: Wiley, 1939.

Graustein, W. C. Introduction to Higher Geometry. New York: Macmillan, 1930.

Heath, Sir Thomas L. A History of Greek Mathematics. Oxford: Clarendon Press, 1960.

_____. The Thirteen Books of Euclid's Elements. New York: Dover, 1956.

_____, et al. "Hellenistic Science and Mathematics" in Cambridge Ancient History, Vol. II. Cambridge: The University Press, 1954.

_____. A Manual of Greek Mathematics. New York: Dover, 1963.

Hilbert, D. The Foundations of Geometry. 3rd edition. Translated by E. J. Townsend. La Salle, Ill. : Open Court, 1938.

Hobson, E. W. "Squaring the Circle, " a History of the Problem. Cambridge: The University Press, 1913.

Kempe, A. B. How to Draw a Straight Line. London: Macmillan, 1877.

Klein, N. F. Famous Problems in Geometry. Translated by W. W. Beman and D. E. Smith. New York: Stechert, 1930.

Mohr, D. Euclides Danicus. Copenhagen: Hølst, 1928.

O'Hara, C. W. , and D. R. Ward. An Introduction to Projective Geometry. Oxford: Clarendon Press, 1937.

Robinson, G. de B. The Foundations of Geometry. Toronto: University of Toronto Press, 1940.

Sanger, R. G. Synthetic Projective Geometry. New York: McGraw-Hill, 1939.

Scott, Joseph F. A History of Mathematics. London: Taylor and Francis, 1960.

Smith, David Eugene. A History of Mathematics. Boston: Ginn, 1923.

Veblen, O. , and J. W. Young. Projective Geometry. Boston: Ginn, 1910.

Young, J. W. Projective Geometry. Chicago: Open Court, 1930.

THE TECHNOLOGICAL AND MATHEMATICAL
DISCOVERIES OF ARCHIMEDES (c. 250 B. C.)

Archimedes (c. 287-212 B. C.), sometimes called "The Thomas Edison of Antiquity, " was a Greek inventor and mathematician.
Although best remembered for his technological discoveries and inventions he was also one of the greatest mathematicians of his day,
ranking with Euclid and Pythagoras.   His major contributions to
mathematics were in the field of geometry.

He was, according to tradition, born in Syracuse, although
this has not been established, very little being known of his early
life.   He was educated in Alexandria where he studied with the astronomers Eratosthenes and Conon of Samos.   The major portion
of his later years was spent in Sicily, in and around Syracuse.   So
far as is known he never held public office, preferring to devote
his life to experiments and research.

Archimedes' kinsman, Hiero II, Tyrant of Syracuse, was
his patron and many of the episodes of his life, some legendary,
are associated with this Greek ruler.   Archimedes is said to have
discovered the law of hydrostatics and applied it in a successful
effort to determine the actual gold content of Hiero's crown.   This
law, sometimes referred to as the "principle of Archimedes, " states
that a body surrounded by a fluid is buoyed up by a force equal to
the weight of the fluid it displaces.   The discovery of this law is
said to have been made when Archimedes was bathing and observed
the overflow of the water displaced by his body.   In his excitement
he ran naked through the streets shouting "Eureka!" (I have found
it!)

When Syracuse was besieged by the Romans in 213 B. C.
Archimedes made his various discoveries and inventions available
to the defending forces.   These included ballistic weapons, grap-
pling hooks, cranes, a system of ropes and pulleys for hauling
heavy ships into the water and other devices.   The use of large
mirrors designed to focus the sun's rays on enemy ships in order
to set them afire has been credited to him.   According to such historians as Polybius, Livy and Plutarch, he was a leader in the defense of Syracuse and his efforts were so successful that Marcus
Claudius Marcellus, the Roman general in command of the invading
forces, found his campaign stalemated for two years.

When Syracuse fell in 212 B. C. Archimedes was killed by
a Roman legionnaire, although Marcellus had issued strict orders
that he was to be captured alive.   It is said that the Syracusan
scientist was drawing a geometrical figure in the sand when the
Roman soldier found him.   He was so absorbed in his calculations
that his only remark to the intruder was "Do not disturb my dia-
grams. "

Archimedes wrote important works on arithmetic, mechanics

and plane and solid geometry.   In mechanics he discovered the
principle of the lever.   He invented a pump (the Archimedean
screw) consisting of a tube wound spirally around an inclined axis
which was used to raise water from a lower to a higher level.   He
invented and constructed a water organ and a model planetarium,
the latter being taken to Rome as booty by Marcellus.

In the field of pure mathematics Archimedes anticipated
many of the discoveries of modern science.   His work on plane
curves augmented Euclidean geometry and predicted integral calculus.   He also studied and wrote on conic sections, pure numbers, the sphere, the circle and other aspects of mathematics.

Suggested Readings

Barker, Stephen F.   Philosophy of Mathematics.   Englewood Cliffs,
    N. J. :   Prentice-Hall, 1964.
Bell, E. T.   Men of Mathematics.   New York: Simon & Schuster,
    1937.
Cajori, Florian.   A History of Mathematics.   New York: Macmil-
    lan, 1922.
Claggett, Marshall.   Archimedes in the Middle Ages.   Madison,
    Wis. :   University of Wisconsin Press, 1964.
_____.   Greek Science in Antiquity.   New York: Abelard-Schu-
    mann, 1955.
Coolidge, J. L.   A History of Geometrical Methods.   Oxford: Clar-
    endon Press, 1940.
Dijksterhuis, E. J.   "Archimedes" in Acta Historica Scientiarum
    Naturalium et Medicinalium, Vol. 12.   Translated by C. Dik-
    shoorn.   Copenhagen: Ejnar Munksgaard, 1956.
Farrington, Benjamin.   Greek Science.   Baltimore: Penguin Books,
    1961.
Heath, Sir Thomas L.   Archimedes.   New York: Macmillan, 1920.
_____.   A History of Greek Mathematics.   Oxford: Clarendon
    Press, 1960.
_____, et al.   "Hellenistic Science and Mathematics" in Cam-
    bridge Ancient History, Vol. II.   Cambridge: The University
    Press, 1954.
_____.   A Manual of Greek Mathematics.   New York: Dover,
    1963.
Hilbert, D.   The Foundations of Geometry.   3rd edition.   Transla-
    ted by E. J. Townsend.   La Salle, Ill. :   Open Court, 1938.
Plutarch.   Parallel Lives of the Noble Greeks and Romans.   Trans-
    lated with an introduction by Bernadotte Perrin.   New York:
    Crowell, 1914-1928 (Originally written c. 105-115 A. D.)
Robinson, G. de B.   The Foundations of Geometry.   Toronto: Uni-
    versity of Toronto Press, 1940.
Scott, Joseph F.   A History of Mathematics.   London: Taylor and
    Francis, 1960.
Smith, David Eugene.   A History of Mathematics.   Boston: Ginn,
    1923.
Ver Eecke, P.   Les Ouevres Completes d'Archimede.   Liege, 1960.

HANNIBAL'S CROSSING OF THE ALPS (218 B. C.)

In the third and second centuries B. C. Rome and Carthage engaged in three wars, known collectively as the Punic Wars. The first of these (264-241 B. C.) was the outcome of the growing political and economic rivalry between the two states and resulted in the cession of the Carthagenian port of Sicily to Rome.

Hamilcar Barca, a great Carthagenian general and father of Hannibal, devoted the remainder of his life to building Carthagenian power in Spain. Hannibal, at the age of nine, had vowed undying hatred of the Romans. When Hamilcar Barca was drowned in 228 B. C. his son-in-law Hasdrubal assumed command of his armies. Hasdrubal was assassinated in 221 B. C. and Hannibal, at 26, was unanimously voted commander-in-chief of the Carthagenian forces.

In 219 B. C. Hannibal, having built up his armies, attacked and, after a seven-month siege, captured Saguntum, a city in Eastern Spain which was allied to Rome. This brought on the Second Punic War.

With an army of 60,000 (some historians say 90,000) infantrymen, 12,000 horsemen and 37 elephants, Hannibal marched out of Cartagena, which had been founded by Hasdrubal, in the spring of 218 B. C. His plan was to invade Italy, proceeding across the Pyrenees, the Rhône River and through the Alps. The trip took five months.

The elephants which accompanied the Carthagenian forces added difficulty to the march. They were not suited for travel over high mountain passes but Hannibal considered them vital to the success of his expedition. As the "tanks of ancient warfare," they would, he knew, create panic among the Roman soldiers who would never have seen such beasts before.

Hannibal did not tell his troops that their destination was Italy. When they were about to cross the Pyrenees on the first leg of their journey they guessed the daunting prospect ahead and a mutiny developed. The young general left about 7,000 of his less reliable men behind and with the others passed over the Pyrenees into Southern Gaul. It would have been possible to make the trip by following the coast. Such a route would have been shorter and the Alpine passes could have been avoided. However, Massalia, a Greek colony which was allied to Rome, would have been encountered and Hannibal did not wish to risk a battle at this point. Instead, he marched his troops up the Rhône Valley west of Massalia.

In due course the Rhône River was crossed. It was necessary to ferry the elephants on rafts. The stream was comparatively shallow and some to the other animals were able to wade across. All made the crossing safely. The troops made the trip by boat or on horseback, the horses swimming or wading from bank to bank.

Polybius, a Greek historian, states that the crossing of the Alps took fifteen days. While he described each day's march he mentioned no place names and consequently the exact route the Carthagenian army took cannot be determined from his or any other records which have come down to us. Sir Gavin De Beer, a British historian, concludes that Hannibal took the southern pass over the Corde la Traversette, east of Gap.

Just before reaching the Alps Hannibal's forces were attacked by members of a hostile local tribe, whom they defeated. They then captured a town and were able to replenish their food supplies for both men and animals.

On their seventh day in the mountains another fight with local tribesmen occurred. Hannibal's army, though losing some men, again overcame the enemy and pressed on.

The eighth and ninth days found the Carthagenians in a snow-covered Alpine pass, 9,000 feet high. From this point the marching was all downhill but the ground was covered with snow and a single misstep could have resulted in a man or animal falling over a precipice to his death. At one point a landslide blocked their path and it was necessary to clear the snow and prepare a rough road. A huge boulder stood in their way. The men felled trees, cut them up, used the wood as fuel for a fire which was lit on top of the rock and then poured sour wine over it, making it friable and permitting it to be broken up with pick axes. The Carthagenians were then able to continue their descent to the plains of Italy.

Hannibal is reported to have lost 36,000 men between the time he crossed the Rhône River and the time he reached Italy. This seems an unusually high percentage of the total strength of his army and some authorities feel that the figure is overstated.

After recruiting additional men to compensate for those he had lost in transit due to snowstorms, landslides and the attacks of hostile mountain tribesmen, Hannibal won a series of victories over the Romans, culminating in the Battle of Cannae, fought in 216 B.C. Following this encounter he needed further reinforcements, which the Carthagenian government refused to furnish. He marched on but failed to take Naples. In 211 B.C. he made an unsuccessful attempt to conquer Rome. He lost Capua which he had originally taken from the Romans. His brother Hasdrubal (possibly the namesake of his late brother-in-law) who attempted to help him, was killed in the Battle of Metaurus River in 207 B.C.

In 202 B.C. Hannibal's troops were defeated by those of the Roman Scipio Africanus at Zama. Carthage capitulated to Rome, ending the Second Punic War. Fifty years later Carthage was completely destroyed. Hannibal, rather than surrender himself to the Romans, committed suicide by taking poison in 183 B.C.

Suggested Readings

Asimov, Isaac. The Roman Empire. Boston: Houghton Mifflin,
   1967.
Baker, G. P. Hannibal. New York: Dodd, Mead, 1929.
Barker, Felix, in collaboration with Anthea Barker. "Hannibal
   Crosses the Alps" and "Hannibal in the Alps" in their The
   First Explorers: Encyclopedia of Discovery and Exploration,
   Vol. I. London: Aldus Books, 1971.
Cottrell, Leonard. Hannibal: Enemy of Rome. New York: Holt,
   Rinehart, 1960.
De Beer, Gavin. Hannibal. New York: Viking Press, 1969.
Dodge, Thomas A. Hannibal. Boston: Houghton Mifflin, 1891.
Flaubert, Gustave. Salammbô (historical fiction). New York: Dut-
   ton, 1971 (Originally published 1862).
Hallward, B. L. "Scipio and Victory" in the Cambridge Ancient His-
   tory, Vol. 8. Cambridge: The University Press, 1928.
Hillyer, V. M. , and E. G. Huey. The Ancient World. New York:
   Meredith Press, 1966.
Liddell Hart, B. A. Greater Than Napoleon, Scipio Africanus.
   Edinburgh: Blackwood, 1926.
Livy. The War with Hannibal, Book XXI. Translated by Aubrey
   de Sélincourt. New York: Penguin Books, 1970.
Russell, Francis H. "The Battlefield of Zama," Archaeology, Ap-
   ril, 1970.
Scullard, Howard Hayes. Scipio Africanus: Soldier and Politician.
   Ithaca, N. Y. : Cornell University Press, 1970.
Sherwood, Robert E. The Road to Rome (play). New York: Scrib-
   ner's, 1928.
Warmington, B. H. Carthage. London: Robert Hall, 1960.

BUILDING THE GREAT WALL OF CHINA (204 B. C.)

The "Great Wall of China," completed in 204 B. C. , is considered the most famous of Emperor Ch'in Shih-huang-ti's achievements. It marks the northern boundary between China and the barbarian steppe.

Ch'in Shih-huang-ti was an extremely despotic ruler. Known
as the "First Emperor" and the "most hated man in China, " he believed in the legalist philosophy which, among other things, declared
the ruler of a state absolute.

For several centuries prior to the "First Emperor's" reign
Mongolian nomads to the north had raided settled lands and towns,
retreating to their own territory on swift horses before the slow-
moving Chinese foot soldiers could close with them. Ch'in Shih-
huang-ti had overcome the independent Chinese princes in 221 B. C.
and, advised by the legalist Li Ssu, resolved to construct a large
wall to keep the Mongolian raiding parties out of his kingdom and

also to keep his subjects in. The Wall, which took twelve years
to construct, stretched 2,000 miles east to west and was built on
shifting sand dunes and rock, and over mountains and deserts. Heavy
taxes were assessed to pay for it, and political and other prisoners were sentenced to labor there. It is said that the "Great
Wall of China was built with men's bones as bricks and men's
blood as mortar. " Most of the Wall was constructed by joining
together and strengthening older walls already in place. Military
garrisons were stationed behind the Wall and defensive watch towers were built every few hundred yards, so designed that archers
could fight off the attacks of enemy horsemen.

    Later Chinese emperors repaired and maintained the Wall
and it is still in existence today. At one section near Peking "a
troop of horsemen can ride abreast on the broad ramp between the
side walls. "

    The Great Wall of China was never really successful in
keeping barbarian invaders out of the country. On occasion they
would enter through less guarded points or go around one end. It
did, however, serve as a boundary to Chinese settlement.

Suggested Readings

Buck, Pearl S. China Past and Present. New York: Day, 1972.
Davis, F. Hadland. "The Great Wall of China" in Hamerton, J. A.,
    ed. Wonders of the Past: The Romance of Antiquity and Its
    Splendours. New York: William H. Wise, 1933.
Eberhard, Wolfram. A History of China. Translated by E. W.
    Dickes. Berkeley, Calif. : University of California Press,
    1960.
Fessler, Loren, and the editors of Life. China. New York: Time,
    Inc. , 1963.
Mitchison, Lois. China. New York: Walker, 1966.
Schafer, Edward H. , and the editors of Time-Life Books. Ancient
    China. New York: Time-Life, 1967.
Seeger, Elizabeth. Pageant of Chinese History. New York: Long-
    mans, Green, 1947.
Silverberg, Robert. Long Rampart: The Story of the Great Wall
    of China. Philadelphia: Chilton, 1966.
Spencer, Cornelia, pseud. Land of the Chinese People. Philadel-
    phia: Lippincott, 1945.
Watson, William. Early Civilization in China. New York: Mc-
    Graw-Hill, 1966.

CAESAR'S CONQUEST OF GAUL (58-51 B. C.)

    Gaius Julius Caesar, a Roman politician, general and man
of letters, became consul in 59 B. C. He and his supporters, Pom-

pey the Great, a Roman general, and Crassus, a wealthy Roman,
formed the political coalition known as the "First Triumvirate."
As consul, Caesar secured the right to recruit an army of three
legions and authority to govern Northern Italy and "the Province,"
an area south of Gaul.

The Gallic people consisted of more than 100 tribes which
were often feuding among themselves.   In the spring of 58 B. C.
the Helvetii, a group of tribes in Western Switzerland, were mi-
grating to richer lands.   They requested permission to pass through
the Roman province in Southern Gaul.   Caesar's reply was an attack on the Helvetii, whose forces he stopped at the Rhône River.
Later that year he and his legions drove a German chief back
across the Rhine in order to forestall his aggressions in Central
Gaul.

That winter he set up quarters in Northwestern Gaul and
the following year conquered what are now Northern France and
Belgium.   The tribes along the Atlantic coast were conquered in
56 B. C. and during the next two years Caesar campaigned in Germany and Britain.   His army seemed victorious in every encounter
despite the fact that Gaul had not been completely conquered.   Although Caesar gained no lasting control in either Germany or Britain his reputation as a successful general made a great impression on his supporters in Rome.

Many of the Gallic tribes refused to submit to Roman rule.
Under the leadership of Ambiorix, a Gallic chieftain, one of Caesar's legions was wiped out.   In 52 B. C. Vercingetorix, another
Gallic leader, unified a tribal coalition.   He employed a scorched
earth policy which forced the Romans to besiege Gallic hill forts.
Finally Caesar cornered Vercingetorix in Alesia where, after a
bitter and bloody siege, the latter surrendered.

By the year 51 B. C. , with the exception of occasional local
rebellions, Caesar's conquest of Gaul was complete.   The country
was devastated.   Its towns and agriculture were badly damaged and
more than half of its men of military age had either been enslaved
or killed in battle.

The conquest of Gaul brought Caesar glory and wealth.   With
his army, which was intensely loyal to him, he was able to return
to Rome where, following a civil war, he seized sole power.

The First Triumvirate dissolved in 53 B. C when Crassus
was killed at the battle of Carrhae and Pompey, who had become
Caesar's rival for power, was murdered in Egypt (48 B. C.) following his defeat by Caesar in the battle of Pharsalus.

Suggested Readings

Balsdon, J. P. V. D. Julius Caesar. New York: Athenaeum, 1967.

Barker, Felix, in collaboration with Anthea Barker. "Caesar Invades Britain" in their The First Explorers: Encyclopedia of Discovery and Exploration, Vol. I. London: Aldus Books, 1971.

Collingwood, R. G., and J. N. J. Myres. Roman Britain and the English Settlements. Oxford: Clarendon Press, 1937.

Cottrell, Leonard. A Guide to Roman Britain. Philadelphia: Chilton, 1966.

Dodge, Thomas A. Caesar: A History of the Art of War Among the Romans. Boston: Houghton Mifflin, 1892.

Duclaux, Mary (A. Mary F. Robinson). A Short History of France from Caesar's Invasion to the Battle of Waterloo. New York: Putnam's, 1918.

Fowler, W. W. Julius Caesar. New York: Putnam, 1891.

Frank, Tenney. An Economic History of Rome. New York: Cooper Square, 1927.

Frere, Sheppard. Britannia: A History of Roman Britain. Cambridge, Mass.: Harvard University Press, 1967.

Fuller, John F. C. Julius Caesar: Man, Soldier, and Tyrant. New Brunswick, N. J.: Rutgers University Press, 1965.

Gelzer, Matthias. Caesar: Politician and Statesman. Translated by P. Needham. Cambridge, Mass.: Harvard University Press, 1968.

Grant, Michael. Julius Caesar. New York: McGraw-Hill, 1969.

H. M. Ordnance Survey. Map of Roman Britain. Chessington: H. M. Ordnance Survey, 1956.

Holmes, Thomas Rice. Ancient Britain and the Invasion of Julius Caesar. Oxford: Clarendon Press, 1907.

_____. The Architect of the Roman Empire. Oxford: Clarendon Press, 1928.

_____. Caesar's Conquest of Gaul. London: Oxford University Press, 1931.

Lewis, Naphtali, and Meyer Reinhold, eds. Roman Civilization. New York: Harper, 1951.

Syme, Ronald. Invaders and Invasions. New York: Norton, 1964.

Tappan, Eva March. "Julius Caesar, the First Emperor of Rome" in her Old World Hero Stories. Boston: Houghton Mifflin, 1937.

Taylor, Lily Ross. Party Politics in the Age of Caesar. Berkeley, Calif.: University of California Press, 1949.

Walter, Gerard. Caesar: A Biography. Translated by Emma Crawford. New York: Scribner's, 1952.

Warrington, John, translator. "Adventures in Ancient Rome" (from "Caesar's War Commentaries") in Thomas, Lowell, ed. Great True Adventures. New York: Hawthorn Books, 1955.

Webb, Robert N. We Were There with Caesar's Legions. New York: Grosset & Dunlap, 1960.

THE BATTLE OF ACTIUM (31 B. C.)

Gaius Julius Caesar was assassinated in 44 B. C. In the

decade following his death a struggle for political power developed
between the Roman general Mark Antony and Octavian, Caesar's
grandnephew.   In 34 B.C. they had become irreconcilable enemies
after Antony, who was married to Octavian's sister Fulvia, repudiated her by openly attaching himself to Cleopatra VII, Queen of
Egypt.

Antony had recruited a large army and Octavian had done
likewise.   War was unavoidable and it became obvious that battle
strategy depended on naval rather than land forces.

In 31 B.C. Octavian declared war on Egypt.   That year he,
with his army, crossed to Epirus, north of Greece.   Antony's
fleet occupied the Ambracian Gulf and his army fortified Actium,
in the Ionian Sea, one of two sandy promontories which pointed
toward each other across the mouth of the gulf.

After several months of skirmishing Antony found that his
supply routes had been cut off by Octavian's fleet, commanded by
Agrippa, a brilliant naval tactician.   On September 1, 31 B.C.,
he held a strategy council with his subordinates.   One Roman faction voted for a retreat by land.   Cleopatra advocated a naval attack or an escape to Egypt.

The two fleets met at the battle of Actium on September 2.
Antony's galleys were large and unwieldy, some having as many as
ten banks of oars.   Octavian's vessels were smaller and more easily maneuvered.

History has given us accounts of the conflict which differ
in some particulars.   It seems probable that Antony's ships, deployed in three formations, advanced through the narrow exit from
the gulf to find their passage blocked by the enemy galleys, also
in three formations.   One squadron of sixty ships, commanded by
Cleopatra, was placed in the rear.   After several hours one wing
of Antony's flotilla was drawn into battle, forcing him to commit
the remainder of his forces.

As the fighting progressed Cleopatra's reserve squadron
suddenly hoisted its purple sails and proceeded through the line of
battle, obviously retreating to Egypt.   Antony abandoned his flagship for a smaller vessel and, with a small portion of his fleet,
followed Cleopatra, leaving the rest of his command to its fate.
Octavian captured about 300 of Antony's ships, many of which he
burned.   A week later Antony's land army surrendered.

Antony and Cleopatra returned to Egypt.   In 32 B.C. Octavian came to Egypt where he met little resistance.   The Egyptian
Queen and her Roman lover committed suicide, leaving Octavian
the undisputed ruler of Rome and the Mediterranean world.

Suggested Readings

Creasy, Edward S. Fifteen Decisive Battles of the World. Harris-
    burg, Pa.: Stackpole Books, 1957.
Falls, Cyril, ed. Great Military Battles. New York: Macmillan,
    1964.
Farmer, Lydia. "Cleopatra" in her A Book of Famous Queens.
    Revised by Willard A. Heaps. New York: Crowell, 1964.
Foster, Genevieve. Augustus Caesar's World, A Story of Ideas
    and Events from B. C. 44 to 14 A. D. New York: Scribner's,
    1949.
Frank, Tenney. An Economic History of Rome. New York: Coop-
    er Square Publishers, 1927.
Fuller, John F. C. A Military History of Western World. New
    York: Funk & Wagnalls, 1954.
Holmes, Thomas Rice. The Architect of the Roman Empire. Ox-
    ford: Clarendon Press, 1928.
Mitchell, Lt.-Col. Joseph B. , and Sir Edward S. Creasy. Twenty
    Decisive Battles of the World. New York: Macmillan, 1964.
Plutarch. "Antony" in his Plutarch's Lives of Themistocles, Per-
    icles, Aristides, Alcibiades, and Coriolanus, Demosthenes,
    and Cicero, Caesar and Antony, in the Translation Called Dry-
    den's. Revised by Arthur Hugh Clough. Edited by Charles
    W. Eliot. New York: Collier, 1909.
Richardson, C. W. "Actium," Journal of Roman Studies, Vol. 27,
    1937.
Shakespeare, William. "Antony and Cleopatra" (play) in Cross,
    E. A. , World Literature. New York: American Book Co. ,
    1935 (Originally written c. 1607-1608).
Tappan, Eva March. "Julius Caesar, the First Emperor of Rome"
    in her Old World Hero Stories. Boston: Houghton Mifflin,
    1937.
Tarn, W. W. "The Battle of Actium," Journal of Roman Studies,
    Vol. 21, 1931.
_____, and M. P. Charlesworth. "The War of the East Against
    the West" in Cambridge Ancient History, Vol. X. Cambridge:
    The University Press, 1934.
Taylor, Lily Ross. Party Politics in the Age of Caesar. Berkeley,
    Calif.: University of California Press, 1949.
Warner, Oliver. Great Sea Battles. New York: Macmillan, 1963.
Weigall, Arthur. The Life and Times of Cleopatra, Queen of Egypt.
    New York: Putnam, 1924.

OVID'S COMPOSITION OF THE
METAMORPHOSES (c. 1-8 A. D.)

"Metamorphoses" is defined as "the transformation (in ancient mythology) of human beings into beasts, fire, water, trees,
stones, or the like. " These metamorphoses furnished a subject
to the Greek poets and writers of the Alexandrine period and to the

Roman poet Ovid.   Ovid (43 B. C. -c. 17 A. D.) was born in Sulmo
(modern Sulmona) in Central Italy, the son of a wealthy man.   Educated for the bar, he developed a great proficiency in the art of
declamation but soon turned to the writing of verses.

After his father's death he went to Athens and later traveled
in Asia and Sicily with the poet Aemilius Macer.   He settled in
Rome where he lived the life of a well-to-do profligate and poet.
In 8 A. D. he was banished to Tomi, on the Black Sea, by the emperor Augustus, where he lived until his death.   The reason for
the banishment is unknown.   One account is that the emperor took
exception to Ovid's Ars Amatoria, an erotic poem on the art of
making love.   Another reason given for the banishment is that Ovid
may have had knowledge of a scandal involving Augustus' profligate
granddaughter Julia and the emperor.   Although the poet wished to
return to the gay life of Rome, he was never permitted to do so.
He died at Tomi at the age of 84.

Ovid's poetry falls into three divisions: the works of his
youth, of his middle age and that composed during his exile at
Tomi.   His youthful writings, such as the Amores, were erotic
poems dealing with love, passion and kindred subjects.   These show
his interest in mythology which was to characterize the fifteen-book
Metamorphoses, his greatest work, written in his middle period,
between 1 and 8 A. D.

The Metamorphoses is concerned with all the transformations
mentioned in mythology, from the Creation down to the time of
Gaius Julius Caesar, who changes to a star.   Critics consider the
poem a definite departure from Ovid's previous writings in both
form and tone.   It is written in the epic meter, the dactylic hexa-
meter which was used by Vergil in the Aeneid and which, like Homer's Iliad, is considered an epic poem.   The Metamorphoses is
classed as narrative rather than epic.   It consists of a series of
stories, connected by "the slenderest of links. "   These stories, in
historical sequence, tell of Cadmus and Thebes, Jason and the
quest for the Golden Fleece, Theseus and the organization of the
separate states at Athens, the fall of Troy in the Trojan War, the
wanderings of Ulysses and the founding of Rome.

Latter day writers based many of their stories, poems and
plays on the Metamorphoses.   Geoffrey Chaucer, William Shakespeare, Edmund Spenser and John Milton, among others, adapted
Ovid's tales of mythology to their own works.   Librettist Ottavio
Rinuccini's opera, Dafne, the first such ever to be performed (1594
or 1597), was based on Ovid's story of Apollo and Daphne in Book
I of the Metamorphoses.

Ovid completed his masterpiece shortly before being exiled
to Tomi.   His writings there are characterized by "melancholy and
despair. "   In the Tristia he describes his unhappy life and entreats
Augustus to permit him to return to Rome, a plea which the emperor ignored.   Other works composed at this time include Epis-
tuloe ex Ponto, the Ibis and the Halieutica.

Aside from being a great poet Ovid was also a born story teller and many of the tales originally appearing in the Metamorphoses are read and enjoyed in modern form today.

Suggested Readings

Auslander, Joseph, and Frank Ernest Hill. The Winged Horse: The Story of the Poets and Their Poetry. Garden City, N. Y.: Doubleday, 1927.

Cross, E. A. "The Latin Poets: Ovid" in his World Literature. New York: American Book Co., 1935.

Frankel, Hermann. Ovid: A Poet Between Two Worlds. Berkeley, Calif.: University of California Press, 1945.

Godolphin, Francis Richard Borroum, ed. The Latin Poets. New York: Modern Library, 1949.

Hadas, Moses. A History of Latin Literature. New York: Columbia University Press, 1952.

Highet, Gilbert. The Classical Tradition. New York: Oxford University Press, 1949.

Macy, John. The Story of World's Literature. New York: Boni & Liveright, 1925.

Otis, Brooks. Ovid as an Epic Poet. Cambridge: The University Press, 1966.

Ovid. The Metamorphoses of Ovid. Translated and with an introduction by Mary M. Innes. Baltimore: Penguin Books, 1945. (Originally written c. 1-8 A. D.).

Rand, Edward K. Ovid and His Influence. New York: Cooper Square, 1925.

Sellar, W. Y. The Roman Poets of the Augustan Age: Horace and the Elegial Poets. Oxford: Clarendon Press, 1891.

Sorley, Herbert T. Exile: Studies of Ovid, Prince Charles Edward, and Victor Hugo. Ilfracombe, England, 1963.

Thibault, John C. The Mystery of Ovid's Exile. Berkeley, Calif.: University of California Press, 1964.

Wilkinson, Lancelot P. Ovid Recalled. Cambridge: The University Press, 1955.

Wright, Frederick A. History of Later Greek Literature from the Death of Alexander in 323 B. C. to the Death of Justinian in 565 A. D. Atlanta, Ga.: Humanities Associates, 1961 (Originally published 1932).

_____. Three Roman Poets: Plautus, Catullus, Ovid: Their Lives, Times and Works. New York: AMS Press, 1938.

THE TRIAL AND EXECUTION
OF JESUS CHRIST (c. 29 A. D.)

One of the most important events in the history of the Christian Church, if not mankind, is the trial, condemnation and execution of Jesus Christ at Golgotha, the hill of Calvary outside Jerusalem, about 29 A. D.

The four canonical gospels (Matthew, Mark, Luke and John) are the principal sources of information concerning Jesus' life and death. These vary in many details but certain particulars are generally agreed upon. Jesus was born in Bethlehem between 8 and 4 B.C., the legal son of Joseph, a carpenter of Nazareth, and Mary, Joseph's wife. As a child he lived at Nazareth and as a young man followed his father's trade. After baptism in the Jordan River by John the Baptist he enlisted twelve disciples. His preaching in Galilee was received with enthusiasm by the common people because of his extraordinary healing powers, effective teaching by parables and the impression of authority which he gave. The Pharisees and privileged classes strongly opposed him because of his interest in the poor and his attacks on hypocrisy. He was thought to preach, not the word of God, but his own, which was regarded as heresy.

Jesus was recognized by some as the long-expected Messiah and this led to further distrust on the part of the ruling classes which suspected him of revolutionary aims against Rome, something he vigorously denied.

After spending some time in Galilee Jesus and his disciples traveled to Jerusalem for the last time, to observe Passover. Here he taught in the temple and drove out the money-changers and traders who, by long-established custom, had been allowed to transact business in the outer court. These, he declared, had made God's house "a den of thieves."

The priests and scribes sought to have him put to death and Judas Iscariot, one of his disciples agreed, for thirty pieces of silver, to help them. On Thursday Jesus ate the Passover supper (the "Last Supper") with his disciples. During the meal he referred to his imminent death as a sacrifice for the sins of mankind. The wine served during the Passover services he called his blood "which shall be shed for the many," and unleavened bread he mentioned as "his body."

Following the meal the group went to Gethsemane, an olive grove where, according to Scripture, Jesus said he would rise again after his death. He then retired for meditation and prayer. Seized by the Roman soldiers, he was taken before the Sanhedrin where he was tried. False witnesses testified against him. Their testimony was contradictory and the high priest, Joseph Caiaphas, placed Jesus under oath and asked him directly if he conceived himself to be "Christ, son of the Blessed." Jesus gave a positive answer, whereupon he was considered blasphemous "and they all condemned him as deserving death" (Mark 14:53-65).

On Friday Jesus was brought before Pontius Pilate, the Roman procurator, for formal condemnation, Pilate being the only authority having the right to inflict capital punishment. The procurator asked Jesus if he were indeed King of the Jews, and the latter answered ambiguously, stating, "Thou sayest it." The crowd, in accordance with the custom of the Passover feast, demanded the release of a prisoner.   Pilate, though feeling Jesus to be innocent, released Barabbas, a convicted murderer.

Finding Jesus to be a Galilean, Pilate sent him to Herod Antipas, ruler of Galilee, who sent him back to Pilate.   Pilate, who is said to have washed his hands symbolically, saying "I find no guilt in this man," nevertheless ordered him executed as a rebel against Rome.   As a preliminary to crucifixion Jesus was scourged, as was customary.   On Saturday he was taken to Golgotha, the place of execution, and crucified between two thieves.

The details of the trial and execution of Jesus, as reported in Holy Scripture, vary in many particulars, as stated above.   These inconsistencies bring up questions over which theologians have argued for centuries.   They are, however, comparatively minor, and the two primary questions which still remain unresolved are (1) Was the condemnation of Jesus legally justified? and (2) Was it the work of the Jews, the Romans, or both?

Suggested Readings

Bannel, Ernst, ed. The Trial of Jesus.   London: Student Christian Movement Press, 1970.

Barton, Bruce. The Man Nobody Knows: A Discovery of Jesus. Indianapolis: Bobbs-Merrill, 1925.

Bishop, Jim. The Day Christ Died.   New York: Harper, 1957.

Blinzler, Josef. The Trial of Jesus.   Translated by Isabel and Florence McHugh.   Cork: Mercier Press, 1959.

Bornkamm, Günther. Jesus of Nazareth.   London: Hodder and Stoughton, 1960.

Brandon, S. G. F. The Trial of Jesus of Nazareth.   New York: Stein and Day, 1968.

Bultmann, Rudolf. Jesus and the World.   New York: Scribner's, 1958 (Originally published 1926).

_____, and Karl Kundsin. Form Criticism: Two Essays in New Testament Research.   New York: Wille H. Clark and Company, 1934.

Debelius, Martin. From Tradition to Gospel.   New York: Scribner's, 1935.

Dix, Gregory, O. S. B. The Shape of the Liturgy.   London: Adam and Charles Black, 1945.

Dodd, C. H. "The Historical Problem of the Death of Jesus" in More New Testament Studies.   Grand Rapids, Mich.: Wm. B. Eerdmans Publishing Co., 1968.

Fuller, Reginald H. The Mission and Achievement of Jesus.   London: Student Christian Movement Press, 1954.

_____. The New Testament in Current Study.   New York: Scribner's, 1962.

Hunter, Archibald M. Paul and His Predecessors.   Philadelphia: Westminster Press, 1961.

Keck, Leander E., and J. Louis Martyn, eds. Studies in Luke--
    Acts. Nashville, Tenn.: Abingdon Press, 1966.
Kilpatrick, G. D. The Trial of Jesus. New York: Oxford Univer-
    sity Press, 1935.
Klausner, Joseph. Jesus of Nazareth: His Life, Times and Teach-
    ings. Boston: Beacon Press, 1965 (Originally published 1925).
Kramer, Werner. Christ, Lord, Son of God. Translated by Brian
    Hardy. London: Student Christian Movement Press, 1966.
Lietzmann, Hans. Mass and Lord's Supper. Leiden: E. J. Brill,
    1953-1964.
Lohse, Eduard. History of the Suffering and Death of Jesus Christ.
    Translated by Martin O. Dietrich. Philadelphia: Fortress
    Press, 1967.
Oesterley, W. O. E. The Jewish Background of the Christian Litur-
    gy. Gloucester, Mass.: Peter Smith, 1965 (Originally pub-
    lished 1925).
Ricciotti, Giuseppe. The Life of Christ. Milwaukee, Wis.: Bruce
    Publishing Co., 1951.
Sherwin-White, A. N. "The Trial of Jesus" in Historicity and Chron-
    ology in the New Testament. London: Society for Promoting
    Christian Knowledge, 1965.
Wilson, W. R. The Execution of Jesus: A Judicial Historical In-
    vestigation. New York: Scribner's, 1970.
Winter, Paul. On the Trial of Jesus. Berlin: Walter de Gruyter,
    1961.

PAUL OF TARSUS' EPISTLE TO THE ROMANS
(55 or 56 A. D.)

Paul, born at Tarsus about 3 A.D. and supposedly in Rome
in 67 or 68 A.D., originally named Saul, was one of Christ's Apostles. He was educated as a rabbi but, having experienced a vision
of Christ crucified, was converted to Christianity. He made three
missionary journeys. The first took him through Cyprus, Pisida
and Lycaonia and the second took him to Philippi, Thessalonica,
Corinth and Antioch. The last took him through Galatia, Phrygia
and parts of Asia to Ephesus. He founded a number of churches,
to which he sent epistles or letters, the "Pauline Epistles," now
part of the New Testament canon. These communications dealt
with practical matters concerning the churches and put forth his
personal theological views.

The most important of the Pauline Epistles was the one
written to the Church at Rome in 55 or 56 A.D. when Paul was
in Corinth at the house of Gaius. This consists of two portions,
marked off respectively by the doxology in Romans 11:36, and by
the benediction in 15:33. Since the fourth century this letter has
stood at the head of the Pauline Corpus in the New Testament.

It would appear that the letter was written as the result of

a theological controversy.   The writer asserts that all persons,
both Gentiles and Jews, will be judged, punished or rewarded, depending on circumstances which he discusses at some length.   He
contrasts faith with legal considerations and holds that, after death,
"sin no longer has control over men since they are not under the
law but under a reign of grace. "

Paul also considers obligations of the Christian life, stating
that charity and tolerance must be universally observed, even though
"talents and gifts are different in different people. " He holds that
such virtues as charity, self-denial, mercy and patience must prevail.

Paul's epistle to the Romans, as an expression of his theological views, has had a great influence on a number of the churchmen who followed him.   These include Origen, Chrysostom, Peter
Abélard, Augustine of Hippo, Thomas Aquinas, Martin Luther, John
Wesley, and others.

Suggested Readings

Barrett, C. K.   A Commentary on the Epistle to the Romans.   New
    York: Harper & Row, 1957.
Barth, Karl.   Epistle to the Romans.   Oxford: The University
    Press, 1968.
Beare, F. W.   "Letter to the Romans" in The Interpreter's Diction-
    ary of the Bible, Vol. IV.   New York: Abingdon Press, 1962.
Bultmann, Rudolf, and Karl Kundsin.   Form Criticism: Two Essays
    in New Testament Research.   New York: Wille H. Clark and
    Company, 1934.
Cross, E. A.   "St. Paul" in his World Literature.   New York:
    American Book Co. , 1935.
Davies, W. D.   Paul and Rabbinic Judaism.   London: Society for
    Promoting Christian Knowledge, 1955.
Debelius, Martin.   From Tradition to Gospel.   New York: Scrib-
    ner's, 1935.
Dix, Gregory, O. S. B.   The Shape of the Liturgy.   London: Adam
    and Charles Black, 1945.
Dodd, C. H.   The Epistle of Paul to the Romans.   New York: Har-
    per & Row, 1932.
Fuller, Reginald H.   The New Testament in Current Study.   New
    York: Scribner's, 1962.
Hunter, Archibald M.   Paul and His Predecessors.   Philadelphia:
    Westminster Press, 1961.
Knox, Wilfred L.   St. Paul and the Church of the Gentiles.   Cam-
    bridge: The University Press, 1961.
Marxsen, W. Introduction to the New Testament.   Translated by
    G. Buswell.   Philadelphia: Fortress Press, 1968.
Nock, Arthur Darby.   St. Paul.   New York: Harper & Row, 1963.
Oesterley, W. O. E.   The Jewish Background of the Christian Lit-
    urgy.   Gloucester, Mass. : Peter Smith, 1965 (Originally pub-
    lished 1925).

Rigaux, Beda. The Letters of Paul: Modern Studies. Edited by
    Stephen Yonick, O. F. M. , S. S. L.   Chicago: Franciscan Herald
    Press, 1968.
Schoeps, H. J.   Paul: The Theology of the Apostle in the Light of
    Jewish Religious History.   Translated by Harold Knight.   Phil-
    adelphia: Westminster Press, 1961.
Whitely, D. E. H.   The Theology of St. Paul.   Philadelphia: For-
    tress Press, 1964.

THE BURNING OF ROME (64 A. D.)

The original site of Rome consisted of a group of low ridges,
known in history as the Seven Hills, on the east side of the Tiber
River.   Legend has it that the city was founded in 753 B. C. by
Romulus and Remus, the twin sons of Mars, god of war, and Rhea
Silvia, a vestal virgin and the daughter of Numitor, king of Alba
Longa.

By the first century A. D. Rome had become a large and
sprawling city.   Many buildings were constructed of highly flammable wood, and the middle and working classes lived in ram-
shackle tenements built in endless rows and having as many as
eight stories.   Sanitation was virtually nonexistent.   The Emperor
Augustus had decreed that any building to be used as a private
dwelling should, as a safety measure, be not more than sixty feet
in height, but this decree had long been disregarded.   Legislation
to modernize the city was, time after time, introduced in the Senate, always to be defeated by those land-owning patricians who had
leased their ground to building speculators at great profit to themselves.   In short, much of Rome was little more than a gigantic
firetrap.

On July 13, 64 A. D. , the inevitable fire occurred.   The
emperor Nero was at his villa at Anzio when a courier reported
to him that Rome was ablaze.   This was not "just another small
fire"; the whole city was burning.

For many weeks no rain had fallen.   The air was sultry
and the wooden buildings were like tinder.   A violent wind was
fanning the flames.   By morning entire districts had been destroyed
and thousands of people had died in the flames.

It was reported that the fire had started simultaneously in
eight different places, and it was reasoned that arsonists rather
than an accident had caused the conflagration.   It was also conjec-
tured that the gods, angered by some act, had ordered the destruction.

Nero, accompanied by Tigellinus, his companion, Epaphroditus,
his secretary, and a detachment of guards, set out for Rome on

horseback.   At the Alban Hills the party saw flames and clouds of
smoke.   Crowds of people were fleeing the burning city, heading
for open country.

   The emperor proceeded to his palace which he found virtually deserted.   For the next several days he made inspection trips
through the burning capital and in doing what he could to direct fire-
fighting operations.

   On the fourth night, the legend goes, Tigellinus suggested
that Nero compose a poem on the Fire of Rome.   The emperor
seized his lyre and walked to the terrace.   There, accompanying
himself on the instrument, he declaimed, but the words were lost
in the noise of the crackling flames.   It is thought that he may
have been reciting verses about the burning of Troy.

   Hilliel, a Gaulonite Jew, shouted that Nero had caused Rome
to be burned "that he might sing to the accompaniment of the flames."
The story spread and others accused the emperor of being the incendiary.   Modern scholars, however, doubt that he had anything
to do with the fire, which burned for a week.   It was finally halted
at the foot of the Esqueline Hill where buildings in its path had
been demolished in order to prevent its further spread.

   Only four of the fourteen districts of Rome were left standing.   Seven were completely burned out and three had been razed
in an effort to contain the flames.

   As mentioned above, Nero was accused of starting the Fire
of Rome.   To offset the charge he placed the blame on the Christians and persecuted them unmercifully.   He rebuilt the city with
great magnificence, constructing for himself a splendid palace,
known as the Golden House.

Suggested Readings

Asimov, Isaac.   The Roman Empire.   Boston: Houghton Mifflin,
    1967.
_____.   The Roman Republic.   Boston: Houghton Mifflin, 1966.
Canfield, L. H.   The Early Persecutions of the Christians.   New
    York: Longmans, Green, 1913.
Franzero, C. M.   The Life and Times of Nero.   London: Alvin
    Redman, 1954.
_____.   "Nero Fiddled" in Corbett, Edmund V., ed.   Great True
    Stories of Tragedy and Disaster.   New York: Archer House,
    1963.
Friend, W. H. C.   Martyrdom and Persecution in the Early Church.
    Garden City, N. Y.: Doubleday, 1967.
Gibbon, Edward.   The History of the Decline and Fall of the Roman
    Empire.   Edited by J. B. Bury.   London: Methuen, 1896-1900
    (Originally published 1776-1778).

Guterman, S. L.   Religious Toleration and Persecution in Ancient
    Rome.   London: Aiglon Press, 1951.
Hardy, E. R.   Christianity and the Roman Government.   London:
    George Allen & Unwin, 1925.
Katz, Solomon.   The Decline of Rome and the Rise of Mediaeval
    Europe.   Ithaca, N. Y. :   Cornell University Press, 1955.
Lanciani, Rodolfo.   Ancient Rome in the Light of Recent Discov-
    eries.   New York: Blom, 1967 (Originally published 1888).
_____.   The Destruction of Ancient Rome: A Sketch of the His-
    tory of the Monuments.   New York: Blom, 1967 (Originally
    published 1901).
_____. New Tales of Old Rome.   New York: Blom, 1967 (Or-
    iginally published 1901).
Mills, Dorothy.   The Book of the Ancient Romans: An Introduction
    to the History and Civilization of Rome from the Traditional
    Date of the Founding of the City to Its Fall in 476 A. D.   New
    York: Putnam's, 1927.
"Nero" in Crime and Criminals, Vol. 11.   Editorial presentation:
    Jackson Morley.   London: BPC, 1973.
Parker, H. M. D.   History of the Roman World from A. D. 138 to
    337: Revised With Additional Notes by B. H. Warmington.   New
    York: Macmillan, 1958.
Payne, Pierre, and the editors of Horizon Magazine.   The Horizon
    Book of Ancient Rome.   New York: American Heritage Pub-
    lishing Co. , 1966.
Ramsay, William.   The Church in the Roman Empire.   London:
    Hoddert & Stoughton, 1907.
Scullard, Howard Hayes.   From Gracci to Nero: Rome from 133
    B. C. to A. D. 68.   New York: Frederick A. Praeger, 1959.
Stobart, John Clarke.   The Grandeur That Was Rome.   New York:
    Hawthorn Books, 1962.
Workman, Herbert B.   The Martyrs of the Early Church.   London:
    Charles H. Kelley, n. d.
_____. Persecution of the Early Church.   London: Epworth
    Press, 1923.

THE MARTYRDOM OF SAINT PETER (c. 67 A. D.)

        In the mid-first century A. D. the Roman emperor Nero ruled
a totalitarian state in which no concept of sovereignty existed outside it.   His political philosophy embraced virtually all aspects of
the lives of the citizens of Rome, including religion.   Here the idea
of an independent church, as exemplified by the teachings of Christ,
was repugnant to the Roman officials, although certain exceptions
were made, as in the case of the religions of conquered peoples.
Generally speaking, Rome was tolerant of other religions so long
as they did not pose a threat to the established totalitarian order.

        Eventually the Christians got into trouble with the Roman
authorities.   Theologians are not agreed concerning the cause of

the difficulties in which the Christians found themselves.   It is, however, an historical fact that in 64 A.D. the city of Rome suffered a severe fire which precipitated persecutions of the Christians by Nero, who accused them of arson.

As a result of this persecution great numbers of Christians suffered martyrdom.   In 95 A.D. Clement of Rome listed the apostles Peter and Paul as victims.   These two men, according to tradition, were put to death in Rome on the same day, and Peter is said to have been crucified head downwards.   That Peter died in Rome, or exactly when he died, has never been conclusively established.

Peter, or Simon Peter, was a native of Bethsaida.   What we know of him and his brother Andrew is derived from the first four books of the New Testament.   He was a disciple of John the Baptist, and later of Jesus.   A fisherman by trade, he was pursuing his calling at Cadernaum when Jesus called him and Andrew to become "fishers of men. "   As one of the Twelve Apostles, he was regarded by Jesus with particular affection.   The latter offered him a primacy not shared by the other apostles, saying, "You are Peter and on this rock I will build my church. " (Matthew 16:18). He is considered the first of a long line of popes.

According to Holy Scripture he was the mover in the election of a new apostle replacing Judas.   After the Resurrection he made Jerusalem his headquarters for preaching and proselyting in Palestine (c. 33-44 A.D.).   With John he was sent from Jerusalem to the Samaritan converts, that they might receive the Holy Ghost.   Later he returned to Jerusalem and from there went to Antioch where, for a time, he worked with Paul.

Students of religious history disagree on Peter's martyrdom. Acts is silent on the matter.   I Peter 5:13 refers to the place of his death as "Babylon" which is taken by some to refer to Rome. John 21:18 indicates that Peter met death by crucifixion, saying "you will stretch out your hands. "   Paul is supposed to have died on the same day as did Peter, and Revelation 11:3, referring to "two witnesses" who are killed by "the beast that ascends from the bottomless pit" has been interpreted to refer to Peter and Paul. Peter's name does not appear on a list of Roman saints addressed by Paul (Romans 16), which is considered evidence that Peter did not live in Rome.

Saint Clement I, the first of the Apostolic Fathers, in his Epistle to the Corinthians (95 or 96 A.D.), states that Peter died as a martyr "because of envy and jealousy. "   From this it is inferred that Peter died in Rome as Clement was writing from that city.   Other churchmen, writing in the second and third centuries A.D., have given theologians fragments of evidence that Peter lived and worked in Rome, founded and organized its church, and suffered martyrdom there by crucifixion.

On December 23, 1950, Pope Pius XII announced that the martyr's grave had been found under the high altar of St. Peter's Basilica in Rome. Some authorities dispute the authenticity of this announcement and the facts concerning the circumstances of the death of the first Roman Catholic pope are still the subject of controversy.

Suggested Readings

Burn-Murdoch, A. The Development of the Papacy. London: Faber & Faber, 1954.

Canfield, L. H. The Early Persecutions of the Christians. New York: Longmans, Green, 1913.

Clarke, W. K. Lowther. The First Epistle of Clement to the Corinthians. New York: Macmillan, 1937.

Cullmann, Oscar. Peter, Disciple, Apostle, Martyr. Translated by Floyd W. Filson. Philadelphia: Westminster Press, 1953.

De Marco, Angelus A. , O. F. M. The Tomb of St. Peter: A Representative and Annotated Bibliography of the Excavations. Leiden: E. J. Brill, 1964.

Friend, W. H. C. Martyrdom and Persecution in the Early Church. Garden City, N. Y. : Doubleday, 1967.

Grant, Robert M. The Apostolic Fathers. New York: Nelson, 1965.

Guarducci, Margherita. The Tomb of St. Peter--New Discoveries in the Sacred Grottoes of the Vatican. Translated by Joseph McLellan. New York: Hawthorne Books, 1960.

Guterman, S. L. Religious Toleration and Persecution in Ancient Rome. London: Aiglon Press, 1951.

Hardy, E. R. Christianity and the Roman Government. London: George Allen & Unwin, 1925.

Jaeger, Werner. Early Christianity and Greek Paideia. Cambridge, Mass. : Harvard University Press, 1961.

Karrer, Otto. Peter and the Church: An Examination of Cullmann's Thesis. New York: Herder and Herder, 1963.

Kirschbaum, Engelbert, S. J. The Tombs of St. Peter and St. Paul. Translated by John Murray, S. J. New York: St. Martin's Press, 1957.

Kleist, James A. The Epistles of St. Clement of Rome and St. Ignatius of Antioch. Westminster, Md. : Newman Press, 1946.

Lawson, J. A. A Theological and Historical Introduction to the Apostolic Fathers. New York: Macmillan, 1961.

Nunn, H. P. V. "St. Peter's Presence in Rome--The Monumental Evidence, " Evangelical Quarterly, April, 1950.

Pfeiffer, Robert H. History of the New Testament Times. New York: Harper & Row, 1949.

Quasten, J. Patrology, Vol. I. Westminster, Md. : Newman Press, 1950.

Ramsay, William. The Church in the Roman Empire. London: Hoddert & Stoughton, 1907.

Toynbee, Jocelyn. "Graffiti Beneath St. Peter's: Prof. Guarducci's Interpretations, " The Dublin Review, Autumn, 1959.

_____, and John Perkins. The Shrine of St. Peter and the Vati-
    can Excavations. New York: Longmans, Green, 1956.
Weltin, E. G. The Ancient Popes. Westminster, Md. : Newman
    Press, 1964.
Workman, Herbert B. The Martyrs of the Early Church. London:
    Charles H. Kelley, n. d.
_____. Persecution of the Early Church. London: Epworth
    Press, 1923.

PLINY THE ELDER'S NATURAL HISTORY (77 A. D.)

Pliny, known as the Elder to distinguish him from his nephew and adopted son Pliny the Younger, was a Roman statesman,
soldier and author. Born in Como, Northern Italy, in 23 A. D. , he
traveled to Rome and at 23 entered the army where he served under Lucius Pomponius Secundus in Germany. In 52 A. D. he returned to Rome where he studied law but abandoned a legal career
for one of study, writing and government service. As a procurator or collector of imperial revenues he served in Spain from about
70 to 72 A. D. In 79 A. D. he was in command of the imperial
fleet stationed in the western Mediterranean when Mount Vesuvius
erupted, burying Pompeii, Herculaneum and Stabiae in volcanic ash.
He visited the scene of the disaster and died of suffocation from
the vapors generated by the eruption.

Aside from his governmental and military duties, Pliny wrote
numerous books of an historical or scientific nature. These include a treatise on the use of the javelin by cavalry, a biography
of his old commander Secundus, treatises on oratory and on declen-
sions and conjugations. He also produced a history of the Germanic wars and a continuation of the Roman history of Aufidius Bassus,
covering the period 41 to 71 A. D. None of these are extant.

Pliny's one writing which has come down to us is his Historia Naturalis, or Natural History, in 37 books. This is an encyclopedia of nature and art. It was dedicated to Titus, son of
the emperor Vespasian, and discusses 20,000 "important facts"
taken from about 2,000 volumes by 100 authors. The first ten
books were published in 77 A. D. and the others after Pliny's death.
They deal with a wide variety of subjects, including astronomy,
anthropology, botany, zoology, medicine, minerology, horticulture
and geography as well as the fine arts, including art history.

Pliny's Natural History, though a momentous achievement,
has been criticized as being incorrect in many respects. The author, it is claimed, gathered his data from earlier writings and
failed to verify the accuracy of such data prior to including it in
his own compilation. It is true that a need for such an encyclopedia existed. During the previous five centuries Greek and Latin
thinkers had discovered many basic scientific principles and it was

appropriate that these should be assembled and discussed in one
writing. Pliny has been characterized as "a reader, rather than
a true investigator ... who relied almost solely on the information
of others whose authority and agreement sometimes led him astray. "
The inaccuracies in Natural History were not recognized as such
until the Renaissance and the book was regarded as an authoritive
source of scientific information for many years. By the fifteenth
century it had been reprinted in at least fifteen editions and three
Italian translations. Today it is considered "another literary relic
of a dead age. "

Suggested Readings

Bailey, K. C. The Elder Pliny's Chapters on Chemical Subjects.
    London: Arnold Publishers, 1929-1932.
Cross, E. A. "The Two Plinys" in his World Literature. New
    York: American Book Co. , 1935.
Dannemann, Friedrich. Plinius und seine Naturgeschichte in ihrer
    Bedeutung für die Gegenwart. Jena, Germany, 1921.
Duff, J. Wright. A Literary History of Rome in the Silver Age
    from Tiberius to Hadrian. New York: Barnes & Noble, 1960.
Hadas, Moses. A History of Latin Literature. New York: Co-
    lumbia University Press, 1952.
Le Bonniec, Henri. Bibliographie de l'histoire naturelle de Pline
    l'Ancien. Paris: 1946.
Plinius Caecilius Secundus. Pliny: Natural History. Translated
    by Harris Rackham, et al. London: Cambridge University
    Press, 1938-1963 (Originally published 77 A. D. and after).
Singer, Charles. A Short History of Science to the Nineteenth Cen-
    tury. Oxford: Clarendon Press, 1941.
Stahl, William H. Roman Science: Origins, Development, and In-
    fluence to the Later Middle Ages. Madison, Wis. : University
    of Wisconsin Press, 1962.
Thorndyke, Lynn. History of Magic and Experimental Sciences
    During the First Thirteen Centuries of Our Era. New York:
    Macmillan, 1929.
Wethered, Herbert N. The Mind of the Ancient World: A Consid-
    eration of Pliny's Natural History. New York: Longmans,
    Green, 1937.

THE DESTRUCTION OF POMPEII (79 A. D.)

On August 24, 79 A. D. , Mount Vesuvius, an Italian volcano
on the Bay of Naples, erupted. The ancient cities of Pompeii, Herculaneum, and Stabiae were completely demolished. Pompeii had
been founded by the Oscans about 600 B. C. and at the time of the
volcanic eruption was a port town and the favorite resort of wealthy
Romans.

Over the years Pompeii was gradually forgotten. Geographical changes in the shore line and the course of the Sarnus River, at the mouth of which it had been located, resulted in Pompeii's exact site becoming temporarily lost.

In 1748 excavations were started by the Neapolitan government. To date, approximately one quarter of the city remains unexcavated and the work is still continuing. The remains found so far are in an unusually good state of preservation, due to the fact that the city was inundated by showers of cinders, lapilli, mud and wet ashes rather than by molten lava. Thus, Pompeii was hermetically sealed when the ashes and cinders dried.

Of the original population of approximately 20,000 persons, only about 2,000 died in the disaster. Most of the residents escaped, taking their most valuable movable possessions with them. After the eruption had ceased they returned, dug down into the ashes, and carried off virtually everything of worth. Consequently, not many objects of real value have been discovered on the site of the ancient city. However, because of the excellent state of preservation of the buildings, artifacts and other items, a remarkably complete picture of life in first century Italy is inferable. Many portable objects, wall paintings and floor mosaics were taken to the National Museum in Naples where they are now on display.

Suggested Readings

Bulwer-Lytton, Sir Edward. The Last Days of Pompeii (fiction). New York: Dodd, Mead, 1946 (Originally published 1834).

Ceram, C. W. Gods, Graves and Scholars. Translated by E. B. Garside. New York: Knopf, 1956.

Corti, E. C. C. Pompeii and Herculaneum. London: Routledge and Kegan Paul. 1951.

_____. "Vesuvius in Eruption" in Corbett, Edmund V. , ed. Great True Stories of Tragedy and Disaster. New York: Archer House, 1963.

Grant, Michael. The Ancient Mediterranean. New York: Scribner's, 1969.

Gusmann, Pierre. Mural Decorations of Pompeii. New York: William Helburn, 1924.

Hall, Jennie. "Pompeii Today" in her Buried Cities. New York: Macmillan, 1922.

Lanciani, Rodolfo. Ruins and Excavations of Ancient Rome. New York: Blom, 1967 (Originally published 1897).

Lepmann, Wolfgang. Pompeii in Fact and Fiction. London: Flek Books, 1968.

Mau, August. Pompeii, Its Life and Art. London: 1889.

Rostovtzeff, Mikhail. The Social and Economic History of the Roman Empire. Revised by P. M. Fraser. Oxford: Clarendon Press, 1957.

Sampson, George, M. A. "Pompeii: As It Was and As It Is Today" in Hammerton, J. A. , ed. Wonders of the Past: The Romance

of Antiquity and Its Splendours, Vol. I.   New York: William
    H. Wise & Co. , 1933.
Schreiber, Hermann, and Georg Schreiber.   Vanished Cities.   New
    York: Knopf, 1957.
Silverberg, Robert.   Lost Cities and Vanished Civilizations.   Phil-
    adelphia: Chilton, 1962.
Tanzer, Helen H.   The Common People of Pompeii: A Study of
    the Graffiti.   Baltimore: Johns Hopkins University Press, 1939.
Van Buren, Albert W.   A Companion to the Study of Pompeii and
    Herculaneum.   Rome, 1938.

PLUTARCH'S PARALLEL LIVES (c. 105-115)

One of the great books of the world is Parallel Lives of Illustrious Greeks and Romans, written by Plutarch, a Greek essayist and biographer, in the early second century A. D.   Plutarch's
plan was to write the biography of a notable Greek and then to follow it by one about a famous Roman whose actions and interests
were similar to those of the Greek.   In all there are 46 biographies arranged in 23 pairs, plus four single biographies.   Included
are both legendary persons (Theseus and Romulus) and actual historical figures (Pericles and Julius Caesar).   Other persons whose
lives are described include Alexander the Great, Lycurgus, Numa
Pompilius, Demosthenes and Cicero.

In his account of Alexander, Plutarch makes it clear that
he considered himself a biographer rather than an historian, and
he felt himself "free to leave more weighty matters and great battles to be treated by others. "   In some cases his accounts of historical events conflict.

In detailing the lives of his biographees Plutarch most often,
but not always, began with a short description of the subject's gene-
alogy.   He then described various character traits, either illustrated by anecdotes concerning the man's childhood or else describing
events in his later life.   His object was to depict his character
through his actions "and thereby inspire virtue in the reader. "

Plutarch's Lives was not particularly popular during his lifetime, but came to be regarded as a primary authority for countless
historical facts after Jacques Amyot translated it into French in
1559 and Sir Thomas North rendered it in English 20 years later.
It is known that the North translation was used by William Shakespeare as a source of material for his Julius Caesar, Coriolanus
and Antony and Cleopatra.   John Dryden, the British poet, dramatist and critic, wrote an introduction to one translation and Oliver
Goldsmith abridged it for young people.   It was highly regarded by
James Boswell, Dr. Samuel Johnson and Alexander Pope.

In addition to Lives, Plutarch wrote a number of essays and

Galen's Writings on Medicine

65

dialogues. The essays, on many subjects, include On the Education of Children, How a Young Man Ought to Hear Poetry, On Superstition, On the Genius of Socrates and On Having Many Friends.

The Lives in translation is still reprinted and widely sold. Rather than being merely consulted by scholars, it is one of the few classical works which are read by the general public.

Suggested Readings

Barrow, Reginald Haynes. Plutarch and His Times. Bloomington, Ind.: Indiana University Press, 1967.
Cross, E. A. "Plutarch" in his World Literature. New York: American Book Co., 1935.
Garraty, John A. The Nature of Biography. New York: Knopf, 1957.
Gossage, A. J. "Plutarch" in Dorey, T. A., ed. Latin Biography. London: Routeledge and Kegan, 1967.
Hembold, William C., and Edward N. O'Neil, eds. Plutarch's Quotations. New York: Interbook, Inc., 1960.
Howard, Martha W. Plutarch in the Major European Literature of the Eighteenth Century. Chapel Hill, N. C.: University of North Carolina Press, 1970.
Jones, C. P. Plutarch and Rome. Oxford: Oxford University Press, 1971.
Jones, Roger M. The Platonism of Plutarch. Menasha, Wis.: Wisconsin Publishing Co., 1916.
Lesky, Albin. A History of Greek Literature. Translated by James Willis and Cornelis de Heer. New York: Crowell, 1966.
Oakesmith, John. The Religion of Plutarch. London: 1902.
Plutarch. Parallel Lives of the Noble Greeks and Romans. Translated with an introduction by Bernadotte Perrin. New York: Crowell, 1914-1928 (Originally written c. 105-115 A. D.)
Russell, D. A. Plutarch. New York: Scribner, 1973.
Stadter, Philip A. Plutarch's Historical Methods: An Analysis of the Mulierum Virtues. Cambridge, Mass.: Harvard University Press, 1965.
Stuart, Duane Reed. Epochs of Greek and Roman Biography. Berkeley, Calif.: University of California Press, 1928.
Thayer, William Roscoe. The Art of Biography. New York: Scribner's, 1920.

GALEN'S WRITINGS ON MEDICINE (c. 180)

Hippocrates (c. 460-377 B. C.), sometimes called "The Father of Medicine," was a Greek physician. He and his predecessor Aristotle (384-322 B. C.) were considered the foremost medical authorities of the ancient world. The former confined his activities to medicine and the latter, aside from his work in the natural sci-

ences, also investigated and wrote about virtually all branches of
knowledge.

Galen (c. 131-c. 201 A.D.), the Greek physician and philosopher, was greatly influenced by the writings of Hippocrates and
Aristotle. Born at Pergamum, Asia Minor, he studied medicine
at Smyrna and then traveled widely, acquiring additional medical
knowledge at Corinth and Alexandria. In 164 A.D. he settled in
Rome where he practiced his profession. His patients included
members of the nobility and he was appointed court physician to the
emperor Marcus Aurelius. He remained in Rome until about 192,
when he returned to Pergamum where he died at seventy.

Next to Hippocrates, Galen was the outstanding physician of
antiquity. Until the sixteenth century he was considered an authority on medical matters by Arabic, Greek and Roman doctors. He
wrote prolifically on medicine, philosophy, religion, logic and ethics, producing some 500 tracts, of which about 100 are extant.

In the period between Hippocrates and Galen experimental
work on anatomy and physiology was conducted at Alexandria by
Herophilus and Erasistratus, two eminent scientists of the day.
Following their deaths in the third century B.C. a decline in general medical research set in, but toward the end of the first century A.D. a revival occurred which helped prepare the way for
Galen.

Galen's writings present both his own views and those of
other medical men with whom he disagreed. A practicing vivisec-
tionist, he recorded the results of his experiments on living animals, together with the conclusions he drew from these experiments.
Only a portion of his medical writings have been published in English translation. However, several translations of his more important works, some of these going back to the sixteenth century when
Galen was considered a medical authority, now exist. His textbook,
Anatomical Procedures, deals with dissection and vivisection. It
describes his research in these areas in which he used swine, apes
and other animals as subjects. It gives detailed instructions on
separating the various parts of the body with surgical instruments
and tells of experiments which can be performed to illustrate the
functions of the body's various organs.

His On the Usefulness of the Parts of the Body describes and
explains all parts of the human anatomy.   On the Natural Faculties
discusses the body's digestive and eliminative functions as Galen
understood them. His contention that the liver transforms food into blood which goes through the body by way of the veins has since
been shown to be erroneous. Some of the other conclusions to
which he came as the result of his experiments and empirical observations have since been corrected by physicians and anatomists.

Galen took great pains with his writings, using as models
the best contemporary Greek authors. The fact that his information

was the best available in its day and that he associated medicine with the other sciences and philosophy resulted in his being considered the supreme authority in his field for fifteen centuries. Today his system of medicine is completely outdated. Lacking the scientific equipment available to modern researchers he was unable to consider such things as the effect of microscopic organisms and chemical changes on the human body. His pioneering work, however, inspired other medical researchers to follow in his footsteps and engage in new investigations which eventually rendered his work obsolete.

Suggested Readings

Brock, A. J. Galen and the Natural Faculties. London: William Heinemann, 1916.

Cheyne, William Watson. Lister and His Achievement. London: Longmans, Green, 1925.

De Kruif, Paul. Microbe Hunters. Edited by Harry G. Grover. New York: Harcourt, Brace, 1932.

Duckworth, W. L. H. , M. C. Lyons and B. Towers. Galen on Anatomical Procedures: The Later Books. Cambridge: The University Press, 1962.

Eberle, Irmengarde. Modern Medical Discoveries. New York: Crowell, 1958.

Glaser, Hugo. The Road to Modern Surgery. New York: Dutton, 1962.

Glasscheib, Hermann S. The March of Medicine. New York: Putnam's, 1964.

Lewis, Sinclair. Arrowsmith (fiction). New York: Modern Library, 1925.

Major, Ralph H. A History of Medicine. Springfield, Ill. : Thomas, 1954.

May, Margaret T. Galen on the Usefulness of the Parts of the Body. Ithaca, N. Y.: Cornell University Press, 1968.

The Merck Manual of Diagnosis and Therapy. 8th edition. Rahway, N. J.: Merck & Co. , Inc. , 1950.

Metchnikov, Ilia Ilich. The Founders of Modern Medicine. New York: Walden Publications, 1939.

Mettler, Cecilia C. History of Medicine. Philadelphia: Blakiston, 1947.

Sarton, George. Galen of Pergamum. Lawrence, Kans. : University of Kansas Press, 1954.

Siegel, Rudolph E. Galen's System of Physiology and Medicine. Basel: S. Karger, 1958.

Singer, Charles. Galen on Anatomical Prodedures. London: Oxford University Press, 1956.

_____, and E. Ashworth Underwood. A Short History of Medicine. New York: Oxford University Press, 1962.

Solmsen, Friedrich. "Greek Philosophy and the Discovery of the Nerves," Museum Helveticum, Vol. XVII, 1961.

Winslow, Charles-Edward Amory. The Conquest of Epidemic Disease. Princeton, N. J.: Princeton University Press, 1943.

Young, Agatha. Scalpel: Men Who Made Surgery. New York:
    Ramdom House, 1956.

THE ALEXANDER LEGENDS (c. 200)

Alexander III, King of Macedon, was one of the greatest
generals of all time.   During the last thirteen years of his life
(336-323 B. C.) he conquered virtually all the ancient world, founded cities which bore his name and inaugurated military tactics
which were so effective that they were copied by succeeding generals for generations.   His victories vastly extended the influence
of Greek civilization and paved the way for the Hellenistic kingdoms and the conquests of the Roman Empire.   He became known
as "Alexander the Great. "

The exploits of such a man inevitably resulted in the appearance of legends exaggerating his actual accomplishments and
mingling idealized fiction with fact.   An account of Alexander's
career was written by Callisthenes, a Greek philosopher, historian
and disciple of Aristotle, who accompanied the Macedonian general
on his campaigns.   This and Callisthenes' other historical works
are no longer extant.   About 200 A. D. an account of Alexander's
adventures, probably originating in Alexandria and sometimes called
the "pseudo-Callisthenes, " appeared.   This account, which was
largely fictitious, became the basis for a number of Middle Age
romances.   Although Alexander was the son of Philip of Macedon,
the pseudo-Callisthenes represents him as the son of Nectanebus,
the last king of Egypt, and credits him with a number of unbelievable exploits.   One of these involves the Gordian Knot, an intricate
knot tied by Gordius, an ancient king of Phrygia, and which was to
be undone only by one who should rule Asia.   Alexander summarily
cut the knot apart with his sword.   This account was translated into Latin early in the fourth century A. D.

Several French poems were based on the Alexander legends.
The best known of these is the "Chanson d'Alexandre (Le Romans
d'Alexandre), " which is ascribed to Alexandre de Bernai, a Pro-
vençal poet.   This is written in a twelve-syllable line divided into
six iambic feet or into thirteen syllables when the end rhyme is
feminine, known as Alexandrine verse.

In the literature of the Middle Ages Alexander the Great is
depicted as a medieval knight.   He became one of four kings in a
deck of playing cards and one of the "nine worthies. "

The Alexander legends found their way into the literature of
the Orient and most European countries.   In the fifth century A. D.
the pseudo-Callisthenes was translated into Syrian and Armenian,
and some slavic forms of the legends have been derived from them.
German versions appeared in the 13th century.   One of the oldest

Spanish poems is the "Libro de Alexandre," another version, and several English adaptations have appeared, the earliest being a poem called "Lyfe of Alisaunder" which was written about 1330.

Suggested Readings

Barker, Felix, in collaboration with Anthea Barker. "Alexander the Great" in their The First Explorers: Encyclopedia of Discovery and Exploration, Vol. I. London: Aldus Books, 1971.

Brunt, P. A. "Persian Accounts of Alexander's Campaigns," Classical Quarterly, Vol. XII, New Series, 1962.

Duggan, Alfred Leo. Besieger of Cities. New York: Pantheon Books, 1963.

Fuller, John F. C. The Generalship of Alexander the Great. New Brunswick, N. J.: Rutgers University Press, 1960.

Hopkinson, Leslie White. "Alexander the Great" in his Greek Leaders. Boston: Houghton Mifflin, 1918.

Jones, A. H. M. The Greek City from Alexander to Justinian. Oxford: Clarendon Press, 1940.

Mercer, Charles E. and the editors of Horizon Magazine. Alexander the Great. New York: American Heritage, 1963.

Myers, Philip van Ness. Ancient History. Boston: Ginn, 1904.

Tarn, W. W. Alexander the Great. Cambridge: The University Press, 1948.

_____. Hellenistic Military and Naval Developments. Cambridge: The University Press, 1930.

Wilcken, Ulrich. Alexander the Great. Translated by G. C. Richards. London: Chatto and Windus, 1932.

THE FOUNDING OF CONSTANTINOPLE (324)

Constantine the Great (c. 280-337) became sole Roman emperor in 324, following the defeat of his rival Licinius, emperor of the east, at Adrianople. He had been converted to Christianity a decade before when, at the battle of Milvain Bridge in which Roman emperor Maxentius was defeated, he had a vision of the cross appearing in the noonday sky. With the cross was the legend written in Greek, "By this conquer!"

As sole governor of the Roman world, Constantine determined to move the capital to the east, Rome being no longer the political or geographical center of the Roman empire. In 324 he chose as a site for "New Rome," or Constantinople, as it came to be called, the ancient city of Byzantium. This was to remain the economic and political center of the Byzantine Empire for a thousand years.

Constantine's choice of Byzantium for his new city was excellent. Like Rome, it was built on seven sloping hills. It was

surrounded on three sides by water, this making it able to resist
attack by enemy military land forces.   The Golden Horn, a bay
seven miles long, protected it on the north and the Bosporus gave
similar protection on the east as did the Sea of Marmora on the
south.   It was intersected by two important trade routes between
Europe and Asia and also controlled trade between the Black Sea
and the Mediterranean.   It was located halfway between the Danube
and the Euphrates and thus was not only more centrally located
than Rome but also was in the most highly developed and prosperous area of the empire.

Constantinople differed from Rome in several particulars.
It did not have a workable senate and was subject to a pro-consul,
although its inhabitants considered themselves Romans.

In May, 330, six years after work on Constantinople was
started, it was dedicated to the Holy Trinity and the Mother of
God.   Immigration to the new city was encouraged by the making
of land grants to settlers in return for which the newcomers were
required to build and maintain houses.   Free bread was given to
several thousand inhabitants on a daily basis, another stimulant to
immigration.   While Constantinople was a Christian city, paganism
was permitted and pagan temples of worship were built there as
well as Christian churches.

Constantinople remained the Roman capital until 1453 when
it fell to the Turks and became the capital of the Ottoman, or
Turkish, Empire.   It was the capital of present-day Turkey until
1923 when the newly-founded Turkish Republic declared Angora
(now Ankara) the capital.   It was occupied by Great Britain, France
and Italy from 1918 to 1923.   Today it is known as Istanbul.

Suggested Readings

Burckhardt, Jacob.   The Age of Constantine the Great.   Translated
    by Moses Hadas.   New York: Doubleday, 1956.
Diehl, Charles.   Byzantium: Greatness and Decline.   Translated
    by Naomi Alford.   New Brunswick, N. J. :   Rutgers University
    Press, 1957.
Eusebius.   The Life of Constantine.   Translated by E. C. Richard-
    son.   Grand Rapids, Mich. :   Wm. P. Eerdmans Publishing
    Co. , 1961.
Hussey, Joan M.   The Byzantine World.   London: Hutchinson &
    Co. , 1957.
Jones, A. H. M.   Constantine and the Conversion of Europe.   New
    York: Crowell, Collier & Macmillan, 1962.
_____ .   The Later Roman Empire, 284-602: A Social, Econom-
    ic and Administrative Survey.   Oxford: Basil Blackwell, 1964.
Lot, Ferdinand.   The End of the Ancient World and the Beginnings
    of the Middle Ages.   New York: Barnes & Noble, 1953 (Orig-
    inally published 1926).
Ostrogorsky, George.   History of the Byzantine State.   Translated

by Joan M. Hussey. New Brunswick, N. J. : Rutgers University Press, 1969 (Originally published 1956).

Parker, H. M. D. History of the Roman World from A. D. 138 to 337. Revised with additional notes by B. H. Warmington. New York: Macmillan, 1958.

Pears, Edwin. The Destruction of the Greek Empire and the Story of the Capture of Constantinople by the Turks. London: Longmans, Green, 1903.

Runciman, Steven. The Fall of Constantinople, 1453. Cambridge: Cambridge University Press, 1965.

Van Loon, Hendrik Willem. The Story of Mankind. New York: Garden City Publishing Co. , 1938.

Vasiliev, Alexander A. The History of the Byzantine Empire, 324-1453. Madison, Wis. : University of Wisconsin Press, 1952.

Vyronis, Speros. Byzantium and Europe. New York: Harcourt, Brace, 1967.

THE CANONIZATION OF THE TALMUD
(c. 375 and c. 480)

The Talmud is the body of Jewish civil and religious law, including commentaries on the law not contained in the Pentateuch. It includes the Mishnah, the collection of oral laws made in 180 by Judah ha-Nasi, a Palestinian religious leader, and a commentary on the Mishnah, called the Gemara. That portion of the Talmud dealing with decisions on disputed questions of law is known as the Halakah, and the anecdotes, sayings and legends in the Talmud illustrative of the traditional law are called the Haggada.

There are two compilations of the Talmud: the Palestinian (Jerusalem) Talmud and the Babylonian Talmud. Both contain the same Mishnah but the Gemaras differ. The Palestinian is the older of the two, having been written by scholars between the third and fifth centuries A. D. The Babylonian Talmud was written between the third and seventh centuries A. D. They were canonized about the years 375 and 480, respectively.

After the first five books of the Old Testament (the Pentateuch) were accepted about 400 B. C. oral tradition began to accumulate. This was, as circumstances warranted, reduced to writing and eventually became the Mishnah, a legal commentary on the Pentateuch. The Talmud, in turn, is a legal commentary on the Mishnah.

For the last fifteen centuries Judaism has been dependent on the Talmud, which gives guidelines for Jewish religious practice, piety and intellectual life. Like the Mishnah it is divided into six sections: seeds, which indicate religious laws dealing with agriculture; seasons, which detail religious laws applying to the Sabbath, fasts and festivals; women, including marriage and divorce; damages,

which pertains to legal procedures; "holy things," including religious
rituals; and purities, in which the laws of ceremonial purity are
set forth.   The discussions in the Talmud are preceded by a passage from the Mishnah in which the various arguments dealing with
the matter under discussion are given, as is a conclusion.

The Talmud and the commentaries concerning it are considered the greatest body of rabbinical literature in the history of Judaism.   One such commentary is the Mishnah Torah, written by
Maimonides, a Spanish-born Jewish philosopher and physician, about
1180.   This is an abstract of all the rabbinical legal literature in
existence at his time.

The Babylonian and Palestinian Talmuds were first printed
by Daniel Bomberg of Venice between 1520 and 1522 and in 1523,
respectively.   The book is today available in an English translation,
edited by Isidore Epstein.   Portions of the Palestinian Talmud are
also to be had in both French and Latin translations.

Suggested Readings

Adler, Morris.   The World of the Talmud.   New York: Schocken
       Books, 1963.
Blunt, A. W. F.   Israel Before Christ, an Account of Social and
       Religious Development in the Old Testament.   London: Oxford
       University Press, 1924.
Chajes, Zebi Hirsch.   The Student's Guide Through the Talmud.
       New York: Philipp Feldheim, 1960.
Herford, Robert T.   Talmud and Apochrypha.   London: Soncino
       Press, 1938.
Jacobs, Lewis.   Studies in Talmudic Logic and Methodology.   Lon-
       don: Valentine, Mitchell, 1961.
Lieberman, Saul.   Hellenism in Jewish Palestine.   New York: Ktav
       Publishing House, 1950.
Moore, George Foote.   Judaism.   Cambridge, Mass. : Harvard
       University Press, 1927.
Neusner, Jacob.   A History of the Jews in Babylonia.   Leiden:
       E. J. Brill, 1965.
Riggs, James Stevenson.   A History of the Jewish People During
       the Maccabean and Roman Periods (Including New Testament
       Times).   New York: Scribner's, 1905.
Stanley, Arthur Penrhyn.   Lectures on the History of the Jewish
       Church.   New York: Scribner's, 1913.
Strack, Hermann L.   Introduction to the Talmud and Midrash.   Phil-
       adelphia: Jewish Publication Society, 1931.
Trattner, Ernest R.   Understanding the Talmud.   New York: Nel-
       son, 1955.

THE EXCOMMUNICATION AND PENANCE
OF THEODOSIUS THE GREAT (390)

During the reign of the Emperor Nero in the first century
A. D. the Christians suffered great persecutions at the hands of
the Romans.   Eventually, however, Rome's power declined and the
Christian Church gathered strength and by the fourth century it was
extremely influential and its high officials wielded great power.
This was demonstrated in the year 390 when Theodosius the Great,
Roman emperor in the east, was required by Ambrose, Bishop of
Milan, to do public penance.

The two men had clashed in the year 388.   This was occasioned by the Bishop of Callinicum who had allowed a group of
Christians to burn a synagogue and a Gnostic (Valentinian) chapel.
Theodosius ordered the bishop to make restitution but Ambrose de-
murred, holding that the Bishop of Callinicum's Christian funds
could not properly be used for a non-Christian purpose.   Theodosius concurred and ordered that money from the imperial treasury
be used.   Again Ambrose objected, arguing that such an action
would, in effect, be an adoption of Judaism as a state religion.

Theodosius disputed this reasoning but acquiesced after Ambrose delivered a sermon threatening to stop the Eucharist unless
the emperor withdrew from the Callinicum matter.

In 390 a charioteer was imprisoned at Thessalonica.   The
man was well liked by the people and a mob appeared at the jail
and demanded his release.   The governor of the town, an imperial official, refused, whereupon he was seized and murdered.   Theodosius, intent on impressing the Thessalonians with the importance
of imperial office holders, had some seven thousand persons massacred by Roman soldiers.   After he had ordered the massacre he
reconsidered and attempted to countermand his instructions but his
message arrived too late.   Then, on August 13, 390, he ordered
that all sentences of death henceforth were suspended for thirty
days and were then to be reconsidered.

About September 10, Bishop Ambrose, horrified at Theodosius' cruel vengeance on the Thessalonians, wrote him a letter
(Letter 51).   This, a secret missive intended for the emperor only, excommunicated him.   It first reviewed the circumstances of
the massacre and then cited the example of David who, as recount-
ed in the Old Testament, performed royal penance.   Emperor Theodosius, said the bishop, must humble his soul before God.

Theodosius did not answer Ambrose's letter but instead sent
Rufinius, his master of offices, to negotiate with the churchman.
Ambrose, however, refused to alter his position and the negotiations
came to nothing.   Late in October, 390, Theodosius agreed to do
public penance.   For several weeks he appeared daily at the church
in Milan where he prayed, wept, abstained from Communion and, to

all intents and purposes, showed himself truly sorry for ordering
the massacre of the Thessalonians.   At the Christian Eucharist
Bishop Ambrose gave him absolution.

The penance done by Emperor Theodosius at the behest of
Bishop Ambrose marked an important turning point in church history in that it established a precedent for church supremacy over
civil authority.   Other monarchs in later days followed the example
of Theodosius and performed public penance, notably Henry IV, King
of Germany and Holy Roman Emperor (1050-1106).

Many rulers resented what they considered undue interference
by the churchmen in affairs of state.   In 1534 Henry VIII of England,
after continued conflict with papal power, obtained from Parliament
the Act of Supremacy creating a national church and appointing the
king protector and sole supreme head of the church and clergy of
England.

Suggested Readings

Ambrose.   "Letter 51.   Early Latin Theology" in Baillie, John,
     John McNeill and Henry Van Dusen, eds.   The Library of
     Christian Classics, Vol. V.   Philadelphia: Westminster Press,
     1961.
Gibbon, Edward.   The Decline and Fall of the Roman Empire.
     Edited by J. B. Bury.   London: Methuen, 1896-1900 (Origin-
     ally published 1776-1778).
Greenslade, S. L.   Church and State from Constantine to Theodo-
     sius.   London: Student Christian Movement Press, 1954.
Huttmann, Maude Aline.   The Establishment of Christianity and the
     Proscription of Paganism.   New York: Columbia University
     Press, 1914.
King, N. Q.   The Emperor Theodosius and the Establishment of
     Christianity.   Philadelphia: Westminster Press, 1960.
Leitzmann, Hans.   "The Era of the Church Fathers" in A History
     of the Early Church, Vol. IV.   Translated by Bertram Lee
     Woolf.   London: Lutterworth Press, 1961.
Momigliano, Arnaldo, ed.   The Conflict Between Paganism and
     Christianity in the Fourth Century.   Oxford: Clarendon Press,
     1963.
Morrison, Carl F.   "Rome and the City of God: An Essay on the
     Constitutional Relationships of Empire and Church in the Fourth
     Century, " Transactions of the American Philological Society,
     1964.
Paredi, Angelo.   Saint Ambrose--His Life and Times.   Translated
     by M. Joseph Costelloe.   Notre Dame, Ind. :   University of
     Notre Dame Press, 1964.
Paulinus the Deacon.   The Life of St. Ambrose.   Translated by
     F. R. Hoare.   New York: Harper and Row, 1965.
Sozomen.   "Church History" in Vol. II, Series 2 of Nicene and
     Post-Nicene Fathers.   Grand Rapids, Mich. :   Eerdmans Pub-
     lishing Co. , 1957.

THE SACK OF ROME BY THE VISIGOTHS (410)

The last Roman emperor to rule over a united empire was Theodosius I, called "The Great," who died in 395 A.D. Following his death the empire broke into eastern and western halves, the split stemming from religious and political disharmony.

Theodosius was succeeded by his two sons, eighteen-year-old Arcadius, who became Augustus (co-ruler) in the east, and Honorius, a mentally retarded child of eleven, who was designated Augustus in the west. General Stilicho, a Vandal, as regent was the actual leader in the west.

Alaric, the Christian leader of the Visigothic allies of the Romans, left the Roman army to be elected king of the Visigoths. In 401, having been appointed "magister militum" (Master of the Soldiers), he invaded Italy but, in 402, was defeated by Stilicho and forced to withdraw. He was defeated again in 403. Stilicho was murdered in 408, following which the Roman soldiers turned on their Gothic allies who deserted to Alaric in large numbers. With Stilicho gone Alaric and his enlarged army were able to invade Italy and strike at the Western Empire. They encountered little opposition.

In 408 and again in 409 Alaric marched on Rome. On the first occasion he permitted himself to be bought off, and on the second he set up his puppet, Priscus Attalus, as a rival emperor to Honorius. The latter had secured supporting troops from the Eastern Empire and refused to capitulate. Alaric then deposed Attalus.

On August 24, 410, Alaric and approximately 40,000 Goths seized Rome and plundered it for three days. They did comparatively little physical damage but made a great impression on contemporaries, Rome not having been taken by an enemy for over 800 years. Thereafter Roman prestige was to be based on the papacy rather than on the Empire.

After his attack on Rome Alaric attempted to invade Africa. This was unsuccessful, his ships being wrecked in a storm before leaving Italy. He died at Cosentia the same year and was buried in the Busento River by followers who were afterwards killed, to prevent anyone from knowing the location of the body and desecrating the remains.

Suggested Readings

Asimov, Isaac. The Roman Republic. Boston: Houghton Mifflin, 1966.

Boak, Arthur E. R., and William B. C. Sinnigen. A History of Rome to A.D. 565. New York: Macmillan, 1965.

Chambers, Mortimer. The Fall of Rome--Can It Be Explained?
    New York: Holt, Rinehart, 1963.
Gibbon, Edward. The History of the Decline and Fall of the Ro-
    man Empire. Edited by J. B. Bury. London: Methuen, 1896-
    1900 (Originally published 1776-1778).
Gwatkin, H. M. , and J. P. Whitney, eds. "The Christian Roman
    Empire and the Foundation of Teutonic Kingdoms" in The Cam-
    bridge Medieval History, Vol. I. New York: Macmillan, 1924.
Jones, A. H. M. The Later Roman Empire, 284-602: A Social,
    Economic and Administrative Survey. Oxford: Basil Blackwell,
    1964.
Katz, Solomon. The Decline of Rome and the Rise of Medieval
    Europe. Ithaca, N. Y. : Cornell University Press, 1955.
Lanciani, Rodolfo. Ancient Rome in the Light of Recent Discover-
    ies. New York: Blom, 1967 (Originally published 1888).
            . The Destruction of Ancient Rome. New York: Blom,
    1967 (Originally published 1901).
            . New Tales of Old Rome. New York: Blom, 1967 (Or-
    iginally published 1901).
Lot, Ferdinand. The End of the Ancient World and the Beginnings
    of the Middle Ages. New York: Barnes & Noble (Originally
    published 1926).
Mills, Dorothy. The Book of Ancient Romans: An Introduction to
    the History and Civilization of Rome from the Traditional Date
    of the Founding of the City to Its Fall in 476 A. D. New York:
    Putnam's, 1927.
Parker, H. M. D. The History of the Roman World from A. D. 138
    to 337. New York: Macmillan, 1958.
Payne, Pierre, and the editors of Horizon Magazine. The Horizon
    Book of Ancient Rome. New York: American Heritage, 1966.
Perowne, Stewart. The End of the Roman World. New York: Cro-
    well, 1966.
Previté-Orton, C. W. "The Later Roman Empire to the Twelfth
    Century" in The Shorter Cambridge Medieval History, Vol. I.
    Cambridge: The University Press, 1953.
Stobart, John Clarke. The Grandeur That Was Rome. 4th edition,
    ed. and rev. by W. S. Maguinness and H. H. Scullard. New
    York: Hawthorn Books, 1962.
Tappan, Eva March. "Alaric the Visigoth Besieges Rome" in her
    Old World Hero Stories. Boston: Houghton Mifflin, 1937.

THE BATTLE OF CHÂLONS (451)

One of the great military encounters of ancient history was
the Battle of Châlons. This was fought near Troyes, northeast
France, in June, 451, between the allied forces of the Romans and
Visigoths and those of Attila the Hun in alliance with the Ostrogoths
under Genseric, king of the Vandals. The Romans, commanded by
General Flavius Aëtius and aided by the Visigoths under their king,
Theodoric I, won the battle. Attila's losses were reported to be

between 200,000 and 300,000 men, although these figures are generally considered to be greatly exaggerated.

Valentinian III became emperor of the west in 423, at the
age of five. His mother, Galla Placidia, sister of the Emperor
Honorius, acted as regent. Aëtius supported a rival claimant to
the throne but was bought off and given command of an army in
Gaul. However, he still remained a threat to the young emperor
and Placidia dismissed him from his military office. He appealed
to the Huns and, with their help, was able to regain his command
in 433. For the next two decades he was the virtual ruler of Gaul.
With the assistance of Hunnish mercenaries he was successful in
holding Roman boundaries in Gaul against attacks by the barbarian
Burgundians, Franks and Goths. The Vandals, meanwhile, took
over North Africa and Britain was occupied by the Saxons.

Attila, having had Bleda, his brother and co-ruler of the
Huns, put to death about 444, united the separate groups of Huns.
He exacted huge sums of money from the Romans in return for
keeping peace, and in 447 he crossed the Danube and made further
demands. These included the hand of Honoria, the emperor's sister, in marriage, with half the western empire as her dowry. Rome
refused to approve the marriage and Attila is said to have used
this refusal as an excuse for further invasion.

Flavius Aëtius lacked sufficient troops to overcome Attila's
threats of additional invasion by force. He decided to ally with
the Visigoths, Rome's traditional enemies, and also to obtain additional help from the Franks. Gaiseric, king of the Vandals, incited Attila against the Visigoths, ruled by Theodoric.

The Battle of Châlons occurred on a plain near Troyes. Attila was unable to get possession of a high position overlooking the
battlefield and ordered an attack on the Roman right flank, composed of Theodoric's Visigoths. Aëtius deployed his Roman troops
and Gothic allies on the left flank, with additional allies from the
Alans at the center.

Casualties were heavy on both sides, but though the Roman
forces were technically victorious, their victory was not clear cut.
Eventually the Huns retreated, with Aëtius' forces pursuing them
as far as the Rhine.

The Battle of Châlons is also known as the Battle of the
Catalaunian Fields, the Battle of Troyes, the Battle of the Mauriac
Plain and the Battle of the Nations. Whatever name it might be
known by, its significance lies in its importance as an illustration
of the complex relations between Rome and the Germanic peoples
of the time.

Attila, in 452, turned his attention to Italy, where he took
several cities and then advanced upon Rome, which was saved when
Pope Leo I intervened. In 453 Attila planned another invasion of

Italy but died of a hemorrhage before his plans could be carried
out. Aëtius became a victim of his own intrigues. In 454 he was
stabbed to death in Rome by Valentinian himself.

Suggested Readings

Asimov, Isaac. The Roman Republic. Boston: Houghton Mifflin,
    1966.
Boak, Arthur E. R., and William B. G. Sinnigen. A History of
    Rome to A. D. 565. New York: Macmillan, 1965.
Chambers, Mortimer. The Fall of Rome--Can It Be Explained?
    New York: Holt, Rhinehart, 1963.
Creasy, Edward S. Fifteen Decisive Battles of the World. Har-
    risburg, Pa. : Stackpole Books, 1957.
Falls, Cyril, ed. Great Military Battles. New York: Macmillan,
    1964.
Fuller, John F. C. A Military History of the Western World. New
    York: Funk & Wagnalls, 1954.
Gibbon, Edward. The History of the Decline and Fall of the Roman
    Empire. Edited by J. B. Bury. London: Methuen, 1896-1900
    (Originally published 1776-1778).
Gordon, C. D. The Age of Attila. Ann Arbor, Mich. : University
    of Michigan Press, 1960.
Jones, A. H. M. The Later Roman Empire, 284-602: A Social,
    Economic and Administrative Survey. Oxford: Basil Blackwell,
    1964.
Katz, Solomon. The Decline of Rome and the Rise of Medieval
    Europe. Ithaca, N. Y. : Cornell University Press, 1955.
Lanciani, Rodolfo. Ancient Rome in the Light of Recent Discover-
    ies. New York: Blom, 1967 (Originally published 1888).
    _____. The Destruction of Ancient Rome: A Sketch of the His-
    tory of the Monuments. New York: Blom, 1967 (Originally
    published 1901).
Lot, Ferdinand. The End of the Ancient World and the Beginnings
    of the Middle Ages. New York: Barnes & Noble, 1953 (Orig-
    inally published 1926).
Mills, Dorothy. The Book of the Ancient Romans: An Introduction
    to the History and Civilization of Rome from the Traditional
    Date of the Founding of the City to Its Fall in 476 A. D. New
    York: Putnam's, 1927.
Mitchell, Lt. -Col. Joseph B. , and Sir Edward S. Creasy. Twenty
    Decisive Battles of the World. New York: Macmillan, 1964.
Perowne, Stewart. The End of the Roman World. New York: Cro-
    well, 1966.
Previté-Orton, C. W. "The Later Roman Empire to the Twelfth
    Century" in The Shorter Cambridge Medieval History, Vol. I.
    Cambridge: The University Press, 1953.
Thompson, E. A. A History of Attila and the Huns. London: Ox-
    ford University Press, 1948.

THE PROMULGATION OF JUSTINIAN'S CODES
(529 and 534)

The earliest code of Roman law, civil, criminal and religious, was the law of the Twelve Tables, drawn up by a group of ten magistrates (decemvirs) about 450 B.C. Originally ten tables of laws were submitted to and accepted by the popular assembly, and two supplementary tables were adopted later. The Twelve Tables, now preserved only in fragmentary form, provided the basis for the development of Roman law.

In the following centuries Roman rule had extended over the Mediterranean and it became necessary for the Romans to develop a new system of law. Each of the conquered territories had its own legal rules and the making of such rules uniform was mandatory. This had been accomplished to some degree between the years 250 and 150 B.C., the praetors defining and interpreting the law in individual cases. In 438 A.D. Theodosius II published a codification of the decrees issued by the emperors. His original plan had been to publish an official digest of the older law, as set forth in the juristic literature, but this was not accomplished.

Justinian, Roman Emperor of the East, mounted the throne in April, 527. He hoped to reunite the Empire territorially and also in terms of religion and law. To the latter end he appointed a committee of ten commissioners, headed by Tribonianus, his chief legal minister, to prepare a legal digest or codex of imperial constitutions. Within a year the Code or Corpus Juris Civilis (Body of Civil Law), containing all of the imperial laws from the reign of Emperor Hadrian (117-138) was assembled and Justinian promulgated it in 529. This publication nullified and replaced all previous laws.

Justinian's own legislative activities soon rendered the Code obsolete and he directed that an amended compilation be prepared. This second Code was promulgated on November 11, 534. While this was in preparation Justinian ordered Tribonianus and his staff to prepare the Digest or Pandects. Published in November, 533, this was a set of abstracts of all writings of Roman jurists. Also published in 533 was Institutes, a textbook for the law students of the time.

Following the publication of Corpus Juris Civilis Justinian issued a long series of statutes known as the Novellae (Amendments). He hoped to consolidate and publish these but no such publication was issued during his reign. Later many of his laws were gathered together and translated into Latin from the original Greek for use in western Europe.

In the twelfth century medieval scholars published a collection of Justinian's constitutions. This, which included legal edicts of certain medieval emperors, is known as the Authentics.

Justinian's Codes are the source of most of today's knowledge of Roman law.   They formed a base upon which latter day
jurists founded systems of public and private law and are the foundation of actual law in most continental Europe today, including France,
Germany and other countries.

Suggested Readings

Baker, G. P. Justinian. London: Thames & Hudson, 1931.
Buckland, W. W. A Textbook of Roman Law from Augustus to Jus-
    tinian. Cambridge: The University Press, 1963.
Burnet, J. Aids to Justinian. London: Thames & Hudson, 1936.
Crook, J. A. Law and Life of Rome. London: Thames & Hudson,
    1967.
Dowley, Glanville. Constantinople in the Age of Justinian. Nor-
    man, Okla. : University of Oklahoma Press, 1968 (Originally
    published 1960).
Gibbon, Edward. The History of the Decline and Fall of the Ro-
    man Empire. Edited by J. B. Bury. London: Methuen, 1896-
    1900 (Originally published 1776-1778).
Jolowicz, H. F. Historical Introduction to the Study of Roman Law.
    Cambridge: The University Press, 1929.
Jones, J. Walter. The Law and Legal Theory of the Greeks: An
    Introduction. Oxford: Clarendon Press, 1956.
Nicholas, Barry. An Introduction to Roman Law. Oxford: Claren-
    don Press, 1962.
Ostrogorsky, George. History of the Byzantine State. Translated
    by Joan M. Hussey. New Brunswick, N. J. : Rutgers Univer-
    sity Press, 1969.
Pringsheim, F. "The Character of Justinian's Legislation, " Law
    Quarterly Review, Vol. LVI, 1940.
Schulz, Fritz. Principles of Roman Law. Oxford: Clarendon
    Press, 1936.
Vasiliev, Alexander A. The History of the Byzantine Empire, 324-
    1453. Madison, Wis. : University of Wisconsin Press, 1952.
Wolff, Hans Julius. Roman Law: An Historical Introduction. Nor-
    man, Okla. : University of Oklahoma Press, 1964 (Originally
    published 1951).

THE DEATH OF KING ARTHUR (c. 537)

King Arthur was a semi-legendary, 6th-century king of Britain.   The son of Uther Pendragon, he was concealed from the public in childhood and raised as the son of a king.   When he assumed
the throne he gathered together a company of knights which he seated at a round table in his palace in order to avoid all questions of
precedence.   In the year 516 he reputedly led his army against the
invading Saxons, and in 520 may have won the victory of Mount Ba-
den.

He fought wars in Continental Europe where he defeated armies of the Roman empire. When his nephew Modred rebelled and seized his kingdom, Arthur returned home to meet Modred's forces.

In the battle of Camlan in Southwest England "the king and the traitor fell, pierced by each other's spears." Modred was killed and Arthur was mortally wounded.

According to Sir Thomas Malory's account, King Arthur, attended by the knights Sir Lucan and Sir Bedwere, realized that he was dying. The two knights attempted to help him, but Sir Lucan expired from wounds received in battle. King Arthur then told Sir Bedwere to take his royal sword Excalibur, throw it into a nearby body of water, and report what followed. Sir Bedwere took the sword but, tempted by the jewels which were mounted on it, hid it beneath a tree. Returning to King Arthur, he reported seeing "nothing but waves and winds." Arthur, knowing the knight to be lying, sent him a second time to throw the sword into the water. Again Sir Bedwere failed to obey, reporting seeing only "waters and waves," and again the king knew him to be lying.

Sir Bedwere went to the water a third time and threw Excalibur "as far into the water as he might. And there came an arm and a hand above the water and met it, and caught it, and so shook it thrice and brandished, and then vanished away the hand and the sword in the water."

Sir Bedwere reported this to the king who now knew he was speaking the truth. The knight carried the dying Arthur to the shore where they were met by "a little barge with many fair ladies in it, and among them all was a queen." Arthur was placed in the barge among the mourning ladies. Sir Bedwere asked, "My lord Arthur, what shall become of me ... among my enemies?" Arthur comforted him, saying that he should do as best he could, "for," said the king, "I will go to the Vale of Avalon, to heal me of my grievous wound. And if thou hear never more of me, pray for my soul."

The barge disappeared in the distant mists and King Arthur disappeared from history, remaining only a legend.

Suggested Readings

Ashe, Geoffrey, et al. The Quest for Arthur's Britain. New York: Frederick A. Praeger, 1968.
Ashley, Maurice. Great Britain to 1688: A Modern History. Ann Arbor, Mich.: University of Michigan Press, 1961.
Chambers, Edmund K. Arthur of Britain. London: Sidgwick & Jackson, 1927.
Clemens, Samuel L. A Connecticut Yankee at King Arthur's Court (fiction). New York: Harper, 1889.

82							Footnotes to World History

Cross, E. A. "European and Oriental Literature Through the Middle Ages" in his World Literature. New York: American Book Company, 1935.
De Camp, L. Sprague, and Catherine C. De Camp. "Tintagel and the Table Round" in their Ancient Ruins and Archaeology. Garden City, N. Y.: Doubleday, 1964.
Edwards, Clayton. "King Arthur of Britain" in his A Treasury of Heroes and Heroines. New York: Hampton Publishing Co., 1920.
Gaster, M. "The Legend of Merlin," Folk-Lore, December, 1905.
Geoffrey of Monmouth. History of the Kings of Britain. New York: Dutton, 1958 (Originally written c. 1139).
Gilbert, Henry F. B. King Arthur. Chicago: Saalfield, n. d.
Giles, J. A., ed. Six Old English Chronicles. London: Henry C. Bohn, 1848.
Giot, P. R. Brittany. London: Thames & Hudson, 1960.
Hibbert, Christopher, and the editors of Horizon Magazine. The Search for King Arthur. New York: American Heritage Publishing Co., 1969.
Holland, Rupert S., ed. King Arthur and the Knights of the Round Table. New York: Grosset & Dunlap, 1919.
Loomis, Roger Sherman. Celtic Myth and Arthurian Romance. New York: Columbia University Press, 1927.
Malone, Kemp. "The Historicity of Arthur," Journal of English and Germanic Philology, Vol. XXIII, 1924.
Malory, Sir Thomas. King Arthur and His Noble Knights; Stories from Morte d'Arthur by Mary Macleod. New York: Burt, n. d.
_____. King Arthur and the Knights of the Round Table. Edited by Clifton Johnson. New York: Macmillan, 1916.
_____. King Arthur: Stories from the Author's Morte d'Arthur, Retold by Mary Macleod. New York: Macmillan, 1936.
Merchant, E. L., compiler. King Arthur and His Knights. Philadelphia: Winston, 1927.
Nash, W. D. Merlin the Enchanter, and Merlin the Bard. Privately printed in Great Britain, 1865.
Ownbey, E. Snydor. "Merlin and Arthur," Birmingham--Southern College Bulletin, January, 1933.
Parry, John J. "The Vita Merlini," Studies in Language and Literature, August, 1925.
Pyle, Howard. The Book of King Arthur. Chicago: Classic Press, 1969.
_____. The Story of the Grail and the Passing of Arthur. New York: Scribner's, 1938.
Robinson, Mabel L. King Arthur and His Knights. New York: Random House, 1953.
Sommer, E. Oskar. Le Roman de Merlin, or the Early History of King Arthur. London: privately printed, 1894.
Tappan, Eva March. "The Legend of King Arthur" in her Old World Hero Stories. Boston: Houghton Mifflin, 1937.
Tennyson, Alfred. Idylls of the King (poems). New York: Crowell, 1885 (Originally written 1859).
_____. Idylls of the King: The King's Henchman, a Play by Edna St. Vincent Millay. Edited by E. M. Ward and E. G. Bernard. New York: Noble, 1945.

THE BIRTH OF ISLAM (622)

Abdul-Kassim, better known as Mohammed, the Arabian prophet and founder of the Mohammedan religion (Islam), was born at Mecca about the year 570. He was the son of Abdallah and his wife Amina, both of the tribe of Koreish, the ruling clan of the town of his birth. His father died about the time his son was born and Mohammed was raised by his uncle, Abu Talib. He became familiar with the religions of the many pilgrims who came to Mecca and also acquired a knowledge of Judaism and Christianity.

At the age of 25 Mohammed was employed as a camel driver by Khadija, a wealthy widow, whom he married in 595. Following his marriage he became an affluent merchant.

Eventually Mohammed was inspired by the religious teacher Waraka, a relative of Khadija, who preached reform and humanitarianism. For the fifteen years following his marriage he had spent much time in meditation, being greatly concerned over the Arab's superstition, ignorance and lack of a national prophet. According to Moslem tradition, when he was 40 years old he received his call from God through the Angel Gabriel. This was about the year 610, during the holy month of Ramadan when he, as was his custom, retired to a cave on Mount Hira to meditate alone. The angel revealed the two primary tenets of the new faith to him in the "word of testimony" that "there is no god but Allah and Mohammed is His prophet. "

He returned to Mecca prepared to teach the new religion. At first he spoke of Islam only to his relatives and friends. He succeeded in converting his wife, his daughters, his adopted son Ali and Abu Bakr, a friend who, after the prophet's death, became the leader of the new cult. Within three years he had gathered some 40 adherents and began preaching his doctrines publicly in Mecca, exhorting his listeners to believe in the one true god.

Other revelations followed the one received from the Angel Gabriel. These were gathered to form the Koran, Islam's sacred scripture. The Islamic creed, as preached by Mohammed and set forth in the Koran, enjoins upon Moslems six articles of faith, to wit: belief in god, in angels, in scripture, in prophets, in the day of judgment and in predestination. In addition, five religious duties are imposed on all Moslems. These, called the "pillars of Islam, " are reciting the creed, the giving of alms, worship, fasting and pilgrimage. This last involves at least one visit to the holy city of Mecca and many pilgrims also visit the tomb of Mohammed at Medina.

Mohammed's preaching in Mecca angered various important persons who saw in him a threat to the profitable pilgrimages to the pagan shrine of the Kaaba. He and his followers were persecuted until 622 when a plot to murder him and his disciples was

discovered. He and Abu Bakr fled from Mecca to Yathrib, later
Medina. This flight, called the "Hegira," established the year 622
as the starting point in the Mohammedan calendar.

The people of Medina welcomed Mohammed and Abu Bakr
and asked the former to restore order in the city which was torn
by internal strife. Mohammed found it necessary to employ force
to overcome the Meccan soldiers over the next two years. By 630,
after successfully defending Medina against a Meccan siege, he attacked and defeated his native city with a force of ten thousand men.
Ultimately he brought all of Arabia under his control, becoming a
judge, lawgiver, social arbiter and increasingly influential religious
leader.

Khadija passed away in 620, following which Mohammed married several wives. The work of Islam, as mentioned above, was
carried on by Abu Bakr after Mohammed's death in 632. He is
buried in Medina, his tomb being considered almost as important
a sacred place as the famous black stone embedded in a wall at
Mecca.

Suggested Readings

Andrae, Tor. Mohammed: The Man and His Faith. Translated by
    Theophil Menzel. Plainview, N.Y.: Books for Libraries, 1936.
Bolitho, William. "Mahomet" in his Twelve Against the Gods: The
    Story of Adventure. New York: Simon & Schuster, 1929.
Dozy, Reinhart Pieter Anne. Spanish Islam: A History of the Mos-
    lems in Spain. Translated by Francis Griffin Stokes. London:
    Chatto and Windus, 1913.
Gibb, Hamilton A. Mohammedanism: An Historical Survey. Ox-
    ford: Oxford University Press, 1953.
Hitti, Philip K. History of the Arabs. London: Macmillan, 1961.
Hoyle, Edwyn. Andalus: Spain Under the Muslims. London:
    Robert Hale, 1958.
King, Noel Quinton. Christian and Muslim in Africa. New York:
    Harper, 1971.
Lane-Poole, Stanley. The Story of the Moors in Spain. New York:
    Putnam's, 1886.
Margoliouth, David S. Mohammed and the Rise of Islam. New
    York: AMS Press, 1905.
Martin, Malachi. The Encounter. New York: Farrar, 1969.
Muir, William. The Life of Mohammed, from Original Sources.
    Edited by Thomas H. Weir. New York: AMS Press, 1975
    (Originally published 1923.)
Ortega y Gosset, José. Invertebrate Spain. New York: Norton,
    1937.
Palmer, E.R., translator. "Chapters from the Koran" in Eliot,
    Charles W., ed. The Harvard Classics. New York: Collier,
    1909.
Payne, Robert. The Holy Sword, the Story of Islam from Muham-
    med to the Present. New York: Harper & Row, 1959.

Pike, E. Royston. Mohammed: Prophet of the Religion of Islam. New York: Frederick A. Praeger, 1969.
Saunders, J. J. A History of Medieval Islam. London: Routledge and Kegan Paul, 1965.
Scott, Samuel Parsons. History of the Moorish Empire in Europe. Philadelphia: Lippincott, 1904.
Stewart, Desmond Stirling, and the editors of Time-Life Books. Early Islam. New York: Time, 1967.

ISIDORE OF SEVILLE'S ETYMOLOGIES (622-633)

At various times in history it has been realized that the knowledge of the past, unless recorded, could become lost, possibly forever. For this reason students and thinkers have, upon occasion, attempted to assemble the knowledge of their ages in encyclopedia form that it might be retrieved when needed by those who would come after them.

One such encyclopedist was Isidore of Seville, a Spanish ecclesiastic and scholar who, between the years 622 and 633, compiled his Etymologies (Origins or Etymologies in Twenty Books). This monumental work is extremely broad in scope and is actually a combined dictionary and encyclopedia. It covers more than 7,000 terms and the compiler obtained his information from over 150 different sources.

The first three books of the Etymologies cover the liberal arts, including grammar, rhetoric, mathematics, astronomy and logic. The next five books deal with medicine, law, librarianship and theology. The ninth book deals with languages and "mankind." It is followed by a list of about a thousand words arranged in alphabetical order, with their etymologies. This, in turn, is followed by discussions of anatomy and physiology.

Book 12 is concerned with zoology, cosmography is dealt with in Book 13, and Book 14 covers physical geography. Book 15 discusses architecture and surveying; minerology, classified as "stones and metals," is treated in Book 16. Book 17 deals with agriculture; discussions of warfare and amusements appear in Book 18; and Book 19 is devoted to ships, houses and clothing. Book 20, the last of the series, covers food, agricultural instruments and furniture.

The Etymologies became a standard medieval reference book and is said to have had influence "second only to the Bible." The material covered is "generally uncritical and unoriginal," Isidore's aim being to compile and report the work of others rather than cover new ground. Unlike many publications of its day, there are nearly a thousand manuscript copies extant and, according to one authority, it was printed at least ten times between 1470 and 1529.

Suggested Readings

Bodmer, Frederick. The Loom of Language. Edited by Lancelot
    Hogben. New York: Norton, 1944.
Brehaut, Ernest. An Encyclopedist of the Dark Ages: Isidore of
    Seville. New York: Burt Franklin, 1967 (Originally published
    1912).
Carlyle, R. W. , and A. J. Carlyle. A History of Medieval Political
    Theory in the West. Edinburgh: William Blackwood and Sons,
    1903-1936.
Cunningham, Robert L. "The Etymologies" in McGill, Frank N. ,
    ed. Masterpieces of Catholic Literature, Vol. I. New York:
    Salem Press, 1965.
"Encyclopedia" in Collier's Encyclopedia. Shores, Louis, editor
    in chief. New York: Crowell-Collier Educational Corporation,
    1972.
Isidore of Seville. Etymologiarum Seu Ariginum Libri XX. Edited
    by W. M. Lindsay. Oxford: Oxford University Press, 1911
    (Originally written 622-633).
    _____. History of the Goths, Vandals and Suevi. Translated
    by Gordon B. Ford, Jr. Louisville, Ky.: Medieval Latin
    Press, 1970 (Originally written 622-633).
Laistner, Max L. W. Thought and Letters in Western Europe, A. D.
    500 to 900. Ithaca, N. Y.: Cornell University Press, 1957.
Thompson, James Westfall. History of Historical Writing. New
    York: Macmillan, 1942.
Thorndyke, Lynn. "Other Early Medieval Learning: Boethius, Isi-
    dore, Bede, Gregory the Great" in his History of Magic and
    Experimental Sciences During the First Thirteen Centuries of
    Our Era, Vol. I. New York: Macmillan, 1929.

THE BATTLE OF TOURS (732 or 733)

One of the most important military encounters of ancient
times was the Battle of Tours, also called the Battle of Poitiers,
fought in October, 732 or 733.   The forces of Charles Martel (the
Hammer), Frankish Mayor of the Palace and grandfather of Charlemagne, checked the Moslem advance into France led by Abd-ar-
Rahman, the Moslem governor of Spain.

In the century following the death of Mohammed in 632, the
Moslems had pushed their way across North Africa and into Spain.
Not content to stop there, they had begun to penetrate north across
the Pyrenees and into Frankish territory.   Through a series of
raids they had, by the year 725, captured Narbonne, Nîmes and
Carcassonne and were advancing further.

Abd-ar-Rahman decided to increase his aggressive tactics.
In 732 he and his Moslem forces took Bordeaux, decisively defeat-
ing Eudes, Duke of Aquitaine.   Eudes then appealed to Charles Mar-

tel for help.   The Frankish Mayor of the Palace agreed to assist
Eudes in return for his agreement to pledge fealty to him.   The
agreement was made and Charles and his army marched to meet
the forces of the invading Moslems.

The two armies fought somewhere between Tours and Poitiers.   For seven days both sides maneuvered, neither attacking.
Then the Moslem cavalry clashed with the Frankish infantry, the
fighting continuing all day.   The Moslems could not break the infantry and the infantry, in turn, were unable to pursue the Moslem horsemen when they were repulsed.

When darkness fell both sides retired.   During the night
the Moslems fled, leaving the field to the Franks.   Charles Martel,
though not able to claim a cleancut victory, prevented the Moslems
from advancing into Western Europe.

For a short time after the Battle of Tours (or Poitiers) the
Moslems made raids into Southern France.   However, the invaders
realized that further aggression would be comparatively unprofitable
and abandoned further attempts to penetrate beyond the Pyrenees.

Suggested Readings

Buckler, F. W.   Harun'l-Rashid and Charles the Great.   Cambridge,
    Mass.:   Medieval Academy of America, 1931.
Bullough, Donald.   The Age of Charlemagne.   New York: Putnam's,
    1966.
Creasy, Edward S.   Fifteen Decisive Battles of the World.   Har-
    risburg, Pa.:   Stackpole Books, 1957.
Dozy, Reinhart Pieter Anne.   Spanish Islam: A History of the Mos-
    lems in Spain.   Translated by Francis Griffin Stokes.   London:
    Chatto and Windus, 1913.
Duclaux, Mary (A. Mary F. Robinson).   A Short History of France
    from Caesar's Invasion to the Battle of Waterloo.   New York:
    Putnam's, 1918.
Falls, Cyril, ed.   Great Military Battles.   New York: Macmillan,
    1964.
Fuller, John F. C.   A Military History of the Western World.   New
    York: Funk & Wagnalls, 1954.
Hale, Edwyn Andalus.   Spain Under the Muslims.   London: Robert
    Hale, 1958.
Lane-Poole, Stanley.   The Story of the Moors in Spain.   New York:
    Putnam's, 1886.
Lewis, Archibald R.   Naval Power and Trade in the Mediterranean,
    A. D. 500-1100.   Princeton, N. J.:   Princeton University Press,
    1951.
Maurois, André.   A History of France.   New York: Farrar, Strauss,
    1956.
Mitchell, Lt.-Col. Joseph B., and Sir Edward S. Creasy.   Twenty
    Decisive Battles of the World.   New York: Macmillan, 1964.
Munz, Peter.   Life in the Age of Charlemagne.   New York: Put-
    nam, 1969.

Oman, Charles. The Art of War in the Middle Ages. Ithaca, N. Y. :
    Cornell University Press, 1953.
Thorndyke, Lynn. The History of Medieval Europe, 3rd edition.
    Edited by William L. Langer. Boston: Houghton Mifflin, 1956.

THE LEGEND OF POPE JOAN (855)

        Whether or not the Catholic Church had a female pope for
a brief period in the ninth century is a matter on which some theologians and historians still speculate.   Leo IV, the 103rd pope,
died in 855 A. D. and was succeeded by Benedict III in the same
year.   However, a few months intervened between the death of Leo
and the accession of Benedict.   According to the legend, myth or,
perhaps, fact, first published by Stephen of Bourbon who died in
1261, during these intervening months the papacy was occupied by
Joan, a former priest and cardinal, who was known as John VIII.
Platina, the Italian humanist and historian, states that she "sat two
years, one month and four days. "

        Joan is said to have been born in either England or in Ger-
many, of English parents.   As a young girl she fell in love with a
Benedictine monk with whom she fled to Athens disguised as a man.
There the monk died and she, retaining her male guise, entered the
priesthood.   In due course she became a cardinal and was elected
to the papacy following the death of Pope Leo IV.

        It is possible that the secret of her sex might never have
become known had she not died in childbirth during a papal procession, so the legend goes.

        Following Stephen of Bourbon's account, several other writ-
ers repeated the story during the next three centuries.   It is interesting to note, however, that the Catholic Church, in 872, elected
a Pope John VIII, only seventeen years after Joan was supposed to
have assumed the papal name.

        The succession of papal Johns became more perplexing.
Some authorities list a Pope John XV as immediately following
Antipope Boniface VII (974 A. D.), which confused the numbering
of the popes called John XV to XXI.   There was no Pope John XX,
the number being given to either John XIX (1024-1032) or John XXI
(1276-1277).

        Emmanuel Rhöides, though presenting the subject in his book
as historical fiction, holds that Pope Joan did exist and quotes a
number of medieval authorities to support his contention.   David
Blondel, a French Calvinist, questioned the authority of the legend.

        In 1863 Johann Dollinger, a German theologian, subsequently
excommunicated from the Catholic Church, attacked and disproved

the story of Pope Joan to the satisfaction of the Church, which denies her existence.

Suggested Readings

Aradi, Zsolt. The Popes: The History of How They Are Chosen,
    Elected and Crowned. New York: Farrar, Straus and Cudahy,
    1955.
Blondel, David. De Joanna Papissa. Paris, 1657.
    _____. Eclaircissement de la question si une femme a été as-
    sise au siège papal de Rome. Paris: 1647.
"Faking It to the Top" in Crimes and Punishment, Vol. 6.   Ed-
    itorial presentation: Jackson Morley. London: BPC, 1973.
Pastor, Ludwig. The History of the Popes. London: Kegan Paul,
    1891.
Rhöides, Emmanuel. Pope Joan (historical fiction). Translated
    by Lawrence Durrell. New York: Dutton, 1961 (Originally
    published 1886).
Stenton, F. M. Anglo-Saxon England. Oxford: Clarendon Press,
    1947.
Synan, E. A. The Popes and the Jews in the Middle Ages.   New
    York: Macmillan, 1965.
Von Dollinger, Johann J. Papstfabelm des Mittelalters.   Berlin:
    1863.
Williams, Michael. The Catholic Church in Action. New York:
    Macmillan, 1935.

THE MIRACLE (MYSTERY) AND MORALITY PLAYS
(c. 1000-c. 1550)

The medieval miracle plays, also known as mystery plays,
were an offshoot of the Roman and earlier Greek dramas.   These
were performed in the English and French languages and had as
subject matter the miracles "performed by saints or scenes from
the Bible. "

Morality plays differed from the miracle or mystery plays
in that they were allegories designed to instruct audiences in the
Christian way of life and the Christian attitude towards death.   Conflict between good and evil was shown, the play ending with the
saving of man's soul.   Characters personifying such abstractions
as Gluttony, Lechery, Pride, Sloth, Envy, Hope, Riches and the
like appear in these plays.   Some moralities were anonymous; others were by authors whose identities are known.   Everyman, adapted into English from the Dutch, is a well known anonymous morality play, as are Castle of Perseverance, Nice Wanton and Mankind.   Sir David Lyndsay wrote Ane Pleasant Satyre of the Three
Estates which was produced in 1540 and Magnificence, printed about
1533, was the work of John Skelton.

Miracle and morality plays existed in crude form throughout Church history. About the end of the 10th century and possibly earlier the Western Church dramatized certain parts of the Latin mass at such times as Easter. Churchmen took part in these dramatizations which, at first, were held inside the churches and cathedrals. Then the performances were held on the church steps with laymen participating. The next development was to move the performances to the market place, away from the church building.

The plays became more sophisticated as time went by. Additional characters were added to the presentations. Extra scenes were used and dialogue was augmented. By the fifteenth and sixteenth centuries the miracle plays reached their zenith. They embodied not only religious matter but also humor, in order to appeal to the commoners who viewed them. The original Latin was replaced with the vernacular. They were given in cycles or series of related scenes. Each scene required only a short time to perform and was acted by members of one of the town's trade guilds. The scene was presented on a wagon or float on wheels which was moved from place to place for repeated performances.

The cycles were named for the towns in which they were presented, some of the better known ones being the Chester plays, Wakefield plays, Coventry plays, York plays and Norwich plays. They were usually performed outdoors on festival days, particularly on Corpus Christi day.

One of the best known of the miracle plays is the Second Shepherd's Play. This is the tale of the shepherds who watched their flocks on the night of Christ's birth and combines religion with a comic episode in which one of the sheep is stolen. The thief hides the animal in a cradle in his home and when apprehended asserts that it is not the stolen sheep but an infant girl.

Other miracle plays were the Play of Adam, the Play of St. Nicholas, the Miracle of Theophilus, the Play of Daniel and Miracles of Our Lady.

In November, 1548, the Parliament of Paris indicted the miracle play because of many protests concerning the comic material which was combined with Biblical texts. By that year a number of playwrights had produced dramas which, in England, became extremely popular. Noblemen and rulers maintained their own companies of players to perform the works of Henry Medwall, John Heywood, Nicholas Udall, George Gascoigne and others. In the Elizabethan era plays by William Shakespeare and his contemporaries, notably John Lyly, George Peele, Robert Greene, Thomas Dekker, Francis Beaumont and John Fletcher, Ben Jonson, Philip Massinger, John Webster, Thomas Kyd, Christopher Marlowe and others were produced, either at court or in theaters especially built for the purpose.

The medieval miracle play survives today in the Passion Play of Oberammergau given in the Bavarian village of that name every ten years. This is a dramatic representation of the passion of Christ.

Suggested Readings

Cawley, Arthur C. , ed. Everyman and Medieval Miracle Plays. New York: Dutton, 1959.
_____. The Wakefield Pageants in the Townley Cycle. Manchester: Manchester University Press, 1958.
Cazamian, L. A History of French Literature. Oxford: Clarendon Press, 1955.
Chambers, Sir Edmund K. "Medieval Drama" in English Literature at the Close of the Middle Ages. Oxford: Clarendon Press, 1945.
Craig, H. English Religious Drama in the Middle Ages. Oxford: Clarendon Press, 1955.
Holmes, Urban T. , Jr. A History of Old French Literature. New York: Russell and Russell, 1962.
Salter, Frederick M. Medieval Drama in Chester. Toronto: University of Toronto Press, 1955.
Sharp, Harold S. , and Marjorie Z. Sharp, compilers. Index to Characters in the Performing Arts. Vol. I: Non-Musical Plays. New York: Scarecrow Press, 1966.
Wickham, Glynne W. Early English Stages, 1300-1660. London: Routledge and Kegan Paul, 1959.
Wild, Sebastian. The Passion Play of Oberammergau. 1662.
Young, Karl. The Drama of the Medieval Church. Oxford: Clarendon Press, 1933.

THE BATTLE OF HASTINGS (1066)

Edward the Confessor, the last Anglo-Saxon King of England, died without heir in 1066. There were then three rivals for the throne of England: The Anglo-Saxon Harold Godwinson, the Norwegian Harold Hardrada, and William, Duke of Normandy, who came to be known as William the Conqueror. All three had some claim to the throne.

Harold Godwinson's force met and defeated the army of Harold Hardrada at Stamford Bridge. Godwinson's soldiers were exhausted as a result of the encounter but word was received that William and his army had, on September 28, landed on the south coast of England. Godwinson, on a forced march of 200 miles, brought his fatigued soldiers to fight the new invading army.

William realized that any delay could be fatal to his campaign. He was unable to furnish food and supplies for his soldiers over an extended period and knew that he must fight before what supplies he had ran out and winter set in.

On October 14, 1066, the two armies met on a field in Sussex, between Hastings and Senlac.   For a while it appeared that
Harold Godwinson's troops would be victorious.   They fought ferociously, depending on a close phalanx formation which was broken
only when William ordered his men to pretend to retreat.   The
Anglo-Saxon soldiers broke ranks to pursue the apparently retreating Normans, who turned and fought with swords, spears and arrows.

Godwinson was killed by a Norman arrow and his army,
though it battled fiercely, was defeated.   William the Conqueror
had won the English throne.

The Battle of Hastings is regarded by some historians as
"the most important single event in English history. " Had Harold
Godwinson defeated William it is possible, if not probable, that
"England might have developed an isolated culture or maintained an
orientation towards Scandinavia. " England has not, since 1066,
been successfully invaded.   By the victory of William at Hastings,
the country "was brought into the European orbit. "

Suggested Readings.

Ashley, Maurice.   Great Britain to 1688: A Modern History.   Ann
      Arbor, Mich. : University of Michigan Press, 1961.
Butler, Denis.   1066: The Story of a Year.   New York: Putnam's,
      1966.
Costain, Thomas Bertram.   William the Conqueror.   New York:
      Random House, 1959.
Creasy, Edward S.   Fifteen Decisive Battles of the World.   Harrisburg, Pa. : Stackpole Books, 1957.
Cross, Arthur Lyon.   A Shorter History of England and Greater
      Britain.   New York: Macmillan, 1929.
Douglas, David C.   William the Conqueror: The Norman Impact
      upon England.   Berkeley, Calif. : University of California
      Press, 1964.
Duggan, Alfred Leo.   Growing Up with the Norman Conquest.   New
      York: Pantheon Books, 1965.
Falls, Cyril, ed.   Great Military Battles.   New York: Macmillan,
      1964.
Feiling, Keith.   A History of England.   New York: McGraw-Hill,
      1948.
Fuller, John F. C.   A Military History of the Western World.   New
      York: Funk & Wagnalls, 1954.
Furneaux, Rupert.   Invasion 1066.   Englewood Cliffs, N. J. : Prentice-Hall, 1966.
Matthews, D. J. A.   The Norman Conquest.   New York: Schocken
      Books, 1966.
Mitchell, Lt. -Col. Joseph B. , and Sir Edward S. Creasy.   Twenty
      Decisive Battles of the World.   New York: Macmillan, 1964.
Setton, Kenneth M.   "900 Years Ago: The Norman Conquest, "
      National Geographic, August, 1966.

Stenton, F. M. Anglo-Saxon England. Oxford: Clarendon Press,
    1947.
Syme, Ronald. Invaders and Invasions. New York: Norton, 1964.
Tappan, Eva March. "William the Conqueror Conquers England"
    in her Old World Hero Stories. Boston: Houghton Mifflin,
    1937.
Terry, Benjamin. A History of England from the Earliest Times
    to the Death of Queen Victoria. Chicago: Scott, Foresman,
    1901.
Trevalyn, George Macaulay. History of England. New York: Dou-
    bleday, 1953.
Van Loon, Hendrik Willem. The Story of Mankind. New York:
    Garden City Publishing Co., 1938.

THE CANOSSA INCIDENT (1077)

For centuries the question of clerical versus lay primacy
was debated by Roman Catholic churchmen and secular authorities.
As early as the fourth century many popes, including Innocent I,
Leo I, Gelasius I and Gregory I, felt that papal authority was superior to that of rulers who were not members of the clergy. Saint
Augustine (354-430) in The City of God, a treatise on the teachings
of the Christian Church, held that the divine will "was intended to
advise the secular arm. "

In 752 Pepin was crowned king of the Franks by the pope,
and his son Charlemagne was similarly crowned as emperor in
800. These crownings were taken by some as acknowledgment of
papal supremacy by the royal rulers.

Henry IV, King of Germany and Holy Roman Emperor, came
to the throne in 1056. About 1065 a struggle began between him
and the pope for temporal power in the Empire. At that time the
land, vitally necessary for sustenance in an agricultural economy,
was owned by the rulers. The use of land was made available to
vassals who were required to swear fealty to the prince who invested them. Often the prince had jurisdiction over churches, abbeys and other ecclesiastical property and appointed both churchmen
and laymen as vassals. It was customary for the unordained prince,
when passing the use of land to a layman, to also appoint him an
abbot or bishop, even though the layman might lack the piety normally expected in the holders of such offices.

In 1074 Pope Gregory VII presided at a council in Rome
which condemned simony and marriage of the clergy and in February, 1075, he issued a decree that lay investiture would be punished by excommunication. Subsequently he issued the Dictatus Pa-
pae in which he declared the right of the pope to remove an emper-
or from office.

King Henry IV understandably took exception to the pope's
decree. A bishopric became vacant in Milan and Henry and the
pope each supported a different candidate for the position. In December, 1075, Gregory admonished the king, accusing him of usurp-
ing papal prerogatives. Henry, in turn, assembled a group of German bishops at Worms. This group sought to depose Pope Gregory
and accused him of sundry crimes, including perjury, immorality
and abuse of papal authority. In February, 1076, the pope retaliated by excommunicating the king, depriving him of all royal authority in Germany.

Henry protested the pope's action. He wrote to him and also to the German bishops. In his message to Gregory he stated
that he, as king, occupied that position, not by usurpation but by
divine right, whereas the pope had been merely elected to his office. In his letter to the German bishops he accused the pope of
"uniting the authority of both priesthood and kingship in his person. "

Henry's excommunication released his subjects from allegiance to him, whereupon the lay and ecclesiastical nobles formed a
coalition threatening not to recognize him unless he could secure
absolution by February, 1077.

In January Pope Gregory was traveling in northern Italy.
He stopped at Canossa, near Reggio (Modenese) at the castle of
Matilda of Tuscany, one of his supporters. King Henry had left
Germany and traveled to Canossa where, barefoot and dressed as
a penitent, he waited three days outside the castle, standing in the
snow and seeking readmission to the communion of the Catholic
Church. Pope Gregory released him from excommunication but
did not restore his kingship.

The German nobles elected Rudolf of Swabia to replace
Henry on the throne, which action resulted in civil war. In 1080
the pope recognized Rudolph as king and Henry was again excommunicated, but on this occasion the nobles remained loyal to him.
Henry then had an antipope, Clement III, elected and after he had
been crowned by Clement, he made a military attack against Rome.
Gregory was forced to flee. Henry's troops were driven from Rome
by an army commanded by Robert Guiscard, a Norman adventurer
and military leader. Pope Gregory died in 1085 in Southern Italy
and Henry, after further difficulties involving his right to occupy
the throne, was again excommunicated, this time by Pope Paschal
II in 1104. He died at Liège in 1106 while enlisting an army with
which he hoped to wrest the kingship from his son Henry V who
had revolted against his father in 1104 and seized the throne two
years later.

Suggested Readings

Barraclough, Geoffrey. The Medieval Papacy. London: Thames
      and Hudson, 1968.

Crusades   95

_____. Studies in Medieval History, Vol. I. Oxford: Basil
     Blackwell, 1938.
Brooke, Zachary N. "Lay Investiture and Its Relation to the Con-
     flict of Empire and Papacy" in Williams, Schaefer, ed. The
     Gregorian Epoch. Boston: Heath, 1964.
Bryce, James. The Holy Roman Empire. New York: Schocken
     Books, 1904.
Cantor, Norman F. "The Crisis of Norman Monasticism, 1050-
     1130," American Historical Review, October, 1960.
Carlyle, R. W., and A. J. Carlyle. A History of Medieval Political
     Theory in the West. Edinburgh: William Blackwood and Sons,
     1903-1936.
Ehler, Sydney Z., and John B. Morrall. Church and State Through
     the Centuries: A Collection of Historic Documents with Com-
     mentaries. London: Burns, Oates, and Washbourne, 1954.
Emerton, Ephraim, translator. The Correspondence of Pope Greg-
     ory VII: Selected Letters from the Registrum. New York:
     Columbia University Press, 1932.
Heer, Frederich. The Holy Roman Empire. New York: Praeger,
     1967.
Morrison, Carl F. "Canossa: A Revision," Traditio, Vol. XVIII,
     1926.
Parker, T. M. Christianity and the State in the Light of History.
     London: Adam and Charles Black, 1955.
Tellenbach, Gerd. Church, State and Christian Society at the Time
     of the Investiture Contest. Translated by K. F. Bennett. Ox-
     ford: Basil Blackwell, 1966.
Tierney, Brian. The Crisis of Church and State, 1050-1300. En-
     glewood Cliffs, N. J.: Prentice-Hall, 1964.
Ullmann, Walter. The Growth of Papal Government in the Middle
     Ages. London: Methuen, 1962.
_____. A History of Political Thought: The Middle Ages. Bal-
     timore: Penguin Books, 1965.
_____. Medieval Papalism: The Political Theories of the Medi-
     eval Canonists. London: Methuen, 1949.
Whitney, J. P. Hildebrantine Essays. Cambridge: The University
     Press, 1932.
Williams, Scafer, ed. The Gregorian Epoch: Reformation, Revo-
     lution, Reaction? Boston: Heath, 1964.

THE CRUSADES (1096-1270)

     The crusades were a series of religious wars waged by the
Christian nations between 1096 and 1270 for the recovery of the
Holy Land from the Moslems. They were eight in number, although some historians regard the Children's Crusade of 1212 as
something apart from the other seven. There were also a number
of similar but less well-known movements which occurred in 1237
and 1458. These expeditions were preceded by earlier armed pilgrimages directed against non-Christians in Spain and other parts
of Europe.

The First Crusade (1096-1099) was advocated by Pope Urban
II.   The Moslems had controlled Jerusalem since the seventh century.   When they attacked the Byzantine Emperor Alexius I Com-
nenus about 1090 the prestige of the Catholic Church had attained
great heights and religious feeling was widespread.   The French
and German nobles were in financial difficulties and combined a
wish for loot with religious feelings.   The peasants were restless
under oppression and the prospect of military adventures, particularly against the Moslems, had great appeal.

Peter the Hermit, Walter the Penniless and others preached
the doctrine of the crusade and inspired many to take the crusader's vow and march on Constantinople.   In the summer and fall
of 1096 organized armies led by Godfrey of Bouillon, his brother
Baldwin, Raymond, Count of Toulouse and others began the long
trip east.   The military leaders disagreed on policy and antagon-
isms resulted.   However, the combined armies attacked and captured the city of Nicaea in May, 1097, and subsequently took Dory-
laeum and Antioch.   Baldwin conquered Edessa, and on July 15,
1099, the crusaders took Jerusalem.   The First Crusade ended later that year when the Egyptians were defeated at Ascalon.

The Second Crusade (1147-1149) resulted from the Moslem
capture of Edessa in 1144.   Pope Eugenius III designated Bernard
of Clairvaux spiritual leader and promised participants remission
of sins, absolution "for transgressions committed in the course of
the crusade," and voiding of personal debts.   Led by Conrad III
of Germany and Louis VII of France, the march started in April,
1147.   The crusaders were not welcome in the Byzantine Empire
and the Turks almost annihilated the Germans in Asia Minor.   The
French fared equally poorly, being defeated at Damascus.   This
crusade was abandoned, although Conrad and Louis established a
base at Jerusalem.

The Third Crusade (1189-1192) was precipitated by the fall
of Jerusalem to Saladin, Sultan of Egypt and Syria.   It was led by
Richard I (Richard the Lion-Hearted) of England, Frederick I, Holy
Roman Emperor, and Philip II of France, and was encouraged by
Pope Gregory VIII.   In this campaign Acre fell to the Christians
in July, 1191.   Frederick had died in 1190 and the other two kings
disagreed.   Philip returned to France and Richard was captured in
Austria and held for ransom, returning to England in 1194.

The Fourth Crusade (1202-1204), like the others, originally
had as its purpose the driving of the Moslems from the Holy Land.
It was initiated by Pope Innocent III and had as its military leaders
Enrico Dandolo, Doge of Venice, and Baldwin I, Count of Flanders.
However, the Venetians had advanced transportation to the crusaders
and imposed their own policies.   Consequently the objective, as
originally announced, was abandoned.   In 1202 the crusaders attacked the city of Zara, a commercial rival of Venice, conquered
and sacked it.   For this "crime against Christendom" the pope excommunicated all involved but later rescinded the penalty.   In 1203

Constantinople was overcome and Isaac II Angeles was restored to the Byzantine throne.   Later he was deposed and the Latin Empire was established, with Baldwin as emperor.

The Children's Crusade (1212) involved, not military forces led by kings and emperors, but unarmed children from France and Germany.   The French children had as their leader Stephen, a shepherd boy, and the German girls and boys were led by Nicholas, another young peasant.   Their objective was to recover the Holy Sepulcher from the Moslems.

The French group left Marseille in August, 1212, in ships provided by unscrupulous slave dealers.   Two of the ships were wrecked and when the others arrived at Alexandria most of the youthful crusaders were sold into slavery.   The German contingent traveled by land over the Alps to Genoa, many of the children dying or deserting en route.

The Fifth Crusade (1228-1229) was organized by the Holy Roman Emperor Frederick II.   Frederick captured Jerusalem in 1228, was crowned the following year, negotiated a ten-year truce with the Sultan of Egypt and returned to Europe.   In 1217 Andrew II, King of Hungary, on the advice of Pope Honorius III, led an expedition which ended in disaster.   Some historians consider this the Fifth Crusade, but the 1228-1229 expedition is generally designated as such.

The Sixth Crusade (1248-1254) was conducted by King Louis IX of France who took the crusader's vow after Jerusalem came under the domination of Islam in 1244.   His army invaded Egypt and captured Damietta in June, 1249, but was defeated at El Mansûra in 1250.   Louis was captured and remained in Syria four years waiting vainly for reinforcements.   He then returned to France.

The Seventh Crusade (1270), like the Sixth, was initiated by Louis IX.   Allied with him was Prince Edward, later King Edward I of England.   Louis died and his army returned to France.   Edward concluded a ten-year truce with the Moslems following victories at Acre and Haifa.

Suggested Readings

Atiya, Asiz. Crusade, Commerce and Culture.   Bloomington, Ind.:
    Indiana University Press, 1962.
Bishop, Morris. The Middle Ages.   New York: American Heritage
    Publishing Co., 1970.
Breasted, James Henry, et al., eds. European History Atlas: An-
    cient, Medieval and Modern European World History.   Chicago:
    Denoyer, 1961.
Brundage, James A. The Crusades: A Documentary Survey.   Mil-
    waukee, Wis.: Marquette University Press, 1962.
_____, ed. The Crusades: Motives and Achievements.   Boston:
    Heath, 1964.

Buehr, Walter. The Crusaders. New York: Putnam, 1959.
Cantor, Norman Frank. Medieval History: The Life and Death of
    a Civilization. New York: Macmillan, 1969.
Diehl, Charles. Byzantium: Greatness and Decline. Translated
    by Naomi Alford. New Brunswick, N. J.: Rutgers University
    Press, 1957.
_____. "The Fourth Crusade and the Latin Empire" in The Cam-
    bridge Medieval History. Cambridge: The University Press,
    1927.
Harding, Samuel Bannister, in consultation with Albert Bushnell
    Hart. Essentials in Mediaeval History (from Charlemagne to
    the Close of the Fifteenth Century). New York: American
    Book Bompany, 1909.
Kerr, Anthony J. C. The Crusades. Exeter: Wheaton, 1966.
Krey, A. C. The First Crusade: The Accounts of Eye-Witnesses
    and Participants. Princeton, N. J.: Princeton University
    Press, 1958.
_____. "Urban's Crusade: Success or Failure?" American
    Historical Review, Vol. LIII, 1948.
Munro, D. C. "The Speech of Pope Urban II at Clermont," Amer-
    ican Historical Review, Vol. XI, 1906.
Palmer, R. R., and others, eds. The Rand McNally Atlas of World
    History. Chicago: Author, 1965.
Robinson, James Harvey. Medieval and Modern Times: An Intro-
    duction to the History of Western Europe from the Dissolution
    of the Roman Empire to the Present Time. Boston: Ginn,
    1919.
Runciman, Steven. Byzantine Civilization. London: E. Arnold &
    Co., 1933.
_____. A History of the Crusades. Cambridge: The Univer-
    sity Press, 1931.
Sellman, R. R. The Crusades. New York: Roy, 1955.
Setton, Kenneth M., editor-in-chief. A History of the Crusades.
    Philadelphia: University of Pennsylvania, 1958.
Tappan, Eva March. "The Crusades" in her Old World Hero Stor-
    ies. Boston: Houghton Mifflin, 1937.
Vasiliev, Alexander A. The History of the Byzantine Empire, 324-
    1453. Madison, Wis.: University of Wisconsin Press, 1952.
Villehardouin, Geoffrey de. Chronicles of the Crusades. Translat-
    ed by M. R. B. Shaw. London: Penguin Books, 1963.
Williams, Jay, in consultation with Margaret B. Freeman and the
    editors of Horizon Magazine. Knights of the Crusades. New
    York: American Heritage Publishing Co., 1962.

THE TRAGIC ROMANCE OF
ABÉLARD AND HÉLOÏSE (1117)

The tragic romance of Peter Abélard, the French scholastic
philosopher, teacher and theologian, and Héloise, the eighteen-year-old
niece of Canon Fulbert, overshadows the importance of Abélard's

contributions to religious thought. A sardonic, brilliant and intellectually arrogant man, he made both friends and enemies. His
students attended his classes at Melun and Corbeil with enthusiasm,
and at least 25 of them became cardinals. He influenced some of
the great thinkers of his age, including the Italian theologian Peter
Lombard and the Italian political reformer, Arnold of Brescia. His
enemies included the French scholastic philosopher Guillaume de
Champeaux, under whom he studied for a time, and Bernard of
Clairvaux, the French ecclesiastic, who accused him of heresy.

Abélard, born in Brittany in 1079, became a teacher of theology. In 1117, at the invitation of Canon Fulbert of Paris, he became tutor to the latter's niece Héloise. The two promptly fell
in love and when Fulbert learned of the affair he attempted to end
it. Abélard, however, sent the girl to his sister's home in Brittany where she gave birth to a son. Later, at Fulbert's insistence,
Héloise and her lover were secretly married in Paris, her uncle
being present at the ceremony. The girl, rather than hinder Abélard's career as a leading teacher and cleric in minor orders, publicly denied her marriage. Abélard, in order to allay scandal, persuaded his wife to enter the convent at Argenteuil, where she subsequently became prioress. Canon Fulbert, believing that Abélard
intended to abandon his niece, arranged for a gang of ruffians to
emasculate him.

Abélard then sought monastic retreat at the abbey of St. Denis in Paris. He visited Héloise frequently and they carried on a
lengthy correspondence which has come down to us. In 1125 she
was appointed abbess of a nunnery at Paraclete. Following their
deaths the two were buried side by side and in 1817 they were en-
tombed at Paris.

Abélard, in his Sic et Non (Thus and Otherwise), produced
in 1121 and 1122, advocated the determining of truth by carefully
weighing the opposing positions of authorities. Judgments should
be based on pure reason, he contended, not blind faith in preconceived ideas. This and other writings were declared heretical by
church authorities and he was imprisoned in 1121. Following his
release from confinement he lived in a series of monasteries, teaching his theories of dialectical discussion, which were based on the
ideas of Johannes Scotus Erigena, the ninth-century philosopher and
theologian.

At the Council of Sens (1141) Bernard of Clairvaux condemned Abélard's teachings. Pope Innocent II ordered Abélard
to remain silent. He was accused of heresy and started to Rome
to defend his doctrine. However, he died at the priory of St. Marcel at Chalon-sur-Saône in 1142 and was never tried.

Besides Sic et Non Abélard wrote the autobiographical Story
of My Calamities and a number of theological and philosophical
treatises. These include Dialects, on logic; Know Thyself, or Eth-

ics, and Christian Theology, the latter being the writing that was
condemned at the Council of Sens and ordered burned.

Suggested Readings

Bishop, Morris. The Middle Ages. New York: American Her-
    itage Publishing Company, 1970.
Butler, Dom Edward Cuthbert. Western Asceticism: The Teach-
    ing of SS Augustine, Gregory and Bernard on Contemplation of
    the Contemplative Life. London: Constable & Company, 1951.
Cantor, Norman Frank. Medieval History: The Life and Death of
    a Civilization. New York: Macmillan, 1969.
Harding, Samuel Bannister, in Consultation with Albert Bushnell
    Hart. Essentials in Mediaeval History (from Charlemagne to
    the Close of the Fifteenth Century). New York: American
    Book Company, 1909.
Heer, Friedrich. The Medieval World: Europe from 1100 to 1350.
    Translated by Janet Sondheimer. London: Weidenfeld and Nic-
    olson, 1961.
James, Bruno S. Saint Bernard of Clairvaux: An Essay in Biog-
    raphy. New York: Harper & Row, 1957.
Knowles, David, O. S. B. The Evolution of Medieval Thought. Bal-
    timore: Helicon Press, 1962.
Lecler, Joseph, S. J. Toleration and the Reformation. Translated
    by T. L. Westow. New York: Associated Press, 1960.
Lloyd, R. B. Peter Abélard: The Orthodox Rebel. London: Lat-
    imer House, 1947.
Meadows, Dennis. A Saint and a Half. New York: Devin-Adair,
    1963.
Murray, A. V. Abélard and St. Bernard. Manchester: Manchester
    University Press, 1967.
Sikes, J. G. Peter Abélard. New York: Russell and Russell, 1965
    (First published 1952).
Vignaux, Paul. Philosophy in the Middle Ages. Translated by
    E. C. Hall. New York: Meridian Books, 1951.
Webb, Geoffrey, and Adrian Walker. St. Bernard of Clairvaux.
    London: A. R. Mowbray and Company, 1961.

THE CONCORDAT OF WORMS (1122)

The word "concordat" is defined as "a solemn agreement
entered into between the Roman Catholic Church and a sovereign
civil state. " It is usually entered into to settle an argument or to
prevent one, and so may be compared to a peace treaty or a non-
aggression pact.

The first formal concordat was probably the Concordat of
Worms, negotiated on September 23, 1122, by Pope Calixtus II and
Henry V, Holy Roman Emperor, which settled the investiture strug-
gle.

The combination of political authority and ownership of land resulted in feudalism making bishops and abbots, as tenants of church land, both political persons and religious leaders. It was necessary for both the church and the state to insist upon the right of appointment to office if they were to maintain the integrity of their respective institutions. This situation led to a bitter struggle over investiture between the papacy and the Holy Roman Empire. On one occasion in 1077 Henry IV, Holy Roman Emperor, was required to wait for three days outside the Castle of Canossa until Pope Gregory VII found it convenient to see him and absolve him of the sin of disobedience. Retaliation followed. When Henry's enemies elected Rudolf, Duke of Swabia, King of Germany and Pope Gregory recognized him as King (excommunicating Henry in 1080), Henry retaliated in 1084 and attacked Rome, deposed Gregory and arranged for antipope Clement III to crown him emperor. Gregory fled, dying in 1085.

The struggle over investiture did not end with Gregory's death. Pope Paschal II suggested a solution which aroused great protest on the part of high churchmen, including bishops and cardinals. Henry V, the new Holy Roman Emperor, captured Paschal who, under duress, granted the right of investiture to all subsequent German kings. This concession was later repudiated by the prelates.

Pope Calixtus II and Henry V finally settled the investiture struggle by signing the Concordat of Worms. Calixtus had expelled Antipope Gregory VIII from Rome in 1121 and was accepted as the true pope. By the Concordat the emperor renounced the right of spiritual investiture of bishops with ring and staff and in turn was given the right of lay investiture with the sceptre, the sign of temporal authority. It was also agreed that the election of bishops and abbots in Germany should take place in the presence of the emperor, who would arbitrate disputes, and that the Catholic Church would have restored to it all possessions taken from it illegally by Henry V and by his father, Henry IV.

Suggested Readings

Barraclough, Geoffrey. The Medieval Papacy. London: Thames and Hudson, 1968.

_____. Studies in Medieval History. Oxford: Basil Blackwell, 1938.

_____, ed. Medieval Germany, 911-1250; Essays by German Historians. Oxford: Basil Blackwell, 1948.

Brooke, C. N. L. The Investiture Disputes. London: Oxford University Press, 1958.

Brooke, Zachary N. "Lay Investiture and Its Relation to the Conflict of Empire and Papacy" in Williams, Schafer, ed. The Gregorian Epoch: Reformation, Revolution, Reaction? Boston: Heath, 1964.

Bryce, James. The Holy Roman Empire. New York: Schocken Books, 1904.

Ehler, Sydney Z. , and John B. Morrall, eds. Church and State
    Through the Centuries: A Collection of Historic Documents
    with Commentaries. London: Burns, Oates, and Washbourne,
    1954.
Ellis, John T. Anti-Pope Legislation in Medieval England (1066-
    1377). Oxford: Basil Blackwell, 1930.
Heer, Frederich. The Holy Roman Empire. New York: Frederick
    A. Praeger, 1967.
Morrison, Carl F. The Investiture Controversy. Huntington, N. Y. :
    Kreiger, 1971.
Parker, T. M. Christianity and the State in the Light of History.
    London: Adam and Charles Black, 1955.
Tellenbach, Gerd. Church, State and Christian Society at the Time
    of the Investiture Contest. Translated by R. F. Bennett. Ox-
    ford: Basil Blackwell, 1966.
Tierney, Brian. The Crisis of Church and State, 1050-1300. En-
    glewood Cliffs, N. J. : Prentice-Hall, 1964.
Ullmann, Walter. The Growth of Papal Government in the Middle
    Ages. London: Methuen, 1962.
            . Medieval Papalism: The Political Theories of the Medi-
    eval Canonists. London: Methuen, 1949.

THE PRESTER JOHN LEGENDS (c. 1122-1540)

        Prester John, i. e. , Priest (or Presbyter) John, was a leg-
endary Christian king and priest whose territory, during the Middle
Ages, was believed to lie either in Asia or Africa. The first mention of him appears in the chronicle (1145) of Otto, Bishop of Frei-
sing. Otto described him as dwelling in the Orient, far beyond
Persia and Armenia, a Nestorian Christian who attempted to come
to the assistance of the Christians during the Crusades. Legends
of about the year 1122 place his mythical kingdom somewhere in
India where it was believed the Nestorian Christians had built up
a large monarchy ruled by the priest-king John. He was believed
to have sent a letter (c. 1165) describing the marvels and wealth
of his territory to the Byzantine emperor, Manuel I. Modern historians consider the story of such a letter to be spurious.

        About 1221 Prester John's many noble deeds and great tri-
umphs were ascribed to the Mongol conqueror Genghis Khan (1162-
1227). Marco Polo, in his account of his travels in the Orient,
mentions Un-khan (Wang Khan), a Tartar king defeated by Genghis
Khan about 1220, whose niece married the latter's fourth son and
was the mother of Kublai Khan. Un-khan is thought by some to
be the one on whom the Prester John legends were based.

        By the end of the twelfth century Asiatic legends concerning
the mythical priest-king died out, being replaced by similar myths
putting his kingdom in Africa, about which little was known at that
time.

In Africa Prester John's kingdom was, in the fourteenth and fifteenth centuries, thought to be in Ethiopia (Abyssinia). For centuries Ethiopian kings had had a chapel and altar at the Church of the Sepulcher in Jerusalem. One of these kings became known as Prester John when Fra Mauro, a Venetian monk of the mid-fifteenth century, published a map so designating him and locating his kingdom in Abyssinia.

King John II of Portugal (1455-1495) encouraged exploration during his reign, sending out Diogo Cam and Bartholomeu Dias, who discovered the mouth of the Congo River in 1484 and the Cape of Good Hope in 1488. Although the Portuguese king's navigators were instructed to communicate with Prester John if at all possible they were unable to do so.

Francisco Alvarez, a Portuguese traveler, lived in Abyssinia between 1520 and 1526. In 1540 he published a book mentioning Prester John by name and describing his kingdom. However, no such kingdom has ever been located and the story of the priest-king and his fabulous realm must be considered nothing more than a myth.

Suggested Readings

Alimen, Henriette. Prehistory of Africa. Translated by Alan H. Broderick. London: Oxford University Press, 1957.

Blake, John William. European Beginnings in West Africa, 1454-1578. Westport, Conn.: Negro University Press, 1937.

Davidson, Basil. Africa: History of a Continent. New York: Macmillan, 1972.

_____. The African Past: Chronicles from Antiquity to Modern Times. Boston: Houghton Mifflin, 1959.

Helleiner, Karl F. "Prester John's Letter: A Medieval Utopia," Phoenix, Vol. XIII, 1959.

Hobley, Leonard Frank. Early Explorers to A.D. 1500. London: Methuen, 1954.

Jones, A.H.M., and Elizabeth Monroe. A History of Ethiopia. Oxford: Basil Blackwell, 1955.

Lamb, Harold. Genghis Khan and the Mongol Horde. New York: Random House, 1954.

Marinescu, Constantin. "Encore une Fois le Problème du prêtre Jean," Académie Roumaine (Bulletin de la Section Historique), Vol. XXVI, 1945.

_____. "Le prêtre Jean, son pays, explication de son non," Académie Roumaine (Bulletin de la Section Historique), Vol. X, 1923.

Nowell, C.E. "The Historical Prester John," Speculum, Vol. XXVIII, 1953.

Oppert, Gustav. Der Presbyter Johannes in Sage und Geschichte. 2nd ed. Berlin: 1870.

Penrose, Boise. Travel and Discovery in the Renaissance, 1420-1620. Cambridge, Mass.: Harvard University Press, 1952.

Polo, Marco. The Book of Marco Polo. New York: Grosset &
    Dunlap, 1931 (Originally written 1298).
_____ . The Travels of Marco Polo (the Venetian). Revised
    from Marsden's translation and edited with introduction by Man-
    uel Komroff. Garden City, N. Y. : Garden City Publishing Co. ,
    1930 (Originally written 1298).
Ross, Sir E. Denison. "Prester John and the Empire of Ethiopia"
    in Newton, A. P. , ed. Travel and Travelers in the Middle Ages.
    New York: Gordon Press, 1926.
Sanceau, Elaine. The Land of Prester John. Hamden, Conn. :
    Shoe String Press, 1944.
Vsevolod, Zarncke. Prester John: The Letter and the Legend.
    Oxford: Oxford University Press, 1959.

THE MURDER OF THOMAS A BECKET (1170)

Thomas à Becket (c. 1118-1170) was an English prelate and
martyr. A protégé of Theobald, Archbishop of Canterbury, he was
able to perform a service for Henry of Anjou, later King Henry II
of England, whose close friend he became. In 1155 Henry appointed him high chancellor and preceptor to his young son, Prince Henry.

Becket had been chancellor for about six years when Theobald died and King Henry, the following year, appointed him Archbishop
of Canterbury, on the assumption that Becket would assist him in
curtailing Church power. Becket is supposed to have accepted the
position with reluctance, realizing that if he did not assist Henry
in his efforts against the Church, the king's friendship towards him
would change to hatred.

In 1163 Becket accused the laity of infringing on the rights
and immunities of the Church. He also excommunicated several
nobles and others who held lands claimed by the Church. He successfully opposed the king on a matter regarding taxation. Henry
wished to abolish certain privileges held by the clergy that excepted
them from the jurisdiction of the civil courts. Becket argued violently against this abolishment but later acquiesced. The king's
proposals were committed to writing as the Constitutions of Clarendon, whereupon Becket refused to sign them, on the grounds that
they violated canon law.

These actions put Becket very much in the king's disfavor.
He twice attempted to leave England but was intercepted on both
occasions. Henry brought lawsuits against him, one for money he
claimed had been lent to Becket and not returned. Becket was nearly condemned as a traitor. He escaped to Flanders and from there
went to France where he spent several years in exile.

By the end of 1169 negotiations for a reconciliation between Becket and the king were well advanced, but received a setback when Prince Henry was crowned in June, 1170, by Roger, Archbishop of York. This ceremony was traditionally performed by the Archbishop of Canterbury and Pope Alexander III, angered at the king's selection of Roger as officiating churchman, suspended him and the other bishops who participated in the coronation.

Becket returned to England, supposing that he and his former friend Henry had reached an understanding. Such was not the case: he was ordered to reinstate the suspended bishops which he refused to do, maintaining that only the pope was authorized to lift the suspensions. Henry is said to have complained angrily concerning Becket's refusal, saying "no one will deliver me from this low-born priest."

Four of the king's barons took him at his word. On December 29, 1170, Reginald Fitzurse, William de Tracy, Hugh de Morbille and Richard le Briton went to Canterbury. There they formally demanded that Becket reinstate the suspended bishops. Becket refused. That evening, accompanied by a troop of soldiers, they returned to the cathedral and repeated their demands, which were again refused. Becket was killed on the spot by repeated blows on the head from his assailants' swords.

The news of the crime sent a shock through England. The Pope refused to see any Englishmen for several weeks and the king feared that his vassals would throw off their allegiance.

Thomas à Becket was canonized in 1173. In 1538 King Henry VIII, who was involved in troubles concerning Church authority, had the shrine built for him by Archbishop Stephen Langton destroyed and his bones burned.

Suggested Readings

Abbott, Edwin A. St. Thomas of Canterbury. London: Adam and Charles Black, 1898.

Anouilh, Jean. Becket, or The Honor of God (play). Translated by Lucienne Hill. New York: Coward-McCann, 1960.

_____. "Becket, or the Honor of God" (play condensation) in Mantle, Burns, ed. The Best Plays of 1960-1961. New York: Dodd, Mead, 1961.

Ashley, Maurice. Great Britain to 1688: A Modern History. Ann Arbor, Mich.: University of Michigan Press, 1961.

Baldwin, Marshall. Alexander III and the Twelfth Century. New York: Newman Press, 1968.

106   Footnotes to World History

Barber, Richard. Henry Plantagenet. London: Barrie and Rock-
    liff, 1964.
Borenus, Tancred. St. Thomas Becket in Art. London: Oxford
    University Press, 1932.
Brooke, Zachary N. The English Church and the Papacy from the
    Conquest to the Reign of John. New York: Macmillan, 1931.
Bryant, Sir Arthur. "The Holy Blissful Martyr" in his The Fire
    and the Rose. Garden City, N.Y.: Doubleday, 1966.
Compton, Piers. The Turbulent Priest. London: Staples Press,
    1957
Dark, Sidney. St. Thomas of Canterbury. London: Macmillan,
    1927.
Duggan, Alfred. The Falcon and the Dove: A Life of Thomas
    Becket of Canterbury. Westminster, Md.: Pantheon Books,
    1966.
_____. My Life for My Sheep. Westminster, Md.: Pantheon
    Books, 1955.
_____. Thomas Becket of Canterbury. London: Faber and
    Faber, 1967.
Eliot, T. S. Murder in the Cathedral (play). New York: Harcourt,
    Brace, 1935.
Fry, Christopher. Curtmantle (play). New York: Oxford Univer-
    sity Press, 1961.
Hutton, William H. Thomas Becket. London: 1900.
Jones, Thomas M. The Becket Controversy. New York: Wiley,
    1970.
Knowles, David. Episcopal Colleagues of Archbishop Thomas Beck-
    et. New York: St. Martin's Press, 1951.
Pain, Nesta. The King and Becket. New York: Barnes & Noble,
    1966.
Smalley, Beryl. The Becket Conflict and the Schools: A Study of
    Intellectuals in Politics in the Twelfth Century. Totowa, N.J.:
    Rowman and Littlefield, 1973.
Speaght, Robert. Thomas Becket. Philadelphia: Richard West,
    1938.
Tennyson, Alfred. Becket, a Tragedy in a Prologue and Four Acts:
    As Arranged for the Stage by Henry Irving & Presented at the
    Lyceum Theatre on 6th February. Folcroft, Pa.: Folcroft
    Library Editions, 1974 (Originally published 1893).
Williamson, Hugh Ross. The Arrow and the Sword: An Essay in
    Detection. London: Duckworth, 1955.
Winston, Richard. Thomas Becket. New York: Knopf, 1968.

THE ROBIN HOOD LEGEND (c. 1180-c. 1210)

One of the figures who appear in history is the all-powerful
hero who helps and defends the oppressed and downtrodden against
the tyrants who persecute them. The concept of a superman whose
sole aim in life is to right the wrongs imposed on the weak by the
strong appeals to the imagination of virtually everyone and is ex-

emplified by such radio and television heroes as the Shadow, Superman, Jack Armstrong and the Lone Ranger.   These modern characters are imaginary but throughout history the idea of the strong,
fearless, unbeatable leader has captured the imagination of many
people and, in some cases, the acts of a real person have furnished
the basis for legends and stories enlarging on that person's actual
accomplishments.   Rodrigo Diaz de Bivar, the 11th-century Spanish
hero and soldier of fortune who was known as El Cid, is an example of this, as is Alexander the Great.

An English hero who "robbed the rich and gave to the poor, "
supposedly a contemporary of the British King John (c. 1167-1216)
and his elder brother Richard I (Richard Coeur de Lion) (1157-1199),
was Robin Hood.   It is possible that the legends surrounding this
man were inspired by the exploits of a single individual or by a
number of men who had certain characteristics in common.   Again,
Robin Hood may be no more than the imaginary fulfillment of the
wish by imposed-upon peasants for a hero who invariably overcame
their enemies, the arrogant noblemen, thieving officials and despotic office holders, as did Till Eulenspiegel, the thirteenth-century
legendary wily peasant and jack-of-all-trades.

The legends of Robin Hood's exploits are legion and in some
cases contradictory.   It is generally agreed that he incurred the
displeasure of King John and was forced to flee to Sherwood Forest
in Nottinghamshire where he organized and led a band of outlaws
who wore clothes of lincoln green, killed the king's deer for food
and robbed passing noblemen.   He was, according to the legend,
an expert archer willing to match his skill with the bow and arrow
"against any man in Christendom. "

Robin Hood is said to have become an outlaw when, as a
young man, he was accosted by a group of the king's foresters
while on the way to Nottingham to compete in an archery contest.
The foresters sneered at "a youth who would shoot against the best
archers in England. " He demonstrated his prowess by killing a
deer.   When the foresters attempted to arrest him he killed one of
them and then fled to the forest.   Another version is that "Robin
Hood" was the name assumed by Robert, Earl of Huntingdon, a
follower of Richard I who quarreled with King John and found it
expedient to retreat to Sherwood Forest until Richard returned
from the Third Crusade.

According to the cycle of English ballads telling of Robin
Hood's exploits, his companions in outlawry included Little John,
Will Scarlet (Scathlok), Friar Tuck and Much the Miller.   Maid
Marian, the daughter of a nobleman, lived with the outlaws in the
forest.   She was Robin's sweetheart or, according to some accounts,
his wife.   His arch enemy was the evil Sheriff of Nottingham who
invariably came off second best whenever he clashed with the merry
men of Sherwood Forest, which was often.

There are many tales relating to the exploits of Robin Hood

and his men.   On one occasion Friar Tuck, at Robin's request,
joined in holy wedlock two lovers who had been forced to part because the girl's father had arranged for her to marry a rich old
nobleman.   The outlaws attended the ceremony uninvited, replaced
the nobleman as groom with the man the girl loved and saw the
ceremony through without further interruption.   Rich noblemen passing through the forest were forced to give up their valuables to the
outlaws but were often invited to dine with them.   Poor people were
helped by Robin and his men, both financially and by force of arms.
The outlaws entered and won archery contests.   Their leader, upon
whose head a price had been put by his enemy the Sheriff of Nottingham, attended at least one in disguise.   Needless to say, he
won the first prize with his fantastic marksmanship.

     King Richard is said to have disguised himself as a monk,
permitted himself to be captured by Robin's men and, after identi-
fying himself, recruiting them into his army as archers.   They,
according to this story, agreed and were unconditionally pardoned
for all the illegal acts they had committed.   Robin Hood is said
to have died following an illness for which his female nurse, an
enemy, bled him and deliberately permitted an excessive and fatal
loss of blood.

     The exploits of Robin Hood are covered in at least forty
ballads which have come down to us.   His name is first mentioned
in the second version of Piers Plowman (c. 1377) and is recorded
historically in Andrew Wyntoun's Oryginale Cronykil of Scotland
(c. 1420) and treated fully in Lyttell Geste of Robyn Hoode (printed
c. 1495 by Wynkyn de Worde).   He is mentioned in Ben Jonson's
pastoral drama The Sad Shepherd, in a comic opera by Reginald
de Koven and in Alfred Noyes' play Sherwood and Tennyson's The
Foresters.   He appears in plays by Anthony Munday, Robert Greene
and Owen Davis and in various anonymous medieval plays.   Several
motion pictures, both silent and talking, have been made concerning
his exploits and he has been the hero of both radio and television
programs.

Suggested Readings

Baskerville, Charles R.   The Elizabethan Jigs and Related Song
     Drama.   Magnolia, Md.: Peter Smith, 1929.
Bryant, Sir Arthur.   "The Grey Goose Feather" in his The Fire
     and the Rose.   Garden City, N. Y.: Doubleday, 1966.
Chambers, Edmund K.   English Literature at the Close of the Mid-
     dle Ages.   Oxford: Oxford University Press, 1945.
Cooke, Donald Edwin.   The Silver Horn of Robin Hood.   Philadel-
     phia: Winston, 1956.
Disney, Walt, Productions, Ltd.   Walt Disney Productions Presents
     Robin Hood and the Great Coach Robbery.   New York: Random
     House, 1974.
_____.   Walt Disney's Adventures of Robin Hood.   New York:
     Simon & Schuster, 1955.

Edwards, Clayton. "Robin Hood" in his A Treasury of Heroes and
    Heroines. New York: Hampton Publishing Co. , 1920.
Gable, J. Harris. Bibliography of Robin Hood. Lincoln, Neb. :
    University of Nebraska Press, 1939.
Gilbert, Henry F. B. Robin Hood. Philadelphia: Winston, n. d.
McGovern, Ann. Robin Hood of Sherwood Forest. New York:
    Crowell, 1968.
Malcolmson, Anne. The Song of Robin Hood. Boston: Houghton
    Mifflin, 1947.
Noyes, Alfred. Sherwood: or, Robin Hood and the Three Kings
    (play). New York: Stokes, 1911.
Prescott, Orville. Robin Hood: The Outlaw of Sherwood Forest.
    New York: Random House, 1959.
Pyle, Howard. Some Merry Adventures of Robin Hood of Great
    Renown in Nottinghamshire. New York: Scribner, 1954 (Or-
    iginally published 1883).
Sargent, Helen C. , and George L. Kittredge, eds. English and
    Scottish Popular Ballads, Nos. 117-154. Boston: Houghton
    Mifflin, 1904.
Stone, Eugenia. Robin Hood's Arrow. Chicago: Wilcox and Fol-
    lett, 1948.
Vance, Eleanor. The Adventures of Robin Hood. New York: Ran-
    dom House, 1953.

THE FOUNDING OF THE ORDER OF FRIARS MINOR
(FRANCISCANS) (1207-1208)

One of the most influential orders of the Roman Catholic
Church is the Order of Friars Minor, generally known as the Franciscans.   Founded in 1207-1208 by St. Francis of Assisi and legally established by Pope Innocent III in 1210, it is rivalled in importance only by the Dominicans or Friars Preachers which received
its pontifical letters in 1205.

As a young man St. Francis, originally Giovanni Francesco
Bernardone, the son of a wealthy merchant of Assisi, "was known
for his leadership in revelry. " The boy had little formal education
but learned French from his father. He served in the army, was
captured by the Perugians and held a prisoner for over a year.
While in captivity he suffered an illness and resolved to lead a better life.

In 1202, having been released by his captors, he returned to
Assisi where he started his charitable work with the lepers. His
father, angered at his son's extravagant donations, legally disin-
herited him. The young man then went to the wilderness of Mount
Subasio where he devoted himself to helping the sick and poor. He
restored a ruined chapel where he held services and here he received a call to go out into the world "to possess nothing and to do
good everywhere. "

He went to Rome and from there back to Assisi where he gained disciples. These became the nucleus of the order he was to found. His first convert was Bernard of Quintavalle, a prosperous businessman. Other members of the group were Brother Giles, his first poor convert, and Brothers Leo, Angelo and Rufino, his famed "three companions" who authored a legend concerning him in 1246. At first these men devoted their time to restoring ruined churches but on St. Matthew's day in 1208 Francis was inspired by a sermon to devote his life to "healing the sick, raising the dead, cleansing lepers and casting out demons."

As wandering mendicant friars Francis and his followers preached the gospel in various towns in northern Italy. When his disciples numbered twelve he sent them out in pairs to spread the word of God.

In 1210 Francis appealed to Pope Innocent III for papal approval of his new order. After some hesitation authorization was given. In 1212 the order of Franciscan nuns known as the Order of Poor Ladies, later called "Poor Clares," was founded by Clare (Clara) of Assisi, an Italian nun. She was the first woman convert to the order and a lifelong friend of Francis.

The Franciscan order grew in size and importance. Cardinal Ugoloino became the "corrector" of the organization. A novitiate was established and the ownership of property was authorized.

Francis remained Minister General, to which position he had been elected, until 1220 when he retired. By then the order had more than 5,000 members. Its founder had spent the previous decade traveling and preaching in Italy, Spain, Egypt and the Holy Land.

In September, 1224, after forty days of fasting, Francis, while praying on Monte Alverno, found that the "stigmata" (marks of the Crucifixion of Christ) had appeared on his body. He died in 1226 and was canonized by Pope Gregory IX in 1228.

The highest offices in the Roman Catholic Church have been filled by Franciscans, including five popes. Father Juan Perez and other Franciscans accompanied Christopher Columbus on his first voyage to America. These priests established the first convents in the New World at Santo Domingo and La Vega. Spanish and French friars accompanied other explorers on their voyages and set up missions throughout the Western Hemisphere.

Suggested Readings

Anonymous. The Little Flowers of St. Francis. Translated by
    T. W. Arnold. London: J. M. Dent & Sons, 1940 (First published 1898, written before 1390).
Bishop, Morris. St. Francis of Assisi. Boston: Little, Brown,
    1974.

Boase, Thomas Shesser Ross. St. Francis of Assisi. London: Duckworth, 1936.

Celand, Thomas. Francis of Assisi. Chicago: Franciscan Herald Press, 1963.

Chesterton, Gilbert K. Saint Francis of Assisi. Garden City, N. Y.: Doubleday, 1957.

Christiani, Leon. St. Francis of Assisi. Boston: Daughters of St. Paul, 1975.

Cunningham, Lawrence S. Saint Francis of Assisi. New York: Twayne, 1976.

De Wohl, Louis. Joyful Beggar (fiction). Philadelphia: Lippincott, 1958.

Dubois, Leo L. Saint Francis of Assisi: Social Reformer. Folcroft, Pa.: Folcroft Library Editions, 1906.

Engelbert, Abbe Omer. St. Francis of Assisi. Translated by E. M. Cooper. Chicago: Franciscan Herald Press, 1965.

Goudge, Elizabeth. My God and My All: The Life of St. Francis of Assisi. New York: Coward-McCann, 1959.

Habig, Marion A., ed. St. Francis of Assisi: Omnibus of Sources of the Life of St. Francis. Chicago: Franciscan Herald Press, 1975.

Hansen, Warren N. St. Francis of Assisi: Patron of the Environment. Chicago: Franciscan Herald Press, 1971.

Jörgensen, Johannes. St. Francis of Assisi. New York: Longmans, Green, 1912.

Kyball, Vlastimil. Francis of Assisi. Notre Dame, Ind.: Ave Maria Press, 1954.

Liversidge, Douglas. Saint Francis of Assisi. New York: Watts, 1968.

Maynard, Theodore. Richest of the Poor. Garden City, N. Y.: Doubleday, 1948.

Petry, Ray C. Francis of Assisi: Apostle of Poverty. Durham, N. C.: Duke University Press, 1941.

Sabatier, Paul. Life of St. Francis of Assisi. Translated by Louise Seymour Houghton. New York: Scribner's, 1922 (Originally published 1894).

Sherley-Price, Leo, translator. St. Francis of Assisi: His Life and Writings. London: A. R. Mowbray, 1959.

THE SIGNING OF THE MAGNA CHARTA (1215)

John I (c. 1167-1216) was the first and last English king to have that name. He was the youngest son of Henry II. When Henry died in 1189, he was succeeded by Richard I, his third son. Richard joined the Third Crusade and during his absence in the Holy Land John attempted unsuccessfully to seize the throne. Richard, who had been a prisoner of Leopold, Duke of Austria, returned to England in 1194 and made peace with John who had been conspiring with Philip Augustus (Philip II) of France. Upon Richard's death in battle in the year 1199, John had himself crowned king, although the legitimate heir was Arthur, the son of Geoffrey, another of his elder brothers.

John was a tyrannical and cruel ruler and disregarded the rights and claims of others. This brought him into violent conflict with both the papacy and the barons of England. He refused to accept as Archbishop of Canterbury the prelate favored by Pope Innocent III, for which the latter issued an interdict against England. This led to further trouble with the Holy Father, to war with France and an overwhelming defeat by that country's army at Bouvines, near Lille, in 1214.

King John was thoroughly detested by his subjects for his high-handed abuses in the administration of justice and his increasing assumption of arbitrary royal powers. The barons saw in his defeat at Bouvines an opportunity to end his tyranny. After considerable prior discussion a group of noblemen drew up a charter which they sent to the king for signature. He refused to sign whereupon the noblemen renounced their allegiance to him. They marched on London and captured it. King John realized that he had no choice but to come to terms with the barons, and on June 15, 1215, he met them at Runnymede and signed the document known as the "Magna Charta." This document guaranteed freedom from certain royal abuses, regularized the judicial system, contained provisions for the abolition of certain arbitrary abuses of feudal tenures and made certain guarantees for the protection of commerce and the procedures for conducting trials.

The last section of the Magna Charta (Chapter 29) sets out the historic basis for English civil liberties, stipulating essentially that life, liberty and property were to be taken only by due legal process and not without the judgment of one's peers.

The Magna Charta was confirmed by Parliament in 1216-17 and in 1297 a Parliament under Edward I confirmed it in a modified and now standard form. Today, although the Magna Charta may be legally refuted by Parliament at any time, the rights established by it "have been given the force of law for over seven centuries and have secured an habitual recognition of validity."

Suggested Readings

Ashley, Maurice. Great Britain to 1688: A Modern History. Ann Arbor, Mich.: University of Michigan Press, 1961.
Bagley, John J. Life in Medieval England. New York: Putnam, 1960.
Breasted, James Henry, et al., eds. European History Atlas: Ancient, Medieval and Modern European and World History. Chicago: Denoyer, 1967.
Cross, Arthur Lyon. A Shorter History of England and Greater Britain. New York: Macmillan, 1929.
Daugherty, James. The Magna Charta. New York: Random House, 1956.

Dickinson, J. C. The Great Charter. London: Historical Asso-
     ciation Publications, 1955.
Halliday, Frank E. A Concise History of England from Stonehenge
     to the Atomic Age. New York: Viking Press, 1964.
Harding, Samuel Bannister, in consultation with Albert Bushnell
     Hart. Essentials in Mediaeval History (from Charlemagne to
     the Close of the Fifteenth Century). New York: American
     Book Company, 1909.
Heyer, Georgette. My Lord John (historical fiction). New York:
     Dutton, 1975.
Holt, J. C. Magna Charta. Cambridge: The University Press,
     1965.
McKechnie, W. S. Magna Charta: A Commentary on the Great
     Charter of King John. Glasgow: J. Maclehose & Son, 1914.
Painter, Sidney. The Reign of King John. Baltimore: Johns Hop-
     kins University Press, 1949.
Parsons, Geoffrey. The Stream of History. New York: Scrib-
     ner's, 1929.
Swindler, W. F. Magna Charta, Legend and Legacy. Indianapolis:
     Bobbs-Merrill, 1965.
Tappan, Eva March. "Magna Charta Signed by King John" in her
     Old World Hero Stories. Boston: Houghton Mifflin, 1937.
Terry, Benjamin. A History of England from the Earliest Times
     to the Death of Queen Victoria. Chicago: Scott, Foresman,
     1901.
Thompson, Faith. The First Century of Magna Charta: Its Role
     in the Making of the English Constitution, 1300-1629. Minne-
     apolis: University of Minnesota Press, 1948.
Webster, Hutton. Early European History. Boston: Heath, 1917.

THE WRITING OF THE ROMANCE OF THE ROSE
(1225-1280)

     One of the most widely read books of the Middle Ages was
The Romance of the Rose, written in the French vernacular by
Guillaume de Lorris and Jean de Meun. These two French authors did not work as collaborators; Lorris composed the first
four thousand lines between the years 1225 and 1240 and the remainder of the work, some 18,000 lines, was written by Meun between 1275 and 1280.

     The Rose is a French love poem or allegorical metrical ro-
mance. The portion written by Lorris describes "the vicissitudes
of a comely youth" who, at the instigation of the God of Love, be-
comes wildly enamored of a rose, symbolizing his enamorata. Various characters, appearing as allegorical abstractions, counsel him
concerning his efforts to "pluck the Rose." Welcome represents
the Rose's natural good nature and other characters, such as Beau-
ty, Joy, Delight, Hope and Generosity are countered by Avarice,
Lust, Covetousness, Slander, Evil Mouth, Fear and others. The

God of Love informs the youth that he must endure "great suffering and all the anguish of Christian courtship before he can be permitted to possess the Rose. " Danger, Shame, Fear and Evil Mouth, who guard the Rose, drive the youth from the garden while Welcome and Hope urge him to continue to seek his prize.   Reason suggests that Rose's petals are not worth her thorns and suggests that he abandon his efforts to "pluck" her.   The youth, aided by Friend, is finally able to kiss the Rose, upon which Evil Mouth reports this to the world, whereupon Jealousy orders both Lorris and the youth imprisoned.   The Rose is then held in close confinement by such characters as Fear, Shame and Slander.

The portion of the Rose written by Guillaume de Lorris ends at this point.   The poem was completed by Jean de Meun half a century later, the latter portion being generally considered inferior to the earlier part.   Meun was a rationalist and iconoclast who produced "a work of chaos and Babylonian confusion. "   Critics of today feel that this second part was used to introduce "three thousand lines of lectures and tirades on various subjects, " at the expense of abandoning the sustained allegory of Lorris' work.

After floundering through the morass of verbiage which comprises some 82 percent of the poem, the youth eventually possesses the Rose.   This is accomplished only after Evil Mouth's tongue is cut out and Venus and the God of Love come to the assistance of the love-smitten young man.

In 1402 Jean de Gerson, a French theologian and chancellor of the University of Paris, attempted to have the Rose suppressed, charging that its frank language, advocacy of sexual intercourse outside of marriage and the author's mingling religious sentiments with the vernacular of bawdy houses rendered the work unfit to read. The poem is considered, by today's standards, to be largely banal, boring and essentially meaningless.   Its value lies in the influence it exerted on French literature for almost three centuries following its publication.   It was translated into English by Geoffrey Chaucer, author of the Canterbury Tales.

Suggested Readings

Auslander, Joseph, and Frank Ernest Hill.   The Winged Horse:
     The Story of the Poets and Their Poetry.   Garden City, N. Y. :
     Doubleday, 1927.
Cohn, N.   The World-View of a Thirteenth Century Parisian Intel-
     lectual: Jean de Meun and the Roman de la Rose.   Newcastle
     upon Tyne: University of Durham Press, 1961.
Cross, E. A.   "Literature Through the Middle Ages" in his World
     Literature.   New York: American Book Co. , 1935.
Goodrich, Norma Loore.   The Ways of Love: Eleven Romances of
     Medieval France.   New York: Beacon Press, 1964.
Holland, Rupert Sargent.   Historic Poems and Ballads.   Philadel-
     phia: G. W. Jacobs & Co. , 1912.

Lewis, Clive Staples. The Allegory of Love: A Study in Medieval
    Tradition. Oxford: Clarendon Press, 1936.
Macy, John. The Story of the World's Literature. New York:
    Boni & Liveright, 1925.
Nichols, Stephen G., ed. Le Roman de la Rose de Guillaume de
    Lorris. New York: Appleton-Century-Crofts, 1967.
Stefferud, Alfred, ed. The Wonderful World of Books. New York:
    New American Library, 1954.
Thuasne, L. Le Roman de la Rose. Paris: E. Malfère, 1929.

THE ESTABLISHMENT OF THE INQUISITION (c. 1233)

The Inquisition was established by the Catholic Church about
1233 for the suppression of heresy, a heretic being virtually anyone who did not share the beliefs of the Church. It was desired
by both Church and lay authorities that unanimity of belief be
achieved; the Church's desire stemmed from religious reasons and
the laymen felt that religious nonconformists were potential rebels
whose activities could undermine the state. Physical force was
used by Christian emperors, particularly Constantine I (c. 280-
337 A.D.) and his sons to achieve uniformity of religious thought,
although the Church Fathers did not all agree that the use of physical coercion could achieve this objective.

About the year 1000 a religious movement known as Catharism or Albigensianism, heretical in the eyes of the Catholic Church,
spread over western Europe. In 1022 thirteen Cathari were burned
at the stake at Orléans on the orders of King Robert II of France.
This was the first execution by fire for heresy. In spite of this,
heresy spread and by the end of the twelfth century it appeared
that Catharism threatened the very existence of the Catholic Church
in southern France. Churchmen became convinced that steps should
be taken to stop the spread of this new belief.

In 1184 it was decreed at the Council of Verona that bishops
were to take aggressive action to locate and do away with heretics
in their dioceses. In 1227 bishops were ordered by the Council of
Narbonne to appoint investigators who were to seek out heresy and
report their findings. Despite these measures heresy was not
checked. Pope Innocent III instigated a crusade against the Albi-
gensians in 1207-1208. This crusade came to an end in 1229, as
agreed upon by the Treaty of Meaux, and in 1233 Pope Gregory IX
issued two bulls establishing the Papal Inquisition. Papal inquisitors
were generally members of the Dominican and Franciscan orders.

The inquisitor was responsible directly to the pope. He and
his company of assistants would conduct inquests based on the testimony of sworn witnesses, the purpose of which was to ascertain
the innocence or guilt of those suspected of heresy. The inquisitor,
upon arriving at a town within his province, received accusations and

confessions. While those accused were not permitted to cross-examine their accusers, they were allowed to draw up a list of the enemies and persons who might benefit from their conviction. Pope Innocent VI authorized the use of torture to extract confessions, but this was abolished by Pope Boniface VIII.

If convicted, the accused heretic was turned over to the secular arm, the clergy being expressly forbidden to shed blood. Sentences ranged from fines, the wearing of distinctive costumes and penances through pilgrimages, to infamy, flagellation, confiscation of property, imprisonment, and death at the stake. These sentences were announced in a solemn religious ceremony, the sermo generalis or auto da fe (act of faith). Held always on a Sunday, the ceremony, to which the public was invited, began with a procession, followed by a sermon, then an announcement of the various sentences, culminating in the carrying out of the sentences. Those condemned to be burned alive and who abjured were often strangled before the fire was lighted.

The Spanish Inquisition, established in 1480 with the approval of Pope Sixtus IV, was designed to root out the secret Jews in the kingdom. Under the direction of Tomás de Torquemada as Inquisitor General, this organization was a responsibility of the Spanish crown which appointed, paid and dismissed the inquisitors. The role of the papacy was one of confirmation only, the king being the master of the Spanish Inquisition. It was finally suppressed in 1834.

Suggested Readings

Blötzer, Joseph. "Inquisition" in The Catholic Encyclopedia. New York: Encyclopedia Press, 1913.

Coulton, George C. Inquisition and Liberty. Boston: Beacon Press, 1959.

Kamen, Henry A. The Spanish Inquisition. New York: American Library, 1965.

Lea, Henry Charles. The History of the Inquisition in Spain. New York: Macmillan, 1906-1907.

_____. The History of the Inquisition in the Middle Ages. New York: Harper, 1888.

Madaule, Jacques. The Albigensian Crusade. New York: Fordham University Press, 1967.

Nickerson, Hoffman. The Inquisition: A Political and Military Study of Its Establishment. Port Washington, N.Y.: Kennikat Press, 1932.

Roth, Cecil. The Spanish Inquisition. New York: Norton, 1964.

Runciman, Steven. The Medieval Manichee. Cambridge: Cambridge University Press, 1947.

Strayer, Joseph R. The Albigensian Crusades. New York: Dial Press, 1971.

Thorndyke, Lynn. The History of Medieval Europe. Edited by William L. Langer. Boston: Houghton Mifflin, 1956.

"Torquemada" in Crimes and Punishment, Vol. 17.   Editorial pre-
   sentation, Jackson Morley.   London: BPC, 1973.
Tuberville, Arthur S.   Medieval Heresy and the Inquisition.   Lon-
   don: Archon Books, 1964.
Vacandard, Elphège.   The Inquisition: A Critical and Historical
   Study of the Coercive Power of the Church.   Translated by
   Bertrand L. Conway.   Merrick, N. Y. :   Richwood, 1940.
Walsh, William T.   Characters of the Inquisition.   New York:
   P. J. Kenedy, 1940.

THE INVENTION OF GUNPOWDER (c. 1250)

     One of the most meaningful of man's inventions was gunpow-
der.   This ranks with such other revolutionary discoveries as the
use of fire, the discovery of the principle of the wheel and the
mining, refining and alloying of metals.   It caused radical changes
in methods of waging war and is still used today in the manufacture
of fireworks and for blasting operations.   It was the only explosive
known to man until about 1628 when fulminating gold, a powerful
explosive, was discovered.

     Gunpowder, or black powder, is a mixture of 75 percent
potassium nitrate (saltpeter), 15 percent carbon and 10 percent
sulfur.   When suitably contained, as in the barrel of a cannon, it
explodes rapidly when ignited, generating sufficient force to propel
a projectile.

     It is not known just when gunpowder was discovered or who
made the discovery, but it is certain that the Chinese used black
powder during the 12th century.   They employed it for religious
purposes, believing that the cracking sound of the exploding powder
drove evil spirits away.   They also used it to propel pebbles and
small rockets and in bombards, the earliest kind of cannon, which
used stone balls as missiles.

     Eventually the secret of making gunpowder came to Western
Europe.   Some authorities feel that the technique came from China
and others are of the opinion that the Europeans discovered it independently.   Roger Bacon (c. 1214-1294), who was an English
Franciscan monk, a philosopher and a man of science who experimented in alchemy and optics, is considered to have known how
to make gunpowder.   One authority claims that a formula for gunpowder and instructions for obtaining saltpeter are contained in "a
puzzling essay by the medieval scientist. " If this contention is
correct, gunpowder was known in Europe by the middle of the 13th
century.   Bacon may have wished to keep his findings secret for
fear of being charged with heresy, as indeed he was in 1257.   In
1268 he admitted to Pope Clement IV that black powder was in widespread use for military purposes.

   The origin of the cannon is shrouded in mystery. Berthold
Schwartz, a legendary German monk and alchemist of the 13th or
14th century, is reputed to have invented such a weapon and also
is thought by some to have discovered gunpowder. Other authorities credit the Moslems with inventing the cannon in the 14th century or earlier. A Florentine document dated 1326 makes a definite reference to a cannon and a picture of such a device appears
in an English book published the following year. It is obvious that
gunpowder must have existed before the cannon but, in any event,
by 1400 virtually all the armies of Europe were using primitive
cannon against their enemies.

   With the adaptation of cannon for military purposes the nature of armed conflict changed. Individual hand-to-hand combat
was replaced with artillery shooting at the foe from a distance. It
was no longer necessary to scale the walls of medieval castles and
forts; these could now be smashed with cannon balls. Sailing ships,
armed with cannon, fired at and sank each other. When rifles
small enough to be carried and fired by individual soldiers were
developed the day of the sword and spear was gone. Horse soldiers were replaced by artillerymen. At the Battle of Trafalgar
in 1805, Admiral Horatio Nelson was killed by a French sharp-
shooter's musket ball which broke his spine.

   Black powder, after about 500 years, was largely supplanted
by newer, more sophisticated explosives. In 1846 nitrocellulose
and nitroglycerin were discovered. Alfred Nobel, the Swedish manufacturer, inventor and philanthropist, invented dynamite in 1866,
making nitroglycerin, a highly unstable compound, safe to handle.
In 1888 he produced ballistite, one of the first smokeless powders.
Since then nitrates, nitro-compounds, fulminates and azides have
been the chief explosive compounds, being used either alone or in
combination with fuels or other agents. The first explosive oxide
was xenon trioxide which was discovered in 1962.

                            Suggested Readings

Akehurst, Richard. The World of Guns. New York: Hamlyn, 1972.
Carman, W. Y. A History of Firearms from the Earliest Times
     to 1914. New York: St. Martin's Press, 1955.
Cipolla, Carlo M. Guns, Sails and Empires. New York: Minerva
     Press, 1965.
Dutton, William S. One Thousand Years of Explosives. Philadel-
     phia: Winston, 1960.
Fuller, John F. C. Armament and History. New York: Scribner's,
     1945.
Guttmann, Oscar. The Manufacture of Explosives. London: 1895.
Marshall, Arthur. Explosives, Vol. I: History and Manufacture.
     London: J. & A. Churchill, 1917.
Nef, John U. Industry and Government in France and England. Ith-
     aca, N. Y.: Great Seal Books, 1957.
Oakeshott, R. Ewart. The Archaeology of Weapons. New York:
     Frederick A. Praeger, 1960.

Partington, James R. A History of Greek Fire and Gunpowder.
    Cambridge: Heffer and Sons, 1960.
Ricketts, Howard. Firearms. London: Octopus, 1964.
Van Gelder, A. P., and H. Schlatter. History of the Explosives
    Industry in America. New York: Arno Press, 1972.
White, Lynn, Jr. Medieval Technology and Social Change. Ox-
    ford: Clarendon Press, 1962.

THE USURY CONTROVERSY (c. 1250)

The lending of money at interest is today an accepted business practice. This, however, was not always the case. Giving
the temporary use of money for a reward was, at one time, considered not only a private sin of injustice but also a civil offense.
Today it is unlawful to charge interest in excess of the amount
fixed by statute, such an excess charge being considered usurious.
In the Middle Ages any payment made to the lender above the amount
loaned constituted usury.

The early Hebrews, Greeks and Romans all were conscious
of the subject of making loans for interest and their ideas descended to the clergy, rulers, businessmen and people of medieval times.
The Hebrews felt that members of the same tribe should not charge
each other for loans but such charges were quite permissible when
dealing with foreigners. This was in spite of the fact that the Talmud declared money to be sterile or unproductive and consequently
no interest should be exacted for lending it. The Greeks also felt
that money was, in this sense, sterile and philosophers such as
Plato held that moneylenders, as creators of social unrest, were
not to be trusted. Both the Greeks and Romans passed legislation
to keep interest rates within prescribed limits. Justinian, in his
digest of Roman legal codes (533-534 A. D.), recognized four different rates of interest legally applicable to loans of different types.

These conflicting ideas which descended to the men of the
Middle Ages resulted in a good deal of confusion concerning the
moral rights or wrongs of usury. Charlemagne, in the early 9th
century, initiated laws declaring that both laymen and clerics who
charged interest for loans were guilty of a civil offense. In the
middle 11th century Edward the Confessor, King of England, decreed that any of his subjects found "guilty of usury" would be deprived of his property and punished in other ways. Similar laws
were promulgated in Germany.

About the year 1100 philosophers, theologians and lawyers
turned their attention to consideration of the anti-usury policies of
the reigning monarchs. Thomas Aquinas, an Italian scholastic philosopher, agreed that usury was contrary to divine law as specified
in the Bible and also to natural law which requires justice for all.
According to Aquinas, money is consumed in its use like food, and

consequently "selling both money and the use of it in a loan" con-
stitutes an unnatural act.   He felt that "usury unnaturally separated
the use and ownership of money. "

Other philosophers felt as Aquinas did but the lawyers were
inclined to disagree with him.   They believed that the profits generated by investments of money were usurious only when the investments were in the form of loans.   Other types of investment, such
as partnerships and annuities, could produce non-usurious profits.
Accursius, an Italian jurist of the 12th century, in commenting on
Roman law, argued that the Justinian Codes permitted usury.

Other legal technicalities existed.   Businessmen were permitted by law to accept interest on loans under certain specified
conditions.   In making a loan the lender could add to the principal
the normal profits he might have made by investing his money elsewhere, the extra sum to be paid back to him by the borrower involving loss of profit.   This meant that the reasonable profit the
lender might have made by an alternate investment was legal, but
claiming an excessive potential profit in some investment other than
the loan was contrary to the statutes.   This led to the modern day
distinction between usury, or illegitimate profit on a loan, and interest, the legitimate profit on a loan.

Many city governments, such as those of Florence, Genoa and
Venice, found themselves in financial difficulties.   Facing bankruptcy,
they solicited loans from businessmen who, while willing to invest in
municipal bonds, expected interest in return.   This led to some
liberalization in the thinking of the Church and governmental authorities.   Moneylenders who charged their customers, often members
of the urban poor, as much as 40 percent for short term loans were
severely criticized.   These usurers were condemned in church sermons and concrete action was taken against them by the establishment of pawnshops by religious orders and city governments.   These
institutions charged a lesser rate of interest than did the moneylenders, but had to make a charge for their loans in order to retrieve
operating costs and overhead.   Jews, forbidden to enter many economic occupations, did a black market type of moneylending for which
they were held up to scorn by the Christian clergymen who hated
the Hebrew religion.   Shakespeare's character Shylock, in The
Merchant of Venice, typified the Jewish moneylender as seen
by contemporary eyes, and today the slang term "Shylock", is
used to refer to pawnbrokers and moneylenders, whether Jewish
or not.

By the year 1500 the literature on usury was considerable
and led to the study of economic theory by such men as Thomas
Robert Malthus, Karl Marx, Friedrich Engels, Adam Smith, John
Maynard Keynes, John Kenneth Galbraith and others.   Some economists feel that the usury controversy helped lead to the development of the capitalistic society.

Suggested Readings

Benvenisti, J. L. The Iniquitous Contract: An Analysis of Usury and Maldistribution. London: Burns, Oates and Washbourne, 1937.

Chandler, Lester V. The Economics of Money and Banking. New York: Harper, 1948.

Cleary, Rev. Patrick. The Church and Usury. London: 1914.

Dempsey, Bernard W. Interest and Usury. Washington, D. C.: American Council on Public Affairs, 1943.

De Rover, Raymond. San Bernardino of Sienna and Sant' Antonio of Florence: The Two Great Economic Thinkers of the Middle Ages. Boston: Harvard Graduate School of Business Administration, 1967.

Divine, Thomas F. Interest: An Historical and Analytical Study in Economics and Modern Ethics. Milwaukee, Wis.: Marquette University Press, 1959.

Kermode, Frank. "Some Themes in the Merchant of Venice" in Barnet, Sylvan, ed. Twentieth Century Interpretations of the Merchant of Venice: A Collection of Critical Essays. Englewood Cliffs, N. J.: Prentice-Hall, 1970.

Kitch, M. J. Capitalism and the Reformation. London: Longmans, Green, 1959.

Nelson, Benjamin. The Idea of Usury. Princeton, N. J.: Princeton University Press, 1949.

Noonan, John T., Jr. The Scholastic Analysis of Usury. Cambridge, Mass.: Harvard University Press, 1957.

Schumpeter, Joseph A. History of Economic Analysis. Edited by Elizabeth Doody Schumpeter. New York: Scribner, 1954.

Shakespeare, William. "The Merchant of Venice" (play) in Clark, W. G., and W. Aldis Wright, eds. The Complete Works of William Shakespeare, Arranged in Their Chronological Order. New York: Halcyon House, n. d. (Originally written c. 1600).

VINCENT OF BEAUVAIS' COMPILATION OF THE SPECULUM MAJUS (c. 1260)

The encyclopedia has been defined as "a work treating separately various topics from all branches of knowledge, usually in alphabetical arrangement." Centuries ago it was realized that information should be assembled and listed in an organized manner, that it might be retrieved when needed. It is believed that Speusippus, a disciple of Plato, compiled the first encyclopedia in the fourth century B. C., although no remnant of this work is extant. Marcus Terentius Varro, a Roman scholar and author, compiled Disciplinarum Libri IX in the second century B. C. This was an encyclopedia of the liberal arts in nine books. He also published Rerum Human Arum et Divinarum Antiquitates in 41 books. This, dealing with Roman antiquities, was similar to Disciplinarum Libri IX. Neither of these works has come down to us.

Pliny, in the first century A.D., compiled Historia Naturalis
which appeared in 27 books and 2493 chapters. Other encyclopedists, including Martianus Capella, Isidore of Seville and Rabanus
Maurus, published compilations of knowledge in succeeding centuries.

The most important of the early encyclopedias was the one
compiled by Vincent of Beauvais, a French Domican scholar. This,
completed about 1260, was the Speculum Majus, also entitled Bibliotheca Mundi and Speculum Triplex. It was in three parts (Spec-
lum Naturale, Speculum Doctrinale and Speculum Historiale) and is
considered the most complete scientific encyclopedia of the thirteenth
century.

Speculum Majus consisted of 80 books, 9,885 chapters and
approximately 3,260,000 words. Subsequently (about 1310-1325)
Speculum Morale was appended to the original work, adding approximately 850,000 words.

The Speculum Naturale (32 books) is "a panorama of natural
or universal being." The Speculum Doctrinale (17 books) sums up
the learning of the author's day, including the liberal, mechanical,
moral and medicinal arts. The Speculum Historiale (31 books)
"surveys the history of mankind from the Creation to 1250."

In putting together his Speculum Majus Vincent drew freely
on the works of many predecessors, including Aristotle, Averroës,
Peter Alfonso, Avicenna, Cicero, Pliny, Albertus Magnus, William
of Conches and many others. The historian Lynn Thorndyke, in
analyzing the Speculum Majus, states that "Vincent's volumes suggest the use of scissors and paste a little too manifestly." However, it has been used as a primary source of information by Geoffrey Chaucer, Jacobus de Voragine, Jean de Meun, Emil Malé
Giovanni Colonna, Benzo of Alessandria and many others.

Until the mid-eighteenth century the Speculum Majus was
the largest and most complete encyclopedia available. It appeared
in a number of manuscripts, translations and, after the invention
of printing from movable type in the mid-fifteenth century, no fewer than six complete editions were produced by this means.

Suggested Readings

Aiken, Pauline. "Vincent de Beauvais and Chaucer's Knowledge of
    Alchemy," Studies in Philology, Vol. XLI, 1944.
Boskoff, P.S. "Quintilian in the Late Middle Ages," Studies in
    Philology, Vol. XXVII, 1927.
Bourgeat, J.B. Etudes sur Vincent de Beauvais. Paris: 1856.
Boutaric, E. Examen des sources Speculum Historiale de Vincent
    de Beauvais (Memoire de l'Academie des Inscriptions et Belles
    Lettres). Paris, 1863.

"Encyclopedia" in Shores, Louis, editor in chief. Collier's Ency-
     clopedia. New York: Crowell-Collier Educational Corporation,
     1972.
Sarton, George.   "Vincent of Beauvais" in his Introduction to the
     History of Science, Vol. II. Baltimore, Md.: Williams &
     Wilkins, 1931.
Thompson, James Westfall. History of Historical Writing.   New
     York: Macmillan, 1942.
Thorndyke, Lynn.   "Vincent of Beauvais" in his A History of Magic
     and Experimental Science During the First Thirteen Centuries
     of Our Era, Vol. II.   New York: Macmillan, 1929.
Ullman, B. L.   "A Project for a New Edition of Vincent of Beau-
     vais, " Speculum, Vol. VIII, 1933.
Weisheip, J. A.   "Vincent of Beauvais" in The New Catholic Ency-
     clopedia, Vol. XIV. New York: McGraw-Hill, 1965.

ROGER BACON'S INTRODUCTION OF
EXPERIMENTAL SCIENCE (c. 1265)

     Although Roger Bacon (c. 1214-1294), the English monk,
writer and philosopher, joined the Franciscan order about the year
1255, his interest and studies centered around scientific rather than
theological matters.   He is known as the exponent, if not the orig-
inator, of the scientific method.   Many legends concerning his discoveries have come down to the present day.   He is popularly
thought to have invented gunpowder and the telescope.   He was believed to have been a conjurer and necromancer who practiced
black magic, and was known as a forward-looking genius who, born
before his time, predicted the automobile and the aeroplane.   By
some he is thought to have been "a martyr of free thought. "   These
concepts are generally untrue but Bacon did much to substitute the
idea of conducting impartial, unbiased scientific experiments for the
blind, unthinking acceptance of "truths" inherited from the past.

     Bacon was educated at Oxford University and the University
of Paris, following which he taught briefly at the latter institution.
He then returned to England where, after becoming a Franciscan
monk, he settled at Oxford to conduct experiments in alchemy and
optics.   These activities caused his superiors to question his religious orthodoxy and in 1257 Bonaventura, the general of the Franciscans, ordered him confined at a religious institution in Paris.
For ten years he was deprived of the use of books, scientific instruments and writing materials.

     In 1265 Pope Clement IV, who had previously heard of Ba-
con's experiments and had expressed a wish to see his writings,
was sent copies of his Opus Majus, Opus Minus and Opus Tertium.
These writings constitute an encyclopedia of all science then known,
embracing mathematics, logic, grammar, physics, experimental research and moral philosophy.   The writer advocated a reformation

in the sciences "through different methods of studying the languages
and nature." They contain criticisms of the scholastic learning of
Bacon's day and strongly advocate the modernization of such learning. They were prepared hurriedly and unfortunately contain errors
of which, Bacon, perhaps, should have been aware. He expressed
a belief in the imaginary philosopher's stone which, it was thought,
could transmute base metals into gold and silver and could also
prolong life. He also believed in the efficacy of astrology. However, his advocacy of experimental science and contributions to the
knowledge of his day more than atone for these shortcomings. His
virulent attacks on the narrow, biased views of his contemporaries
and his challenge of the four "stumbling-blocks of truth": weak authority, established custom, the "sense of the ignorant crowd" and
self delusion make him one of the great scientific researchers of
all time.

Bacon felt that mathematics was the "true key to all sciences." He saw truth in the concrete and practical rather than in
abstract propositions. He carried on the teachings of Robert Grosseteste, his mentor, that arguments, however strong, could never
be conclusive without being followed by impartial, unbiased experiments to test their conclusions.

Bacon advocated the comparative study of languages, that
the Bible could be accurately understood. He felt that many teach-
ers, particularly those at the University of Paris, dealt entirely
too much with theory.

Pope Clement's reaction to Bacon's writings is unknown; he
died shortly after the Opus Majus and the other works reached him.

In 1278 Pope Nicholas III forbade the reading of Bacon's
books and ordered him imprisoned. Following fourteen years' in-
carceration he returned to Oxford. There he wrote a Compendium
Studii Theologioe which was completed shortly before his death in
1294.

Suggested Readings

Bridges, J. H.   The Life and Works of Roger Bacon.   London:
    Williams and Norgate, 1914.
Butterfield, Herbert.   The Origins of Modern Science, 1300-1800.
    New York: Macmillan, 1957.
Crombie, A. C.   Robert Grosseteste and the Origins of Experimen-
    tal Science.   Oxford: Clarendon Press, 1953.
Crowley, Theodore.   Roger Bacon.   Louvain: James Duffy & Co.,
    1950.
Easton, Stewart C.   Roger Bacon and His Search for a Universal
    Science.   New York: Columbia University Press, 1952.
Eastwood, Bruce S.   "Grosseteste's Quantitative Law of Refraction:
    A Chapter in the History of Non-Experimental Science," Journal
    of the History of Ideas, Vol. 28, 1967.

Jaffe, Bernard. Crucibles: The Story of Chemistry from Ancient
    Alchemy to Nuclear Fission. New York: Simon & Schuster,
    1948.
Koryé, Alexandre. From the Closed World to the Infinite Universe.
    Baltimore: Johns Hopkins University Press, 1957.
Little, A. G. , ed. Roger Bacon: Essays. Oxford: Clarendon
    Press, 1914.
Thorndike, Lynn. A History of Magic and Experimental Science
    During the First Thirteen Centuries of Our Era. New York:
    Macmillan, 1929.
White, Andrew Dickson. A History of the Warfare of Science with
    Theology in Christendom. New York: George Braziller, 1955.
Woodruff, F. Winthrop. Roger Bacon: A Biography. Carter Lane:
    James Clarke & Co. , 1938.

THE TRAVELS OF MARCO POLO (1271-1295)

In 1260 Nicolo Polo and his brother Maffeo traveled from
their native Venice to the court of the Khan of the Pipchak Tartars
at Serai. After a year of profitable trading they decided, before
returning home, to visit the court of Kublai Khan, ruler of China,
at Peking.

The Khan welcomed them and, after a pleasant stay, suggested that they return and bring back Christian missionaries from
the West. Returning to Venice they recruited two Dominican friars
who shortly after deserted. However, the two Polo brothers, together with Marco, the fifteen-year-old son of Nicolo, left Venice
in 1271, traveling by sea to Acre and thence by caravan through
Iraq, Persia, Parmir, Samarkand and Yancard, finally arriving at
Peking.

The three Venetians were made welcome, young Marco Polo
making a particularly favorable impression upon the Chinese ruler.
For seventeen years he was the Khan's trusted servant, during
which time he visited virtually every part of China.

He recorded his impressions and adventures in The Book of
Marco Polo. This has since been reproduced in many editions.
He was interested in the manufacturing arts, the commerce, cos-
tume, architecture, customs and habits of the Chinese. The silk
industry was of particular interest to him and his book gives an
excellent description of silk culture, weaving, dyeing and finishing.

Marco Polo did not confine his travels to China. He was
able to visit India and possibly Siberia and the Philippines.

In 1292 Marco, his father and his uncle obtained Kublai Khan's
permission to return to Venice. They escorted the Khan's daughter to Persia where she was to be married to the Khan Arghun.

The trip home took three years, the Venetians traveling primarily by ship. They reached Trebizond on the Black Sea in due course, sailed to Constantinople and thence to Negropont in Greece. They arrived at their native city in 1295 after an absence of 24 years.

In later years Marco Polo served as an officer in the Venetian navy. In 1298 he was captured when the Venetian fleet was defeated by Genoa. While confined in prison he sent for the notes he had made during his travels and dictated his book to a fellow captive, a scribe named Rustigielo of Pisa. He was freed within a year, by which time his book, which was to gain him literary immortality, had been transcribed on parchment. For years it was regarded as a mass of exaggeration and fabrication, but modern French and English scholars have proved its veracity.

Suggested Readings

Bingham, Woodbridge, Hilary Conroy, and Frank W. Iklê. A History of Asia. Boston: Allyn and Bacon, 1964-1965.

Hart, Henry H. Venetian Adventurer. Stanford, Calif.: Stanford University Press, 1942.

Kent, Louise. He Went with Marco Polo; a Story of Venice and Cathay (fiction). Boston: Houghton Mifflin, 1935.

MacDonald, Malcolm Ross. "Merchant Travelers," "The Venetians Return" and "The Polos in China" in his Beyond the Horizon: Encyclopedia of Discovery and Exploration, Vol. 2. London: Aldus Books, 1971.

Napier, William. "The Lure of the East" in his Lands of Spice and Treasure: Encyclopedia of Discovery and Exploration, Vol. 5. London: Aldus Books, 1971.

Olschki, Leonardo. Marco Polo's Asia: An Introduction to his "Description of the World Called 'Il Millione.'" Translated by John A. Scott. Berkeley, Calif.: University of California Press, 1960.

O'Neill, Eugene. "Marco Millions" (play) in his Nine Plays of Eugene O'Neill, Selected by the Author. New York: Liveright, 1932.

Polo, Marco. The Book of Marco Polo. New York: Grosset & Dunlap, 1931 (Originally written 1298).

_____. Marco Polo's Account of Japan and Java. Boston: Directors of the Old South Work, 1896 (Originally written 1298).

_____. The Travels of Marco Polo (The Venetian). Edited and with introduction by Manuel Komroff. Garden City, N.Y.: Garden City Publishing Co., 1930 (Originally written 1298).

Price, Christine. Cities of Gold and Isles of Spice: Travel to the East in the Middle Ages. New York: David McKay, 1965.

Shor, Jean Bowie. After You, Marco Polo. New York: McGraw-Hill, 1955.

Tappan, Eva March. "Marco Polo Visits the Great Khan of China" in her Old World Hero Stories. Boston: Houghton Mifflin, 1937.

DANTE ALIGHIERI COMPOSES THE DIVINE COMEDY
(c. 1306-c. 1321)

The Divine Comedy, an allegorical narrative written by the Italian poet Dante Alighieri sometime between 1306 and 1321, is considered one of the greatest works in the history of literature.

Dante, the son of an Italian member of the lower nobility, was born in Florence in 1265. His mother died during his childhood and his father passed away when he was eighteen. About 1273, when he was nine, he met Beatrice (Bice) Portinari with whom he reputedly fell in love and whom he immortalized in his poems Vita Nuova and the Divine Comedy.

Little is known about his education but he is supposed to have studied at Bologna, Padua, Paris and probably Oxford. He fought on the side of the Guelphs against the Ghibellines and about 1295 entered political life. As a Guelph partisan and member of the Bianchi, or Whites, he was entrusted with several diplomatic missions. Making political enemies of Pope Boniface VIII and high-ranking members of both the Guelph and the Ghibellines resulted in his being tried, in absentia, on trumped up charges while he was in Rome. He was found guilty, banned from Florence for two years and ordered to pay a heavy fine. When he refused to pay he was condemned in 1302, to be burned at the stake if he ever returned to Florence. He never saw his native city again.

Dante spent the last nineteen years of his life as a wanderer, living in Verona, Bologna, Lunigiana, Casentino, Paris, Pisa and Ravenna. It was during this period that he composed his masterpiece, the Divine Comedy.

Little is known about the actual composition of the narrative, called by its author La Commedia. Scholars believe he started work on it at about 1306 or 1307 and completed it in 1321. It is, as mentioned above, considered one of the greatest of all works of literature and is a description of an imaginary four-day journey made by Dante through hell, purgatory and heaven in the year 1300. The Roman poet Vergil, representing Reason, guides the author through hell and purgatory and Beatrice, representing both a manifestation and an instrument of the divine will, conducts him through heaven.

Each section of Dante's masterpiece contains 33 cantos except the first, which has an additional canto which is an introduction. It is written in terza rima in the Italian rather than the Latin language, Dante intending it to be a popular work for his contemporaries.

It is a synthesis of autobiography, history and religion and may be interpreted in many ways. Dante, in a letter to his patron, a young Veronese noble, states that the poem has four levels of

meaning: the literal, allegorical, anagogical or mystic, and moral.
Critics have stated that "the greatness of this work rests on its
multiplicity of meaning even more than on its masterful poetic and
dramatic qualities," and "Dante's imaginary voyage can be understood as an allegory of the purification of man's soul and of his
achievement of inner peace through the guidance of reason and love."

The Divine Comedy has been published in countless editions
in more than 25 languages. Translations have been made by Henry
Wadsworth Longfellow, Laurence Binyon, Dorothy Sayers and John
Ciardi, among others. Many famous artists, including Sandro Bot-
ticelli, Michelangelo, John Flaxman and Gustave Doré, have illustrated some of the editions. Portions have been set to music by
Giocchino Rossini and Robert Schumann as well as by other great
composers.

Suggested Readings

Alighieri, Dante. The Comedy of Dante Alighieri the Florentine.
    Cantica I: "Hell" ("L'Inferno"). Translated by Dorothy L.
    Sayers. Cantica II: "Purgatory" ("Il Purgatoria"). Translated
    by Dorothy L. Sayers. Cantica III: "Paradise" ("Il Paradiso").
    translated by Dorothy L. Sayers and Barbara Reynolds. Har-
    mondsworth, England: Penguin Books, 1949-1962. 3 vols.
    (Originally written c. 1306-c. 1321).
_____. Convivio. Translated by Philip Wicksteed. London:
    Temple Classics, 1903 (Originally written c. 1306-c. 1321).
_____. The Divine Comedy of Dante Aligheri. Translated by
    the Rev. Henry Francis Cary, M. A. New York: Burt, n. d.
    (Originally written c. 1306-c. 1321).
_____. Monarchy and Three Political Letters. London: Wei-
    denfeld and Nicolson, 1954 (Originally written c. 1306-c. 1321).
Auerbach, Erich. Dante, Poet of the Secular World. Translated
    by Ralph Manheim. Chicago: University of Chicago Press,
    1961.
Bergin, Thomas G. Dante. Boston: Houghton Mifflin, 1965.
Chubb, Thomas C. Dante and His World. Boston: Little, Brown,
    1966.
Cosmo, Umberto. Handbook to Dante Studies. Translated by Dav-
    id Moore. Folcroft, Pa.: Folcroft Library Editions, 1950.
Cross, E. A. "Dante: The Divine Comedy" in this World Litera-
    ture. New York: American Book Co., 1935.
d'Entreves, Alessandro Passerin. Dante as a Political Thinker.
    Oxford: Clarendon Press, 1952.
Eliot, T. S. Dante. Brooklyn, N. Y.: Haskell, 1974.
Fergusson, Francis. Dante. New York: Macmillan, 1966.
Gelernt, Jules. Dante's Divine Comedy. New York: Monarch
    Press, 1966.
Pound, Ezra. The Spirit of Romance. New York: New Directions,
    1968.
Priest, Harold Martin. Divine Comedy: Purgatorio, Notes: In-
    cluding General Introduction, Synopsis ... and Essay Topics.
    Lincoln, Neb.: Cliff's Notes, 1971.

Rizzatti, Maria Luisa. The Life and Times of Dante. Translated
    by Salvator Attanasio. Philadelphia: Curtis, 1967.
Rossetti, Dante Gabriel. Dante and His Circle. London: Ellis &
    White, 1874.
Sayers, Dorothy. Further Papers on Dante. Harmondsworth, Eng-
    land: Penguin Books, 1957.
_____. Introductory Papers on Dante. Harmondsworth, England:
    Penguin Books, 1954.
Toynbee, Paget. Dante Alighieri: His Life and Works. 4th ed-
    ition. Gloucester, Mass.: Peter Smith, 1966.

THE BLACK PLAGUE (1347-1351)

Plague has been known for at least 3,000 years. Epidemics
have been recorded in China since 224 B.C. and the last great pandemic began in that country in 1894, spreading through Africa, the
Pacific Islands, Australia and the Americas, reaching San Francisco in 1900. Periodic cases have occurred in the United States during the first half of the 20th century. It is still prevalent in Asia,
Australia, Africa and South America.

The term "plague," though usually referring to bubonic
plague, is applied indiscriminately to all fatal epidemic diseases,
including malaria and typhus. In the medical sense "plague" refers to a particular infectious fever caused by a bacillus called
Pasteurella pestis. It is primarily a disease of wild rodents such
as black rats, marmots and squirrels. Domestic animals and man
are susceptible to this bacillus and unless preventive measures are
taken, an epidemic of plague can occur.

The disease, while suffered by infected rodents, is carried
from one such rodent to another and to man by a vector. In the
case of bubonic plague this carrier is usually a flea called Xeno-
psylla cheopis. These fleas, which live on the blood of those they
bite, transmit the bacillus from infected animals or humans to others who, in turn, become infected.

Today, by the use of pest control techniques and wonder
drugs, epidemics can be largely controlled and eliminated. These,
however, were unknown in medieval days and a number of plague
epidemics were then suffered, one of the worst of which was that
which raged in Europe from 1347 to 1351.

It is believed that the medieval plague originated in China,
being brought to Messina by twelve rat-infested Genoese ships.
From Messina it spread to Venice and Genoa and then on throughout Italy, Hungary and Bavarian Germany. By the end of 1348 it
had penetrated to England and in the following year attacked Scotland, Ireland, Denmark, Norway, Iceland and Greenland. Subsequently it found its way to Sweden, Poland and Russia.

People died by the thousands. Fear and terror were everywhere, with many setting their affairs in order and confessing their
sins to priests. Believing that the plague was transmitted by touch,
those infected were often left to die unattended. Corpses were left
in houses and on streets, abandoned by the living who had fled the
town to areas not yet infected. Those who took flight, in many
cases, were already ill and so took the plague with them to the
communities they descended upon.

The plague struck rich and poor alike. "The palaces of
princes were not less accessible to contagious disease than the
dwellings of the multitude. "

The physicians of the day believed that the plague was caused
by an "evil vapor" which was generated by the sun's rays "falling
on the sea. " As an antidote they prescribed "the kindling of a
large fire of vine-wood, green laurel, or other green wood; worm-
wood or camolile should also be burnt. " This attempt to purify the
air failed to check the pestilence. Jews, suspected of poisoning
wells and somehow spreading the disease, were persecuted.

The Black Plague ended in 1351. This occurred because,
during a plague epidemic, rats tend to die faster than human beings as the carrier fleas find rats' blood more attractive than that
of man. As the rat population decreases insufficient rats remain
alive from which the fleas can carry plague in epidemic proportions.
Thus the plague seems to subside. Unfortunately, infection is firmly intrenched among rats and after a period of re-population plague-
bearing rats and their carrier fleas again appear and the cycle
starts once more. This, in part, accounts for the plague which
struck London in 1665, three centuries after the Black Plague of
the Middle Ages.

Suggested Readings

Ashley, Maurice.   Great Britain to 1688: A Modern History.   Ann
    Arbor, Mich. : University of Michigan Press, 1961.
Bagley, John J.   Life in Medieval England.   New York: Putnam,
    1960.
Bell, Walter George.   The Great Plague in London in 1665.   Lon-
    don: John Lane, 1924.
    _____. "The Plague of London" in Corbett, Edmund V. , ed.
    Great True Stories of Tragedy and Disaster.   New York: Arch-
    er House, 1963.
Campbell, Anna M.   The Black Death and Men of Learning.   New
    York: Columbia University Press, 1931.
Cate, James L.   "The Black Death, or Worse Than Socialized Med-
    icine, " Guthrie Clinical Bulletin, No. 38, April, 1969.
Coulton, George C.   The Black Death.   New York: Robert McBride,
    1930.
Cowie, Leonard W.   Plague and Fire: London, 1665-66.   New York:
    Putnam's, 1970.

Cravens, Gwyneth, and John S. Marr. The Black Death (fiction).
    New York: Dutton, 1977.
Crawfurd, Raymond. Plague and Pestilence in Literature and Art.
    Oxford: Clarendon Press, 1914.
Creighton, Charles. "From A. D. 664 to the Great Plague" in A
    History of Epidemics in Britain. New York: Barnes & Noble,
    1965.
Deaux, George. The Black Death, 1347. New York: Weybright
    and Talley, 1969.
Dorolle, P. "Old Plagues in the Jet Age," World Health Organiza-
    tion Chronicle, March, 1969.
Gallagher, Richard. Diseases that Plague Modern Man. Dobbs
    Ferry, N. Y.: Oceana Publications, 1969.
Gasquet, Francis A., O. S. B. The Black Death of 1348 and 1349.
    London: George Bell & Sons, 1908.
Gaughran, Eugene R. L. "From Superstition to Science: The His-
    tory of a Bacterium," Transactions, New York Academy of Sci-
    ences, January, 1969.
Haggard, Howard W. Devils, Drugs and Doctors. New York:
    Harper, 1929.
Harding, Samuel Bannister. The Story of the Middle Ages. Chi-
    cago: Scott, Foresman, 1912.
Hecker, Justus F. C. The Black Death. New York: Humboldt
    Press, 1885.
_____. The Black Death in the Fourteenth Century. London:
    A. Schloss, 1883.
Hirst, Leonard B. The Conquest of Plague. Oxford: Clarendon
    Press, 1953.
McNeill, William H. Plagues and Peoples. New York: Anchor
    Press, 1976.
Major, Ralph H. A History of Medicine. Springfield, Ill.: Tho-
    mas, 1954.
Marks, Geoffrey J. The Medieval Plague: The Black Death of the
    Middle Ages. Garden City, N. Y.: Doubleday, 1971.
Merliss, Reuben R. The Year of the Death. New York: Double-
    day, 1965.
Mettler, Cecilia C. History of Medicine. Philadelphia: Blakiston,
    1947.
Mullett, Charles F. The Bubonic Plague and England. Lexington,
    Ky.: University of Kentucky Press, 1956.
Nohl, Johannes. The Black Death. London: Allen & Unwin, 1926.
Pirenne, Henri. Economic and Social History of Medieval People.
    New York: Harvest Books, 1937.
_____. Medieval Cities. Princeton, N. J.: Princeton University
    Press, 1950.
Pollitzer, R. Plague. Geneva: World Health Organizations, 1954.
Scott, G. M. The White Poppy. New York: Funk & Wagnalls, 1969.
Trevelyan, G. M. History of England. New York: Doubleday, 1953.
Winslow, Charles-Edward Amory. The Conquest of Epidemic Di-
    sease. Princeton, N. J.: Princeton University Press, 1943.
Witton's Microbiology. New York: McGraw-Hill, 1961.
Ziegler, Philip. The Black Death. New York: John Day, 1969.

THE RELIGIOUS CONDEMNATION OF JOHN WYCLIFFE
(1377, 1378 and 1415)

John Wycliffe, called "The Morning Star of the Reformation,"
was an English religious reformer, theologian and teacher of philosophy.   He was educated at Balliol College, Oxford University,
and spent most of his subsequent career as a member of the Oxford faculty.

England's financial resources had been greatly depleted by
the Hundred Years' War which started in 1337, and the Black Plague
(1347-1351).   King Edward III and the British Parliament were reluctant to pay certain sums demanded by the Catholic Church as
papal tribute.   Wycliffe gained prominence in 1374 as a result of
some pamphlets he had written in Latin refuting the Church's claims
and upholding the right of Parliament to limit Church power.   He
had definite ideas concerning the relationship of Church and State.
He opposed the idea that members of the clergy should own secular
property or hold secular office.   He felt that the Catholic Church
should not interfere in the affairs of Christian rulers who held their
thrones as a matter of divine right.   He opposed the selling of
indulgences by churchmen and argued that rulers had a moral obligation to oppose any clergyman who attempted to "traffic in secular matters. "

Wycliffe not only continued to attack the Church in his pamphlets but also was quite outspoken in his lectures at Oxford.   The
populace of England was in a state of great unrest due to heavy
taxes and oppression of the peasants by the nobility.   The authorities
at Oxford, fearing an uprising by the British commoners, preferred
to permit Wycliffe to continue his attacks on the Church rather than
instruct him to desist.   The Church, for the same reason, hesitated
to take action against him.   Further, he was supported in his views
by such noblemen as John of Gaunt, the son of Edward III, and Henry Percy, Earl of Northumberland.

Finally, on February 19, 1377, Wycliffe was ordered by
Archbishop Sudbury, Archbishop of Canterbury, to appear before
a special convocation at St. Paul's.   The proceedings were can-
celled when a large contingent of Wycliffe's followers appeared at
the meeting place and a near riot resulted.   John of Gaunt, who
had accompanied Wycliffe, got into a personal brawl with an at-
tendee.

Pope Gregory XI took note of Wycliffe's "heretical views"
and ordered an investigation.   He issued several bulls charging the
latter with heresy.   In the autumn of 1377 Wycliffe, at the request
of Parliament, gave his opinion that the shipment of riches belonging to the English Church to another country on instructions from
the pope was illegal.   Early in 1378 he was again summoned to
London, this time to appear at Lambeth Palace.   Once more a hostile crowd gathered and the churchmen, wishing to avoid further trou-

ble, recommended only that Wycliffe desist from preaching.   He
accepted the recommendation and retired to Lutterworth where he
continued to write and publish his pamphlets.   He also initiated
the first complete translation of the Bible into the vernacular.   This
was edited by John Purvey, who completed the work about 1388.

John Wycliffe died from a paralytic stroke in 1384.   In May,
1415, the Council of Constance reviewed his "heresies," condemned
him anew and ordered his body disinterred, burned and the ashes
thrown into the River Swift.

Suggested Readings

Block, Edward A.   John Wycliffe, Radical Dissenter.   San Diego,
    Calif. : San Diego State College, 1962.
Bruce, F. F.   The English Bible: A History of Translations.   New
    York: Oxford University Press, 1961.
Grant, Frederick G.   Translating the Bible.   Greenwich, Conn. :
    Seabury Press, 1961.
Greenslade, S. L. , ed.   The Cambridge History of the Bible: The
    West from the Reformation to the Present Day.   Cambridge:
    The University Press, 1963.
Innis, George S.   Wycliffe: The Morning Star.   Cincinnati: Jen-
    nings & Graham, 1907.
Lechler, Gotthard.   John Wycliffe and His English Precursors.
    London: The Religious Tract Society, 1878.
Leserth, Johann.   Wycliffe and Hus.   Translated by Rev. M. J.
    Evans.   London: Hodder and Stoughton, 1884.
Maxsen, W.   Introduction to the New Testament.   Translated by
    G. Buswell.   Philadelphia: Fortress Press, 1968.
Pfeiffer, Charles F.   The Wycliffe Bible Commentary.   Edited by
    Charles F. Pfeiffer, Old Testament, and Everett F. Harrison,
    New Testament.   Chicago: Moody Press, 1962.
Pope, Hugh, O. P.   English Versions of the Bible.   Revised by Se-
    bastian Bullough, O. P.   St. Louis, Mo. : Herder and Herder,
    1952.
Price, Ira Maurice.   The Ancestry of Our English Bible.   New
    York: Harper & Row, 1956.
Robinson, H. Wheeler, ed.   The Bible in Its Ancient and English
    Versions.   Oxford: Clarendon Press, 1940.
Stacey, John.   John Wyclif and Reform.   Philadelphia: Westminster
    Press, 1964
Workman, Herbert B.   John Wycliffe: A Study of the English Medi-
    eval Church.   Oxford: Clarendon Press, 1926.

THE GREAT (WESTERN) SCHISM (1378-1418)

In the year 1414 the matter of which of three men was the
rightful pope was under dispute.   Since 1378, when the Great, or

Western, Schism began, the papal office had been claimed by Gregory XII, Benedict XIII and John XXIII, and by their predecessors, Urban VI, Boniface IX, Innocent VII and Alexander V.

Following the death of Pope Gregory XI in 1378, the majority of cardinals in a conclave at Rome elected Urban VI to the pontificate. Following this, a number of these cardinals withdrew, declaring the election not to have been free owing to the violence of the Roman factions which, they declared, had "overawed them." They desired a pope who would live in Rome, not return to Avignon where the popes had resided for the previous seventy years. The election was revoked and Clement VII was chosen as another pope. Urban VI lived in Rome and Clement held office in Avignon. Each party had its adherents and in each a rival succession was maintained until 1409, when the Council of Pisa was held. In this assembly both popes, the Roman Gregory XII and Avignon Benedict XIII, were deposed and Alexander V was elected to be the sole and authorized pontiff. Alexander died in 1410 and never reached Rome to occupy the papal throne. He was replaced by John XXIII in that year. Benedict XIII refused to accept the decision of the Council and was later deposed by the Council of Constance in 1417. He died unsubmissive in 1423. Consequently, in 1414, as stated above, there were three claimants to the papacy.

Confusion reigned. Sigismund, King of Hungary and King-elect of the Holy Roman Empire, took the initiative and induced John XXIII to summon a new council, to meet at Constance, Switzerland. John lacked the political strength and personal following outside Italy to refuse, and also, at Sigismund's insistence, took a solemn oath to resign.

The Council of Pisa was followed by the Council of Constance, which lasted from November 1414 to April 1418. It was generally felt that the only way to end the schism was to have the claims of the three rivals considered by an ecumenical council.

John XXIII presided over the first public sessions but it soon became evident that he could not control the meeting. In spite of his oath to step down he abruptly left Constance on March 20, 1415, hoping to disrupt the proceedings and cause the Council to disband. In his absence the group continued to function, enacting the Articles of Constance which promulgated the theory of conciliarism. By this the Council of Constance was authorized to administer the Catholic Church and override the pope.

John XXIII, through Sigismund's efforts, was apprehended, captured, confined in prison and forced to abdicate. Gregory XII, the Roman pope, negotiated with the Council and laid down certain conditions which were accepted. He then abdicated. Pope Benedict XIII secured an interview with Sigismund in which, despite the king's urging, he refused to relinquish his claims to the papacy. His followers, chiefly the Spanish kings, then deserted him and on July 26, 1417, the Council declared him ousted. Following a series of bitter debates the Council of Constance elected Martin V pope on November 11. The Roman Catholic Church then had the first pope to be universally recognized in over forty years.

It was the Council of Constance that tried the Bohemian reformer John Hus and his follower Jerome of Prague for heresy. Both men were found guilty, sentenced to die by burning at the stake, and handed over to the secular arm which carried out the Council's sentences.

Suggested Readings

Barraclough, Geoffrey. The Medieval Papacy. London: Thames and Hudson, 1968.

Cheyney, Edward P. The Dawn of a New Era, 1250-1453. New York: Harper & Row, 1962.

Elliott-Binns, L. The History of the Decline and Fall of the Medieval Papacy. London: Methuen, 1934.

Flick, Alexander C. The Decline of the Medieval Church. Vol. I. London: Kegan Paul, 1930.

Glasfurd, Alec. The Antipope, Peter de Luna, 1342-1423. London: Barrie and Rockliff, 1965.

Hughes, Philip. The Church in Crisis: A History of the General Councils, 325-1870. Garden City, N.Y.: Hanover House, 1961.

Jordon, G. J. The Inner History of the Great Schism of the West. London: Williams and Norgate, 1930.

Locke, Clinton. The Age of the Great Western Schism. Edinburgh: T. & T. Clark, 1897.

Loomis, Louisa Ropes, translator. The Council of Constance. New York: Columbia University Press, 1961.

Mollat, G. The Popes at Avignon. New York: Harper & Row, 1965.

Pastor, Ludwig. The History of the Popes, Vol. I. London: Kegan Paul, 1891.

Schroeder, H. J., O. P. Disciplinary Decrees of the General Councils: Text, Translation and Commentary. St. Louis, Mo.: B. Herder Book Co., 1937.

Spinka, Matthew, ed. Advocates of Reform. Philadelphia: Westminster Press, 1953.

Tierney, Brian. Foundations of the Conciliar Theory: The Contributions of the Medieval Canonists from Gratian to the Great Schism. Cambridge: The University Press, 1955.

Ullman, Walter. The Origin of the Great Schism. London: Burns, Oates and Washbourne, 1948.

Von Ranke, Leopold. History of the Popes of Rome. London: George Bell and Sons, 1902.

Workman, Herbert B. The Dawn of the Reformation. London: C. H. Kelly, 1901-1902.

THE PEASANTS' REVOLT (TYLER'S REBELLION) (1381)

When Richard II of England came to the throne in 1377 his reign was characterized by mounting factionalism on the part of his royal relatives and their followers and by discontent on the part of the peasants. This discontent was caused by the poll or head tax, imposed on rich and poor alike. By law, each person over the age of 15 was taxed one shilling, a sum which meant much to the poverty-stricken peasants, but which was scarcely noticed by the wealthy upper classes. Riots resulted from the attempts to collect this tax and culminated in the Peasants' Revolt of 1381, led by Wat Tyler, an English peasant, and by John Ball, a priest and follower of John Wycliffe.

The insurgents, mostly from Kent, Essex, Middlesex and Sussex, first burned the manor records in order to destroy evidence of their obligations and then marched on London. King Richard, then 15 years old, met with them personally and promised to agree to their demands, which were to remove the poll taxes, abolish restrictions upon freedom of labor and trade, and seize the clerical wealth. John Ball was released from prison where he had been confined for "seditious utterances," and Richard managed to save his own life by offering to lead the peasants himself. However, he failed to keep his promises.

The rebellion failed and reprisals against the peasants were severe. Tyler was killed by Lord Mayor Walworth of London on June 15, 1381, and Ball was executed the same year at St. Alban's in the presence of King Richard.

Suggested Readings

Alderman, Clifford Lindsey. Flame of Freedom: The Peasants' Revolt of 1381. New York: Messner, 1969.

Ashley, Maurice. Great Britain to 1688: A Modern History. Ann Arbor, Mich.: University of Michigan Press, 1961.

Bagley, John J. Life in Medieval England. New York: Putnam, 1960.

Bryant, Sir Arthur. "The Hurling Time" in his The Fire and the Rose. Garden City, N.Y.: Doubleday, 1966.

Cross, Arthur Lyon. A Shorter History of England and Greater Britain. New York: Macmillan, 1929.

Halliday, Frank. A Concise History of England from Stonehenge to the Atomic Age. New York: Viking Press, 1964.

Harding, Samuel Bannister, in consultation with Albert Bushnell Hart. Essentials in Mediaeval History (from Charlemagne to the Close of the Fifteenth Century). New York: American Book Company, 1909.

Parsons, Geoffrey. The Stream of History. New York: Scribner's, 1929.

Terry, Benjamin. A History of England from the Earliest Times to

the Death of Queen Victoria. Chicago: Scott, Foresman, 1901.
Webster, Hutton. Early European History. Boston: Heath, 1917.

THE TRANSLATIONS OF THE BIBLE (1384-1611)

The word "Bible" is defined as "the book of writings accepted by Christians as inspired by God and of divine authority; the
Scriptures. " It is also defined as "the collection of sacred writings of the Christian religion, comprising the Old and the New Testament. "

Prior to the 14th century the only complete Bibles in England
were in the Latin text, used by the clergy, although some passages
were translated into Anglo-Saxon in the 7th century by Caedmon,
the earliest English Christian poet. In the 8th century Bede, an
English scholar, historian and theologian, translated a portion of
the Gospel of St. John. Alcuin, King Alfred and Aelfric also made
translations of various parts of the Bible during the Anglo-Saxon
period.

The first full translation of the Bible was made by John
Wycliffe, an English religious reformer and theologian, in 1384.
Wycliffe's translation was not printed and for a century and a half
was, in manuscript, the only English version of the Bible. The
Church felt that a vernacular Bible was undesirable as laymen who
read it could conceivably misinterpret it "and thus fall into heresy. "

In 1523 William Tyndale, an English cleric, was denied permission by Richard Bancroft, Bishop of London, to make an authorized translation of the Bible. In spite of this he traveled to Ham-
burg, Germany, where he produced such a translation. This was
published in 1525 and in 1530 his translation of the Old Testament
was printed at Antwerp. Copies of the Tyndale Bible were stealth-
ily taken to England where they were sold. Many copies, however,
were impounded and destroyed by the authorities.

In 1534 Henry VIII of England fell out with the Catholic
Church. This led to his making certain religious concessions, in-
cluding the publication of an English Bible. The first complete
Bible to be printed in English was that of the clergyman Miles Cov-
erdale, which was completed in 1535. This was printed at Zurich,
Switzerland, and was authorized for use in the English churches.

In 1537 John Rogers, using the pseudonym Thomas Matthew,
published a complete Bible. This, known as the "Great Bible" and
as "Cranmer's Bible, " was based on those of Tyndale and Cover-
dale and was authorized by the English crown to be used in churches
and became the official Bible of the Anglican Church.

Another Bible published by Protestants who had been exiled

to the Continent during the reign of the Catholic Queen Mary appeared between 1557 and 1560.   This came to be called the Geneva" Bible" after its place of publication.   It was followed by the "Bishop's Bible" in 1568.

Other Bibles were published during the 16th century.   In 1582 the Roman Catholic Church produced an official version of the New Testament.   The complete Bible, published in 1609, is known as the "Douai" or "Douai-Rheims" Bible.

In 1604 James I, King of England, after meeting with John Rainolds who represented the Puritan party at the Hampton Court Conference, authorized the publication of a new translation of the Bible.   Richard Bancroft, Bishop of London and later Archbishop of Canterbury, was assigned to assemble a group of qualified translators and in due course the king approved a list of 54 linguists, one of whom was Lancelot Andrewes, an outstanding Biblical scholar and then Dean of Westminster.   These men were divided into small groups who met at Cambridge, Oxford and Westminster.   Each group was assigned to translate a specific part of the Bible.

The translators worked together, criticizing and correcting each other's work.   When a translated segment was considered satisfactory by the group as a whole it was sent to another group for further consideration.

The "King James Bible" or "Authorized Version," as it came to be called, was completed in 1611.   It was published that year by the king's printer.   After 1611 several more editions of the Geneva Bible appeared, but the Authorized Version soon replaced both it and the Bishop's Bible for reading in churches.

Since its initial publication the King James Bible has appeared in countless editions.   It is considered by many theologians "the most popular and influential single book in the history of the world. "

Suggested Readings

Allen, Ward.   Translating for King James: Notes Made by a Translator of King James's Bible.   Nashville, Tenn. : Vanderbilt University Press, 1969.
Block, Edward A.   John Wycliffe, Radical Dissenter.   San Diego, Calif. : San Diego State College Press, 1962.
Bruce, F. F.   The English Bible: A History of Translations.   New York: Oxford University Press, 1961.
Butterworth, C. C.   The Literary Lineage of the King James Bible. Philadelphia: Westminster Press, 1941.
Daiches, David.   The King James Version of the English Bible. Chicago: University of Chicago Press, 1941.
Grant, Frederick C.   Translating the Bible.   Greenwich, Conn. : Seabury Press, 1961.

Greenslade, S. L. , ed. The Cambridge History of the Bible: The
	West from the Reformation to the Present Day. Cambridge:
	The University Press, 1963.
Lechler, Gotthard. John Wycliffe and His English Precursors. Lon-
	don: The Religious Tract Society, 1878.
Maxsen, W. Introduction to the New Testament. Translated by
	G. Buswell. Philadelphia: Fortress Press, 1968.
Pfeiffer, Charles F. The Wycliffe Bible Commentary. Edited by
	Charles F. Pfeiffer, Old Testament and Everett F. Harrison,
	New Testament. Chicago: Moody Press, 1962.
Pope, Hugh, O. P. English Versions of the Bible. Revised by
	Sebastian Bullough, O. P. St. Louis, Mo. : Herder and Her-
	der, 1952.
Price, Ira Maurice. The Ancestry of Our English Bible. New
	York: Harper & Row, 1956.
Robinson, H. Wheeler, ed. The Bible in Its Ancient and English
	Versions. Oxford: Clarendon Press, 1940.
Workman, Herbert B. John Wycliffe: A Study of the English Medi-
	eval Church. Oxford: Clarendon Press, 1926.

GEOFFREY CHAUCER'S CANTERBURY TALES
(c. 1386-c. 1400)

"Here bygynneth the Book of the Tales of Caunterbury. "
This is the opening sentence of the Prologue to one of the great
works of English literature, Geoffrey Chaucer's Canterbury Tales,
written probably between 1386 and 1400, the year of the author's
death.

Chaucer, considered the first major English poet, was born
in London, the son of a vintner, about 1343. At seventeen he became a court page and two years later a soldier. During his life
he held various offices under the king and had as his patron John
of Gaunt, Duke of Lancaster. Emile Legouis, in his History of
English Literature, says of Chaucer, "his life was active and his
employments diverse. He was page, squire, diplomat and official
in turns. He mingled with courtiers, soldiers and city burghers
and merchants. He had dealings with foreigners in Flanders, France
and Italy. And throughout he remained, for such part of his days
as his official duties left free, an impassioned student and untiring
reader. "

Besides the Canterbury Tales Chaucer translated a portion
of The Romance of the Rose from French to English, and wrote
The Book of the Duchess, the unfinished poem The House of Fame,
The Parliament of Birds, The Legend of Good Women and Troilus
and Criseyde. Some of these were based on the writings of others,
including Giovanni Boccaccio and Francesco Petrarch.

Although Chaucer was familiar with the French, Italian and

Latin languages, he wrote his <u>Canterbury Tales</u> in English.   The
<u>Tales</u> concern a group of thirty pilgrims who set out from the Ta-
bard Inn, Southwark, on the evening of April 16, 1387, for the
tomb of the murdered Thomas à Becket at Canterbury Cathedral.
Harry Bailey, the host of the inn, proposes that in order to pass
the time as they ride, each member of the party tell two stories,
one on the way down and one on the way back.   On the return to
the inn the narrator of the best story shall be given a dinner "at
oure aller cost. "   Bailey was to act as judge and determine the
winner of the contest.

The <u>Canterbury Tales</u> remained unfinished at Chaucer's
death.   Literary historians believe that he had in mind somewhere
between 50 and 60 stories, but when published the book contained
the Prologue, 20 complete, two interrupted and two unfinished stories.   Each story is preceded by its own prologue which links the
stories together, and the author combines prose and verse.

The pilgrims making up the party include a knight, his son
(a squire), their yeoman (or servant), a friar, a monk, a clerk
(or scholar) of Oxford, a prioress, a parson, the parson's brother
(a ploughman), a summoner, a pardoner, a sergeant-at-law, a
"doctor of physic, " a franklin (country gentleman), a merchant, a
shipman, a miller, a cook, a manciple (steward), a reeve (bailiff),
the Wife of Bath, five citizens of London, a nun, a priest, Harry
Bailey and Chaucer himself.   Chaucer, presumably hoping to have
enough stories for 33 people, added "and priestes three, " although
someone else may have appended these words.

The best known tales are those told by the knight, who con-
tributes the first and longest story; the nun's priest's tale, a beast
fable; the pardoner's tale, an illustrative sermon of three revelers
who meet death; and the Wife of Bath's tale in which she condemns
celibacy and describes her life with five successive husbands.   Other tales range from ribald humor to sermons to chivalric romance.

Chaucer gives a picture of the 14th-century England he knew.
He satirizes social class and sex and ridicules human weaknesses.
The <u>Tales</u> were written by a man who understood human nature,
was a master story-teller and poet and whose literary masterpiece
still furnishes enjoyable and worthwhile reading almost six centuries later.

Suggested Readings

Bennett, H. S.   "Chaucer and the Fifteenth Century" in <u>The Oxford
    History of English Literature</u>.   New York: Oxford University
    Press, 1947.
Chaucer, Geoffrey.   <u>Canterbury Tales</u>.   Rendered into Modern Eng-
    lish by J. U. Nicolson.   New York: Covici, Friede, 1934 (Or-
    iginally written c. 1386-1400).
Chute, Marchette.   <u>Geoffrey Chaucer of England</u>.   New York: Dut-
    ton, 1946.

Cross, E. A.   "The Renaissance" in his World Literature.   New
    York: American Book Company, 1935.
Donaldson, E. T. , ed.   Chaucer's Poetry: An Anthology for the
    Modern Reader.   New York: Ronald Press, 1958.
French, Robert Dudley.   A Chaucer Handbook.   New York: Ap-
    pleton-Century-Crofts, 1947.
Kittredge, George L.   Chaucer and His Poetry.   Cambridge, Mass. :
    Harvard University Press, 1915.
Magoun, Francis P. , Jr.   A Chaucer Gazetteer.   Chicago: Uni-
    versity of Chicago Press, 1961.
Manly, J. M.   Some New Light on Chaucer.   New York: Holt, 1926.
Muscatine, Charles.   Chaucer and the French Tradition.   Berkeley,
    Calif. :   University of California Press, 1957.
Robinson, F. N.   The Works of Geoffrey Chaucer.   Boston: Hough-
    ton Mifflin, 1957.
Schoeck, Richard J. , and Jerome Taylor, eds.   Chaucer Criticism:
    The Canterbury Tales.   Notre Dame, Ind. :   Notre Dame Uni-
    versity Press, 1960.
Ward, Henry S.   The Canterbury Pilgrims.   London: Oxford Uni-
    versity Press, 1904.

THOMAS A KEMPIS AND THE
IMITATION OF CHRIST (c. 1400)

Over the centuries a number of churchmen, such as John
Wycliffe, William Tyndale, John Hus, Martin Luther, Girolamo
Savanarola, Ulrich Zwingli and others dissented from the teachings
of the Roman Catholic Church.   One, however, who did not reject
his church's doctrines and had no quarrel with it, was Thomas à
Kempis, a German ecclesiastic and writer who, as a cloistered
monk, produced the famous religious classic the Imitation of Christ.
This book, written about the year 1400, made a profound impression
on Christian readers, both Catholic and Protestant, down through
more than 500 years.

Thomas was born at Kempen, near Düsseldorf, about 1350,
the son of a poor workingman.   His family name was Hammerken
or Hämmerlein.   He was educated at the school in Deventer, the
Netherlands, founded by Gerhard Groote, and studied under Floren-
tius Radewyn.   After graduating he went to the Augustine monastery
of Mount St. Agnes at Zwolle in 1399, where his brother was prior
and of which he, in due course, became sub-prior.   He was ordained a priest in 1413, living an uneventful life at the monastery
and dying in 1471.

The Imitation of Christ begins, "'He that followeth me shall
not walk in darkness, ' saith the Lord.   These are the words of
Christ, and they teach us how far we must imitate His life and
character if we seek true illumination, and deliverance from all
blindness of heart.   Let it be our most earnest study, therefore,

to dwell upon the life of Christ. " Thomas' idea in writing it was essentially to achieve the objectives of Groote's Devotio Moderna (New Devotion), which was an attempt to "return to an idealization of the piety of the early church. " He used examples from the gospels to portray Christ in situations encountered by people in everyday life. By imitating Christ the Christian could merge his human will and spirit with the divine.

In addition to the Imitation of Christ, Thomas à Kempis wrote sermons, devotional books for the young and religious biographies.

Suggested Readings

Cross, E. A.   "Thomas à Kempis" in his World Literature.   New York: American Book Co. , 1935.

De Montmorency, J. E. G.   Thomas à Kempis, His Age and His Book.   Port Washington, N. Y. :   Kennikat Press, 1970 (Originally published 1906).

Ferguson, Wallace K.   Europe in Transition, 1300-1520.   Boston: Houghton Mifflin, 1962.

Hyma, Albert.   The Christian Renaissance.   Hamden, Conn. : Archon Books, 1965.

Kettlewell, S.   Thomas à Kempis and Brothers of Common Life. Philadelphia: Richard West, 1882.

Philips, Margaret Mann.   Erasmus and the Northern Renaissance. London: Hodder & Stoughton, 1949.

Sperry, Willard L.   Strangers and Pilgrims.   Boston: Little, Brown, 1939.

Spinka, Matthew, ed.   Advocates of Reform.   Philadelphia: Westminster Press, 1953.

Thomas à Kempis.   "The Imitation of Christ" in Eliot, Charles W. , ed.   The Harvard Classics.   New York: Collier, 1909 (Originally written c. 1400).

Van Zijil, Rev. Theodore P. , S. V. D.   Gerhard Groote, Ascetic and Reformer, 1340-1384.   Washington, D. C. :   Catholic University of America, 1963.

THE PREACHING AND EXECUTION OF
JOHN HUS (1400-1415)

In the fourteenth and fifteenth centuries the Roman Catholic Church was considered by many to be unduly worldly, interfering without authority in secular matters and assuming prerogatives for which it had no legitimate claim. Such reformers as John Wycliffe, Martin Luther and Girolamo Savonarola preached against Church practices they considered wrong for which, in many cases, they were tried, condemned and executed as heretics. One of these was the Bohemian educator and religious reformer John Hus who steadfastly refused to acknowledge papal authority and was executed in the year 1415 for his views and actions.

Hus was born in Husinetz, near Budweis, about 1369. He was educated at the University of Prague, following which he became a faculty member and lecturer in theology. In 1401 he was ordained a priest and was greatly influenced by the writings of John Wycliffe whose Trialogus he translated into Bohemian in 1403.

After earning his divinity degree he began to preach the doctrine of church reform. His sermons, based on Wycliffe's ideas, were enthusiastically received by the populace which flocked to hear him. He taught that the clergy should not hold property, that shrines, pilgrimages and confession were all valueless, so far as salvation was concerned, and that the pope was not infallible and lacked the authority to excommunicate.

In 1408 the subject of Hus's sermons was made the grounds for a complaint to the Archbishop of Prague and the latter requested authority from the pope to deal with the reformer's heresy. Although Wycliffe's writings were condemned and burned Hus continued to preach and defy the church authorities. In 1410 he was excommunicated for teaching and lecturing on Wycliffe's doctrines. King Wenceslas, King of Bohemia and former Holy Roman Emperor, vacillated, first requesting that Hus be authorized to continue his preaching and then, changing sides, asking that he be censured.

Between 1410 and 1412 the people of Bohemia were divided on the matter of Hus and his theological ideas. Ingrained belief in church teachings was at variance with the thought that being taxed by the Church for self-serving activities "far beyond Bohemian borders" was wrong. In 1414 Hus was summoned to appear before the Council of Constance, a general council at Constance, Switzerland. He was guaranteed a safe conduct by Sigismund, King of Hungary and later of Bohemia and Holy Roman Emperor. In November Hus presented himself before the church officials who charged him with heresy. After seven months confinement he was permitted to answer the charges made against him. The crucial issue in the case was that of papal authority. Hus had contended, from his earliest sermons, that the pope lacked authorization to do many of the things involving discipline, obedience and authority which the reigning pope and his predecessors had considered God-given. His refusal to recant angered both the pope and Emperor Sigismund, the latter finally deserting him. He was found guilty as charged, unfrocked, delivered to the secular arm and, on July 6, 1415, was burned at the stake. Jerome of Prague, his associate and defender, was also tried and condemned as a heretic and was likewise burned on May 30, 1416.

John Hus's execution while supposedly under the protection of Sigismund's safe conduct caused a religious revolt. He was considered a martyr who had been shamefully deceived. Approximately 450 Bohemian noblemen formed a league and defied the decrees

of both the pope and his bishops.   This league received the support of King Wenceslas.

The Hussite Wars, as the conflicts within the Holy Roman
Empire came to be called, lasted from 1415 to 1436.   Hus's chal-
lenging of church authority influenced a number of later reformers,
notably Martin Luther, called "the father of the Reformation in
Germany. "

Suggested Readings

Barraclough, Geoffrey.   The Medieval Papacy.   London: Thames
    and Hudson, 1968.
Bartok, Josef Paul.   John Hus at Constance.   Nashville, Tenn. :
    Cokesbury Press, 1935.
Block, Edward A.   John Wycliffe, Radical Dissenter.   San Diego,
    Calif. :   San Diego State College Press, 1962.
Cheyney, Edward P.   The Dawn of a New Era, 1250-1453.   New
    York: Harper & Row, 1962.
Flick, Alexander C.   The Decline of the Medieval Church, Vol. I.
    London: Kegan Paul, 1930.
Harben, Jan.   Hus and His Followers.   London: G. Bles, 1926.
Hughes, Philip.   The Church in Crisis: A History of the General
    Councils, 325-1870.   Garden City, N. Y. :   Hanover House, 1961.
Leserth, Johann.   Wycliffe and Hus.   Translated by Rev. M. J. Ev-
    ans.   London: Hodder and Stoughton, 1884.
Loomis, Louisa Ropes, translator.   The Council of Constance.   New
    York: Columbia University Press, 1961.
Lutzow, Count.   The Life and Times of Master John Hus.   London:
    J. M. Dent & Sons, 1921.
Roubiczer, Paul, and Joseph Kalmer.   Warrior of God.   London:
    Nicholson and Watson, 1947.
Schroeder, H. J. , O. P.   Disciplinary Decrees of the General Coun-
    cils: Text, Translation and Commentary.   St. Louis, Mo. :
    Herder Book Co. , 1937.
Schwarze, William Nathaniel.   John Hus, the Martyr of Bohemia.
    New York: Fleming N. Revell, 1915.
Spinka, Matthew.   John Hus and the Czech Reformation.   Hamden,
    Conn. :   Archon Books, 1941.
_____, ed.   Advocates of Reform.   Philadelphia: Westminster
    Press, 1953.
_____, translator and editor.   John Hus at the Council of Con-
    stance.   New York: Columbia University Press, 1965.
Stacey, John.   John Wycliffe and Reform.   Philadelphia: Westmin-
    ster Press, 1964.
Tierney, Brian.   Foundations of the Conciliar Theory: The Con-
    tribution of the Medieval Canonists from Gratian to the Great
    Schism.   Cambridge: The University Press, 1955.
Workman, Herbert B.   The Dawn of the Reformation.   London:
    C. H. Kelly, 1901-1902.
_____.   John Wycliffe: A Study of the English Medieval Church.
    Oxford: Clarendon Press, 1926.

THE TRIALS OF JOAN OF ARC (1431 and 1456)

Joan of Arc, the French saint and national heroine, was born of peasant parentage in Domremy on or about January 6, 1412. At the age of thirteen she believed she heard celestial voices sometimes accompanied by visions. She became convinced that the voices were those of St. Catherine, St. Margaret and St. Michael.

In December, 1428, she traveled to Vaucouleurs where she obtained the help of Robert de Baudricourt, the governor, to confer with Charles, Dauphin of France, at Chinon. On March 6, 1429, she had her first interview with the Dauphin and convinced him that she had a divine mission to save France from the English and their allies, the Burgundians, with whom the French were at war.

A board of theologians examined her for heresy and found her "of good faith. " She left Chinon for Orléans where she was provided with armor and a white banner representing God blessing the fleurs-de-lis, the French royal emblem. Having been given troops to command she led them to victory over the English at Orléans, captured Jargeau, drove the enemy from Beaugency and defeated them again at Patay.

Joan and her soldiers conducted the Dauphin to Reims where he was crowned King Charles VII, Joan being in close attendance.

Following the coronation, Joan led several campaigns which culminated in the surrender of Melun. On May 23, 1430, while fighting the English near Compiègne, she was captured by a Burgundian soldier. Imprisoned in the Castle of Beaulieu by John, Duke of Luxemburg, she was sold to the English who sent her to Rouen in chains. Charles VII abandoned her and did not concern himself with subsequent events until 1450.

In Rouen she was confined in prison and preparations for her trial for heresy and sorcery were made, with Pierre Couchon, Bishop of Rouen, as chief judge. On February 21, 1431, she was summoned before Bishop Couchon's tribunal of more than sixty judges for the first time. The bishop attempted to make her confess to a list of seventy articles supposedly based on her testimony. In these charges she was censured for believing she was directly responsible to God rather than to the Catholic Church and for "wearing masculine dress, against the Biblical law. "

During her trial Joan was held in a dungeon rather than in the less disgraceful church prison. At night she was chained to her cot and during the day the chains were not removed from her person. She fell ill, yet managed to parry the confusing questions of the judges, some of whom came to sympathize with her. On May 2, she was threatened with torture for refusing to answer certain questions and was shown the instruments which would be used. On May 24, she was driven into a signing a confession, which she

did with an X, not knowing how to read or write.   Couchon then
condemned her to life imprisonment.

She was returned to her cell and given women's clothing.
On May 27, 1431, this clothing was removed from her cell while
she slept and men's clothing was substituted.   She had no choice
but to put on the substituted garments.   For this she was regarded
as a relapsed heretic.   On May 30, she was condemned to death,
excommunicated and turned over to the secular arm which burned
her at the stake in the Old Market Square.

In 1450 King Charles was advised that his crown, "acquired
by witchcraft," was not legally held and, accordingly, he was not
the King of France.   A retrial of Joan's case was ordered, and
on July 7, 1456, her former judges were censured, their verdict
annulled and her innocence affirmed.   In 1904 she was designated
"venerable," and in 1908-1909 she was beatified.   On May 16, 1920,
she was canonized by Pope Benedict XV.

Suggested Readings

Anderson, Maxwell.   "Joan of Lorraine" (play condensation) in Man-
    tle, Burns, ed.   The Best Plays of 1946-1947.   New York:
    Dodd, Mead, 1947.
Anouilh, Jean.   The Lark (play).   Translated by Christopher Fry.
    Oxford: Oxford University Press, 1956.
Aymar, Brandt, and Edward Sagarin.   "The Trial of Joan of Arc"
    in their A Pictorial History of the World's Great Trials.   New
    York: Crown Publishers, 1967.
Barrett, W. P., translator.   The Trial of Jeanne d'Arc.   London:
    George Routledge & Sons, 1931.
Burk, John Daly.   Female Patriotism; or, The Death of Joan of
    Arc (play).   First produced 1798.
Chartier, Jean.   Joan, the Maid of Orléans.   Translated by Paul-
    ine Sowers.   New York: R. V. Sowers, 1938.
Edwards, Clayton.   "Jeanne d'Arc" in his A Treasury of Heroes
    and Heroines.   New York: Hampton Publishing Co., 1920.
Evans, Joan.   Life in Medieval France.   New York: Phaidon Press,
    1957.
Fabre, Lucien.   Joan of Arc.   Translated by Gerard Hopkins.   New
    York: McGraw-Hill, 1954.
France, Anatole, pseud.   The Life of Joan of Arc.   Translated by
    Winifred Stephens.   London: J. Lane, 1909.
Hagedorn, Hermann.   "Joan of Arc" in his The Book of Courage.
    Philadelphia: Winston, 1920.
Lanéry d'Arc, Pierre.   Le Livre de Jeanne d'Arc.   Paris: 1894.
Lightbody, Charles W.   The Judgments of Joan.   Cambridge, Mass.:
    Harvard University Press, 1961.
Lowell, Francis G.   Joan of Arc.   Boston: Houghton Mifflin, 1896.
McKenna, Marian.   A Pictorial History of Catholicism.   Philadel-
    phia: Philosophical Library, 1962.
McKown, Robin.   "Joan of Arc" in his Seven Famous Trials in His-
    tory.   New York: Vanguard Press, 1963.

Maurios, André. A History of France. New York: Farrar,
    Strauss, 1956.
_____. An Illustrated History of France. New York: Viking
    Press, 1960.
Michelet, Jules. Joan of Arc. Translated by Albert Guérard.
    Ann Arbor, Mich.: University of Michigan Press, 1957.
Myers, A. R. England in the Middle Ages. New York: Penguin
    Press, 1959.
Oman, Charles. A History of the Art of War in the Middle Ages.
    New York: Burt Franklin, 1924.
Paine, Albert Bigelow. The Girl in White Armor: The Story of
    Joan of Arc. New York: Macmillan, 1967.
Pernoud, Régine. Joan of Arc. Translated by Jeanne Unger Duell.
    New York: Grove Press, 1961.
_____. Joan of Arc by Herself and Her Witnesses. Translated
    by Edward Hyams. New York: Stein & Day, 1966.
_____. The Retrial of Joan of Arc. Translated by J. M. Cohen.
    New York: Harcourt, Brace, 1955.
Perroy, Edouard. The Hundred Years' War. London: Eyre &
    Spottiswoode, 1965.
Sackville West, Victoria Mary. Saint Joan of Arc. Garden City,
    N. Y.: Doubleday, 1936.
Shakespeare, William. King Henry VI, Part I (play). Edited by
    John D. Wilson. Cambridge: The University Press, 1952
    (Originally written 1590-1591).
Shaw, George Bernard. "Saint Joan" (play) in The Board of Direc-
    tors of the Theater Guild Anthology. New York: Random
    House, 1936 (Originally published 1923).
Stolpe, Sven. The Maid of Orléans. Translated by Gerard Hop-
    kins. New York: Pantheon Press, 1956.
Tappan, Eva March. "Joan of Arc, the Girl Commander" in her
    Old World Hero Stories. Boston: Houghton Mifflin, 1937.
Twain, Mark, pseud. Personal Recollections of Joan of Arc (his-
    torical fiction). New York: Harper, 1896.
Williams, Jay, and the editors of Horizon Magazine. Joan of Arc.
    New York: American Heritage Publishing Co. , 1963.

THE INVENTION OF PRINTING
FROM MOVABLE TYPE (c. 1450)

It is not known exactly when the art of printing from movable type was invented or who invented it. However, this was one
of the most important discoveries in history and in all probability
exerted as great an influence on man's progress as any other invention.

The Chinese had, by the second century A. D. , developed a
method of printing designs and pictures on textiles, using relief
cuttings on wood blocks. Similar wood block printing was done on
paper which was invented about 105 A. D. In 972 A. D. the Trip-

itaka, the sacred Buddhist scriptures, was printed from wood
blocks. The Chinese also carved characters of their alphabet on
individual wooden blocks from which prints were made, but because
of the tremendous number of characters which are required by the
Chinese method of writing, this proved impractical. The Koreans
made a similar discovery in the 14th century but abandoned it for
the same reason as the Chinese.

The invention of printing from movable type was perfected
in Europe in the 15th century, apparently independently of earlier
developments in the Orient. Johann Gutenberg, born probably in
Mainz about 1400, is traditionally considered the first European to
print, using movable type, although Laurens Janszoon Coster, a
sexton of Haarlem, may possibly have used the process as early
as 1423. Coster's claim is not substantiated by any contemporary
documents and no book now extant carries his name as printer.

Gutenberg, a gem polisher and mirror maker of Mainz, Germany, began experiments in printing before 1439. About 1446 he
formed a partnership with Johann Fust, a goldsmith, to exploit his
invention. Fust had advanced funds to finance the business and
later sued Gutenberg in court. In 1455 the latter made a financial
settlement with Fust, whereby he abandoned his claims to the invention and surrendered his stock in the enterprise. Fust then
took in as a partner Peter Schöffer, his former chief workman.
These two continued the printing business and after 1466, when
Fust died, Schöffer worked alone. Gutenberg, with funds supplied
by his patron Dr. Conrad Humery, reestablished himself in the
printing business. Archbishop Adolph of Nassau, Elector of Mainz,
gave recognition to Gutenberg's works in 1465 and presented him
with a benefice yielding him an income and various privileges.

The best-known publication associated with Gutenberg is the
Gutenberg Bible (or Mazarin Bible), so called because of its discovery, about 1760, in the library of Cardinal Jules Mazarin. Printed in Latin and containing 42 lines to the page, this is considered
by some historians to have been produced by Gutenberg and Humery
between 1450 and 1456. Other authorities feel that it was produced
by Schöffer and Fust. This controversy is due, in part, to the
fact that Gutenberg may have surrendered his type to Fust at the
time of their lawsuit, and the same type may have been used by
both printing firms at different times.

Gutenberg's other works include a 36-line Bible and a 31-line
Indulgence, a theological grammar, and some calendars. Fust and
Schöffer printed a Psalter in 1457, the first book in which the colo-
phon dates and names its printer. They also published a 48-line
Bible and other works.

Printing spread rapidly through Europe during the latter part
of the 15th century. Ulrich Zell entered the business in Cologne
and Anthony Koberger established his press in Nuremberg. Erhard
Ratdoldt printed missals and ecclesiastical books in Augsburg. Print-

ing houses were established in Italy by Konrad Swenheim, Arnold
Pannartz, Aldus Manutius and Nicolas Jenson.   Other printers set
up shop in France, Spain, the Low Countries, and England.

The primitive "wine press" used by the early printers was,
in modern times, improved upon.   Today we have machine-driven
rotary and reciprocating presses, color presses, offset presses,
typesetting machines such as the linotype and monotype and other
methods for the reproduction of written material.   These include
spirit duplicators, motor driven stencil equipment, copper engraving, photographic techniques, the Xerox process and many others.
All of these stemmed from the invention of a 15th-century inventor
who may well have based his idea on the methods used in the Orient
a thousand years earlier.

Suggested Readings

Aldis, Harry G.   The Printed Book.   Revised by John Carter and
    Brooke Crutchley.   Cambridge: The University Press, 1951.
Allen, Agnes.   The Story of the Book.   London: Faber and Faber,
    1952.
Butler, Pierce.   The Origin of Printing in Europe.   Chicago: Uni-
    versity of Chicago Press, 1940.
Carter, Thomas Francis.   The Invention of Printing in China and
    Its Spread Westward.   Revised by L. Carrington Goodrich.
    New York: Ronald Press, 1955.
Chappell, Warren.   A Short History of the Printed Word.   New
    York: Knopf, 1970.
DeVinne, Theodore L.   The Invention of Printing.   Detroit: Gale
    Research, 1969 (Originally published 1878).
Jennett, Sean.   Pioneers in Printing.   London: Routledge and Ke-
    gan Paul, 1958.
McMurtrie, Douglas C.   The Book.   New York: Covici-Friede,
    1937.
_____.   The Invention of Printing: A Bibliography.   New York:
    Burt Franklin, 1971.
Oswald, John Clyde.   A History of Printing.   New York: Appleton,
    1928
Steinberg, Sigfrid H.   Five Hundred Years of Printing.   Baltimore:
    Penguin Books, 1974.

THE FALL OF CONSTANTINOPLE (1453)

Considered one of the most significant events in the history
of the world, the fall of Constantinople to the Turks on May 29,
1453, is listed by some historians as the closing of the Middle
Ages.

Relations between the Greek East and the Latin West were

near the breaking point.   In 1203 Constantinople had been captured
and sacked by members of the Fourth Crusade, something the
Greeks still resented.   Mohammed II, the Turkish sultan, saw in
this situation a chance to defeat the Byzantine Empire and decided,
as part of his campaign, to assault and capture Constantinople.

On April 5, 1453, the Greeks found a Turkish army of more
than 100,000 troops massed before the city's walls.   The Turkish
fleet stood ready to do battle with the much smaller Greek naval
forces.

On April 12, the siege began.   The Turks fired gigantic cannon at the stone walls of the city, and the Greeks were hard pressed
to repair the damage done to their defenses.   In spite of the fact
that they were greatly outnumbered the Greeks, under the leadership of John Giustiniani, won the first two major engagements.   An
attempt by the Turks to scale the walls was defeated on April 18,
and on the following day the Greeks scored a naval victory over a
part of the Turkish fleet.

The siege continued and gradually the Turks wore down their
adversaries.   The Turkish sultan became discouraged when he realized that the Greeks would not surrender but would fight on to
the bitter end.   He also feared that the Greeks might get reinforcements.   On May 27, he considered negotiating a peace but was persuaded to continue the fight by Zagan Pasha, one of his commanders.

The final attack began on May 28.   That night the Greeks
and Latins of Constantinople forgot their differences and celebrated
mass together.   On May 29 the Turks at last forced their way into the city.   Constantine XI, the last Christian emperor of Byzantium, was killed in combat.   Constantinople had fallen to the Ottoman Turks.   It remained the Turkish capital until 1923 when Ankara replaced it as the seat of government.   In 1930 the name of
the city was officially changed to Istanbul.

Suggested Readings

Baynes, North H.   The Byzantine Empire.   London: Hutchinson &
      Co. , 1943.
Brand, Charles M. , ed.   Icon and Minaret: Sources of Byzantine
      and Islam Civilization.   Englewood Cliffs, N. J. :   Prentice-Hall,
      1969.
Cantor, Norman.   Medieval History: The Life and Death of a Civ-
      ilization.   New York: Macmillan, 1969.
Chubb, Thomas Caldecot.   The Byzantines.   Cleveland: World, 1959.
Diehl, Charles.   Byzantium: Greatness and Decline.   Translated
      by Naomi Alford.   New Brunswick, N. J. :   Rutgers University
      Press, 1957.
_____.   "The Fourth Crusade and the Latin Empire" in The
      Cambridge Medieval History.   Cambridge: The University
      Press, 1927.

Franzius, Enno. History of the Byzantine Empire, Mother of Na-
     tions. New York: Funk & Wagnalls, 1967.
Guerdan, René. Byzantium: Its Triumphs and Tragedy. Trans-
     lated by D. L. B. Hartley. New York: Putnam's, 1957.
Harding, Samuel Bannister, in consultation with Albert Bushnell
     Hart. Essentials in Medieval History (from Charlemagne to
     the Fifteenth Century). New York: American Book Co. , 1909.
Hussey, Joan M. The Byzantine World. London: Hutchinson &
     Co. , 1957.
Lot, Ferdinand. The End of the Ancient World and the Beginnings
     of the Middle Ages. New York: Barnes & Noble, 1953 (Or-
     iginally published 1926).
Obolenski, Dimitri. The Byzantine Commonwealth. New York:
     Praeger, 1971.
Ostrogorsky, George. History of the Byzantine State. Translated
     by Joan M. Hussey. New Brunswick, N. J. : Rutgers Univer-
     sity Press, 1969.
Pears, Edwin. The Destruction of the Greek Empire and the Story
     of the Capture of Constantinople by the Turks. London: Long-
     mans, Green, 1903.
Runciman, Steven. Byzantine Civilization. London: E. Arnold &
     Co. , 1933.
          . The Fall of Constantinople, 1453. Cambridge, Mass. :
     Harvard University Press, 1969.
Sherrard, Philip. Byzantium. New York: Time, Inc. , 1966.
Tappan, Eva March. "The Fall of Constantinople" in her Old
     World Hero Stories. Boston: Houghton Mifflin, 1937.
Van Loon, Hendrik Willem. The Story of Mankind. New York:
     Garden City Publishing Co. , 1938.
Vasiliev, Alexander A. The History of the Byzantine Empire,
     324-1453. Madison, Wis. : University of Wisconsin Press,
     1952.
Vyronis, Speros. Byzantium and Europe. New York: Harcourt,
     Brace, 1967.
Zernov, Nicholas. Eastern Christendom. New York: Putnam's,
     1961.

THE OVERTHROW OF THE GOLDEN HORDE (1480-1502)

The "Golden Horde" is the name applied to the army of
Tartars which, under Batu Khan, grandson of Genghis Khan, overran eastern Europe. It additionally designates the empire established by the Tartars on the Volga River, which is also known as
"Kipchak. "

The Tartars crossed the Ural River in 1237 and attacked
and conquered Moscow, Kiev, Ryazan and other cities. Looting,
pillaging, burning and killing were the order of the day. By 1240
Batu had subdued most of the states of central and southern Russia
and made them Mongol possessions.

The year 1300 saw the Khans of the Golden Horde exercising absolute authority in Russia. The rulers of that country paid tribute to the conquerors and were permitted to retain their positions only by sufferance. During the last half of the fourteenth century, however, the Russians began to resist the invaders and the Golden Horde's powers deteriorated, particularly in Moscow, at that time the capital of the Grand Duchy of Vladimir. By 1462, when Ivan III (The Great) ascended the Russian throne, Mongol control over that country had been greatly weakened but not entirely eliminated.

Following his coronation Ivan set about planning a campaign which he hoped would result in destroying the Golden Horde's hold over his country. In this he was opposed by Akhmad Khan, the Mongol leader, who was determined to reimpose the Horde's pristine authority over Moscow. In 1472 Akhmad launched the first of two invasions of Moscow. However, he found it necessary to withdraw because of the effectiveness of the Russian defense. In 1476 Ivan declined flatly to pay any further tribute to the Golden Horde. He opened negotiations for an alliance with Mengli Girey, khan of the Crimean Tartars and an enemy of the Horde. The latter was concerned with an invasion of the Crimea by the Ottoman Turks and consequently the negotiations were not finalized until later.

Akhmad Khan found himself in the position of having either to concede Moscow's independence or enforce his demands on that city. He negotiated an alliance against Ivan with Casimir IV, King of Poland and Grand Duke of Lithuania, and prepared for a second invasion of Russia. In April, 1480, Ivan concluded his alliance with Mengli Girey and that summer the Mongol invasion commenced. Akhmad Khan found the frontier strongly defended. In November he made a stand against the Russians but, for reasons not clear to this day, Ivan did not attack the invading forces, although he was strongly urged to do so by his adviser, Bishop Vassian.

On November 11, 1480, Akhmad ordered his troops to retreat to the south. This "curious and much discussed withdrawal" marked the beginning of the end for the Golden Horde and, in January of the following year, Akhmad Khan was assassinated.

Ivan's soldiers, together with those of Mengli Girey, attacked and overcame the Golden Horde in 1491. In 1502 the Crimean Tartars completed their destruction and the overthrow of the Horde was complete. By 1556 Ivan IV (The Terrible), grandson of Ivan III, succeeded in annexing the lower Volga region.

Suggested Readings

Charques, Richard Denis. A Short History of Russia. New York: Dutton, 1956.

Clarkson, Jesse D. A History of Russia. New York: Random House, 1969.

Fennell, J. L. I. Ivan the Great of Moscow. New York: St. Martin's Press, 1963.

Florinsky, Michael T. Russia: A History and Interpretation. New
    York: Macmillan, 1965.
Graham, Stephen. Ivan the Terrible: The Life of Ivan IV of Rus-
    sia. New Haven, Conn.: Yale University Press, 1933.
Halecki, Oscar. Borderlands of Western Civilization: A History
    of East Central Europe. New York: Ronald Press, 1952.
Hingley, Ronald. Tsars, 1533-1917. New York: Macmillan, 1968.
Kluchevsky, Vasily O. A History of Russia. Translated by C. J.
    Hogarth. New York: Russell and Russell, 1960 (Originally
    published 1913).
Lamb, Harold. Genghis Khan and the Mongol Horde. New York:
    Random House, 1954.
Pares, Bernard. A History of Russia. New York: Knopf, 1960.
Riasanovsky, Nicholas Valentine. A History of Russia. New York:
    Oxford University Press, 1963.
Utechin, S. V. Russian Political Thought: A Concise History. New
    New York: Frederick A. Praeger, 1964.
Vernadsky, George. A History of Russia. New Haven, Conn.:
    Yale University Press, 1954.
Wren, Melvin C. The Course of Russian History. New York:
    Macmillan, 1968.

THE TOWER DEATHS OF THE TWO
ENGLISH PRINCES (1483 or 1486)

One of the most ambitious and unscrupulous kings of England
was Richard III, the former Duke of Gloucester. According to some
accounts, he obtained his throne by chicanery and the ordered murder of his nephews, the two young princes who stood between him
and the kingship.

King Edward IV died on April 9, 1483, leaving the care of
his heir, thirteen-year-old Edward V and Edward's younger brother
Richard to the duke, who was also charged with the administration
of the kingdom. Edward IV's queen was Elizabeth Woodville, a
commoner and widow with two children, and she and her relatives
attempted unsuccessfully to control the government. Because Elizabeth had been previously married, many felt that she, "not being
a virgin, was not the legitimate wife of the king. " George, Duke
of Clarence, King Edward's second brother and heir-presumptive,
had a claim to the throne if Edward's marriage to Elizabeth was
illegal, as Edward's progeny could not then succeed him. Edward
had his brother imprisoned in the Tower of London where he was
murdered, being drowned, according to legend, in a butt of malm-
sey.

Earl Rivers, a member of the Woodville family, engaged
with Richard in a struggle for power. Richard sent young Edward
to the Tower, there to be kept under "protective custody" until his
coronation. On June 16 Prince Richard, on his uncle's orders, fol-

lowed his brother to the Tower.   Neither prince was ever seen
alive again and it is believed that they were smothered to death on
instructions from their paternal uncle.   Hugh Ross Williamson, in
his Historical Whodunits, puts forth the theory that the two boys
were murdered in 1486 by order of Henry Tudor, Earl of Richmond and later King Henry VII of England.

Richard was crowned king of England on June 26, 1483, Parliament having declared the marriage of his brother, Edward IV, to
Elizabeth Woodville illegal.   King Richard III ruled until 1485 when
he was killed at the Battle of Bosworth Field and Henry became
king.

Sir Thomas More (1478-1535), the British statesman and
author, in his History of Richard III, expressed his belief that the
two princes had been suffocated in the Tower by order of their uncle.
This account is regarded by many historians as substantially correct.   In 1674 a wooden box containing human bones was found in
the Tower.   These are presumed to be the bones of the two murdered boys.   They were subjected to a careful scientific examination in 1933 and the results of this examination confirm More's
suppositions.

It is generally agreed that Richard III was a man without
scruples or conscience who permitted nothing to stand in the way
of his ambitions.   "While many of the accusations of his enemies
are unfounded, the murder of his two nephews in the Tower is
quite generally ascribed to Richard's orders. "

The news of the murder of the two boys aroused great indignation and Henry, taking advantage of this, crossed over from
Brittany to England, landing at Milford Haven on August 7, 1485.
Here he gathered an army of supporters numbering about 5,000
men.   Richard's forces totaled more than 15,000.   The Battle of
Bosworth Field was fought on August 22.   In spite of the numerical superiority of Richard's army it was decisively defeated.   About
100 of Henry's men and several hundred of Richard's were lost.
Richard's troops were unenthusiastic and he learned, too late, that
many of the subordinates upon whom he had counted for support
were disloyal.   He was killed in the fighting and when he fell Sir
William Stanley, a defecting Yorkist officer, retrieved the royal
crown and placed it upon Henry's head, proclaiming him king.   Several weeks later his kingship was ratified, he becoming Henry VII,
effecting the transfer of the throne from one family to another.   He
and his descendants ruled England until 1603 when Elizabeth I, the
last of the Tudor line, died and was replaced by James I (James VI
of Scotland), bringing the first of the Stuarts to the English throne.

Suggested Readings

Bagley, John J.   Life in Medieval England.   New York: Putnam,
      1960.

Bindoff, S. T. Tudor England. Baltimore: Penguin Books, 1950.

Clark, George. Early Modern Europe from About 1450 to About
    1720. New York: Oxford University Press, 1960.

Cross, Arthur Lyon. A Shorter History of England and Greater
    Britain. Rev. ed. New York: Macmillan, 1929.

Elton, Geoffrey Rudolf. England Under the Tudors. Edited by Sir
    Charles Oman. New York: Putnam, 1955.

Feiling, Keith. A History of England. New York: McGraw-Hill,
    1948.

Fisher, H. A. L. The History of England from the Accession of
    Henry VII to the Death of Henry VIII. London: Longmans,
    Green, 1906.

Harding, Samuel Bannister, in consultation with Albert Bushnell
    Hart. Essentials in Mediaeval History (from Charlemagne to
    the Close of the Fifteenth Century). New York: American
    Book Co. , 1909.

Lander, J. R. The War of the Roses. London: Secker and War-
    burg, 1965.

Lockyer, Roger. Tudor and Stuart Britain, 1471-1714.   London:
    Longmans, Green, 1964.

Mackie, John Duncan. The Earlier Tudors. Edited by Sir George
    N. Clark. Oxford: Clarendon Press, 1952.

More, Sir Thomas. History of Richard III. 1557.

Rowse, Alfred L. Bosworth Field: From Medieval to Tudor Eng-
    land. Garden City, N. Y. : Doubleday, 1966.

Shakespeare, William. The Tragedy of Richard III (play). New York:
    American Book Co. , 1912 (Originally written c. 1592-1593).

Terry, Benjamin. A History of England from the Earliest Times
    to the Death of Queen Victoria. Chicago: Scott, Foresman,
    1901.

Trevalyn, George Macaulay. History of England. New York: Dou-
    bleday, 1953.

Williamson, Hugh Ross. "The Princes in the Tower" in his His-
    torical Whodunits. New York: Macmillan, 1955.

Williamson, James A. The Tudor Age. London: Longmans, Green,
    1957.

THE DIAS EXPEDITION (1487-1488)

Prince Henry the Navigator, Prince of Portugal, though never making any voyages of exploration himself, was extremely interested in geography. In 1418 he took up residence at Sagres,
Cape St. Vincent. He established an observatory and a school of
navigation and spent his life directing voyages of discovery along
the African coast and collecting accounts of journeys to Africa and
Asia. He sent navigators south almost annually, beginning in 1418
and hoped to establish contact with Prester John, a legendary Christian king whose domain was supposed to exist in Ethiopia.

Henry died in 1460. Under John II, King of Portugal, who

ascended the throne in 1481, the voyages of exploration were continued. Diogo Cam (or Cão) reached the mouth of the Congo River
in 1484 and explored the West African coast to the 22nd parallel.
Until the Dias expedition of 1487-1488 he had gone farther along the
coast of Africa than any other explorer.

In August, 1487, an expedition ordered by King John and
headed by Bartholomeu Dias de Novaes, a Portuguese navigator,
left Lisbon and headed south. It was believed that "ships which
sailed down the coast of Guinea might be sure to reach the end of
land by persisting in a southward direction." The three caravels
which composed Dias' fleet sailed southward, arriving at Angra Pequeña, now called Lüderitz Bay, in early December. There one of
the three caravels, which carried stores for the expedition, was
anchored and the other two continued down the African coast. A
storm which lasted thirteen days caught the two vessels and carried them around the Cape of Good Hope at the tip of the African
continent.

In February, 1488, the expedition arrived at Mossel Bay,
its first landfall after rounding the Cape. It was realized that the
southernmost point of the African continent had been passed.

Dias' crew, as that of Christopher Columbus was to do four
years later, demanded to return home. The two vessels, having
sailed over 500 miles eastward from the Cape, turned westward,
probably somewhere in the vicinity of the Great Fish River. They
remained near present day Capetown for several months and then
rejoined the store ship at Angra Pequeña. The reunited fleet then
returned to Lisbon, arriving in December, 1488.

The Dias Expedition is considered one of the most important
events in maritime history. It reinforced the belief that an all-
water route to India had been discovered. On the strength of it
King John broke off negotiations with Christopher Columbus who
hoped to establish a route to Asia by sailing due west. Columbus,
as every schoolboy knows, obtained a charter from King Ferdinand
and Queen Isabella of Spain and, on October 12, 1492, discovered
the hitherto unsuspected North American continent.

Dias' 1487-1488 expedition was followed by those of Vasco
da Gama. In 1497 he sailed with four vessels from Lisbon, rounded the Cape of Good Hope, reached Malindi on the east coast of
Africa and from there sailed across the Indian Ocean to Calicut.
This was the first voyage from Western Europe around Africa to
the east. He made a second journey in 1502-1503 and established
Portuguese colonies at Mozambique and Sofala.

The pioneer explorations of Dias and his predecessors, followed by those of da Gama, made it unnecessary for European merchants, trading with Asia, to pay tribute to Eastern Mediterranean
Turks. These voyages also eliminated the need to carry goods overland through areas dominated by the hostile Ottomans at Constantinople.

Suggested Readings

Beaglehole, J. C.   The Exploration of the Pacific.   New York: Macmillan, 1934.

Boxer, Charles R. C.   The Portuguese Seaborne Empire, 1415-1825. New York: Knopf, 1969.

Hale, J. R. , and the editors of Time-Life.   The Age of Exploration. New York: Time, Inc. , 1967.

Hart, Henry H.   Sea Road to the Indies.   New York: Macmillan, 1950.

Hobley, Leonard Frank.   Early Explorers to A. D. 1500.   London: Methuen, 1954.

Mitchell, Carleton.   Beyond Horizons: Voyages of Adventure and Discovery.   New York: Norton, 1953.

Parry, J. H.   The Age of Renaissance.   New York: Mentor Books, 1964.

_____ . Europe and the Wider World, 1415-1715.   London: Hutchinson & Co. , 1949.

Penrose, Boies.   Travel and Discovery in the Renaissance, 1420-1620.   Cambridge, Mass. : Harvard University Press, 1952.

Prestage, Edgar.   The Portuguese Pioneers.   New York: Barnes & Noble, 1967.

Sykes, Percy.   A History of Exploration from the Earliest Times to the Present.   New York: Harper & Row, 1961 (Originally published 1934).

THE LAMBERT SIMNEL AND PERKIN WARBECK IMPOSTURES
(1487 and 1491-1499)

On August 22, 1485, the army of Henry Tudor, Earl of Richmond, defeated that of Richard III, the reigning king of England and member of the House of York, at Bosworth Field. This battle ended the Wars of the Roses. Richard was killed in combat and his crown, found under a bush, was placed on the head of Henry, who became King Henry VII. This effected the transfer of the kingship from one family to another.

The Yorkists did not take their defeat easily and made efforts to regain the crown. In their attempts to do this two impostors, Lambert Simnel and Perkin Warbeck, were presented as legal claimants to the English throne.

Simnel was the son of an Oxford joiner. He came to the attention of Richard Symonds, a priest whose sympathies were with the House of York. Symonds determined to exploit young Simnel, passing him off as Edward, Earl of Warwick.

Symonds took the boy to Ireland which was strongly Yorkist and in May, 1487, the latter was accepted as Warwick and crowned in Dublin as Edward VI. This was despite the fact that the real

Earl of Warwick was very much alive. In June Simnel landed in
Lancashire, supported by 2,000 German mercenaries supplied by
Margaret of Burgundy, sister of the late King Edward IV. Accompanying him was John de la Pole, a former Tudor supporter and
pretender to the throne. The Battle of Stoke was fought the same
month. Henry's forces were victorious and Simnel and Symonds
were captured. Symonds was imprisoned and Simnel, whom Henry
realized to have been little more than a harmless dupe, was assigned to perform menial tasks in the royal kitchen.

     Perkin Warbeck impersonated Richard, Duke of York, the
younger of the two princes imprisoned by Richard, Duke of Gloucester, in the Tower of London. He was the Flemish-born son of
a poor man. In 1491, having traveled to Ireland, he was, because
of his lavish clothes and aristocratic manner, taken by the natives
to be of royal descent. Assured of Irish support, he went to the
continent to raise an army with which to invade England. Charles
VIII of France considered participating in the scheme but withdrew
his support when he made peace with Henry VII. Maximilian I
and Margaret of Burgundy assisted in the plot to put Warbeck on
the English throne.

     The conspiracy was discovered and quashed. Warbeck, how-
ever, continued to aspire to the crown of England, having apparently convinced himself that his claims were genuine. He gained some
support in both Scotland and Ireland but was not able to invade England until 1497. His forces engaged those of King Henry at Taunton. Defeated, he surrendered and was imprisoned in the Tower of
London. An attempt to escape in 1489 was unsuccessful, as was a
second similar attempt. For this and for his efforts to cause a rebellion he was executed at Tyburn on November 23, 1499. Also executed was Edward, the genuine Earl of Warwick and the last Yorkist of the male line.

Suggested Readings

Ashley, Maurice. Great Britain to 1688: A Modern History. Ann
    Arbor, Mich.: University of Michigan Press, 1961.
Bacon, Francis. The History of Henry VII. Edited by J. R. Lumby.
    London: 1876 (Originally published 1622).
Bagley, John J. Life in Medieval England. New York: Putnam,
    1960.
Bindoff, S. T. Tudor England. Baltimore: Penguin Books, 1950.
Cross, Arthur Lyon. A Shorter History of England and Greater
    Britain. New York: Macmillan, 1929.
Elton, Geoffrey Rudolph. England Under the Tudors. Edited by
    Sir Charles Oman. New York: Putnam, 1955.
Fisher, H. A. L. The History of England from the Accession of
    Henry VII to the Death of Henry VIII. London: Longmans,
    Green, 1906.
Ford, John. Perkin Warbeck (play). New York: Harper, 1915
    (Originally published 1634).

Halliday, Frank. A Concise History of England from Stonehenge
    to the Atomic Age. New York: Viking Press, 1964.
Harding, Samuel Bannister, in consultation with Albert Bushnell
    Hart. Essentials in Mediaeval History. New York: American
    Book Company, 1909.
Lander, J. R. The War of the Roses. London: Secker and War-
    burg, 1965.
Mackie, John Duncan. The Earlier Tudors. Edited by Sir George
    N. Clark. Oxford: Clarendon Press, 1952.
Parsons, Geoffrey. The Stream of History. New York: Scribner's,
    1929.
Rowse, Alfred L. Bosworth Field: From Medieval to Tudor Eng-
    land. Garden City, N. Y.: Doubleday, 1966.
Terry, Benjamin. A History of England from the Earliest Times
    to the Death of Queen Victoria. Chicago: Scott, Foresman,
    1901.
Webster, Hutton. Early European History. Boston: Heath, 1917.
Williamson, Hugh Ross. "The Identity of Perkin Warbeck" in his
    Historical Whodunits. New York: Macmillan, 1955.
_____. "The Princes in the Tower" in his Historical Whodunits.
    New York: Macmillan, 1955.
Williamson, James A. The Tudor Age. London: Longmans,
    Green, 1957.

THE SURRENDER OF GRANADA (1492)

The province of Granada in Andalusia, Southern Spain, was
founded by the Moors in the eighth century. Its capital city, also
called Granada, located at the confluence of the Genil and Darro
rivers, lies at the root of the Sierra Nevada mountains. The
Moors had come from Africa, crossing the strait between that continent and the Iberian Peninsula. By 719 the Moslem power was
supreme in Spain but their armies were unable to subdue France.
They were defeated by the Frankish ruler Charles Martel at the
battle of Tours in 732 or 733 and from that time on concentrated
on developing the area south of the Pyrenees.

Between 1036 and 1234 Granada was part of the kingdom of
Córdoba. When, at the end of that period, the Moors had been
deprived of most of their Spanish possessions by the Christian kings
of Northern Spain, the city of Granada became the capital of their
remaining territory. It was a rich trading and cultural center.

In 1469 Isabella, Queen of Castile, married her cousin Ferdinand, King of Aragon, thus uniting two great Spanish Christian
powers. While the royal husband and wife continued to exercise
sovereign power over their respective kingdoms, administration
was centralized and the two worked together in a common cause:
the establishment of the supreme power of the throne. They also
determined to complete the work done by their forebears and drive
the Moors from Granada.

Muley Hacen, Emir of Granada since 1466, was old and senile. An internal struggle for his throne had developed and by the last decade of the fifteenth century Granada was on the verge of civil war. The aging Emir was replaced by his son Boabdil, a weak and incompetent man.

Ferdinand and Isabella prepared to attack Granada. With this in mind, in 1484 they organized the most modern and efficient military force of its time. The Moorish town of Ronda in Southern Spain was attacked and on May 15, 1485, surrendered to the Christian forces. The town of Losa followed and was overcome, following which Malaga was besieged. After several months of fighting the Christians had done little more than subdue part of the suburbs. Ferdinand summoned his wife to the scene of battle and she so greatly inspired the invading Christian troops by her presence that they renewed the attack and Malaga fell.

The capture of Malaga meant that the western portion of the kingdom of Granada was in Christian hands. However, the eastern part had still to be conquered. In May, 1489, Ferdinand attacked the mountain city of Baza on the eastern front. As in the siege of Malaga, the Christians were unable to subdue Baza until Queen Isabella again appeared on the scene to inspire the troops. Before the town could be taken by assault the Emir of Baza, after some negotiations, decided to surrender. El Zagel, Emir of Almeria, followed suit, and the Christians took over the eastern portion of the kingdom of Granada.

The next step in the campaign was to take the city of Granada. Boabdil vacillated. Granada was crowded with refugees and food and supplies were running low. Ferdinand and Isabella forbade any armed attack on the city while their envoys negotiated with the Moors. On October 28, 1491, Boabdil agreed to surrender his city within sixty days. His military and government officials protested what they considered his treachery and on January 1, 1492, fearing reprisal, the last Emir of Granada offered immediate surrender. The Spanish monarchs accepted his offer and entered the city. Boabdil met them and handed them the keys to Granada. He then crossed the strait to Africa and retired to Fez where he died in 1533 or 1534.

Suggested Readings

Davies, Reginald Trevor. The Golden Century of Spain, 1501-1621. London: Macmillan, 1937.

Dozy, Reinhart Pieter Anne. Spanish Islam: A History of the Moslems in Spain. Translated by Francis Griffin Stokes. London: Chatto and Windus, 1913.

Elliott, John H. Imperial Spain, 1469-1716. New York: St. Martin's Press, 1964.

Hale, Edwyn Andalus. Spain Under the Muslims. London: Robert Hale, 1958.

Irving, Washington. A Chronicle of the Conquest of Granada. New
    York: The Cooperative Publication Society, n. d. (Originally
    published 1829).
Lane-Poole, Stanley. The Story of the Moors in Spain. New York:
    Putnam's, 1886.
Mariejol, Jean Hippolyte. The Spain of Ferdinand and Isabella.
    Translated and edited by Benjamin Keen. New Brunswick,
    N. J. : Rutgers University Press, 1961.
Miller, Townsend. The Castles and the Crown. New York: Cap-
    ricorn Books, 1964.
Parsons, Geoffrey. The Stream of History. New York: Scrib-
    ner's, 1929.
Plunket, Ierne Arthur Lifford. Isabel of Castile and the Making
    of the Spanish Nation, 1451-1504. New York: Putnam's, 1915.
Prescott, William H. History of the Reign of Ferdinand and Isa-
    bella the Catholic. Edited by John Foster Kirk. Philadelphia:
    Lippincott, 1873 (Originally published 1838).
Robinson, James Harvey, and Charles A. Beard. The Development
    of Modern Europe: An Introduction to the Study of Current His-
    tory. Boston: Ginn, 1907-1908.
Scott, Samuel Parsons. History of the Moorish Empire in Europe.
    Philadelphia: Lippincott, 1904.
Thorndyke, Lynn. The History of Medieval Europe. Edited by
    William L. Langer. Boston: Houghton Mifflin, 1956.

THE EXPULSION OF THE SPANISH JEWS (1492)

The term "Jew" refers to the cultural descendants of the
Hebrews and Israelites, from the time of their return from the so-
called Babylonian Captivity to the present. They are members of
a separate ethnic community or fellowship rather than a race. A
people of the Diaspora, they have lived through most of their history without a country of their own. In spite of incessant persecution the Jew has maintained his group identity for almost nineteen centuries. This cohesion is attributed to Judaism, the religious system which "governs Jewish life in its every aspect. "

The Jews settled in Spain as early as the year 300. Even
at this early date they "aroused the suspicions" of the Christians.
In 313 the Council of Elvira advocated a separation of Christians
and Jews, and during the succeeding centuries this distrust increased.

In 711 the Moslems invaded Spain from Morocco and by 719
their power was supreme as far north as the Pyrenees. The Spanish Jews, hoping to improve their religious and political positions,
welcomed them. By the eleventh century, however, disputes regarding dynastic successions and other matters weakened the Moslems to the extent that Christians in Northern Spain resolved to
take back their country. Toledo fell to the armies of Alfonso VI

in 1085 and it became obvious that once again the Spanish Jews
would have to deal with a hostile Christian environment.

In 1145 or 1150 the Almohades, an African sect, invaded
Spain and within five years dominated the Moslem areas.   In 1212
another battle at Toledo resulted in a victory by the Christian forces and the Almohades were expelled from Spain shortly thereafter.
The Moorish power was then restricted to Cadiz and the kingdom
of Granada, and in 1492 the Moors were expelled from the Spanish
peninsula.   During the reign of the Almohades the Jews in Spain
suffered such persecution that many of them converted, at least
outwardly, to Islam, and others fled the country.

During the Crusades many Jews were massacred and in the
Middle Ages persecution was the rule, many Christians believing
that every Jew had participated in the Crucifixion.   The Inquisition,
introduced into Spain by papal bull about 1233, worsened the lot of
the "heretic" Jew.   Mobs killed thousands of Jews and some of
these, seeking safety, converted to Christianity.   Others, called
Marranos, professed to have adopted the Christian religion but
practiced Judaism in secret.

Isabella of Castile and Ferdinand of Aragon, both devout
Catholics, were married in 1469.   This resulted in centralization
of the joint administration of their separate kingdoms and fanned
Christian religious fervor to feverish pitch.   The Jewish "Christians" were special objects of this augmented fanaticism, particularly those who professed to have been converted but actually remained faithful to their own religion.   Tomás de Torquemada, a
Spanish Dominican monk, was appointed by Ferdinand and Isabella
as first inquisitor general for all the Spanish possessions in 1483.
In 1487 Pope Innocent VIII made him grand inquisitor.   Known as
the "Scourge of the Jews," he resolved to stamp out all heresy
within his jurisdiction.   He became notorious for the severity of
his judgments and the cruelty of his punishments.   Jews were required to wear clothing disclosing them for what they were.   The
Auto-da-fê (act of faith), a public execution, was inaugurated in
1481 when twelve Marranos, six of whom were men and six were
women, were burned at the stake for heresy.

Granada surrendered to the forces of Ferdinand and Isabella
in 1492 and the rulers felt that all that remained necessary to save
Spain for the Catholics, now that the Moors were defeated, was to
subjugate all non-Christians.   By a royal edict of March 30, 1492,
the Jews were ordered to leave Spanish territory no later than July 30, unless they submitted to baptism.   Those who refused were
to be summarily executed.   Despite the efforts of Abraham Senior,
chief Rabbi of Castile and Isaac Abrabanel, a Portuguese theologian
and financial adviser to the Spanish monarchs to have the edict revoked, the Jews were expelled.   They migrated chiefly to North
Africa.   Some went to Portugal but were driven from that country
because of a pending marriage between the son of King John II and
the daughter of Ferdinand and Isabella.

In 1497 Ferdinand invaded Italy and in 1512 acquired all
of Navarre south of the Pyrenees. Funds to finance his military
expeditions were obtained by the confiscation of the property of the
Jews.

Suggested Readings

Baer, Yitzhak. A History of the Jews in Christian Spain. Phil-
adelphia: Jewish Publication Society, 1966.
Benardete, M. J. Hispanic Culture and Character of the Sephardic
Jews. New York: Hispanic Institute of the United States, 1953.
Borchsenius, Paul. The Three Rings. Translated by Michael Her-
on. London: George Allen and Unwin, 1963.
Elliott, John H. Imperial Spain, 1469-1716. New York: St. Mar-
tin's Press, 1964.
Gratz, H. History of the Jews, Vol. III, IV. Philadelphia: Jewish
Publication Society, 1893.
Mariejol, Jean Hippolyte. The Spain of Ferdinand and Isabella.
Translated and edited by Benjamin Keen. New Brunswick, N. J.:
Rutgers University Press, 1961.
Miller, Townsend. The Castles and the Crown. New York: Cap-
ricorn Books, 1964.
Minkin, Jacob S. Abrabanel and the Expulsion of the Jews from
Spain. New York: Behrman's, 1938.
Neuman, Abraham A. The Jews in Spain. Philadelphia: Jewish
Publication Society, 1942.
Plunket, Ierne Arthur Lifford. Isabel of Castile and the Making of
the Spanish Nation, 1451-1504. New York: Putnam's, 1915.
Prescott, William H. History of the Reign of Ferdinand and Isa-
bella the Catholic. Edited by John Foster Kirk. Philadelphia:
Lippincott, 1873 (Originally published 1838).
Roth, Cecil. A History of the Marranos. Philadelphia: Jewish
Publication Society, 1941.
_____. The Spanish Inquisition. New York: Norton, 1964.

THE REFORM OF THE SPANISH
CATHOLIC CHURCH (c. 1495)

        In the late fifteenth century many persons were unhappy with
the various conditions existing in the Spanish Catholic Church. It
was felt that worldliness had replaced piety on the part of churchmen who, despite priestly vows, were "grossly addicted to sins of
the flesh. " The bishops enjoyed excessively large revenues and
many of the benefices were too richly endowed. Spanish clerics,
in many cases, demonstrated a "want of learning" and the illegitimate sons of the nobility were frequently elevated to high church
positions, sometimes while they were still mere infants. These
abuses, which had continued for many years, were not confined to
Spain but it was in that country that Isabella, Queen of Castile and

a great advocate of Catholicism, decided that reforms were needed
and set about making them.

By the year 1492 Isabella and her husband Ferdinand, King
of Aragon, had driven the Moors from Granada, the last Moorish
stronghold on the Iberian Peninsula, and had made Spain a single
political entity. Since her childhood the queen had hoped to reform
the Spanish clergy. This hope became a possibility after 1492 and
she, a determined woman, set about realizing it. In Jiménez de
Cisneros she found a man who, she felt, could and would help her
achieve the church reforms she believed necessary.

Jiménez, born in 1437, was a Spanish prelate and statesman
and a member of the Franciscan order who ultimately became a
cardinal. In 1482 Pedro González de Mendoza, Archbishop of Toledo, suggested Jiménez as confessor to the queen. Following an
interview she accepted him in this capacity and, after the death of
Mendoza in 1495, nominated him to fill the latter's office. The
nomination was confirmed by Pope Alexander VI.

The new archbishop and primate of Spain accepted his appointment reluctantly, preferring to live as a humble churchman.
However, he set about reforming the Catholic Church. The Franciscan Conventuals were particularly corrupt and Jiménez turned
his attention to the conduct of the members of this order. He made
unannounced personal inspections of their abbeys and monasteries.
These inspections were thorough and merciless. When he had gathered sufficient evidence to support his charges of unchurchly conduct he gave the monks and priests involved the choice of immediate
reform or dismissal from the order. In some cases persons obviously unsuited to the religious life were pensioned. Queen Isabella approved and supported his reforming activities and, on occasion, personally admonished those nuns who, in her opinion, had
shown insufficient piety or religious zeal.

Jiménez' attacks on the Franciscans aroused the ire of its
higher members and in due course complaints were lodged with the
pope. Alexander VI sent Gil Delfini, General of the Franciscan
Order, from Rome to Spain to investigate the situation and report
back to him. Delfini protested Jiménez' policies to Isabella who
upheld the latter's actions. He then submitted an unfavorable report to Pope Alexander but in spite of this Jiménez continued his
crusade. Following the reformation of the Franciscans he turned
his attention to the other religious orders, including the Augustin-
ians, Benedictines and Dominicans, who soon "entered into the fold
of the reformed."

Having done with the various orders Jiménez next turned his
attention to the members of the cathedral clergy. These were required to send their mistresses away, live lives of austerity, sell
their luxurious houses and practice celibacy. His efforts were encouraged and supported by the queen.

The work of Jiménez and his royal supporter, though not complete, was highly effective in giving Spain a clergy worthy of the faith it professed. It paved the way for other Spanish reformers, including Theresa of Avila, John of the Cross and Ignatius Loyola.

Suggested Readings

Davies, Reginald Trevor. The Golden Century of Spain, 1501-1621. London: Macmillan, 1937.

Elliott, John H. Imperial Spain, 1469-1716. New York: St. Martin's Press, 1964.

Mariejol, Jean Hippolyte. The Spain of Ferdinand and Isabella. Translated and edited by Benjamin Keen. New Brunswick, N. J. : Rutgers University Press, 1961.

Merton, Reginald. Cardinal Jiménes and the Making of Spain. London: Kegan Paul, 1934.

Miller, Townsend. The Castles and the Crown. New York: Capricorn Books, 1964.

Parsons, Geoffrey. The Stream of History. New York: Scribner's, 1929.

Plunket, Ierne Arthur Lifford. Isabel of Castile and the Making of the Spanish Nation. New York: Putnam's, 1915.

Prescott, William H. History of the Reign of Ferdinand and Isabella the Catholic. Edited by John Foster Kirk. Philadelphia: Lippincott, 1873 (Originally published 1838).

Robinson, James Harvey, and Charles A. Beard. The Development of Modern Europe: An Introduction to the Study of Current History. Boston: Ginn, 1907-1908.

Thorndike, Lynn. The History of Medieval Europe. Edited by William L. Langer. Boston: Houghton Mifflin, 1956.

Von Hefele, The Rev. Dr. The Life of Cardinal Ximenes. Translated by The Rev. Canon Dalton. London: Catholic Publishing and Bookselling Company, 1860.

THE DEATH OF GIROLAMO SAVONAROLA (1498)

Girolamo Savonarola was an Italian preacher, monk and reformer who attacked what he considered the sinfulness of the Catholic Church, thereby making an enemy of the dissolute and licentious Pope Alexander VI. He paid for his convictions and actions with his life.

Savonarola joined the Dominican Order in 1474 at the age of 22. In July, 1491, he became prior of San Marco in Florence. His sermons were largely attacks on the sinfulness of the times and criticisms of the policies of the pope. In 1493 he proposed a reform of the Dominican Order, which was approved by Rome, and he was appointed Vicar-general.

His preaching became both political and prophetic. He fore-
cast the advent of the French under Charles VIII and, in due course,
the French expedition arrived in Florence. Savonarola and other
deputies welcomed the French monarch. When Charles' forces departed and a republic was formed the Dominican monk became the
virtual dictator of Florence, although he had no political functions.

For a while Pope Alexander tolerated Savonarola's attacks on
him and on the Catholic Church, regarding him as little more than
a nuisance. However, his patience reached its limit and in July,
1495, Savonarola was summoned to Rome to answer a charge of
heresy. When he failed to appear he was forbidden to preach. He
was offered a promotion to the rank of cardinal if he would change
his style of preaching. The offer was indignantly refused and he
was again forbidden to deliver sermons.

Savonarola incurred the antipathy of the powerful Medici family by his criticisms of the papacy and the church's emphasis on
ceremony, art and political rather than spiritual matters. He
caused a bonfire, known as the Bonfire of the Vanities, to be lit
in the Piazza della Signoria. Here paintings, books, carnival masks,
costumes and musical instruments were destroyed.

Although discharged as Vicar-general by the pope, he continued to function in that capacity. Finally, on May 13, 1497,
Pope Alexander excommunicated him. He asked for a pardon and
his request went unanswered. He defied the pope's edict by conducting a mass on Christmas Day. He preached on February 11
of the following year, stating that "anyone who accepts my excommunication as valid is a heretic. "

Savonarola's followers began to desert him, fearing that if
they remained in his coterie Pope Alexander would retaliate by excommunicating all the citizens of Florence. He sealed his doom
when he charged Alexander with buying the votes which had elected
him to office and that he was, for that reason, not a valid pope.
On Palm Sunday he and two Dominican followers, Domenico da
Pescia and Silvestro Maruffi, were arrested. The three monks
were interrogated under torture. Being subjected to the strappado,
Savonarola confessed to error, sinning, and anything else that was
demanded of him, but once the torture was stopped he promptly
recanted. His fellow-monks were able to withstand the agony of
the torture chamber and maintained their innocence.

Pope Alexander sent Judge Romolino and another commissioner from Rome to examine the three churchmen. Romolino's
observation concerning Savonarola was that "we shall make a good
bonfire of him. " Further torture under the direction of the pope's
commissioners proved useless. Brothers Domenico and Silvestro
refused to admit any error. Savonarola, confessing while on the
strappado, invariably withdrew the statements made under torture
as soon as the pain subsided.

The three monks were cited before the Council, found guilty of heresy and seditious teaching and sentenced to die. The pope confirmed the sentence and Savonarola and his two disciples were turned over to the secular arm. On May 23, 1498, the three churchmen were publicly hanged in the Piazza della Signoria. The executioner then burned the suspended bodies in a huge bonfire.

Suggested Readings

Clark, William. Savonarola: His Life and Times. Philadelphia: Richard West, 1890.

De La Bedoyère, Michael. The Meddlesome Friar and the Wayward Pope. Garden City, N. Y.: Doubleday, 1958.

Fusero, Clemente. The Borgias. New York: Frederick A. Praeger, 1972.

Hagedorn, Hermann. "Savonarola" in his The Book of Courage. Philadelphia: Winston, 1920.

MacHardy, George. Savonarola. Philadelphia: Richard West, 1901.

Ridolfi, Roberto. The Life of Girolamo Savonarola. Translated by Cecil Grayson. New York: Knopf, 1959.

Roeder, Ralph. "Savonarola" in his The Man of the Renaissance: Four Lawgivers, Savonarola, Machiavelli, Castiglione, Aretino. New York: Viking Press, 1933.

_____. Savonarola: A Study in Conscience. New York: Bretano's, 1930.

Symonds, John Addington. The Age of the Despots. New York: Putnam, 1960.

Van Paassen, Pierre. A Crown of Fire. New York: Scribner, 1960.

Van Wyck, William. Savonarola (play). New York: Random House, 1926.

"We Shall Make a Good Bonfire of Him" in Crimes and Punishment, Vol. 6. Editorial presentation, Jackson Morley. London: BPC, 1973.

Weinstein, Donald. Savonarola and Florence: Prophecy and Patriotism in the Renaissance. Princeton, N. J.: Princeton University Press, 1971.

NICCOLO MACHIAVELLI'S THE PRINCE (1513)

Niccolò Machiavelli, an Italian statesman, historian, playwright and political philosopher, was born in Florence in 1469. Not much is known of his early years. He was the son of a family which, though not wealthy, was not without means. His father, a lawyer, gave him a good education which included instruction in Latin.

Following a short period during which he served as a minor clerk in the chancery he became, in 1498, a secretary to the Flor-

entine Republic, responsible to "The Ten," whose concerns were
war and internal affairs.   He held this position until 1512 and during his tenure went on diplomatic missions to France, Forli, Romagna, Blois, Bolzano and elsewhere.   He first met Cesare Borgia in 1502 on his first mission to Romagna and in 1504 had further
contacts with him both there and in Rome.   His work as diplomatic representative gave him a wide knowledge of political intrigue.

In 1512 the Medici regained power in Florence.   The Republic fell and Machiavelli lost his position with the state.   He sought
an appointment worthy of his talents with the Medici but, being suspected of conspiracy against the new regime was, in 1513, arrested,
imprisoned and tortured.   Upon the accession of Pope Leo X in the
same year he was banished from Florence for a year.   He retired
to his villa at San Casciano outside the city and there devoted himself to writing.   His best-known literary effort, The Prince,
was completed in 1513 and published in 1532, five years after
his death.

The Prince, written in the first person, is essentially a
manual of practical statecraft, developed from Machiavelli's own
experiences and from deductions based on Roman history.   A major aim of the book was to urge the salvation of Italy as a national
entity through the control of a strong despot and the establishment
of a national army of conscripts rather than mercenaries.   It was
dedicated to Lorenzo de' Medici, who is said to have read the book
in manuscript and declared it to be too theoretical.   Historians are
generally of the opinion that the prince whom the author praised
most unstintingly was Cesare Borgia.   Count Carlo Sforza declared
that The Prince "made Machiavelli famous and infamous."   John
Addington Symonds, the English poet, essayist and literary historian, considers the book to contain "the foundations of modern political science."

Machiavelli's opinion of human nature was negative and pessimistic.   He advised the prince or ruler to emulate both the lion and
the fox, combining boldness and fearlessness with cunning and deception in order to gain his objectives.

He states that a "new province" should be colonized rather
than be kept under subjugation by garrisons.   His reasoning is that
colonizing a territory makes enemies only of the few whose lands
have been taken from them and given to the colonists and the other
inhabitants who, "having suffered no loss are easy to keep quiet" as
they do not relish the possibility of "being deprived of their land
also."   Large bodies of armed men, on the other hand, are
expensive to maintain and antagonize the natives of the "new
province."

This and other examples illustrate Machiavelli's philosophy
that the prince should make his decisions only in terms of their ef-

fectiveness, ignoring any ethical considerations.   He felt that the
end invariably justified the means required to attain that end.   Lying should be avoided if possible, but promises should be broken and
treaties ignored when expedient.

The Prince is divided into 26 chapters.   Some of the chapter
headings are illustrative of Machiavelli's theme: how to be a successful ruler.   These headings include: "On Those Who Have
Become Princes by Crime," "Generosity and Meanness," "Cruelty and Clemency and Whether It Is Better to Be Loved or
Feared," "In What Manner Princes Should Keep Their Word,"
and "How a Prince Should Conduct Himself in Order to Acquire
Prestige. "

Suggested Readings

Beuf, Carlo M.   Cesare Borgia, the Machiavellian Prince.   New
    York: Macmillan, 1942.
Bradford, Sarah.   Cesare Borgia.   New York: Macmillan,
    1976.
Butterfield, Herbert.   The Statecraft of Machiavelli.   New York:
    Macmillan, 1956.
Chabod, Federico.   Machiavelli and the Renaissance.   Translated
    by David Moore.   London: Bowes and Bowes, 1958.
Fester, Richard.   Machiavelli.   New York: Bury Franklin,
    1904.
Fusero, Clement.   The Borgias.   New York: Frederick A. Prae-
    ger, 1972.
Gilbert, Allan H.   Machiavelli's Prince and Its Forerunners.   Dur-
    ham, N. C. :   Duke University Press, 1938.
Gilbert, Felix.   Machiavelli and Guicciardini: Politics and History
    in Sixteenth Century Florence.   Princeton, N. J. :   Princeton
    University Press, 1965.
Hale, J. R.   Machiavelli and Renaissance Italy.   New York: Mac-
    millan, 1960.
Jensen, De Lamar, ed.   Machiavelli: Cynic, Patriot or Political
    Scientist?   Boston: Heath, 1960.
Macaulay, Thomas Babington.   "Machiavelli" in Eliot, Charles W. ,
    ed.   The Harvard Classics.   New York: Collier, 1909.
Machiavelli, Niccolò.   Lettere Familiari.   Edited by Eduardo
    Alvisi.   Florence: 1883 (Originally written early 16th cen-
    tury).
_____.   The Prince.   Translated and edited by T. G. Bergin.
    New York: Clifts, 1947 (Originally written 1513).
Marcu, Valeiru.   Accent on Power: The Life and Times of Machia-
    velli.   Translated by Richard Winston.   New York: Farrar &
    Rhinehart, 1939.
Morley, John.   Machiavelli.   Folcroft, Pa. : Folcroft Library Ed-
    itions, 1897.
Muir, Dorothy E.   Machiavelli and His Times.   Westport, Conn. :
    Greenwood Press, 1976.

Ridolfi, Roberto.   The Life of Niccolò Machiavelli.   Translated
     by Cecil Grayson.   Chicago: University of Chicago Press,
     1963.
Roeder, Ralph.   "Machiavelli" in his The Man of the Renaissance:
     Four Lawgivers, Savonarola, Machiavelli, Castiglione, Aretino.
     New York: Viking Press, 1933.
Symonds, John Addington.   The Age of the Despots.   New York:
     Putnam, 1960.
Whitfield, John H.   Machiavelli.   Oxford: Basil Blackwell,
     1947.
Woodward, William H.   Cesare Borgia.   London: 1913.

SIR THOMAS MORE'S UTOPIA (1516)

One of the all-time great works of political theory is Sir
Thomas More's Utopia, published in Louvain, the Netherlands, in
1516.   Written in Latin by an English statesman, student, playwright and humanist, it describes the author's conception of the
ideal state and was the forerunner of such books as Voltaire's Candide, Samuel Butler's Erewhon, Jonathan Swift's Gulliver's Travels
and Edward Bellamy's Looking Backward.

Sir Thomas More, the son of a judge, was born in London
in 1478.   After attending Canterbury Hall, now Christ Church, Oxford University, he studied law.   He wrote comedies and studied
Greek and Latin literature and in 1499 decided to become a Car-
thusian monk.   Four years later he abandoned the idea of a career
in the Church and entered Parliament.   In 1510 he was made under-
sheriff of London.   While an envoy to Flanders he sketched a description, in Latin, of an imaginary island called Utopia (Greek for
"no place") which he completed and published in 1516.   This was
printed in the Netherlands because English printing was then in its
infancy.   Desiderius Erasmus, a Dutch scholar and More's friend,
saw the book through the press.   In England it was extremely popular and widely read.

Utopia exploits the popular credulity of the 16th century regarding remote lands and peoples.   Written in two parts, it is essentially a satire on the government and society of England as More
knew it.   It includes a long conversation with Ralph Hythloday (Hyth-
lodaye) whose name means "disseminator of nonsense."   Hythloday
was an imaginary sailor who was supposedly a member of the crew
of Amerigo Vespucci, the Italian navigator, and whom More "claimed"
to have met in the Netherlands.

In Utopia Hythloday compares the social and economic conditions prevailing in Western Europe with those of the imaginary island of Utopia, which he says he has recently visited.   The interests of the individual on More's island are subordinate to those of

society at large.   All persons residing there must do some work and the land is owned in common.   Universal education and religious toleration are practiced.

Conditions in Utopia are contrasted with those of Europe, to the substantial disadvantage of the latter.   Warmongering of European rulers is disparaged as is the greed of those wealthy land holders who "close off common land and tear down peasant villages to facilitate sheep raising. "

Other matters discussed by Hythloday include the republican system of government in which all men are permitted to vote and to hold office and the fact that the more important posts are given to those who are the best educated.

Private property does not exist in Utopia.   Each family receives what it needs for a frugal but adequate existence.   War is avoided whenever possible and only unoccupied territories are colonized.   The ranks of Utopia's armies are filled with mercenaries rather than conscripts, "that their own citizens may be spared. " Enemies are overcome by diplomacy and trickery rather than by force and war, being destructive of property, is not permitted to break out on Utopia's own land.   The death penalty does not exist and criminals are enslaved and made to work for the commonwealth.   Only the terminally ill may legally commit suicide.

Ralph Hythloday states that, compared to Utopia, all other kingdoms he has seen seem like "conspiracies of rich men. " More feels that he cannot accept all the customs and practices of the Utopians but hopes that some could be adopted in England.

Utopia was translated into English in 1551, sixteen years after the author's death.   The Latin version was widely read and admired but did not cause any great changes in English politics or contemporary life.

In 1518 More came to the attention of King Henry VIII, one of whose favorites he became.   He held several important political posts under Henry, including that of Lord Chancellor.   He eventually fell out with the king over the latter's decision to divorce Catherine of Aragon.   In 1534 he was imprisoned in the Tower of London, and was tried the following year.   He refused to take an Oath of Supremacy, holding that Parliament lacked the right to usurp papal authority in favor of the king.   For this stand he was condemned and on July 7, 1535, was beheaded.   The Roman Catholic Church canonized him in 1935.

Suggested Readings

Ames, Russell.   Citizen Thomas More and His Utopia.   Princeton,

N. J. : Princeton University Press, 1949.

Bellamy, Edward. Looking Backward. New York: New American
Library, 1960 (Originally published 1888).

Bestor, Arthur. Backwoods Utopias. Philadelphia: University of
Pennsylvania Press, 1950.

Butler, Samuel. Erewhon, or Over the Range, and Erewhon Revisited. New York: Modern Library, 1927 (Originally published 1872 and 1901, respectively).

Campbell, William E. More's Utopia and Its Social Teaching. London: Eyre and Spottiswoode, 1930.

Chambers, Robert W. Thomas More. London: Jonathan Cape,
1951.

Hexter, J. H. More's Utopia: Biography of an Idea. Princeton,
N. J. : Princeton University Press, 1952.

Kautsky, Karl. Thomas More and His Utopia. New York: Russell and Russell, 1959 (Originally published 1890).

More, Sir Thomas. Utopia. Based on a translation by Ralph Robinson. London: J. M. Dent & Sons, 1957 (Originally published
1516).

_____. Utopia of Sir Thomas More. Edited by H. B. Cot-
terill. New York: St. Martin's Press, 1908 (Originally
published 1516).

Negley, Glenn, and J. Max Patrick. The Quest for Utopia. Washington, D. C. : Consortium Press, 1972.

Seebohm, Frederic. The Oxford Reformers. London: Longmans,
Green, 1887.

Surtz, Edward, S. J. The Praise of Pleasure. Cambridge, Mass. :
Harvard University Press, 1957.

_____. The Praise of Wisdom. Chicago: Loyola University
Press, 1957.

Swift, Jonathan. Gulliver's Travels. New York: Pocket Books,
1957 (Originally published 1726).

Voltaire, pseud. Candide. New York: Random House, 1975 (Originally published 1759).

MARTIN LUTHER'S 95 THESES (1517)

Martin Luther, a German law student turned Augustinian
monk, found himself beset with doubts concerning many of the teachings of the Catholic Church. He was particularly concerned with
the custom of selling indulgences which, according to Pope Leo X,
wiped out punishments for past sins and lessened the time a deceased sinner must spend in purgatory. The pope commissioned
John Tetzel, a Dominican friar, to sell indulgences, the money
derived to be used for the building of St. Peter's Basilica in
Rome.

On the evening of All Saint's Day, October 31, 1517, Luther
nailed his "Ninety-Five Theses" to the door of the Castle Church

at the University of Wittenberg. This document contained 95 paragraphs for discussion and was a blast against the sale of indulgences and other practices of the Catholic Church.

Luther's document had essentially three parts. The first of
these denounced papal venality. The second stated that the pope had
no jurisdiction over purgatory, "and if he did he should empty the
place free of charge." The third part asserted that forgiveness
of sin comes from God and that this cannot be purchased with
money.

Tetzel and other Dominicans denounced Luther to the pope
and he was summoned to Rome. His secular lord Frederick the
Wise was able to insist that Luther's hearing take place on German
soil and he was examined by Cardinal Cajetan at Augsburg in October, 1518.

A political situation saved Luther from the stake, the normal punishment for those who refused to recant ideas opposed to
those of the Church. Luther was able to maintain his position,
engaging in a debate with Johann Eck at Leipzig in July, 1519.
Here he proposed several radical theories, such as one contending that papal authority was only a human invention and
that the Bible alone was an infallible authority in matters of
religion.

Luther published a number of theological treatises which
attacked the Church and its abuses and which called for papal
reform. Leo X condemned him as a heretic in the bull Ex-
surge Domine, which Luther later burned in a public ceremony.

Appearing before the Diet of Worms in 1521, Luther again
refused to recant. He then went into hiding at Wartburg Castle. He was condemned for heresy in absentia. Emerging
from the castle a year later he found that he had gained a
tremendous following. Many Germans had broken with the Catholic Church. Hundreds of priests and nuns renounced their vows
and accepted the new theology. Many of these married, as
Luther did in 1525.

Today the Lutheran Church is worldwide. Historians believe
that the Protestant movement is the direct result of Martin Luther's
posting his "Ninety-Five Theses" on the church door at Wittenberg
in 1517.

Suggested Readings

Bainton, Roland H. The Age of the Reformation. Princeton, N. J. :
    Van Nostrand, 1956.
        . Here I Stand: A Life of Martin Luther. New York:
    Abingdon, 1950.

_____. The Reformation of the Sixteenth Century. Boston:
    Beacon Press, 1956.
Boehmer, Heinrich. Martin Luther: Road to Reformation. New
    York: Living Age Books, 1957.
Bornkamm, Heinrich. Luther's World of Thought. St. Louis, Mo.:
    Concordia Publishing House, 1958.
Chadwick, Owen. The Reformation. Baltimore: Penguin Books,
    1964.
Clark, George. Early Modern Europe from About 1450 to About
    1720. New York: Oxford University Press, 1960.
Cowie, Leonard. The Reformation of the Sixteenth Century. New
    York: Putnam, 1970.
Dickens, Arthur G. Reformation and Society in Sixteenth-Century
    Europe. New York: Harcourt, Brace, 1966.
Dillenberger, John, ed. Martin Luther: A Selection from His
    Writings. New York: Doubleday Anchor Books, 1961.
Elliott-Binns, L. The History of the Decline and Fall of the Medi-
    eval Papacy. London: Methuen, 1934.
Erikson, Erik H. Young Man Luther. New York: Norton Library,
    1962.
Fosdick, Harry Emerson. Martin Luther. New York: Random
    House, 1956.
Friedenthal, Richard. Luther: His Life and Times. Translated
    by John Nowell. New York: Harcourt, Brace, 1967.
Grisar, Hartmann. Martin Luther: His Life and Work. West-
    minster, Md.: The Newman Press, 1950.
Hagedorn, Hermann. "Martin Luther" in his The Book of Courage.
    Philadelphia: Winston, 1920.
Harbison, E. Harris. The Age of Reformation. Ithaca, N.Y.:
    Cornell University Press, 1955.
_____. The Christian Scholar in the Age of the Reformation.
    New York: Scribner's, 1956.
Holl, Karl. The Cultural Significance of the Reformation. New
    York: Meridian Books, 1959.
Jones, Rufus M. Spiritual Reformers in the 16th and 17th Centur-
    ies. Boston: Beacon Press, 1959.
Kooiman, Willem Jan. By Faith Alone: The Life of Martin Luther.
    New York: Philosophical Library, 1955.
Lau, Franz. Luther. Translated by Robert Fisher. Philadelphia:
    Westminster Press, 1963.
Lecler, Joseph, S.J. Toleration and the Reformation. Translated
    by T. L. Westow. New York: Associated Press, 1960.
Lortz, Joseph. How the Reformation Came. New York: Herder
    & Herder, 1964.
Luther, Martin. "The Ninety-Five Theses: Address to the German
    Nobility Concerning Christian Liberty." Translated by R. S.
    Grignon in Eliot, Charles W., ed. The Harvard Classics,
    Vol. 36. New York: Collier, 1910 (Originally written 1517).
_____. Three Treatises. Philadelphia: Fortress Press, 1960
    (Originally written 1517).
McGiffert, A.C. Protestant Thought Before Kant. New York: Har-
    per & Row, 1962.

Mueller, William A.   Church and State in Luther and Calvin.   Garden City, N. Y.:   Doubleday, 1965.

Osborne, John.   "Luther" (play condensation) in Mantle, Burns, ed. The Best Plays of 1963-1964.   New York: Dodd, Mead, 1964.

Pelikan, Jaroslav.   Obedient Rebels.   New York: Harper & Row, 1964.

Rupp, E. Gordon.   Luther's Progress to the Diet of Worms.   New York: Harper & Row, 1964.

_____.   The Righteousness of God.   New York: Philosophical Library, 1953.

Schwiebert, Ernst G.   Luther and His Times.   St. Louis, Mo.: Concordia Publishing House, 1950.

Spitz, Lewis W., ed.   The Protestant Reformation.   Englewood Cliffs, N. J.: Prentice-Hall, 1966.

_____.   The Reformation: Material or Spiritual?   Boston: Heath, 1962.

Wakeman, Henry Offley.   An Introduction to the History of the Church of England, from the Earliest Times to the Present Day.   5th edition.   London: Rivingtons, 1898.

Watson, Philip S.   Let God Be Good.   London: Epworth Press, 1960.

Whale, J. S.   The Protestant Tradition.   Cambridge: The University Press, 1962.

THE MAGELLAN EXPEDITION (1519-1522)

By the end of the 15th century the eastern Mediterranean was dominated by the Turks and the land routes were obstructed by the Ottomans at Constantinople.   This made the East-West trade routes both costly and dangerous to use and consequently Portugal and Spain sought other routes to the East.   The voyages of exploration made by Christopher Columbus, Bartholomeu Dias and Vasco da Gama all had as an objective the finding of new ways to reach the East.   Columbus sailed west and the other two proceeded south and east around the continent of Africa.

In 1519-1522 Ferdinand Magellan, a Portuguese navigator in the service of Charles V, King of Spain, completed Columbus' scheme by sailing west, around what is now called Cape Horn, and across the Pacific Ocean which had been discovered by the Spanish explorer Vasco Nuñez de Balboa in 1513.

Late in 1518 Magellan sought and received authorization and financial aid from King Charles to undertake his voyage.   He went to Seville where he spent more than a year readying his five-ship fleet.   The ships assigned to him were old, small and in poor repair.   They ranged in size from the 120-ton San Antonio to the 75-ton Santiago.   The other three vessels were the Trinidad, the Concepción and the Victoria.

Crews were difficult to recruit but eventually this was accomplished. On September 20, 1519, Magellan set sail from Seville. After a voyage lasting two months he arrived off the coast
of Brazil. He then headed south, hoping to find a strait or passage to the Pacific. No such strait was found and when the
summer of 1520 ended in March, Magellan dropped anchor in
the waters off Patagonia, there to spend the winter. Mutiny
broke out, the San Antonio deserted and the Santiago was wrecked
on a reef.

In August he resumed the voyage with his three remaining
ships. On October 1, he discovered a strait between Argentina
and Tierra del Fuego which has since been named after him. On
November 28, the reduced fleet emerged in the Pacific, 320
miles from the Atlantic through the strait. It proceeded westward, arriving at Guam in the Ladrone Islands on March 6,
1521. The voyage was one of great difficulty. Food ran out and
Magellan and his men were reduced to eating rats and chewing
leather.

From Guam Magellan resumed his westward journey and discovered the Philippines, landing on the island of Cebu on April 7.
There he made an alliance with the local ruler, agreeing to
assist him in an attack on the natives of Mactan, a neighboring island. During this expedition Magellan was killed, dying on
April 27.

Following the leader's death the voyage continued under
guidance of Juan Sebastián del Cano, a Basque seaman. Many of
the crewmen had died and the Concepción was burned for want of
a crew and the remaining two vessels separated. The Trinidad
sailed for Panama but was captured by the Portuguese. The Victoria, under the command of del Cano, crossed the Indian Ocean
and headed for South Africa. The Cape of Good Hope was sighted
in May, 1522. The 22 men aboard del Cano's ship were suffering
from scurvy and starvation. However, they managed to complete
the trip, arriving at Seville on September 8, 1522, three years
less twelve days after their departure.

While Magellan did not live to complete the journey he did
circumnavigate the globe. On a previous voyage he had reached
the Banda Islands in the Molucca archipelago at longitude 130° east
of Greenwich. When he was killed on Mactan he had sailed west
to longitude 124° east of Greenwich, thus going six degrees beyond
the complete circumnavigation of the globe. The cargo of spices
brought to Spain by the Victoria was sufficiently valuable to pay the
expenses of the voyage.

The route around Cape Horn was used by navigators for the
next 400 years. In 1914 the Panama Canal was completed, providing a shorter means of passage between the Atlantic and Pacific
Oceans.

Suggested Readings

Beaglehole, J. C. The Exploration of the Pacific. New York:
   Macmillan, 1934.
Bourne, Edward Gaylord. Spain in America. New York: Barnes
   & Noble, 1962.
Guillemard, F. H. H. The Life of Ferdinand Magellan and the Great
   Circumnavigation of the Globe, 1480-1521. New York: Dodd,
   Mead, 1891.
Hale, J. R. , and the editors of Time-Life. The Age of Exploration.
   New York: Time, Inc. , 1967.
Hart, Henry H. Sea Road to the Indies. New York: Macmillan,
   1950.
Mitchell, Carleton. Beyond Horizons: Voyages of Adventure and
   Discovery. New York: Norton, 1953.
Nowell, Charles E. , ed. Magellan's Voyage Around the World.
   Evanston, Ill. : Northwestern University Press, 1962.
Parr, Charles McKew. Ferdinand Magellan, Circumnavigator.
   New York: Crowell, 1964 (Originally published 1953 as So
   Noble a Captain).
Parry, J. H. The Age of Renaissance. New York: Mentor Books,
   1964.
_____ . Europe and the Wider World, 1415-1715. London:
   Hutchinson & Co. , 1949.
Penrose, Boies. Travel and Discovery in the Renaissance, 1420-
   1620. Cambridge, Mass.: Harvard University Press, 1952.
Pond, Seymour Gates. Ferdinand Magellan, Master Mariner. New
   York: Random House, 1957.
Sykes, Percy. A History of Exploration from the Earliest Times
   to the Present. New York: Harper & Row, 1961 (Originally
   published 1934).

THE CONQUEST OF MEXICO (1519-1540)

By the end of the decade following the discovery of America
by Christopher Columbus on October 12, 1492, the Spanish had established colonies in the New World. One of these was at Santo
Domingo on the Caribbean island of Hispaniola. Here Hernando
Cortés, a 19-year-old immigrant from Spain, settled in 1504. He
acquired property and profited from his activities in farming, mining and the raising of livestock.

In 1517 Diego de Vélasquez, who had been sent out from Hispaniola to conquer Cuba and had become governor of that island the
same year, dispatched Francisco Fernández de Córdoba to explore
the west and search for treasure.

Córdoba discovered Yucatan where the Maya Indians drove
him and his party away. He took with him a few specimens of
gold. In 1518 Velásquez sent out a second expedition to follow up

Córdoba's discoveries.   This expedition, headed by Juan de Grijalva, reached Tabasco where they found the Indians prepared to par-
ley.

Montezuma II, Aztec emperor, had been following the progress of Grijalva and his men.   Runners acting as spies kept him
advised of the movements of the Spaniards.   It had been prophesied
that Quetzalcoatl, an Aztec god, would return to his country in the
Aztec year Ce Acatl.   This was to be 1519, the following year.
Montezuma assumed that the white-skinned intruders were representatives of the god and made overtures to them.

Grijalva sailed back to Cuba with samples of gold, precious
stones and feather work the Indians had given him.   These substantiated the rumor that a fabulously wealthy kingdom existed in
the west.

Velásquez appointed Hernando Cortés to lead an expedition
to the new kingdom.   He and Cortés financed the venture and, although Velásquez had a change of heart and decided to place another man in charge, Cortés ignored the orders to return.   He set
sail on February 18, 1519, with a force of about 550 soldiers, 11
ships, 16 horses, four small cannon and ten brass guns.   Pedro
de Alvarado, one of his captains, landed at Cozumel Island and
robbed the Indians of many of their possessions.   Cortés ordered
the stolen property returned.

At Tabasco Cortés fought a battle with hostile Indians, de-
feating them.   Valuable gifts were presented to the Spaniards.   These
included 20 Tabascan girls, one of whom, Malinche, became Cortés'
devoted mistress.   She soon learned the Spanish language and,
along with Jeronimo de Aguilar, a Spanish castaway who had been
enslaved by the Indians and rescued by Cortés, acted as interpreter.

Cortés and his men proceeded to a point on the coast near
the island of San Juan de Ulua.   There he was greeted by emis-
saries of Montezuma who was by that time firmly convinced that
Cortés was indeed the god Quetzalcoatl.   The Spaniards were presented with many valuable gifts of gold and precious stones.   Montezuma hoped to persuade Quetzalcoatl to leave until he, Montezuma,
should die, following which the god could assume the throne of the
Aztec empire.   Cortés, however, decided to meet the Aztec emper-
or face to face.   He disavowed allegiance to Velásquez, established
the municipality of Veracruz and had himself elected governor, responsible only to Charles V, King of Spain.   In order to prevent
any of his men from deserting and returning to Cuba he sank his
ships and set out for Tenochtitlán, the Aztec capital.   His forces
were augmented by many Totonac Indians who had fallen out with
Montezuma and joined forces with the Spaniards.   On the way to
the capital they were attacked by Indians of the Tlaxcala tribe,
whom they defeated in battle, following which these Indians allied
themselves with the Spaniards.

At Cholula Cortés and his army defeated the warriors of that city. They then proceeded to Tenochtitlán which was situated on an island in a lake and connected to the mainland by three stone causeways. They traveled through the 17,000 foot pass between the volcanoes Popocatépetl and Ixtacihuatl and in due course arrived at their destination. There they were welcomed by Montezuma in person. Cortés, though treated graciously by the Aztec emperor, decided to take him prisoner and assume the leadership of the Aztec people with Montezuma, as his puppet, remaining emperor in name only.

The Spaniards seized Montezuma and placed him under house arrest, forcing him to swear allegiance to King Charles of Spain. This, as well as Cortés' attacks on the Aztec religion, incited the natives to rebellion against the invaders. A force headed by Panfilo de Narváez, sent from Cuba to overthrow the rebellious Cortés, was attacked and defeated by the latter. Many of Narvárez' soldiers defected to Cortés and returned with him to Tenochtitlán.

During Cortés' absence Pedro de Alvarado, who had been left in command, massacred a number of Aztecs who were engaged in a religious ceremony. Cortés, in an effort to appease the natives, released Montezuma's brother Cuitlahuac who had been arrested with him. On the following day the Aztecs, led by Cuitlahuac, attacked. After five days Cortés instructed Montezuma to address his people, telling them that the Spanish would leave if guaranteed a safe conduct from the city. Montezuma attempted to persuade the Aztecs to agree to Cortés' proposal but was stoned and fatally injured when he started to speak.

Cortés decided to break through to the mainland. On June 30, 1520, shortly before midnight, he and his army attempted to leave. The Aztecs sounded the alarm and attacked in great numbers. They had removed the eight bridges from the causeways and Cortés had had a portable bridge constructed to enable his men to cross the gaps. This proved ineffective but some Spaniards, including Cortés, Alvarado and Malinche, Cortés' Indian mistress, escaped by scrambling over the dead bodies which had piled up in the spaces from which the bridges had been removed. More than two thirds of the Spanish forces were destroyed on this occasion, which came to be known as La Noche Triste.

Following another encounter with the Aztecs, Cortés and his remaining men escaped to Tlaxcalan territory. In May, 1521, he attacked Tenochtitlán, laying siege to the city and cutting off supplies of water, food and other necessities. On August 13, 1521, the city was captured. The Spaniards had reduced it to rubble.

Cortés proceeded to rebuild the city. Colonists were brought over from Spain and the former Aztec capital became the principal European city in America. On October 15, 1522, Cortés was named governor and captain general of New Spain. Eventually, fearing his ambition, the Spanish court ordered his goods confiscated and his

followers imprisoned. Between 1528 and 1539 he made several
trips to Spain but was gradually stripped of his responsibilities
and possessions. After participating in the unsuccessful 1541 expedition against the buccaneers of Algiers he retired to a small
estate near Seville where he died in 1547.

Suggested Readings

Beals, Carleton. Land of the Mayas: Yesterday and Today. Lon-
don: Abelard-Schuman, 1966.
Blacker, Irwin R. , and the editors of Horizon Magazine. Cortés
and the Aztec Conquest. New York: American Heritage Pub-
lishing Co. , 1965.
Collis, Maurice. Cortés and Montezuma. New York: Harcourt,
Brace, 1954.
Cortés, Hernán. Fernando Cortés--His Five Letters of Relation
to the Emperor Charles V. Translated by Francis Augustus
MacNult. New York: The Hakluyt Society, 1908 (Originally
written 1519-1526).
De Gómara, Francisco López. Cortés: The Life of the Conqueror.
Translated and edited by Lesley Byrd Simpson. Berkeley, Calif. :
University of California Press, 1964.
De Madariaga, Salvador. Hernán Cortés, Conqueror of Mexico.
New York: Macmillan, 1941.
Diaz del Castillo, Bernal. The Discovery and Conquest of Mexico.
Translated by A. P. Maudslay and edited by Irving A. Leonard.
New York: Farrar, Straus and Giroux, 1956 (Originally written
in 3rd quarter of 16th century).
_____. The Fall of the Aztecs. Edited by Shirley Glubok. New
York: St. Martin's Press, 1965 (Originally written in 3rd quar-
ter of 16th century).
Dresner, Simon. "The Lure of Gold" and "Rivers of Destiny" in
his Encyclopedia of History and Exploration, Vol. 6. London:
Aldus Books, 1971.
Gardiner, C. Harvey. Naval Power in the Conquest of Mexico.
Austin, Texas: University of Texas Press, 1956.
_____, ed. History of the Conquest of Mexico. Chicago: Uni-
versity of Chicago Press, 1966.
Garst, Doris. Three Conquistadors: Cortés, Coronado, Pizarro.
New York: Messner, 1947.
Godwin, John. "The Vanishing Treasures" in his Unsolved: The
World of the Unknown. Garden City, N. Y. : Doubleday, 1976.
Hale, J. R. , and the editors of Time-Life. The Age of Exploration.
New York: Time, Inc. , 1967.
Hordern, Nicholas. "God, Gold and Glory" in his Encyclopedia of
History and Exploration, Vol. 4. London: Aldus Books, 1971.
Morris, J. Bayard, translator. Hernando Cortés: Five Letters,
1519-1526. London: George Routledge & Sons, 1928.
Padden, R. C. The Hummingbird and the Hawk: Conquest and Sov-
ereignty in the Valley of Mexico, 1503-1541. Columbus, Ohio:
Ohio State University Press, 1967.
Parsons, Geoffrey. The Stream of History. New York: Scribner's
1929.

Prescott, William H. History of the Conquest of Mexico. New
     York: Modern Library, 1970 (Originally published 1843).
     _____ . The World of Aztecs. Geneva: Minerva, 1970 (Orig-
     inally published 1847).
Sharp, Hal. The Aztec Vase (fiction). Oakland, Calif. : Univer-
     sity High Press, 1937.
Soustelle, Jacques. Daily Life of the Aztecs on the Eve of the
     Spanish Conquest. Translated by Patrick O'Brian. New York:
     Macmillan, 1961.
Syme, Ronald. Cortés of Mexico. New York: Morrow, 1951.

THE PEASANTS' WAR (1524-1526)

The "Peasants' War" consisted of a revolt of German peasants and members of the lower classes against their feudal over-
lords. As was so often the case in medieval days, the German
nobles of the sixteenth century subjected the proletariat to excessive economic, judicial and religious oppression, much against the
latter's will.

In 1524 fighting broke out between the peasants and the soldiers of the noblemen in Germany, near the Swiss border. The
conflict rapidly spread over much of the rest of Germany and Austria. The peasants, in 1525, formulated their demands, which included the abolishment of serfdom, the granting of fishing and hunting rights, guarantees of fair treatment in the law courts and the
reduction of feudal dues.

In Thuringia the religious issue was particularly strong, with
the Anabaptist Thomas Münzer leading the attack. He was successful in overthrowing the feudal regime and in establishing a cooperative community for his peasant followers, but in 1525 he was defeated at Frankenhausen, captured and beheaded. By the end of
that year the nobles had succeeded in putting down the rebellion in
Germany but it continued in Austria in 1526.

The revolt in Germany was unsuccessful and the peasants
won no concessions from the nobility as a result of it. In Austria
a few of the injustices and evils that led to the Peasants' War were
abolished.

Suggested Readings

Armstrong, E. Emperor Charles V. New York: Gordon Press,
     1976.
Bainton, Roland H. The Age of the Reformation. Princeton, N. J. :
     Van Nostrand, 1956.
Bax, Ernest Belfort. The Peasants' War in Germany, 1525-1526.
     London: Swan Sonnenschein, 1899.

Brandi, Karl. The Emperor Charles Five: The Growth and Des-
    tiny of a Man and of a World Empire. Atlantic Highlands,
    N. J.: Humanities Press, 1968.
Cowie, Leonard W. Reformation of the Sixteenth Century. New
    York: Putnam, 1970.
Engels, Friedrich. The Peasant War in Germany. Translated by
    Moissaye J. Olgin. New York: International Publishers, 1926.
Franz, Günther. Der deutsche Baurenkrieg. 4th edition. Darm-
    stadt, 1956.
Grimm, Harold J. The Reformation Era, 1500-1650. Revised ed-
    ition. Edited by James J. Carroll. New York: Macmillan,
    1965.
Harbison, E. Harris. The Age of Reformation. Ithaca, N. Y.:
    Cornell University Press, 1955.
Holborn, Hajo. A History of Modern Germany. Vol. I: The Re-
    formation. New York: Knopf, 1959.
Janssen, Johannes. History of the German People at the Close of
    the Middle Ages. New York: AMS Press, 1925.
Thompson, James M. Feudal Germany. New York: Frederick
    Ungar, 1962.

THE SEARCH FOR THE NORTHWEST PASSAGE
(1524-1850/1854)

In 1494 King John II of Portugal was dissatisfied with the
Papal Bull Inter Caetera which gave Spain certain rights in the
lands newly discovered by Christopher Columbus in the New World.
He persuaded the Spanish crown, by the Treaty of Tordesillas, to
give Portugal a claim to Brazil. This, in turn, annoyed King Francis I of France, who felt that "a mere piece of parchment" gave
Spain and Portugal "exclusive rights to all the world's newly discovered lands. "

In 1497 and 1498 John Cabot, under patent from King Henry VII of England, made voyages to the New World in search of a
sea route to Asia. He did not find one but did explore the North
American coast. Equally unsuccessful were the two Corte-Real
brothers who sailed under the Spanish flag three years later.

When Hernando Cortés made his successful conquest of the
Aztec empire in the early 1500's and gold, silver and precious
stones were transported to Spain in huge quantities, King Francis
resolved to break what he considered an unjust monopoly and sent
explorers of his own to find and claim a western sea route to the
Orient. In 1524 he commissioned Giovanni da Verrazano, an Italian navigator, to find the fabled Northwest Passage.

Verrazano explored the coast of North America from present-
day North Carolina to Newfoundland and spent some time near the
mouth of the Hudson River. His voyage, however, failed to produce
any information concerning the strait he sought.

In 1533 Jacques Cartier, a French adventurer, proposed to King Francis that a new voyage of exploration be made to the New World. The king agreed and in 1534 furnished Cartier with two vessels and a crew of 120 men. Altogether Cartier made three voyages to Canada and sailed up the St. Lawrence river to the site of present-day Montreal. He did not find the Northwest Passage.

In 1533 Sir Hugh Willoughby was appointed by a company of English merchants to look for the Passage. He and his navigator Richard Chancellor left for Norway from Deptford, England, in May of that year. Willoughby and his men died during the voyage. Chancellor, who had escaped death and who had traveled overland from the port of Vardo to Moscow, returned to England in 1554. His dealings with the Russians resulted in the formation of the Muscovy Company, a trading organization which took over the search for the Northwest Passage.

In 1576 Sir Martin Frobisher left England to seek the Passage. He explored the coast of Canada and returned there the following year to search for gold. He found neither gold nor the Passage.

John Davis, another English seaman, made three Arctic voyages between 1585 and 1588. He discovered Davis Strait, named after him, into Baffin Bay but was unsuccessful in his search for the Passage.

Other navigators and explorers sought the elusive Passage. Willem Barents, sailing for the Dutch, made three voyages. In 1596 he discovered Spitzbergen but did not find the Passage. In 1610 Henry Hudson, representing the Muscovy Company, looked for another route, the Northeast Passage. Like the others, his search was unsuccessful.

Between 1612 and 1616 William Baffin, an English navigator, served as pilot on several expeditions looking for the Passage. He, too, was unsuccessful.

Vitus Bering, the Danish navigator, was employed by Peter the Great of Russia in 1725. He was to determine whether or not North America is joined to Asia or if they are separated by a passage. He discovered the Bering Sea and Bering Strait, both named after him, but not the elusive Passage.

Sir John Ross, Sir Edward Parry, James Clark Ross and Sir John Franklin all sought the Passage without success. The members of Franklin's last party were lost and several expeditions were sent in search of them. Sir Robert John McClure, a British naval officer, headed one such expedition (1850-1854) and in the course of the search discovered the Passage. In between 1903 and 1906 Roald Amundsen, the Norwegian explorer, became the first man to navigate the new route. In his 45-foot sloop Gjöa he sailed from the Atlantic to the Pacific Ocean. The Gjöa was on exhibition

at Golden Gate Park, San Francisco, for several years and was
then sent to Norway.   In 1969 the Humble Oil Company tanker Manhattan Expedition successfully navigated the Passage through Lancaster Sound to Prince of Wales Strait and Amundsen Gulf, ending
at the oil fields of Point Barrow on Alaska's North Slope.

Suggested Readings

Amundsen, Roald.   The North East Passage.   Norwood, Pa. : Nor-
    wood Editions, 1908.
_____. The North West Passage: Being the Record of a Voyage
    of Exploration in the Ship "Gjöa, " 1903-1906.   New York: AMS
    Press, 1908.
_____. To the North Magnetic Pole Through the Northwest Pas-
    sage.   Seattle: Shorey Publications, 1906.
Commager, Henry Steele, ed.   "The Papal Bull Inter Caetera
    (Alexander VI), " (Doc. No. 2) in his Documents of American
    History, 8th edition.   New York: Appleton, 1968.
_____. "The Treaty of Tordesillas" (Doc. No. 3) in his Docu-
    ments of American History, 8th edition.   New York: Appleton,
    1968.
Dresner, Simon.   "Seeking the Northwest Passage" in his Rivers
    of Destiny: Encyclopedia of Discovery and Exploration, Vol. 6.
    London: Aldus Books, 1971.
Hale, J. R. and the editors of Time-Life.   The Age of Exploration.
    New York: Time, Inc. , 1967.
Hart, Henry H.   Sea Road to the Indies. New York: Macmillan, 1950.
Hobley, Leonard Frank.   Early Explorers to A. D. 1500.   London:
    Methuen, 1954.
Mitchell, Carleton.   Beyond Horizons: Voyages of Adventure and
    Discovery.   New York: Norton, 1953.
Newbolt, Sir Henry John.   "Sir John Franklin" in his Book of the
    Long Trail. New York: Longmans, Green, 1919.
Parry, J. H.   Europe and the Wider World, 1415-1715.   London:
    Hutchinson & Co. , 1949.
Penrose, Boies.   Travel and Discovery in the Renaissance, 1420-
    1620.   Cambridge, Mass. : Harvard University Press, 1952.
Sykes, Percy.   A History of Exploration from the Earliest Times
    to the Present.   New York: Harper & Row, 1961 (Originally
    published 1934).
Willis, Thayer.   "A Northern Passage to Cathay" in his The Frozen
    World: Encyclopedia of Discovery and Exploration, Vol. 14.
    London: Aldus Books, 1971.

THE CONQUEST OF PERU (1526-1535)

        Francisco Pizarro came to America from his native Spain
in 1502.   He took part in a number of exploring expeditions, including the one of 1513 headed by Vasco Nuñez de Balboa which re-

sulted in the discovery of the Pacific Ocean. About 1520 he settled in Panama, becoming a partner of the adventurer Diego de Almagro and Fernando de Luque, a priest, in a project to explore and
conquer territory south of Panama.

In November, 1524, Pizarro sailed from Panama on the Pacific Coast, with Almagro following in a second ship. This expedition
was a failure and the explorers, having run out of supplies, returned to their home port.

A second expedition, consisting of two vessels carrying 160
men and five horses, financed by the mayor of Panama, Gaspar
de Espinosa, sailed south in March, 1526. Pizarro and his men
landed on the coast of Colombia where they found Indian settlements
and gold. They were assisted by Bartolome de Ruiz, a distinguished
navigator.

Almagro returned to Panama to recruit additional men and
obtain needed provisions. Ruiz sailed south to survey the coast
and Pizarro led a party inland to search for gold and treasure.
Pizarro's group found little in the way of spoil but when Ruiz returned he reported finding a highly developed Indian civilization at
a point just below the equator. Almagro returned with new re-
cruits and a stock of provisions and then went once more to Panama to enroll sufficient troops to insure the success of the forthcoming expedition into the land of the Incas.

Pedro de los Ríos was the new governor of Panama. He
believed that the proposed expedition was doomed to failure and
sent two vessels to Gallo Island where Pizarro and his men had
camped, with orders to bring them home. Pizarro refused to obey.
He drew a line in the sand with his sword and stated that he proposed to sail south. Thirteen of his men, by stepping over the
line, indicated their willingness to sail with him. The others returned to Panama.

Eventually Pizarro, Almagro and a small band of followers
started southward, landing at the city of Tumbes on the Gulf of
Guayaquil. Here they found treasure and a temple sheathed with
gold.

After further explorations the expedition returned to Panama.
Governor Ríos was still unimpressed with the project and Pizarro
went to Spain where Emperor Charles V authorized further explorations. Pizarro recruited his three half-brothers, Gonzalo, Hernando, and Juan and Martin de Alcantara, to join the enterprise.

In January, 1531, Pizarro led his third and final expedition
to Peru, landing there in 1532. A civil war was raging. The last
emperor, Huayna Capac, had died in 1527, leaving half of his kingdom to each of his two sons, Atahualpa and Huáscar. These two
engaged in a bitter struggle to obtain each other's share of the kingdom, and Atahualpa had defeated Huáscar, whom he imprisoned.

Atahualpa was at the small unfortified town of Cajamarca recovering from a wound received in battle.

Pizarro, with a small force, marched on Cajamarca. Atahualpa had been advised of his coming and, feeling that there was no reason to fear a small band of Spaniards, made him welcome. The following day Atahualpa was seized by the Spaniards and many of his followers, being unarmed, were massacred.

As a prisoner Atahualpa offered to buy his freedom by filling a room, 22 feet long and 17 feet wide, with gold as high as he could reach--about seven feet. Pizarro accepted the offer and the Inca emperor fulfilled his side of the bargain. The Spanish, however, were afraid to release the emperor, believing that he would then rally his followers and wipe the intruders out. Accordingly, they accused him of "treason," incest (the recognized legal marriage with his sister) and heresy, as well as other trumped up offenses. He was tried, found guilty and condemned to die by burning at the stake. Just before the execution his sentence was commuted to strangulation and the lesser sentence was carried out.

On November 15, 1533, Pizarro entered Cusco (Cuzco) with a force of 480 men. The city was plundered of everything of value and the inhabitants were tortured, raped and murdered.

Cusco, located high in the Andes, was too far inland to serve as a center of trade with Spain. Realizing this, Pizarro, in 1535, founded what is now the city of Lima near the mouth of the Rimac River.

By 1535 the conquest of Peru was complete. Conflicts over territorial jurisdiction broke out between Pizarro, supported by his brothers, and Almagro. The latter was defeated and Pizarro had him put to death in July, 1538. Pizarro was assassinated in 1541 by a group which was still loyal to Almagro.

Suggested Readings

Beals, Carleton. Land of the Mayas: Yesterday and Today. London: Abelard-Schuman, 1966.

Bourne, Edward Gaylord. Spain in America. New York: Barnes & Noble, 1962.

Garst, Doris. Three Conquistadors: Cortés, Coronado, Pizarro. New York: Messner, 1947.

Godwin, John. "The Vanishing Treasures" in his Unsolved: The World of the Unknown. Garden City, N.Y.: Doubleday, 1976.

Hale, J.R., and the editors of Time-Life. The Age of Exploration. New York: Time, Inc., 1967.

Hordern, Nicholas. "God, Gold and Glory" in his Encyclopedia of Exploration and Discovery, Vol. 4. London: Aldus Books, 1971.

Howard, Cecil, and the editors of Horizon Magazine. Pizarro and

the Conquest of Peru. New York: American Heritage Publishing Co. , 1968.
Parsons, Geoffrey. The Stream of History. New York: Scribner's, 1929.
Prescott, William H. The History of the Conquest of Peru. New York: Dutton, 1963 (Originally published 1847).
_____. The World of Aztecs. Geneva: Minerva, 1970 (Originally published 1847).
Soustelle, Jacques. Daily Life of the Aztecs on the Eve of the Spanish Conquest. Translated by Patrick O'Brian. New York: Macmillan, 1961.
Syme, Ronald. Invaders and Invasions. New York: Norton, 1964.

THE ACT OF SUPREMACY (1534)

Henry VIII, King of England, had married his brother Arthur's widow, Catherine of Aragon, shortly after his accession in 1509. Pope Julius II had granted a dispensation in order to make it legally possible for Henry to marry the woman who had been married to his brother. Catherine had produced a daughter, the future Queen Mary in 1516 but, although pregnant several times, had not given birth to a son who survived infancy. By 1520 she was beyond the age of childbearing and Henry, who wished for a son and heir to secure a Tudor succession and to insure the future stability of his kingdom, grew tired of her. He had become infatuated with Anne Boleyn, one of Catherine's ladies-in-waiting. Anne had declined to become his mistress and wished to be Queen of England.

In 1527 Henry began proceedings for the annulment of his marriage and also sought permission from Pope Clement VII to marry Anne. The ecclesiastical courts could not grant a divorce but only an annulment, the pope having made sure that the marriage was valid.

Henry appealed to Rome through his chancellor, Cardinal Wolsey. Clement VII was a virtual prisoner of Holy Roman Emperor Charles V, Catherine's nephew, and did not wish to antagonize either Charles or Henry. He and his officials delayed decisive action for six years. Henry, disgusted at the long delay, dismissed Wolsey in 1529 and attempted to put pressure on the pope by reducing, through parliamentary legislation led by Sir Thomas More, the legal rights of the pope in England. Clement, however, stood firm. In 1533 Thomas Cranmer, the newly appointed Archbishop of Canterbury, in a court he convened in May of that year, declared the marriage of Henry and Catherine to be invalid. Thomas Cromwell, a royal secretary, along with Cranmer, had consulted the universities of Europe on the question of the royal marriage and had found no impediment to the annulment.

In 1530 Pope Clement, free of Charles V's control, forbade Henry to remarry and also forbade further discussion of the subject. Henry replied by arranging for the English nobility to send a missive to the pope urging an annulment and predicting civil war if Henry did not father a male heir.

Henry made further moves against Rome in 1531 and 1532, curtailing the independence of the Catholic Church in England and placing ecclesiastical courts above canon law.

Cranmer was appointed Archbishop of Canterbury by Henry in 1532 after William Warham, the incumbent, died. He was consecrated the following year. Cranmer granted a dissolution to Henry's marriage on May 23, 1533. Henry had been secretly married to Anne Boleyn since January and she was pregnant with the future Queen Elizabeth I. Pope Clement excommunicated Henry, Anne and Cranmer and in 1534 gave a negative decision on the annulment.

Thomas Cromwell continued to draft anti-church legislation in 1533 and 1534. This legislation denied the pope all legal jurisdiction in England and all appeals from the church courts were to be made to the royal courts.

On November 11, 1534, Parliament voted the Act of Supremacy. This was the most significant statute of the English Reformation in that "it climaxed all that had gone before." This Act, formally accepted by Henry on December 18, did not declare him "Supreme Head of the Church" (in England) but stated that he already held that position. As Head he was authorized to supervise the conduct of the clergy and charged with the responsibility of maintaining doctrinal purity in England. Anyone denying these powers to the king was to be declared guilty of treason, punishable by death.

The validity of Henry's marriage to Anne Boleyn was further recognized by the Oath of Succession, passed by Parliament. This could be required of anyone but was especially applicable to such persons as schoolmasters, lawyers, public officials and the clergy. John Fisher, a bishop, refused to take the oath, as did Sir Thomas More. Both men, as well as a number of monks who likewise refused to accept it, were tried for treason, found guilty and executed in 1535.

Suggested Readings

Ashley, Maurice. Great Britain to 1688: A Modern History. Ann Arbor, Mich.: University of Michigan Press, 1961.

Bindoff, S. T. Tudor England. Baltimore: Penguin Books, 1950.

Bowle, John. Henry VIII. London: George Allen & Unwin, 1964.

Chambers, Robert W. Thomas More. London: Jonathan Cape, 1951.

Coulton, George G. Five Centuries of Religion. Cambridge: The University Press, 1950.

Cross, Arthur Lyon. A Shorter History of England and Greater
    Britain. New York: Macmillan, 1929.
Dickens, Arthur G. The English Reformation. New York: Schock-
    en Books, 1964.
_____. Thomas Cromwell and the English Reformation. Lon-
    don: English Universities Library, 1959.
Elton, Geoffrey Rudolph. England Under the Tudors. Edited by
    Sir Charles Oman. New York: Putnam, 1955.
Fisher, H. A. L. The History of England from the Accession of
    Henry VII to the Death of Henry VIII. London: Longmans,
    Green, 1906.
Gairdner, James H. The English Church in the Sixteenth Century,
    from the Accession of Henry VIII to the Death of Mary, 1509-
    1558. London: Macmillan, 1912.
Gee, Henry, and W. J. Hardy. Documents Illustrative of English
    Church History. London: Macmillan, 1896.
Hackett, Francis. Henry VIII. New York: Liveright, 1929.
Halliday, Frank E. A Concise History of England from Stonehenge
    to the Atomic Age. New York: Viking Press, 1964.
Hughes, Philip. A Popular History of the Reformation. Garden
    City, N. Y. : Hanover House, 1956.
_____. The Reformation in England. New York: Macmillan,
    1963.
Mackie, John Duncan. The Earlier Tudors. Edited by Sir George
    N. Clark. Oxford: Clarendon Press, 1952.
Mattingly, Garrett. Catherine of Aragon. Boston: Little, Brown,
    1941.
Pollard, A. F. Henry VIII. London: Longmans, Green, 1951.
_____. Wolsey. London: Longmans, Green, 1929.
Ridley, Jasper. Thomas Cranmer. Oxford: Clarendon Press,
    1966.
Rival, Paul. The Six Wives of Henry VIII. Translated by Leo
    Gurko. New York: Putnam, 1936.
Scarisbrick, J. J. Henry VIII. Berkeley, Calif. : University of
    California Press, 1968.
Smith, H. Maynard. Henry VIII and the Reformation. London:
    Macmillan, 1964.
Smith, Lacey B. Tudor Prelates and Politics. Princeton, N. J. :
    Princeton University Press, 1953.
Terry, Benjamin. A History of England from the Earliest Times
    to the Death of Queen Victoria. Chicago: Scott, Foresman,
    1901.
Williams, Neville. Henry VIII and His Court. New York: Mac-
    millan, 1971.
Williamson, James A. The Tudor Age. London: Longmans, Green,
    1957.

THE SUPPRESSION OF THE ENGLISH
MONASTERIES (1535-1540)

In 1534 Henry VIII, King of England, obtained from Parlia-

ment the Act of Supremacy which created a national church separate
from the Roman Catholic Church and stated that he was protector
and sole supreme head of the church and clergy of England.   This
break with the Vatican was brought about by the king's matrimonial
problems.   He wished to divorce his wife, Catherine of Aragon, the
widow of his brother Arthur, and marry Anne Boleyn.

In January of the following year he named Thomas Cromwell,
his secretary, vicar general.   Cromwell, who had boasted that he
would make Henry "the richest prince in Christendom," took immediate steps to suppress over 550 religious houses in England,
confiscating their assets and turning them over to the royal treasury.   This suppression, according to some historians, was the
result of the king's insatiable need for new sources of revenue plus
the "almost inevitable flowering of a materialistic age in which ...
monasticism could not withstand the growing power of the monarchy."

Cromwell appointed lawyers Richard Layton, Thomas Legh
and John Ap Rice to a royal commission whose function was to inspect monasteries and convents and make recommendations concerning the spiritual and material status of each.   The commission
reported its findings to Cromwell in late 1535 and early 1536.   Six
of the smaller monasteries surrendered to the crown and were suppressed.   In March, 1536, Parliament enacted legislation doing
away with all religious houses having an annual income of less than
two hundred pounds, it being argued that such small organizations
could not, for lack of adequate funds, carry out their functions satisfactorily.   It was also felt that the morals and spiritual lives of
the inmates of these small organizations were inferior to those of
the larger establishments.   By this act of Parliament about 160
monasteries and 60 convents were suppressed, the priests and nuns
involved being permitted, should they so desire, to enter larger
organizations which had not been suppressed.   As an alternative,
the dispossessed were allowed to return to the outside world, being
furnished with small pensions.   Committees of local laymen assessed the various church properties and assisted with the transfer
of the inmates.

In some cases the suppression of the monasteries met with
resistance.   A brief uprising in Lincolnshire was put down in October, 1536 and another, called the Pilgrimage of Grace, led by Robert Aske, occurred in Yorkshire.   Almost 40,000 persons were involved in this latter rebellion, which was eventually put down.   Over
200 persons, including Aske and several monks who had been involved, were tried and executed.

Having done away with the smaller houses, King Henry and
Cromwell turned their attention to the larger ones.   Rather than
resort to parliamentary edicts, they decided to try coercion.   Pressure was brought on superiors to surrender voluntarily and in most
cases the churchmen bowed to the inevitable and complied.   By
March 23, 1540, approximately 250 of the larger institutions had
been done away with in this manner, and only three houses rejected

the royal overtures.   These were the Franciscans of Greenwich, the Carthusians of London and the Bridgettine Nuns of Sion.   This defiance resulted in the executions of the leaders of the orders and the dispersing of the members.

Some 32 of the suppressed monasteries survived in other forms, such as educational centers and cathedral foundations.   Members who had been dismissed were granted pensions from the incomes of the suppressed houses, but most of this income found its way into the royal treasury.   The thousands of acres of land which had been confiscated were eventually sold or leased to private individuals.

Suggested Readings

Ashley, Maurice.   Great Britain to 1688: A Modern History.   Ann
    Arbor, Mich.: University of Michigan Press, 1961.
Baskerville, Geoffrey.   English Monks and the Suppression of the
    Monasteries.   London: Jonathan Cape, 1937.
Bindoff, S. T.   Tudor England.   Baltimore: Penguin Books, 1950.
Bowle, John.   Henry VIII.   London: George Allen & Unwin, 1964.
Coulton, George G.   Five Centuries of Religion.   Cambridge: The
    University Press, 1950.
Cross, Arthur Lyon.   A Shorter History of England and Greater
    Britain.   New York: Macmillan, 1929.
Dickens, Arthur G.   The English Reformation.   New York: Schock-
    en Books, 1964.
_____.   Thomas Cromwell and the English Reformation.   Lon-
    don: English Universities Library, 1959.
Dodds, M. H., and R. Dodds.   The Pilgrimage of Grace, 1536-7,
    and the Exeter Conspiracy, 1538.   Cambridge: The University
    Press, 1915.
Elton, Geoffrey Rudolph.   England Under the Tudors.   Edited by
    Sir Charles Oman.   New York: Putnam, 1955.
Fisher, H. A. L.   The History of England from the Accession of
    Henry VII to the Death of Henry VIII.   London: Longmans,
    Green, 1906.
Gairdner, James H.   The English Church in the Sixteenth Century,
    from the Accession of Henry VIII to the Death of Mary, 1509-
    1558.   London: Macmillan, 1912.
Gasquet, Francis, O. S. B.   Henry VIII and the English Monasteries.
    London: John Hodges, 1902.
Gee, Henry, and W. J. Hardy.   Documents Illustrative of English
    Church History.   London: Macmillan, 1896.
Hackett, Francis.   Henry VIII.   New York: Liveright, 1929.
Halliday, Frank.   A Concise History of England from Stonehenge
    to the Atomic Age.   New York: Viking Press, 1964.
Hughes, Philip.   A Popular History of the Reformation.   Garden
    City, N. Y.: Hanover House, 1956.
_____.   The Reformation in England.   New York: Macmillan,
    1963.
Knowles, David, O. S. B.   The Religious Orders of England.   Cam-
    bridge: The University Press, 1959.

Mackie, John Duncan. The Earlier Tudors. Edited by Sir George
    N. Clark. Oxford: Clarendon Press, 1952.
Pollard, A. F. Henry VIII. London: Longmans, Green, 1951.
    _____. Wolsey. London: Longmans, Green, 1929.
Savine, Alexander. English Monasteries on the Eve of Their Dis-
    solutions. Oxford: Oxford University Press, 1909.
Scarisbrick, J. J. Henry VIII. Berkeley, Calif. : University of
    California Press, 1968.
Smith, H. Maynard. Henry VIII and the Reformation. London:
    Macmillan, 1964.
Smith, Lacey B. Tudor Prelates and Politics. Princeton, N. J. :
    Princeton University Press, 1953.
Terry, Benjamin. A History of England from the Earliest Times
    to the Death of Queen Victoria. Chicago: Scott, Foresman,
    1901.
Williams, Neville. Henry VIII and His Court. New York: Mac-
    millan, 1971.
Williamson, James A. The Tudor Age. London: Longmans,
    Green, 1957.

THE COPERNICAN SYSTEM (1543)

In the second century A. D. the Greek astronomer Ptolemy
advanced his theory that the earth is the stationary center of the
universe and that the other planets revolve around it in circles or
epicycles.   The planet closest to the earth, he contended, is the
moon and beyond it, extending outward in a straight line are Mercury, Venus and the sun.   These are followed successively by Mars,
Jupiter and Saturn and the so-called "fixed stars. "

Later astronomers supplemented the Ptolemaic System, which
was generally accepted by scientists until the 16th century, when it
was abandoned for that of Nicolaus Copernicus.

Copernicus was born at Torún (then Thorn, Prussia) in 1473.
He was educated in mathematics, science, astronomy, canon law
and medicine and in 1505 traveled to Poland where he remained the
rest of his life, practicing medicine, performing his religious duties and holding various minor political offices.   He also devoted
a good deal of time to the study of astronomy.   His observations
were neither numerous nor particularly accurate and he was primarily concerned with analyzing the results of experiments performed by others.   His research demonstrated conclusively that the
astronomical evidence could be explained only on the assumptions
that first, the earth and planets are all revolving in orbits around
the sun and second, the earth is spinning on its North-South axis
from west to east, performing one revolution each 24 hours.   These
two hypotheses formed the basis of the Copernican System which
explained most of the contradictions of the centuries-old Ptolemaic
System.

Copernicus' findings were published in Nüremberg, Germany, in 1543, shortly before his death.   The author left the book untitled. Andreas Osiander, a German Lutheran minister, edited it and entitled it Six Books Concerning the Revolutions of the Heavenly Spheres (De Revolutionibus Orbium Coelestium).

Because Copernicus insisted that only circular motion of the planets was possible his system was imperfect.   However, his book inspired later scientists such as Tycho Brahe, Galileo Galilei, Johannes Kepler and Isaac Newton to work on what became the Heliocentric Theory.

From its inception the Copernican System was disputed by theologians and philosophers as well as by scientists.   Such churchmen as Philipp Melanchthon and John Calvin quoted the Bible in refutation, particularly Ecclesiastes 1:5 which reads, "the sun rises and the sun goes down." Copernicanism became identified with atheism by many students of religion.   Nevertheless, the Six Books, as a stepping stone to further inquiry, was a major breakthrough in astronomical thinking.   It is considered a work of monumental significance in man's search for scientific truth.

Suggested Readings

Armitage, Angus. Copernicus: The Founder of Modern Astronomy.
    London: G. Allen and Unwin, 1938.
_____. John Kepler. London: Faber and Faber, 1966.
_____. The World of Copernicus. New York: Mentor Books,
    1961.
Brodrick, James, S. J. Galileo, the Man, His Work, His Misfor-
    tunes. New York: Harper & Row, 1964.
Burke-Gaffney, M. W. , S. J. Kepler and the Jesuits.   Milwaukee,
    Wis. : Bruce Publishing Co. , 1944.
Butterfield, Herbert.   The Origins of Modern Science, 1300-1800.
    New York: Macmillan, 1957.
Caspar, Max. Kepler, 1571-1630.   Translated by Doris Hellman.
    New York: Collier Books, 1962.
Dreyer, John L. E. A History of Astronomy from Thales to Kepler.
    New York: Dover Publications, 1953.
Fermi, Laura, and Gilberto Bernardini. Galileo and the Scientific
    Revolution. New York: Macmillan, 1961.
Galilei, Galileo. Dialogue on the Two Great World Systems.   Trans-
    lated and edited by Giorgio de Santillana.   Chicago: University
    of Chicago Press, 1953 (Originally written 1632).
Geymonat, Ludovico. Galileo Galilei.   Translated by Stillman
    Drake. New York: McGraw-Hill, 1965.
Golino, Carlo L. , ed. Galileo and His Precursors.   Berkeley,
    Calif. : University of California Press, 1966.
_____. Galileo Reappraised.   Berkeley, Calif. : University of
    California Press, 1966.
Kesten, Hermann. Copernicus and His World.   New York: Roy
    Publishers, 1945.

Knight, David C.   Johannes Kepler and Planetary Motion.   New
    York: Franklin Watts, 1962.
Koestler, Arthur.   The Watershed.   Garden City, N. Y. :   Anchor
    Books, 1960.
Koryé, Alexandre.   From the Closed World to the Infinite Universe.
    Baltimore: Johns Hopkins University Press, 1957.
Kuhn, Thomas S.   The Copernican Revolution.   Cambridge, Mass. :
    Harvard University Press, 1957.
Langford, Jerome J.   Galileo, Science and the Church.   New York:
    Desclee Company, 1966.
Lecler, Joseph, S. J.   Toleration and the Reformation.   Translated
    by T. L. Westow.   New York: Associated Press, 1960.
Santillana, Giorgio de.   The Crime of Galileo.   Chicago: Univer-
    sity of Chicago Press, 1955.
Sarton, George.   Six Wings: Men of Science in the Renaissance.
    Bloomington, Ind. :   Indiana University Press, 1957.
Shapley, Harlow, and Helen E. Howarth.   A Source Book of As-
    tronomy.   New York: McGraw-Hill, 1929.
Taylor, F. Sherwood.   Galileo and the Freedom of Thought.   Lon-
    don: Watts and Company, 1938.
Wallis, Charles G.   Great Books of the Western World.   Chicago:
    Encyclopaedia Britannica, 1955.
White, Andrew Dickson.   A History of the Warfare of Science with
    Theology in Christendom.   New York: George Braziller, 1955.

THE COUNCIL OF TRENT (1545-1563)

Although the Roman Catholic Church was well entrenched by
the sixteenth century, it had been subjected to severe criticism by
such religious reformers as John Wycliffe, John Hus, Girolamo
Savonarola, Martin Luther and others.   Some popes, including Alexander VI and Julius II, had conducted themselves in a most unchurchly manner and it was realized that reforms within the Church were
urgently required.   As had been customary for centuries, a council
of bishops was eventually summoned to consider the Church's needs
"from every aspect. "   The idea of this council was proposed by
Charles V, Holy Roman Emperor, who hoped the Church would reinforce the measures he had decreed against the Lutherans.

In 1537 Pope Paul III appointed a committee of high ranking
churchmen to study the abuses of the Church.   Their report laid
the blame for most of these on the papacy.   It led to the Council
of Trent, the eighteenth ecumenical council of the Roman Catholic
Church which, under the pontificates of Paul III, Julius III and
Pius IV, was held, with intermissions, from 1545 to 1563.

The Council opened at Trent, in northern Italy, on December
13, 1545.   Two major issues were to be discussed: the reform
of abuses in the Church and "a restatement of Catholic doctrine in
clear distinction to Protestantism. "   Martin Luther had questioned

the worth of the books of Judith and Maccabees and the epistle of James. The members of the Council agreed on the acceptance of the Latin Vulgate as the official Bible of the Catholic Church, including the books mentioned above. They also determined that sacred tradition was to be put on a par with Scripture. The doctrine of justification was, after much discussion, laid down and Lutheran teachings were emphatically condemned. Laws regarding episcopal residence were considered at great length. It was officially declared that there are seven sacraments established by Christ, a doctrine which had been taught since the twelfth century but which had been rejected by most Protestants, with the exception of baptism and the Eucharist.

In 1547 the Council was moved to Bologna and it reassembled for the second session in Trent in 1551-1552. Here it was declared that, despite the belief of many Protestants that the presence of Christ in the Eucharist is merely symbolic, He is, in fact, "really and physically present." Decrees on the Sacraments of penance and extreme unction were also issues at this session.

Pope Pius IV summoned the third session of the Council to Trent in 1561. A decree on the mass stated that this was the same sacrifice as the sacrifice made by Christ on the cross. A decree pertaining to marriage was also put forth, and the question of episcopal residence was again considered, with a decree dealing with this being issued. It was decided to discontinue efforts to control the influence of secular rulers over church offices.

Pope Pius IV confirmed the decrees of the entire Council on January 25, 1564, which set the standard of Roman Catholic faith and practice to the present day. Since the Council of Trent the only things added have been the definition of the Infallibility of the pope and the two definitions of Immaculate Conception.

Suggested Readings

Bainton, Roland H. The Reformation of the Sixteenth Century. Boston: Beacon Press, 1956.

Burns, Edward McNall. The Counter-Reformation. Princeton, N. J.: Van Nostrand, 1964.

Cowie, Leonard W. The Reformation of the Sixteenth Century. New York: Putnam, 1970.

Denzinger, Heinrich. Enchiridion Symbolorum No. 1500-1835. 10th edition. Freiburg: 1922.

Dickens, Arthur. Reformation and Society in Sixteenth-Century Europe. New York: Harcourt, Brace, 1966.

Elliott-Binns, L. The History of the Decline and Fall of the Medieval Papacy. London: Methuen, 1934.

Fichter, Joseph H., S. J. James Laynez, Jesuit. St. Louis, Mo.: B. Herder Book Co., 1944.

Grisar, Hartmann. Martin Luther: His Life and Work. Westminster, Md.: Newman Press, 1950.

Hughes, Philip. The Church in Crisis: A History of the General
    Councils, 325-1870. Garden City, N. Y. : Hanover House, 1961.
    _____. A Popular History of the Reformation. Garden City,
    N. Y. : Hanover House, 1956.
Janelle, Pierre. The Catholic Reformation. Milwaukee, Wis. :
    Bruce Publishing Co. , 1948.
Jedin, Hubert. A History of the Council of Trent. Translated by
    Ernest Graf, O. S. B. London: Nelson, 1961.
Jones, Rufus M. Spiritual Reformers in the 16th and 17th Centur-
    ies. Boston: Beacon Press, 1959.
Kidd, B. J. The Counter-Reformation, 1550-1600. London: Society
    for Promoting Christian Knowledge, 1913.
Raab, Clement, O. F. M. The Twenty Ecumenical Councils of the
    Catholic Church. London: Longmans, Green, 1937.
Schroeder, H. J. , O. P. Disciplinary Decrees of the General Coun-
    cils: Text, Translation and Commentary. St. Louis, Mo. :
    B. Herder Book Co. , 1937.
    _____. Canons and Decrees of the Council of Trent. St. Louis,
    Mo. : B. Herder Book Co. , 1950.
Spinka, Matthew, ed. Advocates of Reform. Philadelphia: West-
    minster Press, 1953.
"Trento" in Enciclopedia Cattolica. Vatican City: 1954.

THE ARDEN MURDER (1551)

Thomas Arden, Mayor of Feversham, England, was an unscrupulous, miserly businessman. He married Alice North, sister
of Sir Thomas North, the translator of Plutarch's Lives. It is
generally thought that he chose Alice for his wife because of her
connection with a prominent family rather than for reasons of sen-
timent. His primary interest was, and continued to be, the amass-
ing of money and property and increasing his already considerable
holdings.

For several years Arden and his wife lived together, she
finding married life dull and dreary. Then she met a tailor named
Morsby whose mistress she became. What evidence has come down
to us indicates that her husband not only did not object to the illicit liaison but actually encouraged it. Possibly he may have welcomed anything that would divert his wife's thoughts from her unhappy married state to other things, leaving him more freedom to
conduct his business affairs. It is known that Arden invited Morsby to stay in his house while he was away on business, "to protect
his wife from danger. "

The tailor was quite content with this arrangement but it
did not suit Alice Arden. She did not love her husband and may
have thought that, with him out of the way, her lover would marry
her. In any event she persuaded Morsby that Arden should be killed.
Reluctantly, Morsby agreed and sought the aid of a man named Greene

who had been defrauded of some of his land by the mayor.   Greene, in turn, hired two assassins to perform the murder.

One evening in 1551 Morsby and the two hired killers came to Thomas Arden's house where he and his wife were eating supper. They stabbed and strangled him, and Morsby struck him with an iron.   The body was then dragged to a nearby field.

Unfortunately for the killers, the ground was covered with a light coating of snow.   The authorities were able to follow the footsteps and bloodstains from the body in the field to Arden's house.

Morsby, Alice, one of the assassins and two servants who had helped drag the body of the murdered man to the field were arrested.   Later, Morsby's sister, who had become implicated in the affair, was also taken into custody.

The murderers were tried and found guilty.   Alice Arden, a maidservant and the one assassin who was caught were burned alive at Canterbury on March 14, 1551.   Morsby and his sister were hanged at Smithfield and a manservant was hanged in chains at Feversham.

The Arden murder inspired the Elizabethan drama Arden of Feversham which, some authorities feel, may have been written by William Shakespeare.

Suggested Readings

Abrahamson, David, M. D.   The Murdering Mind.   New York: Harper & Row, 1973.

Bromberg, Walter.   Mold of Murder: A Psychiatric Study of Homicide.   New York: Grune & Stratton, 1961.

Catton, Joseph.   Behind the Scenes of Murder.   New York: Norton, 1940.

Guttmacher, M. S.   The Mind of the Murderer.   Freeport, N. Y. : Books for Libraries, 1960.

"The Husband Killers" in Crimes and Punishment, Vol. 6.   Editorial presentation: Jackson Morley.   London: BPC, 1973.

Jesse, F. Tennyson.   Murder and Its Motives.   London: Harrap, 1952.

Lester, David, and Gene Lester.   Crime of Passion: Murder and the Murderer.   Chicago: Nelson Hall, 1975.

McDade, Thomas M. , compiler.   The Annals of Murder.   Norman, Okla. : University of Oklahoma Press, 1961.

Marshburn, J. H.   Murder and Witchcraft in England, 1550-1640, as Recorded in Pamphlets, Ballads, Broadsides, and Plays.   Norman, Okla. : University of Oklahoma Press, 1971.

Reinhardt, James Melvin.   The Psychology of Strange Killers. Springfield, Ill. : Thomas, 1962.

Sparrow, Gerald.   Women Who Murder.   New York: Abelard, 1970.

Unknown (possibly William Shakespeare).   "Arden of Feversham"
     (play) in McIlwraith, A. K. , ed.   Five Elizabethan Tragedies.
     London: Oxford University Press, 1963 (Originally acted be-
     fore 1592; printed 1592).
Wilson, Colin, and Patricia Pitman.   Encyclopedia of Murder.   New
     York: Putnam, 1962.
Wolfgang, Marvin E. , compiler.   Studies in Homicide.   New York:
     Harper & Row, 1967.

THE DEATH OF AMY ROBSART (1560)

Whether Amy Robsart Dudley, better remembered by her
maiden name, the 28-year-old wife of Robert Dudley, later Earl of
Leicester, committed suicide, died accidentally or was murdered
by the order of Queen Elizabeth I of England, is still unresolved
after 400 years.

Dudley was an English courtier, Master of the Queen's
Horse and one of Elizabeth's favorites.   Historians have stated
that she fell in love with him "and would marry no other. "   It was
rumored that she had borne him an illegitimate child, although this
has never been substantiated.   Throughout Dudley's career, which
lasted until 1588, he remained in the Queen's good graces, except
for occasional disagreements as when, in 1563, he "offended her
with his presumptuousness. "

While Queen Elizabeth was Dudley's "good friend, " if not
more, he was otherwise generally unpopular.   A Spanish envoy
described him as "the worst young fellow I have ever encountered;
heartless, spiritless, treacherous and violent. "

On September 8, 1560, Amy Robsart had given her servants
permission to attend a village fair.   When they returned to her
home at Cummor Hall, Oxfordshire, they found her dead at the foot
of a staircase.   James Anthony Froude, the English historian, has
determined that on September 4, four days prior to Amy's death,
Elizabeth had stated to the Spanish ambassador that the girl was
dead.   Froude feels that this is definite evidence that the Queen
was an accessory to a murder.   A year previously the same ambassador had told the Spanish king that Dudley was planning to kill
his wife with poison.

News of his wife's death was sent to Dudley who was at
Windsor, thirty miles away.   Rather than go to Cummor Hall he
sent his cousin, with orders to impanel a jury "of discreet and
substantial men, to conduct an inquest. "   The jury, in due course,
determined that Dudley's wife's death was accidental.

Rumors flew through England that Elizabeth had ordered Amy
Robsart killed that she might marry her favorite.   Their nuptials

never came about and Elizabeth never married, having rejected other suitors and remaining Dudley's protector until his death.

In 1564 Dudley obtained an "excellent sinecure" for Amy's half-brother. In 1567 the half-brother stated that he had "covered up the murder for Dudley's sake. " Later he amended this to declaring only that "he had never been satisfied with the jury's verdict of accidental death. "

Various historians have done research on the question of the death of Dudley's wife. A. L. Rowse, in writing of the incident, states positively that Amy was dying of cancer of the breast when she tripped and fell downstairs. This statement is confirmed by a letter written by the Spanish ambassador eighteen months before her death. In this letter he speaks of her suffering from cancer.

There the matter rests. If the cancer story is true, it would seem logical that Dudley would have made that fact known, if only to scotch the rumors concerning his relationship with Queen Elizabeth. Amy may have accidentally tripped and fallen down the stairs. She may have, in her illness or because she felt her husband loved the Queen rather than herself, deliberately committed suicide. She may have been killed by orders of the Queen, or by her husband, with the Queen's connivance and knowledge. The record of the inquest no longer exists, and the truth, in all probability, will never be known.

Suggested Readings

Abrahamsen, David, M. D. The Murdering Mind. New York: Harper & Row, 1973.

Anthony, Katharine. Queen Elizabeth. New York: Knopf, 1929.

Ashley, Maurice. Great Britain to 1688: A Modern History. Ann Arbor, Mich.: University of Michigan Press, 1961.

Black, J. B. The Reign of Elizabeth, 1558-1603. 2nd edition. Oxford: Oxford University Press, 1959 (Originally published 1936).

"Blue Blooded Murder" in Crimes and Punishment, Vol. 5. Editorial presentation, Jackson Morley. London: BPC, 1973.

Bromberg, Walter. Mold of Murder: A Psychiatric Study of Homicide. New York: Grune & Stratton, 1961.

Catton, Joseph. Behind the Scenes of Murder. New York: Norton, 1940.

Creighton, Mandell. Queen Elizabeth. New York: Crowell, 1966.

Dark, Sidney. Queen Elizabeth. New York: Doran, 1927.

Farmer, Lydia. "Elizabeth I" in her A Book of Famous Queens. Revised by Willard A. Heaps. New York: Crowell, 1964.

Guttmacher, M. S. The Mind of the Murderer. Freeport, N. Y.: Books for Libraries, 1960.

Jenkins, Elizabeth. Elizabeth the Great. New York: Coward-McCann, 1958.

Jesse, F. Tennyson. Murder and Its Motives. London: Harrap, 1952.

Lester, David, and Gene Lester. Crime of Passion: Murder and
    the Murderer. Chicago: Nelson Hall, 1975.
Levine, Joseph M. , compiler. Elizabeth I. Englewood Cliffs,
    N. J. : Prentice-Hall, 1969.
McDade, Thomas M. , compiler. The Annals of Murder. Norman,
    Okla. : University of Oklahoma Press, 1961.
Marshburn, J. H. Murder and Witchcraft in England, 1550-1640, as
    Recorded in Pamphlets, Ballads, Broadsides, and Plays. Nor-
    man, Okla. : University of Oklahoma Press, 1971.
Neale, John E. Queen Elizabeth First: A Biography. Garden City,
    N. Y. : Doubleday, 1957.
Plowden, Alison. Young Elizabeth. New York: Stein, 1971.
Reinhardt, James Melvin. The Psychology of Strange Killers.
    Springfield, Ill. : Thomas, 1962.
Scott, Sir Walter. Kenilworth (historical fiction). New York: Dodd,
    Mead, 1956 (Originally written 1821).
Smith, Lacey B. The Elizabethan World. Boston: Houghton Miff-
    lin, 1967.
Verney, Sir Harry, ed. The Verneys of Claydon. Elmsford, N. Y. :
    Pergamon Press, 1968.
Williams, Neville. Elizabeth I, Queen of England. New York: Dut-
    ton, 1967.
Williamson, Hugh Ross. "The Death of Amy Robsart" in his His-
    torical Whodunits. New York: Macmillan, 1955.
Wilson, Colin, and Patricia Pitman. Encyclopedia of Murder. New
    York: Putnam, 1962.
Wolfgang, Marvin E. , compiler. Studies in Homicide. New York:
    Harper & Row, 1967.

THE BATTLE OF LEPANTO (1571)

The Battle of Lepanto, a naval engagement, was fought in
the Gulf of Corinth, located between Thessaly and Morea, on October 7, 1571. This battle marked the climax of the conflict between Christians and Moslems which had existed for fifteen centuries. It is considered the most decisive naval battle fought since
the Battle of Actium in 31 B. C.

The Turks had captured Constantinople in 1453 and had destroyed a number of cities as well as securing control of much of
the Mediterranean coast. Europe was disunited and Turkish sea
power, virtually unchallenged, posed a serious threat to the Christians.

Pope Pius V, Philip II of Spain and the Doge of Venice
formed an alliance to organize a fleet which would be able to destroy the Turkish armada and protect Christian Europe by defeat-
ing Islam.

The Christian fleet was commanded by Don Juan of Austria,

Philip's illegitimate half-brother.   Though only 26 years old he was
an experienced soldier and capable naval commander.   The Spanish
ships were combined with the papal fleet of Marco Antonio Colonna,
the Venetian fleet commanded by Agostino Barbarigo and the Genoese
galleys under Giovanni Andrea Doria.   Altogether Don Juan had
command of approximately 205 oar-propelled galleys.   Part of his
fleet consisted of six Venetian galleasses, so large and unwieldy
that they had to be towed into position.   The Turkish fleet, commanded by Ali Pasha, consisted of more than 250 galleys and 88,000
men.

Don Juan put to sea on September 16, 1571.   The various
admirals and captains quarreled among themselves and could not
agree on a course of action until, on October 6, word was received
that the Turks had attacked Cyprus and killed its Venetian defend-
ers.   This news unified the Christian commanders and they sailed
immediately to attack the Turkish fleet.

Ali Pasha, following the attack on Cyprus, together with his
subordinate admirals Uluch Ali and Mohomet Sirocco, anchored
their galleys near Lepanto.

On October 7 the two forces met.   Don Juan placed his galleasses in front, supporting them with 167 galleys in line abreast,
with a reserve of 38 galleys.   The Christian fleet entered the gulf
from the north, to find the Turkish fleet bearing down, with 100
ships at the center, 55 on the right and an assault force of 95 on
the left flank.   Both fleets held additional galleys in reserve.   The
Turks stopped to furl their sails and heavy fire from the galleasses
mowed their oarsmen down.

The two fleets came together, grappled, and the encounter
became one of fierce hand-to-hand fighting in the style of a land
battle rather than a naval conflict.

The fighting continued for three hours, especially on the
left wing where Agostino Barbarigo's Venetians routed the Turks.
In the center Ali Pasha made for Don Juan's flagship.   For a
while he and his men appeared to have the advantage, but this was
lost when Colonna came to the rescue.   The Turk was decapitated
and his head raised on a pike.   Genoese fighters under Giovanni
Andrea Doria were engaged with the Turkish left when Christian
reserves arrived and the Turks fled, badly beaten.   They lost over
30,000 men.

Only forty of the Turkish ships ever returned to Constantinople, over 100 being captured, the others being burned or sunk.
The Christians lost seventeen ships and 8,000 of their men were
killed.

While the Turkish fleet was not completely destroyed at the
Battle of Lepanto, Turkish sea power never again threatened the
western Mediterranean nations as it had previously.   The Christian

alliance of Spain, Italy and the papacy crumbled after the battle
but Islamic hopes for further conquest were lost and from then on
Turkish power steadily declined.

Suggested Readings

Anderson, R. C. Naval Wars in the Levant. Princeton, N. J.:
    Princeton University Press, 1925.
Bishai, Wilson B. Islamic History of the Middle East: Back-
    grounds, Development and Fall of the Arab Empire. Boston:
    Allyn, 1968.
Creasy, Edward S. Fifteen Decisive Battles of the World. Har-
    risburg, Pa.: Stackpole Books, 1957.
Falls, Cyril, ed. Great Military Battles. New York: Macmillan,
    1964.
Fuller, John F. C. A Military History of the Western World. New
    York: Funk & Wagnalls, 1954.
Mitchell, Lieut. Col. Joseph B., and Sir Edward S. Creasy. Twen-
    ty Decisive Battles of the World. New York: Macmillan, 1964.
Potter, Elmer B., and Chester W. Nimitz, eds. Sea Power: A
    Naval History. Englewood Cliffs, N. J.: Prentice-Hall, 1960.
Rodgers, William L. Naval Warfare Under Oars, Fourth to Six-
    teenth Centuries. Annapolis, Md.: U. S. Naval Institute, 1939.
Stirling, Maxwell William. Don Juan of Austria. London: Long-
    mans, Green, 1883.
Walsh, William. Philip II, King of Spain, 1527-1598. London:
    Sheed and Ward, 1937.
Warner, Oliver. Great Sea Battles. New York: Macmillan, 1963.

THE ST. BARTHOLOMEW'S EVE MASSACRE (1572)

      The Protestants of France, from about 1560 to 1629, were
known as "Huguenots," a word of uncertain origin. Protestantism
had been introduced into France between 1520 and 1523 and had
been accepted by a large number of members of the nobility, in-
telligentsia and middle classes. Originally protected by royalty,
the Huguenots eventually were persecuted by Francis I and his successor, Henry II. In spite of this persecution the Huguenots increased in number, which alarmed the French Roman Catholics and
incited their hatred.

      Catherine de' Médici, Regent of France and mother of young
Charles IX, allied herself with the Huguenots at times for political
reasons, but generally sided against them. Religious intolerance
brought about further persecution of the French Protestants and led
to reprisals by them on the Catholics. In France no fewer than
eight civil wars involving the Catholics and the Protestants were
fought between 1562 and 1598. The treaties which terminated these
wars "usually granted the Huguenots some measure of toleration,

but always after the signing of a treaty the government's attempts to repudiate or ignore its terms led to a renewal of hostilities. "

The St. Bartholomew's Eve Massacre was precipitated by the marriage of Margaret of Valois, daughter of Catherine de' Médici and Henry II of France, to Henry of Navarre, later King Henry IV. Catherine and Charles IX had, two years previously, signed a treaty with the Huguenots allowing them freedom of worship. The Huguenots had been lulled into a false sense of security. On the evening of St. Bartholomew's Day, August 24, 1572, Catherine and her son caused thousands of Huguenots to be massacred. Estimates of the number killed ranged from 2,000 to 100,000. Admiral Gaspard de Coligny, a Huguenot leader, was killed by the Duc de Guise, a leading Catholic, who sought him out. Henry Condé and Henry of Navarre reportedly saved themselves by renouncing the Protestant religion. Catherine induced her son Charles to accept sole responsibility for the massacre. The pope ordered a medal struck in commemoration of the event and sent Cardinal Orsini to convey in person his felicitations to the Queen Mother.

Suggested Readings

Baird, Henry M. The Huguenots and Henry of Navarre. New York: Scribner's, 1903.

England, Sylvia Lennie. "The Massacre of St. Bartholomew" in Corbett, Edmund V., ed. Great True Stories of Tragedy and Disaster. New York: Archer House, 1963.

Erlanger, Philippe. St. Bartholomew's Night. Translated by Patrick O'Brien. New York: Pantheon Books, 1962.

Farmer, Lydia. "Catherine de' Médici" in her A Book of Famous Queens. Revised by Willard A. Heaps. New York: Crowell, 1944.

Kingdon, Robert M. Geneva and the Consolidation of the French Protestant Movement, 1564-1572. Madison, Wis.: University of Wisconsin Press, 1967.

"Les Huguenots" (opera in five acts). Music: Giacomo Meyerbeer; libretto, Eugène Scribe and Emile Deschamps. First presented at the Académie, Paris, February 29, 1836. Condensation in Victor Talking Machine Company. The Victor Book of the Opera. Camden, N.J.: 1912---.

Neale, John E. The Age of Catherine de' Medici. London: Jonathan Cape, 1943.

Noguères, Henri. The Massacre of St. Bartholomew. Translated by Claire Elaine Engel. New York: Macmillan, 1962.

Sedgwick, Henry. Henry of Navarre. Indianapolis: Bobbs-Merrill, 1931.

Thompson, James Westfall. The Wars of Religion in France, 1559-1576. New York, Frederick Ungar, 1909.

Van Dyke, Paul. Catherine de' Médicis. New York: Scribner's 1923.

Whitehead, A.W. Gaspard de Coligny, Admiral of France. London: Methuen, 1904.

Williamson, Hugh Ross. Catherine de' Medici. New York: Viking
    Press, 1973.
Zoff, Otto. The Huguenots. New York: L. B. Fischer, 1942.

THE DEFEAT OF THE SPANISH ARMADA (1588)

The Spanish Armada was a formation of combat ships sent
by King Philip II of Spain in 1588 to attack England in a final effort to carry out a papal request to destroy the Anglican Church.
Known also as the "Invincible Armada," it consisted of 129 armed
vessels commanded by the Duke of Medina Sidonia who had been
placed in charge following the deaths of the original leaders, Don
Alvarez de Bazan, Marquis of Santa Cruz, and his vice-admiral.
Of the 129 vessels, 65 were over 700 tons and the fleet carried
8,000 sailors and 19,000 soldiers.

The Armada was opposed by the British navy, under the
command of Lord Charles Howard. Serving under him were, among
other famous sailors, Sir Francis Drake, Sir John Hawkins, Sir
Martin Frobisher and Lord Seymour. Howard's command consisted
of eighty ships, of which only thirty were ships of the line.

In spite of the huge size of the Armada, it was decisively
defeated by the smaller British fleet. This was due, in part, to
the superior maneuverability of the smaller British vessels and
the outstanding seamanship of their commanders. Drake distinguished himself in the encounter. Stationed off Ushant with one of
the three divisions of the English fleet, he defeated and pursued
the Spanish ships to the north of Scotland.

The destruction of the Spanish Armada was completed by
storms, and of the original 129 vessels, only 54 were able to return to Spanish ports. This sea battle between the British and
Spanish forces initiated the fall of Spain as a major sea power and
saved English Protestantism and independence. Sir Francis Drake
referred to it as "singeing the King of Spain's beard."

Suggested Readings

Anthony, Katharine. Queen Elizabeth. New York: Knopf, 1929.
Ashley, Maurice. Great Britain to 1688: A Modern History. Ann
    Arbor, Mich.: University of Michigan Press, 1961.
Bindoff, S. T. Tudor England. Baltimore: Penguin Books, 1950.
Black, J. B. The Reign of Elizabeth, 1558-1603. 2nd edition. Ox-
    ford: Oxford University Press, 1959 (Originally published 1936).
Creasy, Edward S. Fifteen Decisive Battles of the World. Har-
    risburg, Pa.: Stackpole Books, 1957.
Creighton, Mandell. Queen Elizabeth. New York: Crowell, 1966.

Cross, Arthur Lyon. A Shorter History of England and Greater
    Britain. New York: Macmillan, 1929.
Dark, Sidney. Queen Elizabeth. New York: Doran, 1927.
Elliott, John H. Imperial Spain, 1469-1716. New York: St. Mar-
    tin's Press, 1964.
Elton, Geoffrey Randolph. England Under the Tudors. Edited by
    Sir Charles Oman. New York: Putnam, 1955.
Falls, Cyril, ed. Great Military Battles. New York: Macmillan,
    1964.
Farmer, Lydia. "Elizabeth I" in her A Book of Famous Queens.
    Revised by Willard A. Heaps. New York: Crowell, 1964.
Feiling, Keith. A History of England. New York: McGraw-Hill,
    1948.
Fuller, John F. C. A Military History of the Western World. New
    York: Funk & Wagnalls, 1954.
Hagedorn, Hermann. "Francis Drake" in his The Book of Courage.
    Philadelphia: Winston, 1920.
Jenkins, Elizabeth. Elizabeth the Great. New York: Coward-
    McCann, 1958.
Levine, Joseph M. , compiler. Elizabeth I. Englewood Cliffs,
    N. J. : Prentice-Hall, 1969.
Lewis, Michael. Armada Guns: A Comparative Study of English
    and Spanish Armaments. London: George Allen & Unwin, 1961.
Lockyer, Roger. Tudor and Stuart Britain, 1471-1714. London:
    Longmans, Green, 1964.
Lynch, John. Spain Under the Habsburgs. Vol. I: "Empire and
    Absolutism, 1516-1598. " New York: Oxford University Press,
    1964.
McFee, William. The Life of Sir Martin Frobisher. New York:
    Harper, 1928.
Mattingly, Garrett. The Armada. Boston: Houghton Mifflin, 1959.
Mitchell, Lt. -Col. Joseph B. , and Sir Edward S. Creasy. Twenty
    Decisive Battles of the World. New York: Macmillan, 1964.
Neale, John E. Queen Elizabeth First: A Biography. Garden City,
    N. Y. : Doubleday, 1957.
Potter, Elmer B. , and Chester W. Nimitz, eds. Sea Power: A
    Naval History. Englewood Cliffs, N. J. : Prentice-Hall, 1960.
Richmond, Herbert. The Navy as an Instrument of Policy, 1558-
    1727. Cambridge: The University Press, 1953.
Smith, Lacey B. The Elizabethan World. Boston: Houghton Mif-
    flin, 1967.
Tappan, Eva March. "The Invincible Armada Is Defeated" in her
    Old World Hero Stories. Boston: Houghton Mifflin, 1937.
Terry, Benjamin. A History of England from the Earliest Times
    to the Death of Queen Victoria. Chicago: Scott, Foresman,
    1901.
Trevalyn, George Macaulay. History of England. New York: Dou-
    bleday, 1953.
Walsh, William T. Philip II, King of Spain, 1527-1598. London:
    Sheed and Ward, 1937.
Warner, Oliver. Great Sea Battles. New York: Macmillan, 1963.
Williams, Jay. Spanish Armada. New York: American Heritage
    Publishing Co. , 1966.

Williams, Neville.   Elizabeth I, Queen of England.   New York:
    Dutton, 1967.
Williamson, James A.   The Tudor Age.   London: Longmans,
    Green, 1957.
Woodroofe, Thomas.   Vantage at Sea: England's Emergence as an
    Ocean Power.   New York: St. Martin's Press, 1958.

THE EDICT OF NANTES (1598)

Henry IV, the first Bourbon king of France, brought to an
end the religious wars which had devastated his country during the
second half of the sixteenth century.   He was raised a Calvinist
and in 1562 when his father died he became King of Navarre and
titular head of the Huguenot faction.

Since 1562 a religious war had raged in France between the
Roman Catholics and the Huguenots.   Henry had attempted to put
down the Catholics, who were led by members of the Guise family
who resolved to use the resources of the Holy League to prevent
the accession of Henry as king.   Pope Sixtus V was persuaded to
excommunicate Henry and rule that no heretic could become King
of France.   Finding that his military forces were unable to conquer Paris, the chief center of League strength, Henry decided in
1593 to convert to Catholicism, having assumed the French throne
in 1589 following the death of Henry III.   This maneuver almost
destroyed the League in France and Henry occupied Paris in 1594.

In 1598 Henry was able to restore peace in France, having
been at war with Spain and the powerful Guise family.   On April
13 he issued the Edict of Nantes which confirmed Roman Catholicism
as the official religion of France but granted the Huguenots certain
rights, including freedom of worship.   The Edict contained 92 general articles, plus 56 particular "secret" articles signed on May 2,
and three "secret" briefs.   In addition to guaranteeing the Huguenots
the right to worship as they saw fit in many cities and towns it declared them eligible to hold public office and to be admitted to colleges and academies.   It permitted synods and political meetings,
gave the Huguenots tribunals in several parliaments and ceded them
about 200 towns.   They gained the right to trade freely and to inherit property.   They were exempted from arrears of taxes and
promised restitution of all property lost during the wars.   The
three "secret" briefs granted subsidies to the Huguenots of 248,000
crowns annually.

Henry IV was assassinated in 1610 by François Ravaillac, a
fanatical French schoolmaster.   Following his death the religions
and political positions of the Huguenots once more became precarious.   The Edict of Alais, issued in 1629 by Louis XIII on the advice of Cardinal Richelieu, deprived them of both their strongholds
and their political rights.   The Edict of Nantes was abrogated by

Louis XIV on October 18, 1685, depriving them of their religious liberties.

Suggested Readings

Baird, Henry M.   The Huguenots and Henry of Navarre.   New York: Scribner's, 1903.

Cowie, Leonard W.   Seventeenth Century Europe.   London: George Bell & Sons, 1960.

Guérard, Albert.   France: A Modern History.   Ann Arbor, Mich. : University of Michigan Press, 1959.

Harris, R. W.   Absolutism and Enlightenment.   London: Blandford Press, 1964.

Lecler, Joseph, S. J.   Toleration and the Reformation.   Translated by T. L. Westow.   New York: Associated Press, 1960.

Neale, John E.   The Age of Catherine de' Médici.   London: Jonathan Cape, 1943.

Ogg, David.   Europe in the Seventeenth Century.   New York: Macmillan, 1961.

Pearson, Hesketh.   Henry of Navarre.   New York: Harper & Row, 1963.

Sedgwick, Henry.   Henry of Navarre.   Indianapolis: Bobbs-Merrill, 1931.

Thompson, James Westfall.   The Wars of Religion in France, 1559-1576.   New York: Frederick Ungar, 1909.

Tilley, Arthur.   The French Wars of Religion.   London: Society for Promoting Christian Knowledge, 1919.

_____, ed.   Modern France.   2nd edition.   New York: Russell & Russell, 1967.

Wolf, John B.   Louis XIV.   New York: Norton, 1968.

Zoff, Otto.   The Huguenots.   New York: L. B. Fischer, 1942.

THE MURDER OF FRANCESCO CENCI (1598)

A sixteenth century murder which inspired several literary works (among them a tragedy by Percy Bysshe Shelley) was that of Francesco Cenci, in 1598.   The murdered man was extremely wealthy, licentious, vicious and cruel.   He had twelve children by his first wife, one of whom was Beatrice, who grew up to be a beautiful woman.   Cenci's wife died and he transferred Beatrice from his home in Rome to La Petrella, a castle near Naples.   He also remarried.

According to some accounts he had determined to have an incestuous relationship with his daughter.   Modern historians are inclined to think that the relationship did not extend that far and that he was determined only to keep her under his wing and forbid her to marry.

Abbé Guerra, a rich young noble, wished to marry Beatrice
Cenci. Her father declined to give his permission, stating to the
suitor, "She is my mistress." Guerra said to Beatrice, "He de-
serves to die," and the girl agreed with him, as did two of her
brothers, Bernardo and Giacomo. The latter arranged with Olim-
pio Calvetti, Beatrice's friend and former lover, and a hired assassin named Marzio, to kill Francesco. Marzio, infatuated with
the girl, readily agreed to be a party to the scheme.

During the night of September 9, 1598, Beatrice and her
stepmother drugged Francesco's wine with opium. He passed out
and was put to bed. Marzio and Calvetti then entered the bed-
chamber, killed him by driving spikes into his throat and brain,
then throwing the body out the window where it was caught in the
branches of a tree below.

The authorities sent a commission to investigate Francesco
Cenci's death. At first it was supposed that he had accidentally
fallen from his bedroom window while in a drunken stupor. Some
evidence of murder existed and the commissioner decided to examine the Cencis under torture. The Abbé Guerra, learning of the
intentions of the authorities, hired two more assassins to do away
with Calvetti and Marzio. Calvetti was assassinated at Terni but
Marzio was arrested. Under torture he confessed.

Beatrice, her brothers and her stepmother were arrested.
Marzio, upon seeing her, withdrew his confession. He was tortured further and died under it. The two brothers confessed under
similar circumstances but Beatrice, although subjected to the strappado, refused to talk. The four were convicted of murder and sentenced to death.

Appeals were made to Pope Clement VIII. He was on the
verge of granting a pardon but changed his mind and confirmed the
sentence. On September 11, 1599, the Cencis went to the scaffold.
A last minute reprieve saved the life of Bernardo, whose sentence
was reduced to life imprisonment. Giacomo's head was smashed
with a mace and the two women were beheaded. The Abbé Guerra
escaped. He left Italy and was never heard of again.

Suggested Readings

Abrahamson, David, M.D. The Murdering Mind. New York: Har-
    per & Row, 1973.
Artaud, Antonin. The Cenci, A Play. Translated by Simon Watson
    Taylor. New York: Grove Press, 1970.
Bertolotti, A. Francesco Cenci e la sua famiglia. Rome: 1877.
Borowitz, A.I. "The Cenci Affair," Opera News, March 17, 1973.
Bromberg, Walter. Crime and the Mind: A Psychiatric Analysis
    of Crime and Punishment. New York: Macmillan, 1965.
————. Mold of Murder: A Psychiatric Study of Homicide. New
    York: Grune & Stratton, 1961.

Catton, Joseph. Behind the Scenes of Murder. New York: Norton, 1940.

Crawford, F. Marion. "The True Story of a Misunderstood Tragedy," Century, January, 1908.

Dumas, Alexandre Davy de la Pailleterie. "The Cenci" in his Celebrated Crimes. Boston: Houghton Mifflin, 1910.

Guttmacher, M. S. The Mind of the Murderer. Freeport, N. Y.: Books for Libraries, 1960.

Jesse, F. Tennyson. Murder and Its Motives. London: Harrap, 1952.

Kirchner, Susanne. Roman Scandal: The Story of Beatrice Cenci (fiction). New York: Mason/Charter, 1976.

Larousse, M. "Beatrice Cenci; a Daughter of Tragedy," The Mentor, November, 1927.

Lester, David, and Gene Lester. Crime of Passion: Murder and the Murderer. Chicago: Nelson Hall, 1975.

"Let's Murder Father," Time, July 25, 1955.

McDade, Thomas M., compiler. The Annals of Murder. Norman, Okla.: University of Oklahoma Press, 1961.

Moravia, Alberto, pseud. Beatrice Cenci (play). Translated by Augustus Davidson. New York: Farrar, Straus, 1966.

"Parent Killers" in Crimes and Punishment, Vol. 7. Editorial presentation: Jackson Morley. London: BPC, 1973.

Prokosch, Frederick. Tale for Midnight (fiction). Boston: Little, Brown, 1955.

Reinhardt, James Melvin. The Psychology of Strange Killers. Springfield, Ill.: Thomas, 1962.

Ricci, Corrado. Beatrice Cenci. Translated by Morris Bishop and Henry Logan Stuart. New York: Liveright, 1933.

Shelley, Percy Bysshe. "The Cenci" (play) in Tatlock, John S. P. and Robert G. Martin, eds. Representative English Plays from the Middle Ages to the End of the Nineteenth Century. New York: Century, 1916 (Originally published 1819).

Simeon, S. L. "Death of the Cenci in Rome," Nineteenth Century and After, December, 1917.

Sparrow, Gerald. Women Who Murder. New York: Abelard, 1970.

Wilson, Colin, and Patricia Pitman. Encyclopedia of Murder. New York: Putnam, 1962.

Wolfgang, Marvin E., compiler. Studies in Homicide. New York: Harper & Row, 1967.

THE FALSE DIMITRY (1603-1606)

Russia had become an absolute monarchy during the reign of Ivan Vasilyevich (Ivan IV) (Ivan the Terrible) who reigned from 1533 until 1584. As a boy he had been neglected and pushed aside and he conceived an undying hatred of the boyars, the powerful aristocratic landed nobles. He waged political war against them and by the use of his powerful secret police which had unlimited power of life and death over his subjects ended the boyars' pretensions of independent political power in Russia.

Ivan the Terrible was a violent, unstable, mentally unbalanced man. In 1581 he killed his eldest son Ivan in a fit of rage. Feodor Ivanovich, his eldest surviving son, a physical and mental weakling, became tsar when his father died in 1584. The new tsar was dominated by various power-seeking boyars who hoped to obtain the Russian throne for themselves. In September, 1598, Boris Godunov, regent during Feodor's reign and brother of Irene, Feodor's wife, became tsar in his own right despite the opposition of the boyars and the leaders of the Russian Orthodox Church.

When famine caused widespread disorders throughout the kingdom in 1601-1603, the boyars began to consider means by which Boris could be removed from the throne. The situation was further complicated by Boris' realization that friends and relatives of the tsarina, mother of Dimitry Ivanovich, youngest son of Ivan the Terrible, would attempt to place him on the throne following the death of Feodor. Some years before Boris had sent Dimitry, his mother and certain relatives to the convent of Uglich on the Volga River. There, in 1591, nine-year-old Dimitry died under circumstances which have never been explained. His death may have been self-inflicted, although many people believed that he had been killed on Boris' order.

In 1603 the "False Dimitry" appeared. A young adventurer, apparently a runaway monk named Grigori Otrepyev, declared himself the tsarevitch Dimitry. He found asylum in Poland and received the backing of King Sigismund of that country. He knew a great deal about the background of the tsarevitch he purported to be and some historians feel that he actually believed himself to be the son of Ivan the Terrible and also Feodor's half-brother. He married the daughter of a Polish nobleman and became a member of the Roman Catholic Church.

In October, 1604, the False Dimitry led an "army" of fewer than 4,000 Polish runaway peasants and freebooting nobles to Russia where he gained the support of the cossacks, peasants and disaffected small landowners. Boris Godunov died suddenly in 1605 and his supporters were murdered. Vasily Shuisky, a boyar who had conducted an investigation into the 1591 death of the tsarevitch and who was later to become tsar himself, declared that the new arrival was indeed Dimitry.

Shuisky and the other boyars refused to swear allegiance to Boris' son and Shuisky personally administered the oath to the False Dimitry. Russia, desperate for a ruler, accepted him.

Once installed as tsar, the False Dimitry's support literally evaporated. As a Roman Catholic he offended the adherents to the Russian Orthodox Church. He was considered too frivolous and worldly by the Muscovites who felt that the gay parties and balls which he attended were unbecoming to the tsar of Russia. Shuisky and the other boyars who had supported him as tsar, hoping to use him as a tool to further their own interests, found in him a man of independence and strong will who refused to be their cat's paw.

Further, it was feared that he might put the interests of his friend, King Sigismund of Poland, ahead of those of Russia.

Shuisky and his accomplices arranged for the murder of the False Dimitry on May 17, 1606.   Following the murder, Shuisky assumed the title of tsar, remaining in precarious control for four years.   A second pretender, called Dimitry II, the "Thief of Tushino," also claimed to be the murdered tsarevitch.   Shuisky and his adherents appealed to Sweden for help and Dimitry II and his followers were driven away.   In 1610 Shuisky was deposed by the boyars and forced to enter a monastery.

Suggested Readings

Almedingen, Martha Edith von.   The Romanovs: Three Centuries of an Ill-Fated Dynasty.   New York: Holt, 1966.

Barbour, Philip L.   Dimitry, Called the Pretender, Tsar and Great Prince of All Russia, 1605-1606.   London: Macmillan, 1967.

"Boris Godounow" (opera in three acts).   Music: Modeste Moussorgsky; text arranged by Moussorgsky, based on an historical drama by Alexander Pushkin.   First presented in its entirety January 24, 1874.   Condensation in The Victor Book of the Opera.   Camden, N. J. :   Victor Talking Machine Co. , 1912--.

Charques, Richard Denis.   A Short History of Russia.   New York: Dutton, 1956.

Cherniavsky, Michael.   Tsar and Empire: Studies in Russian Myths. New York: Random House, 1969.

Clarkson, Jesse D.   A History of Russia.   New York: Random House, 1969.

Florinsky, Midhael T.   Russia: A History and Interpretation.   New York: Macmillan, 1965.

Graham, Stephen.   Ivan the Terrible: The Life of Ivan IV of Russia. New Haven, Conn. :   Yale University Press, 1933.

Hingley, Ronald.   Tsars, 1533-1917.   New York: Macmillan, 1968.

Howe, Sonia E.   The False Dimitry, a Russian Romance and Tragedy Described by British Eye-Witnesses.   New York: Stokes, 1916.

Moscow, Henry, and the editors of Horizon Magazine.   Russia Under the Czars.   New York: American Heritage Pub. Co. , 1962.

Pushkin, Alexander.   Boris Godunov (historical drama).   Russian text with Translation and Notes by Philip L. Barbour.   New York: Columbia University Press, 1953 (Completed 1825, originally published 1831).

Riasanovsky, Nicholas Valentine.   A History of Russia.   New York: Oxford University Press, 1963.

Vernadsky, George.   A History of Russia.   New Haven, Conn. : Yale University Press, 1954.

THE GUNPOWDER PLOT 91605-1606)

King James I of England had inaugurated a number of anti-

Catholic laws which made him exceedingly unpopular with the Roman Catholics of his day. A group of prominent Catholics, led by Robert Catesby, conspired to blow up the king, the House of Lords and the House of Commons at the opening of Parliament as a protest against these laws.

Catesby recruited his cousin Robert Winter and his friend John Wright, both fellow Catholics. Then Thomas Bates, Thomas Percy, Robert Keyes, Francis Tresham, John Grant, Ambrose Rokewood and Robert Winter's brother Thomas were added. Finally Guy Fawkes, an English Protestant soldier and adventurer who had been converted to Catholicism, became a member of the group.

Thirty-six barrels of gunpowder were stored in a vault or cellar directly beneath the House of Lords. This vault had been rented by the conspirators. November 5, 1605, was the date on which the gunpowder was to be set off. Fawkes was to ignite it and then flee to Flanders. The plot, however, was exposed. Fawkes was apprehended as he came from the vault. He was carrying fuses on his person. In the vault were found a lighted lantern and the barrels of gunpowder.

Fawkes was arrested. At first he claimed to be "John Johnson, servant of Mr. Percy," but under severe torture he identified himself correctly, confessed his guilt and named his accomplices. Nearly all of these were killed upon being taken or executed, along with Fawkes, on January 31, 1606.

Guy Fawkes Day is now remembered in England and other parts of the British Empire by an annual celebration on November 5. Fireworks are set off and bonfires are lit to commemorate the discovery of the plot. At one time it was also customary to burn Fawkes in effigy.

Suggested Readings

Ainsworth, William Harrison. Pictorial Life and Adventures of Guy Fawkes. Philadelphia: T. B. Peterson & Brothers, 184?

Anonymous. Guy Fawkes: A Legend of the Tower of London. London: John Williams, 1840.

Ashley, Maurice. Great Britain to 1688: A Modern History. Ann Arbor, Mich. : University of Michigan Press, 1961.

Barlow, Thomas. The Gunpowder-Treason with a Discourse of the Manner of Its Discovery. London: T. Newcomb and H. Hills, 1679.

Brandt, Aymar, and Edward Sagarin. "Guy Fawkes" in their A Pictorial History of the World's Great Trials. New York: Crown Publishing Co. , 1967.

Carswell, Donald, ed. The Trial of Guy Fawkes and Others (The Gunpowder Plot). London: W. Hodge & Co. , 1934.

Cross, Arthur Lyon. A Shorter History of England and Greater Britain. New York: Macmillan, 1929.

Gardiner, Samuel Rawson. History of England from the Accession of James I to the Outbreak of the Civil War. London: Longmans, Green, 1884.

Garnett, Henry. Portrait of Guy Fawkes. London: R. Hale, 1962.

"Guy Fawkes" in Crimes and Punishment, Vol. 5. Editorial presentation: Jackson Morley. London: BPC, 1973.

Halliday, Frank. A Concise History of England from Stonehenge to the Atomic Age. New York: Viking Press, 1964.

Jardine, David. The Gunpowder Plot. London: C. Knight, 1835.

Langdon-Davies, John. The Gunpowder Plot. New York: Grossman, 1964.

Parsons, Geoffrey. The Stream of History. New York: Scribner's, 1929.

Spink, Henry H. The Gunpowder Plot and Lord Mounteagle's Letter. London: Simpkin, Marshall & Co., 1902.

Terry, Benjamin. A History of England from the Earliest Times to the Death of Queen Victoria. Chicago: Scott, Foresman, 1901.

Williamson, Hugh Ross. "The Gunpowder Plot" in his Historical Whodunits. New York: Macmillan, 1955.

JOHANNES KEPLER AND HIS LAWS OF
PLANETARY MOTION (1609 and 1619)

Nicolaus Copernicus published his De Revolutionibus Orbium Coelestium in 1543. This put forth the theory that the earth rotates daily on its axis and that planets revolve in orbits around the sun. His hypotheses were challenged by theologians on the grounds that they were contrary to the teachings of the Bible and by astronomers and mathematicians because many of his calculations were at variance with observation. One of the astronomers who rejected the Copernican system was Tycho Brahe, a Dane.

Brahe's theory was a compromise between the older Ptolemaic hypothesis and that of Copernicus. He conceded that planets revolve around the sun rather than the earth but considered the earth the stationary center of the universe around which the sun and its satellite planets revolved.

Johannes Kepler, a German astronomer who had been influenced by the teachings of Copernicus and who had held the chair of astronomy and mathematics at the University of Graz from 1594 until 1600, became Brahe's assistant at the latter's observatory near Prague in 1601. Brahe died later in the same year and Kepler was appointed his successor as mathematician and court astronomer to Rudolf II, the Holy Roman Emperor. In 1612 he became mathematician to the states of Upper Austria and in 1627 he moved to Ulm. There he completed and published the Rudolphine Tables, a set of astronomical tables started by Brahe. He also edited astrological almanacs and made contributions to the field of optics as well as developing a system of mathematics which was the forerunner of the calculus.

A prolific writer in his field, Kepler's best known publication is Astronomia Nova de Motibus Stelloe Martis ex Observationibus Tychonis Brahe, called, in shortened form, The New Astronomy. This was financed by Rudolf II and completed in 1609. In this work Kepler enumerated the first two of his three laws of the motion of planets, the third being announced in his Harmonice Mundi (The Harmony of the World) in 1619. These laws are: 1) Planets travel in elliptical paths around the sun, the sun being one of the foci. 2) The areas described in a planetary orbit by the straight line joining the center of the planet and the center of the sun are equal for equal time intervals. That is, the closer a planet comes to the sun the more rapidly it moves. 3) The squares of the times required for different planets to describe a complete orbit are proportional to the cubes of their mean distances from the sun.

Kepler's other mathematical accomplishments include confirming some of the theories of Galileo Galilei, the Italian astronomer and physicist, and forecasting transits, such as that of Venus across the sun. In 1628 he became mathematician to Albrecht Wallenstein, the Austrian general officer. He died in 1630.

Suggested Readings

Armitage, Angus. Copernicus: The Founder of Modern Astronomy. London: G. Allen and Unwin, 1938.
_____. John Kepler. London: Faber and Faber, 1966.
_____. The World of Copernicus. New York: Mentor Books, 1961.
Brodrick, James, S. J. Galileo, the Man, His Work, His Misfortunes, New York: Harper & Row, 1964.
Burke-Gaffney, M. W. , S. J. Kepler and the Jesuits. Milwaukee, Wis.: Bruce Publishing Co. , 1944.
Butterfield, Herbert. The Origins of Modern Science, 1300-1800. New York: Macmillan, 1957.
Caspar, Max. Kepler, 1571-1630. Translated by C. Doris Hellman. New York: Collier Books, 1962.
Dreyer, John L. E. A History of Astronomy from Thales to Kepler. New York: Dover Publications, 1953.
Fermi, Laura, and Gilberto Bernardini. Galileo and the Scientific Revolution. New York: Macmillan, 1961.
Galilei, Galileo. Dialogue on the Two Great World Systems. Translated and edited by Giorgio de Santillana. Chicago: University of Chicago Press, 1953 (Originally written 1632).
Geymonat, Ludovico. Galileo Galilei. Translated by Stillman Drake. New York: McGraw-Hill, 1965.
Golino, Carlo L. , ed. Galileo and His Precursors. Berkeley, Calif.: University of California Press, 1966.
_____. Galileo Reappraised. Berkeley, Calif.: University of California Press, 1966.

Kesten, Hermann. Copernicus and His World. New York: Roy
    Publishers, 1945.
Knight, David C. Johannes Kepler and Planetary Motion. New
    York: Franklin Watts, 1962.
Koestler, Arthur. The Watershed. Garden City, N. Y. : Anchor
    Books, 1960.
Koryé, Alexandre. From the Closed World to the Infinite Universe.
    Baltimore: Johns Hopkins University Press, 1957.
Kuhn, Thomas S. The Copernican Revolution. Cambridge, Mass. :
    Harvard University Press, 1957.
Langford, Jerome J. Galileo, Science and the Church. New York:
    Desclee Company, 1966.
Lecler, Joseph, S. J. Toleration and the Reformation. Translated
    by T. L. Westow. New York: Associated Press, 1960.
Pauli, W. "The Influence of Archetypal Ideas of the Scientific Theo-
    ries of Kepler" in Silz, Priscilla, translator. The Interpreta-
    tion of Nature and Psyche. New York: Pantheon Books, 1955.
Santillana, Giorgio de. The Crime of Galileo. Chicago: Univer-
    sity of Chicago Press, 1955.
Sarton, George. Six Wings: Men of Science in the Renaissance.
    Bloomington, Ind. : Indiana University Press, 1957.
Shapley, Harlow, and Helen E. Howarth. A Source Book of As-
    tronomy. New York: McGraw-Hill, 1929.
Taylor, F. Sherwood. Galileo and the Freedom of Thought. Lon-
    don: Watts and Company, 1938.
Wallis, Charles G. Great Books of the Western World. Chicago:
    Encyclopaedia Britannica, 1955.
White, Andrew Dickson. A History of the Warfare of Science with
    Theology in Christendom. New York: George Braziller, 1955.

THE OVERBURY POISONING (1613)

Robert Carr (or Kerr), a handsome young Scotchman, attracted the attention of James I of England and became the King's
court favorite. He was made Viscount Rochester and later Earl
of Somerset. Little is known of his early background but his relationship with King James was undoubtedly homosexual.

Sir Thomas Overbury, secretary to the King, became an
associate of Rochester, both men seeking to maximize their positions by pandering to James's vices. Rochester contracted an adul-
terous intrigue with Lady Frances Howard, wife of the Earl of Essex, and Overbury assisted him in the affair. According to historians, Lady Frances was "a person of violent passions, and lost to
all sense of shame. " Her husband was in her way and she brought
suit for divorce on embarrassingly shameful grounds. The divorce
was granted and she immediately proceeded with her plans to marry
Rochester. Overbury felt that a marriage by Rochester would dis-
please King James and retard further advancement for both of them.
He attempted to dissuade Rochester from the marriage but succeeded
only in angering him.

Lady Frances was advised of Overbury's stand in the matter and she, like Rochester, became his enemy. Rochester arranged for Overbury to decline a diplomatic appointment, upon which King James ordered him confined in the Tower of London.

Rochester then managed to have Sir Jervis Elwes, one of his followers, appointed Lieutenant of the Tower, and another follower, Richard Weston, made under-keeper. Pretending to feel sympathy for Overbury, Rochester wrote him friendly letters and, as did Lady Frances, sent presents of food, "pastries and other delicacies," which had been poisoned. These poisons were procured by a former brothel keeper named Mrs. Turner and prepared by a Dr. Forman and an apothecary named Franklin.

The poisons, including blue vitriol, cantharides, mercury and arsenic, were so prepared that they worked slowly. Overbury stubbornly refused to die and finally Lady Frances ordered him killed immediately. Weston administered a fatal dose of corrosive sublimate in October, 1613, after Overbury had been confined for more than six months. Immediately after his death his body was buried without ceremony in a pit in the cellar of the Tower.

Shortly after the fatal poisoning Rochester and Lady Frances were married, with King James present at the ceremony. Rochester stood high in the King's favor but this did not remain the case for long. Rumors that Overbury had been murdered spread and George Villiers, Duke of Buckingham, had come to the King's attention and was soon to replace Rochester as the royal favorite. Buckingham encouraged Overbury's relatives to prosecute their inquiries into his strange death.

Sir Jervis Elwes, Weston, Franklin and Mrs. Turner were arrested and eventually Lady Frances and Rochester (by this time the Countess and Earl of Somerset) were confined, all by order of the King. Late in 1615 Weston, Elwes, Franklin and Mrs. Turner were tried, found guilty of poisoning, and executed. The Earl and Countess of Somerset were tried in May of the following year. Sir Francis Bacon prosecuted the case against them. The Countess pleaded guilty and was sentenced to death. The Earl, tried separately, pleaded not guilty but was convicted and, like his wife, received the death penalty. King James, however, was afraid to sign their death warrants, fearing that their dying speeches would compromise him. The Earl and the Countess were sent to the Tower where they remained for nearly five years, and were then granted royal pardons. Although the Earl's estates had been confiscated, King James granted him an income of four thousand pounds per year.

Suggested Readings

Abrahamsen, David, M. D. The Murdering Mind. New York: Harper & Row, 1973.

Anderson, Fulton H. Francis Bacon. Los Angeles: University of
    Southern California Press, 1962.
"Blue Blooded Murder" in Crimes and Punishment, Vol. 5. Ed-
    itorial presentation: Jackson Morley. London: BPC, 1973.
Bromberg, Walter. Mold of Murder: A Psychiatric Study of Hom-
    icide. New York: Grune & Stratton, 1961.
Catton, Joseph. Behind the Scenes of Murder. New York: Nor-
    ton, 1940.
Gardiner, Samuel Rawson. History of England from the Accession
    of James I to the Outbreak of the Civil War. London: Long-
    mans, Green, 1884.
Guttmacher, M. S. The Mind of the Murderer. Freeport, N. Y. :
    Books for Libraries, 1960.
Jesse, F. Tennyson. Murder and Its Motives. London: Harrap,
    1952.
Lester, David, and Gene Lester. Crime of Passion: Murder and
    the Murderer. Chicago: Nelson Hall, 1975.
McDade, Thomas M. , compiler. The Annals of Murder. Norman,
    Okla. : University of Oklahoma Press, 1961.
McElwee, William Lloyd. The Murder of Sir Thomas Overbury.
    New York: Oxford University Press, 1952.
Mackay, Charles. "The Slow Poisoners" in his Memoirs of Extra-
    ordinary Popular Delusions and the Madness of Crowds. Lon-
    don: Office of the National Illustrated Library, 1852. Re-
    printed by L. C. Page & Co. , Boston, 1932.
Patrick, John M. Francis Bacon. London: Longmans, Green, 1961.
Reinhardt, James Melvin. The Psychology of Strange Killers.
    Springfield, Ill. : Thomas, 1962.
Williamson, Hugh Ross. George Villiers, First Duke of Bucking-
    ham. London: Duckworth, 1940.
_____. "The Murder of Sir Thomas Overbury" in his Historical
    Whodunits. New York: Macmillan, 1955.
Wilson, Colin, and Patricia Pitman. Encyclopedia of Murder. New
    York: Putnam, 1962.
Wolfgang, Marvin E. , compiler. Studies in Homicide. New York:
    Harper & Row, 1967.

THE INVENTION OF LOGARITHMS (1614)

One of the greatest mathematical inventions of all time was
the logarithm, conceived by John Napier, a Scottish mathematician.
Described in his book Canonis Descriptio (1614), the logarithm
simplified the arithmetic processes of multiplication, division, expansion to powers and extraction of roots.

Napier's system of logarithms is based upon the correspondence of a geometrical and arithmetical series of numbers. The
common and natural systems of logarithms now used do not employ
the same base that Napier used, although natural logarithms are
sometimes referred to as Napierian logarithms.

In 1615 Henry Briggs, an English mathematician and then professor of geometry at Gresham College, having developed a simplification of Napier's original logarithms, traveled to Edinburgh to discuss them with their inventor in person. Following his visit he set about calculating the logarithms of numbers to the base of ten. The first table of such logarithms, including values for 30,000 numbers and accurate to 14 significant digits, was published in 1624, although Justus Byrgius, a Swiss mathematician, put out a table of logarithms in 1620. The logarithm using the base of ten is now called "common" or "Briggsian."

The concept of logarithms may be illustrated by considering a series of powers of the number 2: 2^1, 2^2, 2^3, 2^4, 2^5, and 2^6. These correspond to the series 2, 4, 8, 16, 32, and 64. The exponents 1, 2, 3, 4, 5 and 6 are considered the logarithms of these numbers to the base 2. Thus, when it is desired to multiply any two numbers in the series it is necessary only to add the exponents of both numbers and then locate, in the tables, the antilogarithm, i.e., the number corresponding to the sum. For example, if one wished to multiply 8 (2^3) by 4 (2^2) the logarithm of 8 being 3 and the logarithm of 4 being 2, he merely adds 3 and 2. The sum, 5, is the antilogarithm of 32, the product sought.

In dividing by using logarithms, one is subtracted from another. Thirty-two may be divided by 8 by subtracting the exponent of 8, which is 3, from that of 32, which is 5, resulting in a difference of 2. This is the logarithm of the quotient 4.

To expand a number to any power, it is necessary only to multiply its logarithm by the power desired and then find (in the tables) the antilogarithm of the product. For example, to find 4^3: log (logarithm) 4 = 2; 3 X 2 = 6; antilogarithm (antilog) 6 = 64, which is the third power of 4.

A root may be extracted by dividing the logarithm by the desired root. To find $\sqrt[5]{32}$: log 32 = 5; 5÷5 = 1; the antilog of 1 = 2, which is the 5th root of 32.

Other mathematical problems may be solved by the use of logarithms.

In addition to inventing logarithms, Napier is credited with being the first to use the decimal point to express decimal fractions scientifically. He invented a mechanical device known as "Napier's bones" which applied the logarithmic principle and was the forerunner of the modern slide rule or "slip stick."

In addition to compiling the tables of logarithms mentioned above, Briggs published Arithmetica Logarithmica (1624) and Trigonometria Britannica, the latter being completed by Henry Gellibrand, the English mathematician and astronomer, following Briggs' death in 1631.

Suggested Readings

Barker, Stephen F. Philosophy of Mathematics. Englewood Cliffs,
    N. J. : Prentice-Hall, 1964.
Bell, E. T. The Development of Mathematics. New York: McGraw-
    Hill, 1940.
_____. Men of Mathematics. New York: Simon & Schuster,
    1937.
Boyer, C. B. The Concepts of the Calculus. New York: Colum-
    bia University Press, 1939.
Boyer, Lee Emerson. "Logarithms" in his An Introduction to Math-
    ematics: An Historical Development. Revised edition. New
    York: Holt, 1955.
Cajori, Florian. A History of Mathematics. New York: Macmil-
    lan, 1922.
Claggett, Marshall. Archimedes in the Middle Ages. Madison,
    Wis. : University of Wisconsin Press, 1964.
Courant, Richard. Differential and Integral Calculus. Translated
    by E. J. McShane. New York: Nordemann, 1940.
_____, and Herbert Robbins. "The Calculus" in their What Is
    Mathematics? London: Oxford University Press, 1941.
Hardy, G. H. A Course in Pure Mathematics. Cambridge: The
    University Press, 1938.
Heath, Sir Thomas L. A History of Greek Mathematics. Oxford:
    Clarendon Press, 1960.
Merrill, Arthur A. How Do You Use a Slide Rule? New York:
    Dover, 1961.
Scott, Joseph F. A History of Mathematics. London: Taylor and
    Francis, 1960.
Selby, Peter H. Logarithms Self-Taught. New York: McGraw-
    Hill, 1964.
Smith, David Eugene. A History of Mathematics. Boston: Ginn,
    1923.
Snodgrass, Burns. Teach Yourself the Slide Rule. New York:
    Dover, 1955.

THE PUBLICATION OF FRANCIS BACON'S
NOVUM ORGANUM (1620)

Francis Bacon, 1st Baron Verulam and Viscount St. Albans,
was a British philosopher, statesman, essayist and author. He is
remembered for his Essays, History of Henry VII, Advancement of
Learning and certain legal writings, but his Novum Organum (The
New Logic), published in 1620, is considered his masterpiece.
Written in Latin, this work was called by Thomas Babington Macaul-
ay, "Bacon's greatest performance. " It was dedicated to James I,
King of England, who dismissed it, saying that it was beyond his
comprehension. William Harvey, the court physician, remarked that
"Bacon writes philosophy like a lord chancellor. "

The Novum Organum was intended to form the second book
of a greater treatise, Instauratio Magna, a review of encyclopedias
of all knowledge, which was to appear in six parts, but was never
completed.   The Novum Organum was concerned with Bacon's "doctrine of idols," a term he used "as a picture taken from reality;
a thought mistaken for a thing." Errors (prejudices, preconceived
attitudes and the like) come under this head and Bacon felt that "the
first problem of logic is to trace and dam the sources of these errors." He enumerated them as, first, "Idols of the tribe"--falla-
cies natural to humanity in general.   Then came "Idols of the cave"
--errors peculiar to the individual man. Thirdly, "Idols of the
market place," "arising from the commerce and association of men
with one another." Finally he designated "Idols of the theater,"
which come from tradition.   These are "Idols which have migrated
into men's minds from the various dogmas of philosophers, and
also from wrong laws of demonstration ... all the received systems of philosophy are but so many stage plays representing worlds
of their own creation after an unreal and scenic fashion."

Bacon's belief, laid down in his masterpiece, was that the
traditional philosophy of Aristotle, as well as such other ancient
thinkers as Plato, was false and misleading.   He believed that
"man is the servant and interpreter of nature, that truth is not
derived from authority, and that knowledge is the fruit of experience." He challenged Aristotle's induction by simple enumeration,
i. e., drawing general conclusions from a number of particular data.   His method was "to infer by use of analogy, from the characteristics or properties of a single datum, the characteristics or
properties of the larger group to which that datum belonged." He
felt that later experience would make it possible to correct evident
errors.

While Bacon professed respect for the ancient Greek scientists and philosophers he felt that the classic age of Greek philosophy, from Socrates on, "marked a regression from true knowledge, as men became more turned in upon themselves and ignored
nature." Men following the precepts of the ancients, he contended,
were fitted only to deal with words and subtle theories while the
actual content of human knowledge had made very little progress.

Bacon felt that theology should be kept separate from philosophy, as "the truths of religion are indisputable and rational inquiry cannot unlock the secrets of God but only the secrets of nature."

The fourth part of Novum Organum is concerned with descrip-
tions of certain experiments Bacon had performed and with the analysis of axioms which might be derived from experiment.   The
book did much toward imbuing science with a spirit of unbiased
and accurate observation and experimentation.   It exerted great
influence on such philosophers and scientists as René Descartes
who came after him.

Suggested Readings

Anderson, Fulton H. Francis Bacon. Los Angeles: University of
    Southern California Press, 1962.
_____. The Philosophy of Francis Bacon. Chicago: University
    of Chicago Press, 1948.
Bacon, Francis. "Preface to Novum Organum" in Eliot, Charles
    W., ed. The Harvard Classics. New York: Collier, 1909
    (Originally written 1620).
_____. Selected Writings. With an introduction and notes by
    Hugh G. Dick. New York: Modern Library, 1955 (Originally
    written early 17th century).
Bochenski, Innocenty M. A History of Formal Logic. Notre Dame,
    Ind. : Notre Dame University Press, 1961.
Boole, George. An Investigation of the Laws of Thought. Glou-
    cester, Mass. : Peter Smith, 1966 (Originally published 1854).
Chase, Stuart. Guides to Straight Thinking: With Thirteen Com-
    mon Fallacies. New York: Harper, 1956.
Cohen, Morris R. , and Ernest Nagel. Logic and the Scientific
    Method. New York: Harcourt, Brace, 1934.
Crowther, James G. Francis Bacon, the First Statesman of Sci-
    ence. London: Casset Press, 1960.
Descartes, René. The Discourse on Method. Edited by Laurence
    J. Lafleur. New York: Liberal Arts Press, Bobbs-Merrill,
    1956 (Originally written 1637).
Durant, Will. "Francis Bacon" in his The Story of Philosophy.
    Garden City, N. Y. : Garden City Publishing Co. , 1926.
Eiseley, Loren. Francis Bacon and the Modern Dilemma. Lincoln,
    Neb. : University of Nebraska Press, 1962.
Elliott, John W. Writings of Sir Francis Bacon. New York: Mon-
    arch, 1966.
Enriques, F. The Historic Development of Logic. Translated by
    J. Rosenthal. New York: Holt, 1929.
Farrington, Benjamin. Francis Bacon: Philosopher of Industrial
    Science. London: Lawrence and Wishart, 1951.
_____. The Philosophy of Francis Bacon. Liverpool: Univer-
    sity Press of Liverpool, 1961.
Ferguson, John. Aristotle. New York: Twayne, 1972.
Green, Adwin Wigfall. Sir Francis Bacon. New York: Twayne,
    1966.
Lloyd, G. E. R. Aristotle: The Growth and Structure of His Thought.
    Cambridge: The University Press, 1968.
Lukasiewicz, Jan. Aristotle's Syllogistic from the Standpoint of
    Modern Formal Logic. Oxford: The University Press, 1957.
Patrick, John M. Francis Bacon. London: Longmans, Green,
    1961.
Tarski, Alfred. Introduction to Logic and to the Methodology of
    Deductive Sciences. Oxford: Oxford University Press, 1965.

THE FALL OF CHARLES I (1625-1649)

When Charles I ascended the English throne in 1625 following the death of his father, James I, the financial affairs of the country were in a state of chaos. Charles, who believed in the "divine right of kings," desperately needed funds and attempted to get them by any means he could.

Speculators had built houses on the outskirts of London. Charles ordered these torn down unless the builders paid three years' rent into the royal treasury. He revived the Star Chamber, founded originally by Henry VII over a century earlier. This was essentially a royal court, presided over by judges sympathetic to the king, who imposed gigantic fines, often for comparatively trivial offenses or on trumped-up charges.

Charles appointed George Villiers, Duke of Buckingham, an incompetent soldier and former favorite of his father, a general in his army. Buckingham's military campaigns resulted in disaster, and in 1628 he was assassinated by John Felton, a Puritan fanatic, after having been saved from impeachment by the intervention of the king.

Charles then decided to rule without Parliament, which he did from 1629 until 1640. At the urging of Archbishop William Laud he attempted to require the Scots to use the English Prayer Book, thus precipitating a revolt. It was necessary for him to recall Parliament in order to get money to establish an army. Parliament declined to vote the necessary funds and Charles dissolved it again, only to reassemble it once more after the Scots had invaded England.

Thomas Wentworth, Earl of Strafford, became the king's favorite. At first an opponent of Charles' policies, he changed sides and became the king's supporter and adviser. An enemy of Parliament and all that it represented, he was arrested, imprisoned in the Tower of London, tried under a bill of attainder, convicted of plotting to coerce Parliament and beheaded on Tower Hill in 1641. Charles reluctantly signed the death warrant.

Parliament then outlawed the Star Chamber and declared many of Charles' methods for raising money illegal. Archbishop Laud was arrested, tried, convicted of high treason and beheaded in 1645.

The king's next step was to attempt to arrest John Pym, a Parliamentary leader who had consistently opposed his course of action. Oliver Cromwell, who had become Lord Protector of England, led the four-year civil war that followed. He was victorious and Charles surrendered to the Scots, who eventually handed him over to the English. He escaped to Carisbrooke, on the Isle of Wight. Fighting broke out again and Cromwell defeated the Scots at Preston.   Charles was removed to London in January, 1648, where Parliament impeached him.   He was accused of treason, tried and sentenced to death by beheading.   The sentence was carried out on January 30, 1649.

Suggested Readings

Ashley, Maurice.   Great Britain to 1688:   A Modern History.   Ann Arbor, Mich.:   University of Michigan Press, 1961.

Birkenhead, Frederick Edwin Smith.   "The Trial of Thomas Wentworth (Earl of Strafford)" in his Famous Trials of History.   Garden City, N. Y.:   Garden City Publishing Co., 1928.

Cowie, Leonard W.   The Trial and Execution of Charles I.   New York: Putnam, 1972.

Cross, Arthur Lyon.   A Shorter History of England and Greater Britain.   New York: Macmillan, 1929.

Davies, Godfrey.   "The Early Stuarts, 1603-1660" in The Oxford History of England.   Oxford: Clarendon Press, 1956.

Feiling, Keith.   A History of England.   New York: McGraw-Hill, 1948.

Friedrich, Carl J.   The Age of the Baroque.   New York: Harper & Row, 1952.

Gardiner, Samuel Rawson.   History of England from the Accession of James I to the Outbreak of the Civil War.   London: Longmans, Green, 1884.

Halliday, Frank E.   A Concise History of England from Stonehenge to the Atomic Age.   New York: Viking Press, 1964.

"Impeachment" in Crimes and Punishment, Vol. 17.   Editorial presentation: Jackson Morley.   London: BPC, 1973.

Judson, Margaret A.   The Crisis of the Constitution.   New Brunswick, N. J.:   Rutgers University Press, 1949.

Mosse, George L.   The Struggle for Sovereignty in England.   East Lansing, Mich.:   Michigan State University Press, 1950.

Taylor, Philip A. M.   The Origins of the English Civil War: Conspiracy, Crusade or Class Conflict?   Boston: Heath, 1960.

Terry, Benjamin.   A History of England from the Earliest Times to the Death of Queen Victoria.   Chicago: Scott, Foresman, 1901.

Trevalyn, George Macaulay.   History of England.   New York: Doubleday, 1953.

Wedgwood, Cicely V.   A Coffin for King Charles: The Trial and Execution of Charles I.   New York: Macmillan, 1964.

————.   The King's War, 1641-1647.   New York: Macmillan, 1959.

————.   The Life of Cromwell.   New York: Collier, 1966.

————.   Oliver Cromwell.   London: Gerald Duckworth & Co., 1939.

Wingfield-Stratton, Esme.   Charles, King of England, 1600-37.   London: Hollis & Carter, 1949.

THE PETITION OF RIGHT (1628)

Charles I, King of England, succeeded to the throne in 1625. England was at war with Spain and also became involved in an unsuccessful war with France. These wars could not be waged without money voted by the House of Commons, and the king found himself desperately in need of funds. The early parliaments of his reign were in a strong position to enforce their wishes against the king and to air both old and new grievances.

The leaders in the House of Commons blamed George Villiers, Duke of Buckingham, the king's chief minister and head of the navy, as well as other "evil advisers," for the country's war policy against Spain and the incompetent manner in which it was being administered. As an expression of its dissatisfaction the House voted, at the Third Parliament in March, 1628, the "tunnage and poundage" tax for only one year rather than for the king's entire reign, as had been done in the past. This tax involved the levying of customs duties and the House's action in voting it for one year only was a definite indication that Charles did not enjoy its confidence and trust. It was also an attempt to force the king to accede to its wishes by refusing him money.

The House complained of the king's policy of levying forced loans on the more financially substantial men in his kingdom and jailing them when they refused to pay. It also protested the forced billeting of soldiers in households and maintained that the king lacked the right to imprison his subjects without showing cause. Further, it declared that martial law should not be declared in peace time.

It was resolved to demand from Charles a formal concession of the rights and privileges claimed by the House and to refuse any grant of money until he gave his royal assent. These rights were embodied in a statute, known as the Petition of Right, so called because the grievances were presented in the form of a petition.

The Petition was presented to the king on May 28, 1628. The king quibbled and hesitated but finally agreed to it on June 7. The House of Commons remained in session and voted Charles the funds he needed. Buckingham was assassinated on August 28 by John Felton, a disappointed office seeker and Puritan fanatic. His death removed one of Parliament's major grievances. When that body met again in 1629 Charles ordered it adjourned. Leading members, led by Sir John Eliot, held the Speaker down in his chair while they voted three actions of the monarchy illegal. Charles countered by adjourning Parliament and, for the next eleven years, ruled without calling another.

Suggested Readings

Ashley, Maurice.   Great Britain to 1688:   A Modern History.

Ann Arbor, Mich.: University of Michigan Press, 1961.

Cowie, Leonard W. The Trial and Execution of Charles I. New York: Putnam, 1972.

Cross, Arthur Lyon. A Shorter History of England and Greater Britain. New York: Macmillan, 1929.

Davies, Godfrey. "The Early Stuarts, 1603-1660" in The Oxford History of England. Oxford: Clarendon Press, 1956.

Feiling, Keith. A History of England. New York: McGraw-Hill, 1948.

Friedrich, Carl J. The Age of the Baroque, 1610-1660. New York: Harper & Row, 1952.

Gardiner, Samuel Rawson. History of England from the Accession of James I to the Outbreak of the Civil War. London: Longmans, Green, 1884.

_____, ed. The Constitutional Documents of the Puritan Revolution. Oxford: Clarendon Press, 1958.

Halliday, Frank E. A Concise History of England from Stonehenge to the Atomic Age. New York: Viking Press, 1964.

Hulme, Harold. The Life of Sir John Eliot. New York: New York University Press, 1957.

Judson, Margaret A. The Crisis of the Constitution. New Brunswick, N.J.: Rutgers University Press, 1949.

Mosse, George L. The Struggle for Sovereignty in England. East Lansing, Mich.: Michigan State University Press, 1950.

Notestein, Wallace. The Winning of the Initiative by the House of Commons. Oxford: Clarendon Press, 1924.

Relf, Francis H. The Petition of Right. Minneapolis: University of Minnesota Studies in the Social Sciences, 1917.

Terry, Benjamin. A History of England from the Earliest Times to the Death of Queen Victoria. Chicago: Scott, Foresman, 1901.

Trevalyn, George Macaulay. History of England. New York: Doubleday, 1953.

Wedgwood, Cicely V. A Coffin for King Charles: The Trial and Execution of Charles I. New York: Macmillan, 1964.

Willson, David Harris. The Privy Councillors in the House of Commons, 1604-1629. Minneapolis: University of Minnesota Press, 1940.

Wingfield-Stratton, Esme. Charles, King of England, 1600-37. London: Hollis & Carter, 1949.

THE "DAY OF THE DUPES" (1630)

Following the assassination of Henry IV of France in 1610, his nine-year-old son assumed the throne as Louis XIII. Louis' widowed mother, Marie de' Medici, became regent. Marie was not popular with the French people as she relied on the Spanish ambassador for political advice and was herself a foreigner, having descended from the Medici family of Florence, Italy.

An ambitious French prelate, Armand Jean du Plessis, managed to insinuate himself into the favor of the regent who made
him grand almoner and Secretary of State for War and Foreign Affairs.   In 1622 she exerted her influence to have him made cardinal.
Du Plessis is best remembered as Cardinal Richelieu.

The French court was then a maze of intrigue.   Plots and
counterplots were the order of the day.   Louis ended the regency
in 1617 by rebelling against his mother and her Italian favorite,
Concino Concini, Marquis d'Ancre.   Marie was imprisoned, Concini was murdered and Charles d'Albert, Louis' friend, who con-
nived with him in the murder, became a duke and peer and later,
constable of France.

Richelieu attacked the Huguenots and, in other ways, began
systematically to extend the power of the French crown.   Louis,
though disliking Richelieu personally, appreciated his ability as a
statesman and realized that he could not rule without him.

Marie de' Medici escaped from imprisonment and inspired
two revolts, both of which were ended by negotiation.   In 1621 and
1622 Louis led his forces against the Huguenots.

In 1624 another crisis resulted in Louis making Richelieu
his minister, although he still disliked him.   The cardinal remained the dominant figure at the French court until Louis' death
in 1643.

Between 1627 and 1628 Richelieu took the last two Huguenot
strongholds, including La Rochelle, the most important, commanding the army in person.   His next step was to remove Marie from
court, to which she had returned.   She had become his enemy and
was plotting his downfall.   She argued incessantly against the cardinal and prevented him from seeing the king.   Louis' wife, Anne
of Austria, joined with Marie in denouncing Richelieu as she resented his influence over her royal husband.

On November 10, 1630, Louis was in conference with his
mother at Versailles and had left strict orders that they were not
to be disturbed.   Although the king had refused to grant Richelieu
an audience, Marie had taken the added precaution of locking the
doors to her son's chambers.   One door, however, had inadvertently been left unlocked.   The cardinal, entering through this unlocked
door, fell on his knees before the king and begged forgiveness for
any offense he might have given.   The queen-mother, infuriated at
the intrusion, screamed with rage and Louis left the room in dis-
gust.

Later in the day Louis sent for Richelieu, who offered to
resign.   The king refused to accept the proffered resignation, saying he valued the Cardinal's services highly and that his mother had,
without authority, meddled in the affairs of state.   That evening
Louis met with his council, said that the conspiracy against Riche-

lieu had disrupted official business for the past year, and ordered Michel de Marillac, Richelieu's opponent, to resign. De Marillac died in prison some months later. Michel's brother, Louis de Marillac, was charged with "corruption" and beheaded.

Marie de' Medici was banished to Compiègne and some of her friends were confined to the Bastille. One of the courtiers remarked, "This is the day of the dupes." The phrase came to be accepted as an appropriate description of the king's change of heart.

Suggested Readings

Barrière, J. F. Memoirs of the Duke de Richelieu. New York: 1904.

Batiffol, Louis. Marie de' Medici and the French Court in the Seventeenth Century. Translated by Mary King. London: Chat-to and Windus, 1908.

Boulenger, Jacques. The Seventeenth Century in France. New York: Capricorn Books, 1963 (Originally published in French, 1911).

Bulwer-Lytton, Sir Edward. "Richelieu: or, The Conspiracy" (play) in Matthews, Brander, and Paul Robert Lieder, eds. The Chief British Dramatists, Excluding Shakespeare. Boston: Houghton Mifflin, 1924 (Originally produced 1839).

Burckhardt, Carl J. Richelieu: His Rise to Power. Translated and abridged by Edwin and Villa Muir. London: George Allen & Unwin, 1940.

Duclaux, Mary (A. Mary F. Robinson). A Short History of France From Caesar's Invasion to the Battle of Waterloo. New York: Putnam's, 1918.

Huxley, Aldous. Grey Eminence. New York: Harper & Row, 1941.

Lodge, Richard. Richelieu. London: Longmans, Green, 1896.

Lough, John. An Introduction to Seventeenth Century France. New York: David McKay, 1954.

Maurios, André. A History of France. New York: Farrar, Strauss, 1956.

———. An Illustrated History of France. New York: Viking Press, 1960.

Perkins, J. B. Richelieu and the Growth of French Power. New York: 1900.

Wedgwood, Cicely V. Richelieu and the French Monarchy. New York: Macmillan, 1949.

GALILEO'S DIALOGUE CONCERNING THE TWO GREAT WORLD SYSTEMS (1632)

Galileo Galilei (1564-1642), an Italian scientist commonly re-ferred to only by his first name was, in a sense, the first modern physical scientist. His method was to apply mathematics, exper-

imentation and inductive reasoning to the understanding of physical
phenomena.   He studied logic, Greek and Latin at the monastery of
Vallombrosa, near Florence, and following this entered the University of Pisa where he studied medicine.

Resigning from the university in less than a year, he returned to Florence.   There he made certain scientific discoveries
regarding the pendulum, invented a hydrostatic balance and wrote
a treatise on the center of gravity in solids.   As a member of the
faculty of the University of Pisa he continued his research and made
a number of scientific discoveries concerning falling bodies and the
parabolic path taken by a projectile.   Later, at Padua, he made astronomical observations with the newly-invented telescope.   These
observations led to a number of discoveries in this field.

In 1543 Nicolaus Copernicus had published his ideas concerning heliocentricity, which clashed with the beliefs of the theologians
of his time.   These people felt that such theories were contrary to
the teachings of the Bible and therefore heretical.   Both Copernicus
and his successor, Johannes Kepler, whose ideas amplified those
of Copernicus, avoided sharp conflict with the authorities of the
Christian Church.   Galileo, however, was not so fortunate.   He
had, in 1610, published Sidereus Nuncius (Starry Messenger) in
which he put forth some unorthodox opinions.   However, at Rome
he was received with honor by Pope Paul V and Cardinal Maffeo
Barberini, later Pope Urban VIII.   Cardinal Robert Bellarmine,
however, was suspicious of Galileo's doctrine and began an investigation into the latter's affairs.

In 1616 Galileo was summoned to Rome for questioning.   A
letter he had written, in which he attempted to reconcile Copernicus' theory with the Bible by declaring that the Bible often speaks
metaphorically, had come to the attention of the Inquisition.   Cardinal Bellarmine, in a private interview with Galileo, secured his
promise not to teach Copernicanism as truth.   No action was taken
against Galileo although Copernicus' book was placed on the Index
of Forbidden Books and in 1616 the Inquisition condemned Copernicanism as being contrary to scripture.

Galileo returned to Florence and continued his work.   Barberini became pope in 1623 and Galileo, whose friend he was, visited him at the Vatican.   During this visit he received the impression that the pontiff had authorized him to resume teaching the Copernican theory.   In 1631 he received permission to publish his
Dialogue Concerning the Two Great World Systems and this, with
a preface written by the ecclesiastical censors, appeared in 1632.

This book is a fictional conversation between two of Galileo's
deceased friends and former students, Giovanni Francesco Sagredo
and Filippo Salviati.   These two uphold the Copernican theory and
debate with a fictional character named Simplicio who sides with
the traditionalists.   Salviati argues for Galileo and defends the Copernican theory brilliantly.

Although publication of the book had been authorized, permission was withdrawn and the sale of the Dialogue was forbidden. Galileo was summoned before the Inquisition at Rome in 1633. The case against him was based on the warning he had received in 1616 not to teach the "heretical theory" in any form. Galileo maintained that he had received nothing more than a private warning from Cardinal Bellarmine and produced a certificate from the late cardinal substantiating this.

Galileo agreed to plead guilty to the lesser included offense of "disobedience arising from vanity" rather than to the much more serious one of heresy, the penalty for which would have been, in all probability, death by burning at the stake. He made a formal recantation of the Copernican theory and affirmed his belief in the teachings of Ptolemy and Aristotle. The book was placed in the Index, from which it was not removed until 1922. He was sent to prison for a short time and then placed under house arrest at his villa near Florence. Until his death in 1642 he continued his researches and wrote and published other less controversial works.

Suggested Readings

Armitage, Angus. Copernicus: The Founder of Modern Astronomy. London: G. Allen and Unwin, 1938.

_____. John Kepler. London: Faber and Faber, 1966.

_____. The World of Copernicus. New York: Mentor Books, 1961.

Brodrick, James, S. J. Galileo, The Man, His Work, His Misfortunes. New York: Harper & Row, 1964.

Burke-Gaffney, M. W. , S. J. Kepler and the Jesuits. Milwaukee, Wis.: Bruce Publishing Co., 1944.

Butterfield, Herbert. The Origins of Modern Science, 1300-1800. New York: Macmillan, 1957.

Caspar, Max. Kepler, 1571-1630. Translated by C. Doris Hellman. New York: Collier Books, 1962.

Dreyer, John L. E. A History of Astronomy from Thales to Kepler. New York: Dover Publications, 1953.

Fermi, Laura, and Gilberto Bernardini. Galileo and the Scientific Revolution. New York: Macmillan, 1961.

Galilei, Galileo. Dialogue Concerning the Two Great World Systems. Translated and edited by Giorgio de Santillana. Chicago: University of Chicago Press, 1953 (Originally published 1632).

Geymonat, Ludovico. Galileo Galilei. Translated by Stillman Drake. New York: McGraw-Hill, 1965.

Golino, Carlo L. , ed. Galileo and His Precursors. Berkeley, Calif.: University of California Press, 1966.

_____. Galileo Reappraised. Berkeley, Calif.: University of California Press, 1966.

Kesten, Hermann. Copernicus and His World. New York: Roy Publishers, 1945.

Knight, David C. Johannes Kepler and Planetary Motion. New York: Franklin Watts, 1962.

230   Footnotes to World History

Koestler, Arthur. The Watershed. Garden City, N. Y. : Anchor
    Books, 1960.
Koryé, Alexandre. From the Closed World to the Infinite Universe.
    Baltimore: Johns Hopkins University Press, 1957.
Kuhn, Thomas S. The Copernican Revolution. Cambridge, Mass. :
    Harvard University Press, 1957.
Langford, Jerome J. Galileo, Science and the Church. New York:
    Desclee Company, 1966.
Lecler, Joseph, S. J. Toleration and the Reformation. Translated
    by T. L. Westow. New York: Associated Press, 1960.
McKown, Robin. "Galileo" in his Seven Famous Trials in History.
    New York: Vanguard Press, 1963.
Pauli, W. "The Influence of Archetypal Ideas on the Scientific
    Theories of Kepler" in Silz, Priscilla, translator. The In-
    terpretation of Nature and Psyche. New York: Pantheon Books,
    1955.
Roth, Cecil. The Spanish Inquisition. New York: Norton, 1964.
Santillana, Giorgio de. The Crime of Galileo. Chicago: University
    of Chicago Press, 1955.
Sarton, George. Six Wings: Men of Science in the Renaissance.
    Bloomington, Ind. : Indiana University Press, 1957.
Shapley, Harlow, and Helen E. Howarth. A Source Book of As-
    tronomy. New York: McGraw-Hill, 1929.
Taylor, F. Sherwood. Galileo and the Freedom of Thought. Lon-
    don: Watts and Company, 1938.
Tuberville, Arthur S. Medieval Heresy and the Inquisition. Lon-
    don: Archon Books, 1964.
Vacandard, Elphège. The Inquisition: A Critical and Historical
    Study of the Coercive Power of the Church. Translated by
    B. L. Conway. London: Longmans, Green, 1908.
Wallis, Charles G. Great Books of the Western World. Chicago:
    Encyclopaedia Britannica, 1955.
White, Andrew Dickson. A History of the Warfare of Science With
    Theology in Christendom. New York: George Braziller, 1955.

THE HOLLAND TULIPOMANIA (1634-1636)

        The tulip is a "flowering bulbous herb of the genus tulipa
belonging to the lily family. There are about sixty species native
to Asia and the Mediterranean region, and thousands of varieties are
cultivated as garden flowers. "

        The garden tulip was introduced into Western Europe from
Constantinople about the middle of the sixteenth century. It soon
achieved great popularity, especially in Holland, and by the year
1634 a craze known as "Tulipomania" developed. Wealthy Holland-
ers ordered bulbs direct from Constantinople, paying extravagant
prices for them. One Haarlem trader paid half his fortune for a
single tulip root, not to resell it at a profit but to plant in his own
conservatory.

The rage to possess tulips became so great that much ordinary business was neglected and both the poor and the wealthy speculated in tulip bulbs. Prices rose as the mania increased and by the year 1635 it became necessary to sell tulip bulbs by their weight in perits, a unit of weight less than a grain. A tulip of the Admiral Liefken variety, weighing 400 perits, brought 4,400 florins and one of the Semper Augustus variety, an extremely sought after bulb weighing 200 perits, sold for 5,500 florins.

By 1636 the demand for rare tulips was such that regular markets for their sale were established on the stock exchanges of many Dutch cities, including Amsterdam, Rotterdam, Leyden, Alkmaar and others. Stock jobbers dealt largely in tulips and price rigging was common. The trade became so extensive that a code of laws and regulations was drawn up. People from all walks of life converted their property into cash, often at a fraction of its value, and speculated in the tulip market.

Eventually it became obvious to the more conservative people that tulip prices would not increase indefinitely. Those who had originally purchased tulip bulbs for planting now held them to sell at a profit. It was realized that someone must eventually suffer a serious speculative loss. As this conviction spread, prices fell drastically and stayed down. Purchasers defaulted and others found themselves owning bulbs which they had bought at high prices and which no one would buy from them. Many speculators were bankrupted.

Government regulation of the tulip trade was required. Contracts made prior to November, 1636, were declared null and void. Further, on contracts made after that date, purchasers were legally freed from their contracts by paying 10 percent to the seller. This did not solve the problem. The Provincial Council at the Hague considered the situation but failed to act. Courts found that tulip speculation was actually gambling and refused to interfere, on the grounds that "debts contracted in gambling were no debts in law."

The Holland Tulipomania rested there. Those buyers who had purchased tulip bulbs at high prices took their losses. Those who had profited through speculation were permitted to keep their gains.

Suggested Readings

Biagioni, P. "Tulip Bubble: The Story of Holland's Tulip Boom,"
    Commonweal, April 28, 1939.
Blunt, Wilfrid. Tulipomania. Middlesex, England: Penguin Books,
    1950.
Borah, R. "Some Odd Pages from the Annals of the Tulip," National Geographic Magazine, September, 1933.
Bourne, L.M. "Tulipomania," Horticulture, May, 1963.

Hall, Sir Alfred Daniel. The Book of the Tulip. New York:
    Stokes, 1929.
Hodge, H. "King Tulip: Rich in History and Once the Cause of
    a Great Speculative Orgy," Nature Magazine, October, 1938.
Howard, C. "The Flower That Set a Nation Mad," Ladies' Home
    Journal, May, 1900.
Jacob, J. "Some Tales of the Tulip," Garden Magazine, September,
    1920.
Mackay, Charles. "The Tulipomania" in his Memoirs of Extraor-
    dinary Popular Delusions and the Madness of Crowds. London:
    Office of the National Illustrated Library, 1852. Reprinted by
    L. C. Page & Co., Boston, 1932.
Murray, W. S. "Tulips and Tulipomania," Journal of the Royal
    Horticultural Society, March, 1909.
Solms-Laubach, Count H. Weizen und Tulpe. Leipzig, 1899.
"Tulip" in Seymour, E. L. D., B. S. A., ed. The Wise Garden En-
    cyclopedia. New York: Wm. H. Wise & Co., 1951.

RENÉ DESCARTES' DISCOURSE ON METHOD (1637)

One of the many-sided geniuses of all time was René Descartes (1596-1650), the French philosopher, scientist and mathematician. As a philosopher he attempted to apply the rational inductive methods of science to philosophy. He rejected the then-pop-
ular method of scholasticism which involved comparing the different
views of recognized authorities. He held nothing true until he had
established grounds for believing it true, saying, "in our search
for the direct road to truth we should busy ourselves with no object about which we cannot attain a certitude equal to that of the
demonstrations of arithmetic and geometry. "

Descartes' investigations started from the single fact of
which he was sure. This was expressed in his well known words,
"cogito, ergo, sum" ("I think, therefore I am"). He believed that
a clear consciousness of his thinking proved his existence. His
philosophy, known as cartesianism, reinstated the idea of God. It
proceeds to establish the idea that God is all-good and all-truthful
and, as such, would not allow man to be "systematically deceived,
so the physical world must, in fact, exist. "

As a scientist Descartes abandoned the Copernican theory of
the universe with its set of planets spinning around the sun. He
took this action when the Church declared Copernicus' statements
to be heretical, substituting for it a theory of vortices in which
space was filled with matter whirling around the sun. He also
did pioneer work in optics and discovered a fundamental law of reflection, that the angle of incidence equals the angle of reflection.

As a mathematician Descartes systematized analytical geometry, attempted to classify curves according to types of equations

which produce them, added to man's knowledge of the theory of
equations and proved the impossibility of doubling the cube and trisecting the angle.   He invented the method of indices to express
the powers of numbers and formulated Descartes' rule of signs for
finding the number of positive and negative roots for any algebraic
equation.

   As a student of law and medicine in France Descartes became convinced of the unreliability of traditional philosophy.   He
was, for a while, a professional soldier and following this spent
the rest of his life performing scientific experiments, doing research in mathematics and meditating on philosophy.   He was influenced in these areas by Isaac Beekman, a Dutch scientist.   By
1627 he had formulated his idea of "unifying all the sciences into
a single system" and, at the encouragement of Cardinal Pierre
deBeruelle, prepared to publish his findings.   His Rules for the
Direction of the Mind was privately printed and was published posthumously.   In 1637 he published his famous Discourse on Method,
the full title of which is Discourse on the Method of Rightly Conducting the Reason and Seeking the Truth in the Sciences.   In this
he explained his basic principles.   It begins with the statement that
in all his travels he had encountered only one thing which seemed
to him unquestionably true.   This was the set of principles upon
which geometry is based.   It was, in other words, a denial of the
thought that the sources of truth were in theology and the literature
of the Humanists, but in science.

   Discourse on Method was followed by other philosophical
works, including Meditations on First Philosophy, published in 1641,
and The Principles of Philosophy which came off the press in 1644.
In all his writings Descartes holds that "the essence of the material
world is 'extension' as the essence of the self is thought.   Extension
is the thought that physical bodies occupy space and everything else
about them is derived from this fundamental fact. "

Suggested Readings

Armitage, Angus.   Copernicus: The Founder of Modern Astronomy.
      London: G. Allen and Unwin, 1938.
   _____.   The World of Copernicus.   New York: Mentor Books,
      1961.
Balz, Albert G.   Descartes and the Modern Mind.   New Haven,
      Conn. : Yale University Press, 1952.
Barker, Stephen F.   Philosophy of Mathematics.   Englewood Cliffs,
      N. J. : Prentice-Hall, 1964.
Beck, Leslie J.   The Metaphysics of Descartes.   Oxford: Claren-
      don Press, 1965.
Bochenski, Innocenty M.   A History of Formal Logic.   Notre Dame,
      Ind. : Notre Dame University Press, 1961.
Boole, George.   An Investigation of the Laws of Thought.   Glouces-
      ter, Mass. : Peter Smith, 1966 (Originally published 1854).
Cajori, Florian.   A History of Mathematics.   New York: Macmil-
      lan, 1922.

234 Footnotes to World History

Daley, Leo Charles. The Philosophy of René Descartes. New
York: Monarch, 1965.
Descartes, René. The Discourse on Method. Edited by Laurence
J. Lafleur. New York: Liberal Arts Press, Bobbs-Merrill,
1956 (Originally published 1637).
_____. "Discourse on the Method of Rightly Conducting the
Reason and Seeking the Truth in the Sciences" in Eliot, Charles
W., ed. The Harvard Classics. New York: Collier, 1909
(Originally published 1637).
_____. The Method, Meditations and Philosophy of Descartes.
New York: Tudor, 1901 (Originally published 1641).
Enriques, F. The Historic Development of Logic. Translated by
J. Rosenthal. New York: Holt, 1929.
Haldane, Elizabeth S. Descartes, His Life and Times. London:
John Murray, 1905.
Keeling, S. V. Descartes. London: Ernest Benn, 1934.
Scott, Joseph F. A History of Mathematics. London: Taylor and
Francis, 1960.
_____. The Scientific Work of René Descartes. London: Tay-
lor and Francis, 1952.
Smith, David Eugene. A History of Mathematics. Boston: Ginn,
1923.
Smith, Norman Kemp. New Studies in the Philosophy of Descartes.
London: Macmillan, 1952.
Versfeld, Marthinus. An Essay on the Metaphysics of Descartes.
London: Methuen, 1940.

THE CATALONIAN REVOLT (1640)

Catalonia is a region of Northeast Spain, comprising the
provinces of Tarragona, Lérida, Barcelona and Genoa. Spain,
which had flourished during the sixteenth century, due largely to
the gold brought from the New World following the conquest of
Mexico by Hernando Cortés and of Peru by Francisco Pizarro, had
commenced to decline in power and prestige. English corsairs had
captured much booty from the Spanish treasure galleons and diverted it to their country. The defeat of the Spanish Armada in 1588
had crippled Spain's sea power and the Hapsburg wars in central
Europe had depleted the Spanish treasury.

When Philip III of Spain died in 1621 he was succeeded by
his eldest son, Philip IV. During the latter's reign Spain's industry and commerce continued to decline and the country was impoverished by disastrous foreign wars, especially with France, Germany and Holland.

The new king followed his father's policy of assigning a
court favorite to administer government affairs while he performed
the social duties required of the reigning monarch. Gaspar De
Guzmán, Count-Duke of Olivares, was appointed chief minister. A

conscientious, honest man, he set about instigating policies and reforms which, he hoped would rescue Spain from her economic doldrums.

Olivares' plan for reform was in two major areas.   First, he proposed to overhaul the tax system that it might produce revenue equitably and also to achieve administrative reform by doing away with all regional privileges.   The second part of the chief minister's plan concerned the principality of Catalonia, in the kingdom of Aragon.   Like Spain, Catalonia and its principal city, Barcelona, had steadily declined during the previous century.   The natives had, over the years, obtained a number of concessions, including self-taxation and making payments to the crown at their own discretion.   They were also authorized to establish their own armed forces and to refuse to quarter the troops of foreign powers, including Castile.

Olivares, for over a decade, attempted to persuade the Catalans to give up their concessions, offering inducements such as official positions in the Castilian administration in return.   However, with the exception of a few small subsidies to the crown, they declined to accede to his wishes.

In 1639 Catalonia was invaded by French forces and the Count of Santa Coloma, Viceroy of Catalonia, following instructions from Madrid, sent troops to oppose them.   In the encounter that followed the French were defeated but Catalonian losses were heavy and Olivares was forced to send Castilian troops to Catalonia to oppose further invasions from France.   These "foreign" soldiers were billeted among the Catalonian peasants, much against the latter's will.

In Barcelona, in the spring of 1640, a mob of peasants, following a minor provocation, revolted and killed Santa Coloma.   Pau Claris, canon of the cathedral chapter of Urgel, took over control of the city.   Olivares sent troops to Barcelona to overcome the revolt and offered some concessions to the Catalans.   Claris, finding himself in an impossible position, took what seemed to him the only way out.   In January, 1641, he declared Catalonia independent of Spain and allied it to France, then ruled by Louis XIII.

In 1640 Portugal declared her independence from Spain and John, Duke of Braganza, became king.   Olivares had no troops available to send to Portugal and for this reason was unable to take military action against the rebels.   Like Catalonia, Portugal did not wish to pay taxes to the Spanish crown, feeling that if Spain could not protect the Portuguese empire from her enemies, the Portuguese had no reason to support Spain against her enemies.

A similar movement for independence sprang up in Andalusia and in 1643 Olivares was dismissed from his post as chief minister, being replaced by Luis de Haro, nephew of Philip IV.

Suggested Readings

Altamira, Rafael. A History of Spain. Translated by Muna Lee.
    New York: Van Nostrand, 1949.
Crow, John A. Spain: The Root and the Flower. New York: Har-
    per & Row, 1963.
Davies, Reginald Trevor. Spain in Decline, 1621-1700. New York:
    St. Martin's Press, 1961.
Elliott, John H. Imperial Spain, 1469-1716. New York: St. Mar-
    tin's Press, 1964.
_____. The Revolt of the Catalans. Cambridge: The Univer-
    sity Press, 1963.
Hume, Martin. The Court of Philip IV. New York: Brentano's,
    1928.
_____. Imperial Spain, 1469-1716.
Livermore, Harold V. A History of Spain. New York: Grove
    Press, 1958.
_____. A New History of Portugal. Cambridge: The Univer-
    sity Press, 1966.
Nowell, Charles E. A History of Portugal. Princeton, N. J. : Van
    Nostrand, 1952.
Pattee, Richard. Portugal and the Portuguese World. Milwaukee,
    Wis. : Bruce Publishing Co. , 1957.
Smith, Rhea Marsh. Spain: A Modern History. Ann Arbor, Mich. :
    University of Michigan Press, 1965.
Trend, John P. Portugal. London: Ernest Benn, Ltd. , 1957.

JOHN MILTON'S AREOPAGITICA (1644)

John Milton, regarded as "the greatest Puritan writer and,
perhaps, the greatest poet of his time," is remembered primarily
for his epic poems, particularly Paradise Lost and Paradise Regained, as well as his sonnets, his masque Comus and his poetic
drama Samson Agonistes. However, he also devoted some twenty
years of his life to the writing and publishing of religious and political pamphlets, the most important of which was Areopagitica,
an impassioned plea for freedom of the press.

In 1642 Charles I of England, having attempted unsuccessfully to maintain his royal prerogatives while dealing with a dom-
inantly Puritan Parliament, precipitated the civil war which led to
the establishment of the Commonwealth under the leadership of Oliver Cromwell. In June, 1643, the House of Commons passed the
Ordinance for the Regulation of Printing. This required that all
books and pamphlets be submitted to censorship prior to printing,
and that they be licensed by the government. Further, the names
of both author and printer were to appear on the title page, and
publications which did not conform were to be confiscated and the
authors and publishers subjected to punishment. Censors were appointed and the Stationer's Company, the guild of booksellers, en-

forced the Ordinance.   The Moderate Presbyterians who controlled the House of Commons intended the Ordinance to deal with Royalist tracts and the religious pamphlets of the Extreme Puritans.

One of the first to oppose the new law was John Milton, whose political sympathies were anti-Royalist and whose writings reflected his views on the subject.   He had previously published pamphlets attacking the institution of bishops and urging the carrying of the Reformation farther than it had gone under the Elizabethan settlement.   He also wrote on divorce, urging that marriage was instituted for intellectual as well as physical association and that divorce should be granted for incompatibility.   The unlicensed Areopagitica, published on November 23, 1644, assailed the Ordinance for the Regulation of Printing.   This was published anonymously and only one edition appeared during Milton's lifetime.   The title is derived from a speech made by the Athenian orator Isocrates about 335 B.C. which was addressed to the Athenian assembly.   In his speech Isocrates urged the reform of the court of Areopagus.

Milton's pamphlet first extols the Parliament and then suggests that to such an august body the censorship ordinance is a "mere lapse" and the parliamentarians will prove their high-mindedness by revoking it.   He then declares that throughout history only two types of writing were censored: the aesthetic and the libelous, and that total censorship changed only with the Inquisition. From this he argues that "the Puritan censors thus unwittingly imitate the detested Romans. "

Milton's argument continues.   "Books, " he says, "are not absolutely dead things ... they do preserve ... the purest efficacy and extraction of that living intellect that bred them. "   Later he says, "who kills a man kills a reasonable creature, God's image; but who destroys a good book kills reason itself. "   He holds that if one fears the evil in books it follows that the Holy Bible itself must be banned because both good and evil are closely mixed in it.   He states that the safest way to learn about evil is to read about it.   He questions the qualifications of "those who would act as censors" and points out that "censors, by the very nature of their office, will approve only those ideas which are already commonly accepted. "

In his Areopagitica Milton suggests that the Stationer's Company was prompted by ulterior motives, hoping to monopolize all printing in England rather than act as a distributor of Truth.   The Company complained to Parliament concerning this "slander" but that body did not alter its policy of censorship.

Milton continued to publish.   When Charles I was beheaded in 1649 the poet was offered and accepted a post with the government.   He continued to write, did editorial work and published additional pamphlets.   When Charles II assumed the English throne in 1660 Milton resigned his position and went into hiding.   He was found, fined and imprisoned for a short time and then returned to

London where he lived the remainder of his life in seclusion.   He
had become blind in 1652 and wrote by dictating to his daughters.
He died in 1674.

Suggested Readings

Ashley, Maurice.   Great Britain to 1688:   A Modern History.   Ann
    Arbor, Mich.:   University of Michigan Press, 1961.
_____.   Life in Stuart England.   New York: Putnam's, 1964.
Barker, Arthur E.   Milton and the Puritan Dilemma.   Toronto:
    University of Toronto Press, 1942.
Davies, Godfrey.   "The Early Stuarts, 1603-1660" in The Oxford
    History of England.   Oxford: Clarendon Press, 1956.
Feiling, Keith.   A History of England.   New York: McGraw-Hill,
    1948.
Fletcher, Harris F.   The Intellectual Development of John Milton.
    Urbana, Ill.:   University of Illinois Press, 1956.
Gardiner, Samuel Rawson.   History of England from the Accession
    of James I to the Outbreak of the Civil War.   London: Long-
    mans, Green, 1884.
Hutchinson, Francis E.   Milton and the English Mind.   London:
    Hodder & Stoughton, 1946.
Lockyer, Roger.   Tudor and Stuart Britain, 1471-1714.   London:
    Longmans, Green, 1964.
Masson, David.   The Life of John Milton.   New York: Peter Smith,
    1946.
Saillens, Émile.   John Milton: Man, Poet and Polemicist.   Oxford:
    Basil Blackwell, 1964.
Sensabaugh, George F.   The Grand Whig.   Palo Alto, Calif.:   Stan-
    ford University Press, 1952.
Terry, Benjamin.   A History of England from the Earliest Times
    to the Death of Queen Victoria.   Chicago: Scott, Foresman,
    1901.
Wolfe, Don M.   Milton in the Puritan Revolution.   London: Cohen
    and West, 1941.
_____, et al., eds.   The Complete Prose of John Milton.   New
    Haven, Conn.:   Yale University Press, 1959 (Originally written
    mid-17th century).

THE PEACE OF WESTPHALIA (1648)

The Peace of Westphalia consisted of the treaties concluded
at Münster and Osnabrück, Westphalia, which ended the Thirty
Years' War.   This war began with a revolt in Bohemia, spread to
Germany and, in addition, involved Britain, Spain, the Netherlands,
Denmark, France and Sweden.   The major battleground was Germany
and the Holy Roman Empire and the war lasted from 1618 to 1648.

Two separate sets of negotiations were necessary, one be-

tween the Bourbons and the Hapsburgs (Münster) and the other between Sweden and the Holy Roman Empire (Osnabrück). Both treaties were concluded on October 24, 1648, although negotiations had
begun in 1641 and were actively pursued from 1643 on.

Religious issues played an important part in the War. The
underlying cause was the deep-seated hostility between the German
Protestants and the German Catholics. Before the war was over
most of the nations of Europe were involved, with all concerned
struggling for political power and additional territory.

The Thirty Years' War has been divided by historians into
four periods: the Bohemian period (1618-1620), the Danish period
(1625-1629), the Swedish period (1630-1635) and the Swedish-French
period (1635-1648). The Bohemian period involved a revolt by the
Protestants when the Archbishop of Prague, a Catholic, ordered a
Protestant church destroyed. Emperor Matthias refused to take action and the revolt followed. This was unsuccessful and cost the
Bohemians their independence. Catholicism became the state religion.

The Danish period began when Protestant countries other
than Bohemia began to realize the possibility of being overwhelmed
by Catholics. Christian IV, Protestant King of Denmark, was repeatedly defeated in battle, being opposed by Ferdinand II, Holy
Roman Emperor, who was aided by the troops of General Wallenstein. Christian IV finally signed the Treaty of Lübeck (1629) and
withdrew from Saxony.

The Swedish period began in 1630 when Sweden, led by King
Gustavus Adolphus and subsidized by the French minister Cardinal
Richelieu, entered the conflict. The Swedes were, at first, vic-
torious but, following the death of the king in 1632 in the Battle
of Lützen, finally succumbed when their army was destroyed in the
Battle of Nördlingen in 1634.

The Swedish-French period was characterized by political
rather than religious considerations. Richelieu, determined to
block the growth of Hapsburg power, interfered on the side of the
Protestants. In 1635 he sent a French army into Germany which
joined with a new Swedish army. The Protestants and their French
allies won a series of victories. Ferdinand III, Holy Roman Emperor, agreed to peace.

In 1644 the European countries sent representatives to a
peace conference. The negotiations dragged on for four years before the Peace of Westphalia was signed. By it Alsace and Lor-
rain were acquired by France and Sweden gained control of the
Elbe, Oder and Weser Rivers. Calvinism was put on an equal
footing with Lutheranism and Catholicism.

The Reformation and Counter-Reformation had ended. Sweden
emerged a great power in Northern Europe. The Holy Roman Em-

pire, however, lost ground, as did Spain. Under Louis XIV France became the leading continental power, "anxious to challenge anew its old adversaries, the Spanish and Austrian Hapsburgs."

Suggested Readings

Ashley, Maurice. Louis XIV and the Greatness of France. London: English Universities Press, 1955.

Bryce, James. The Holy Roman Empire. New York: Schocker Books, 1904.

Burckhardt, Carl J. Richelieu: His Rise to Power. Translated and abridged by Edwin and Villa Muir. London: George Allen & Unwin, 1940.

Cronin, Vincent. Louis XIV. Boston: Houghton Mifflin, 1965.

Ergang, Robert Reinhold. The Myth of the All-Destructive Fury of the Thirty Years' War. Pocono Pines, Pa.: Craftsmen Press, 1956.

Friedrich, Carl J. The Age of the Baroque, 1610-1660. New York: Harper & Row, 1952.

Hertz, Frederick. The Development of the German Public Mind: A Social History of German Political Sentiments, Aspirations, and Ideas, Vol. I: The Middle Ages and the Reformation. New York: Macmillan, 1937.

Holborn, Hajo. A History of Modern Germany, Vol I: The Reformation. New York: Knopf, 1959.

Huxley, Aldous. Grey Eminence. New York: Harper & Row, 1941.

Ogg, David. Europe in the Seventeenth Century. New York: Macmillan, 1961.

Rabb, Theodore K., ed. "The Thirty Years' War: Problems of Motive, Extent and Effect" in Problems of European Civilization. Boston: Heath, 1964.

Schiller, Johann Christoph von. "The Camp of Wallenstein" (play) in Bates, Alfred, editor in chief. German Drama. London: Smart and Stanley, 1903 (Originally published 1798-99).

Steinberg, Sigfrid H. The Thirty Years' War. New York: Norton, 1966.

Thomson, S. Harrison. Europe in Renaissance and Reformation. New York: Harcourt, Brace, 1963.

Ward, A. W. "The Peace of Westphalia" in Ward, A. W., et al, eds. The Cambridge Modern History. Cambridge: The University Press, 1906.

Wedgwood, Cicely V. Richelieu and the French Monarchy. New York: Macmillan, 1949.

_____. The Thirty Years' War. Gloucester, Mass.: Peter Smith, 1962.

THE FRONDE INSURGENCE (1648-1653)

The Thirty Years' War (1618-1648), fought chiefly in Germany and involving most of the countries of western Europe, was one of the most destructive conflicts in European history.   It imposed a serious financial drain on many countries, including France.   In 1648 it triggered a strong opposition movement, called the Fronde, against the administration of Cardinal Jules Mazarin, the French prime minister who succeeded Cardinal Richelieu in that post in 1642.

King Louis XIV of France was, at this time, a minor and his mother, Anne of Austria, was Queen Regent, although behind-the-scenes power was actually wielded by Mazarin.   The Insurgence involved the Parlement of Paris, an ancient court of law and appeals, of which Matthieu Molé was president.

The Fronde Insurgence precipitated in January, 1648, when Omer Talon, advocate general of France, ordered the Parlement to register seven royal edicts, six of which increased taxes.   Molé advised Queen Anne that the Parlement was legally entitled to examine all edicts and to present arguments or remonstrances to the ruler concerning their content.   While stipulating that the king had final authority, the queen agreed with President Molé's contention.

Following this the Parlement considered modifications of the royal edicts which it had received from Talon, although the queen made it clear that if modifications were made "she would be compelled to take strong measures. "   The Parlement then warily agreed to present remonstrances only, and not modifications.   This however, did not end the matter.   For some time many French citizens had felt that the idea of absolute monarchism was wrong and that the subjects of any ruler should not accede to his dictates unquestioningly.   This attitude was furthered by the general dislike in which Mazarin and his policies were held.   During the spring of 1648 opposition to the French court grew in spite of threats from Baptiste, Duke of Orléans and brother of Louis XIII, who later conspired against the prime minister and who joined the Fronde.   In June criticisms of royal policy were extended to include public affairs in general.   The government was unable to put down what it considered a rebellion as the soldiers who would normally be used to police the French capital were engaged in a war with Spain and hence were unavailable.

In July, 1648, the Parlement presented the French court with several demands.   These proposed a number of reforms and also sought to establish the Parlements as legislative bodies, having the function of making laws rather than merely acting as courts and sitting in judgment.   The reforms demanded that no new taxes be imposed without the approval of the courts, that all personal taxes be reduced, that certain royal officials be dismissed and that no person charged with the commission of a crime be imprisoned for more than 24 hours without appearing before a magistrate.

The government met these demands with a series of delaying tactics, hoping that force could be applied to the "rebels" once the military situation had been clarified and soldiers had become available. In August Louis II, the French military leader known as "the Great Condé," having achieved a victory at Lens, was re-called to Paris to put down the Fronde. He had trouble with Ma-zarin and later fought on the side of the Fronde against Marshal Turenne who had joined that body in 1649 but subsequently was re-conciled with the court.

Mazarin ordered the arrest of two members of the Parlement of Paris and others were, on his instructions, sent into exile. This maneuver was unsuccessful; Mazarin was threatened with death and the prisoners were released and the exiles permitted to return to Paris. Debates between the royal government and the courts con-tinued through the year 1648 and on October 22 the Fronde issued a declaration which, at least on paper, limited the powers of the royal ruler.

In January, 1649, King Louis and the royal family traveled to the suburb of St. Germain. Members of the Fronde were then notified that Paris would be besieged unless they submitted to royal authority without question.

At this time the royalists were supported by the Great Condé. Although some noblemen sided with the members of the Parlement, King Louis' military forces were able to achieve a partial victory over the insurgents and an agreement was eventually reached.

Mazarin finally crushed the Fronde in 1653, thus ending what remained of French feudalism and laying the basis for the despotism of the last of the Bourbons, who were to rule France until the time of the French Revolution, which erupted in 1793.

Suggested Readings

Ashley, Maurice. Louis XIV and the Greatness of France. Lon-
    don: English Universities Press, 1955.
Bailly, Auguste. Mazarin. Paris: 1935.
Boulenger, Jacques. The Seventeenth Century in France. New
    York: Capricorn Books, 1963 (Originally published in French,
    1911).
Cronin, Vincent. Louis XIV. Boston: Houghton Mifflin, 1965.
Doolin, Paul Rice. The Fronde. Cambridge, Mass.: Harvard
    University Press, 1935.
Ergang, Robert Reinhold. The Myth of the All-Destructive Fury of
    the Thirty Years' War. Pocono Pines, Pa.: Craftsmen Press,
    1956.
Friedrich, Carl J. The Age of the Baroque, 1610-1660. New York:
    Harper & Row, 1952.
Guérard, Albert. The Life and Death of an Ideal. New York:
    George Braziller, 1956.
Hassal, Arthur. Mazarin. London: 1903.
Lough, John. An Introduction to Seventeenth Century France. New
    York: David McKay, 1954.

Ogg, David. Europe in the Seventeenth Century. New York: Mac-
    millan, 1961.
Rabb, Theodore K., ed. "The Thirty Years' War: Problems of
    Motive, Extent and Effect" in Problems of European Civiliza-
    tion. Boston: Heath, 1964.
Steinberg, Sigfrid H. The Thirty Years' War. New York: Nor-
    ton, 1966.
Wedgwood, Cicely V. The Thirty Years' War. Gloucester, Mass.:
    Peter Smith, 1962.

THE CROMWELLS AND THE ENGLISH
COMMONWEALTH (1649-1659)

For centuries the English kings believed that they held their
royal offices by divine right and that God had bestowed absolute
sovereignty on them. This view was held by the Stuart rulers,
James I and his son Charles I, who found themselves at odds with
Parliament, the members of which felt that they should have a
voice in government.

While firm believers in the divine right of kings, the Tudor
sovereigns had consulted Parliament on various occasions, as in
legalizing the Anglican Reformation. From the ascension of James
I to the English throne in 1603 to his death in 1625 and from that
year until 1649 when Charles I was king, Parliament repeatedly
defied the rulers. It made a number of demands, including the
rights of freedom of speech and freedom from arrest when engaged
in parliamentary duties. It also insisted that the king could not
levy taxes without Parliament's consent, something with which the
Stuarts, father and son, did not agree. In 1629 Charles dismissed
Parliament and ruled without it for eleven years.

On April 13, 1640, he convened Parliament for the purpose
of dealing with the Bishop's War over Scotland's refusal to accept
Anglicanism. This body, which came to be called the "Short Parliament," was dismissed three weeks later as its members refused
to vote funds with which to conduct the war until their demands were
met. The situation with Scotland did not abate and Charles, much
against his will, found it necessary to reconvene Parliament. This,
the "Long Parliament," first met in November, 1640. A peace with
Scotland was achieved but the Radical Presbyterian majority stripped
the king of most of his power. It also tried to convert the Church
of England to Presbyterianism but without success. This latter move
resulted in converting a High Church element in Parliament from
opposition to siding with Charles in 1642 as a royalist faction. Civil
war erupted in August of that year, with the Presbyterians opposing
the Royalists.

Oliver Cromwell, who was to become Lord Protector of England, had been raised a Puritan. He was elected to Parliament and

when the civil war broke out he, as captain of a crack cavalry
regiment known as the Ironsides, upheld the parliamentary cause.
In 1644 he was appointed a lieutenant general and a member of
Parliament for both kingdoms, which directed military and civil
policies.   In the Battle of Marston Moor, July 2, he commanded
the final cavalry charge that defeated the Royalist forces in the
first civil war.   During the war the Presbyterians, while fighting
King Charles, were also opposed by Cromwell and his Independents
who wished to do away with the monarchy and any organized church,
be it Anglican or Presbyterian.

A second civil war broke out with Royalist uprisings in
Wales.   Cromwell, the acknowledged leader of the army, defeated
the Scots at Pembroke Castle in July, 1648, and again in August,
at Preston in Lancashire.

The Presbyterians, as a result of the gradually increasing
power of the Independents, attempted to resolve their differences
with the king.   Cromwell then took Charles prisoner in 1647, recaptured him when he escaped, ordered Colonel Thomas Pride (December, 1648) to purge the House of Commons of all but sixty Independents when it refused to depose the king, and tried the latter
for treason.   Charles was found guilty by the 67 judges and was
beheaded at Whitehall on January 30, 1649.

Colonel Pride's action in reducing the Long Parliament to
the "Rump Parliament" was known as "Pride's Purge."   This, plus
the execution of the king, were the major steps in the formation of
the Commonwealth.   Cromwell and his followers were forced to
consolidate their power.   The Rump Parliament did this by enacting
legislation which did away with the House of Lords and the monarchy.
It further declared anyone who criticized the new government guilty
of treason.   Religious toleration was granted to all, with the exception of Catholics and certain supporters of the former king.   England was declared by the Rump Parliament to be a "Commonwealth
and Free State" on May 19, 1649.

Oliver Cromwell ruled England as a military dictator, something completely foreign to English tradition.   Both he and his reign
were unpopular with the British public.   He put down rebellions by
the Irish and the Scots with military force.   He also fought wars
with Holland and Spain.   His attempts to secure popular support
were unsuccessful.

In 1653 he dissolved the Rump Parliament, substituting oth-
ers for it between 1654 and 1656.   In the same year he adopted the
"Instrument of Government," a written constitution which made the
Commonwealth a Protectorate, with himself as Lord Protector.

In March, 1657, Parliament drafted a new constitution, "The
Humble Petition and Advice."   This called for a restoration of the
monarchy with Cromwell as king, a title he refused, although he
did accept the other parts of the Petition.   In 1658 the new two-house

Parliament met.   Quarrels arose concerning the Petition and the
Protector dissolved the Parliament.

Cromwell called a Parliament for December, 1658, but did
not live to meet with it, having died on September 3.   Richard, his
eldest surviving son, succeeded to the Protectorate.   Lacking his
father's political ability and iron will, he retired the following May,
following which he lived in seclusion in France under the name of
John Clarke until 1680.

General George Monck, governor of Scotland, realized that
order must be restored to English government.   He, Sir John
Grenville, Edward Hyde, later Earl of Clarendon and others negotiated with Charles Stuart, son of the executed king, who was living
in the Netherlands in exile.   It was proposed that he mount the
British throne as Charles II.   In 1660 the third Stuart king proceeded to London which he entered on May 29.   The Commonwealth was
no more and England was once again a monarchy.

Suggested Readings

Ashley, Maurice.   Great Britain to 1688:   A Modern History.   Ann
        Arbor, Mich. :   University of Michigan Press, 1961.
_____.   The Greatness of Oliver Cromwell.   New York: Collier,
        1962.
_____.   Life in Stuart England.   New York: Putnam's, 1964.
_____.   Oliver Cromwell and the Puritan Revolution.   Mystic,
        Conn. :   Verry, Laurence, Inc. , 1958.
_____.   The Stuarts in Love.   New York: Macmillan, 1964.
Boyer, Richard E.   Oliver Cromwell and the Puritan Revolt: Fail-
        ure of a Man or a Faith?   Boston: Heath, 1966.
Clark, George.   "The Later Stuarts, 1660-1714" in The Oxford His-
        tory of England.   Oxford: Clarendon Press, 1956.
Cooper, Thompson.   "General Monck" in Lee, Sidney, ed.   Diction-
        ary of National Biography.   London: Smith, Elder & Co. , 1894.
Cross, Arthur Lyon.   A Shorter History of England and Greater
        Britain.   New York: Macmillan, 1929.
Davies, Godfrey.   "The Early Stuarts, 1603-1660" in The Oxford
        History of England.   Oxford: Clarendon Press, 1956.
Feiling, Keith.   A History of England.   New York: McGraw-Hill,
        1948.
Firth, Charles H.   The Last Years of the Protectorate, 1656-1658.
        New York: Russell and Russell, 1964.
_____.   Oliver Cromwell and the Rule of the Puritans in England.
        New York: Putnam's, 1900.
Friedrich, Carl J.   The Age of the Baroque, 1610-1660.   New York:
        Harper & Row, 1952.
Gardiner, Samuel Rawson.   History of England from the Accession
        of James I to the Outbreak of the Civil War.   London: Long-
        mans, Green, 1884.
_____.   History of the Commonwealth and Protectorate, 1649-
        1956.   New York: AMS Press, 1965.

_____, ed. The Constitutional Documents of the Puritan Revo-
    lution. Oxford: Clarendon Press, 1958.
Halliday, Frank. A Concise History of England from Stonehenge to
    the Atomic Age. New York: Viking Press, 1964.
Shaw, W. A. "The Commonwealth and the Protectorate (1648-59)"
    in The Cambridge Modern History. Edited by A. W. Ward, et
    al. Cambridge: The University Press, 1906.
Taylor, Philip A. M. The Origins of the English Civil War: Con-
    spiracy, Crusade or Class Conflict? Boston: Heath, 1960.
Terry, Benjamin. A History of England from the Earliest Times
    to the Death of Queen Victoria. Chicago: Scott, Foresman,
    1901.
Wedgwood, Cicely V. A Coffin for King Charles: The Trial and
    Execution of Charles I. New York: Macmillan, 1964.
_____. The King's War, 1641-1647. New York: Macmillan,
    1959.
_____. The Life of Cromwell. New York: Collier, 1966.
_____. Oliver Cromwell. London: Gerald Duckworth & Co.,
    1939.

THE RESTORATION OF CHARLES II (1659-1660)

Charles I, King of England, was beheaded on January 30, 1649, having been condemned as a traitor by Parliament. England was then ruled during the period of the Commonwealth and Protectorate by Oliver Cromwell, a general in the Parliamentary army which had deposed Charles.

After Cromwell's death in September, 1658, his son Richard ruled as Lord Protector until May, 1659. However, Richard lacked his father's strength and could not govern effectively, and a group of political and army leaders forced him to resign.

It was vital that England have a government of some sort. The Scots had, in 1649, a month after Charles' execution, proclaimed his son Charles their king. He was crowned as Charles II at Scone on January 1, 1651, but ruled only a few months. In August he led a Scottish army into England where he was overwhelmingly defeated at the Battle of Worcester. He spent the next nine years wandering about Europe.

General George Monck was commander of the army in Scotland. Following Oliver's death and Richard Cromwell's resignation Monck set himself to quietly effect the Stuart Restoration. In January 1660 he brought his army to London and used his influence to restore the Long Parliament. His next step was to dissolve this Parliament and provide for elections to a Convention Parliament, following which Charles II was to be recalled from the Netherlands where he was then in exile.

Following the dissolution of the Long Parliament Monck conferred with Sir John Grenville who was extending his efforts to restore the monarchy. Caution was mandatory as the election for the Convention Parliament had not yet been held and no one knew how it would turn out. Monck dispatched Grenville to Charles with a message, which Grenville memorized. At Breda in the Netherlands Grenville and Charles awaited the outcome of the election. When the new Parliament had been voted in it indicated that it was willing to call Charles to the throne. Grenville delivered Charles' statement, known as the Declaration of Breda, to Parliament. The Declaration made known Charles' intention to work closely with Parliament and his willingness to agree with its decisions in such important matters as religious toleration, pay of soldiers and settlement of Royalist property.

Parliament then declared Charles II King of England and preparations were made to bring him home from Breda. In 1660 he assumed the throne in a bloodless revolution meeting general approval. The Stuart dynasty had been restored.

Suggested Readings

Airy, Osmond. Charles II. London: 1904.
Ashley, Maurice. Great Britain to 1688: A Modern History. Ann Arbor, Mich.: University of Michigan Press, 1961.
_____. The Greatness of Oliver Cromwell. New York: Collier, 1962.
_____. Life in Stuart England. New York: Putnam's, 1964.
_____. The Stuarts in Love. New York: Macmillan, 1964.
Belloc, Hilaire. Charles II: The Last Rally. New York: Harper & Row, 1939.
Bryant, Sir Arthur. Charles II. London: R. Hale, 1962.
_____. "The Miraculous Providence" in his The Fire and the Rose. Garden City, N. Y.: Doubleday, 1966.
Clark, George. "The Later Stuarts, 1660-1714" in The Oxford History of England. Oxford: Clarendon Press, 1956.
Cooper, Thompson. "General Monck" in Lee, Sidney, ed. Dictionary of National Biography. London: Smith, Elder & Co., 1894.
Cross, Arthur Lyon. A Shorter History of England and Greater Britain. New York: Macmillan, 1929.
Davies, Godfrey. The Restoration of Charles II, 1658-1660. San Marino, Calif.: Huntington Library, 1955.
Feiling, Keith. A History of England. New York: McGraw-Hill, 1948.
Firth, Charles H. The Last Years of the Protectorate, 1656-1658. New York: Russell and Russell, 1964.
Friedrich, Carl J. The Age of the Baroque, 1610-1660. New York: Harper & Row, 1952.
Gardiner, Samuel Rawson. History of the Commonwealth and Protectorate, 1649-1656. New York: AMS Press, 1965.
Halliday, Frank. A Concise History of England from Stonehenge to the Atomic Age. New York: Viking Press, 1964.

Loth, David. _Royal Charles, Ruler and Rake_. New York: Bren-
    tano's, 1930.
Norman, Charles. _The Flight and Adventures of Charles II_. New
    York: Random House, 1958.
Ogg, David. _England in the Reign of Charles II_. Oxford: Claren-
    don Press, 1955.
Pepys, Samuel. _Memoirs of Samuel Pepys_. Edited by Richard
    Lord Braybrooke. London: Frederick Warne & Co., 1825
    (Originally written 1660-1669).
Terry, Benjamin. _A History of England from the Earliest Times
    to the Death of Queen Victoria_. Chicago: Scott, Foresman,
    1901.
Trevalyn, George Macaulay. _History of England_. New York: Doub-
    leday, 1953.
Wedgwood, Cicely V. _A Coffin for King Charles: The Trial and
    Execution of Charles I_. New York: Macmillan, 1964.
_____. _The Life of Cromwell_. New York: Collier, 1966.
_____. _Oliver Cromwell_. London: Gerald Duckworth & Co.,
    1939.

THE GREAT LONDON FIRE (1666)

Early on the morning of Sunday, September 2, 1666, a fire,
breaking out in the home of Thomas Farriner, a baker of Thames
Street, London, rapidly went out of control. Before it was finally
extinguished it had reached Pie Corner in Smithfield. In the three
days that it burned it destroyed most of the walled section of the
city. More than 12,000 homes and public buildings were burned,
as was "the greatest part of the furniture and merchandise that
were in them." The fact that London had experienced a long drought
and that the wooden buildings were highly flammable enabled the
fire, once started, to spread rapidly.

London was just recovering from a severe epidemic of plague
which, in 1665, had swept the city. Nearly 70,000 Londoners had
succumbed to the disease and the devastating fire which followed
seemed to some to be evidence of God's wrath.

Much of the information we have concerning the Great London
Fire of 1666 comes from the written accounts of such eyewitnesses
as Samuel Pepys, John Evelyn, Daniel DeFoe, Richard Baxter and
the Earl of Clarendon. Pepys was advised of the fire on Sunday
morning by Jane, a maid employed in his home. That day he made
an inspection trip and went to Whitehall. As an important naval
official and highly regarded by both King Charles II and the king's
brother James, Duke of York, he was able to suggest to them that
"unless his Majesty did command houses to be pulled down nothing
could stop the fire." King Charles instructed Pepys to "go to my
Lord Mayor ... and command him to spare no houses, but to pull
down before the fire every way." The Lord Mayor, on receiving

the king's order, protested that he had been pulling down houses, "but the fire overtakes us faster than we can do it. "

The Duke of York, who had been placed in charge of the fire fighters, supervised the demolition of houses, but the official account in the London Gazette reported that this failed to stop the the flames. "Many attempts were made to prevent the spreading of it by pulling down houses, and making great intervals, but all in vain, the fire seising upon the timber and rubbish and so continuing itself. "

According to the Earl of Clarendon's account, it was suspected that the fire had been deliberately set by the Dutch, French and Roman Catholics of the town. Robert Hubert, a Frenchman, was accused of starting the fire. He was hanged in October, 1666, although it was found later that he was not even in England when the conflagration began.

Pepys observed that people were more interested in saving what possessions they could than in fighting the flames. He found "the streets full of nothing but people and horses and carts loaden with goods. " Many Londoners fled to Highgate Fields outside the town where they camped, waiting for the fire to subside.

Eventually the wind, which had been fanning the flames, abated. The fire gradually burned itself out. The Rebuilding Act of 1667 "stipulated that only stone and brick were to be employed, with the result that the new buildings which rose from the ruins bore little resemblance to the quaint wooden building of Old London.

Suggested Readings

Ashley, Maurice. Great Britain to 1688: A Modern History. Ann Arbor, Mich.: University of Michigan Press, 1961.

_____. Life in Stuart England. New York: Putnam's, 1964.

Bell, Walter George. The Great Plague in London in 1665. London: John Lane, 1924.

_____. "The Plague of London" in Corbett, Edmund V., ed. Great True Stories of Tragedy and Disaster. New York: Archer House, 1963.

Bryant, Sir Arthur. Charles II. London: R. Hale, 1931.

Cowie, Leonard W. Plague and Fire: London, 1665-66. New York: Putnam's, 1970.

_____. Seventeenth Century Europe. London: George Bell & Sons, 1960.

DeFoe, Daniel. A Journal of the Plague Year. London: 1721.

Feiling, Keith. A History of England. New York: McGraw-Hill, 1948.

Halliday, Frank E. A Concise History of England from Stonehenge to the Atomic Age. New York: Viking Press, 1964.

Henty, G. A. When London Burned (historical fiction). New York: Scribner's, 1897.

Leasor, James. The Plague and the Fire. New York: Pan Books,
    1962.
Loth, David. Royal Charles, Ruler and Rake. New York: Bren-
    tano's, 1930.
Marê, Eric de. London's Riverside. New York: Reinhardt, 1958.
Mitchell, R. J., and M. D. R. Leyes. A History of London Life.
    Baltimore: Penguin Books, 1963.
Ogg, David. England in the Reign of Charles II. Oxford: Claren-
    don Press, 1955.
Pepys, Samuel. Memoirs of Samuel Pepys. Edited by Richard
    Lord Braybrooke. London: Frederick Warne & Co., 1825
    (Originally written 1660-69).
Verney, Sir Harry, ed. The Verneys of Claydon. Elmsford, N. Y.:
    Permagon Press, 1968.

THE HOPE DIAMOND CURSE (1668-1911)

One of the legends which is now and then revived is that
concerning the stolen jewel, generally a diamond bearing a curse,
which brings misfortune to its owner or wearer. One such stone,
the Hope Diamond, has a history of apparently causing bad luck and
violent death. This is said to be attributed to its original owners,
the priests of a Burmese temple, who prayed that death, destruction
or disaster might strike whoever had the diamond in his possession.

In 1668 Jean Baptiste Tavernier, a French traveler, was
shown a large blue diamond which formed the center eye of Rama-
Sita, the twin gods in the temple of the ancient Burmese city of
Pagan. He was allowed by the Grand Mogul to handle the stone,
which he described as "weighing 279 of our carats and presenting
the form of an egg cut in half. "

Tavernier stole the diamond and carried it to Paris. There
he sold it to Louis XIV, King of France, "for a goodly fortune and
a title. " The money he received was used largely to pay his son's
debts, and after several years of financial difficulties he made a
last trip to the Orient where he was attacked and killed by a pack
of wild dogs.

King Louis had the stone, now called the "French Blue,"
cut to 65 carats. During his reign France was engaged in a series
of disastrous wars, saw her prestige diminish and found herself
saddled with debt. The Marquise de Montespan, his mistress, wore
the jewel at times. Louis grew tired of her and she was replaced
by Madam Scarron.

Louis died in 1715 and his son, Louis XV, inherited the
throne and the diamond. During his reign France was embroiled
in the Seven Years' War which cost her losses in Canada and India and in other wars which were equally disastrous. French fi-

nances were chaotic and the reign was characterized by domestic unrest and hatred of the king by the masses.

Louis XVI, who next ascended the throne was, with his wife Marie Antoinette, guillotined in 1793.   Marie de Lamballe, a friend of the Queen, sometimes wore the French Blue.   She was killed by a mob of revolutionists in a Paris street

In the fall of 1792 the diamond was stolen from the Garde-Beuble, along with other crown jewels.   These were later recovered, but the French Blue was not.   A nameless Indian brilliant was among the articles stolen and when a blue diamond of 44. 5 carats turned up in Amsterdam it was thought to be a portion of the French Blue, cut once more.   Now called the "Diamond of Death, " the gem was taken to London by Francis Beauliew who sold it to Daniel Eliason, a jeweler, Beauliew being practically bankrupt.   Eliason kept the stone until 1830, when he sold it to the English banker, Henry Thomas Hope, for a fraction of its value.   When the banker died the diamond, now known as the "Hope Diamond, " came into the possession of his descendant, Lord Francis Hope.

Lord Francis married May Yohe, an actress, in 1894.   She left him for another man and divorced him in 1902, the year in which he sold the jewel in an effort to avoid bankruptcy.   Miss Yohe attributed the desertion of her husband to the baleful influence of the stone.

The Hope Diamond passed from owner to owner, and each in turn had reason to dispose of it.   It came into the possession of Prince Kanitousky, a Russian nobleman, who gave it to his mistress, Mademoiselle Ladue, an actress.   She was shot by a spurned lover and two days later the Prince was stabbed to death.   It was owned by the Turkish sultan Abdul Hamid, whose wife and family were killed in an accident on the day he purchased the gem.   The sultan gave it to a friend, Kulub Bey, who was mysteriously strangled shortly afterwards.   Hamid died violently in a revolution.

Edward B. McLean, a Washington, D. C. , millionaire, purchased the stone in 1911.   His son was killed in an automobile accident.   Following McLean's death in 1947 the Russian government attempted to purchase the Hope Diamond but the transaction was not consummated.   The stone became the property of Harry Winston, a New York dealer in precious gems.   Winston donated it to the Smithsonian Institution in Washington, to form the nucleus of an American jewel collection.

Suggested Readings

"Big Blue, " New Yorker, May 7, 1949.
"Big Rocks: Hope Diamond, " Time, April 18, 1949.
"Big Start for a U. S. Gem Collection: Hope Diamond, " U. S. News and World Report, November 21, 1958.

"By Registered Mail: The Hope Diamond," Life, November 24, 1958.

"The Curse of the Diamond," Newsweek, November 17, 1958.

Dunsany, Edward John Moreton Drax Plunkett. "A Night at an Inn" (play) in Cerf, Bennett, and V. H. Cartmell, eds. Thirty Famous One Act Plays. New York: Random House, 1943.

"Famous Diamonds of the World," Technical World Magazine, July, 1912.

"The Gem and the Curse: Hope Diamond," Newsweek, April 18, 1949.

Godwin, John. "The Gems of Doom" in his Unsolved: The World of the Unknown. Garden City, N. Y.: Doubleday, 1976.

"Great Diamonds," Scientific American, February 10, 1900.

"Great Diamonds of All Countries," Scientific American, January 25, 1902.

Harrell, D. T. "History and Legend Regarding the Diamond," Hobbies, May, 1955.

"The Hope Diamond," Hobbies, February, 1943, and March, 1959.

"Hope Diamonds" in Crime and Punishment, Vol. 7. Editorial presentation: Jackson Morley. London: BPC, 1973.

Kunz, G. F. "Six Famous Diamonds," The Mentor, December, 1925.

Patch, Suzanne Steinem. Blue Mystery: The Story of the Hope Diamond. Washington, D. C.: Smithsonian Institute Press, 1976.

Ross, Leonard. "Profiles: Harry Winston," New Yorker, May 15, 1954.

Schloss, E. "Diamonds and Bad Luck," Good Housekeeping, April, 1945.

Stevenson, Robert Louis. "The Rajah's Diamond" (fiction) in his The Complete Short Stories of Robert Louis Stevenson. Edited and with an introduction by Charles Neider. Garden City, N. Y.: Doubleday, 1969 (Originally published 1882).

"Stories About the Diamond," Hobbies, September, 1945.

THE MAN IN THE IRON MASK (1669-1703)

One of the most baffling mysteries of the late 17th and early 18th centuries was the affair of the "man in the iron mask." The man, a prisoner in the Bastille at Paris for 34 years, though held in high esteem, was never permitted to show his face, which was concealed behind a mask. This mask was not metal but velvet. The French satirist Voltaire described him as wearing a mask of iron and it is by this appellation that he is remembered today.

The man was imprisoned by order of Louis XIV, King of France. Louis, called the "Sun King" and the "Grand Monarch," was an absolute ruler, fully convinced that he held his exalted position by virtue of the divine right of kings. He was inordinately ambitious and used his monarchial authority despotically. His idea of government was summed up in the words attributed to him: "I am the state!"

King Louis was merciless in dealing with his enemies and considered anyone an enemy who in any way threatened his royal position. He did not hesitate to order the execution or imprisonment of anyone who incurred his displeasure.

In 1669 a "tall, well-dressed man of courtly bearing" was delivered to Monsieur Saint-Mars, governor of the Bastille. As a prisoner, this man was lodged in comfortable quarters and shown the greatest respect by the few who came in contact with him. He was permitted the comfort of a priest, books and musical instruments. His food was the best obtainable. However, he was never allowed, at any time during his imprisonment, to remove the velvet mask from his face. When he died in 1703, still a prisoner, he was buried in St. Paul Cemetery, Paris, under the name of Ercole Antonio Mattioli.

To this day it is not known why Louis XIV condemned the man to spend the remainder of his life in the Bastille. It is not known why the king spared his life or why he went to such great lengths to hide the prisoner's identity which, three centuries later, remains unknown.

Some historians have hazarded the conjecture that the man may have been the illegitimate son of Anne of Austria, the king's mother, and that the Duke of Buckingham was the man's father. If this theory is correct, Louis may well have ordered the imprisonment to stifle scandal, sparing the man's life out of consideration for his mother. It has also been surmised that the man was Louis' twin brother, confined to the Bastille in order to avoid a contest for the French throne. In either case such a person of noble blood would be treated with dignity. The mask was ordered that any facial resemblance between the prisoner and the royal family would not be seen.

In The Man in the Iron Mask Alexandre Dumas père romanticized the story of the unknown prisoner and the episode has sparked a number of novels, short stories and at least two motion pictures.

Suggested Readings

Barnes, A. S. Man of the Mask: A Study in the Byways of History. London: Smith, 1912.

Cronin, Vincent. Louis XIV. Boston: Houghton Mifflin, 1965.

Dover, George James. The True Story of the State Prisoner Commonly Called the Iron Mask ... from ... the French Archives. London: Murray, 1827.

Dumas, Alexandre. The Man in the Iron Mask (fiction). New York: Dodd, Mead, 1944. Adapted by Emile van Vliet from Dumas' novel Vicomte de Bragelonne, or Twenty Years Later (1848-1850).

Funck-Brentano, Franz. Legendes et archives de la Bastille. Paris: Hachette, 1914.

Hart, Harold H. "The Man in the Mask" in his From Bed to Verse.
    New York: Hart Publishing Co. , 1966.
Hopkins, T. "The Man in the Iron Mask, " Athenaeum, May 18,
    1901.
Lang, Andrew. "The Man in the Iron Mask, " Athenaeum, July 6,
    1901.
_____. "Velvet Mask, " Independent, August 15, 1901.
Lucas, W. J. The Man with the Iron Mask (melodrama). 1842.
Nolan, J. C. "Prisoner" (short story), St. Nicholas, June, 1929.

THE POPISH PLOT (1678-1681)

The Popish Plot, an imaginary conspiracy against the Roman Catholics in Restoration England, was "uncovered" by Titus Oates, Israel Tongue and others.

Oates, the principal informer, was employed by Tongue, an English divine who was obsessed with the notion of popish plots. The English public was, in 1678, generally hostile towards the Catholic Church. The conspirators, instigated by Anthony Ashley Cooper, Earl of Shaftesbury, a political Machiavelli, took advantage of this hostility by inducing Christopher Kirkby, a Lancashire gentleman, to reveal to the persons interested the details of a fictitious plot of Roman Catholics to murder King Charles II, burn London, destroy English trade, "massacre all Protestants in their beds, " and make the Catholic James Stuart, Duke of York, king. The alleged plot involved the pope, King Louis XIV of France, the General of the Jesuits, the Archbishop of Dublin, and others.

Prior to the fabrication of the Popish Plot Oates, the son of an Anibaptist preacher, had pretended to be converted to Catholicism, been expelled from two Jesuit seminaries, had returned to Protestantism and had been implicated in various affairs of an unsavory nature. He reported the details of the alleged plot to King Charles who detected several discrepancies in his story and literally laughed in his face, refusing to take seriously the "wild tale of a man who had twice changed his religion. " Shaftesbury's agents spread rumors concerning the plot and while Charles and his officials regarded the matter as nonsense and Oates a "mischevious fraud, " many of the English populace took it seriously.

Oates, realizing that his efforts to cause the king to take action against the Catholics had failed, decided to report the matter at a lower level. On September 6, 1678, he made a false deposition before Sir Edmund Berry Godfrey, a magistrate, to the truth of the plot. Shortly thereafter Godfrey was murdered. His murderer was never discovered.

The Godfrey murder caused a great panic. His funeral in London drew large crowds and Charles, fearful of further demon-

strations if not actual civil war, reluctantly signed death warrants
for 35 Catholics who, though probably innocent, were executed.
One historian attributes the murder to Philip Herbert, Earl of Pembroke, a violent man who had been indicted for the murder of a
drinking companion by a jury headed by Godfrey. Herbert was
tried before the House of Lords which released him on a technicality. He was known to have committed at least six other murders
and may well have revenged himself on Godfrey by killing him.
Others feel that Oates instigated the murder.

Miles Prance, an informer, confessed that he was present
when Godfrey was murdered by hirelings in the courtyard of Somerset House, London, while Roman Catholic priests looked on. On
his evidence Robert Green, Lawrence Hill and Henry Berry were
tried and hanged in 1697. Prance later admitted that he had per-
jured himself.

Oates accused the Catholic Queen Catherine of Braganza,
wife of Charles, of intending to poison her husband and of complicity in the Popish Plot. He accused the queen's physician of
being involved. Queen Catherine was shielded from Oates' attacks
by the king and the physician was acquitted.

At first Oates lived in Whitehall Palace and was granted a
pension. However, a reaction set in and, after calling the Duke
of York a traitor he was, in 1684, imprisoned. In 1685, following
the accession of James II, he was tried and found guilty of perjury.
He was sentenced to be pilloried, whipped at the cart's tail and
afterward confined for life. In 1689, after William III became king,
he was pardoned and again granted a pension.

Suggested Readings

Airy, Osmond, Charles II. London: 1904.
Ashley, Maurice. Great Britain to 1688: A Modern History. Ann
    Arbor, Mich.: University of Michigan Press, 1961.
            . Life in Stuart England. New York: Putnam's, 1964.
Belloc, Hilaire. Charles II, The Last Rally. New York: Harper
    & Row, 1939.
Birkenhead, Frederick Edwin Smith. "The Trial of Green and Oth-
    ers for the Murder of Sir Edmundbury Godfrey" in his Famous
    Trials of History. Garden City, N.Y.: Garden City Publishing
    Co., 1928.
Brown, L. F. The First Earl of Shaftesbury. London: 1933.
Carr, John Dickson. The Murder of Sir Edmund Godfrey. West-
    port, Conn.: Hyperion Press, 1975 (Originally published 1936).
Christie, W. D. A Life of Anthony Ashley Cooper, First Earl of
    Shaftesbury. London: 1871.
Clark, George. "The Later Stuarts, 1660-1714" in The Oxford His-
    tory of England. Oxford: Clarendon Press, 1956.
Dakers, Elaine Kidner. Titus Oates. London: Oxford University
    Press, 1949.

Feiling, Keith. A History of England. New York: McGraw-Hill,
     1948.
Lane, Jane. Titus Oates. New York: International Publications
     Service, 1949.
Lang, Andrew. The Mystery of Sir Edmund Berry Godfrey. Phil-
     adelphia: Richard West, 1901.
Loth, David. Royal Charles, Ruler and Rake. New York: Bren-
     tano's, 1930.
Ogg, David. England in the Reign of Charles II. Oxford: Claren-
     don Press, 1955.
Pollock, Sir John. The Popish Plot. London: Oxford University
     Press, 1944.
Terry, Benjamin. A History of England from the Earliest Times
     to the Death of Queen Victoria. Chicago: Scott, Foresman,
     1901.
Trevalyn, George Macaulay. History of England. New York: Doub-
     leday, 1953.
Williamson, Hugh Ross. "The Murder of Sir Edmund Berry God-
     frey" in his Historical Whodunits. New York: Macmillan, 1955.

THE RYE HOUSE PLOT (1683)

The Rye House Plot was a conspiracy hatched in 1683, its
object being to assassinate King Charles II of England and his brother the Duke of York, later King James II.

The Whig party sprang up in 17th-century England during the
great contest respecting the royal prerogatives and the rights of
the people. Those persons involved in the Rye House Plot were
members of the Whig party.

Lord William Russell, Algernon Sidney, Arthur Capel and
others had, for some time, been considering the possibility of an
armed uprising to depose Charles, but while an assassination was
planned, these men had no part in it. The victims were to be done
away with as they were passing Rumbold's Rye House, located on
the road between London and Newmarket.

The assassination plot failed as the royal party had passed
by earlier than had been expected. After the plot was revealed to
the authorities by an informer the conspirators were arrested. Tried
before Judge Jeffreys, Russell, Sidney, Capel and the actual plotters
were found guilty of high treason. Russell and Sidney were executed
and Capel, having been sent to the Tower, was found with his throat
cut, probably a suicide.

Suggested Readings

Airy, Osmond. Charles II. London, 1904.

Ashley, Maurice. Great Britain to 1688: A Modern History. Ann
    Arbor, Mich.: University of Michigan Press, 1961.
_____. Life in Stuart England. New York: Putnam's, 1964.
_____. The Stuarts in Love. New York: Macmillan, 1964.
Belloc, Hilaire. Charles II, The Last Rally. New York: Harper
    & Row, 1939.
Bryant, Sir Arthur. Charles II. London: R. Hale, 1931.
Clark, George. "The Later Stuarts, 1660-1714" in The Oxford His-
    tory of England. Oxford: Clarendon Press, 1956.
Cross, Arthur Lyon. A Shorter History of England and Greater
    Britain. New York: Macmillan, 1929.
Feiling, Keith. A History of England. New York: McGraw-Hill,
    1948.
Halliday, Frank. A Concise History of England from Stonehenge to
    the Atomic Age. New York: Viking Press, 1964.
Helm, Peter James. Jeffreys: A New Portrait of England's Hang-
    ing Judge. New York: Crowell, 1966.
Loth, David. Royal Charles, Ruler and Rake. New York: Bren-
    tano's, 1930.
Ogg, David. England in the Reign of Charles II. Oxford: Claren-
    don Press, 1955.
Trevalyn, George Macaulay. History of England. New York: Doub-
    leday, 1953.

THE MONMOUTH REBELLION (1685)

James Scott, Duke of Monmouth, was the natural son of
Charles II of England and the King's mistress, Lucy Walter. He
was born in Rotterdam in 1649 and raised a Protestant by the diplomat William Crofts. In 1662 he was brought to England where
Charles acknowledged him as his son and created him Duke of Monmouth. In 1663 he married Anne Scott, Countess of Buccleuch, and
took her surname. On the death of the British general officer
George Monck in 1670 King Charles appointed him captain general
of his troops.

Monmouth's right to succeed Charles on the English throne
was upheld by the Earl of Shaftesbury. Charles fell ill in 1679 and,
at the insistence of his brother James, afterwards King James II,
banished Monmouth. The latter left England, returning only to flee
again in 1683 after the arrest of the Whig leaders of the Rye House
Plot, in which he was involved. This was a conspiracy to assassinate King Charles and his brother.

Charles died in 1685 and Monmouth, feeling himself to have
a "legitimate and legal" claim to the throne, arranged to join Lord
Argyll and Robert Ferguson's expedition to England. With some 82
followers they captured Axminster and Taunton but were defeated by
Lord Louis de Durfort of Feversham and John Churchill at Sedge-
moor.

Monmouth was captured, "made a cringing confession of
wrongdoing, wrote contrite letters to James and offered to turn
Catholic. " He was tried for treason, convicted and beheaded on
Tower Hill in 1685. His followers and supporters were cruelly
and indiscriminately punished by the Bloody Assizes treason trials
conducted by Lord Chief Justice George Jeffreys. Over three hundred persons were sentenced to death and more than eight hundred
were transported to America.

Suggested Readings

Ashley, Maurice. Great Britain to 1688: A Modern History.   Ann
    Arbor, Mich. : University of Michigan Press, 1961.
    _____. Life in Stuart England. New York: Putnam's, 1964.
    _____. The Stuarts in Love. New York: Macmillan, 1964.
Bryant, Sir Arthur. Charles II. London: R. Hale, 1931.
Clark, George. "The Later Stuarts, 1660-1714" in The Oxford His-
    tory of England. Oxford: Clarendon Press, 1956.
Cross, Arthur Lyon. A Shorter History of England and Greater
    Britain. New York: Macmillan, 1929.
Feiling, Keith. A History of England. New York: McGraw-Hill,
    1948.
Halliday, Frank E. A Concise History of England from Stonehenge
    to the Atomic Age. New York: Viking Press, 1964.
Helm, Peter James. Jeffreys: A New Portrait of England's Hang-
    ing Judge. New York: Crowell, 1966.
Lodge, Richard. "The History of England from the Restoration to
    the Death of William III, 1660-1702" in The Political History
    of England. London: Longmans, Green, 1910.
Loth, David. Royal Charles, Ruler and Rake. New York: Bren-
    tano's, 1930.
Ogg, David. England in the Reign of Charles II. Oxford: Claren-
    don Press, 1955.
    _____. Europe in the Seventeenth Century. New York: Mac-
    millan, 1961.
Terry, Benjamin. A History of England from the Earliest Times
    to the Death of Queen Victoria. Chicago: Scott, Foresman,
    1901.
Trevalyn, George Macaulay. History of England. New York: Doub-
    leday, 1953.

THE "GLORIOUS REVOLUTION" (1688-1689)

James II, King of England, was converted to Catholicism
sometime between 1668 and 1671. When he assumed the throne
following the death of his brother, Charles II in 1685, he was a
staunch Catholic, a firm believer in the divine right of kings, and
a man of little tact. Charles had, following his restoration in 1660,
achieved a satisfactory working arrangement with Parliament and had

ruled responsibly through his nation's representatives.   James, by his attitude and actions, tore down the acceptable relationship built up by Charles and so precipitated a situation which climaxed in the "Glorious Revolution" of 1688-1689.

James' major goal was to restore Roman Catholicism in England.   He attempted to persuade Parliament to repeal the Test Acts of 1673 and 1678 which required holders of public offices to take Communion as prescribed by the Church of England, something a Catholic could not conscientiously do.   Parliament refused to repeal the Acts.   James retaliated by packing the Court of King's Bench with judges of his own selection who rendered decisions according to his wishes.

Although opposition to his pro-Catholic policies mounted, James attempted to strengthen his position.   In 1687 he issued a declaration of indulgence in England.   This suspended all penal laws against Dissenters and Roman Catholics, thus granting both groups freedom of worship.   Other similar manifestations of Catholic despotism followed.   On April 27, 1688, he issued a second declaration and ordered that it be read from all pulpits of the Church of England.   Seven bishops, including the Archbishop of Canterbury, petitioned James to rescind the order which he refused to do, countering by bringing charges of seditious libel against the churchmen involved.   On June 30 the churchmen were acquitted and on the same day seven high ranking English Whig and Tory leaders sent a secret letter to William of Orange, James' Protestant son-in-law, asking him to "come to England to secure their liberties" and to assume the English throne.

William complied, invading Southern England.   James' standing army and sizable fleet could not drive the foreigners out.   By mid-December, 1688, William had triumphed over James, who fled to France.

On January 22, 1689, Parliament formally bestowed the crown of England jointly on William and his wife Mary.   The two were recognized as joint sovereigns in both England and Scotland. Ireland, however, capitulated only after James, supported by French troops, was defeated by those of William at the Battle of the Boyne on July 1, 1690.

James returned to France, to write on the subject of religion, spending much time meditating in Catholic retreats and waiting in vain for his restoration.   He died September 6, 1701.

Suggested Readings

Ashley, Maurice.   The Glorious Revolution of 1688.   New York:
      Scribner, 1966.
_____.   Great Britain to 1688:   A Modern History.   Ann Arbor,
      Mich.:   University of Michigan Press, 1961.

_____ . Life in Stuart England. New York: Putnam's, 1964.
_____ . The Stuarts in Love. New York: Macmillan, 1964.
Clark, George. "The Later Stuarts, 1660-1714" in The Oxford History of England. Oxford: Clarendon Press, 1956.
Cross, Arthur Lyon. A Shorter History of England and Greater Britain. New York: Macmillan, 1929.
Feiling, Keith. A History of England. New York: McGraw-Hill, 1948.
Halliday, Frank E. A Concise History of England from Stonehenge to the Atomic Age. New York: Viking Press, 1964.
Lodge, Richard. "The History of England from the Restoration to the Death of William III, 1660-1702," in The Political History of England. London: Longmans, Green, 1910.
Loth, David. Royal Charles, Ruler and Rake. New York: Brentano's, 1930.
Ogg, David. "England in the Reigns of James II and William III" in The Political History of England. London: Longmans, Green, 1910.
Pinkham, Lucille. William III and the Respectable Revolution: The Part Played by William of Orange in the Revolution of 1688. Cambridge, Mass.: Harvard University Press, 1954.
Straka, Gerald M., ed. The Revolution of 1688: Whig Triumph or Palace Revolution? Boston: Heath, 1963.
Tanner, J. R. "The Revolution of 1688" in English Constitutional Conflicts of the Seventeenth Century, 1603-1689. Cambridge: Cambridge University Press, 1962.
Temperley, Harold W. "The Revolution and Revolution Settlement in Great Britain" in Ward, A. W., et al, eds. The Cambridge Modern History. Cambridge: Cambridge University Press, 1908.
Terry, Benjamin. A History of England from the Earliest Times to the Death of Queen Victoria. Chicago: Scott, Foresman, 1901.
Trevalyn, George Macaulay. History of England. New York: Doubleday, 1953.
Wolf, John B. The Emergence of the Great Powers, 1685-1715. New York: Harper & Row, 1951.

THE PETRINE REFORMS (1689-1725)

Peter I, called "The Great," Tsar of Russia, is considered the founder of the Russian Empire. The reforms he instituted provided the basis for a national framework, particularly in the areas of governmental and social structure. These remained essentially unchanged until the 1917 Revolution. According to the historian B. H. Sumner, "Before Peter the Great Russia rested as a slumbering backward giant on the eastern marshes of Europe; since his reign Russia has played a leading role in the affairs of Europe."

Peter ascended the Russian throne in 1682. Until 1689, under the regency of his half-sister Sophia, he ruled jointly with his mentally deficient older half-brother Ivan. Peter was designated Junior Tsar and Ivan, as Ivan V, was Senior Tsar. Sophia attempted to deprive Peter of his right to the throne, and when this failed she sought to have him and his mother assassinated. The plot failed, Peter's partisans at court installed him as sole ruler and, in 1689, Sophia was required to resign all power and enter a convent.

As a youth Peter was taught by private tutors and later he studied craft trades, often incognito. Soon he came to realize that Russia would remain a semi-backward country unless she adopted a program of "Westernization."

Once Peter became sole ruler of Russia he inaugurated his program of reform. This included abolition of the power of the boyars and the subordination of those nobles and of the church to the throne. He modernized the obsolete Russian army, in which he was assisted by Patrick Gordon, a Scottish soldier of fortune who became general-in-chief and led Russian troops to victories against their enemies. In this area Peter was also assisted by Alexander Menshikov, a close friend. Alexis Kurbatov carried out financial reforms and used methods similar to those employed in Western Europe to increase tax revenues.

The administrative apparatus of the state was overhauled and reorganized to make it more modern and efficient. In the year 1700 the old Russian calendar was eliminated, being replaced by the Julian, then eleven days behind the Gregorian calendar. Tsar Peter turned his personal attention to the Russian alphabet, simplifying it. He also was concerned with the editing of Russia's first newspaper. Arabic numerals were introduced and the Academy of Sciences was augmented.

As a regimented state, every occupation in Russia was controlled by a strictly enforced set of regulations and penalties for non-compliance were swift and severe. While some Russians viewed their ruler's thoroughgoing reforms with admiration, others, especially those concerned with religion, viewed them with suspicion and distrust. By 1710 the opposing forces had found a champion in Peter's disgruntled son Alexis. Matters came to a head in 1718 when Peter, convinced that Alexis was involved in a plot to repeal certain of the reforms, forced him to renounce his succession to the throne. Then, by Peter's order, Alexis was arrested and sent to prison where he died under torture. By the tsar's will his second wife ascended the throne as Catherine I following his death in 1725.

The series of weak rulers who succeeded Peter failed to continue his reforms until Catherine II published her Instruction in 1767. This document, intended to be a general statement of basic philosophical principles concerning various facets of Russian life, was so amended by her advisers that no workable code could be produced.

Suggested Readings

Almedingen, Martha Edith von. The Romanovs: Three Centuries
    of an Ill-Fated Dynasty. New York: Holt, 1966.
Blum, J. G. Lord and Peasant in Russia from the Ninth to the
    Nineteenth Century. Princeton, N. J.: Princeton University
    Press, 1961.
Charques, Richard Denis. A Short History of Russia. New York:
    Dutton, 1956.
Cherniavsky, Michael. Tsar and Empire: Studies in Russian Myths.
    New York: Random House, 1969.
Clarkson, Jesse D. A History of Russia. New York: Random
    House, 1969.
Florinsky, Michael T. Russia: A History and Interpretation. New
    York: Macmillan, 1965.
Goodwin, Albert, ed. The European Nobility in the Eighteenth Cen-
    tury. New York: Harper & Row, 1953.
Hingley, Ronald. Tsars, 1533-1917. New York: Macmillan, 1968.
Kluchevsky, Vasily O. A History of Russia. Translated by C. J.
    Hogarth. New York: Russell and Russell, 1960 (Originally
    published 1913).
Moscow, Henry, and the editors of Horizon Magazine. Russia Un-
    der the Czars. New York: American Heritage Publishing Co.,
    1962.
Pares, Bernard. A History of Russia. New York: Knopf, 1960.
Raeff, Marc, ed. Peter the Great: Reformer or Revolutionary?
    Boston: Heath, 1963.
Riasanovsky, Nicholas Valentine. A History of Russia. New York:
    Oxford University Press, 1963.
Rogger, Hans. National Consciousness in Eighteenth Century Rus-
    sia. Cambridge, Mass.: Harvard University Press, 1960.
Sumner, B. H. Peter the Great and the Emergence of Russia. New
    York: Collier Books, 1962.
Thompson, G. S. Catherine the Great and the Expansion of Russia.
    London: Macmillan, 1955.
Trowbridge, W. R. H. "Catherine II, Empress of Russia, 1729-
    1796" in his Seven Splendid Sinners. London: T. F. Unwin,
    1908.
Vernadsky, George. A History of Russia. New Haven, Conn.:
    Yale University Press, 1954.
Wolf, John B. The Emergence of the Great Powers, 1685-1715.
    New York: Harper & Row, 1951.
Wren, Melvin C. The Course of Russian History. New York:
    Macmillan, 1968.

THE GREAT NORTHERN WAR (1700-1721)

The Battle of Narva, fought by Russia, Poland and Denmark
who were united against Sweden, occurred on November 20, 1700.
It resulted in an overwhelming victory for the Swedes, led in per-

son by King Charles XII, and was the first encounter of the Great
Northern War which was to continue until 1721.

Charles, who had ascended the Swedish throne in 1697 at
the age of fifteen, is considered by military historians to be one
of the greatest generals of all time.   He commanded the armies
of his country during the Great Northern War.   Soon after Charles'
assumption of the Swedish throne his country, which had extensive
possessions on the shores of the Baltic Sea, was threatened by a
coalition of Frederick IV of Denmark, Augustus the Strong, Elector
of Saxony and King of Poland, and Peter I (the Great) of Russia.
These three hoped to recover territories they had lost to Sweden
in the seventeenth century.   The war which resulted was, at first,
a war of defense on Sweden's part.   Then, following Charles' success at the Battle of Narva, it became a war of conquest, and finally, through his failure, a struggle for existence.

In 1700, when the Great Northern War broke out, Frederick
of Denmark concentrated his forces against the German provinces
of Sweden, his objective being to eliminate Swedish influence in
Holstein-Gottorp.   At the same time Polish-Saxon forces commenced
an assault on Swedish positions in Livonia in the eastern Baltic.
Charles landed his troops, numbering some 11,000 men, in northern
Denmark and on August 18, 1700, Frederick capitulated at the Peace
of Travendal.

Russia, which had only entered the war on August 9, having
been engaged in peace negotiations with the Turks, replaced Denmark in the conflict.   Peter the Great and Augustus the Strong offered to negotiate with Charles but he, as confident following his
victory over the Danes as Peter and Augustus were impressed by
it, rejected their proposals.   He marched to Riga in Latvia where
he compelled the Poles to raise their siege of that city and then,
by forced marches, brought his troops to Narva, a fortress in
Swedish Esthonia on the Gulf of Finland where he won the victory
mentioned above.

Following the Swedish victories over Denmark and Russia
Charles, rather than follow up the second victory, turned to conquer Poland which was soon overrun by Swedish troops.   Augustus
was deposed and driven into Saxony and in 1705 Charles obtained
the election of Stanislas Leszczynski as king of Poland.

Charles next turned his attention to Russia.   He and his
army of 46,000 men penetrated the interior of that country.   On
July 8, 1709, while besieging Poltava he suffered an overwhelming
defeat at the hands of the Russians.   He and 300 of his guard
barely escaped into Turkish territory.   He then persuaded the sultan to declare war on Russia.   He spent the next three years plotting further attacks on that country, was imprisoned by the Turks
at Bender and Dimtika, and escaped back to Sweden in 1714.   Finding his country in a deplorable state he raised another army with
which he invaded Norway in 1717 and 1718.   He was killed by a

cannonball at the siege of Fredrikshald in the latter year.

Russia became the dominant power in the Baltic. By the treaties of Stockholm and Mystadt, signed in 1721, Sweden lost much of her German territory. She also ceded Livonia, Estonia, Ingermanland, part of Karelia and a number of Baltic islands to Russia.

Suggested Readings

Bain, R. Nisbet. Charles XII and the Collapse of the Swedish Empire, 1682-1719. New York: Putnam's, 1895.
_____. "Charles XII and the Great Northern War" in The Cambridge Modern History. Edited by A. W. Ward, et al. Cambridge: The University Press, 1908.

Charques, Richard Denis. A Short History of Russia. New York: Dutton, 1956.

Clarkson, Jesse D. A History of Russia. New York: Random House, 1969.

Florinsky, Michael T. Russia: A History and Interpretation. New York: Macmillan, 1965.

Holborn, Hajo. A History of Modern Germany, Vol. II: 1648-1840. New York: Knopf, 1964.

Kluchevsky, Vasily O. A History of Russia. Translated by C. J. Hogarth. New York: Russell and Russell, 1960 (Originally published 1913).

Ogg, David. Europe in the Seventeenth Century. New York: Macmillan, 1961.

Pares, Bernard. A History of Russia. New York: Knopf, 1960.

Riasanovsky, Nicholas Valentine. A History of Russia. New York: Oxford University Press, 1963.

Roberts, Penfield. The Quest for Security, 1715-1740. New York: Harper, 1947.

Sumner, B. H. Peter the Great and the Emergence of Russia. New York: Collier Books, 1962.

Vernadsky, George. A History of Russia. New Haven, Conn. : Yale University Press, 1954.

Wolf, John B. The Emergence of the Great Powers, 1685-1715. New York: Harper & Row, 1951.

Wren, Melvin C. The Course of Russian History. New York: Macmillan, 1968.

BACH'S INAUGURATION OF MODERN MUSIC (c. 1700-1750)

The many compositions and innovations of the German organist, violinist, master contrapuntist and conductor Johann Sebastian Bach established what are today regarded as musical landmarks. Although during his lifetime Bach remained an obscure church musician and teacher, he is now considered the greatest of all compo-

sers of organ music and the one who most fully realized the possibilities of counterpoint. His works marked the end of the Baroque Era which began about 1600 and continued until 1750, the year
of Bach's death.

Bach was born of a musical family. His father was a violinist in the Eisenach town band and his elder brother, Johann
Christoph Bach, was an organist. Young Johann Sebastian Bach
received music lessons from both these relatives. In 1700 he
moved to Lüneberg where he served as chorister at the Church of
St. Michael. In 1703 he became a violinist at Weimar and later
in the same year was appointed organist of the New Church in Arn-
stadt.

For the following twenty years he traveled, studied, held
a number of positions in various court orchestras and churches
and composed prolifically. During this period he developed an
outstanding organ technique. He married Maria Barbara Bach, a
second cousin, in 1707. His wife died in 1720 and in 1721 he married again, this time to Anna Magdalena Wilcken, the daughter of
a court musician.

In 1717 he was kapellmeister at the court of Prince Leopold
of Anhalt-Köthen. While there he composed some of his finest
secular instrumental numbers and completed Part I of The Well-
Tempered Clavier. This, finished in 1740, consisted of 48 preludes
and fugues for the keyboard, ranging through all keys, both major
and minor. It was written to demonstrate the practicability of the
now standard equally tempered keyboard, in which the octave is
divided into twelve equidistant semitones.

In 1723 Bach moved to Leipzig where he lived the remaining
27 years of his life, occupying the position of musical director and
choirmaster of St. Thomas' church and church school. His employers criticized his work, considering it old fashioned. Bach himself
was regarded as "a stuffy old man who clung stubbornly to obsolete
forms of music." In spite of this, compositions continued to pour
from his pen. These included 295 cantatas, of which 202 survive,
as well as Goldberg Variations, Part II of The Well-Tempered Clavier and The Art of the Fugue.

For decades after his death the greatness of Bach's work
remained unrecognized. Three of his sons, musicians in their own
right, tended to be patronizing toward their father. For almost a
hundred years "the voice of Johann Sebastian Bach was silenced."
His genius, however, was realized by such great masters as Beetho-
ven, Mozart, Liszt, Haydn, Schumann, Brahms, Mendelssohn and
even Wagner. Mendelssohn arranged a performance of the Passion
of St. Matthew in 1829 which was instrumental in arousing popular
interest in Bach. The Bach Gesellschaft, organized in 1850, dedicated itself to locating, editing and publishing Bach's works. In the
20th century Albert Schweitzer, the French musician, did much to
bring the eighteenth-century composer's music to the attention of the
world.

Bach's music, a catalog of which would fill several volumes, "simultaneously grips the emotions and fascinates the intellect . . . . Once understood his music develops an infinitely rich experience. "

Suggested Readings

Blom, Eric, ed. "Johann Sebastian Bach" in Grove's Dictionary of Music and Musicians. 5th edition. New York: St. Martin's Press, 1954.

Blumme, Friedrich. Two Centuries of Bach: An Account of Changing Taste. Translated by Stanley Godman. Oxford: Oxford University Press, 1950.

Davey, Henry. "Some Points in Bach's Treatment of the Chorale, " Proceedings of the Musical Association, Vol. XXIV, 1897.

Davison, Archibald T. Bach and Handel: The Consummation of the Baroque in Music. Cambridge: Cambridge University Press, 1951.

Dickinson, A. E. F. The Art of Bach. Washington, D. C. : Duckworth, 1936.

Geiringer, Karl. Symbolism in the Music of Bach. Washington, D. C. : Library of Congress, 1956.

_____, and Irene Geiringer. Johann Sebastian Bach: The Cumulation of an Era. New York: Oxford University Press, 1966.

Hindemith, Paul. J. S. Bach: Heritage and Obligation. New Haven, Conn. : Yale University Press, 1952.

Newman, Ernest. "Johann Sebastian Bach" in Thompson, Oscar, ed. The International Cyclopedia of Music and Musicians. New York: Dodd, Mead, 1939.

Rüber, Johannes. Bach and the Heavenly Choir (fiction). Translated by M. A. Michael. Cleveland: World, 1956.

Schweitzer, Albert. J. S. Bach. Translated by Ernest Newman. London: A. C. Black, 1952.

Spitta, Philipp. Johann Sebastian Bach. New York: Dover Publications, 1951 (Originally published 1873-1880).

Terry, C. S. Bach: A Biography. Oxford: Oxford University Press, 1928.

THE BATTLE OF BLENHEIM (1704)

The Battle of Blenheim, fought on August 13, 1704, was the Duke of Marlborough's most famous victory and one of the most decisive battles in history.

Louis XIV of France wished to place his grandson, Philip of Anjou, on the Spanish throne which was empty following the death of Charles II in 1700. This was part of the French king's ambitious objective of "placing members of his family on every throne in Europe. "

Louis' plans were hampered by the Grand Alliance of Austria, England and Holland.   The Dutch and English fleets blocked him at sea but he felt that his army could help him achieve his goal.   By taking Vienna the Grand Alliance would be destroyed and he would have a free hand to do as he wished with Europe.

To prevent an Austrian collapse, John Churchill, Duke of Marlborough, commanding the armies of England and Holland, made a surprise march to the Danube River to join the Austrians, led by Prince Eugène of Savoy.   Once there, Marlborough destroyed everything of military value and then sought a decisive battle with the French and Bavarians, commanded by Marshals Tallard and Marsin and the Elector of Bavaria, whose forces were camped along the Nebel River.

On August 13, 1704, when the fog lifted, the Grand Alliance army deployed, ready to attack.   Their adversaries were taken completely by surprise.

The Allies attacked vigorously and were repelled with equal force.   Prince Eugène's men were in line before the French left flank, confronting the troops of Marsin and the Elector of Bavaria. Marlborough's soldiers faced those of Tallard.

As the fighting progressed Marlborough, by repeated attacks, drew the French reserves in the center of their line off towards their flanks.   Then, feeling that the time was ripe, he ordered a combined cavalry and infantry charge through the enemy's weakened center.   Tallard's troops broke before the charge.

Marlborough's cavalry, having ridden through the French lines, made a wheeling movement to the right.   This maneuver forced some thirty French squadrons into the Danube and many men were drowned.   Tallard was captured and his remaining infantry was forced into the village of Blenheim where, after suffering great losses, it surrendered.

The Allies lost 7,000 killed and as many wounded out of a total of 52,000 men.   The French army lost 21,000 killed in battle or drowned in the Danube, 7,000 wounded and 14,000 taken prisoner.

The victory at Blenheim is considered by historians to be England's greatest since that at Agincourt.   It ended the French king's ambitious plans to control Europe as a maker of kings and it made a hero of Marlborough who led Grand Alliance armies for a decade without suffering a defeat.

In 1711 he and his wife incurred the animosity of Queen Anne.   He was accused of embezzlement, was relieved of his military post as commander-in-chief and stripped of his public offices. His military rank was restored to him following the accession of George I to the English throne.

268 Footnotes to World History

Suggested Readings

Atkinson, Christopher T. Marlborough and the Rise of the British
  Army. New York: Putnam's, 1930.
Churchill, Winston S. Marlborough, His Life and Times. New
  York: Scribner's, 1933-1938.
Core, William C. Memoirs of the Duke of Marlborough with His
  Original Correspondence. London: Henry G. Bahn, 1847-1848.
Creasy, Edward S. Fifteen Decisive Battles of the World. Har-
  risburg, Pa.: Stackpole Books, 1957.
Falls, Cyril, ed. Great Military Battles. New York: Macmillan,
  1964.
Fortescue, John W. A History of the British Army. New York:
  St. Martin's Press, 1899.
Fuller, John F. C. A Military History of the Western World. New
  York: Funk & Wagnalls, 1954.
Mitchell, Lt. Col. Joseph B., and Sir Edward S. Creasy. Twenty
  Decisive Battles of the World. New York: Macmillan, 1964.
Montross, Lynn. War Through the Ages. New York: Harper &
  Row, 1960.
Murray, George, ed. Letters and Dispatches of J. Churchill, First
  Duke of Marlborough from 1702-1712. London: Henry C. Bahn,
  1845.
Taylor, Frank. The Wars of Marlborough, 1702-1709. London:
  Oxford University Press, 1921.
Wolf, John B. The Emergence of the Great Powers, 1685-1715.
  New York: Harper & Row, 1951.
_____. Louis XIV. New York: Norton, 1968.

THE SOUTH SEA BUBBLE (1711-1720)

In 1711 the British floating national debt amounted to more
than $50,000,000, an extremely large sum for that time. Robert
Harley, 1st Earl of Oxford and newly appointed Chancellor of Exchequer and Lord Treasurer, originated a plan by which this debt,
he felt, could be eliminated.

In essence, Harley's idea was to have the debt taken over
by merchants. In turn, the British government was to guarantee
an annual interest payment of $3,000,000. This interest was to
be generated by placing duties on imports.

The merchants were incorporated as the South Sea Company
and were guaranteed a trade monopoly with South America. Shares
were sold and in 1717 the Company advanced $25,000,000 to the
government which had spread the rumor that Spain intended to permit Company members to participate in a portion of its South American trade.

By 1720 the British national debt had increased to more than

$150,000,000, and the Company proposed to take over a large portion of this. Other companies came into existence, some of which were prosecuted by the original South Sea Company, under the Bubble Act. Intense speculation in the stock of the Company caused the price to rise tenfold, with shares originally subscribed to for $500 bringing as much as $5,000.

At this time the chairman and some of the executives of the Company sold their holdings which, in turn, created a feeling of caution on the part of many speculators. Shares were thrown on the market and on September 17, 1720, the price fell to $2,000. Later that year they fell further, causing the financial ruin of many stockholders.

Subsequent investigations by Parliament disclosed complicity on the part of certain members of the cabinet, and only a comparatively small portion of the original investment was saved for the shareholders.

Suggested Readings

Brown, V. L. "South Sea Company and Contraband Trade," American Historical Review, July, 1926.

Carswell, John. The South Sea Bubble. Stanford, Calif.: Stanford University Press, 1960.

Clapham, Sir John. The Bank of England: A History by Sir John Clapham. New York: Macmillan, 1945.

"Con-Men" in Crimes and Punishment, Vol. 8. Editorial presentation: Jackson Morley. London: BPC, 1973.

Cowles, Virginia Spencer. The Great Swindle: The Story of the South Sea Bubble. New York: Harper, 1960.

Forbes, H. T. S. "Financial Boom of the Last Century," Cornhill Magazine, June 27, 1896.

Giuseppi, John. Bank of England: A History from Its Foundation in 1694. Chicago: Henry Regnery, 1966.

Mackay, Charles. "The South-Sea Bubble" in his Memoirs of Extraordinary Illusions and the Madness of Crowds. London: Office of the National Illustrated Library, 1852. Reprinted by L. C. Page & Co., Boston, 1932.

Morgan, W. T. "Origins of the South Sea Company," Political Science Quarterly, March, 1929.

Nelson, G. H. "Contraband Trade Under the Asiento, 1730-1739," American Historical Review, October, 1945.

Samuel, A. M. "War-Debt Conversion: A Warning from 1720," Pan-American Magazine, February, 1922.

"South Sea Bubble" in Crimes and Punishment, Vol. 16. Editorial presentation: Jackson Morley. London: BPC, 1973.

Thiers, Louis Adolphe. Mississippi Bubble: A Memoir of John Law; To Which Are Added Authentic Accounts of the Darien Expedition and the South Sea Scheme. Translated and edited by Frank S. Fiske. Westport, Conn.: Greenwood Press, 1969 (Originally published 1859).

THE PEACE OF UTRECHT (1713)

One of the great international peace settlements of history was the Peace (or Treaty) of Utrecht. This marked the end of the War of the Spanish Succession and resulted in many changes in the map of Europe. It also achieved some balance of power between the nations of Europe.

In 1701 England, Holland and the Austrian Hapsburgs agreed to undertake a joint effort against the French king Louis XIV, who had attempted to place his grandson, Philip of Anjou, on the Spanish throne following the demise of Charles II, who had died childless in 1700. The Dutch and the British supported the Austrian claimant, the Archduke Charles. Further, both countries were concerned with maintaining the European balance of power which Louis' dynastic union with Spain would destroy.

War broke out in May. England, Holland and Austria allied with several of the German states against France and Spain. In 1704 armies under the Duke of Marlboro and Prince Eugène of Savoy defeated the French at the Battle of Blenheim. In 1711 the Archduke Charles became the Holy Roman Emperor. Some prospect of a union between Austria and Spain existed, which was feared as much as a union between France and Spain.

Negotiations were started and the Peace of Utrecht was signed on April 11, 1713, by Great Britain, France, the Netherlands, Savoy and Prussia. According to the provisions of the treaty, the French Duke of Anjou was recognized as King of Spain but France agreed that Spain and France should never be united under one ruler. Great Britain's colonial and commercial powers were increased. She acquired Gibraltar and the island of Minorca from Spain, who also gave her the assiento (contract) for supplying the Spanish colonies with African slaves. The Duke of Savoy assumed control of Sicily. Austria received Milan, Naples, Sardinia and the Catholic Netherlands, all from Spain. Holland, in the so-called "Barrier Agreements," received the right to arm frontier towns against French aggression.

In America, France ceded Nova Scotia, Newfoundland and the Hudson Bay Territory to Great Britain, but retained Quebec. As a result of the Peace of Utrecht Great Britain emerged as the world's leading colonial and commercial power.

Suggested Readings

Churchill, Winston S. Marlborough, His Life and Times. New York: Scribner's, 1933-1938.
Clark, George. "The Later Stuarts, 1660-1714" in The Oxford History of England. Oxford: Clarendon Press, 1956.
Cross, Arthur Lyon. A Shorter History of England and Greater Britain. New York: Macmillan, 1929.

Halliday, Frank E. A Concise History of England from Stonehenge
    to the Atomic Age. New York: Viking Press, 1964.
Hertz, Frederick. The Development of the German Public Mind:
    A Social History of German Political Sentiments, Aspirations,
    and Ideas. Vol. II: The Age of Enlightenment. London:
    George Allen & Unwin, 1962.
Holborn, Hajo. A History of Modern Germany. Vol. II: 1648-
    1840. New York: Knopf, 1964.
Israel, Frederick L., ed. Major Peace Treaties of Modern His-
    tory, 1648-1966. New York: Chelsea House, 1967.
Lindsay, J. O. "International Relations" in Lindsay, J. O., ed.
    The New Cambridge Modern History. Cambridge: Cambridge
    University Press, 1957.
Maurois, André. A History of France. New York: Farrar,
    Strauss, 1956.
Ogg, David. Europe in the Seventeenth Century. New York: Mac-
    millan, 1961.
Ward, A. W. "The Peace of Utrecht and the Supplementary Pac-
    ifications" in Ward, A. W., et al, eds. The Cambridge Mod-
    ern History. Cambridge: Cambridge University Press, 1908.
Wolf, John B. The Emergence of the Great Powers, 1685-1715.
    New York: Harper & Row, 1951.
_____. Louis XIV. New York: Norton, 1968.

THE MISSISSIPPI BUBBLE (1717-1720)

The Mississippi Bubble was promoted by John Law, a Scottish speculator and financier. Having studied banking in Amsterdam, he moved to Paris in 1715 where, under the patronage of
the Duke of Orleans, he founded the Banque Générale. This bank
was the first to be established in France and was authorized to
issue paper notes, which it did in great quantities. In 1719 this
became the Banque Royale and its paper currency was guaranteed
by the King of France, Louis XV.

Law originated his Mississippi scheme in 1717, his object
being to raise funds for France. He organized the Compagnie de
la Louisiane ou d'Occident which had control over large land grants
in the Mississippi delta region and also had exclusive trade rights
in the area for 25 years. The Compagnie took over the East India and China Company in 1719 and also merged with the Banque
Royale. Shortly thereafter it was granted the management of the
French mint and coin issue for a period of nine years. It also
arranged to receive government debts.

Shares in the project were offered to the public. Speculation ran rife and the price of these shares rose astronomically.
At the same time huge amounts of paper money were being issued.
The inevitable collapse occurred in 1720 after the French king had,
by royal decree, reduced the value of paper currency by 50 percent.

Prices of commodities skyrocketed and metal coins disappeared
from circulation.

The Banque Royale was forced to suspend payments. The
price of shares in Law's Compagnie plummeted. Law was held generally responsible for the debacle and left France for Venice where
he died in poverty and obscurity in 1729.

Suggested Readings

Bishop, Morris. "The Scoundrel Who Invented Credit," Horizon,
    Spring, 1971.
"Con-Men" in Crimes and Punishment, Vol. 8. Editorial presen-
    tation: Jackson Morley. London: BPC, 1973.
Costain, Thomas Bertram. The Mississippi Bubble. New York:
    Random House, 1955.
Hough, Emerson. The Mississippi Bubble. Indianapolis, Ind.:
    Bobbs-Merrill, 1902.
Hunt, William R. Dictionary of Rogues. New York: Philosophical
    Library, 1970.
Hyde, Harford Montgomery. John Law: The History of an Honest
    Adventurer. London: Horne and Van Thal, 1948.
Mackay, Charles. "The Mississippi Scheme" in his Memoirs of
    Popular Delusions and the Madness of Crowds. London: Of-
    fice of the National Illustrated Library, 1852. Reprinted by
    L. C. Page & Co., Boston, 1932.
"Masters of Money," Fortune, April, 1948.
Minton, Robert W. John Law: The Father of Paper Money. New
    York: Association Press, 1975.
_____. "John Law: The Man Who Blew the Mississippi Bubble,"
    Bankers Magazine, Spring, 1971.
_____. "John Law's Bubble: Bigger, Bigger and Then Bust!
    Crisis of 1720," Smithsonian, January, 1976.
Rand, Clayton. Stars in Their Eyes: Dreamers and Builders in
    Louisiana. Gulfport, Miss.: Dixie Press, 1953.
Sabatini, Rafael. Gamester (fiction). Boston: Houghton Mifflin,
    1949.
Thiers, Louis Adolphe. Mississippi Bubble: A Memoir of John
    Law; To Which Are Added Authentic Accounts of the Darien
    Expedition and the South Sea Scheme. Translated and edited
    by Frank S. Fiske. Westport, Conn.: Greenwood Press, 1969
    (Originally published 1859).

THE INVENTION OF THE FLYING SHUTTLE (1733)

The term "Industrial Revolution" designates, in economic history, the rapid changes in methods of production and technology
which began to appear in England about the year 1760. These resulted in the replacement of the domestic or putting-out system by

the factory system.   New scientific conceptions, such as those formulated by Sir Isaac Newton, found profitable application in industry,
as exemplified by the steam engine, perfected by James Watt and
patented in 1769.   Other inventions which hastened the coming of
the factory system were the spinning jenny (James Hargreaves,
1764) and the power loom (Edmund Cartwright, 1785).

One of the more significant inventions which preceded those
of Hargreaves and Cartwright and which contributed to the mechan-
ization of the British textile industry, was the flying shuttle, invented by John Kay and patented in 1733.   As a youth he was ap-
prenticed to a reed-maker, a man who fashioned the tools used
for separating the threads in the warp of the weaving process.   In
1730 he took out a patent for a thread-twisting device.

Prior to the invention of the flying shuttle, also known as
the "wheel shuttle," hand weaving was done by two persons, one
standing at each side of the loom.   The shuttle was passed by one
operator to another on the opposite side, who then returned it to
the first operator.   Kay's invention made it possible for a similar
loom to be operated by one person who, sitting at the front, man-
ipulated a lever which caused the shuttle to fly back and forth between the warp threads.   This speeded up the weaving process and
reduced the number of persons required to operate the loom.

Kay took his shuttle to Colchester, a textile manufacturing
center in southern England, where he hoped to introduce it.   He
planned to license his invention to textile manufacturers and, with
this in mind, formed partnerships with various entrepreneurs, including Solomon Smith, Henry Abbott and William Carter.   The
partners asked fifteen shillings per year for the use of the shuttle
but found that many textile mills had pirated the idea and were using it without authorization and without paying for such use.   Lawsuits for patent infringement were brought but none was ever settled.

The inventor's troubles increased.   The flying shuttle ran
into mechanical difficulties and often broke threads in the loom.
Kay improved his device and by 1735 had overcome this malfunction.
Once again the proprietors of British textile mills pirated his invention, using the shuttle but not paying royalties to its inventor.
Kay's right to the basic patent was challenged and it was contended
that the idea of the flying shuttle was not original with him but had
been known in the textile industry for decades.   Between 1737 and
1743 John Kay was engaged in over fifty patent infringement lawsuits.

In 1747 Kay traveled to France.   The cost of his numerous
court actions and his unsuccessful attempts to realize a profit from
leasing his invention had impoverished him.   His English partners
no longer supported him.   The weavers, fearing that use of the
flying shuttle would lead to unemployment in the textile trade, resisted its introduction.   Kay, on several occasions, found his life
threatened by mobs of angry weavers.

In Abbeville, France, the unlucky inventor became an associate of Daniel and Moses Scalonge, proprietors of a firm which
manufactured woollen textiles. He was able to obtain French patents on his flying shuttle and on some other devices applicable to
the weaving of cloth. However, his financial affairs did no better
in France than they had in his native England and he died a bankrupt man in 1779.

Suggested Readings

Burlingame, Roger. Inventors Behind the Inventor. New York:
    Harcourt, Brace, 1947.
Cressy, Edward. A Hundred Years of Mechanical Engineering.
    New York: Macmillan, 1937.
Finch, James K. Engineering and Western Civilization. New York:
    McGraw-Hill, 1951.
Kirby, Richard S., et al. Engineering in History. New York:
    McGraw-Hill, 1956.
Lipson, E. The History of the Woollen and Worsted Industries.
    London: Frank Cass & Co., 1963.
Mantoux, Paul. The Industrial Revolution in the Eighteenth Century.
    New York: Macmillan, 1961 (Originally published 1928).
Moffitt, Louis W. England on the Eve of the Industrial Revolution.
    London: Frank Cass & Co., 1963.
Singer, Charles, et al., eds. A History of Technology. Oxford:
    Clarendon Press, 1954-1958.
Usher, Abbott P. A History of Mechanical Inventions. New York:
    McGraw-Hill, 1929.
Wadsworth, Alfred P., and Julia De Lacy Mann. The Cotton Trade
    and Industrial Lancashire, 1600-1780. Manchester: Manches-
    ter University Press, 1931.
Walton, Perry. The Story of Textiles. New York: Tudor Pub-
    lishing Co., 1925.
Wolf, Abraham. A History of Science, Technology, and Philosophy
    in the Eighteenth Century. New York: Macmillan, 1939.

THE EUGENE ARAM MURDER (1745)

The English village of Knaresborough, Yorkshire, was the
scene of a brutal murder on the morning of February 7, 1745.
Daniel Clark, a shoemaker, William Houseman, a linen-weaver,
and Eugene Aram, a schoolmaster, had spent the night drinking
and carousing together. Aram and Houseman were in need of money, but Clark habitually carried 300 pounds, a portion of his wife's
dowry, on his person. Aram and Houseman lured Clark to the
Nidd River where he was killed by a blow with a pickaxe. The two
murderers then divided the money and buried the body of their late
companion in nearby St. Robert's Cave.

The three men had shady reputations in their village, and all had been in trouble with the authorities for drunkenness and petty thievery. Clark had obtained goods without paying for them, and after his disappearance his creditors offered a cash reward for the return of their merchandise "and no questions asked." It is not known if any of these goods were ever recovered, but Aram, fearing that he might become involved in the murder, deserted his wife and seven children and went to London. An accomplished self-taught linguist, he obtained employment giving instruction in foreign languages. He also led a dissolute life in the English capital.

For twelve years Aram remained in London. He then moved to King's Lynn in Norfolk where he acquired a mistress and a position as teacher of Latin in a local school. In June, 1758, he was seen and recognized by a native of his old village. When greeted as a fellow-townsman he denied his identity and declared he knew nothing of Knaresborough.

Aram imprudently remained in King's Lynn. When a laborer discovered a skeleton while excavating on the bank of the Nidd River it was taken for that of the long-missing Daniel Clark. Houseman was arrested. Following interrogation he took the police to St. Robert's Cave and showed them where Clark's body had been buried. At the inquest the man who had seen Aram in King's Lynn told the authorities of the encounter and two deputies were sent to arrest him and return him to Knaresborough.

Eugene Aram's trial was held in August, 1759. He had spent a year in York jail preparing his defense, which he handled personally. He contended that the bones found were those of religious martyrs and he denied all accusations of murder. The prosecutor, Fletcher Norton, secured a conviction and Aram was sentenced to hang. The night before his execution he attempted unsuccessfully to commit suicide by slashing his wrists, and was dragged "half alive and half dead" to the gallows at Tyburn where the death sentence was duly carried out. Following his execution his body was suspended in chains at Knaresborough.

Suggested Readings

"A-Z of Crime: Eugene Aram" in Crimes and Punishment, Vol. 1. Editorial presentation: Jackson Morley. London: BPC, 1973.
Birkenhead, Frederick Edwin Smith. "The Trial of Eugene Aram" in his Famous Trials of History. Garden City, N. Y.: Garden City Publishing Co., 1928.
Bromberg, Walter. Crime and the Mind: A Psychiatric Analysis of Crime and Punishment. New York: Macmillan, 1965.
_____. Mold of Murder: A Psychiatric Study of Homicide. New York: Grune & Stratton, 1961.
Guttmacher, M. S. The Mind of the Murderer. Freeport, N. Y.: Books for Libraries, 1960

Hood, Thomas. "The Dream of Eugene Aram" (poem) in Stephens,
    James, et al, eds. English Romantic Poets. New York: Amer-
    ican Book Co. , 1933.
Jesse, F. Tennyson. Murder and Its Motives. London: Harrap,
    1952.
Lester, David, and Gene Lester. Crime of Passion: Murder and
    the Murderer. Chicago: Nelson Hall, 1975.
Lytton, Edward Bulwer. "Eugene Aram" (fiction) in The Works of
    Edward Bulwer Lytton. East Saint Clair Shores, Mich.: Schol-
    arly Press, 1976 (Originally published 1832).
McDade, Thomas M. , compiler. The Annals of Murder. Norman,
    Okla.: University of Oklahoma Press, 1961.
Reinhardt, James Melvin. The Psychology of Strange Killers.
    Springfield, Ill.: Thomas, 1962.
Wilson, Colin, and Patricia Pitman. Encyclopedia of Murder. New
    York: Putnam, 1962.
Wolfgang, Marvin E. , compiler. Studies in Homicide. New York:
    Harper & Row, 1967.

THE DIDEROT ENCYCLOPEDIE (1751-1780)

The word "encyclopedia" is defined as "a work in which the
various branches or fields of learning are treated in separate articles. " The earliest encyclopedia extant is Pliny's first century
A. D. Historia Naturalis in which an attempt was made to consolidate the learning of the time. Pliny was preceded by earlier encyclopedists, such as Speusippus who lived in the 4th century B. C.
and Marcus Terentius Varro, whose Disciplinarum Libri IX and
Rerum Humanarum et Divinarum Antiquitates appeared in the 2nd
century B. C. All traces of these early forms of encyclopedia have
been lost.

Other encyclopedias were produced by Martianus Capella in
the 5th century A. D. , by Isidore of Seville in the 6th century A. D.
and by Vincent of Beauvais, whose Bibliotheca Mundi appeared in the
13th century A. D. Still other encyclopedias, designed for continuous reading and study, were compiled in succeeding centuries.
They represented the accumulated learning of their individual authors, differing from modern encyclopedias which are the product of
the cooperation of many subject specialists and authorities.

The transition from the old to the modern type of encyclopedia was due, among other things, to the Enlightenment, a cultural movement of the 18th century "characterized by a questioning
of authority, a creative interest in political and cultural matters
and emphasis on the experimental method in science. " This movement, which flourished particularly in France, inspired such men
as Voltaire, Etienne Bonnot de Condillac and the encyclopedists
Denis Diderot and his helper Jean Le Rond d'Alembert, a French
mathematician.

In 1728 Ephraim Chambers had published his two volume Cyclopaedia which went through several editions during his lifetime. This was translated into Italian in 1748-1749 and a French translation was made from the original English by John Mills and Gottfried Sellius. This last, commonly called The Encyclopedia, was the foundation for Denis Diderot's Encyclopédie.

Diderot was a philosopher, writer, translator and encyclopedist. He had been imprisoned because of certain material appearing in his Lettre sur les Aveugles, published in 1749. He was released in 1751 in order to be able to work with d'Alembert and others to compile what was to become the famous Encyclopédie, ou Dictionaire raisonné des sciences, des artes et des métiers, par une societé de gens de lettres, the first modern encyclopedia, on which he worked for over two decades. When completed in 1765 it consisted of seventeen volumes of text. Eleven additional volumes of plates and illustrations came off the press in 1772 and five supplementary volumes appeared in 1776-1777. These contained over 200 plates. In 1780 a two-volume table of contents was published. Subsequently many editions followed, with the work being modified and updated. The articles were arranged alphabetically and cross-references, as in Chambers' 1728 Cyclopaedia, were employed. Diderot's contributors included d'Alembert, Anne Robert Jacques Turgot, François Quesnay, the Comte de Buffon, Jean-Jacques Rousseau, Louis Jean Marie Daubenton and many other distinguished scholars of the 18th century. Besides editing the mathematical articles d'Alembert wrote the now famous preface.

The Encyclopédie was considered unduly radical and materialistic. It was subjected to condemnation and Diderot was imprisoned on two occasions. Twice the French government forbade further publication but Chrêtien-Guillaume de Malesherbes, the official censor, who was in sympathy with the encyclopedists, and Andrê-François le Breton, the publisher, hid page proofs on several occasions. It is felt that without le Breton's assistance Diderot's work would never have seen the light of day.

The editors of today's encyclopedias tend to be dispassionate, neither editorializing nor taking sides on controversial subjects. Such was not the case with the Encyclopédie. This work editorialized openly, being extremely critical of religion, government policies and of some aspects of science and technology.

In 1781 Diderot's Encyclopédie was followed by Charles Joseph Panckoucke's Encyclopédie Méthodique et par orde des Matières. This was designed to break Diderot's work down into a series of independent subject "dictionaries." It was completed in 1832, being published in 167 volumes. It had 51 parts, each covering a separate subject.

Today there are a number of standard general encyclopedias as well as others dealing with particular facets of human knowledge. These are, in most cases, updated frequently as technologies change and new discoveries are made.

Suggested Readings

Barker, Joseph Edmund. Diderot's Treatment of the Christian Re-
     ligion in the Encyclopédie. New York: King's Crown Press,
     1941.
Cassirer, Ernst. Philosophy of the Enlightenment. Translated by
     Fritz C. A. Koelln and James P. Pettegrove. Boston: Beacon
     Press, 1955.
Crocker, Lester G. Diderot's Chaotic Order: Approach to Syn-
     thesis. Princeton, N. J.: Princeton University Press, 1974.
          . The Embattled Philosopher: A Biography of Denis Di-
     derot. London: Neville Spearman, 1955.
Diderot, Denis. Rameau's Nephew and Other Works. Translated
     by Jacques Barzun and Ralph H. Bowen. Garden City, N. Y.:
     Doubleday, 1956 (Originally written latter part of 18th century).
"Encyclopedia" in Collier's Encyclopedia. Shores, Louis, editor
     in chief. New York: Crowell-Collier Educational Corporation,
     1972.
Fellows, Otis E. Diderot Studies. Westport, Conn.: Greenwood
     Press, 1971 (Originally published 1949).
Fredman, Alice G. Diderot and Sterne. New York: Octagon
     Books, 1972.
Gillispie, Charles Coulston. A Diderot Pictorial Encyclopedia of
     Trades and Industry. New York: Dover, 1959.
Gordon, Douglas H. , and Normand L. Torrey. The Censoring of
     Diderot's Encyclopédie and the Re-Established Text. New York:
     Columbia University Press, 1947.
Morley, John. Diderot and the Encyclopedists. Detroit: Gale,
     1971 (Originally published 1878).
Rodgers, Gary B. Diderot and the Eighteenth Century Press. For-
     est Grove, Ore.: International Scholarly Book Services, 1973.
Vartanian, Aram. Diderot and Descartes. Westport, Conn.: Green-
     wood Press, 1975 (Originally published 1953).
Wilson, Arthur M. Diderot: The Testing Years, 1713-1759. New
     York: Oxford University Press, 1957.

THE MAD MONKS OF MEDMENHAM ABBEY (1752)

The "Mad Monks of Medmenham Abbey" were members of
the Hell-Fire Club, founded by Sir Francis Dashwood in 1752. Other members of the Club were such notables as John Wilkes, George
Bubb Dodington, Lord Sandwich, John Stuart, Earl of Bute, Thomas Potter, Paul Whitehead and Charles Churchill.

Dashwood was born in London in 1708 to a noble English
family. As a youth he and his tutor traveled through Europe during which time he became enchanted with "the unholy, the forbidden,
the perverse." Returning to England, he set about putting together
an organization which would satisfy his desire for "a sexual establishment with its own clientele, apparel and costumes."

In 1752 he leased the twelfth century Medmenham Abbey. This he had renovated, to include a "chapel" appropriate for the orgies he contemplated. He had little difficulty in recruiting a number of profligates like himself from the English nobility. The Hell-Fire Club had two degrees: the Superiors, which included Dashwood and twelve "apostles" and the Inferiors, representing the balance of the membership.

The Club members met at the Abbey to indulge in obscene parodies of Roman Catholic ritual. Satan was implored to appear and join in the festivities. Sacrificial wine was drunk from human skulls. Prostitutes dressed as nuns joined in the revelry.

John Wilkes became fed up with the "whole silly business" and hid a baboon, dressed in a devil's mask and suit, in a chest in the chapel. That evening when the Mad Monks were carousing and entreating the Evil One to appear, he released the animal, terrifying his fellow club members to a point where Lord Sandwich fainted.

Some members of the Club attained high political positions during the reign of George III. Dashwood became Chancellor of the Exchequer and was made Baron Le Despencer. Bute became Prime Minister and Dodington wound up as a nobleman and entered the peerage as Baron Melcombe. Wilkes founded the North Briton in which he attacked Bute and charged George III with falsehood (issue No. 45, published in 1763). He was prosecuted for libel but obtained a verdict, with damages for illegal arrest, against the secretary of state in 1769. He was elected to the House of Commons from which he was expelled and to which he was re-elected several times. He also became Chamberlain of the city of London. Charles Churchill, the poet, was a frequent contributor to Wilkes' newspaper.

The Hell-Fire Club gradually disintegrated. Dashwood transferred its headquarters to a cave in High Wycombe but he, like his fellow members, was "too old, too tired and too dissipated to enjoy further devil worship. "

Suggested Readings

Bamberger, Bernard Jacob. Fallen Angels. Philadelphia: Jewish
    Publication Society of America, 1952.
Basham, Don. Deliver Us from Evil. Washington Depot, Conn. :
    Chosen Books, 1972.
Boyd, Mildred. Man, Myth and Magic. New York: Criterion
    Books, 1969.
Carus, Paul. History of the Devil and the Idea of Evil, from the
    Earliest Times to the Present Day. New York: Land's End
    Press, 1969 (Originally published 1900).
Cavendish, Richard. Powers of Evil in Western Religion Magic and
    Folk Belief. New York: Putnam, 1975.

Cohen, Daniel. Voodoo, Devils and the New Invisible World. New
    York: Dodd, Mead, 1972.
Cruz, Nicky. Satan on the Loose. Old Tappan, N. J. : Revell,
    1973.
Garden, Nancy. Devils and Demons. Philadelphia: Lippincott,
    1976.
Hagee, J. C. Invasion of Demons. Old Tappan, N. J. : Revell,
    1973.
"Hell-Fire Club" in Crimes and Punishment, Vol. 6. Editorial
    presentation, Jackson Morley. London: BPC, 1973.
Kemp, Betty. Sir Francis Dashwood, an 18th Century Independent.
    New York: St. Martin's Press, 1967.
_____. "Some Letters of Sir Francis Dashwood, Baron Le Des-
    pencer, as Joint Postmaster General, 1766-81, " John Rylands
    Library Bulletin, September, 1954.
Remi, Nicolas. Demonolatry. Translated by E. A. Ashwin. Lon-
    don: J. Rodker, 1930 (Originally published 1595).
Rhodes, Henry Taylor Fowkes. The Satanic Mass: A Sociological
    and Criminological Study. New York: Citadel Press, 1955.
Townsend, James. The Oxfordshire Dashwoods. Oxford: Oxford
    University Press, 1922.

THE DISAPPEARANCE AND RETURN OF
ELIZABETH CANNING (1753)

        One of the unexplained mysteries of the eighteenth century
was that of Elizabeth Canning, an English servant girl, who disappeared from her place of employment in the Hounsditch area of
London on New Years Day, 1753.   Her family organized an intensive search for her but were not able to find any trace of the eighteen-year-old girl.   Then, one month later, she returned, wearing
only a night shift.   She was hungry, filthy and exhausted and had
a bleeding wound in her ear.   She told a story of having been kid-
naped and held prisoner in a bordello until she was able to escape
and find her way home.

        Elizabeth told her family that, as she walked down the street,
two men had seized her, ripped off most of her clothes and forced
her to walk several miles to a house of prostitution.   There, one
of three women present, according to her story, had slashed her
stays with a knife and stolen her corset.   She was then asked to
participate in the activities at the brothel and when she refused
was imprisoned in an upstairs room.   There she remained, living
only on bread and water until she made her escape by prying loose
a wall panel and climbing down to the ground.   She then walked
home, a distance, she said, of about ten miles.

        The girl was unable to say who the men and women she had
met might be and was vague and confused concerning the location
of the house in which she claimed to have been held prisoner.   Rob-

ert Scarratt, a neighbor, spoke of a house owned by a woman
named Susannah Wells which might have been the one she described. Elizabeth then said she remembered someone mentioning
the name "Susannah Wells" while she was being held.

Next day the girl repeated her story to the authorities. A
warrant was issued for the arrest of the Wells woman and Elizabeth was taken to the former's home by several policemen. There
she identified Mary Squires, an ugly, deformed gypsy, as the one
who had cut her stays. In spite of their protestations that they
had never set eyes on Elizabeth Canning before, the five women and
three men found in the house were arrested and lodged in jail.
Mary Squires maintained that she had been in Dorset, over a hundred miles away, when the girl first disappeared from home. Virtue Hall, one of the inmates of Susannah Wells' brothel, in an effort to save helself, repudiated her original denials of complicity
in the affair and turned state's evidence, saying that Elizabeth Canning's story was true.

Mary Squires and Mrs. Wells were tried and convicted. The
former was sentenced to be hanged for stealing the Canning girl's
corset, and the latter was to have the letter "T" branded on her
hand for harboring and protecting a thief. The sentence of branding was carried out, but Sir Crispe Gascoyne, Lord Mayor of London, instituted a postponement of the hanging of Mary Squires until
further investigation could be made.

For fifteen months Mary Squires remained in prison while
the authorities sought witnesses who could substantiate her alibi.
It gradually became evident that she had told the truth and that the
Canning girl had lied, having never been in the Wells house until
she went there with the police.

In the spring of 1754, Mary Squires was released. Elizabeth Canning was charged with perjury, tried, convicted and sentenced to seven years transportation to America. She was taken
to the New World by ship where she met John Treat, marrying
him in 1756. She died in 1773 without ever telling how she had
actually spent the month she had been missing from home. It was
rumored that she had run away with a lover who had robbed and
abandoned her, and also that she had disappeared in order to have
an illegitimate child of which her family was in ignorance. Neither
of these theories, however, was ever proved. She has come down
in history as the "Canning Wonder," an appellation bestowed upon
her by the people of her day.

Suggested Readings

De La Torre, Lillian. "Elizabeth Is Missing," University of Col-
orado Studies, October, 1945.
_____. Elizabeth Is Missing; or, Truth Triumphant; An Eigh-
teenth Century Mystery, Being a True and Complete Relation

of Her Mysterious Disappearance.   San Mateo, Calif.:   Joseph
Publishing Co., 1947.
       , compiler.   "The Disappearing Servant Wench" (fiction)
in her Villainy Detected.   New York: Appleton-Century, 1947.
Fielding, Henry.   Enquiry into the Causes of the Late Increase of
Robbers, &c.   New York: AMS Press, 1975 (Originally pub-
lished 1751).
Lang, Andrew.   "Historical Mysteries: The Case of Elizabeth Can-
ning," Cornhill Magazine, May, 1904.
Machen, Arthur.   The Canning Wonder.   New York: Knopf, 1926.
Pearson, Edmund Lester.   "The First Great Disappearer" in De
La Torre, Lillian, compiler.   Villainy Detected.   New York:
Appleton-Century, 1947.
      .   More Studies in Murder, New York: Random House,
1936.
Rush, Philip.   More Strange People.   North Tarrytown, N.Y.:
Hutchinson, 1958.
"They Cheated the Gallows" in Crimes and Punishment, Vol. 15.
Editorial presentation, Jackson Morley.   London: BPC, 1973.

THE BLACK HOLE OF CALCUTTA (1756)

The Black Hole of Calcutta is located at Fort William, at
one time the stronghold of the East India Company.   On June 20,
1756, the fort was captured by Sirajud-Ud-Daula, Nawab of Bengal
and leader of a group of native insurrectionists.

The British garrison was overpowered by the natives and,
according to an official of the East India Company, writing in 1758,
146 British soldiers were confined in a virtually unventilated cell
measuring eighteen feet by fourteen feet ten inches.   The prisoners
remained in the cell overnight, at the end of which time only 23
remained alive, the others having perished of heat, thirst, and
suffocation.

The truth of this report has never been established.   The
Home Office of the East India Company was never officially advised of the incident and the commander of the British forces in
India, so far as is known, took no retaliatory measures against
the natives.

It is true that the fort was attacked, and that 114 men died
defending it.   Nine British officers were held overnight in a small
room following the fort's capture and three of these officers died,
two of them from wounds received during the encounter.

Suggested Readings

Barber, Noël.   The Black Hole of Calcutta: A Reconstruction.
London: Collins, 1965.

Barber, W. J.   British Economic Thought and India, 1600-1858.
    Oxford: Clarendon Press, 1975.
Corbett, Edmund V.   "The Black Hole of Calcutta" in his Great
    True Stories of Tragedy and Disaster. New York: Archer
    House, 1963.
Davies, A. Mervyn.   Clive of Plassey: A Biography. New York:
    Scribner's, 1939.
Forrest, Sir G. W.   Life of Lord Clive. London: Cassell, 1918.
Foster, William.   The East India House: Its History and Associa-
    tions. London: John Lane, 1924.
Great Britain India Office.   A Guide to the India Office Records,
    1600-1858. By William Foster, C. I. E., Registrar and Super-
    intendent of Records. London: Eyre and Spottiswoode, 1919.
Minney, R. J.   Clive. London: Jarrolds, 1931.
Mottram, R. H.   Traders' Dream: The Romance of the East India
    Company. New York: Appleton, 1939.
Russell, Jack.   Clive of India. New York: Putnam, 1965.
Wilson, Colonel Sir Charles.   Lord Clive. New York: Macmillan,
    1905.

THE PUBLICATION OF ROUSSEAU'S
JULIE, OU LA NOUVELLE HELOISE (1760)

Jean-Jacques Rousseau was a French-Swiss philosopher,
moralist and author. He published a number of significant novels,
one of which, Julie, ou la Nouvelle Héloise, became what might
be called one of the first best sellers. This, written between 1756
and 1758, was published in the year 1760.

Rousseau was born in Geneva, Switzerland, in 1712. His
mother died at his birth and he was brought up by an aunt and an
uncle. After a brief apprenticeship to an engraver he ran away,
to become secretary to Madam Louise Éléonore de Warens at
Annecy and Chambéry. He went to Paris in 1742 where he supported himself by teaching and copying music and working as a
political secretary. At this time he met Denis Diderot and contributed articles on music and political economy to the latter's Encyclopédie as well as writing an opera, Les Muses Galantes.

He continued his literary efforts, producing essays and an
operetta. In Montmorency he wrote Julie, which was followed by
Le Contrat Social (1762) and Émile, ou Traité de l'Éducation, published in the same year. Of the three, Julie was the most popular.
It is a sentimental and moralizing romance written in the form of
letters and telling the story of the daughter of a nobleman who
falls in love with Saint-Preux, her tutor, with whom she has an
illicit affair. Saint-Preux then leaves to escape the anger of Julie's
father and she, in accordance with her father's wishes, marries
Wolmar, a Russian gentleman. In due course Julie confesses her
affair with the tutor to her husband. The latter denies that any sin

was involved and employs Saint-Preux as tutor for his and Julie's
children.   Following this all live together in happiness and the love
between Julie and Saint-Preux "is not diminished but is now platon-
ic. "   At the end of the novel the heroine dies.

The plot of Julie is simple.   It is based, in part, on the
true life story of Peter Abélard, the twelfth-century philosopher-
teacher and his pupil and wife Héloise.   Rousseau's heroine is a
composite of several women in his life, particularly Madam de
Warens and Madam d'Houdetot.   Julie and his other writings "introduced a new style of extreme emotional expression, concern
with intense personal experience, and exploration of the conflicts
between moral and sensual values. "   Rousseau exerted an enormous
influence on romanticism in literature and philosophy in the early
nineteenth century and also "affected the development of the psy-
chological literature, psychoanalytic theory and philosophy of exis-
tentialism of the twentieth century. "

Rousseau's own feelings are expressed in his novel.   He
indicates his idealization of marriage, his ideas on the proper
raising of children, his views on religion and "emphasizes the beau-
ties of nature as compared to the corrupting influences of civilization and progress. "   His most remarkable work was the autobiographical Confessions, published in 1782.   It had a tremendous influence on the course of literature and psychology.

Julie, though extremely popular with the reading public, was
condemned by a number of authorities, notably Voltaire, who may
have suspected that the Age of Reason, which they endorsed, might
well be replaced by an age which would reject classicism/rational-
ism for romanticism.

Jean-Jacques Rousseau died in 1778 and was undoubtedly
partly insane during the last ten or fifteen years of his life.

Suggested Readings

Broome, J. H.   Rousseau: A Study of His Thought.   London: Ed-
     ward Arnold, 1963.
Cross, E. A.   "Eighteenth-Century Prose Fiction" in his World Lit-
     erature.   New York: American Book Co. , 1935.
Durant, Will, and Ariel Durant.   Rousseau and Revolution.   New
     York: Simon and Schuster, 1967.
Einaudi, Mario.   The Early Rousseau.   Ithaca, N. Y. : Cornell
     University Press, 1967.
Havens, George R.   The Age of Ideas.   New York: Holt, Rinehart
     and Winston, 1955.
Johnson, Edward W.   Jean-Jacques Rousseau and the 18th-Century
     Political Philosophers.   New York: Monarch, 1965.
Martin, Kingsley.   French Liberal Thought in the Eighteenth Century.
     London: Phoenix House, 1962.
Osborn, Annie Marion.   Rousseau and Burke.   New York: Russell
     and Russell, 1964.

Rousseau, Jean-Jacques. Julie, ou la Nouvelle Héloise. New
    York: French and European Publications, 1963 (Originally pub-
    lished 1760).
Sahakian, Mabel Lewis. Rousseau as an Educator. New York:
    Twayne, 1974.
Smith, Horatio. "Rousseau" in his Masters of French Literature.
    New York: Scribner's, 1937.
Winwar, Frances. Jean-Jacques Rousseau, Conscience of an Era.
    New York: Random House, 1961.

BECCARIA'S TREATISE ON CRIMES
AND PUNISHMENTS (1764)

For centuries communities have set up rules of conduct which must be obeyed by their members and for violations of which punishments are designated. These rules, or laws, emanate from a government and apply to the people subject to that government. Until comparatively recent times the punishments inflicted on law violators were extremely severe. Many offenses, often compara- tively trivial in nature, were legally punishable by death. Torture was used to extract confessions from suspected wrong-doers. Flog- ging, mutilation, branding and other painful punishments were com- monplace.

This situation of legally sentencing convicted criminals to punishments far out of proportion to the crimes committed was the practice as recently as the eighteenth century. Certain re- formers felt that the cruel punishments of the day were far more barbaric than was appropriate in a world which, in other areas, had made tremendous progress. Of the eighteenth century reform- ers, three were pioneers in the field of humanizing criminal laws. These were Cesare Bonesana, Marchese di Beccaria (1738-1794), Jeremy Bentham (1748-1832) and Sir Samuel Romilly (1757-1818). Legal historians consider these men "the three most important re- formers of criminal law" and feel that Beccaria topped the other two in terms of influence and importance.

Beccaria, an Italian economist and jurist, published his famous Treatise on Crimes and Punishments in 1764. In this book, originally produced anonymously at Monaco with an introduction written by Voltaire, he condemns confiscation, capital punishment and torture and advocates the prevention of crime by education. He argues against the severities and abuses of criminal law and asserts that "good laws are needed to assist the weak and the oppressed. "

In his book Beccaria points out that "every act of authority which is not absolutely necessary is a tyrannical act. " Human justice, he says, is not the same as God's justice and consequent- ly any punishment going beyond what the laws provide is unjust. Punishment is useless if it does not discourage crime.

Beccaria holds that the function of a judge is to decide cases brought before him in terms of laws "interpreted by the sovereign. " He feels that Aristotle's three steps of syllogistic logic should be applied by judges, with the major premise being the law itself, the minor premise "the conformity or opposition of an act to the law" and the conclusion either to punish or release the accused.

The author considers trial procedures, maintaining that "the credibility of witnesses should be more and more questioned as the crime is more atrocious. " Half the jury should consist of peers of the accused and the other half should be peers of the person offended. Under no circumstances, he says, can secret accusations be justified. Anyone accused of a crime must be considered innocent until his guilt is proven beyond a reasonable doubt and torture, administered to secure confessions, is unjustified and should not be permitted. Long pretrial imprisonments should be prohibited and immediate punishment of the guilty is to be desired. The death sentence should be imposed "only when there is great danger if a criminal be allowed to live. "

Treatise on Crimes and Punishments became extremely popular and was translated into virtually all European languages. It exerted a great influence on the reforming of the penal codes of Russia, France and other European nations. Beccaria died in 1794 and his ideas were given additional impetus by Bentham, Romilly and others, including the writers of the Constitution of the United States.

Suggested Readings

Beccaria, Cesare Bonesana. Treatise on Crimes and Punishments. Translated by Henry Paolucci. Indianapolis: Bobbs-Merrill, 1963 (Originally published 1764).
Bromberg, Walter. Crime and the Mind: A Psychiatric Analysis of Crime and Punishment. New York: Macmillan, 1965.
Commager, Henry Steele, ed. "The Constitution of the United States" (Doc. No. 87) in his Documents of American History, 8th edition. New York: Appleton, 1968.
Helm, Peter James. Jeffreys: A New Portrait of England's Hanging Judge. New York: Crowell, 1966.
Johnston, Norman Leonard Savitz, and Marvin Wolfgang, eds. The Sociology of Punishment and Correction: A Book of Readings. New York: Wiley, 1962.
Laurence, John. A History of Capital Punishment. New York: Citadel Press, 1960.
Maestro, Marcello T. Voltaire and Beccaria as Reformers of Criminal Law. New York: Columbia University Press, 1942.
Phillipson, Coleman. Three Criminal Law Reformers: Beccaria, Bentham, Romilly. London: J. M. Dent & Sons, 1923.
Pugh, Ralph Bernard. Imprisonment in Medieval England. London: Cambridge University Press, 1968.

Society of Friends.   What Do the Churches Say on Capital Punish-
ment?   Philadelphia: Friends World Committee, 1960.
Twain, Mark, pseud.   The Prince and the Pauper (fiction).   New
York: Macmillan, 1962 (Originally published 1881).

THE INSTRUCTION OF CATHERINE THE GREAT (1767)

Catherine II of Russia, known as Catherine the Great, was
married in 1745, at the age of sixteen, to Peter of Holstein-Gottorp, heir to the Russian throne.   The Russian court was then
coarse and immoral and ridden with intrigue.   Catherine's husband,
who became Tsar Peter III on the death of Empress Elizabeth in
1762, was weak and sensual.   He lost interest in his wife, humiliated her publicly and threatened to divorce her, marry his mistress the Princess Vorontsova, and declare his son Paul illegitimate.

Though Catherine's moral character was no better than that
of her husband she was, by contrast, a strong-willed, capable person.   In July, 1762, Peter was seized, imprisoned and strangled
by a group of young nobles led by Catherine's current lover, Count
Grigori Grigorievich Orlov, and Catherine assumed the throne.

The new ruler found her country to be composed of two primary classes: the nobility and the peasantry.   No middle class,
as such, existed.   Russia had recently entered the world of European power politics and was at a distinct disadvantage.   Though
rich in mineral resources she had no way of turning them to practical account.   Her peasants were largely uneducated serfs, existing on small farms and, for the most part, were shamelessly exploited by the land-owning nobles.   Her army was sadly lacking in
competent officers and her trade was only a fraction of its potential.
Tsar Peter III had freed the nobility from all military service obligations except in time of war and had made this highly privileged
class a number of other concessions.   Taxes were extremely difficult to collect.   Improvements in several fields were necessary
if Russia was to achieve the position she had enjoyed under Peter I
more than half a century before, and which had been lost by the
weak, dilatory rulers who succeeded him.

On July 30, 1767, Catherine published her Instruction.   This
document, which contained 653 sections and took over two years to
prepare, was intended to be "a statement of her basic philosophical
principles of the political, social, economic and cultural life of
Russia."   She hoped that the application of principles enumerated
in the Instruction would make it possible for Russia to compete successfully with the more advanced Western countries.   This involved
a statement of basic legal principles by which the service of Russia's nobility could be regularized and a viable middle class developed.

Catherine had been greatly influenced by the writings of the French political philosopher Baron de Montesquieu and the Instruction was, to a great extent, based on his ideas as well as those of Cesare Bonesana, Marchese di Beccaria, the Italian economist and jurist, and the Russian historian and novelist Nikolai Mikhailovich Karamzin. However, she had submitted her version of the Instruction to several of her most trusted advisers who had edited and amended it to the point where it had been "emasculated by qualification." The legislative commission had further considered the document over a period of time without producing a code that was in any way practical. It was not possible to transform Catherine's principles into laws that would fit the realities of life in eighteenth century Russia.

As originally conceived, the Instruction was intended to pave the way for the creation of a prosperous middle class, to encourage the growth of private industry and to expand foreign commerce. While Russia was to remain an autocracy, it was to be governed by laws which would apply equally to everybody, whether rich or poor, aristocrat or peasant. Population increase was urged so that there would be sufficient Russian citizens to exploit the country's natural wealth. Within reasonable limits religious toleration was to be observed, as was freedom of the press.

Catherine's attempt to improve conditions in her country was idealistic but, unfortunately, the provisions of the Instruction could not, in spite of the best efforts of her advisers, be formed into a workable code of laws. Historians feel that, despite Catherine's desire to solve the problems facing her country, she achieved very little in the way of overcoming them.

Suggested Readings

Almedingen, Martha Edith von. The Romanovs: Three Centuries of an Ill-Fated Dynasty. New York: Holt, 1966.

Blair, Lowell, translator. The Memoirs of Catherine the Great. New York: Bantam Books, 1957.

Blum, J. G. Lord and Peasant in Russia from the Ninth to the Nineteenth Century. Princeton, N. J.: Princeton University Press, 1961.

Charques, Richard Denis. A Short History of Russia. New York: Dutton, 1956.

Clarkson, Jesse D. A History of Russia. New York: Random House, 1969.

Duke, Paul. Catherine the Great and the Russian Nobility. Cambridge: The University Press, 1967.

Florinsky, Michael T. Russia: A History and Interpretation. New York: Macmillan, 1965.

Gooch, George P. Catherine the Great and Other Studies. Hamden, Conn.: Shoe String Press, 1954.

Goodwin, Albert, ed. The European Nobility in the Eighteenth Century. New York: Harper & Row, 1953.

Hingley, Ronald. Tsars, 1533-1917. New York: Macmillan, 1968.
Hötzsch, Otto. "Catherine II" in The Cambridge Modern History.
    Edited by A. W. Ward, et al. Cambridge: The University
    Press, 1909.
Kluchevsky, Vasily O. A History of Russia. Translated by C. J.
    Hogarth. New York: Russell and Russell, 1960 (Originally
    published 1913).
Moscow, Henry, and the editors of Horizon Magazine. Russia Un-
    der the Czars. New York: American Heritage Publishing Co.,
    1962.
Oldenbourg, Zoé. Catherine the Great. New York: Random House,
    1965.
Pares, Bernard. A History of Russia. New York: Knopf, 1960.
Reddaway, W. F., ed. Documents of Catherine the Great. Cam-
    bridge: The University Press, 1931.
Riasanovsky, Nicholas Valentine. A History of Russia. New York:
    Oxford University Press, 1963.
Rogger, Hans. National Consciousness in Eighteenth Century Rus-
    sia. Cambridge, Mass.: Harvard University Press, 1960.
Thompson, G. S. Catherine the Great and the Expansion of Russia.
    London: Macmillan, 1955.
Trowbridge, W. R. H. "Catherine II, Empress of Russia, 1729-
    1796" in his Seven Splendid Sinners. London: T. F. Unwin,
    1908.
Vernadsky, George. A History of Russia. New Haven, Conn.:
    Yale University Press, 1954.
Wolf, John B. The Emergence of the Great Powers, 1685-1715.
    New York: Harper & Row, 1951.
Wren, Melvin C. The Course of Russian History. New York:
    Macmillan, 1968.

THE JAMES WATT STEAM ENGINE (1769)

The idea of converting heat into work through the medium of steam is by no means a modern concept. Hero of Alexandria, a Greek scientist of the 3rd century A. D. or earlier, designed and built a primitive form of steam engine. Thomas Savery, an English military engineer, patented the first commercially successful steam engine, an atmospheric device used for pumping water, in 1698. Thomas Newcomen, an English blacksmith, entered into partnership with Savery and improved the Savery engine. In 1705, in association with John Calley (Cawley), he invented an engine in which steam admitted to a cylinder was condensed by a jet of cold water and the piston was driven by atmospheric pressure.

For half a century the Newcomen engine was considered the marvel of the age. Then, in the winter of 1763-1764 James Watt, a Scottish instrument maker and engineer, was asked to repair a model of the Newcomen engine and had an opportunity to study its construction at first hand. He realized that the Newcomen engine

was horribly inefficient.   The alternate heating and cooling of the
cylinder wasted 99 percent of the fuel and, as someone observed,
"it took an iron mine to build a Newcomen engine and a coal mine
to keep it going. "

James Watt set about improving the steam engine.   What he
accomplished made the atmospheric engine obsolete.   After exper-
imenting to determine the properties of steam he invented a separate condenser which prevented the loss of steam in the cylinder.
He patented this device in 1769, along with such other improvements as a closed cylinder and steam-jacketing to prevent radiation of heat.

Watt went into partnership with John Roebuck, the Scottish
owner of the Carron Iron Works, who had financed his research.
They manufactured steam engines until 1775, when Roebuck was
replaced as Watt's business partner by Matthew Boulton, owner of
the Soho Engineering Works in Birmingham.   In the meantime Watt
continued to improve the engine, adding such refinements as the
piston ring and an air pump for exhausting condensed steam.   Further improvements included the throttle, the centrifugal governor,
the recording steam indicator and the double-acting engine.

The firm of Watt and Boulton continued in business until
1800, when Watt retired to devote himself to scientific research.
The pioneering work of James Watt was continued by others, particularly after his patents expired in 1800, by which time there
were over 500 Watt and Boulton engines in service.   Robert Fulton
adapted the steam engine to boats, making a successful round trip
between New York and Albany with the Clermont.   Compound steam
engines were built by the British inventor Arthur Woolf at the beginning of the 19th century.   In these devices steam at high pressure is used in one cylinder and then, after it has expanded and
consequently lessened in pressure, it is piped to another cylinder
where it expands still further.   Woolf's engines were originally
equipped with two cylinders but later compound engines used triple
and even quadruple expansion.

Richard Trevithick in England and Oliver Evans in the United States built successful non-condensing engines.   George Stephenson applied the steam engine to locomotives, later manufacturing
them and using them on the railroads with which he became associated.

Research on steam power continued through the 19th and
20th centuries.   Nikola Tesla, Sir George Parsons, Gustaf de La-
val and others developed the steam turbine.   Small steam engines
have been used successfully as power sources for automobiles.
Electrical generators operated by steam power are found in many
parts of the world.   Hugh Longbourne Callendar, the English physicist, did much research relating to steam and thermometry and has
published extensively on these subjects.

It is felt that James Watt, with his inventions and improvements on the Newcomen atmospheric engine, contributed more than
any other individual to the age of industrial power. Aside from
his work in steam he was an outstanding civil engineer, invented
an attachment to telescopes which adapted them for use in the measurement of distance and also invented a copying press and a device for reproducing sculpture.

Suggested Readings

Asimov, Isaac. "James Watt: He Started Two Revolutions, " Sen-
ior Scholastic, November 14, 1958.
Baron, Denys Bradford. The Cornish Beam Engine. Truro, Corn-
wall, England: Author, 1966.
Burlingame, Roger. Inventors Behind the Inventor. New York:
Harcourt, Brace, 1947.
Cardwell, D. S. L. Steam Power in the Eighteenth Century. Lon-
don: Sheed and Ward, 1963.
Cooper, Lettice. James Watt. London: A. & C. Black, 1963.
Dickinson, Henry W. James Watt, Craftsman and Engineer. Cam-
bridge: The University Press, 1935.
_____. A Short History of the Steam Engine. London: Frank
Cass & Co. , 1963.
Duncan, John. Steam and Other Engines. New York: St. Martin's
Press, 1956.
Farey, John. Treatise on the Steam Engine: Historical, Practical,
Descriptive. Newton, Mass. : Abbott, David, 1971 (Originally
published 1827).
Finch, James K. Engineering and Western Civilization. New York:
McGraw-Hill, 1951.
Hart, Ivor B. James Watt and the History of Steam Power. New
York: Henry Schuman, 1949.
Rolt, L. T. C. James Watt. New York: Arco Publishing Co. , 1963.
_____. Thomas Newcomen: The Prehistory of the Steam En-
gine. Dawlish, England: David and Charles, 1963.
Wise, David Burgess. Steam on the Road. New York: Hamlyn,
1973.

ADAM SMITH AND THE WEALTH OF NATIONS (1776)

An Inquiry into the Nature and Causes of the Wealth of Nations, published in 1776 by Adam Smith, the Scottish philosopher
and economist, is considered to have exerted a greater influence
on political and economic theory than any other book. It is required reading in many college level economics courses today.

Smith was educated at the University of Glasgow and at Balliol College, Oxford. In 1751 he was appointed professor of logic
at Glasgow and in 1752 was made professor of moral philosophy.

He was influenced in his thinking by David Hume, the Scottish philosopher whose lifelong friend he became.

His first major publication was Theory of Moral Sentiments which appeared in 1759. He resigned from the university in 1763 to become tutor to the young Duke of Buccleuch with whom he made an eighteen-month tour of France and Switzerland. In France he met Anne Robert Jacques Turgot and François Quesnay whose economic ideas impressed and influenced him.

In 1766 Smith returned to Kirkcaldy, his birthplace, and spent the next decade writing his best known work, popularly known as The Wealth of Nations. This book, in five parts, shows that Smith was dependent on the thinking of others for many of the ideas embodied in his treatise. However, as the first serious attempt to separate the study of political economy from ethics, politics and law, it earned its writer the sobriquet of "father of the science of political economy."

Smith, in The Wealth of Nations, puts forth the thesis that the fundamental sources of all income, i. e., the basic forms in which wealth is distributed, are rent, profits and wages. Following this, the author studies the historical development of European commerce and industry and considers the nature of capital. He maintains that capital is most efficiently employed for the distribution of wealth under conditions of free trade and governmental non-interference. Private enterprise, he feels, works most efficiently when not hampered by government regulation and control.

Since Smith's day this view has been modified by economists in the light of historical developments. Nevertheless, many of his basic precepts still constitute the starting points for theoretical studies in political economy. During the nineteenth century Smith's advocacy of the "economic system of natural liberty" had many followers, notably William Pitt, the British prime minister, who sought to introduce free trade principles in his country's economic policy.

In 1778 Adam Smith was appointed commissioner of customs in Edinburgh, a position he retained until his death in 1790. He was made lord rector of the University of Glasgow in 1787.

Suggested Readings

Cropsey, Joseph. Polity and Economy. The Hague: Martinus Nijhoff, 1957.
Dillard, Dudley E. The Economics of John Maynard Keynes. New York: Prentice-Hall, 1948.
Due, John F. Intermediate Economic Analysis. Homewood, Ill.: Richard D. Irwin, 1953.
Fay, C. R. Adam Smith and the Scotland of His Day. Cambridge: Cambridge University Press, 1956.
_____. The World of Adam Smith. Cambridge: The University Press, 1960.

Fusfeld, Daniel Roland. The Age of the Economist. Glenview, Ill.: Scott, Foresman, 1966.

Gide, Charles, and Charles Rist. A History of Economic Doctrines. Translated by R. Richards. Boston: Heath, n. d.

Ginzberg, Eli. The House of Adam Smith. New York: Columbia University Press, 1934.

Halévy, Elie. The Growth of Philosophic Radicalism. Translated by Mary Morris. Boston: Beacon Press, 1955.

Haney, Lewis H. History of Economic Thought. New York: Macmillan, 1912.

Hansen, Alvin H. Monetary Theory and Fiscal Policy. New York: McGraw-Hill, 1949.

Heilbroner, Robert L. The Worldly Philosophers: The Lives, Times and Ideas of the Great Economic Thinkers. New York: Simon & Schuster, 1953.

Jenkins, Arthur Hugh. Adam Smith Today. New York: R. R. Smith, 1948.

Jevons, W. Stanley. Theory of Political Economy. London: 1878.

Keynes, John Maynard. The General Theory of Employment, Interest, and Money. New York: Harcourt, Brace, 1936.
_____. A Treatise on Money. New York: Harcourt, Brace, 1930.

Kimmel, Lewis. Federal Budget and Fiscal Policy, 1789-1958. Washington, D. C.: Brookings Institution, 1959.

Marshall, Alfred. Principles of Economics. London: 1890.

Ricardo, David. Principles of Political Economy. London: 1817.

Ruggles, Richard. An Introduction to National Income and Income Analysis. New York: McGraw-Hill, 1949.

Smith, Adam. An Inquiry into the Nature and Causes of the Wealth of Nations. Edited and annotated by Edwin Cannan. New York: Random House, 1937 (Originally published 1776).

Stephen, Sir Leslie. The English Utilitarians. London: Gerald Duckworth & Co., 1900.

THE DEATH OF CAPTAIN JAMES COOK (1779)

The Pacific Ocean, the largest and deepest of the five oceans, was discovered by Vasco Nuñez de Balboa, a Spanish explorer, on September 25, 1513. On September 29, he took formal possession of it and all the lands in it for Spain, calling it "El Mar del Sur" (The South Sea).

For three centuries following the original discovery by Balboa the Pacific was explored by navigators from various European countries. In 1520 Ferdinand Magellan, a Portuguese sailing in the service of Spain, traveled through the strait at the southern tip of Cape Horn, which strait was named after him, and on March 16 discovered the Philippine Islands. Magellan's explorations were followed by more than two dozen navigators, all seeking to learn more about the huge ocean. Some of these made important new discoveries and others corroborated earlier findings.

One of the many important discoveries was that of the Hawaiian Islands, made by Captain James Cook, an English navigator, who landed at Kauai on January 18, 1778. He named the archipelago the "Sandwich Islands," in honor of the Earl of Sandwich.

James Cook had enlisted in the British navy as a common seaman in 1755 and although a man without property or political connections had risen, by sheer merit, to the rank of captain. He had impressed his commanding officer, Captain Hugh Palliser, with whom he sailed on the Eagle. Palliser, with others gave him the opportunity to learn navigation, surveying and charting. He surveyed the St. Lawrence Channel (1759) and the coast of Newfoundland and Labrador (1763-1767). In 1768 he captained the ship Endeavour on an expedition to the South Pacific Ocean and at Tahiti observed the transit of Venus the following year. He also charted the coasts of New Zealand, Australia and New Guinea, and returned to England in 1771. A second expedition to the Pacific in 1772-1775, conducted in the ships Resolution and Adventure, resulted in the discovery of New Calendonia. It was on his last expedition, made in the Resolution and the Discovery, that he discovered the Hawaiian (Sandwich) Islands.

The islanders assumed that Cook was a reincarnation of Lono, an ancient Hawaiian god, whose return to the Islands had been prophesied. At the instigation of the native priests and chiefs the officers and crews of the two English ships were furnished with food and gifts, which greatly depleted the local stores. After needed repairs had been made to the ships Cook and his men left, to the general relief of the natives. However, the Resolution developed serious trouble with her masts and rigging and it was necessary to return to the islands where further repairs could be made. During this second visit William Watman, one of the British sailors, died and was buried ashore. The natives realized that the visitors were mortals, not gods, and incidents of thievery occurred. Natives prized iron nails from the bottoms of the ships by diving under them. Small articles were pilfered. One native who ignored warnings was flogged as an example but the thefts went on, growing more and more serious.

One night the Discovery's cutter was stolen from her moorings close by the ship. Cook decided to seize the highest chief available and hold him as a hostage until the cutter was returned. He and an armed guard of marines commanded by Lieutenant Phillips were rowed ashore. A second detachment, led by Lieutenant King, accompanied them in another boat. Cook, in full uniform, was armed with a double-barreled shotgun.

Reaching shore, the Englishmen proceeded to the house of King Kalaniopu'u, who was to be the hostage. The king, when told of the theft, of which he had no previous knowledge, agreed to go to the Resolution and remain there until the cutter was returned. Cook, the king, two of his sons and the marines started to walk to the boats in which the landing parties had come ashore. When they reached a point on the beach a few yards from the boats the two sons ran ahead and jumped in.

Some of the native canoes in the bay had been stopped by British sailors who had fired at them from the ships. A large, excited crowd assembled on the beach. The king's favorite wife, screaming hysterically, begged her husband not to go with Cook to the Resolution. The crowd grew angry. Some natives picked up stones and others ran into houses where they obtained clubs, spears and woven fiber war mats, designed to be worn as protective armor. Two young chiefs gently pushed the king down so that he could not continue to walk towards the boats. The crowd's anger increased when it was learned that an important chief had been killed by gunshots in the bay. Cook left the king, feeling that serious bloodshed would result from any further effort to take him aboard the Resolution. A native warrior menaced Cook with a stone and a dagger. Cook ordered him to discard his weapons and when the warrior started to throw the stone Cook killed him with his shotgun.

A general riot followed. Shots were fired by the marines and four of them were killed by the natives while other marines were wounded before they had time to reload their muskets. Captain Cook did not reload his shotgun. He raised his hand to order a cease fire and turned to the beach. As he reached the water's edge a warrior rushed up to him and struck him from behind with a war club. He sank to his knees. Other warriors clubbed and stabbed him. The marines then opened fire on the mob, virtually annihilating it.

Cook's body was taken back to the Resolution. It was returned to England and buried in the center aisle of Great St. Andrews Church, not far from Christ's College.

Suggested Readings

Beaglehole, J. C. , ed. Journals of Captain James Cook. Cambridge: The University Press, 1966.

Bellis, Hannah. Captain Cook. New York: McGraw-Hill, 1968.

Kippis, A. Captain Cook's Voyages, with an Account of His Life and Intervening Periods. New York: Knopf, 1925 (Originally written 1788).

Lloyd, Christopher. Captain Cook. New York: Roy, 1955.

MacLean, Alistair. Captain Cook. Garden City, N. Y. : Doubleday, 1972.

Mitchell, Carleton. Beyond Horizons: Voyages of Adventure and Discovery. New York: Norton, 1953.

Moorehead, Alan. Fatal Impact: An Account of the Invasion of the South Pacific, 1767-1840. New York: Harper, 1966.

Swenson, Eric. The South Sea Shilling: Voyages of Captain Cook, R. N. New York: Viking Press, 1952.

Sykes, Percy. A History of Exploration from the Earliest Times to the Present. New York: Harper and Row, 1961 (Originally published 1934).

Syme, Ronald. Captain Cook, Pacific Explorer. New York: Mor-
    row, 1960.
Villiers, Alan. Captain James Cook. New York: Scribner, 1967.
Warner, Oliver, and the editors of Horizon Magazine. Captain
    Cook and the South Pacific. New York: American Heritage
    Publishing Co. , 1963.

THE MONTGOLFIER BALLOON FLIGHTS (1783)

The first successful flight of a manned balloon was held at
Paris, France, on November 21, 1783. Jean François Filâtre de
Rozier and the Marquis d'Arlandes stayed aloft for 25 minutes in
a hot-air balloon designed by the Montgolfier brothers, Joseph Michel and Jacques Étienne. The 75-foot-high craft, 49 feet in diameter
and constructed of cloth and paper, rose 280 feet over the Château
La Muette and traveled to Butte-Aux-Cailles where it landed safely.

This flight was the culmination of a series of experiments
with lighter-than-air craft which began in November, 1782, at Avignon. Joseph Montgolfier constructed a small hot-air balloon which
made its first flight in his lodgings. At Annonay he continued to
experiment with larger balloons and on April 25, 1783, he and his
brother Jacques launched a balloon which rose over a thousand feet.
Encouraged, the brothers planned a public demonstration of their invention.

On June 5, 1783, the first public flight of a hot-air balloon
was staged at Annonay's town square. This craft, which was unmanned, rose to a height of 6,000 feet and remained in the air
about ten minutes.

The Academy of Sciences at Paris heard of the Annonay
flight and, feeling that the triumph of the Montgolfier brothers reflected adversely on their scientific prowess, decided to stage a
demonstration with a balloon of their own, designed by Jacques
Alexandre César Charles, with hydrogen rather than hot air as the
lifting agent. Such a balloon was built by Aîné Robert and his brother Cadet. These brothers developed a rubber coating for fine silk,
designed to keep the gas from leaking out of its container.

The Montgolfier brothers were in Paris on the day of the
launching but were denied admittance to the enclosure at the Champ
de Mars where the ascension was to take place. The unmanned
hydrogen balloon, christened the Globe, rose 3,000 feet and traveled
to Gonesse where it landed in a field 45 minutes later. Peasants,
terrified by the strange contraption, destroyed it with pitchforks.

In September the Montgolfier brothers prepared for a demonstration of a large spherical balloon which would carry as passengers a sheep, a rooster and a duck. This, like their other bal-

loons, used hot air as a lifting agent.   The demonstration, which
took place on September 19, was witnessed by King Louis XVI and
Marie Antoinette.   The flight was successful.

On November 21, 1783, de Rozier and the Marquis d'Arlandes made their flight.   A wicker basket suspended below the gas
bag held the two pioneer balloonists, who stoked a fire in a metal
basket with straw, thus keeping the air in the balloon hot.

This successful flight inspired others to emulate it.   Until
well into the twentieth century balloon ascensions were featured at
fairs and carnivals.   The simple hot-air and hydrogen-filled balloons were the forerunners of such gigantic engine-propelled zep-
pelins as the Hindenburg and the Shenandoah.

Suggested Readings

Blanchard, Jean Pierre.   The First Air Voyage in America: The
    Times, the Place, and the People of the Blanchard Balloon
    Voyage of January 9, 1793 (Philadelphia to Woodbury).   Phil-
    adelphia: Penn Mutual Life Insurance Co. , 1943.
Dollfus, Charles.   The Orion Book of Balloons.   New York: Orion
    Press, 1960.
Duke, Neville Frederick, ed.   The Saga of Flight.   New York:
    John Day, 1961.
Dwiggins, Don.   The Air Devils: The Story of Balloonists, Barn-
    stormers and Stunt Flyers.   New York: Lippincott, 1966.
Hyde, Margaret Olroyd.   Flight Today and Tomorrow.   New York:
    Whittlesey House, 1962.
Josephy, Alvin M. , Jr. , ed.   The American Heritage History of
    Flight.   New York: American Heritage Publishing Co. , 1962.
Lewellyn, John Bryan, and Irwin Shapiro.   The Story of Flight.
    New York: Golden Press, 1959.
Poe, Edgar Allan.   "The Balloon-Hoax" (science fiction) in Com-
    plete Stories and Poems of Edgar Allan Poe.   Garden City,
    N. Y. :   Doubleday, 1966 (Originally published 1844).
Rolt, L. T. C.   The Aeronauts: A History of Ballooning, 1783-1903.
    New York: Walker & Co. , 1966.
Singer, Charles, et al, eds.   A History of Technology.   Oxford:
    Clarendon Press, 1954-1958.
Twain, Mark, pseud.   Tom Sawyer Abroad (fiction).   New York:
    Harper, 1894.
Whitehouse, Arch.   The Early Birds.   Garden City, N. Y. :   Double-
    day, 1965.

THE AFFAIR OF THE QUEEN'S DIAMOND NECKLACE
(1784-1786)

The "affair of the Queen's diamond necklace" was a confidence game by which Monsieur Boehmer, a Paris jeweler, was bilked of a diamond necklace valued at 1,600,000 francs and Cardinal de Rohan was also victimized.

In 1784 the Cardinal was "enamored of the charms" of Marie Antoinette, Queen of France, but the Queen did not reciprocate his feelings. One of the Queen's ladies of honor was Comtesse Jeanne de la Motte, a French adventuress, and the Cardinal made her his confidante.

The Comtesse had been present at an interview which Marie Antoinette had granted Monsieur Boehmer. The jeweler had attempted to sell her a diamond necklace which the Queen admired but, pleading poverty, did not purchase. Comtesse de la Motte conceived a plan by which she could gain possession of the necklace, using the Cardinal as a dupe. She told de Rohan of the Queen's admiration for the necklace and of her inability to purchase it. The Cardinal, a wealthy man, offered to buy and present it to the Queen in the hope that such a gift might alter her feelings for him.

Comtesse de la Motte suggested that he instead persuade the jeweler to give the Queen credit and accept her promissory note, to be paid on a date to be agreed upon later. The Cardinal had such a note drawn up and delivered it to the Comtesse who returned it to him shortly afterwards with an acceptance, apparently in the Queen's handwriting but which was later found to be a forgery, on the margin. She also told him that the Queen was greatly pleased and would shortly arrange a rendezvous with him in the gardens at Versailles and would then present him with a flower as a token of her regard.

The Cardinal obtained the necklace from the jeweler and delivered it at the Comtesse's home to a man disguised as a valet of the Queen. The Comtesse then arranged for a young Frenchwoman named D'Olive, who bore a strong resemblance to the Queen, to keep the evening rendezvous with the Cardinal in the garden. The meeting proceeded according to plan, the Cardinal received his flower and was overjoyed.

In due course the forgery was discovered. The jeweler named the Comtesse and Cardinal de Rohan as the persons with whom he had dealt. The two then were arrested and imprisoned in the Bastille. There the Comtesse implicated Giuseppe Balsamo, better known as Count Cagliostro, an Italian charlatan, swindler, and soldier of fortune. Cagliostro and his wife, Seraphina, were arrested and imprisoned. The Comtesse's husband fled to England and it was suspected that he had taken the diamond necklace with him, to be broken up and sold. The Comtesse, however, insisted that she had delivered it to Cagliostro, who was to dispose of it piecemeal.

Cagliostro, de Rohan and the Comtesse were put on trial. Cagliostro, in an impassioned speech, declared his innocence of any

wrongdoing. Cardinal de Rohan was found to have been himself a
victim of the conspiracy and he and Cagliostro were acquitted.
Comtesse de la Motte was found guilty. She was condemned to be
publicly whipped while naked, branded on the back, and imprisoned.
Her husband was sentenced, in absentia, to the galleys. The Comtesse, however, escaped.

The Italian charlatan and his wife were ordered to leave
Paris within 24 hours. They proceeded to London where they met
Lord George Gordon. The latter inserted a letter in the newspapers, charging Marie Antoinette with being implicated in the affair
of the necklace and asserting that she was the guilty party. Gordon was, for his accusation, tried, found guilty of libel and sentenced to pay a fine and serve a long prison sentence.

Suggested Readings

Bolitho, William. "Cagliostro (and Seraphina)" in his Twelve Against
    the Gods: The Story of Adventure. New York: Simon & Schus-
    ter, 1929.
"Cagliostro" in Crimes and Punishment, Vol. 2. Editorial presen-
    tation: Jackson Morley. London: BPC, 1973.
Carlyle, Thomas. The French Revolution: A History. New York:
    William Kerr & Co., 1841 (Originally published 1837).
Castelot, André. Queen of France: A Biography of Marie Antoin-
    ette. Translated by Denise Folliot. New York: Harper &
    Row, 1957.
_____. The Turbulent City: Paris, 1783-1871. Translated by
    Denise Folliot. New York: Harper & Row, 1962.
Deeson, A. F. L. Great Swindlers. New York: Drake Publishers,
    1972.
Farmer, Lydia. "Marie Antoinette" in her A Book of Famous
    Queens. Revised by Willard A. Heaps. New York: Crowell,
    1964.
Faÿ, Bernard. Louis XVI; or, The End of a World. Chicago:
    Henry Regnery, 1968.
Finger, Charles J. "Three Splendid Scoundrels: 'Count' St. Ger-
    main, 'Count' Cagliostro, Jeanne de Valois" in his Romantic
    Rascals. New York: McBride, 1927.
Gershoy, Leo. From Despotism to Revolution, 1763-1789. New
    York: Harper, 1944.
Gottschalk, Louis R. The Era of the French Revolution, 1715-1815.
    Boston: Houghton Mifflin, 1957.
Lang, Andrew. "Historical Mysteries: The Cardinal's Necklace,"
    Cornhill Magazine, July, 1904.
Mackay, Charles. "The Alchymists" in his Memoirs of Extraor-
    dinary Delusions and the Madness of Crowds. London: Office
    of the National Illustrated Library, 1852. Reprinted by L. C.
    Page & Co., Boston, 1932.
Padover, Saul K. The Life and Death of Louis XVI. New York:
    Taplinger Publishing Co., 1963.
Photaidès, Constantin. "The Queen's Necklace" in his Count Cag-

liostro: An Authentic Story of a Mysterious Life. London:
Rider & Co. , 1932.
Trowbridge, W. R. H. "The Comtesse de la Motte, 1756-1791" in
his Seven Splendid Sinners. London: T. F. Unwin, 1908.

THE WARREN HASTINGS IMPEACHMENT TRIAL
(1788-1795)

The English East India Company was a commercial concern
chartered originally by Queen Elizabeth I of England on December
31, 1600, under the title of "The Governor and Company of Merchants of London Trading Into the East Indies. " The Company's
charter was renewed a number of times and it became the most
important of all such companies, of which there were several, chartered by France, Denmark and the Netherlands. It remained in existence until January 1, 1874, when the East India Stock Dividend
Redemption Act went into force.

During its lifetime the Company was authorized to perform
not only mercantile but governmental functions, including the acquisition of territory, the issuing of currency, the negotiation of
treaties, the collection of taxes, the waging of war and the administration of justice.

Warren Hastings went to India as a clerk for the Company
at the age of eighteen. A decade later he had been promoted to
membership in the Calcutta Council. He retired briefly and then
was appointed to a high company position at Madras and, in 1772,
became governor and president of the Bengal Council. In 1773
the British government appointed him the first governor-general of
Bengal and India. Here he was presiding officer of the four-mem-
ber Bengal Council.

One of the members of the Council was Sir Philip Francis,
a ruthlessly ambitious man and a bitter personal enemy of Hastings.
The two men fought a duel in which Francis was severely injured.
The latter returned to England where he made accusations of mis-
management, corruption and the accepting of bribes against Hastings. Edmund Burke, the crusading Irish-born politician, writer
and orator, listened to Francis and after hearing his accusations
urged the House of Commons to take action.

In 1787, by which time Hastings had resigned from his gov-
ernor-generalship, Parliament agreed to his impeachment. This
was in spite of the fact that, upon Hastings' return to England, he
had been congratulated by King George III on "a fine job, well done, "
and also was commended by the officials of the Company.

The impeachment trial of Warren Hastings began on February
13, 1788, in Westminster Hall before the House of Lords. It was

to last for seven years. The proceedings opened with a four-day
oration by Burke, in which he charged Hastings with a long list of
administrative crimes. Hastings pleaded "not guilty" to all charges.

Richard Brinsley Sheridan, playwright, theater manager and
orator, joined the prosecution, making a three-day speech. Then,
for the next two years, the charges were considered. At the end
of the third year Parliament was dissolved and the new Parliament,
in due course, continued the trial.

The proceedings continued until April 23, 1795, when the 29
peers still sitting found Warren Hastings not guilty. By this time
Burke had retired from the House of Commons and from politics.
Hastings' expenses for his defense came to 71,080 pounds, the payment of which would virtually bankrupt him. His old employers,
the English East India Company, came to his rescue, voting him a
pension of 4,000 pounds a year and making immediate payment of
the first ten years.

Following the seven-year trial Hastings retired to a home
in the country. In 1813 he appeared before the House of Commons
to give evidence concerning the renewing of the Company's charter.
He died in 1818.

Suggested Readings

Birkenhead, Frederick Edwin Smith. "The Trial of Warren Hast-
    ings" in his Famous Trials of History. Garden City, N.Y.:
    Garden City Publishing Co., 1928.
Davies, A. Mervyn. Strange Destiny: A Biography of Warren Hast-
    ings. New York: Putnam's, 1935.
Durant, Jack Davis. Richard Brinsley Sheridan. Boston: Twayne,
    1975.
Feiling, Keith G. Warren Hastings. Hamden, Conn.: Shoe String
    Press, 1967 (Originally published 1954).
Foster, William. The East India House: Its History and Associa-
    tions. London: John Lane, 1924.
Gleig, Rev. G.R. Memoirs of the Life of Warren Hastings. Lon-
    don: 1841.
Kramnick, Isaac, ed. Edmund Burke. Englewood Cliffs, N.J.:
    Prentice-Hall, 1974.
Lyall, Alfred. Warren Hastings. Plainview, N.Y.: Books for
    Libraries, 1889.
Marshall, Peter James. The Impeachment of Warren Hastings.
    London: Oxford University Press, 1965.
Monckton Jones, M.E. Warren Hastings in Bengal, 1772-74. Lon-
    don: 1918.
Moon, Penderel. Warren Hastings and British India. London: Ox-
    ford University Press, 1947.
"An Old Colonial Score" in Crimes and Punishment, Vol. 17. Ed-
    itorial presentation: Jackson Morley. London: BPC, 1973.

Sutherland, Miss Stuart. "Lord Shelburne and East India Company
    Politics, 1766-9, " English Historical Review, July, 1934.
Trotter, Lionel J. Warren Hastings. Mystic, Conn. : Verry,
    1962 (Originally published 1890).

THE BOUNTY MUTINY (1789)

In 1787 the British government decided that breadfruit plants,
the source of an excellent starch food, should be transported from
Tahiti, where they grew in profusion, to the British West Indies.
There they were to be transplanted and the fruit used to feed Negro
slaves.

The H. M. S. Bounty a British 215-ton merchant vessel originally named the Bertha, was assigned to perform the mission and
Lieutenant William Bligh was placed in command. Bligh was a
professional naval officer, a man of choleric temper who obeyed
the orders given him by his superiors and who expected instant
obedience from his subordinates. Surprisingly, however, he was
concerned for the happiness and comfort of the members of his
command. He was an efficient navigator, seaman and officer.

The Bounty left Spithead in December, 1787, arriving at
Tahiti on October 25, 1788. After a six-month sojourn the ship
started its return trip. The natives of Tahiti had welcomed the
voyagers who were loath to leave the pleasures of shore life for
a dreary year-long sea voyage.

Fletcher Christian, Bligh's 24-year-old mate, had been accused by the captain of stealing coconuts. Other brushes had occurred between the two men. It was Christian, together with Matthew Quintal, John Adams (Alexander Smith), William Musprat, Peter Heywood, James Morrison and other members of the company
who, wishing to return to Tahiti, incited a portion of the crew to
mutiny. Bligh and eighteen loyal crew members were cast adrift
in a small launch.

Bligh and his men, after an incredible 41-day voyage of
3,618 miles in the open boat, reached Kupang on the island of Timor, only one man being lost. He returned to England and, on October 22, 1790, a formal courtmartial concerning the loss of the
Bounty cleared him of responsibility and found that the vessel "was
violently and forcibly seized by Fletcher Christian and certain other
mutineers. "

Christian and his followers returned to Tahiti and from there
had, with several native men and women, sailed to Pitcairn Island.
There the Bounty was sunk. Christian was killed by a native. Fourteen of the mutineers were captured at Pitcairn and shipped to England on the frigate Pandora commanded by Captain Edward Edwards.

The <u>Pandora</u> was wrecked on the Great Barrier Reef off the coast of Australia and four of the mutineers were lost. The remaining ten finally arrived in England and were tried for mutiny on September 12, 1792, the trial lasting until the eighteenth. Four of the men were acquitted, six were found guilty but three were later pardoned and three were hanged on October 29.

Suggested Readings

Anthony, Irvin, ed. <u>The Saga of the Bounty: Its Strange History as Related by the Participants Themselves.</u> New York: Putnam's, 1935.

Ball, Ian M. <u>Pitcairn: Children of Mutiny.</u> Boston: Little, Brown, 1973.

Barrow, Sir John, bart. <u>Description of Pitcairn's Island and Its Inhabitants. With an Authentic Account of the Mutiny of the Ship Bounty and the Subsequent Fortunes of the Mutineers.</u> New York: Haskell House, 1972 (Originally published 1900).

_____. <u>The Mutiny and Piratical Seizure of H. M. S. Bounty,</u> by Sir John Barrow. London: H. Milford, 1914

Belcher, Diana Joliffe, Lady. <u>Mutineers of the Bounty and Their Descendants in Pitcairn and Norfolk Islands.</u> London: J. Murray, 1870.

Bligh, William. <u>Bligh and the "Bounty:" His Narrative of the Voyage to Otaheite with an Account of the Mutiny and of His Boat Journey to Timor.</u> New York: Dutton, 1936 (Originally written late 18th or early 19th century).

_____. <u>A Book of the "Bounty"</u> by William Bligh and Others. New York: Dutton, 1952 (Originally written late 18th or early 19th century).

Daneilsson, Bengt. <u>What Happened on the "Bounty."</u> Translated by Alan Tapsell. London: Allen, 1962.

Evatt, Herbert V. <u>Rum Rebellion.</u> Sydney, Australia: 1938.

Fuller, Edmund. <u>Mutiny!</u> New York: Crown Publishers, 1953.

Herbert, David. <u>Great Historical Mutinies, Comprising the Mutiny of the Bounty, the Mutiny at Spithead, the Mutiny at the Nore, Mutinies in Highland Regiments and the Indian Mutiny.</u> London: Nimmo, 1876.

Hough, Richard. <u>Captain Bligh and Mr. Christian: The Men and the Mutiny.</u> New York: Dutton, 1973.

Mackaness, George. <u>The Life of Vice-Admiral William Bligh, R. N, F. R. S.</u> Sydney, Australia: Angus & Robertson, 1931.

McKee, Alexander. <u>H. M. S. Bounty.</u> New York: Morrow, 1961.

Michener, James A., and A. Grove Day. <u>Rascals in Paradise.</u> New York: Random House, 1957.

Montgomerie, Hastings Seton. <u>William Bligh of the "Bounty" in Fact and Fable.</u> London: Williams, 1937.

Nordhoff, Charles, and James Norman Hall. <u>The "Bounty" Trilogy Comprising Three Volumes: Mutiny on the "Bounty," Men Against the Sea, Pitcairn's Island</u> (historical fiction). Boston: Little, Brown, 1932.

Rawson, Geoffrey. <u>"Pandora's" Last Voyage.</u> New York: Harcourt, Brace, 1964.

THE TENNIS COURT OATH (1789)

In 1789 France, although one of the most prosperous nations in Europe, found the royal government on the verge of bankruptcy. This was due primarily to the inequity of the tax system, although inefficient management of the royal monopolies contributed to the dismal financial situation.

Neither the clergy nor the nobility paid taxes to the crown, which meant that the peasants found themselves saddled with a heavy tax burden. Many wealthy bourgeoisie paid a smaller percentage of their income in taxes than did the commoners.

The royal government, in order to avoid going bankrupt, attempted to impose taxes which would be paid by the hitherto exempt clergy and nobility. This led to a struggle between King Louis XVI and the privileged classes.

The Parlement of Paris reflected the views of the aristocracy, and Louis finally announced that the States-General would convene in May, 1789. This body, which had not met since 1614, was composed of the clergy (first estate), the nobility (second estate) and the commoners (third estate). These three groups had traditionally met and voted separately, with the consensus being expressed by the majority vote of two of the three estates. The Parlement declared that the States-General would meet in three separate groups. This meant that the first and second estates could outvote the third estate in any matters pertaining to their taxes.

The third estate requested King Louis to increase their numbers that they might be numerically equal to the other two. The king agreed, reasoning that the 2/3 majority vote would still prevail regardless of the number of persons voting in each estate. Further, he desired the support of the third estate in the forthcoming assembly.

The clergy and the nobility met in their separate halls, preparing to organize as separate orders. The third estate, wishing to meet with the two others as one combined body, instituted delaying tactics and refused to organize itself. The first estate, in sympathy with the commoners, postponed its own organization.

Further delaying tactics were used by the commoners. They demanded that the credentials of the three orders be verified at a joint meeting. This the nobility refused, so the commoners retaliated by declining to verify their own credentials.

On June 10, 1789, the Abbé Emmanuel Joseph Sieyes, leader of the third estate, proposed that the three meet together, that a combined rollcall be taken and that those not responding be eliminated. The rollcall began on June 12. Five days later the third estate assumed the name "National Assembly." Many of the clergy

voted to join the third estate and the king called a royal session,
to meet on June 23.   On June 20, when the third estate attempted
to meet in their assigned hall, the members found it closed on
Louis' orders, he wishing to prevent further meetings until the
23rd.   They then decided to meet at a nearby indoor tennis court.

Jean-Joseph Mounier, a member of the third estate, proposed that they bind themselves together in a common oath, to
which they agreed.   The members resolved, in the Tennis Court
Oath, not to separate, but to meet whenever necessary until France
had a constitution.   All members signed the declaration except Martin Dauch.

On June 23 the king ordered the deputies to meet in three
bodies and to limit the discussion to financial matters.   These instructions were ignored, indicating that the deputies considered
themselves not one order of the States-General but a national convention representing the French people.   This was tantamount to
revolution and was one of the factors leading to the French Revolution of 1789.

Suggested Readings

Aulard, Alphonse.   The French Revolution: A Political History,
    1789-1804.   Translated by B. Miall.   New York: Russell and
    Russell, 1955.
Bourne, Henry Eldridge.   The Revolutionary Period in Europe
    (1763-1815).   New York: Century, 1917.
Brinton, Crane.   A Decade of Revolution, 1789-1799.   New York:
    Harper & Row, 1934.
Carlyle, Thomas.   The French Revolution: A History.   New York:
    William Kerr & Co. , 1841 (Originally published 1837).
Castelot, André.   The Turbulent City: Paris, 1783-1871.   Trans-
    lated by Denise Folliot.   New York: Harper & Row, 1962.
Dawson, John Philip.   The French Revolution.   Englewood Cliffs,
    N. J. : Prentice-Hall, 1967.
Duclaux, Mary (A. Mary F. Robinson).   A Short History of France
    from Caesar's Invasion to the Battle of Waterloo.   New York:
    Putnam's, 1918.
Eimerl, Sarel.   Revolution! France, 1789-1794.   Boston: Little,
    Brown, 1967.
Faÿ, Bernard.   Louis XVI; or, The End of a World.   Chicago:
    Henry Regnery, 1968.
Fisher, John.   Six Summers in Paris, 1789-1794.   New York: Har-
    per & Row, 1966.
Gershoy, Leo.   From Despotism to Revolution, 1763-1789.   New
    York: Harper, 1944.
Goodwin, Albert.   The French Revolution.   New York: Harper,
    1962.
Gottschalk, Louis R.   The Era of the French Revolution, 1715-1815.
    Boston: Houghton Mifflin, 1957.
Higgins, E. L.   The French Revolution Told by Contemporaries.   Lon-
    don: Harrap, 1939.

Johnson, Douglas W. J.   The French Revolution.   New York: Put-
     nam's, 1970.
Lefebvre, Georges.   The Coming of the French Revolution.   New
     York: Vintage Books, 1957.
_____.   The French Revolution from Its Origins to 1793.   New
     York: Columbia University Press, 1961.
Legg, Wickham, ed.   Documents Illustrative of the History of the
     French Revolution.   Oxford: Clarendon Press, 1905.
Lofts, Norah, and Margery Weiner.   Eternal France: A History
     of France, 1789-1944.   Garden City, N. Y. :   Doubleday, 1968.
Mathiez, Albert.   The French Revolution.   New York: Grosset
     and Dunlap, 1946.
Michelet, Jules.   History of the French Revolution.   Edited by Gor-
     don Wright.   Chicago: University of Chicago Press, 1967.
Montague, F. C.   "The National Assembly and the Spread of An-
     archy" in Ward, A. W. , et al. , eds.   The Cambridge Modern
     History.   Cambridge: Cambridge University Press, 1904.
Morris, Gouverneur.   A Diary of the French Revolution.   Boston:
     Houghton Mifflin, 1939.
Padover, Saul K.   The Life and Death of Louis XVI.   New York:
     Taplinger Publishing Co. , 1963.
Palmer, R. R.   Twelve Who Ruled.   Princeton, N. J. :   Princeton
     University Press, 1941.
Rudé, George.   The Crowd in the French Revolution.   Oxford:
     Clarendon Press, 1959.
Stephens, H. Morse, ed.   The Principal Speeches of the Statesmen
     and Orators of the French Revolution.   Oxford: Clarendon
     Press, 1892.
Stewart, John Hall.   A Documentary Survey of the French Revolu-
     tion.   New York: Macmillan, 1951.
Thompson, James M.   The French Revolution.   New York: Ox-
     ford University Press, 1966.

THE FALL OF THE BASTILLE (1789)

     The fall of the Bastille, a fortress-prison in Paris, was
triggered by the dismissal and exile of Jacques Necker, France's
popular director general of finances.   He had been exiled in 1787
as the result of a published article responding to one attacking his
administration, but was recalled in 1788, by popular demand, to
his former post.

     Necker supported the convocation of the States-General and
double representation therein for the third estate.   When he refused
to support a court-projected coup against the National Assembly he
was again dismissed and exiled.   It was this second dismissal which
caused the uprising and storming of the Bastille on July 14, 1789.

     Rumors had been rampant in Paris that King Louis XVI was
planning to dissolve the National Assembly, which had been meeting

in Versailles for the previous month.   When the king began moving Swiss and German mercenary troops to Versailles and Paris, the people feared that this posed a serious threat to the National Assembly and to the revolutionary movement.   Necker was dismissed on July 11.   The news reached Paris on the 12th and the citizens promptly revolted, the uprising lasting until July 14.

The people began a search for arms with which to defend themselves against the king's mercenaries.   The more conservative element realized that it was necessary to preserve law and order. A Central Committee was elected, and Jacques de Flesseles was chosen chairman.   The Committee organized a National Guard whose functions were to prevent rioting and protect private property.

Crowds roamed the streets in search of arms, fearing a massacre of patriots similar to the St. Bartholomew's Eve massacre of 1572.   On July 14 a mob marched on the Bastille, intending to seize arms and powder which had been placed there for safekeeping.   The original intention was not to attack the prison or release the inmates.

The mob demanded that Bernard René de Launay, military governor of the prison, withdraw his cannon and turn over his supply of powder and arms to the people.   While de Launay was negotiating some members of the mob pushed their way into the inner court.   De Launay panicked and opened fire, whereupon fighting broke out.   After two hours the National Guard brought up cannon, upon which de Launay surrendered.   Shortly thereafter he and de Flesseles were murdered, the latter being charged with misdirecting the search for arms.

The revolutionists then turned on the Bastille itself and proceeded to demolish it.   The royal troops had been driven from Paris.   Rioters roamed the streets and were eventually disarmed by members of the National Guard.

On July 15 Necker was recalled once more.   Though he was received with great popular acclaim, he proved unequal to the crisis, being distrusted by both the court and the National Assembly. He resigned in September, 1790, and retired to Coppet.

Suggested Readings

Aulard, Alphonse.   The French Revolution: A Political History,
     1789-1804.   Translated by B. Miall.   New York: Russell and
     Russell, 1955.
Bourne, Henry Eldridge.   The Revolutionary Period in Europe
     (1763-1815).   New York: Century, 1917.
Brinton, Crane.   A Decade of Revolution, 1789-1799.   New York:
     Harper & Row, 1934.
Carlyle, Thomas.   The French Revolution: A History.   New York:
     William Kerr & Co., 1841 (Originally published 1837).

Castelot, André. The Turbulent City: Paris, 1783-1871. Translated by Denise Folliot. New York: Harper & Row, 1962.

Dawson, John Philip. The French Revolution. Englewood Cliffs, N. J. : Prentice-Hall, 1967.

Duclaux, Mary (A. Mary F. Robinson). A Short History of France from Caesar's Invasion to the Battle of Waterloo. New York: Putnam's, 1918.

Eimerl, Sarel. Revolution! France, 1789-1794. Boston: Little, Brown, 1967.

Faÿ, Bernard. Louis XVI; or, The End of a World. Chicago: Henry Regnery, 1968.

Fisher, John. Six Summers in Paris, 1789-1794. New York: Harper & Row, 1966.

Gershoy, Leo. From Despotism to Revolution, 1763-1780. New York: Harper, 1944.

Godechot, Jacques. The Taking of the Bastille, July 14, 1789. New York: Scribner's, 1970.

Goodwin, Albert. The French Revolution. New York: Harper, 1962.

Gottschalk, Louis R. The Era of the French Revolution, 1715-1815. Boston: Houghton Mifflin, 1957.

Higgins, E. L. The French Revolution Told by Contemporaries. London: Harrap, 1939.

Johnson, Douglas W. J. The French Revolution. New York: Putnam's, 1970.

Lefebvre, Georges. The French Revolution from Its Origins to 1793. New York: Columbia University Press, 1961.

Legg, Wickham, ed. Documents Illustrative of the History of the French Revolution. Oxford: Clarendon Press, 1905.

Lofts, Norah, and Margery Weiner. Eternal France: A History of France, 1789-1944. Garden City, N. Y. : Doubleday, 1968.

Mathiez, Albert. The French Revolution. New York: Grosset and Dunlap, 1946.

Michelet, Jules. History of the French Revolution. Edited by Gordon Wright. Chicago: University of Chicago Press, 1967.

Montague, F. C. "The National Assembly and the Spread of Anarchy" in Ward, A. W. , et al. , eds. The Cambridge Modern History. Cambridge: Cambridge University Press, 1904.

Morris, Gouverneur. A Diary of the French Revolution. Boston: Houghton Mifflin, 1939.

Padover, Saul K. The Life and Death of Louis XVI. New York: Taplinger Publishing Co. , 1963.

Rudé, George. The Crowd in the French Revolution. Oxford: Clarendon Press, 1959.

Stephens, H. Morse, ed. The Principal Speeches of the Statesmen and Orators of the French Revolution. Oxford: Clarendon Press, 1892.

Stewart, John Hall. A Documentary Survey of the French Revolution. New York: Macmillan, 1951.

Thompson, James M. The French Revolution. New York: Oxford University Press, 1966.

THE EXECUTION OF LOUIS XVI (1793)

Louis XVI, King of France, is considered by historians to have been a victim of circumstances rather than a despot such as Louis XIV or Louis XV.   He was, as a ruler, incapable and pre-ferred hunting and lock-making to affairs of state.   Not overly in-telligent, he was dominated unduly by his wife, the extremely un-popular Marie Antoinette.

At the time of his accession to the throne in 1774 France was much disturbed by misery and discontent.   Louis, aided by such capable ministers as Anne Robert Jacques Turgot, Chrétien Guillaume de Lamoignon de Malesherbes and Comte de Vergennes, remitted objectionable taxes and abolished evil laws.   Conditions improved to some extent but the king was overruled by the extrav-agant queen and court.   Turgot, as minister of finance, was forced to resign, being replaced by Jacques Necker.   Necker, after trying in vain to help France out of the financial morass into which she had fallen was, like his predecessor, relieved of his position.   The new finance minister, Charles Alexandre de Calonne, appointed in 1783, borrowed money for the queen and court until 1786 at which time the borrowing limit was reached.   Necker was recalled in 1788 but was unable to prevent the bankruptcy of the French gov-ernment.   He was dismissed again and this was the immediate cause of the storming of the Bastille on July 14, 1789, and the start of the French Revolution.

Louis found himself unable to reconcile the revolutionary changes inaugurated by the National Assembly.   He sought means of annulling the Revolution and considered using force against the Assembly but did not do so.   By the terms of the constitution of 1791 France became a constitutional monarchy.   This constitution authorized veto power to the king but Louis was unable to dominate the new government which controlled fiscal matters and had the loyalty of the army.

When Pope Pius VI denounced the religious enactments of the revolutionary government which had been reluctantly accepted by the king, the latter attempted to escape to Austria with the roy-al family.   On June 20, 1791, the party left Paris by coach.   It was apprehended at Varennes and returned to the French capital. Louis and his family became political prisoners.

During the last half of 1791 France drifted toward war.   Both the king and the Girondins, the major political faction in the Nation-al Assembly, felt that a war would consolidate the nation.   On Ap-ril 20, 1792, war was declared against Austria and Prussia.   This led to the downfall of the king and the Girondins and the rise of the Jacobins.   That summer a Prussian army commanded by Karl Wilhelm Ferdinand, Duke of Brunswick, invaded France and marched toward Paris.   On July 25 Ferdinand issued a manifesto which stated, in essence, that he intended to do away with anarchy in France and

"stop the attacks directed against the throne and altar. " Further,
he indicated that if any harm came to the royal family the city of
Paris would be completely destroyed.

The manifesto indicated to the French people that King Louis was an ally of their enemies. On August 10 the king's residence
was attacked by a mob and Louis, who took refuge with the National Assembly, was deposed. A new Constitutional Assembly met on
September 21 and on September 22 France was declared a republic,
following which it was decided that the king should be tried for treason.

The Girondins defended Louis at his trial. The Jacobins,
led by Maximilien de Robespierre, prosecuted him and demanded
the death penalty. The trial lasted for over a month and in January, 1793, the king was condemned to death. He was beheaded
on the Place de la Révolution on January 21. Marie Antoinette was
also tried, found guilty of treason, and followed her husband to the
guillotine on October 16.

Suggested Readings

Aulard, Alphonse. The French Revolution: A Political History,
    1789-1804. Translated by B. Miall. New York: Russell and
    Russell, 1955.
Bourne, Henry Eldridge. The Revolutionary Period in Europe (1763-
    1815). New York: Century, 1917.
Brinton, Crane. A Decade of Revolution, 1789-1799. New York:
    Harper & Row, 1934.
Carlyle, Thomas. The French Revolution: A History. New York:
    William Kerr & Co. , 1841 (Originally published 1837).
Castelot, André. Queen of France: A Biography of Marie Antoin-
    ette. Translated by Denise Folliot. New York: Harper &
    Row, 1957.
_____. The Turbulent City: Paris, 1783-1871. Translated by
    Denise Folliot. New York: Harper & Row, 1962.
Dawson, John Philip, compiler. The French Revolution. Englewood
    Cliffs, N. J. : Prentice-Hall, 1967.
Duclaux, Mary (A. Mary F. Robinson). A Short History of France
    from Caesar's Invasion to the Battle of Waterloo. New York:
    Putnam's, 1918.
Eimerl, Sarel. Revolution! France, 1789-1794. Boston: Little,
    Brown, 1967.
Farmer, Lydia. "Marie Antoinette" in her A book of Famous
    Queens. Revised by Willard A. Heaps. New York: Crowell,
    1964.
Faỹ, Bernard. Louis XVI; or, The End of a World. Chicago: Hen-
    ry Regnery, 1968.
Fisher, John. Six Summers in Paris, 1789-1794. New York: Har-
    per & Row, 1966.
Gershoy, Leo. The French Revolution and Napoleon. New York:
    Appleton, 1934.

_____. From Despotism to Revolution, 1763-1789. New York: Harper, 1944.

Goodwin, Albert. The French Revolution. New York: Harper, 1962.

Gottschalk, Louis S. The Era of the French Revolution, 1715-1815. Boston: Houghton Mifflin, 1957.

Hazen, Charles Downer. The French Revolution and Napoleon. New York: Holt, 1917.

Higgins, E. L. The French Revolution Told by Contemporaries. London: Harrap, 1939.

Johnson, Douglas W. J. The French Revolution. New York: Putnam's, 1970.

Lefebvre, Georges. The Coming of the French Revolution. New York: Vintage Books, 1957.

_____. The French Revolution from Its Origins to 1793. New York: Columbia University Press, 1961.

_____. The French Revolution from 1793 to 1799. New York: Columbia University Press, 1964.

Legg, Wickham, ed. Documents Illustrative of the History of the French Revolution. Oxford: Clarendon Press, 1905.

Lofts, Norah, and Margery Weiner. Eternal France: A History of France, 1789-1944. Garden City, N. Y.: Doubleday, 1968.

Mathiez, Albert. The French Revolution. New York: Grosset and Dunlap, 1946.

Michelet, Jules. History of the French Revolution. Edited by Gordon Wright. Chicago: University of Chicago Press, 1967.

Montague, F. C. "The National Assembly and the Spread of Anarchy" in Ward, A. W., et al., eds. The Cambridge Modern History. Cambridge: Cambridge University Press, 1904.

Morris, Gouverneur. A Diary of the French Revolution. Boston: Houghton Mifflin, 1939.

Padover, Saul K. The Life and Death of Louis XVI. New York: Taplinger Publishing Co., 1963.

Palmer, R. R. Twelve Who Ruled. Princeton, N. J.: Princeton University Press, 1941.

Rudé, George. The Crowd in the French Revolution. Oxford: Clarendon Press, 1959.

Stephens, H. Morse, ed. The Principal Speeches of the Statesmen and Orators of the French Revolution. Oxford: Clarendon Press, 1892.

Stewart, John Hall. A Documentary Survey of the French Revolution. New York: Macmillan, 1951.

Thompson, James M. The French Revolution. New York: Oxford University Press, 1966.

_____. Robespierre and the French Revolution. New York: Collier Books, 1965.

THE ASSASSINATION OF JEAN-PAUL MARAT (1793)

The French Revolution resulted in the overthrow of the Bour-

bon monarchy, among other things, and the establishment of the
First Republic.   During its ten-year life (1789-1799) the Revolution
was dominated by a series of political parties, including the Girondins, the Jacobins and the Cordeliers.   These parties, in turn,
were led by politicians who were characterized by idealism in some
cases, by unreasoning fanaticism in others and by ruthless ambition
in still others.

One of the earlier political organizations was the moderate
republican Girondin party, formed in the French Legislative Assembly in 1791.   Its members were largely impractical idealists who
favored transformation of the constitutional monarchy into a federal
republic similar to the United States.   The Montagnards, consisting
of Jacobins and Cordeliers, favored the establishment of a highly
centralized indivisible republic.

The political differences between the Girondins and the Montagnards attained gigantic proportions after King Louis XVI vetoed
certain legislation, which then brought the Girondins into power.

Jean-Paul Marat, a Swiss-born physician, journalist, radical,
political agitator, Jacobin and violent anti-Girondist, established a
Paris newspaper, L'Ami du Peuple, in which he attacked his political enemies without mercy.   The Montagnards, led by the lawyer-
politician Georges Jacques Danton, dominated a new Parisian government, achieving control over the Legislative Assembly.   Marat,
because of his inflammatory writings in his newspaper, is generally
considered responsible for instituting the Paris massacre of September 2-7, 1792.   Mobs attacked and murdered priests in the
streets.   Girondins were arrested and subjected to farcical trials
in which the sentence of death was invariably imposed.   On June 2,
1793, a Paris mob "arrested" a number of Girondins, deputies from
the Convention, most of whom were executed.

Charlotte Corday, a 25-year-old resident of the town of Caen
in Normandy, was a passionate admirer of the Girondins.   The
daughter of an impoverished nobleman, she followed the downfall of
the Girondins with dismay.   She, as an idealist and avid reader of
Corneille, Plutarch and Cicero, came to believe that Marat was an
enemy of the state and a monster who must be destroyed before he
did France further damage.   When she read of the June massacre
she resolved to travel to Paris and kill the man who, she felt, was
responsible for the carnage.

On July 11, 1793, Charlotte Corday arrived in Paris where
she engaged a room at the Hôtel de la Providence.   She visited
Lauze Duperret, a deputy from Caen, for the purpose of enlisting
his assistance in connection with a business matter for a friend.
Duperret was unable to help her.

On Saturday, July 13, she arose early.   She went to the
market and purchased a six-inch kitchen knife for which she paid
two francs.   At nine o'clock she took a coach to Marat's residence,

the knife concealed in her clothing.   Arriving at her destination, she asked to speak with Marat, stating that she had some "secret and important information to give him. "   She was told that Marat was ill and saw no one.   Disappointed, she left, returning to her hotel where she wrote and dispatched a note to the man she planned to kill.   The note, which hinted at plots and implied that she could inform him of them, was delivered.

Having received no reply from Marat, Charlotte Corday wrote another note which she put in her pocket, hoping that if she was refused admittance a second time she could send this note to him and that, on reading it, he would admit her.   She then returned to Marat's home and was permitted to enter.

Marat, who suffered from eczema and other ailments, was in his bathtub, a copper contraption shaped something like a high shoe.   A vinegar-soaked bandanna was around his head and his chest was bare.   A wooden board lay across the front of the tub in such a way that he could use it as a writing desk.

The girl, at Marat's request, seated herself on a small stool and spoke of an "uprising" in Caen.   Marat proceeded to take notes as she talked.   While he wrote she rose, produced her knife and drove the blade into his chest.   The blow was fatal but before he died Marat was able to shout for help.

Members of the dying man's household seized the girl.   One grabbed a chair and struck her over the head.   She was arrested and taken to police headquarters.   There she stated calmly that she had come to Paris for the express purpose of killing Marat, feeling that he was about to precipitate civil war.

Charlotte Corday was tried immediately for the murder of Jean-Paul Marat.   At no time did she deny her guilt or ask for mercy.   She was sentenced to die by the guillotine and the sentence was carried out in Paris on the evening of July 17, 1793.

Suggested Readings

Abrahamsen, David, M. D.   The Murdering Mind.   New York: Harper & Row, 1973.
Aulard, Alphonse.   The French Revolution: A Political History, 1789-1804.   Translated by B. Maill.   New York: Russell and Russell, 1955.
Bourne, Henry Eldridge.   The Revolutionary Period in Europe (1763-1815).   New York: Century, 1917.
Brinton, Crane.   A Decade of Revolution, 1789-1799.   New York: Harper & Row, 1934.
Bromberg, Walter.   Mold of Murder: A Psychiatric Study of Homicide.   New York: Grune & Stratton, 1961.
Carlyle, Thomas.   The French Revolution: A History.   New York: William Kerr & Co. , 1841 (Originally written 1837).

314   Footnotes to World History

Castelot, André. The Turbulent City: Paris, 1783-1871. Trans-
    lated by Denise Folliot. New York: Harper & Row, 1962.
Dawson, John Philip, compiler. The French Revolution. Engle-
    wood Cliffs, N. J. : Prentice-Hall, 1967.
Eimerl, Sarel. Revolution! France, 1789-1794. Boston: Little,
    Brown, 1967.
Faÿ, Bernard. Louis XVI; or, The End of a World. Chicago: Hen-
    ry Regnery, 1968.
Fisher, John. Six Summers in Paris, 1789-1794. New York:
    Harper & Row, 1966.
Gershoy, Leo. From Despotism to Revolution, 1763-1789. New
    York: Harper, 1944.
Goodwin, Albert. The French Revolution. New York: Harper,
    1962.
Gottschalk, Louis R. The Era of the French Revolution, 1715-
    1815. Boston: Houghton Mifflin, 1957.
Higgins, E. L. The French Revolution Told by Contemporaries.
    London: Harrap, 1939.
Johnson, Douglas W. J. The French Revolution. New York: Put-
    nam's, 1970.
Lefebvre, Georges. The French Revolution from 1793 to 1799.
    New York: Columbia University Press, 1964.
Legg, Wickham, ed. Documents Illustrative of the History of the
    French Revolution. Oxford: Clarendon Press, 1905.
Lenotre, G. The Guillotine. Paris: Librarie Académique, Perrin
    et Cie, 1916.
_____. Paris Révolutionaire. Paris: Librarie Académique,
    Perrin et Cie, 1916.
Lofts, Norah, and Margery Weiner. Eternal France: A History
    of France, 1789-1944. Garden City, N. Y. : Doubleday, 1968.
Loomis, Stanley. "The Murder of Marat" in his Paris in the Ter-
    ror, June, 1793-July, 1794. Philadelphia: Lippincott, 1964.
Mathiez, Albert. The French Revolution. New York: Grosset and
    Dunlap, 1946.
Michelet, Jules. History of the French Revolution. Edited by Gor-
    don Wright. Chicago: University of Chicago Press, 1967.
Morris, Gouverneur. A Diary of the French Revolution. Boston:
    Houghton Mifflin, 1939.
Padovar, Saul K. The Life and Death of Louis XVI. New York:
    Taplinger Publishing Co. , 1963.
Palmer, R. R. Twelve Who Ruled. Princeton, N. J. : Princeton
    University Press, 1941.
Reinhardt, James Melvin. The Psychology of Strange Killers.
    Springfield, Ill. : Thomas, 1962.
Rudé, George. The Crowd in the French Revolution. Oxford: Clar-
    endon Press, 1959.
Sparrow, Gerald. Women Who Murder. New York: Abelard, 1970.
Stephens, H. Morse, ed. The Principal Speeches of the Statesmen
    and Orators of the French Revolution. Oxford: Clarendon
    Press, 1892.
Stewart, John Hall. A Documentary Survey of the French Revolu-
    tion. New York: Macmillan, 1951.
Thompson, James M. The French Revolution. New York: Oxford
    University Press, 1966.

_____. Robespierre and the French Revolution. New York:
    Collier Books, 1965.
Vatel, C. Dossiers du Proces Charlotte Corday. Paris, 1861.

THE OAK ISLAND AND COCOS ISLAND TREASURES
(1795 and 1821)

Throughout the centuries the thought of finding a long-lost treasure has fascinated mankind. Stories concerning lost mines, sunken treasure galleons and buried pirate loot are legion. In some cases the treasure is only legendary. In others the existence of the lost valuables is well documented. Two such treasures which are known to exist but, at this writing, have not yet been recovered despite many efforts to do so, are those on Oak Island, off the coast of Nova Scotia, and on Cocos Island, a possession of the government of Costa Rica.

In 1795 three young men, McGinnis, Smith and Vaughn, were picnicking on Oak Island. In a clearing they found an ancient oak tree from which a limb had been sawed off, presumably for use as a derrick. On the trunk of the tree were marks apparently caused by a block and tackle. Nearby was a hollow in the ground resembling a filled-in well. The three men also discovered a rusty ring-bolt attached to a large stone, a boatswain's whistle and a copper coin dated 1713.

The trio commenced excavating the "old well." It was found to be a circular shaft with the marks of picks and shovels still visible on the sides. At ten feet they encountered a layer of oak planks. These they removed and continued digging through the soft loam.

At the twenty-foot level another layer of oak planks was found, and a bulkhead was discovered thirty feet from the surface. The three diggers, unable to remove this last obstruction, ceased their efforts and returned home.

In 1801 McGinnis, Smith and Vaughn, with a Dr. Lynds of Truro, Nova Scotia, formed a company to conduct further excavations on Oak Island. The digging was extended to a depth of 95 feet. As before, obstructions were encountered at each ten-foot level. Some were wooden planks, others were layers of coconut matting and a layer of putty-like material. An engraved stone, since lost, was found and it is thought that this might have contained information concerning the mysterious man-made "well."

During the night following the reaching of the 95-foot level some seventy feet of water entered the shaft from some outside source. Refusing to be discouraged, the excavators dug two additional shafts. These, like the original one, became flooded and the treasure-seekers abandoned the search.

A century later another group of diggers determined to secure the treasure thought to have been buried on the island. These
people sank several shafts simultaneously, their object being to
drain the water from the central well where it was thought the buried treasure might be.   This group, using drill bits, encountered
a soft metal thought to be gold, but this was never determined, the
metal not adhering to their excavating equipment. The shafts they
dug, like the others, filled with water, and this group eventually
gave up the search.

In 1910 the Bath Wrecking and Salvage Association of New
York, using the most modern equipment available, drilled to a
depth of 170 feet. Again the shaft filled with water and the project was abandoned.

In 1913 a detailed study of the problem was made by Professor Welling, a member of the faculty of the University of Wisconsin at Madison. He found that the builders of the "money pit,"
as it came to be called, had constructed a tunnel connecting the
pit with the ocean. This would account for the flooding of the well,
but difficulties developed. Welling placed red dye in the flooded
main shaft, reasoning that the dye would penetrate to the tunnel's
opening in the ocean. Once located by this dye method the tunnel
could be plugged, thus preventing further flooding of the shaft. The
colored water, however, remained in the shaft, which led the professor to reason that the original builders had installed a cut-off
valve, which caused the water to remain in the pit. The location
of the valve, if there was one, has never been discovered.   To
this day the Oak Island treasure remains unclaimed.

No fewer than three separate treasures were, according to
history, hidden on Cocos Island. A Captain Edward Davis is said
to have cached a hoard of gold there and the pirate Benito Bonito
is also supposed to have hidden a store of loot there early in the
nineteenth century.   The third Cocos Island treasure is that buried
there by Captain Thompson, master of the Mary Dier.

When Simón Bolívar, the Venezuelan soldier, statesman and
revolutionary leader, led his forces against Peru, the wealthy citizens arranged to have their assets shipped to Spain.   In 1821 the
Mary Dier, loaded with treasure, departed Lima harbor.   Thompson joined forces with Bonito and sailed for Cocos Island where the
ship's fabulously valuable cargo was buried.

After leaving the island the Mary Dier encountered the British frigate Espiegle. A battle ensued in which Bonito was killed
and Captain Thompson was taken prisoner.   Thompson promised
his captors, in return for his life, to disclose to them the site of
the stolen treasure.   The Espiegle proceeded to Cocos Island where
Thompson managed to escape into the jungle.   The British left him
marooned and he was later rescued by a passing ship.

Twenty years later Thompson organized an expedition to retrieve the treasure, estimated to total about sixty million dollars, but he died before the group could start. He willed the chart showing the location of the treasure to his partner, a man named Keating.

Keating set sail with a Captain Boag. When the crew of the vessel learned of the object of the voyage it mutinied, demanding a share of the treasure. Keating and Boag escaped to the jungle and the crew sailed away. Captain Boag died on the island and Keating, like Thompson, was rescued by a passing vessel. The treasure remained on the island. In 1867 Keating made another attempt, in which his ship was wrecked. He died a few years later, leaving the chart to a sailor named Fitzgerald. Fitzgerald, in turn, died in 1894, leaving the chart to Commodore Curzon Howe, R. N. In 1929 the chart was given by the commodore's heirs to an Englishman named Campbell who, with an associate named Guinness, sailed in the latter's yacht to Cocos Island, hoping to locate the long-lost treasure.

Campbell and Guinness, having arrived at the island, followed the instructions on the chart meticulously. However, they found nothing. A German named Gessler searched for sixteen years without success. The Costa Rican government, using convict labor, has literally dug up every foot of Cocos Island but none of the three treasures have been found.

Suggested Readings

Burney, James. History of the Buccaneers of America. London: G. Allen & Company, 1912.

Hart, Harold H. "Cocos Island" and "The Money Pit of Oak Island" in his From Bed to Verse. New York: Hart Publishing Company, 1966.

Jameson, John Franklin. Privateering and Piracy in the Colonial Period. New York: Macmillan, 1923.

Karraker, Cyrus H. Piracy Was a Business. Durham, N. C. : R. R. Smith, 1953.

Nesmith, Robert I. Dig for Pirate Treasure. New York: Devin-Adair, 1958.

Paine, Ralph D. The Book of Buried Treasure. New York: Sturgis and Walton, 1911.

Poe, Edgar Allan. "The Gold Bug" (fiction) in Complete Stories and Poems of Edgar Allan Poe. Garden City, N. Y. : Doubleday, 1966.

Pyle, Howard. Book of Pirates. New York: Harper, 1921.

Reisberg, Harry E. Adventures in Underwater Treasure Hunting. New York: F. Fell, 1965.

_____. Treasure! New York: Holt, 1957.

Sherwell, Guillermo Antonio. Simón Bolívar (The Liberator) Patriot, Warrior, Statesman, Father of Five Nations, a Sketch of His Life and His Work. Caracas?: Bolivarian Society of Venezuela, 1921.

Snow, Edgar Rowe. Pirates and Buccaneers of the Atlantic Coast.
    Boston: Yankee, 1944.
_____ . True Tales of Buried Treasure. New York: Dodd,
    Mead, 1951.
Wilkins, Harold T. Hunting Hidden Treasure. New York: Dutton,
    1929.

THE SPITHEAD AND POST-SPITHEAD MUTINIES (1797)

Today's merchant marine sailors have the protection of union rulings backed by law to protect them from exploitation by the
owners and officers of the ships upon which they serve.   Members
of the navy are subject to the rules of the Code of Military Justice
which sets up guide lines for the conduct of officers and men alike
and provides appropriate punishments for those who transgress its
regulations.

Such was not the case in 1797 when the sailors of the British navy were virtual slaves, often on ships that were "floating
hells, ruled by some sadistic tyrant, with drunken, flogging officers. . . . " This did not always hold true: such captains as Horatio
Nelson, Adam Duncan and James Cook were liked and respected by
the men who served under them.   However, the lot of the common
sailor was not something to be envied, even under the better captains.   Often dragged from their families by press gangs, seamen
were "recruited" into a life of poor food, backbreaking labor, brutal surroundings, floggings for minor infractions of rules and voyages which often lasted three years or longer.   Upon occasion the
sailors retaliated by staging a mutiny.   These generally involved
a single ship, as exemplified by the Bounty mutiny of 1789 when
a group of sailors, led by mate Fletcher Christian, cast Captain
William Bligh and eighteen of his crew adrift in an open boat on
the Pacific Ocean, 3,618 miles from Timor.

In 1797 England was at war with France which was aided by
Holland and Spain.   Ireland was on the verge of revolution and England's only real protection from invasion by her enemies was the
royal navy.   The navy, under Admiral Sir John Jervis, had defeated the Spanish in a sea battle in February, 1797.   However, in
April of that year the British Channel Fleet struck.

The primary demand of the striking sailors was for more
money.   For nearly a century naval pay had stood at ten shillings
a month for an ordinary seaman and 24 shillings for an A. B.   These
wages were no longer adequate, as inflation, even as today, had
caused the prices of commodities to rise until naval sailors could
no longer support their families on what they were paid.   Salaries
for merchant seamen, soldiers and a few naval officers had been
increased but the sums paid the sailors serving in the navy remained unchanged.

In March, 1797, the men of the Channel Fleet had combined to send anonymous round robins to Lord Richard Howe, Admiral of the Fleet, politely requesting a raise in pay and stating their reasons therefore. Howe, then an invalid and about to hand his command over to his deputy, Alexander Hood, Lord Bridport, forwarded the petitions to the Admiralty, where they were ignored. When the fleet returned to Spithead following the spring cruise the men, learning that their request had remained unanswered, became angry.

Lord Bridport was not aware of the situation, the Admiralty having failed to advise him of it. When he learned about it on April 12 he, being personally sympathetic with the men's demands, became highly incensed with the Admiralty. This body, determined to sidetrack the matter, ordered him to send the fleet to sea.

On the morning of April 16, Easter Sunday, Bridport ordered the fleet to weigh anchor. His order was ignored. Sailors from the Queen Charlotte, Howe's former flagship, put off in boats and rowed to the other vessels of the fleet, telling them to send two delegates each to a meeting to be held on the Queen Charlotte that evening. Bridport then ordered his captains to muster their men that they might state their grievances.

That evening the delegates from sixteen ships met on the Queen Charlotte to "draw up rules for regulation of the fleet." The mutiny was to be an orderly one. Officers were to be shown respect, watches were to be kept and drunkenness and disorderly conduct were to be punished by flogging. However, no anchor was to be raised until the demands of the sailors were satisfied. They did agree to sail and "do their duty" should England be attacked by the French and they prevented cargo ships from participating in the mutiny "lest the country's trade should suffer."

Rear Admiral Pole was sent to the Admiralty, there to inform its members of the mutiny. He talked with Earl George Spencer, First Lord who, in turn, talked with the Prime Minister. On April 18 the Admiralty Board of Inquiry held a series of interviews at the Fountain Inn, Portsmouth. It used flag officers as go-betweens with the delegates. This led to a drawing-out of the negotiations which, in turn, caused the delegates to increase their demands. In addition to the original request for wage increases, they added stipulations for changes in the food rations, provision for the care of sick and wounded sailors and shore leave when in port.

In the end these demands, which were entirely reasonable, were granted. This, however, was not accomplished until Earl Spencer obtained a royal pardon for all men involved in the mutiny. The royal proclamation of pardon was read to the sailors, whereupon the Spithead mutiny ended and the sailors returned to their duties.

Following the Spithead mutiny a fresh outbreak occurred at Portsmouth, when the primary grievance was not money but the ex-

treme brutality with which the officers frequently treated the men.
Further, the rumor, though false, had spread that Parliament
would not approve the bill for supplementary naval pay.   Lord Howe,
after seeing that the bill was approved, went to Portsmouth in person.   There he visited each ship of the fleet and negotiated a reconciliation between the fleet and the Admiralty.   Unpopular officers
were transferred to other ships and once again the fleet stood ready to sail.

     A third mutiny followed, this one engineered by Richard
Parker, an ex-schoolmaster and tradesman of unsavory reputation
who had "taken the King's quota money" to extricate himself from
debtor's prison.   Assigned to the depot ship Sandwich, he stirred
up trouble in ships lying in the Little Nore River.   Parker's demands were, for the most part, completely unreasonable and disregarded the agreements made at Spithead.   His mutiny "proceeded
on its own momentum and degenerated into rebellion for the sake
of rebellion. "

     The Admiralty declined to consider Parker's ultimatum and
eventually the sailors sickened of his presumptuousness and refused
to follow him.   On June 15, 1797, the crew of the Sandwich repudiated Parker's authority and handed him over to the military.   He
was courtmartialed, found guilty and, on June 30, hanged from the
yardarm of his ship.   Twenty-eight others were also executed and
thirty more were sentenced to flogging or imprisonment.   Of the
412 ringleaders found guilty, 300 were pardoned.

     Historians are generally agreed that the mutinies, though
seeming terrible at the time, called the country's attention to the
abuses which were impairing England's military might and did much
to improve the conditions of sailors everywhere.

Suggested Readings

Anthony, Irvin, ed.   The Saga of the "Bounty;" Its Strange History
     as Related by the Participants Themselves.   New York: Put-
     nam's, 1935.
Bryant, Sir Arthur.   "The Revolt of Tom Bowling" in his The Fire
     and the Rose.   Garden City, N. Y. :   Doubleday, 1966.
Campbell, John.   Naval History of Great Britain.   London: 1813.
Clowes, William L.   The Royal Navy: A History.   London: 1899.
Dugan, James.   The Great Mutiny.   New York: Putnam, 1965.
Fuller, Edmund.   Mutiny!   New York: Crown Publishers, 1953.
Gill, Conrad.   Naval Mutinies of 1797.   Manchester: Manchester
     University Press, 1913.
Herbert, David.   Great Historical Mutinies, Comprising the Mutiny
     of the "Bounty, " the Mutiny at Spithead, the Mutiny at the Nore,
     Mutinies in Highland Regiments and the Indian Mutiny.   London:
     Nimmo, 1876.
Hutchinson, J. R.   The Press Gang, Afloat and Ashore.   New York:
     Dutton, 1914.

James, Sir William Milburne. Old Oak, the Life of John Jervis,
    Earl of St. Vincent. New York: Longmans, Green, 1950.
Neale, W. J. Mutiny at Spithead and the Nore. London: 1842.

THE BATTLE OF THE NILE (1798)

One of the decisive engagements in naval history was the
Battle of the Nile, also known as the Battle of Abukir (Aboukir)
Bay, fought by English and French fleets on August 1-2, 1798.
The English fleet, commanded by Horatio Nelson, then a rear ad-
miral, decisively defeated the French flotilla under Vice Admiral
François Paul Brueys.

Napoleon Bonaparte had made peace with Austria (1797-98)
which resulted in a temporary halt to hostilities on the Continent.
However, France and England remained at war but the situation
had reached a stalemate as France, lacking control of the English
Channel, could not invade England and England had no army of any
size.   Napoleon suggested to the Directory a scheme by which the
French could possibly defeat England by attacking her trade routes
to the East.

The Directory authorized Napoleon's proposal and on May 19,
1798, he sailed from Toulon for Egypt with a fleet of seventeen
ships carrying an army of 36,000 men.   Early in July the troops
landed at Alexandria, attacked and conquered the city and then
marched to Cairo.   On July 24 Napoleon's forces, having put the
Egyptian army to rout, occupied the capital.

Following the capture of Alexandria the French used the harbor as an unloading port for supplies and military equipment.   In
the meantime Nelson, with a fleet of fourteen ships, searched the
Mediterranean for the French fleet and on the afternoon of August
1 found it anchored in Abukir Bay, some fifteen miles northeast of
Alexandria.

Admiral Brueys, feeling that the harbor at Alexandria was
too shallow to accommodate deep-draft ships of the line, had moved
his fleet to the new location.   There he anchored thirteen ships in
line parallel to one shore of the bay, with two frigates between the
shore and the last ship at each side.   Believing that the English
fleet would approach from seaward he ordered the guns on the seaward side of his ships made ready for action and neglected those
on the landward side.   Nelson, taking a calculated risk that the
water would be sufficiently deep, maneuvered part of his fleet between the French ships and the shore and part of it on the seaward
side of the French.   He was thus able to attack the enemy from
both sides at the same time.

The battle began on the afternoon of August 1 and soon the

French fleet found itself under heavy bombardment. The French
flagship L'Orient was blown up when a shot from a British ship
penetrated its powder magazine.

The Battle of the Nile continued through the night and into
the following morning, resulting in victory for the British. Admiral Brueys was killed and Nelson received a serious wound in
the head. All but four of the French ships were either captured
or destroyed and the four which did escape were later overcome
by Nelson's forces. The British casualties were about 700 wounded
and 200 killed and the French losses amounted to approximately
5,000 killed, wounded and taken prisoner. The English victory
gave Great Britain control of the entire Mediterranean Sea and cut
off Napoleon Bonaparte's line of communication to France. This,
in due course, caused him to withdraw from the Near East in spite
of his military victories there. Napoleon laid the blame for the
French defeat on Admiral Brueys, stating on one occasion that he
had ordered the admiral to enter the Old Harbor at Alexandria if
at all possible. On another occasion he asserted that Brueys had
been instructed to leave Egypt and sail to the island of Corfu and
that he had failed to do so.

Suggested Readings

Bolitho, William. "Napoleon I" in his Twelve Against the Gods:
    The Story of Adventure. New York: Simon & Schuster, 1929.
Chandler, David. The Campaigns of Napoleon: The Mind and Meth-
    od of History's Greatest Soldier. New York: Macmillan, 1966.
Fisher, H. A. L. Napoleon. New York: Holt, Rinehart and Winston,
    1913.
Geyl, Pieter. Napoleon: For and Against. New Haven, Conn. :
    Yale University Press, 1949.
Herold, J. Christopher. Bonaparte in Egypt. New York: Harper
    & Row, 1962.
Hutt, Maurice, compiler. Napoleon. Englewood Cliffs, N. J. :
    Prentice-Hall, 1972.
Kennedy, Ludovic H. C. Nelson's Captains. New York: Norton,
    1951.
Ludwig, Emil. Napoleon. Translated by Eden and Cedar Paul.
    New York: Boni & Liveright, 1926.
MacDonell, A. G. Napoleon and His Marshals. New York: Mac-
    millan, 1934.
Mahan, Alfred T. Influence of Sea Power Upon the French Revolu-
    tion and Empire, 1793-1812. Boston: Little, Brown, 1918.
    _____ . The Life of Nelson. Boston: Little, Brown, 1897-1900.
Markham, Felix. Napoleon. New York: American Library, 1964.
Masefield, John. Sea Life in Nelson's Time. New York: Macmil-
    lan, 1925.
Oman, Charles. Nelson. New York: Doubleday, 1946.
Rodger, A. B. The War of the Second Coalition, 1798-1801. Ox-
    ford: Clarendon Press, 1964.
Rose, John Holland. Life of Napoleon I. London: Macmillan, 1901.

Southey, Robert. The Life of Nelson. Boston: Houghton Mifflin,
    1916 (Originally published 1813).
Warner, Oliver. The Battle of the Nile. London: B. T. Batsford,
    1960.
_____. Great Sea Battles. New York: Macmillan, 1963.
_____. Victory, the Life of Lord Nelson. Boston: Little,
    Brown, 1958.
_____, and the editors of Horizon Magazine. Nelson and the
    Age of Fighting Sail. New York: American Heritage Publish-
    ing Co. , 1963.
Whipple, Addison Beecher Colvin. Hero of Trafalgar: The Story
    of Lord Nelson. New York: Random House, 1963.

THE MALTHUSIAN THEORY (1798 and 1803)

One of the most controversial economic theories was that of
Thomas Robert Malthus, an English curate, economist and educator.
He wrote several books on political economy but his most famous
was An Essay on the Principles of Population, published in 1798.
In this he held that population, when unchecked, tends to increase
in a geometric ratio while the means of subsistence tend to increase only in an arithmetic ratio.   Consequently, preventive checks
on increase of population are necessary as an alternative to the
exclusive operation of positive checks, such as overcrowding, poverty, disease, war and vice.

In 1803 Malthus published a second edition of his book.   In
this he documented his argument, relinquished the question of mathematical ratios, recognized the influence of moral restraint as a
preventive check and remained pessimistic concerning the possibilities of the future progress of mankind.

Malthus' theory contradicted the optimistic belief in economic
progress which prevailed in the 19th century.   Such men as William
Godwin, the English philosopher, reformer and writer, and the Marquis de Condorcet, the French philosopher, mathematician and politician, held views concerning universal progress which differed
from those of Malthus, and whose views the latter attacked in his
book.

Although pessimistic, Malthus did not believe his theory
denied all hope of progress.   He recommended a policy of "moral
restraint" of "the passion between the sexes" to prevent the increase of the population to a point where it became unmanageable.
He felt, however, that human nature being what it is and seeing
little hope of any change in sexual passion, such a suggestion was
basically impractical.   He advocated limiting help to the poor, on
the assumption that such assistance leads them to reproduce beyond
the means of subsistence.   He also favored encouraging the production of food and educating the populace that they might realize the
"virtue of prudence. "

Malthus' writings encouraged the study of demography and influenced the thinking of such men as David Ricardo and Charles Darwin. During the second half of the 19th century the population theory was, for a time, invalidated in both Europe and the United States. This was due to technological advances in agriculture and industry and the opening of new lands to cultivation. However, after World War II the high rate of population growth became a matter of vital importance in world affairs. Malthus' theory is particularly applicable to underdeveloped countries in Asia and Africa which are characterized by a rapid population growth and widespread starvation. The United Nations is studying the problem and advocating such measures as birth control and methods of increasing food production.

Suggested Readings

Due, John F. Intermediate Economic Analysis. Homewood, Ill. : Richard D. Irwin, 1953.

Fusfeld, Daniel Roland. The Age of the Economist. Glenview, Ill. : Scott, Foresman, 1966.

Gide, Charles, and Charles Rist. A History of Economic Doctrines. Translated by R. Richards. Boston: Heath, n. d.

Glass, David Victor, ed. Introduction to Malthus. London: Watts, 1953.

Halévy, Elie. The Growth of Philosophic Radicalism. Translated by Mary Morris. Boston: Beacon Press, 1955.

Haney, Lewis H. History of Economic Thought. New York: Macmillan, 1912.

Heilbroner, Robert L. The Worldly Philosophers: The Lives, Times and Ideas of the Great Economic Thinkers. New York: Simon & Schuster, 1953.

Jevons, W. Stanley. Theory of Political Economy. London: 1878.

Malthus, Thomas R. An Essay on the Principles of Population. London: 1798 and 1803.

_____. Principles of Political Economy. London: 1820.

Marshall, Alfred. Principles of Economics. London: Macmillan, 1890.

Paglin, Morton. Malthus and Lauderdale: The Anti-Ricardian Tradition. New York: Augustus M. Kelley, 1961.

Ricardo, David. Principles of Political Economy. London: 1817.

Stephen, Sir Leslie. The English Utilitarians. London: Gerald Duckworth & Co. , 1900.

THE BATTLE OF TRAFALGAR (1805)

Viscount Horatio Nelson, considered one of England's greatest admirals and naval heroes, had distinguished himself in the Indies, at Toulon, Calvi, Cape St. Vincent, Tenerife and the Battles of the Nile and of Copenhagen. He had risen from midshipman to admiral and had lost his right eye and his right arm in the service of his country.

The Peace of Amiens (1802-1803) temporarily ended the fighting between England and France.   In spite of this Napoleon Bonaparte prepared to invade England.   He built ships, purchased surplus war supplies, often from his recent enemy, and billeted troops along the French coast across the channel from England

Nelson was living in Merton, near London and when war broke out again in 1803 he was made commander of the British Mediterranean fleet.   A large French flotilla under Vice-Admiral Pierre Charles de Villeneuve was at anchor at Toulon, where Nelson had served previously.   Villeneuve's ships were preparing to invade England.   Nelson kept them blockaded there for two years before they escaped and fled to the West Indies.   Nelson pursued the French ships which eluded him and returned to Europe, taking refuge at the port of Cadiz.   There they were joined by a fleet of Spanish ships, Spain having entered the war on the French side in December, 1804.

The British blockaded the port but the French Vice-Admiral was able to break out of the harbor and on October 21, 1805, the English engaged the combined French and Spanish fleets, totaling 46 ships carrying a total of 2,640 guns.   This engagement was the Battle of Trafalgar, fought at Cape Trafalgar, off the southwest coast of Spain.

Nelson's fleet consisted of 33 ships carrying, altogether, 2,138 guns.   He directed the battle from his flagship Victory, commanded by Captain Sir Thomas Hardy.

As the English fleet carried fewer guns than did Villeneuve's combined fleet, Nelson decided against a broadside-to-broadside attack.   His plan, worked out weeks before, was to divide his command into three divisions, with his ships sailing down on the enemy in three separate lines.   The object of this maneuver was to break through and split the enemy forces, confusing the commanders of the combined fleet and putting the leader of each of the three British columns on his own.   This was a departure from traditional naval strategy, as previously one commander had directed the entire battle through signal flags flown from his flagship.   Nelson was thus substituting three separate actions for a single one involving one coordinated fleet.

On the morning of October 20, the combined fleet started to leave the port of Cadiz.   The news was sent by signal flag to Nelson aboard the Victory.   The breeze, coming from the west, was slight and gusty, making it difficult for the gigantic sailing ships to navigate.

As dawn broke on October 21, the combined fleet was sighted, coming from the east in a single line.   Nelson ordered his ships to

swing into battle order. He had decided to attack the enemy in
two columns rather than three, with the Victory leading the northern column and the Royal Sovereign, commanded by Vice-Admiral
Cuthbert Collingwood, leading the one on the south. Nelson then
ordered Lieutenant John Pasco, his signal officer, to send a flag
message to the fleet: "England expects that every man will do his
duty. "

The Royal Sovereign, a faster ship than the Victory, reached
the line of battle first, hitting the center and firing at the enemy,
cutting its line in two. The Victory fired a broadside into the
French ship Bucentaure, causing tremendous damage. The enemy
line was thus cut in two places. The Victory then collided
with the French ship Redoubtable, and the rigging of the two ships
became entangled. The French ship had riflemen hidden behind
canvas screens on her masts and from there riflemen were delivering a withering fire to the decks of the Victory. Nelson was wearing his uniform coat, complete with decorations. Captain Hardy
suggested that these made him easy for the enemy marksmen to
identify and that he should leave the quarterdeck and change to a
coat which was less conspicuous. Nelson declined to leave and he
and the captain remained topside.

A marksman on the Redoubtable fired a shot which entered
Nelson's spine. The wounded man was carried below. Dr. William
Beatty, the Victory surgeon, was unable to extract the bullet. Captain Hardy reported that "twelve or fourteen of the enemy's ships"
had surrendered and that none of the British vessels were lost. Later he announced a complete victory for Nelson's fleet.

Midshipman John Pollard shot and killed two French riflemen
who had been firing at the Victory from the masthead of the Redoubtable. One of these may well have been the man who killed Nelson.

The admiral died aboard his flagship. His last words were,
"Thank God, I have done my duty. " He had saved England from
invasion by the French and her allies. Napoleon's greatest threat
was overcome. Not one English ship surrendered and the few French
and Spanish ships which escaped were so badly damaged that they
were never used in combat again.

Lord Nelson was buried at St. Paul's. The Victory was badly damaged but was able to make the return voyage to England. Today, having been restored, she is on display at Portsmouth.

Suggested Readings

Bryant, Sir Arthur. "Touch and Take: Trafalgar" in his The Fire
     and the Rose. Garden City, N. Y. : Doubleday, 1966.
Fisher, H. A. L. Napoleon. New York: Holt, Rinehart and Winston,
     1913.
Hutt, Maurice, compiler. Napoleon. Englewood Cliffs, N. J. : Pren-
     tice-Hall, 1972.

Kennedy, Ludovic H. C. Nelson's Captains. New York: Norton,
   1951.
Legg, Stuart, compiler. Trafalgar: An Eye-Witness Account of a
   Great Battle. New York: John Day, 1966.
Ludwig, Emil. Napoleon. Translated by Eden and Cedar Paul.
   New York: Boni & Liveright, 1926.
Mahan, Alfred T. The Life of Nelson. Boston: Little, Brown,
   1897-1900.
Masefield, John. Sea Life in Nelson's Time. New York: Mac-
   millan, 1925.
Oman, Charles. Nelson. New York: Doubleday, 1946.
Parsons, Geoffrey. The Stream of History. New York: Scribner's,
   1929.
Pope, Dudley. Decision at Trafalgar. Philadelphia: Lippincott,
   1960.
Ramos Oliveira, Antonio. Politics, Economics and Men of Modern
   Spain, 1808-1946. Translated by Teener Hall. London: Vic-
   tor Gollancz, 1946.
Rodger, A. B. The War of the Second Coalition, 1798-1801. Ox-
   ford: Clarendon Press, 1964.
Southey, Robert. The Life of Nelson. Boston: Houghton Mifflin,
   1916 (Originally published 1813).
Warner, Oliver. Great Sea Battles. New York: Macmillan, 1963.
   _____. Trafalgar. London: B. T. Batsford, 1959.
   _____. Victory, the Life of Lord Nelson. Boston: Little,
   Brown, 1958.
   _____, and the editors of Horizon Magazine. Nelson and the
   Age of Fighting Sail. New York: American Heritage Publish-
   ing Co., 1963.
Whipple, Addison Beecher Colvin. Hero of Trafalgar: The Story
   of Lord Nelson. New York: Random House, 1963.

THE BATTLE OF AUSTERLITZ (1805)

The Battle of Austerlitz, fought on December 2, 1805, between a combined Russian and Austrian force of approximately
85,000 men and a French army of approximately 73,000 resulted
in an overwhelming victory for the French, commanded in person
by Napoleon Bonaparte. This historic military encounter is considered an extremely important point in Napoleon's military career
because of "the numerical inferiority of his forces, the audacity of
his plan, the precision with which it was executed, and the victory
won." England's prime minister, William Pitt, upon receiving
news of the battle, is said to have remarked, "Roll up the map of
Europe; we shall not be needing it for the next ten years."

The Third Coalition, formed in 1805 by Great Britain, Austria, Russia and Sweden, opposed France and continued the wars
against that country. Austria and Russia declared war on Napoleon's
newly-created empire. For some time Napoleon had been consider-

ing an invasion of England but realizing that, because of the weakness of the French navy, such an invasion could not be accomplished, he decided instead on a military campaign against Austria.   On October 20, 1805, he defeated their army, commanded by Baron Karl Mack von Leiberich, at Ulm and captured Vienna in mid-November.

By the end of the month the Russian army had assembled in Moravia, north of Vienna, where it was joined by some troops from the Austrian army.   The principal Austrian forces, under the command of Archduke Charles, were far to the south of the Danube River, retiring towards the east.   Alexander I, Tsar of Russia, decided to send his soldiers into action against the French, despite the fact that his military advisers opposed the idea.   The Russian troops outnumbered the French and the Tsar, for this reason, anticipated a victory.

Napoleon's forces took up a position behind Goldbach Brook, stretching over a five-mile front between Brünn--Austerlitz Road to Menitz Pond.   On the morning of December 2, 1805, the Allied army attacked the French.   The Russians massed against Napoleon's right flank, being aware that he had concentrated his strength on his left flank and center.   The French Third Corps, under the command of Marshal Louis Nicholas Davout, though greatly outnumbered by the enemy, stood fast.   Napoleon realized that the Russians were determined to overcome his right flank and he ordered an attack on his opponent's weakened center.   The French left flank moved forward and at the same time the Fourth Corps, led by Marshal Nicholas Jean de Dieu Soult, attacked the Pratzen Heights. This maneuver resulted in the splitting of the Allied army into two parts and soon both were in full retreat.

Soult and Davout's soldiers proceeded to high ground in the center and then performed a pivot action on the latter's men, thus forcing the enemy troops into the ice-covered lakes of Menitz and Satschan, which had been on the French right flank.

The French scored a complete victory.   An armistice was requested by Francis II, the Holy Roman Emperor, and Austria was compelled to sign the Treaty of Pressburg, by which she was forced out of the Third Coalition.   Tsar Alexander did not sign a peace treaty but returned the remains of his battered army to Russia.   The Prussians, on hearing of the French victory and who had been intending to enter the conflict on the side of the Allies, sent envoys to Napoleon to discuss terms.   Napoleon then organized the Confederation of the Rhine.   This, a league of German principalities, renounced allegiance to the Holy Roman Empire which thereupon came to an end.   Napoleon was virtually master of the Continent but Lord Horatio Nelson's naval victory over the French and Spanish at the Battle of Trafalgar on October 21, 1805, had given Great Britain supremacy on the seas and made the thought of any immediate French invasion of the British Isles an impossibility.

Suggested Readings

Brunn, Geoffrey. Europe and the French Imperium, 1799-1814. New York: Harper & Row, 1938.

Bryant, Sir Arthur. "The Grey Goose Feather" in his The Fire and the Rose. Garden City, N. Y. : Doubleday, 1966.

Chandler, David G. The Campaigns of Napoleon: The Mind and Method of History's Greatest Soldier. New York: Macmillan, 1966.

Creasy, Edward S. Fifteen Decisive Battles of the World. Harrisburg, Pa. : Stackpole Books, 1957.

Esposito, Vincent J. , and John Robert Elting. A Military History and Atlas of the Napoleonic Wars. New York: Frederick A. Praeger, 1964.

Falls, Cyril, ed. Great Military Battles. New York: Macmillan, 1964.

Fisher, H. A. L. Napoleon. New York: Holt, Rinehart and Winston, 1913.

Fuller, John F. C. A Military History of the Western World. New York: Funk & Wagnalls, 1954.

Gagnon, Paul A. France Since 1789. New York: Harper & Row, 1962.

Gershoy, Leo. The French Revolution and Napoleon. New York: Appleton, 1934.

Geyl, Pieter. Napoleon: For and Against. New Haven, Conn. : Yale University Press, 1949.

Gottschalk, Louis R. The Era of the French Revolution, 1715-1815. Boston: Houghton Mifflin, 1957.

Herold, J. Christopher, and the editors of Horizon Magazine. The Horizon Book of the Age of Napoleon. New York: American Heritage Publishing Co. , 1963.

Hobsbawm, E. J. The Age of Revolution: Europe from 1789-1848. New York: New American Library, 1962.

Lefebvre, Georges. Napoleon: From 18 Brumaire to Tilsit, 1799-1807. New York: Columbia University Press, 1969 (Originally published 1936).

Ludwig, Emil. Napoleon. Translated by Eden and Cedar Paul. New York: Boni & Liveright, 1926.

Manceron, Claude. Austerlitz: The Story of a Battle. Translated by George Unwin. New York: Norton, 1966.

Markham, Felix. Napoleon. New York: American Library, 1964.

Marshall-Cornwall, James. Napoleon as Military Commander. Princeton, N. J. : Van Nostrand, 1967.

Mitchell, Lt. Col. Joseph B. , and Sir Edward S. Creasy. Twenty Decisive Battles of the World. New York: Macmillan, 1964.

Montross, Lynn. War Through the Ages. New York: Harper & Row, 1960.

Thompson, James M. Napoleon Bonaparte: His Rise and Fall. New York: Oxford University Press, 1952.

Wright, Gordon. France in Modern Times: 1760 to the Present. Chicago: Rand McNally, 1960.

THE "DOS DE MAYO" INSURRECTION (1808)

In the year 1700 Charles II, the last of the Hapsburg kings of Spain, passed away. He was succeeded by his grandnephew Philip of Anjou (Philip V of Spain), grandson of the Bourbon Louis XIV of France. A close alliance between France and Spain resulted which lasted for the following hundred years. Although the two countries often fought together against their common enemies, the relationship changed when the French Revolution broke out in 1789 and Spain sided with the French monarchy rather than the revolutionists. When Louis XVI of France was executed in 1793 Spain joined the First Coalition against France.

Charles III of Spain (1716-1788) is considered by historians "the greatest of the Bourbon kings," but his son, Charles IV, who ascended the Spanish throne in 1788, was weak and vacillating. He was dominated by his wife Maria Louisa of Parma and her favorite and lover, Manuel de Godoy who, at the queen's insistence, had been appointed prime minister. Godoy, a self-aggrandizing, greedy, scheming opportunist, concluded alliances with France in the early 1800's after Napoleon Bonaparte had come to power in 1799 and made himself Emperor of the French in 1804. As a result of Godoy's political maneuvering Spain became closely allied with France and subservient to Napoleon who, ambitious to control Europe, saw in Godoy's ruthless greed a means of dominating Spain.

In 1807 Napoleon concluded an alliance with Godoy which permitted French troops to pass through northern Spain into Portugal, his object being to take over both countries. Late that year French troops occupied part of northern Spain and drove the Portuguese royal family out of their country.

The Spanish people resented this pro-French policy and turned against King Charles, Queen Maria Louisa and Prime Minister Godoy. Charles' son Ferdinand, heir to the throne, who was popular with his father's subjects, hoped to obtain help from Napoleon in overthrowing his parents and Godoy. Napoleon, however, intended to do away with all Spanish Bourbon rulers and install his brother Joseph Bonaparte as king. In February, 1808, a French force commanded by Marshal Joachim Murat was sent to Madrid. The Spaniards, believing that the French intended to help Ferdinand replace Charles on the throne, welcomed them. They demanded the resignation of Godoy and the abdication of Charles in favor of Ferdinand.

Charles submitted his resignation and made plans to go to America. Napoleon instructed Murat not to recognize Ferdinand as the new king because, as mentioned above, he wished to place his brother Joseph on the Spanish throne. Murat then persuaded Charles to revoke his abdication and to transfer his right to Napoleon, following which Charles and Ferdinand were promised estates in France. They agreed and Joseph Bonaparte was named King of Spain.

The Spanish people were highly incensed by the double de-
throning.   On May 2, 1808, the "Dos de Mayo" (Second of May)
insurrection occurred in Madrid.   A large crowd stood by as the
royal family prepared to leave the palace.   Suddenly a riot broke
out, with the crowd, now a mob, attacking the French military
guard.   Marshal Murat ordered his troops to fire on the rioters
and martial law was declared.   Disorder spread and by the end of
the month virtually all of Spain was in rebellion.   Napoleon was
forced to dispatch additional troops to fight the Spaniards but was
unable to overcome them.   Joseph Bonaparte remained on the Spanish throne until 1813 and in 1814 Ferdinand, ruling as Ferdinand
VII, was reinstated by Napoleon.

Suggested Readings

Altamira, Rafael.   A History of Spain.   Translated by Muna Lee.
    New York: Van Nostrand, 1949.
Brunn, Geoffrey.   Europe and the French Imperium, 1799-1814.
    New York: Harper & Row, 1938.
Carr, Raymond.   Spain, 1808-1839.   Oxford: Clarendon Press,
    1966.
Chandler, David G.   The Campaigns of Napoleon: The Mind and
    Method of History's Greatest Soldier.   New York: Macmillan,
    1966.
Chastenet, Jacques.   Godoy, Master of Spain.   Translated by J. F.
    Huntington.   London: Batchworth Press, 1953.
Clarke, H. Butler.   Modern Spain, 1815-1898.   Cambridge: The
    University Press, 1906.
Crow, John A.   Spain: The Root and the Flower.   New York:
    Harper & Row, 1963.
De Madariaga, Salvador.   Spain: A Modern History.   New York:
    Frederick A. Praeger, 1958.
Esposito, Vincent J. , and John Robert Elting.   A Military History
    and Atlas of the Napoleonic Wars.   New York: Frederick A.
    Praeger, 1964.
Fisher, H. A. L.   Napoleon.   New York: Holt, Rinehart and Wins-
    ton, 1913.
Fuller, John F. C.   A Military History of the Western World.   New
    York: Funk & Wagnalls, 1954.
Geyl, Pieter.   Napoleon: For and Against.   New Haven, Conn. :
    Yale University Press, 1949.
Herold, J. Christopher, and the editors of Horizon Magazine.   The
    Horizon Book of the Age of Napoleon.   New York: American
    Heritage Publishing Co. , 1963.
Lefebvre, Georges.   Napoleon: From 18 Brumaire to Tilsit, 1799-
    1807.   New York: Columbia University Press, 1969 (Originally
    published 1936).
Lovett, Gabriel H.   Napoleon and the Birth of Modern Spain.   New
    York: New York University Press, 1965.
Ludwig, Emil.   Napoleon.   Translated by Eden and Cedar Paul.
    New York: Boni & Liveright, 1926.
Markham, Felix.   Napoleon.   New York: American Library, 1964.

Oman, Charles. A History of the Peninsula War. Oxford: The
      University Press, 1902-1922.
Ramos Oliveira, Antonio. Politics, Ecomonics and Men of Modern
      Spain, 1808-1946. Translated by Teener Hall. London: Vic-
      tor Gollancz, 1946.
Ross, Michael. The Reluctant King. New York: Mason/Charter,
      1977.
Smith, Rhea Marsh. Spain: A Modern History. Ann Arbor, Mich. :
      University of Michigan Press, 1965.
Thompson, James M. Napoleon Bonaparte: His Rise and Fall.
      New York: Oxford University Press, 1952.

THE PRINCESS CARIBOO AFFAIR (1812)

In the winter of 1812 an elaborate hoax and swindle was
played on the people of Bristol, England. The Princess Cariboo,
apparently a member of a wealthy Oriental ruling family, appeared
at the White Lion Hotel. She was accompanied by a large retinue
of native servants and a great quantity of personal baggage. She
spoke no English and her representative, a Chinese, spoke it only
imperfectly. She engaged the best suite of rooms at the hotel and
tipped the servants lavishly in gold, ate only exotic dishes prepared
for her by her own chef, and wore extravagant oriental costumes.

Little was said about the object of her visit to England, but
one morning the Bristol Mirror published a story to the effect that
she had "come from her home in the remotest East to proffer His
Majesty George III the unobstructed commerce of her realm, which
was as remarkable for its untold wealth as for its marvelous beau-
ty. " Another paper, Felix Farley's Journal, disclosed further fas-
cinating facts about the Princess Cariboo and her country but did
not indicate exactly where in the East it might be located. In the
Journal's account it was stated that the Princess had fallen in love
with a sailor who had been shipwrecked on her coast and had since
returned to his native England, where she had come in search of
him. Later the source of these news stories was traced to the
Princess's garrulous agent.

Such a distinguished visitor in Bristol caused great excitement. The local citizenry vied for her attention. "The street in
front of the White Lion was day after day blocked up with elegant
equipages, and her reception-rooms thronged with 'fair women and
brave men'. " Presents were thrust upon her by jewelers, perfumers
and florists. Dressmakers and milliners sent examples of their
most fashionable creations, hoping to solicit her patronage. Would-
be admirers sent her pictures, engravings, sketches and paintings
of themselves, hoping to supplant her English sailor sweetheart.

The aristocracy gave magnificent entertainments in her honor,
and eventually Mr. Worrall, the Recorder of Bristol, arranged a

grand municipal reception at the town hall.   People thronged to this reception by the thousands.

At last the Princess Cariboo announced, through her agent, that she intended to leave Bristol for London.   Her mountains of baggage were shipped by water and she planned to travel to the capital by coach.   Declining offers of the use of privately owned carriages and teams, she and her retinue departed Bristol in hired vehicles.

The Princess Cariboo never reached London.   Somewhere along the road she and her servants disappeared from sight and from history.   The landlord of the White Lion had approved a thousand pound draft on a Calcutta firm, which draft was found to be worthless.   Mr. Worrall had spent large sums of money for the municipal reception which he had arranged.   The merchants who had given the Princess expensive presents realized that they had been bilked.   The young admirers had lost not only their pictures and engravings but had lost face as well.

While the Princess Cariboo has never been identified, it is thought that she may have been "a certain actress of more notoriety than note, humbly born in the immediate vicinity" of Bristol, and that she was assisted in her hoax by "a set of dissolute young noblemen and actors" who had financed her and helped her carry her scheme out.   The net profit to those involved in the affair was estimated to be at least ten thousand pounds.

Suggested Readings

Barnum, Phineas Taylor.   The Life of Barnum, the World-Renowned Showman ... to Which Is Added the Art of Money Getting; or, Golden Rules for Making Money.   Philadelphia: Ariel Book Co. , n. d.
_____.   "The Princess Cariboo" in Klein, Alexander, ed.   The Double Dealers: Adventures in Grand Deception.   Philadelphia: Lippincott, 1958.
Bloom, Murray Teigh.   Money on Their Own.   New York: Scribner's, 1957.
Deeson, A. F. L.   Great Swindlers.   New York: Drake Publishers, 1972.
Gibson, Walter Brown, ed.   The Fine Art of Swindling.   New York: Grosset & Dunlap, 1966.
Hancock, Ralph, and Henry Chafetz.   The Compleat Swindler.   New York: Macmillan, 1968.
Klein, Alexander.   Grand Deception: The World's Most Spectacular and Successful Hoaxes, Impostures, Ruses and Frauds.   Philadelphia: Lippincott, 1955.
MacDougall, Curtis D.   Hoaxes.   New York: Macmillan, 1940.
McKelway, St. Clair.   True Tales from the Annals of Crime and Rascality.   New York: Random House, 1957.
Mehling, Harold.   The Scandalous Scamps.   New York: Holt, 1956.

Smith, H. Allen. The Compleat Practical Joker. Garden City,
    N. Y. : Doubleday, 1959.
Wade, Carlson. Great Hoaxes and Famous Imposters. Middle
    Village, N. Y. : David, 1976.

THE BATTLE OF WATERLOO (1815)

The Battle of Waterloo, fought on June 18, 1815, constituted
the final military defeat of Napoleon Bonaparte, Emperor of the
French, and ended the war in Europe between Revolutionary France
and her neighbors.   The war had started in 1792 and persisted in-
termittently for nearly a quarter of a century.

Napoleon abdicated in 1814 and was exiled to the island of
Elba, in the Mediterranean off the Italian coast.   He escaped in
1815 and on March 1 returned to France, hoping to regain his old
position of power.   The European political situation at that time
was clarifying.   Great Britain and Austria had opposed the plan of
Prussia and Russia to divide Poland and Saxony between themselves.
The four nations had reached an agreement and decided to join forces against Napoleon.

The former French emperor recruited an army of about
74,000 troops commanded by himself, Marshal Michel Ney and Marquis Emmanuel de Grouchy.   The Allies were led by Arthur Wellesley, Duke of Wellington, who was assisted by Prussian troops
commanded by General Gebhard Leberecht von Blücher.   Wellington had approximately 67,000 troops immediately available, plus
some 73,000 others scattered to the east of France.

Napoleon planned to attack the enemy before it could unite
to oppose his army with a superior force, a technique which had
worked well for him in the past.   Wellington's conglomerate army
of British, Belgians and Germans was located in Belgium, near
Brussels.   Blücher's Prussian force was to the east, three days'
march away.   Napoleon planned to move into Belgium and hit each
force individually before they could combine into a single unit.

The French commander divided his army into three divisions.
Ney, in command of the left wing, was to attack Wellington.   Grouchy, in charge of the right wing, was to seek out Blücher's forces.
The center, commanded by Napoleon, was to reinforce whichever
wing turned out to need assistance.   The battle was fought at Waterloo, a small town near Brussels.

Grouchy's men made contact with Blücher's army near Ligny
and defeated it.   Blücher ordered a retreat and Napoleon, thinking
that the Prussians were retreating eastward, rested his own troops
through June 17.   At noon on the 18th the French started a fierce
attack, which Wellington's troops resisted.   Historians feel that Na-

poleon might have won at Waterloo had he attacked earlier in the day. His delay permitted Blücher to arrive with his Prussian troops and reinforce Wellington. The battle was a stalemate until the arrival of Blücher's forces, which helped turn the tide against the French.

Napoleon made one more effort to win. He sent his best troops, the "Old Guard," commanded by Marshal Ney, against the enemy. Ney's men were repulsed by Wellington's entrenched soldiers time after time. As darkness fell "the last hour of daylight converted a repulse into a rout." Both sides lost many killed and wounded, the French suffering about 40,000 casualties and the Allies 23,000.

Following the Battle of Waterloo Napoleon returned to Paris on June 21 and attempted to raise a fresh army. His marshals declined to serve and the legislature demanded that he abdicate a second time. He surrendered to the British and was incarcerated on the island of St. Helena where he died May 5, 1821.

Suggested Readings

Belloc, Hilaire. Waterloo. London: S. Swift & Co., 1912.
Bolitho, William. "Napoleon I" in his Twelve Against the Gods: The Story of Adventure. New York: Simon & Schuster, 1929.
Bryant, Sir Arthur. "Waterloo" in his The Fire and the Rose. Garden City, N.Y.: Doubleday, 1966.
Buchan, Susan. The Sword of State: Wellington After Waterloo. Boston: Houghton Mifflin, 1928.
Chandler, David G. The Campaigns of Napoleon: The Mind and Method of History's Greatest Soldier. New York: Macmillan, 1966.
Cotton, Edward. A Voice from Waterloo. Brussels: 1854.
Creasy, Edward S. Fifteen Decisive Battles of the World. Harrisburg, Pa.: Stackpole Books, 1957.
Duclaux, Mary (A. Mary F. Robinson). A Short History of France from Caesar's Invasion to the Battle of Waterloo. New York: Putnam's, 1918.
Falls, Cyril. Great Military Battles. New York: Macmillan, 1964.
Fisher, H. A. L. Napoleon. New York: Holt, Rinehart and Winston, 1913.
Fortescue, John W. A History of the British Army. New York: St. Martin's Press, 1899.
Geyl, Pieter. Napoleon: For and Against. New Haven, Conn.: Yale University Press, 1949.
Gottschalk, Louis R. The Era of the French Revolution, 1715-1815. Boston: Houghton Mifflin, 1957.
Guedella, Philip. Wellington. New York: Harper, 1931.
Guérard, Albert. Napoleon I: A Great Life in Brief. New York: Knopf, 1956.
Hazen, Charles Downer. Europe Since 1815. New York: Holt, 1917.

_____. The French Revolution and Napoleon. New York: Holt, 1917.

Herold, J. Christopher, and the editors of Horizon Magazine. The Horizon Book of the Age of Napoleon. New York: American Heritage Publishing Co., 1963.

Howarth, David. Waterloo: Day of Battle. New York: Atheneum, 1968.

Hutt, Maurice, compiler. Napoleon. Englewood Cliffs, N. J.: Prentice-Hall, 1972.

Kennedy, General Sir John Shaw. Notes on the Battle of Waterloo. London: John Murray, 1865.

Longford, Elizabeth. Wellington: The Years of the Sword. New York: Harper, 1969.

Ludwig, Emil. Napoleon. Translated by Eden and Cedar Paul. New York: Boni & Liveright, 1926.

MacDonnell, A. G. Napoleon and His Marshals. New York: Macmillan, 1934.

Markham, Felix. Napoleon. New York: American Library, 1964.

Maurios, André. A History of France. New York: Farrar, Straus, 1956.

_____. An Illustrated History of France. New York: Viking Press, 1960.

_____. Napoleon, a Pictorial Biography. New York: Viking Press, 1964.

Mitchell, Lt. Col. Joseph B., and Sir Edward S. Creasy. Twenty Decisive Battles of the World. New York: Macmillan, 1964.

Naylor, John. Waterloo. London: B. T. Batsford, 1960.

Phillips, Major Thomas, R., ed. "The Military Maxims of Napoleon" in his Roots of Strategy. Harrisburg, Pa.: Military Service Publishing Co., 1940.

Rose, John Holland. The Life of Napoleon I. London: Macmillan, 1901.

Sutherland, John. Men of Waterloo. Englewood Cliffs, N. J.: Prentice-Hall, 1966.

DECIPHERING THE ROSETTA STONE (1822)

The Rosetta Stone, found near Rosetta, North Egypt, in 1799 by French troops serving under Napoleon Bonaparte, is a slab of black basalt bearing an inscription in Greek and Egyptian in both its hieroglyphic and demotic forms. It presents a long text in two different periods of the Egyptian language together with a Greek translation, thus furnishing a means by which the tongue of ancient Egypt, long lost, could be regained. This made it possible to decipher other Egyptian writings which had hitherto been incomprehensible.

This tremendously valuable artifact measures 3' 9" in height, 2' 4½ " in breadth and is eleven inches thick. Its inscriptions are dated March 27, 195 B. C. In all three languages it identically publishes a decree of the Egyptian priesthood commemorating the coronation of Ptolemy V Epiphanes in his ninth year, 196 B. C., listing the good deeds he performed during his reign.   Of the hieroglyphic inscription, fourteen mutilated lines--about half the text--remain.   The demotic text of 32 lines is almost complete and the 54 lines of Greek writing are well preserved, with only a small portion missing.

The Rosetta Stone was originally set up in Memphis but was later taken to Rosetta.   In 1801 it was ceded to the British government along with some other archaeological finds.   It was brought to England where it was placed in the British Museum by King George III.   It is now displayed on a pedestal at the entrance of the Egyptian Sculpture Gallery.

Following its discovery the Rosetta Stone attracted the attention of scholars because its multilingual character promised the possibility of decipherment.   Baron Anton Isaac Silvestre de Sacy, a French Orientalist and Jean David Akerblad, a Swedish Egyptologist, were able to identify the royal names of the demotic text because of their correspondence in position to the Greek names. Jørgen Zoëga, a Danish archaeologist, correctly assumed that the groups in the hieroglyphic text enclosed within an oval line or cartouche were, because of this distinction, royal names.   Thomas Young, a British physician, physicist and Egyptologist, proved the correctness of this assumption.   He deciphered the name Ptolemy on the Rosetta Stone and that of Berenike (Berenika), an Egyptian princess, on another similarly inscribed piece of basalt.   Young was the first to take for granted that signs with the cartouches were not purely symbolic as had been previously supposed but, rather, were alphabetic or quasi-alphabetic.

Young, a man of many interests, did not carry his research as far as he, perhaps, could have but his work inspired that of Jean François Champollion, a French Egyptologist.   Champollion wrote several books dealing with his findings, including Grammaire Égyptienne (1836) and Dictionnaire Égyptienne (1841), both published posthumously.   In 1824 he published Précis du Système Hiéroglyphique des Anciens Égyptiens.

Champollion, following up the earlier work of Young, found that the hieroglyphics outside the cartouches were in the form of the Coptic language.   This was the language used liturgically by the Egyptian Christians and thus it was realized that Coptic was a later form of the earlier Egyptian tongue.

Young had determined that a name within a cartouche corresponded in position to the Greek ΠΤΟΛΕΜΑΙΟΣ or Ptolemaios (Ptolemy), being depicted by the signs (□ 𝑓 ⬯ 𝔮𝔮 ⌐) which were read P-T-O-L-M-I-S, the vowels E and A, and in other instances O, being omitted, a principle known to students of the Semitic languages.

A similar bilingual inscription found at Philae, an island in the Nile River, confirmed Young's discovery. The name ΚΛΕΟΠΑΤΡΑ (Cleopatra) was found to be shown as ⟨ ⟩. In the case of the Egyptian queen it was obvious that the letters L, O and P occurred essentially in their proper places. The bird sign following ▫ (P) and the second bird were taken to be A. This was confirmed by the position of the same symbol in the name Berenike (Berenika). From this it was deduced that must equal TR and must equal K, which meant that would necessarily equal E. Here the vowels were given, not the case with Ptolemy, except O and unless (I or Y) is regarded as a vowel. Young had observed that the signs usually followed a female name and that they could be omitted as nothing more than a feminine termination.

Having progressed this far, the word ⟨ ⟩ was analyzed. This should have been the Egyptian form of Alexander. The bird sign was correct for A, for L, for S, for TR, and should be E. This cryptographic deduction was progressing correctly, as AL. SE. TR. was in all probability ΑΛΕΞΑΝΔΡΟΣ or Alexandros (Alexander). The unknown signs , , were no doubt an alternate form of K, the sign for N and a second form of S. Putting it together, it read ALKSENTRS. Once again, as sometimes in Ptolemaios, the vowel O was omitted as was the E. Greek Ξ (X) was represented by KS and could be either A or E, while would represent a T or a D.

With the deciphering of the Rosetta Stone well started it was realized that many signs did not spell out words but, rather, expressed whole ideas, on the order of such Oriental languages as Japanese, Chinese and Korean. Eventually scholars were able to read and understand the inscriptions on ancient clay tablets, tomb walls and papyrus, the forerunner of paper. From this discovery much has been learned about the life and customs of the ancient world.

Suggested Readings

Aldred, Cyril. Egypt to the End of the Old Kingdom. New York: McGraw-Hill, 1965.
_____. The Egyptians. London: Thames and Hudson, 1961.
Asimov, Isaac. The Egyptians. Boston: Houghton Mifflin, 1967.
Barker, Felix, in collaboration with Anthea Barker. "Into the Unknown" in their The First Explorers: Encyclopedia of Discovery and Exploration, Vol. I. London: Aldus Books, 1971.
Baumann, Hans. The World of the Pharaohs. New York: Pantheon Books, 1960.
Casson, Lionel, and the editors of Time-Life books. Ancient Egypt. New York: Time, Inc., 1965.

Champollion, Jean François. Dictionnaire Égyptienne. Edited by Jean Jacques Champollion-Figeac. Paris: 1841.
_____. Grammaire Égyptienne. Paris: 1836.
_____. L'Égypte, sous les Pharaons. Paris: 1814.
_____. Précis du Système Hiéroglyphique des Anciens Égyptiens. Paris: 1824.
Cleator, P. E. Lost Languages. New York: John Day, 1961.
Cohen, Daniel. Secrets from Ancient Graves: Rulers and Heroes of the Past Whose Lives Have Been Revealed Through Archaeology. New York: Dodd, Mead, 1968.
Cottrell, Leonard. Digs and Diggers: A Book of World Archaeology. Cleveland: World, 1964.
_____. Land of the Pharaohs. Cleveland: World, 1960.
Davies, Nina M. Picture Writing in Ancient Egypt. New York: Oxford University Press, 1958.
Diringer, David. The Alphabet: A Key to the History of Mankind. New York: Funk & Wagnalls, 1968.
_____. Writing. New York: Frederick A. Praeger, 1962.
Doblhofer, Ernst. Voice in Stone: The Decipherment of Ancient Scripts and Writings. Translated by Mervyn Savill. New York: Viking Press, 1961.
Doyle, Arthur Conan. "The Adventure of the Dancing Men" (short story) in Bond, R. T., ed. Famous Stories of Code and Cipher. New York: Rinehart, 1947 (Originally published 1905).
Driver, Godfrey R. Semitic Writing. Oxford: The University Press, 1954.
Edwards, Amelia B. Egypt and Its Monuments. New York: Harper, 1891.
Falls, C. B. The First 3,000 Years: Ancient Civilizations of the Tigris, Euphrates, and Nile River Valleys and the Mediterranean Sea. New York: Viking Press, 1960.
Farmer, Lydia. "Nefertiti" in her A Book of Famous Queens. Revised by Willard A. Heaps. New York: Crowell, 1964.
Gardiner, Alan H. Egypt of the Pharaohs. New York: Oxford University Press, 1966.
_____. Egyptian Grammar: Being an Introduction to the Study of Hieroglyphics. New York: Oxford University Press, 1957.
_____. The Kadesh Inscriptions of Ramses II. Oxford: The University Press, 1960.
Gelb, I. J. A Study of Writing. Chicago: University of Chicago Press, 1952.
Gleason, H. A. An Introduction to Descriptive Linguistics. New York: Holt, Rinehart and Winston, 1965.
Hall, H. R., D. Litt, F. S. A. "The Rosetta Stone: Master Key to Egypt's Lore" in Hamerton, J. A., ed. Wonders of the Past: The Romance of Antiquity and Its Splendours, Vol. IV. New York: William H. Wise, 1933.
Hawkes, Jacquetta, and the editors of Horizon Magazine. Pharaohs of Egypt. New York: American Heritage Publishing Co., 1965.
Mason, W. A. A History of the Art of Writing. New York: Macmillan, 1928.
Mertz, Barbara. Red Land, Black Land: The World of the Ancient Egyptians. London: Hodder and Stoughton, 1967.

_____. Temples, Tombs and Hieroglyphs: The Story of Egyptol-
ogy. New York: Coward-McCann, 1964.
Moorhouse, A. C. The Triumph of the Alphabet. New York: Henry Schuman, 1953.
Moran, H. A., and D. H. Kelley. The Alphabet and the Ancient Cal-
endar Signs. Palo Alto, Calif.: Daily Press, 1969.
Petrie, Sir W. M. Flinders. Seventy Years in Archaeology. London: Sampson, Low, Marston & Co., 1931.
Poe, Edgar Allan. "The Gold Bug" (fiction) in Complete Stories
and Poems of Edgar Allan Poe. Garden City, N. Y.: Doubleday, 1966.
Sewell, Barbara. Egypt Under the Pharaohs. New York: Putnam,
1968.
Warren, Ruth. The Nile: The Story of Pharaohs, Farmers and
Explorers. New York: McGraw-Hill, 1968.
Woolley, C. Leonard. Digging Up the Past. New York: Scrib-
ner's, 1931.

THE DECEMBRIST REVOLT (1825)

Russia's first modern attempt at revolution was the Decembrist Revolt of December 26, 1825, at St. Petersburg when a group
of Russian officers sought to overthrow the autocracy of the tsars
and to establish political and social reforms following the death of
Alexander I. It developed from the political and intellectual unrest
generated by the French Revolution and the Napoleonic era.

The revolutionists were largely military officers who had
served in the anti-Napoleonic campaigns of 1813-14. These men,
mostly aristocrats, formed a secret society known as the Union of
Salvation in 1816. It was reorganized as the Union of Welfare the
following year. This, in turn, evolved into two branches, the
Northern Society and the Southern Society, led respectively by Nikita Muravyov and Paul Pestel. The purpose of these organizations was to replace the autocratic Russian government with a constitutional monarchy or a republic.

On December 1, 1825, Tsar Alexander I of Russia died at
Taganrog. Grand Duke Constantine Pavlovich, his elder brother,
was next in line of succession but had renounced his rights two
years previously. Unaware of this, the Russian officials swore
allegiance to him. When Constantine refused to accept the throne
Nicholas, his younger brother, the next in line, agreed to become
tsar.

Nicholas appeared to be a usurper, Constantine not having
made any public explanation of his refusal to accept the Russian
throne. The Northern Society saw in this situation a chance to
seize control of the state. Nicholas, as incoming tsar, was to
swear the new oath on December 26. On the 25th the leaders of

the Society met at the home of Kondraty Ryleiev to plan their strategy. Unfortunately for them none of the group were professional revolutionists and Muravyov was away from St. Petersburg, leaving the group virtually leaderless.

On December 26 the officers led some 3,000 troops into the Senate Square to protest the taking of the oath of allegiance by the tsar designate. Nicholas had mustered 15,000 soldiers to oppose the forces of the Society. After some hours of indecision he ordered cannon to be fired, first over the heads and then into the ranks of the revolutionists. The rebellion became a massacre. Pestel was arrested, along with other Society leaders. After an investigation a 72-man court tried the rebels. A total of 579 then were indicted and 121 received sentences. The five considered most guilty were condemned to be drawn and quartered, and 31 were sentenced to be hanged, with others being sent to exile in Siberia. Tsar Nicholas commuted the hanging sentences to exile and imprisonment and reduced the drawing and quartering to hanging. On July 21, 1826, Pestel, Muravyov, Ryleivev, Mikhail Bestuzhev-Ryumin and Peter Kakhovsky were hanged.

Suggested Readings

Blum, J. G.   Lord and Peasant in Russia from the Ninth to the Nineteenth Century.   Princeton, N. J.:   Princeton University Press, 1961.
Charques, Richard Denis.   A Short History of Russia.   New York: Dutton, 1956.
Clarkson, Jesse D.   A History of Russia.   New York: Random House, 1969.
Florinsky, Michael T.   Russia: A History and Interpretation.   New York: Macmillan, 1965.
Grunwald, Constantin de.   Tsar Nicholas I.   Translated by Brigit Patmore and Douglas Saunders.   London: MacGibbon and Kee, 1954.
Hingley, Ronald.   Tsars, 1533-1917.   New York: Macmillan, 1968.
Kluchevsky, Vasily O.   A History of Russia.   Translated by C. J. Hogarth.   New York: Russell and Russell, 1960 (Originally published 1913).
Kornilov, A. A.   Modern Russian History.   Translated by Alexander S. Kaun.   New York: Knopf, 1952.
Mazour, Anatole G.   The First Russian Revolution: The Decembrist Revolt.   Berkeley, Calif.:   University of California Press, 1937.
Moscow, Henry, and the editors of Horizon Magazine.   Russia Under the Czars.   New York: American Heritage Publishing Co., 1962.
Pares, Bernard.   A History of Russia.   New York: Knopf, 1960.
Pushkarov, Serge.   The Emergence of Modern Russia.   Translated by Robert H. McNeal and Tova Ledlin.   New York: Holt, Rinehart, 1963.
Rogger, Hans.   National Consciousness in Eighteenth Century Rus-

sia.   Cambridge, Mass. :   Harvard University Press, 1960.
Tompkins, S. R.   The Russian Mind.   Norman, Okla. :   University
    of Oklahoma Press, 1953.
Vernadsky, George.   A History of Russia.   New Haven, Conn. :
    Yale University Press, 1954.
Wren, Melvin C.   The Course of Russian History.   New York:
    Macmillan, 1968.
Zetlin, Mikhail.   The Decembrists.   Translated by George Panin.
    New York: International Universities Press, 1958.

THE BURKE AND HARE MURDERS (1828)

In the early nineteenth century anatomists and medical students found it very difficult to obtain dead human bodies for dissection and study because of legal restraints then on the statute books.
Consequently, a trade in "body snatching" came about, where fresh
corpses were exhumed and sold to medical schools "with no questions asked. "

In 1828 William Burke and James Hare were living in the
slums of Edinburgh.   Hare and his wife, Margaret, rented rooms
in their home to lodgers.   Burke, a bachelor, shared one of these
rooms with his mistress, Helen McDougal.

On November 29, 1827, one of Hare's lodgers died of natural causes, owing his landlord four pounds back rent.   Burke and
Hare sold the corpse to Dr. Ronald Knox, a professor of anatomy
at Surgeon's Square, for seven pounds and ten shillings.   Knox indicated that he would pay ten pounds each for additional bodies.

Two of Hare's lodgers became ill.   The two men smothered
them, delivered the bodies to Dr. Knox and collected the promised
ten pounds for each.

The murderers then conceived the idea of luring people into
the lodging house, killing them by suffocation, and selling the corpses
to Knox.   With the assistance of Margaret Hare and Helen Mc-
Dougal, who had become involved in the scheme, they invited an
old beggar named Abigail Simpson into the house, got her drunk,
suffocated her and delivered the body in a tea chest.   Again they
collected their fee, the money being spent for whiskey for the men
and gaudy clothes for the women.

Other victims followed.   Two old women, prostitutes named
Mary Paterson and Janet Brown, were lured into the trap.   Janet
made her escape when Helen McDougal, in a jealous rage, attacked
them.   Mary Paterson, however, was too drunk to realize what was
happening and so went the way of the other victims.

Burke and Hare next killed an old Irish woman and her twelve-

year-old grandson, thereby becoming richer by twenty pounds. Ann
McDougal, a distant relative of Burke's, followed them, with Mrs.
Mary Haldane and her daughter Peggy being killed shortly afterwards. Next came Daft Jamie, an eighteen-year-old mentally retarded boy.

On October 31, 1828, Burke met Mrs. Mary Docherty, an
impoverished Irish beggar. He invited her to a Halloween party at
the lodging house. She accepted the invitation and accompanied
him. When the party got under way Hare, not wishing witnesses
to what was to follow, ejected two new lodgers, James Gray and
his wife Ann.

Acting on a tip from an informer, who was later found to
be James Gray, the police raided Surgeon's Square early on the
morning of November 2. They found the naked body of Mary Docherty crammed into a tea chest. Burke and Hare were arrested,
as were Mrs. Hare and Helen McDougal. Hare, in order to save
his life, turned king's evidence, as did his wife, and Burke and
Helen McDougal went on trial. While at least fifteen persons had
been killed the only charge made was for the murder of Mary Docherty.

The trial lasted over 24 hours. Ann Gray testified for the
prosecution, saying that when she returned to the lodging house
following the Halloween party she found the naked body of Mary
Docherty covered with straw. She also said that Helen McDougal
had offered her money to say nothing about it. John McCulloch,
a porter who had taken the tea chest containing the body to Surgeon's Square, also testified. The statements made by Burke,
Hare, Hare's wife and the McDougal woman were contradictory.
Burke was found guilty of murder and hanged on January 28, 1829.
Helen McDougal's guilt was "not proven" and she was released.
She emigrated to Australia.

Margaret Hare went to Ireland where she dropped from sight.
Hare became blind and ended his days as a match-seller on the
London streets. Dr. Knox left Edinburgh in disgrace, his medical
career at an end. Gray died in poverty shortly after the trial.

In 1832 the Anatomy Act was passed. This legalized the
use of dead bodies for medical research under certain specified
conditions. The Act served to put an end to body snatching and
the murderous activities of such men as Burke, Hare and their female accomplices.

Suggested Readings

Abrahamsen, David, M. D. The Murdering Mind. New York: Har-
    per & Row, 1973.
Bromberg, Walter. Mold of Murder: A Psychiatric Study of Hom-
    icide. New York: Grune & Stratton, 1961.

"Burke and Hare" in Crimes and Punishment, Vol. 20. Editorial
    presentation: Jackson Morley. London: BPC, 1973.
Catton, Joseph. Behind the Scenes of Murder. New York: Nor-
    ton, 1940.
Griffiths, Arthur. Mysteries of Police and Crime. London: 1901.
Guttmacher, M. S. The Mind of the Murderer. Freeport, N. Y. :
    Books for Libraries, 1960.
Jesse, F. Tennyson. Murder and Its Motives. London: Harrap,
    1952.
Lester, David, and Gene Lester. Crime of Passion: Murder and
    the Murderer. Chicago: Nelson Hall, 1975.
McDade, Thomas M. , compiler. The Annals of Murder. Norman,
    Okla. : University of Oklahoma Press, 1961.
Reinhardt, James Melvin. The Psychology of Strange Killers.
    Springfield, Ill. : Thomas, 1962.
Wilson, Colin, and Patricia Pitman. Encyclopedia of Murder. New
    York: Putnam, 1962.
Wolfgang, Marvin E. , compiler. Studies in Homicide. New York:
    Harper & Row, 1967.

PUBLICATION OF PRINCIPLES OF GEOLOGY
AND THE ORIGIN OF SPECIES (1830-1833 and 1859)

For centuries the manner in which the world was created,
as described in Genesis, was accepted as literally true. Those
who dared to question the teachings of the Bible risked persecution
by the Church. Such was the case with Galileo Galilei who, having
propounded "heretical views" in his writings, was denounced and
admonished by Pope Paul V. Persisting in his publication of doctrines which conflicted with Christian teachings he was tried in
1633 by the Inquisition and ordered to recant or suffer torture.
He elected to recant.

Over the succeeding centuries many persons sought to ex-
plain various phenomena in terms of reason rather than God's will.
A list of men and women who made and proved basic scientific discoveries would be endless. However, two who did extremely important pioneer work in natural science were Sir Charles Lyell, a
Scottish geologist, and Charles Darwin, an English naturalist. Both
were instrumental in establishing the principle of natural selection,
defined as "the elimination of the unfit and the survival of the fit
in the struggle for existence, depending on the adjustment of an
organism to a special environment. "

Neither of these men originated the idea of natural selection.
Aristotle, in his Physicae Auscultationes, touches on the idea, though
obliquely. Georges Louis Buffon and Jean Baptiste Lamarck, French
naturalists, suggested a theory of evolutionary biology half a century
before Darwin published The Origin of Species in 1859. Others wrote
on the subject, including Patrick Matthew, Christian Leopold von

Buch, Constantine Samuel Rafinesque, Samuel Steman Haldeman and M. J. d'Omalius d'Halloy. These and others influenced the thinking of both Lyell and Darwin.

Lyell, the son of an amateur botanist, became interested in geology after attending lectures by William Buckland at Oxford. He practiced law for several years and then, in 1827, turned his attention to geological studies and made several geological expeditions to various parts of the world. He published his Principles of Geology in three volumes between 1830 and 1833. This book, which appeared in eleven editions during Lyell's lifetime, implied evolutionary doctrines and was a refutation of the catastrophic theory which maintained that geological change had always been the result of great natural upheavals. Lyell maintained that the forces then slowly operating to change the earth's crust had been operating in the same way and at the same rate throughout the entire history of the earth. This theory, based on the 1795 book Theory of the Earth, authored by the Scottish geologist James Hutton, is known as uniformitarianism.

Lyell's book, read by Charles Darwin while traveling as a naturalist on the ship Beagle, had a great influence on the latter's thinking, and later he and Lyell became close friends. It was on this five-year voyage that Darwin, originally a student of geology, became interested in flora and fauna. His grandfather, Erasmus Darwin, had written on the subject of evolution but the younger Darwin's theory, when resolved, did not coincide with that of his ancestor.

Charles Darwin was impressed with the fact that the animal life of the Galapagos Islands, off the coast of South America, differed from that of the mainland although the climates of both areas were similar. When he returned to England he had no particular ideas about evolution but was convinced that it was a fact. He was aware that it was possible, by the selective breeding of animals, to modify certain forms of animal life, and wondered if some mechanism in nature might not perform in a like manner. Thomas Malthus' An Essay on the Principles of Population, published in 1798 and in a second edition in 1803, suggested an answer. Malthus' contention was that population, when unchecked, tends to increase in a geometric ratio while the means of subsistence tend to increase only in an arithmetic ratio, and that preventive checks on the increase of population are necessary as an alternative to the exclusive operation of positive checks, such as overcrowding, disease, war, poverty and vice.

Darwin reasoned that if population tended to outrun the sustenance available to support it in man-made society, a similar situation could exist in nature, corresponding to the selective breeding of animals. Thus, in their struggle for existence, animals which develop variations helpful for their survival will replace those of the same species which did not adapt to the environment and eventually new species will evolve.

In 1858 Alfred Russel Wallace, a Scottish naturalist, independently originated the theory of natural selection and communicated with Darwin concerning his findings. Papers by both men
on the subject were read at the same meeting of the Linnaean Society in London and were published jointly in the Society's Transactions for 1858. In the following year Darwin, at the urging of
his friend Lyell, published his Origin of Species by Means of Natural Selection. This, as a denial of the prevailing interpretation
of the Scriptures, created a great sensation. Darwin added to the
controversy by putting forth the idea that apes and men were descended from a common ancestor. His views were endorsed by
Thomas Henry Huxley, a famous English biologist, and by others.

The controversy persisted for many years. As recently as
1925 a lawsuit at Dayton, Tennessee, pitted the fundamentalists,
led by William Jennings Bryan, against the advocates of Darwinism,
headed by the attorney Clarence Darrow. This, the "Scopes Monkey
Trial," was concerned not with the accuracy of the theory of natural selection but with the legality of teaching doctrines contrary
to the Bible in the public schools.

Suggested Readings

Adams, Frank Dawson. The Birth and Development of the Geologi-
    cal Sciences. London: Ballière, Tindall and Cox, 1938.
Bailey, Edward. Charles Lyell. Garden City, N. Y.: Doubleday,
    1963.
Barlow, Nora, ed. The Autobiography of Charles Darwin, 1809-
    1882. Edited with Appendix and Notes by his Granddaughter,
    Nora Barlow. New York: Harcourt, Brace, 1958.
    _____. Charles Darwin and the Voyage of the "Beagle." New
    York: Philosophical Library, 1946.
Barnett, Samuel Anthony, ed. A Century of Darwin. Cambridge,
    Mass.: Harvard University Press, 1958.
Barzun, Jacques. Darwin, Marx, Wagner: Critique of a Heritage.
    Garden City, N. Y.: Doubleday, 1958.
Darwin, Charles. The Origin of Species by Means of Natural Se-
    lection or the Preservation of Favored Races in the Struggle
    for Life, and the Descent of Man, and Selection in Relation to
    Sex. New York: Modern Library, 1958 (Originally published
    1859).
    _____. The Voyage of the "Beagle." New York: Bantam Books,
    1958 (Originally written 1840-1843).
Darwin, Francis, ed. The Life and Letters of Charles Darwin.
    New York: Appleton, 1896.
De Beer, Gavin. Charles Darwin: Evolution by Natural Selection.
    Garden City, N. Y.: Doubleday, 1964.
Dickinson, Alice. Charles Darwin and Natural Selection. New York:
    Franklin Watts, 1964.
Eiseley, Loren. Darwin's Century. Garden City, N. Y.: Double-
    day, 1958.
Gillispie, Charles Coulston. The Age of Objectivity. Princeton,
    N. J.: Princeton University Press, 1960.

_____. Genesis and Geology. Cambridge, Mass.: Harvard
    University Press, 1951.
Ginger, Ray. Six Days or Forever? Tennessee v. John Thomas
    Scopes. Boston: Beacon Press, 1958.
Glass, Bentley, ed., with Oswei Temkin and William Straus, Jr.,
    under the auspices of the Johns Hopkins History of Ideas Club.
    Forerunners of Darwin: 1745-1859. Baltimore: Johns Hop-
    kins University Press, 1959.
Greene, Carla. Charles Darwin. New York: Dial Press, 1968.
Greene, John C. Darwin and the Modern World View. New York:
    Mentor Books, 1963.
Himmelfarb, Gertrude. Darwin and Darwinian Revolution. New
    York: Doubleday, 1962.
Huxley, Julian. Evolution: The Modern Synthesis. New York:
    Harper, 1942.
_____, and H.B.D. Kettlewell. Charles Darwin and His World.
    New York: Viking Press, 1965.
Irvine, William. Apes, Angels and Victorians: The Story of Dar-
    win, Huxley and Evolution. New York: McGraw-Hill, 1955.
Karp, Walter, and the editors of Horizon Magazine. Charles Dar-
    win and the Origin of Species. New York: American Heritage
    Publishing Co., 1968.
Lack, David. Darwin's Finches. New York: Harper, 1961.
Lane, Carroll, and Mildred Harris Fenton. Giants of Geology.
    Garden City, N.Y.: Doubleday, 1956.
Lawrence, Jerome, and Robert E. Lee. Inherit the Wind (play).
    New York: Random House, 1955.
_____. Inherit the Wind (play condensation) in Mantle, Burns,
    ed. The Best Plays of 1954-1955. New York: Dodd, Mead,
    1955.
Moore, Ruth. Charles Darwin. New York: Knopf, 1955.
_____. The Earth We Live On. New York: Knopf, 1956.
_____, and the editors of Life Magazine. Evolution. New York:
    Time, Inc., 1962.
Moorehead, Alan. Darwin and the "Beagle." New York: Harper
    & Row, 1969.
Murray, Robert H. Science and Scientists in the 19th Century.
    London: Sheldon Press, 1925.
Ong, Walter, S.J. Darwin's Vision and Christian Perspectives.
    New York: Macmillan, 1960.
Raverat, Gwen. Period Piece. New York: Norton, 1953.
Reinfeld, Fred. Young Charles Darwin. New York: Sterling Pub-
    lishing Co., 1956.
Simpson, George Gaylord. The Meaning of Evolution. New Haven,
    Conn.: Yale University Press, 1959.
White, Andrew Dickson. A History of the Warfare of Science
    with Theology in Christendom. New York: George Braziller,
    1955.
Willis, Marcia. "Darwin in South America" in her Jungle Rivers
    and Mountain Peaks: Encyclopedia of Discovery and Exploration,
    Vol. 9. London: Aldus Books, 1971.
The World's Most Famous Court Trial: Tennessee Evolution Case.
    Cincinnati: National Book Co., 1925.

THE BRITISH EMANCIPATION ACT (1833)

The institution of slavery has been known since ancient times. It is a condition similar to vassalage or serfdom but is distinguished from them in that it represents "the most absolute and involuntary form of human servitude. " Here human beings are regarded as chattels, owned by other humans, to be bought and sold in the same manner as any other tangible property. Slavery existed in the English colonies until 1833 when it was legally abolished by the British Emancipation Act.

England entered the slave trade in 1533 and was followed by France in 1624 and later by Holland, Denmark and the American Colonies. Since 1787 William Wilberforce, an English philanthropist and anti-slavery crusader, had led agitation in the House of Commons against the slave trade. He was supported in this by Thomas Clarkson, William Pitt and members of the Quaker religious sect. In 1807 he won legal outlawing of the dealing in slaves and urged the complete abolition of slavery itself. In January, 1823, the Society for the Mitigation and Abolition of Slavery Throughout the British Dominions, popularly known as the Anti-Slavery Society, was founded. This organization had a number of socially and politically prominent members. Its president was the Duke of Gloucester, a nephew of the late King George III, and vice presidents included several peers and members of the House of Commons. On the roster of officers were Wilberforce, Clarkson, Henry Peter Brougham and Thomas Fowell Buxton, all members of Parliament. Zachary Macaulay edited its monthly journal, Anti-Slavery Monthly Reporter, in which news pertaining to the cause was published.

On May 5, 1823, Buxton, a British philanthropist and advocate of abolition, in an address to Parliament, stated that slavery was "repugnant alike to the British constitution and Christian principles" and should be gradually abolished. The plan he suggested for achieving such abolition provided that all children born after a certain date be declared free, and that reform measures be taken for those who were then slaves. George Canning, prime minister and leader of the House of Commons, in replying, presented a counter-proposal which provided for the amelioration and eventual abolition of slavery. Buxton withdrew his proposal and Canning's resolutions were approved. These constituted the basis of British governmental policy on the slavery question until 1833 when, as mentioned above, the British Emancipation Act was passed.

Canning's proposals on governmental policy were strongly opposed by the planters of the West Indies. These men felt that without slave labor they would not be able to operate their sugar plantations profitably. Political pressure was brought to bear on Parliament and by 1830 it was realized that the idea of gradual emancipation of slaves was inoperable. An attempt was made to resurrect the policy of amelioration. Slave codes were ordered

reformed and, although the planters were promised a lower duty
on sugar, they resisted all such efforts.

In June, 1831, the Agency Committee was formed by such
abolitionists as James Stephen and Joseph Sturge. This organization sought to bring the anti-slavery message to the British people
by means of lectures, hoping thereby to force Parliament to accede
to the public's wishes on the issue.

When Parliament met in February, 1833, Buxton decided to
press the matter. King William IV, in opening the session, had
failed to make any mention of the slavery question and this spurred
Buxton to action. Parliament was flooded with petitions. A convention of anti-slavery delegates was held at Exeter Hall on April
18. Buxton, in a speech to Parliament, proposed immediate emancipation and the government indicated that it would present its plan
on April 23. On May 14, after additional information had been
gathered and evaluated, Colonial Secretary Edward Stanley gave the
government's answer. In his speech Stanley proposed that (1) all
children born after the Act, or under six years of age, should be
declared free. (2) An apprentice system leading to ultimate freedom in no longer than twelve years, was to be instituted. (3) Compensation to the slave-owning planters, in the form of a loan, was
to be arranged.

These proposals came before Parliament as a bill and, after
some modifications, including the substitution of an outright money
gift for the originally proposed loan, was passed as the British
Emancipation Act. It received the required royal assent on August
28, 1833, and became law. As a result some 800,000 slaves in
the British empire became free, an outstanding triumph for the
abolitionists.

Suggested Readings

Coupland, Reginald. The British Anti-Slavery Movement. London:
        Frank Cass & Co., 1964.
Howard, Richard Christopher. Black Cargo. London: Wayland,
        1972.
Hurd, John C. The Law of Freedom and of Bondage. Westport,
        Conn.: Negro University Press, 1858-1862.
Klingberg, Frank J. The Anti-Slavery Movement in England: A
        Study in English Humanitarianism. New Haven, Conn.: Yale
        University Press, 1926.
Lloyd, Arthur Young. The Slavery Controversy, 1831-1860. Chap-
        el Hill, N.C.: University of North Carolina Press, 1939.
McPherson, James M. The Struggle for Equality. Princeton, N.J.:
        Princeton University Press, 1964.
Mathieson, William Law. British Slave Emancipation, 1838-1849.
        New York: Octagon Books, 1967 (Originally published 1932).
_____. British Slavery and Its Abolition, 1823-1838. New York:
        Octagon Books, 1967 (Originally published 1926).

Mellor, George R. British Imperial Trusteeship, 1783-1850. Lon-
    don: Faber and Faber, 1951.
Ward, William E. The Royal Navy and the Slavers: The Suppres-
    sion of the Atlantic Slave Trade. New York: Pantheon Books,
    1969.
Williams, Eric. Capitalism and Slavery. New York: Capricorn
    Books, 1966.

THE CANADIAN REBELLION (1837)

By the terms of the Treaty of Paris in 1763 virtually the
entire French domain on the North American mainland was ceded
to Great Britain. Excepted were the territories west of the Mississippi River and New Orleans, which had been previously ceded
to Spain. Also excepted were the islands of St. Pierre and Mique-
lon, which continued to be held by France. All of Canada became
a British dominion.

British rule over Canada caused widespread grievances. In
Upper Canada the primary cause of discontent was the arbitrary
conduct of the British official appointees, most of whom represented
commercial or landed interests. Other sources of unrest were the
ineffectuality of the popularly elected legislative assembly, the distribution of crown lands and the favoritism shown the Anglican
Church.

Grievances in Lower Canada stemmed from essentially the
same causes and were compounded by the British policy of restrict-
ing official posts to persons of British extraction.

In 1837 a group of lower Canadians, under the leadership
of Louis Joseph Papineau, a French-Canadian insurgent, revolted
against British rule. In Upper Canada the Scottish-born insurrec-
tionist William Lyon Mackenzie led 800 men in a Toronto uprising
with the intention of setting up a provisional government. Neither
uprising received significant support and both were quickly overcome by the authorities. Captured rebels were given exceedingly
lenient treatment by John George Lambton, Earl of Durham, the
newly-appointed Governor General and Lord High Commissioner of
Canada.

Mackenzie fled to the United States, organized supporters
in Buffalo, N. Y. , and fortified Navy Island in the Niagara River
where he was involved in the "Caroline Affair. " He was imprisoned
in the United States until 1840 for violating neutrality laws.

Suggested Readings

Commager, Henry Steele, ed.   "The 'Caroline' Affair" (Doc. No.

156) in his Documents of American History, 8th edition.   New
York: Appleton, 1968.
Crawford, Michael, compiler.   1837:   Mackenzie.   Toronto: Clarke,
    Irwin, 1968.
De Celles, A. D.   "Papineau, Cartier" in The Making of Canada
    Series, anniversary edition, Vol. V.   New York: Oxford Uni-
    versity Press, 1926.
Field, John L., and Lloyd A. Dennis.   From Sea to Sea: The
    Story of Canada in the Nineteenth and Twentieth Centuries.
    New York: Abelard, 1965.
Flint, David.   William Lyon Mackenzie, Rebel Against Authority.
    New York: Oxford University Press, 1971.
Gates, L. F.   "Mackenzie's Gazette: An Aspect of W. L. Macken-
    zie's American Years," Canadian Historical Review, December,
    1965.
Guillet, Edwin C.   The Lives and Times of the Patriots.   Toronto:
    University of Toronto Press, 1968.
Kilbourn, William M.   "Epilogue to the Firebrand," Ontario Library
    Review, November, 1961.
_____.   Firebrand: William Lyon Mackenzie and the Rebellion
    in Upper Canada.   Toronto: Clarke, Irwin, 1956.
Lambton, John George.   Report on the Affairs of British North
    America.   London: 1839.
Leacock, Stephen B.   "Mackenzie, Baldwin, La Fontaine, Hincks"
    in The Making of Canada Series, anniversary edition, Vol. V.
    New York: Oxford University Press, 1926.
Lindsey, Charles.   The Life and Times of William Lyon Mackenzie.
    Philadelphia: J. W. Bradley, 1862.
Mackenzie, William Lyon.   The Life and Times of Martin Van Bur-
    en.   Boston: Cooke & Co., 1846.
Peck, Anne Merriman.   The Pageant of Canadian History.   New
    York: Longmans, Green, 1943.
Rasporich, Anthony W., compiler.   William Lyon Mackenzie.   New
    York: Holt, 1972.
Romney, P.   "William Lyon Mackenzie as Mayor of Toronto," Ca-
    nadian Historical Review, December, 1975.
Wrong, George M.   The Canadians: The Story of a People.   New
    York: Macmillan, 1938.

THE INVENTION OF PHOTOGRAPHY (1839)

        Louis Jacques Mandé Daguerre, a French painter, is gen-
erally thought of as the inventor of photography, the "process, science and art of producing images of objects on sensitized surfaces
by the chemical action of light or of other forms of radiant energy."
It is true that Dominique François Jean Arago, the French director
of the Paris Observatory, announced to the Academy of Sciences on
January 9, 1839, that Daguerre had perfected a practical method
for capturing the images of three-dimensional objects on the surface
of a metal plate held in a specially adapted camera obscura.   How-

ever, Daguerre's invention, though a significant milestone in the development of photography, was both based on and followed by the work of others

The camera obscura was known as early as the eleventh century. This is a darkened box-like device in which the images of external objects, received through an aperture, are exhibited in their natural colors on a surface arranged to receive them. In the late eighteenth century the British scientists Sir Humphry Davy and Thomas Wedgwood conducted experiments in the recording of photographic images. They succeeded in producing impressions of various objects on paper coated with silver chloride. These pictures, however, were not permanent as the entire surface of the paper turned black when exposed to light.

About 1829 Daguerre, who had worked as a scene painter for the opera and who had evolved and exhibited the diorama in 1822, began corresponding with Joseph-Nicéphore Niépce, the inventor of the heliograph. In August, 1829, the two men entered into a partnership. It was understood that Daguerre's function was to improve on Niépce's invention, his primary objective being to find a way of reducing the required exposure time from eight hours to a few minutes.

Niépce died in 1833 and his place was temporarily taken by Isidore Niépce, his nephew. At this time Daguerre had not solved the problem of the long exposure and he worked independently following the death of his original partner.

Daguerre concentrated on finding a suitable coating for his photographic plates and a technique for developing them once they had been exposed to light. He learned how to reduce the required time of exposure by the use of mercury vapor. In May, 1835, he announced that he had discovered a practical process for capturing and fixing projected images. However, his developed photographs persisted in fading and it was not until 1837 that he learned that such fading could be prevented by coating the developed plate with a strong solution of ordinary table salt. This fixing process had been originated by William Henry Fox Talbot, a British scientist and inventor who discovered and described "photogenic drawing" in 1839. Daguerre's process had as an end product a single photograph on a silver plate for each exposure. Talbot's method involved the use of a paper negative from which any number of prints could be made. His method, called the "calotype" or "Talbotype process," patented in 1841, improved on Daguerre's method. Talbot found that paper covered with silver iodide could be made more sensitive to light if dampened by a solution of silver nitrate and gallic acid before exposure, and that the solution could also be used to develop the paper negative after exposure. The negative image was made permanent after exposure by immersion in "hypo" (sodium thiosulphate). The calotype method permitted pictures to be taken with exposures lasting about 40 seconds, and in 1851 Talbot discovered a method of instantaneous photography.

The original inventions of Daguerre, Niêpce, Talbot and their predecessors were improved upon over the succeeding decades by such men as Frederick Scott Archer, Richard Kennett, James Clerk Maxwell, George Eastman and others. Today photography is used in countless commercial and military applications. The motion picture, color photography, the "instant" camera developed by Dr. Edwin H. Land, aerial surveying and such photomechanical processes as photoengraving, lithography, gravure and serigraphy have all evolved from the medieval camera obscura.

Suggested Readings

Boni, Albert. Photographic Literature. New York: R. R. Bowker, 1962.

Burlingame, Roger. Inventors Behind the Inventor. New York: Harcourt, Brace, 1947.

Eder, Josef Maria. The History of Photography. Translated by Edward Epstean. New York: McGraw-Hill, 1945.

Focal Encyclopedia of Photography. 32nd revised edition. New York: McGraw-Hill, 1960.

Gernsheim, Helmut. The History of Photography from the Earliest Use of the Camera Obscura in the Eleventh Century up to 1914. London: Oxford University Press, 1955.

_____, and Alison Gernsheim. L. J. M. Daguerre: The History of the Diorama and the Daguerrotype. New York: Dover, 1968.

Harrison, W. Jerome. History of Photography Written as a Practical Guide and an Instruction to Its Latest Developments. New York: Arno Press, 1887.

Jammes, André, and Robert Sobieszek. "French Primitive Photography, " Aperture, Spring, 1970.

Larmore, Lewis, Ph. D. Introduction to Photographic Principles. Englewood Cliffs, N. J. : Prentice-Hall, 1958.

Marino, T. J. Pictures Without a Camera. New York: Sterling Publishing Co. , 1974.

Morgan, Willard D. , general editor. The Encyclopedia of Photography. New York: Greystone Press, 1963.

Newhall, Beaumont. The Daguerrotype in America. New York: Dover, 1976.

_____. The History of Photography from 1839 to the Present. New York: Museum of Modern Art, 1949.

_____. Latent Image: The Discovery of Photography. New York: Doubleday, 1967.

Rhode, Robert B. , and Floyd H. McCall. Introduction to Photography. 2nd edition. New York: Macmillan, 1971.

Usher, Abbott P. A History of Mechanical Inventions. New York: McGraw-Hill, 1929.

THE IRISH POTATO FAMINE (1845-1849)

The Irish potato famine, caused by the failure of the potato

crop of 1845, lasted until 1849 because of the failures of succeeding crops. The direct cause of the disaster was a fungus, phytoph-
thora infestans, a microscopic organism. This, in all probability, came by ship from North America where, in 1842, outbreaks
of potato blight had occurred. The wind-borne fungus spores had
invaded the potato plant, germinated and reproduced. The Irish
crop for 1845 was planted with diseased seed potatoes, resulting
in the complete loss of the vegetable for that year. This was disastrous for the Irish peasants whose primary source of sustenance
was the potato. When the crop failed the only alternative for many
was starvation.

In the 18th and 19th centuries the Irish peasants lived a
miserable existence. Many were illiterate and poverty-stricken.
Exploited by the agents of absentee landlords, they were charged
excessive rents for the tiny patches of land they occupied and cultivated. Payment of rent was made in potatoes raised by the peasants who seldom saw or handled specie. When, because of crop
failures they were unable to pay their rent, they were summarily
evicted, with virtually no hope of legal redress.

In 1843 the Devon Commission, organized to investigate the
situation, found that the primary cause of the peasants' miserable
lot was bad relations between them and their landlords. Another
cause of distress was the peasants' apallingly low standard of living. Entire families occupied one-room huts which they frequently
shared with the pigs they raised. When evicted from these miserable quarters they sought shelter in ditches and bog holes. The
tragic situation was compounded by the wide failure of crops other
than potatoes throughout Europe. Some landlords converted their
estates to grazing farms or else switched to other crops the raising of which did not require the services of the potato peasants.
Diseases such as scurvy, dysentery, dropsy, cholera and typhus
claimed the lives of over 700,000 Irish tenants between 1846 and
1849.

Sir Robert Peel, Conservative Prime Minister of Great
Britain, organized the Relief Commission for Ireland in November,
1845. His relief program was fourfold. Local committees, consisting of sympathetic landlords, magistrates and members of the
clergy, were to raise money with which to buy food for the needy
and landlords were to increase the number of workers employed
on their estates. The Irish Board of Works was to inaugurate a
program of road building, hiring potato peasants to perform the labor. Arrangements were to be made to care for the sick. In addition, Peel ordered the purchase of over a million pounds of corn
from the United States, this to be distributed by local relief com-
missions. Further, he worked for the repeal of the centuries-old
Corn Laws, high tariffs protecting British grain. By this he hoped
to encourage the importation of grain. This last was successful,
the Corn Laws being repealed in June, 1846. However, a combination of Liberals and Protectionist Tories felt that the Laws should
stand and Peel was replaced as Prime Minister by the Liberal John
Russell in the same year.

Unfortunately the reforms inaugurated by Peel did not achieve their objectives. Charles Edward Trevelyan, the British treasury's financial secretary who sought to make Ireland financially self-sufficient, rejected Peel's foreign grain and public works programs. He did, however, find it necessary to place additional orders for American corn. What public works had been completed were found to be substandard and unsatisfactory. Russell's cabinet phased out this part of Peel's program in 1847, replacing it with soup kitchens established to feed the starving Irish peasants. The Irish Fever Bill was passed by Parliament to provide medical care for the sick.

The Irish potato famine caused thousands of peasants to emigrate, many of them to America. The population declined from 8,000,000 in 1841 to 6,500,000 ten years later, much of this attributable to deaths from disease and starvation.

In 1849 Parliament passed the Encumbered Estates Act, designed to assist ruined landowners. William Smith O'Brien, who headed the Young Ireland Party, precipitated the Tipperary Insurrection in July of 1848. He hoped that the local peasants would support him but the uprising was put down by the police and O'Brien was deported to Tasmania.

Suggested Readings

Barnes, Donald G. A History of the English Corn Laws, 1660-1846. New York: F. S. Croft, 1930.

Burton, W. G. The Potato. Waginingen, Holland: H. Veenman and Zonen N. V. , 1966.

Curtis, Edmund. A History of Ireland. 6th edition. London: Methuen, 1950.

Edwards, R. Dudley, and T. Desmond Williams, eds. The Great Famine: Studies in Irish History, 1845-52. New York: New York University Press, 1957.

Eversley, George John Shaw-Lefevre. Peel and O'Connell: A Review of the Irish Policy of Parliament from the Act of Union to the Death of Sir Robert Peel. Port Washington, N. Y. : Kennikat Press, 1970.

Hobsbawm, E. J. The Age of Revolution: Europe from 1789-1848. New York: New American Library, 1962.

Langer, William L. Political and Social Upheaval, 1832-1852, Vol. XIV. New York: Harper & Row, 1969.

McCord, Norman. The Anti-Corn Law League, 1838-1846. London: George Allen & Unwin, 1958.

McIntosh, Thomas P. The Potato, Its History, Varieties, Culture, and Diseases. London: Oliver and Bond, 1927.

Pomfret, John E. The Struggle for Land in Ireland, 1800-1923. Princeton, N. J. : Princeton University Press, 1930.

Ramsay, Anna A. W. Sir Robert Peel. London: T. Constable & Co. , 1928.

Rich, E. E. , and C. H. Wilson, eds. The Cambridge Economic History of Europe, Vol. IV. Cambridge: The University Press, 1967.

Salaman, Redcliffe N.   The History and Social Influence of the Po-
    tato. Cambridge: The University Press, 1949.
Schrier, Arnold.   Ireland and the American Emigration, 1850-1900.
    Minneapolis: University of Minnesota Press, 1958.
Uris, Leon.   Trinity (fiction). New York: Bantam Books, 1977.
Woodham-Smith, Cecil B.   The Great Hunger: Ireland, 1845-1849.
    New York: Harper & Row, 1962.
Woodward, Llewellyn.   "The Age of Reform, 1815-1870" in The
    Oxford History of England, Vol. XIII, 2nd edition.   Oxford:
    Clarendon Press, 1962.

THE TAIPING REBELLION (1848-1864)

In the 1840's Hung Hsiu-ch'üan, a fanatical Chinese mystic,
precipitated a popular revolution against the Chinese imperial government.   This was called the Taiping Rebellion because its leaders sought to replace the Manchu dynasty of Chinese emperors with
a Taiping dynasty.

Hung was born in 1812.   As a young man he taught school
and learned something of Christianity.   He suffered a long illness
during which he had strange religious visions and about 1840 became the leader of a mystic society in Kwangsi.   Here he gained
converts to his cause which was based, in part, on Christian doctrine and aimed at idolatry.   By 1848 he and his followers began
to challenge the imperial authority.

Between 1848 and 1850 the movement was confined to sporadic local outbursts.   In the latter year the insurgents commenced
a general offensive against the national Manchu government.   A
series of victories in the south encouraged Hung and his forces to
invade North China and Nanking, which fell to the insurgents in
1853, becoming Hung's headquarters.   From this stronghold he issued edicts and directed his military subordinates and, for the next
seven years, his armies defeated the imperial troops repeatedly.
However, the rebel forces became lawless and destructive.   They
failed to consolidate their conquests and administrative weakness
and lack of military discipline accounted for their failure to crush
the Manchu regime.

In 1860 the imperial government commissioned Frederick
Townsend Ward, an American military adventurer, to organize and
lead the imperial forces against the rebels.   His command, called
the "Ever-Victorious Army," won a number of battles during the
next two years.   Ward was wounded in action and died the following day, September 21, 1862.   Command of the army was then giv-
en to the British general Charles George Gordon and the Chinese
statesman Li Hung-chang.   Gordon suppressed the Taiping Rebellion
in 33 actions and by July, 1864, Nanking had been recaptured and
the rebel armies soundly defeated.

Hung, realizing that his cause was lost and, facing retaliation from the Manchus, committed suicide by taking poison. Gordon died at the siege of Khartoum in 1885.

Suggested Readings

Anderson, Lady Flavia G. The Rebel Emperor. Garden City, N. Y. : Doubleday, 1959.

Boardman, Eugene Powers. Christian Influence upon the Ideology of the Taiping Rebellion, 1851-1864. Madison, Wis. : University of Wisconsin Press, 1952.

Brine, Lindeasy. Taeping Rebellion in China: A Narrative of Its Rise and Progress, Based Upon Original Documents and Information Obtained in China. London: Murray, 1862.

Cahill, Holgel. A Yankee Adventurer: The Story of Ward and the Taiping Rebellion. New York: Macaulay, 1930.

Chien, Yu-wen, with the editorial assistance of Adrienne Suddard. Taiping Revolutionary Movement. New Haven, Conn. : Yale University Press, 1973.

Elton, Godfrey Elton. Gordon of Khartoum: The Life of General Charles George Gordon. New York: Knopf, 1954.

Gregory, James Stothert. Great Britain and the Taipings. New York: Frederick A. Praeger, 1969.

Hake, A. E. The Story of Chinese Gordon. London: Remington, 1884.

MacFarlane, Charles. The Chinese Revolution. London: 1853.

Michael, Franz H. The Taiping Rebellion: History and Documents. Seattle: University of Washington Press, 1966.

Moule, Arthur Evans. Half a Century of China. London: 1911.

Têng, Ssü-Yü. New Light on the History of the Taiping Rebellion. New York: Russell & Russell, 1950.

Wortham, H. E. Chinese Gordon. Boston: Little, Brown, 1933.

THE COMMUNIST MANIFESTO (1848) AND DAS KAPITAL (1867, 1885 and 1894)

Two of the most influential men in world history were Karl Marx (1818-1883) and Friedrich Engels (1820-1895). These German revolutionists and co-founders of scientific socialism, both prolific writers in the field of political economy, are best known for The Communist Manifesto and the three-volume Das Kapital. These writings had a profound effect on modern socialist doctrine. The theories expounded by Marx and Engels, though revised by most socialists after Marx's death, were revived by Nikolai Lenin, the Russian communist leader, in the 20th century and became the core of the theory and practice of bolshevism and the Third International.

Marx, following graduation from college, became editor of the Cologne newspaper Rheinische Zeitung. His writings in the

Zeitung led to his forced resignation and shortly afterwards the paper suspended publication.   He moved to Paris in 1844, and Friedrich Engels, whom he had met some years earlier, visited him.
The two men found that they had independently arrived at identical
views on the nature of revolutionary problems.   They decided to
join forces and organize an international working-class movement
dedicated to the principles of communism.

Engels came from a wealthy Protestant family with interests
in the textile manufacturing industry.   As a youth he was influenced
by the writings of Heinrich Heine and Georg Hegel and in 1842 he
was converted to communist beliefs by Moses Hess, the German
Jewish socialist.   He wrote for a number of publications and studied
political economy, becoming convinced that politics and history
could be explained only in terms of the economic development of
society.   He, like Marx, felt that the social evils of his time were
the result of the institution of private property and that these could
be eliminated only by a class struggle leading to a communist society.   In 1844 he published Condition of the Working Class in England in which he expounded his ideas.

The collaboration of Marx and Engels continued until the
former's death in 1883.   Marx did the lion's share of the work on
their joint efforts but Engels' contributions were extremely important.   The Communist Manifesto, published in 1848, influenced all
subsequent communist literature and is considered a classic exposition of the modern communist viewpoint.   This, written by Marx,
was based on a draft prepared by Engels and is the first systematic statement of modern socialist doctrine.   It ends with the still
remembered words, "Workers of the world unite!"

In 1859 Marx followed the Manifesto with his Critique of Political Economy.   In these publications Marx contends that the history of society is a history of class struggles between the ruling
(exploiting) classes and the social (exploited) classes.   He predicted that the capitalists would be overthrown in a world-wide working-class revolution and the two-class system would be replaced
by a classless communist society.

Following the publication of the Manifesto revolution broke
out in France and Germany and Marx was banished from Belgium.
He went first to Paris and thence to the Rhineland.   In Cologne he
engaged in publishing a newspaper advocating communism and also
busied himself with communistic organization activities.   He was
expelled from Germany and later from France, and for the balance
of his life lived and worked in London.   Here he continued the publication of communistic propaganda and wrote Das Kapital, which is
considered his greatest work.   It appeared in three volumes, the
first being published in 1867.   The second and third volumes (1885
and 1894), edited by Engels, appeared posthumously.   These are a
systematic and exhaustive historical analysis of the capitalist economy and cover Marx's theory of the exploitation of the working classes by the employers through the appropriation by the latter of the
"surplus value" produced by the workers.

Marx and Engels continued to write and publish until their deaths. They wrote as a team and also made individual contributions to the literature of communism and political science.

Suggested Readings

Barzun, Jacques. Darwin, Marx, Wagner: Critique of a Heritage. Garden City, N. Y.: Doubleday, 1958.

Berlin, Isaiah. Karl Marx: His Life and Environment. New York: Oxford University Press, 1935.

Bober, M. M. Karl Marx's Interpretation of History. Cambridge, Mass.: Harvard University Press, 1948.

Cole, G. H. D. Socialist Thought: Marxism and Anarchism, 1850-1890. New York: St. Martin's Press, 1964.

Coser, Lewis A., and Irving Howe. The American Communist Party. Boston: Beacon Press, 1957.

Daniels, Robert V. The Conscience of the Revolution: Communist Opposition in Soviet Russia. Cambridge, Mass.: Harvard University Press, 1960.

Eastman, Max. Marxism: Is It Science? New York: Norton, 1940.

Fromm, Erich. Beyond the Chains of Illusion: My Encounter with Marx and Freud. New York: Pocket Books, 1963.

Gyorgy, Andrew. Communism in Perspective. Boston: Allyn and Bacon, 1964.

Hunt, R. Carew. The Theory and Practice of Communism. London: Geoffrey Bles, 1950.

Landauer, Carl. European Socialism: A History of Ideas and Movements. Berkeley, Calif.: University of California Press, 1959.

Lichtheim, George. Marxism: An Historical and Critical Study. New York: Frederick A. Praeger, 1961.

Mehring, Franz. Karl Marx. Ann Arbor, Mich.: University of Michigan Press, 1962.

Meyer, Alfred G. Communism. New York: Random House, 1962.

Ponomaryov, Boris N., et al. History of the Communist Party of the Soviet Union. Moscow: Foreign Languages Publishing House, 1960.

Schapiro, Leonard. The Communist Party of the Soviet Union. New York: Random House, 1960.

Wetter, Gustav A. Dialectical Materialism. Translated by Peter Heath. New York: Frederick A. Praeger, 1958.

THE CRYSTAL PALACE EXHIBITION (1851)

Exhibitions, also called "expositions," are defined as "public displays of commercial products, or of fine arts." Exhibitions are usually short-term displays of products or arts, while expositions are for a longer period and on a larger scale. Either may

be regional, national or international and may show the products
of a single industry or "all products of civilized endeavor. "

   The forerunner of the exhibition/exposition of today was the
medieval fair. These fairs were essentially commercial in nature
and were held in conjunction with religious festivals. They developed in areas where quantities of goods had accumulated and potential purchasers were present. While trade was the principal
purpose of fairs, entertainment, provided by jugglers, acrobats,
magicians and puppet shows, was also an important feature.

   Prior to 1851 exhibitions were regional, as was the Paris
Exhibition of 1849. Henry Cole, assistant keeper of the British
Public Record Office, had visited this exhibition and learned that
a proposal to make it international had been rejected. He, as an
advocate of free trade, suggested that a similar exhibition, international in scope, be held in England. He presented the idea to
the Royal Society of Arts, of which Prince Albert, consort of Queen
Victoria, was president. The prince approved the suggestion and
a royal commission, consisting of members of the Society, was appointed to look into the proposal. Members of the commission included Richard Cobden, Sir Robert Peel and Lord John Russell.

   It was necessary for the sponsors of the exhibition to overcome the objections of some English manufacturers who opposed
the idea, fearing that foreign competitors might learn their trade
secrets. Others felt that visitors from the Continent might introduce "revolutionary ideas" into England. It had been proposed that
Hyde Park, a wooded area of London, be the site of the exhibition.
This was opposed by Henry Peter Brougham, former Lord Chancellor, Colonel Charles Sibthorp and others who argued that such
a project would ruin the district and attract "bad characters. "

   Realizing that government funding of the project was out of
the question, the sponsors sought private individuals to invest in
it. Eventually, with the support of Prince Albert, such financing
was arranged for and the Crystal Palace Exhibition became a practical
proposition. It was to be the first of many international expositions
of technology.

   Two hundred and thirty three designs for the building to
house the exhibits were submitted, all of them being rejected by
the building committee. The design finally accepted was the work
of Joseph Paxton. This was a single shed with a lofty arched nave
and transept and many side aisles. The walls and roof were made
entirely of glass supported by wrought iron lattice girders. Douglas Jerrold, the English playwright and humorist, writing in Punch,
called it the "crystal palace. " It covered 22 acres and housed the
entire exhibition, being completed in January, 1851.

   Queen Victoria opened the exhibition on May 1. By the time
it closed on October 15, more than six million people had visited
it. It was successful financially, showing a surplus of 186,000

pounds, and was followed by many other international exhibitions. Among these were the Dublin and New York City Exhibitions of 1853 and the Exposition Universelle, held in Paris in 1855. Others were those of 1862 (London), 1867 (Paris), 1889 (Paris), 1893 (Chicago), 1900 (Paris), 1904 (St. Louis), 1915 (San Francisco), 1926 (Philadelphia), 1933-1934 (Chicago), 1937 (Paris) 1939-1940 (New York City), 1958 (Brussels), 1962 (Seattle), 1964-1965 (New York City), 1967 (Montreal) and 1976 (Moscow).

After the Crystal Palace Exhibition closed, the glass and iron building was moved from Hyde Park to Sydenham Hill, south of London. In 1936 it was destroyed by fire.

Suggested Readings

Augur, H. A. Trade Fairs and Exhibitions. New York: International Publications, 1967.

Bentley, Nicolas. Victorian Scene: A Picture Book of the Period 1837-1901. London: Weidenfeld, 1968.

Briggs, Asa. Victorian People: A Reassessment of Persons and Themes, 1851-67. Chicago: University of Chicago Press, 1955.

Farmer, Lydia. "Victoria" in her A Book of Famous Queens. Revised by Willard A. Heaps. New York: Crowell, 1964.

Fay, C. R. Palace of Industry, 1851: A Study of the Great Exhibition and Its Fruits. London: Cambridge University Press, 1951.

Ferguson, Eugene S. "Expositions and Technology" in Kranzberg, Melvin, and Carroll W. Pursell, eds. Technology in Western Civilization. New York: Oxford University Press, 1967.

French, Yvonne. The Great Exhibition: 1851. London: Harville Press, 1950.

Hobhouse, Christopher. 1851 and the Crystal Palace. London: John Murray, 1950 (Originally published 1937).

Howarth, Patrick. The Year Is 1851. London: Collins & Co., 1951.

Luckhurst, Kenneth W. The Story of Exhibitions. New York: Studio Publications, 1951.

Walford, Cornelius. Fairs, Past and Present. Clifton, N. J.: Augustus M. Kelley, 1968.

Young, G. M. Victorian England: Portrait of an Age. New York: Oxford University Press, 1964 (Originally published 1936).

THE AUSTRALIAN GOLD RUSH (1851-1854)

On January 24, 1848, James Wilson Marshall discovered gold in a mill race at Coloma, California, on the American River. It was this discovery which set off the California gold rush of 1849. Emigrants from virtually every part of Europe, China, Australia

and the South American countries found their way to San Francisco
and from there to the mines in the Sierras beyond Sacramento.

Some of the miners struck it rich; many others did not. One
of the latter was Edward Hammond Hargraves, an Englishman who
came to San Francisco from Australia on the Elizabeth Archer
in 1849, hoping to make his fortune.

He returned to Australia in 1851, arriving in Sydney on
January 7, no richer than when he had left. He was convinced
that although he had not made a strike in California, gold existed
in Australia and he was the man to find it. This belief was not
unreasonable. Small amounts of gold had been found there as early as 1823 and as recently as 1848.

Hargraves sent two letters to Deas Thomson, secretary to
Governor Charles FitzRoy, stating that he could find gold in Australia. These letters remained unanswered, the administration
feeling that a gold strike would attract criminals and other unde-
sirables, as had been the case in San Francisco. It suppressed
news of all gold discoveries "for fear of agitating the public mind. "
However, Hargraves obtained a grubstake of 105 pounds from William Northwood, a Sydney alderman. By this arrangement Northwood was to be reimbursed with half of any gold Hargraves found.

In early February, 1851, Hargraves traveled by horseback
from Sydney to Bathurst, some 125 miles west, across the Blue
Mountains. He talked with Thomas Icely, the owner of a gigantic
cattle, sheep and horse ranch and a respected man of means who
was, as a sideline, mining copper on his lands and who had found
samples of gold there. Icely directed him to Guyong Inn, 21 miles
from Bathurst. Near there he and Johnnie Lister, the son of the
proprietress of the inn, panned a few specks of gold, the only gold
that Hargraves was to discover in Australia.

He returned to Sydney, arriving on March 29. There he
obtained an interview with Thomson, but received no encouragement
concerning his mining project. He then was granted an interview
with Governor FitzRoy, who referred him back to Thomson, from
whom he asked a reward of 500 pounds for his "discovery. " As
Hargraves had brought no gold with him to substantiate his story,
Thomson remained skeptical and suggested that Hargraves submit
his request in writing, following which the colonial government
would give it "proper consideration. "

Hargraves enlisted the aid of Enoch William Rudder, a fellow goldseeker who had been to California. Rudder published a
story concerning Hargraves' "discovery" in the Sydney Morning
Herald and on the same day that this appeared (April 4, 1851) Secretary Thomson received the letter he had requested from Hargraves.
On April 15 Thomson wrote, saying that the colonial government
would not award Hargraves the 500 pounds he requested but that,
if a valid discovery was made, "a reward would undoubtedly

be granted, the amount depending on the field's nature and value. "

In the meantime Johnnie Lister and his friend William Tom had gone prospecting in the area near the Guyong Inn and on April 7 had made a sizeable strike. Hargraves was advised of this, the news appeared in the Herald on April 29 and Governor FitzRoy authorized the 500 pound reward to Hargraves, who later received considerably more. Hargraves paid William Northwood 250 pounds as agreed under the grubstake arrangement, but insisted on having the partnership papers returned to him, thus relieving himself of the necessity of making any further payments to his former associate.

Hargraves announced the gold discovery far and wide and shortly thereafter the rush to Bathurst began. Gold was found there in great abundance, one "poor but honest Scot" panning a lump of the precious metal weighing 46 3/4 ounces. Fantastic but true tales of immense individual strikes were published in the Herald and these induced thousands of persons, first from Australia and then from virtually all parts of the world, to seek their fortunes "down under. "

Additional strikes were made at Ballarat, Bendigo and other Australian areas. Ballarat became the richest alluvial gold field ever known. By 1853 it had produced more than 300 million dollars worth of gold, more than California's total production by 1870. Bendigo, 75 miles to the north, produced an unbelievable amount of wealth.

During the decade which followed 1850 the Australian population increased by nearly 300 percent. Large numbers of Chinese were among the immigrants and several race riots broke out. As a consequence the Australian government imposed severe restrictions on immigration from China which led to the so-called "white Australia" policy.

The increased population generated an augmented demand for foodstuffs and other consumer goods. The industrial structure, accordingly, lost its generally one-sided pastoral character and became more diversified. The huge land holdings of the pastoralists were gradually broken up, becoming comparatively small farms. Protective tariffs replaced the old free trade policies and industrial expansion led to trade unionism.

Suggested Readings

Anderson, R. S. Australian Gold Fields. Edited by George Mackaness. Sydney: 1956.
Australian Encyclopedia. East Lansing, Mich. : Michigan State College Press, 1958.
Barrett, Charles L. , ed. Gold in Australia. London: Oxford University Press, 1951.
Blainey, Geoffrey. The Rush That Never Ended. Melbourne: 1963.

Churchward, L. G.   "The American Contribution to the Victorian
    Gold Rush," Victorian Historical Magazine, June, 1942.
    _____. Australia and America (unpublished M. A. dissertation,
    University of Melbourne, 1941).
Clacy, Mrs. Charles.   A Lady's Visit to the Gold Diggings of Au-
    stralia in 1852-53.   London: 1853.
Crawford, R. M. , and G. F. James.   "The Gold Rushes and the
    Aftermath, 1851-1901" in Grattan, A. Hartley, ed.   Australia.
    Berkeley, Calif. :   University of California Press, 1947.
Davison, Simpson.   The Discovery and Geognosy of Gold Deposits
    in Australia.   London: 1860.
Earp, G. B.   The Gold Colonies of Australia and Gold Seeker's
    Manual.   London: 1852.
Erskine, John Elphinstone.   A Short Account of the Late Discov-
    eries of Gold in Australia.   London: 1852.
Glasson, W. R.   Australia's First Goldfield.   Sydney: 1944.
Jackson, Joseph Henry.   Anybody's Gold: The Story of California's
    Mining Towns.   New York: Appleton, 1941.
Monagham, Jay.   Australians and the Gold Rush: California and
    Down Under, 1849-1854.   Berkeley, Calif. :   University of Cal-
    ifornia Press, 1966.
Paul, Rodman W.   California Gold: The Beginning of Mining in the
    Far West.   Cambridge, Mass. :   Harvard University Press,
    1947.
    _____. Mining Frontiers in the Far West.   New York: Holt,
    Rinehart, 1963.
Place, Marian T.   Gold Down Under: The Story of the Australian
    Gold Rush.   New York: Crowell-Collier Press, 1969.
Pyke, N. O. P.   Foreign Immigration to the Gold Fields (unpublished
    M. A. dissertation, University of Sydney, 1946).
Sherer, John.   The Gold-Finder of Australia.   London: 1853.
Swift, David, and Heinz Marcuse.   "The Golden Century," Mining
    and Geological Journal, September, 1951.

THE CRIMEAN WAR (1853-1856)

The Crimean War of 1853-1856 between the Russian Empire
and Turkey, supported by France, Great Britain and Sardinia, was
the result of the aggressive policy of Tsar Nicholas I of Russia toward the Ottoman Empire.   The Tsar believed the collapse of Turkey (the Ottoman Empire) to be imminent.   He wished to destroy
the Anglo-French alliance on the Eastern Question and suggested to
the British that they and Russia agree on the division of Turkish
territory prior to the breakdown of the Ottoman Empire.   The British, in turn, feared that the dissolution of the Empire would upset
stability in the Near East and thus threaten their control in India.
Accordingly, they supported the Turks.

The immediate cause of the war was the Russian assertion,
in May, 1853, of a protectorate over Greek Christians in the Turk-

ish dominions. France was the traditional protector of the Latin, or Roman Catholic, Church in the Holy Land and Russia considered herself the protector of the Greek Orthodox Church in the same region. Louis Napoleon (Napoleon III), who had been elected president of the Second French Republic, negotiated with the Turks and agreed to allot equal authority over the holy places to both Latins and Greeks, but Russia remained firm in her demands for Greek control.

Russia's demands brought most of the European powers into extended diplomatic negotiations. Great Britain and France sided with Turkey, as they felt that Russia posed a threat to their positions in the Near East. When Prince Alexander Menshikov, the Russian diplomat and military leader, appeared in Constantinople and demanded that Turkey accept his country as the protector of all the Greek Christians in the Ottoman Empire, the Turks indignantly refused to comply.

On October 23, 1853, Turkey declared war on Russia and in March of the following year France and Great Britain entered the conflict, siding with Turkey. An Anglo-French force was sent to the Crimea, the British troops being commanded by General Fitzroy Raglan and the French serving under Marshal Armand Saint-Arnaud. The Battle of Alma River, fought on September 20, resulted in the defeat of the Russian forces commanded by Menshikov. The siege of Sevastopol by the French and British began in early October and on October 25 the Russians attacked a British unit at Balaklava. It was here that the disaster which inspired Alfred, Lord Tennyson's 1854 poem, "The Charge of the Light Brigade," occurred. The Russians were defeated in the following battle which occurred on November 5.

The winter of 1854-1855 was severe and further hostilities were postponed until spring. The sufferings of the Allied troops from hunger, cold and disease were intensified by incompetent supply planning on the part of the high command. Their sufferings would have been worse had it not been for the activities of Florence Nightingale, the English nurse, hospital reformer and philanthropist who, in 1854, took 38 nurses to Scutari. She organized barrack hospitals, introduced sanitation and thereby reduced the number of cases of typhus, cholera and dysentery.

In January, 1855, Sardinia declared war on Russia and in April Allied armies, reinforced with additional troops and serving under new commanders, resumed hostilities. The siege of Sevastopol continued throughout the summer and a Russian army was defeated at Tchernaya on August 16. Sevastopol fell to the Allies on September 8 and the Russians were forced to withdraw, virtually ending the war.

A peaceful settlement was concluded in February, 1856, by the Treaty of Paris, with all the belligerents cooperating. Russia made a number of concessions to the Allied powers, including re-

nunciation of her protectorate over the Danubian principalities and
the withdrawal of her warships from the Black Sea. European interests in the Ottoman Empire were further defined and Count Ca-
millo di Cavour of Sardinia was able to air the Italian Question.

Suggested Readings

Aubry, Octave.   The Second Empire.   Philadelphia: Lippincott,
    1940.
Bolton, Sarah K.   "Florence Nightingale, Nurse (1820-1908)" in
    her Lives of Girls Who Became Famous.   New York: Crowell,
    1949.
Case, Lynn M.   French Opinion on War and Diplomacy During the
    Second Empire.   Philadelphia: University of Pennsylvania Press,
    1954.
Corley, Thomas A. B.   Democratic Despot: A Life of Napoleon III.
    London: Barrie and Rockliff, 1961.
Cross, Arthur Lyon.   A Shorter History of England and Greater
    Britain.   New York: Macmillan, 1929.
Fuller, John F. C.   A Military History of the Western World.   New
    York: Funk & Wagnalls, 1954.
Gooch, Brison D.   The New Bonapartist Generals in the Crimean
    War: Distrust and Decision-Making in the Anglo-French Alli-
    ance.   The Hague: Martinus Nijhoff, 1959.
Gooch, George P.   The Second Empire.   London: Longmans,
    Green, 1960.
Guérard, Albert.   Napoleon III.   Cambridge, Mass. :   Harvard
    University Press, 1943.
Hallbert, Charles W.   Franz Joseph and Napoleon III, 1852-1864:
    A Study of Austro-French Relations.   New York: Bookman
    Associates, 1955.
Henderson, Gavin B.   Crimean War Diplomacy and Other Historical
    Essays.   Glasgow: Glasgow University Press, 1947.
Hingley, Ronald.   Tsars, 1533-1917.   New York: Macmillan, 1968.
Kinglake, Alexander William.   The Invasion of the Crimea.   Lon-
    don: William Blackwood & Sons, 1863-1887.
Puryear, Vernon J.   England, Russia, and the Straits Question,
    1844-1856.   Berkeley, Calif. :   University of California Press,
    1931.
Riasanovsky, Nicholas Valentine.   A History of Russia.   New York:
    Oxford University Press, 1963.
Sencourt, Robert.   Napoleon III, the Modern Emperor.   New York:
    Appleton-Century, 1934.
Syme, Ronald.   Invaders and Invasions.   New York: Norton, 1964.
Temperley, Harold W.   England and the Near East: The Crimea.
    London: Longmans, Green, 1936.
Tennyson, Alfred.   "The Charge of the Light Brigade" in The Com-
    plete Poetical Works of Tennyson.   Boston: Houghton Mifflin,
    1898 (Originally written 1854).
Terry, Benjamin.   A History of England from the Earliest Times
    to the Death of Queen Victoria.   Chicago: Scott, Foresman,
    1901.

Williams, Roger. The World of Napoleon III, 1851-1870 (Gaslight
    and Shadow). New York: Collier Books, 1962.
Zeldin, Theodore. The Political System of Napoleon III. New
    York: St. Martin's Press, 1958.

THE PALMER POISON CASE (1855)

Dr. William Palmer, an English surgeon, gambler and wom-
anizer, may or may not have also been a mass poisoner. In November, 1855, he was arrested and charged with the murder of
John Parsons Cook, his friend. He was convicted, largely on circumstantial evidence, and was hanged the following year. It was
suspected, though never proved, that he was responsible for the
poison deaths of fourteen other people.

Palmer was the son of an alcoholic, profligate mother and
a dishonest businessman father. When his mother was widowed each
of her seven children received seven thousand pounds from the father's estate, the money to be paid to each when he reached the age
of 21. Jane Widnall, a fortune-hunter who thought Palmer had already come into his inheritance, seduced him and he stole money
from his employer to pay for an abortion. Prosecution was avoided
only because Palmer's mother made financial restitution.

A man named Abley, with whose wife Palmer was said to
be involved, died. Palmer was suspected of being responsible, although this was never proved. In 1845 he studied surgery at Bart's
Hospital in London. Here he became addicted to gambling. Though
qualified as a medical man his financial affairs were chaotic and
he decided to marry for money. His wife was Annie Brooks, the
daughter of a colonel whose four brothers had all committed suicide,
and who later shot himself.

Annie was devoted to her husband who built up a thriving
medical practice, only to lose his money at the race track. He also had several mistresses. Annie and Palmer had a son, Willy.
She wanted nothing further except the society of her mother who
had, since her husband's suicide, become an alcoholic. The mother
came to live with her daughter and son-in-law, and in two weeks
she was dead. Palmer had inherited nine houses from her estate
and it was whispered that he had "done her in" in order to inherit,
even though the houses were in disrepair and rehabilitating them
cost the doctor a good deal of money.

The rumors continued. Palmer visited his uncle and the
next day the old man died. He had two illegitimate children, both
of whom died shortly after their father visited them. Annie had
four children after Willy, these dying in convulsions while still infants. A friend named Bladon visited Palmer and died a week later. The purpose of his visit was to collect some money the doc-

tor owed him. Bladon's death was followed by that of a man named
Bly, to whom Palmer owed 800 pounds.

The next to die was Palmer's wife Annie, who had caught
a slight cold. Dr. Bamford, who treated her, diagnosed her ail-
ment as "English cholera. " The rumors that Palmer was a poisoner persisted.

Nine months after Annie's death Palmer's housekeeper gave
birth to his illegitimate son. The baby died. The doctor's financial affairs worsened and he attempted to recoup by gambling but
lost more than he won. He fell into the hands of usurers. Then
his brother Walter, an alcoholic and gambler, entered the picture.
His health was poor and his money had gone largely for gin. Dr.
Palmer proposed that he insure his brother's life and keep him
supplied with liquor, with the understanding that after Walter passed
on he would "get it back in full. " Walter agreed, and William in-
sured his brother's life for 13,000 pounds. He had attempted to
purchase a policy worth 82,000 pounds but the insurance officials,
suspicious since the death of Annie Palmer, refused to approve the
larger sum.

Shortly afterwards Walter Palmer was found dead. The coroner stated that the death was due to apoplexy. William put in a
claim on the insurance policy and the insurance company instituted
an investigation. Payment on the policy was held up.

Dr. Palmer met an old friend, John Parsons Cook, at the
racetrack. Cook had won some substantial bets and was in funds.
He treated Palmer and some other friends to supper, followed by
brandy. Cook became ill and Palmer took him to his home in
Rugeley "where he could look after him. " Dr. Bamford was called
in and under his ministrations Cook began to improve. In the meantime Palmer had taken Cook's money and paid some of his more
pressing financial obligations. A day or two later Cook was dead.
Dr. Bamford, who signed the death certificate, certified that the
death was due to an "apoplectic seizure. " The dead man's step-
father arrived. He became suspicious when Palmer told him that
Cook owed him 4,000 pounds.

A post-mortem revealed that Cook had died of tetanus. No
strychnine was found in the body but a witness testified that Palmer
had purchased strychnine from him. When it was suggested that
this substance can cause death by tetanus Palmer was arrested and
charged with the murder of his friend Cook.

The bodies of his brother and wife were exhumed and examined, and no poison was found in either. He was not indicted for
his brother Walter's death as the evidence was insufficient.

Dr. William Palmer was tried in London. The medical men
called to testify disagreed among themselves, some contending that
Cook's body contained strychnine and others holding that it did not.
Nevertheless, Palmer was found guilty of murder and hanged.

Suggested Readings

Abrahamsen, David, M. D.   The Murdering Mind.   New York: Harper & Row, 1973.

Bromberg, Walter.   Mold of Murder: A Psychiatric Study of Homicide.   New York: Grune & Stratton, 1961.

Catton, Joseph.   Behind the Scenes of Murder.   New York: Norton, 1940.

"The Doctor Who Prescribed Death" in Crimes and Punishment, Vol. 4.   Editorial presentation: Jackson Morley.   London: BPC, 1973.

Guttmacher, M. S.   The Mind of the Murderer.   Freeport, N. Y. : Books for Libraries, 1960.

Jesse, F. Tennyson.   Murder and Its Motives.   London: Harrap, 1952.

Lester, David, and Gene Lester.   Crime of Passion: Murder and the Murderer.   Chicago: Nelson Hall, 1975.

McDade, Thomas M. , compiler.   The Annals of Murder.   Norman, Okla. : University of Oklahoma Press, 1961.

Reinhardt, James Melvin.   The Psychology of Strange Killers. Springfield, Ill. : Thomas, 1962.

Scott, Sir Harold, with Philippa Pearce.   From Inside Scotland Yard.   New York: Macmillan, 1965.

Thompson, Laurence Victor.   The Story of Scotland Yard.   New York: Random House, 1954.

Wilson, Colin, and Patricia Pitman.   Encyclopedia of Murder.   New York: Putnam, 1962.

Wolfgang, Marvin E. , compiler.   Studies in Homicide.   New York: Harper & Row, 1967.

THE DISCOVERY OF THE NEANDERTHAL MAN (1856)

The exact chronology of the development of the modern human species, Homo sapiens, is uncertain.   Paleontologists and anthropologists differ in their conclusions on many points but are generally agreed that the first European race of true men was the Cro-Magnon, so-called after the fossil bones found in the Cro-Magnon Cave in Dordogne, France.   Other similar finds in various parts of the world have provided information concerning extinct species which are regarded as direct or collateral evolutionary ancestors of the modern human species.

One of the more important of such discoveries was that of the skull and portions of a human skeleton found in the Feldhofen Cave of the Neanderthal Ravine near Düsseldorf, Germany, in 1856. Professor Johann Carl Fuhlrott of the Realschule in Elberfeld was able to obtain fourteen separate pieces.   The skull was considered human but not so fully developed as the skull of 20th-century humans, being somewhat apelike.

When reconstructed the head was exceedingly long (dolicho-
cephalic), had virtually no chin, a rounded, sloping forehead and
eyes that were large and set wide apart. The eyes were surmount-
ed by a prominent ridge, not unlike that of apes. The Neanderthal's
hands were prehensile and he was comparatively short, being less
than 5' 4" in height. Some anthropologists feel that he walked with
an ape-like crouch and others believe that he walked completely
erect. His feet were similar to those of modern man and not prehensile, as is the case with apes' feet. He is supposed to have
lived on earth from 150,000 years ago until as recently as 25,000
years ago.

Professor Fuhlrott's discovery precipitated a great controversy in European scientific circles. This concerned the exact
nature of the being whose skull had been found. One school, headed by Rudolf Virchow, a German pathologist and anthropologist, contended that the skull was that of an individual who had suffered
from a bone disease which caused the cranium to become deformed.
Others felt that it was that of "an ordinary savage of ancient days"
who had been born with a malformed skull.

Thomas Henry Huxley, an English biologist and author, took
issue with Virchow and his associates. In his book, Man's Place
in Nature (1863) he emphasized the apelike characteristics of the
Neanderthal skull, calling it "the most pithecoid cranium yet discovered. " He did not feel, however, that the Neanderthal fossils
"represented an intermediate type between men and apes. "

The French surgeon and anthropologist Paul Broca, a pioneer in the science of modern craniology who accepted the theories
of Charles Darwin, maintained that the Neanderthal skull was a possible key to human evolution. The contention of the Huxley-Broca
school that the Neanderthal skull "must have belonged to an 'early
man'" was substantiated in 1886 when two similar skeletons were
found in the Cave of Spy, in Belgium. Also found were some chipped
tools, made from stone, from which scientists infer that the
two skeletons were of beings more man than ape.

In 1887-1895 Marie Eugène F. T. Dubois, a Dutch anatomist
and paleontologist, served as a military surgeon in the Dutch East
Indies. Excavating in Java he discovered, on the bank of the Solo
River, bones of an animal apparently intermediate between man and
the existing anthropoid apes. This "Java Man" he named Pithecan-
thropus erectus. Scientists concluded that the Java Man had been
"closer to human type than to ancient ones, " which served to establish the Neanderthal Man as belonging to a similar catagory.

Other evidence of man's evolution came to light with the discoveries of such fossils as those of the Cro-Magnon Man, the Hei-
delberg Man, the Saldanha Man and the Peking Man. It was learned
that the Neanderthal Man was comparatively numerous and skeletal
fossils of this genus have been found in Europe, North Africa and
Western Asia.

Suggested Readings

Andrews, Roy Chapman. Meet Your Ancestors. New York: Viking Press, 1963.
Bastian, Hartmut. And Then Came Man. New York: Viking Press, 1963.
Borer, Mary Cathcart. Mankind in the Making. London: Frederick Warne, 1962.
Boyd, William C. , Ph. D. , and Isaac Asimov, Ph. D. Races and People. New York: Abelard-Schuman, 1955.
Breuil, Henri, and Raymond Lantier. The Men of the Old Stone Age. New York: St. Martin's Press, 1965.
Constable, George, and the editors of Time-Life. The Neanderthals. New York: Time-Life Books, 1973.
Day, Michael H. Fossil Man. New York: Grosset & Dunlap, 1970.
De Chardin, Pierre Teilhard. The Appearance of Man. New York: Harper & Row, 1965.
Huxley, Thomas Henry. Man's Place in Nature. Ann Arbor, Mich. : University of Michigan Press, 1959 (Originally published 1863).
McKern, Thomas W. , and Sharon McKern. Human Origins: An Introduction to Physical Anthropology. Englewood Cliffs, N. J. : Prentice-Hall, 1969.
Megaw, Vincent, and Rhys Jones. The Dawn of Man. New York: Putnam, 1972.
Morris, Desmond. The Naked Ape: A Zoologist's Study of the Human Animal. New York: McGraw-Hill, 1967.
Pfeiffer, John E. The Emergence of Man. New York: Harper & Row, 1969.
Silverberg, Robert. The Morning of Mankind. New York: Graphic Society Publishers, 1967.
Vlahos, Olivia. Human Beginnings. New York: Viking Press, 1966.

THE BACONIAN THEORY (1857)

William Shakespeare is considered one of the greatest dramatists and poets of all time. His plays, written between c. 1590 and 1613, are constantly being performed and his life and works have been the subjects of a vast amount of research. He was preceded by Robert Greene, Henry Medwall, John Heywood, Nicholas Udall, William Stevenson and George Gascoigne, among others, whose works still live. His contemporaries included such great playwrights as Ben Jonson, Thomas Dekker, John Webster, Francis Beaumont, John Fletcher, Christopher Marlowe and Philip Massinger. However, when Tudor or Jacobean drama is mentioned, it is Shakespeare who comes first to mind.

Not much is known about Shakespeare's life. He was born at Stratford-upon-Avon in 1564, the son of a glover and dealer in farm produce. He was educated in the Stratford Grammar School

where he studied Latin, Greek and the plays of Plautus and Terence.
By 1592 he was established in London as an actor-playwright and
prospered financially.   He and his associate Richard Burbage performed at the Globe Theater which they had organized.   After his
death in 1616 Henry Condell and John Heminges, actors at the
Globe, decided to print, in more accurate versions than were then
available, the plays already published and eighteen additional plays
not previously published in quarto.   This, the famous First Folio,
was printed by Isaac Iaggard and Ed. Blount in 1623.   It did not
include Pericles.   Three other folios were published between 1632
and 1685.   The Third Folio added six other plays ascribed to Shakespeare, but these are apocryphal.

About the middle of the nineteenth century it was suggested
that the plays attributed to Shakespeare were not, in fact, written
by him but by Sir Francis Bacon, the English philosopher, statesman and essayist.   In 1857 Delia Salter Bacon, an American author,
published The Philosophy of the Plays of Shakespeare Unfolded.   This
book, which had a preface by Nathaniel Hawthorne, credited Bacon
with the authorship of the plays.   This, the "Baconian Theory," has
attracted its adherents but most students of English literature and
history have rejected it.

The Baconian Theory is two-fold.   It attempts to show that
Shakespeare, with only a grammar school education, could not possibly have written the plays attributed to him.   Second, it seeks to
demonstrate Bacon's authorship.

No manuscript of any play in Shakespeare's writing has survived and little, as mentioned above, is known of his life.   Consequently, the supporters of the Baconian Theory argue, there is little to identify Shakespeare as the author of the dramas.

The contention that Bacon wrote the plays is based on the
fact that certain passages in Bacon's writings are similar to passages in the plays.   Also, Ignatius Donnelly, an American politician
and writer, in The Great Cryptogram, published in 1888, hoped to
prove that a cipher or code containing cryptic disclosures of Bacon's
authorship can be detected in the plays.

Scholars feel that the parallel passages consist of phrases
in common use at the time, and the cryptic disclosures are so obscure and tenuous that many Baconians deny their authenticity.

In 1957 William F. Friedman and his wife Elizabeth, both
cryptographers, made an analysis of the evidence furnished by the
Baconians to support the cipher theory.   In their book, The Shakespearean Ciphers Examined, they conclude that no evidence in Shakespeare's literary output exists which would support rival claims to
authorship.

People other than Bacon have been suggested as the true
authors of Shakespeare's plays.   These include Edward de Vere,

17th Earl of Oxford, and Sir Walter Raleigh, the English author and navigator. In his 1955 book Murder of the Man Who Was Shakespeare, Calvin Hoffman, an American dramatic critic, maintains that Christopher Marlowe, author of Tamburlaine the Great, The Jew of Malta and other plays, was not killed by Ingram Frisar in a tavern brawl in 1593 but after that date lived incognito, writing under Shakespeare's name. Drama authorities do not take any of these proposals seriously.

Suggested Readings

Anderson, Fulton H. Francis Bacon. Los Angeles: University of Southern California Press, 1962.

Bacon, Delia Salter. The Philosophy of the Plays of Shakespeare Unfolded. New York: AMS Press, 1970 (Originally published 1857).

Bacon, Francis. Selected Writings. With an introduction and notes by Hugh G. Dick. New York: Modern Library, 1955 (Originally written early 17th century).

Churchill, R. C. Shakespeare and His Betters. Bloomington, Ind. : Indiana University Press, 1959.

Chute, Marchette. Shakespeare of London. New York: Dutton, 1949.

_____. Stories from Shakespeare. New York: New American Library, 1956.

Crowther, James G. Francis Bacon, the First Statesman of Science. London: Cresset Press, 1960.

Donnelly, Ignatius. The Great Cryptogram: Francis Bacon's Cipher in the So-Called Shakespeare Plays. East Saint Claire Shores, Mich: Scholarly Press, 1970 (Originally published 1888).

Durant, Will. "Francis Bacon" in his The Story of Philosophy. Garden City, N. Y. : Garden City Publishing Co. , 1926.

Eiseley, Loren. Francis Bacon and the Modern Dilemma. Lincoln, Neb. : University of Nebraska Press, 1962.

Elliott, John W. Writings of Sir Francis Bacon. New York: Monarch, 1966 (Originally written early 17th century).

Farrington, Benjamin. Francis Bacon: Philosopher of Industrial Science. London: Lawrence and Wisehart, 1951.

Friedman, William F. , and Elizabeth Friedman. The Shakespearean Ciphers Examined. London: Cambridge University Press, 1957.

Frye, Roland Mushat. Shakespeare: The Art of the Dramatist. Boston: Houghton Mifflin, 1970.

Green, Adwin Wigfall. Sir Francis Bacon. New York: Twayne, 1966.

Hart, J. C. "Who Wrote Shakespeare? " Chambers's Journal, June, 1852.

Hoffman, Calvin. The Murder of the Man Who Was Shakespeare. London: Messner, 1955.

Holmes, Judge Nathaniel. The Authorship of Shakespeare. London: 1866-1886.

374　　　　　　　　　　　　Footnotes to World History

Lang, Andrew.　Shakespeare, Bacon and the Great Unknown.　New
　　York: AMS Press, 1912.
Patrick, John M.　Francis Bacon.　London: Longmans, Green,
　　1961.
Rowse, Alfred L.　Shakespeare the Man.　New York: Harper &
　　Row, 1973.
Smith, William Henry.　Bacon and Shakespeare: An Enquiry Touch-
　　ing Players, Playhouses, and Playwriters in the Days of Eliz-
　　abeth.　London: 1857.
Wadsworth, Frank W.　The Poacher from Stratford: A Partial Ac-
　　count of the Controversy Over the Authorship of Shakespeare's
　　Plays.　Berkeley, Calif.: University of California Press, 1958.
Wright, Louis B.　"The Anti-Shakespeare Industry and the Growth
　　of Cults," Virginia Quarterly Review, Vol. XXXV, 1959.

THE INDIAN (SEPOY) MUTINY (1857-1859)

　　　　The Indian (or Sepoy) Mutiny was a rebellion against British
authority by Indian natives and sepoys (native troops employed by
the East India Company) lasting from May, 1857 to July, 1859.
British rule in India, exercised by the Company, was generally resented by the natives for a number of reasons.　The annexation of
Indian territory by the Company and British disregard for Hindu
and Moslem religious customs were major contributing factors.

　　　　Sepoys were equipped with breech-loading Enfield rifles, the
cartridges for which were greased with tallow and lard, substances
taboo to them.　The requirement that the native troops come into
contact with these greases met with great opposition and led to a
number of minor mutinies at various military posts.

　　　　On May 10, 1857, a native garrison at Meerut, near Delhi,
mutinied rather than handle the greased cartridges.　This mutiny
resulted in the massacre of British officers and Europeans in the
area.　The following morning Delhi was attacked and many Europeans were killed.

　　　　The revolt spread under the leadership of Bahadur Shah II,
emperor of the Mogul Empire.　Natives in many parts of India
joined the uprising, led by Nana Sahib who declared himself to be
the adopted son of Baji Rao II, the last Peshwa of Poona.

　　　　In June, 1857, General Sir Hugh Wheeler, military commander at Cawnpore, surrendered to Nana Sahib.　The captives, approximately 780 in all, including women and children, were massacred
although they had been promised safe conduct to Allahabad.

　　　　On July 16 Cawnpore was relieved by a detachment under
Sir Henry Havelock.　The British Residency at Lucknow was relieved by Sir Colin Campbell on November 17, having been besieged

since June 30. Delhi had also been recaptured by the British, and
by June, 1858, the mutineers were virtually overcome, although
sporadic fighting continued until 1859. Tantia Topa, a Brahman
leader, was captured and executed in April, 1859. Bahadur Shah
II had been captured and sentenced to life imprisonment in 1858.

As a result of the mutiny, the East India Company lost its
governmental authority in India, which was assumed by the British
crown.

Suggested Readings

Chattopadhyaya, Haraprasad. The Sepoy Mutiny, 1857: A Social
    Study and Analysis. New York: Bookland, 1957.
Dangerfield, George. Bengal Mutiny: The Story of the Sepoy Re-
    bellion. New York: Harcourt, Brace, 1933.
Doyle, A. Conan. "The Sign of the Four" (fiction) in his Tales of
    Sherlock Holmes. New York: Grosset & Dunlap, n. d. (Orig-
    inally published 1890).
Edwards, Michael. A Season in Hell: The Defense of the Lucknow
    Residency. New York: Taplinger, 1973.
Embree, Ainslee T., ed. 1857 in India: Mutiny or War of Inde-
    pendence? Boston: Heath, 1963.
Farmer, Lydia. "Victoria" in her A Book of Famous Queens. Re-
    vised by Willard A. Heaps. New York: Crowell, 1964.
Fortescue, John W. A History of the British Army. New York:
    St. Martin's Press, 1899.
Foster, William. The East India House: Its History and Associa-
    tions. London: John Lane, 1924.
Herbert, David. Great Historical Mutinies, Comprising the Mutiny
    of the "Bounty," the Mutiny at Spithead, the Mutiny at the Nore,
    Mutinies in Highland Regiments, and the Indian Mutiny. Lon-
    don: Nimmo, 1876.
Hilton, Major-General Richard. The Indian Mutiny. London: Hol-
    lis & Carter, 1957.
_____. "The Massacre of Cawnpore" in Corbett, Edmund V.,
    ed. Great True Stories of Tragedy and Disaster. New York:
    Archer House, 1963.
Mallison, George B., ed. Kaye's and Mallison's History of the
    Indian Mutiny of 1857-58. Westport, Conn.: Greenwood Press,
    1968 (Originally published 1898).
Masters, John. The Nightrunners of Bengal (fiction). New York:
    Viking Press, 1951.
Metcalf, Thomas R. The Aftermath of Revolt: India, 1857-1870.
    Princeton, N. J.: Princeton University Press, 1964.
Sen, Surendra Nath. Eighteen Fifty-Seven. New York: Luzak,
    1957.
Spear, Thomas George. India: A Modern History. Ann Arbor,
    Mich.: University of Michigan Press, 1961.
Thompson, Edward J. The Other Side of the Medal. New York:
    Harcourt, Brace, 1926.

Trotter, Captain Lionel J. The Bayard of India: A Life of General Sir James Outram. New York: Dutton, 1909.
_____. History of India Under Queen Victoria from 1836 to 1880. London: Allen, 1886.

THE LAYING OF THE TRANSATLANTIC CABLE (1858-1866)

Samuel F. B. Morse perfected his invention, the electric telegraph, in 1837. After it was introduced he considered the possibilities of running his telegraph lines under rivers and larger bodies of water. In 1850 such an underwater line was laid between Calais and Dover, beneath the surface of the English Channel, and other similar lines were laid in the Mediterranean and Scandinavia.

In 1854 Cyrus W. Field, a wealthy American merchant, became interested in the project of laying a telegraph cable under the Atlantic Ocean. In that year the New York, Newfoundland and London Telegraph Company was organized, as was a European counterpart, known as the Atlantic Telegraph Company.

In 1857 an attempt was made to lay a submarine cable between Ireland and Newfoundland, but after some 350 miles of line had been paid out the cable broke. Two more attempts to lay the cable were made in 1858, the second of which was successful. On August 5, 1858, Queen Victoria sent a message of congratulation to President James Buchanan by way of Valentia, Ireland, to Trinity Bay, Newfoundland. The insulated cable, made of copper, was about 1,950 miles long and extended through water as much as two miles deep. Three weeks after the Queen's message had been transmitted the cable ceased to function because of inadequate insulation.

Over the next seven years, work financed by Field was performed to improve the electrical and mechanical aspects of marine cables. Such prominent engineers as Sir William Thompson (Lord Kelvin) worked on the problem and contributed much to its ultimate successful solution. In 1865 the Atlantic Telegraph Company chartered the gigantic steamship Great Eastern to lay a cable west from Valentia to Newfoundland. The work was supervised by Sir Daniel Gooch who was financially interested in the project. The cable broke after 1,200 miles had been laid and the venture was temporarily abandoned.

This failure resulted in the withdrawal of the backers from the Atlantic Telegraph Company. Field and Gooch organized a new corporation, the Anglo-American Company. On July 13, 1866, the laying of a new cable started, and two weeks later it stretched from Ireland to Newfoundland. The Great Eastern then grappled for and retrieved the lost 1865 cable. An extension was spliced to it and it was continued to Newfoundland.

Since 1866 telegraphic communication between the two continents has been continuous. The underwater cable remained the
fastest means of communication between the widely separated continents and is still used, although radio, the telephone and satellite
television now provide alternate means of transmitting information.

Suggested Readings

Bright, Charles. The Story of the Atlantic Cable. New York:
    1903.
_____. Submarine Telegraphs: Their History, Construction and
    Working. New York: Arno Press, 1974 (Originally published
    1898).
Carter, Samuel, III. Cyrus Field: Man to Two Worlds. New York:
    Putnam, 1968.
Clarke, Arthur C. Voice Across the Sea. New York: Harper &
    Row, 1958.
Dibner, Bern. The Atlantic Cable. Norwalk, Conn. : The Burndy
    Library, 1959.
Field, Henry Martyn. The History of the Atlantic Telegraph. Plain-
    view, N. Y. : Books for Libraries, 1972 (Originally published
    1867).
_____. The Story of the Atlantic Telegraph. New York: Arno
    Press, 1972 (Originally published 1892).
Garnham, S. A. and Robert L. Hadfield. The Submarine Cable.
    London: S. Low, Marston & Co. , 1934.
Haigh, Kenneth R. Cableships and Submarine Cables. London:
    Adlard Coles, 1958.
Judson, Isabella Field, ed. Cyrus W. Field, His Life and Work,
    1819-1892. New York MssInformation Corp. , 1972 (Originally
    published 1896).
McDonald, Philip B. A Saga of the Seas: The Story of Cyrus W.
    Field and the Laying of the First Atlantic Cable. New York:
    Wilson-Erickson, 1937.
Mullay, John. The Laying of the Telegraph Cable. New York:
    1858.
Reid, James D. The Telegraph in America. New York: 1886.

THE FOUNDING OF THE INTERNATIONAL
WORKINGMEN'S ASSOCIATION (1864)

The International Workingmen's Association, also known as
the "First International, " was founded at St. Martin's Hall, London,
on Wednesday, September 28, 1864. It was "the first society of
workingmen to be organized on an international scale for the establishment of socialism throughout the world. "

The London meeting had been preceded by other meetings between British and French trade unionists in 1862 and 1863. In 1862

preliminary contacts were made in London. In July of 1863 a
French delegation met with British labor unionists to protest Russia's suppressive actions against the Poles after the Polish uprising in January. At this 1863 meeting the idea of Anglo-French cooperation was suggested and the St. Martin's Hall meeting of 1864,
which was attended by representatives of Germany, Poland and Italy
as well as Great Britain and France, saw the formal organization
of the Association.

     Karl Marx, the German political philosopher, attended the
meeting and became a member of the executive committee. Although he had not taken an active part in the formation of the Association, he soon became its foremost member. He gave the in-
augural address, in which he advocated political action rather than
revolution, pointing out that the workers possessed a great advantage over the capitalists in that they far outnumbered them. He
declared the goal of the Association to be the amelioration of "the
misery of the toiling masses" through the "application of the simple
laws of mortality and justice. " He made the point that, although
production and wealth had greatly increased between 1848 and 1864,
the workers reaped no benefits from such increase. Like the Communist Manifesto, his address ended with the words, "Workers of
the world, unite!"

     Marx realized that the idea of revolution was distasteful to
many of the trade unionists. Generally speaking, the British members were concerned primarily with the banning of strike breakers
and considered the Association a means of preventing employers
from importing such "scabs. " The French, many of whom were
followers of Pierre Joseph Proudhon, a socialist who opposed political action, were mutualists.

     Annual meetings were held after 1866 at Geneva, Lausanne,
Brussels and Basel successively. The attendees advocated such
measures as nationalization of the means of production and communication in each country and a general strike in any country which
should "embark on an imperialist war. " From 1864 to 1870 the
size and scope of the membership of the Association increased from
the original 70,000 to an estimated 450,000, with members from
Belgium, Holland, Denmark, Switzerland, Spain, Austria-Hungary
and the United States swelling its ranks.

     By 1872 the Association had experienced a turning point for
the worse. After the victory of Prussia in the Franco-Prussian
War (1870-1871) the French workers established the Paris Commune,
a revolutionary government. The leaders of the Association gave
its support to the Commune and as a result of this action many of
the less radical members, primarily the British trade unionists,
resigned. When the Commune was overthrown in May, 1871, French
sections of the Association were suppressed, causing a further decline in membership.

     In the following year the Association was split when Mikhail

Aleksandronovich Bakunin, a Russian exile and anarchist who had
differed with Marx at the 1869 Basel congress, clashed with Marx
and the Association's leaders on matters of policy. Bakunin wished
the Association to be "a loose federal organization that would attack
authority in all its forms, particularly the state." Marx, in turn,
wished to operate the Association as a centralized organization which
would "capture the state and use it for the proletariat rather than
dissolve it." In 1872 Marx was able to have Bakunin and his followers expelled from the organization, following which its headquarters were established in New York City. It was formally dissolved at a congress held in Philadelphia in 1876.

The International Workingmen's Association was significant
in that it was "the first international organization to formulate and
attempt to apply the doctrines of revolutionary socialism." Socialist and Communist leaders in many countries later adopted these
doctrines. This was particularly true of the Second, or Labor and
Socialist, International, and the Third (Communist) International.

Suggested Readings

Berlin, Isaiah. Karl Marx: His Life and Environment. New York:
    Oxford University Press, 1935.
Carr, E. H. Michael Bakunin. New York: Random House, 1961
    (Originally published 1937).
Checkland, Sydney George. The Rise of Industrial Society in Eng-
    land, 1815-1885. London: St. Martin's Press, 1964.
Cole, G. H. D. Socialist Thought: Marxism and Anarchism, 1850-
    1890. New York: St. Martin's Press, 1964.
Flanders, Allan, and H. A. Clegg, eds. The System of Industrial
    Relations in Great Britain. London: Oxford University Press,
    1960.
Kitson Clarke, George S. R. The Making of Victorian England.
    Cambridge, Mass.: Harvard University Press, 1962.
Landauer, Carl. European Socialism: A History of Ideas and
    Movements. Berkeley, Calif.: University of California Press,
    1959.
Lichtheim, George. Marxism: An Historical and Critical Study.
    New York: Frederick A. Praeger, 1961.
Mehring, Franz. Karl Marx. Ann Arbor, Mich.: University of
    Michigan Press, 1962.
Nicolaevsky, Boris I. "Secret Societies and the First International"
    in Drachkovitch, Milorad M., ed. The Revolutionary Interna-
    tionals, 1864-1943. Palo Alto, Calif.: Stanford University
    Press, 1966.
Pelling, Henry. A History of British Trade Unionism. London:
    Oxford University Press, 1963.
_____. A Short History of the Labour Party. New York: St.
    Martin's Press, 1972.
Phelps Brown, Ernest H. The Economics of Labor. New Haven,
    Conn.: Yale University Press, 1962.
_____. The Growth of British Industrial Relations. London: Ox-
    ford University Press, 1959.

Thompson, David. England in the Nineteenth Century. Harmonds-
    worth, England: 1967.
United Kingdom Ministry of Labour. Industrial Relations Handbook.
    London: Her Majesty's Stationery Office, 1961.
Woodward, Sir Llewellyn. The Age of Reform, 1815-1870. Oxford:
    Oxford University Press, 1962.

THE MEXICAN ADVENTURE OF MAXIMILIAN (1864-1867)

Following Mexico's acquisition of independence from Spain
in 1821 the conservatives, with minor exceptions, ruled until the
overthrow of Antonio López de Santa Anna by the liberals, led by
Juan Alvarez Benito Juárez, in 1855. The Juárez reign was characterized by financial and political instability and the situation was
one of great concern to the governments of England, France and
Spain. Nationals of these powers living in Mexico suffered great
financial losses and it was feared that the United States might an-
nex a portion, if not all, of that country.

In 1861 Juárez became president, having emerged victorious
in the civil war known as the War of Reform. His bankrupt government published a decree suspending payment of the foreign debt for
two years. England, France and Spain immediately entered into an
alliance of intervention. It was agreed to send an allied expedition
to force Juárez to honor his country's financial obligations, but Napoleon III, Emperor of France, who had been won over by Mexican
royalists, decided to establish a monarchy in Mexico.

Napoleon chose as ruler Archduke Ferdinand Maximilian Joseph, brother of Francis Joseph I, Emperor of Austria, and husband of Princess Charlotte (Carlota), daughter of Leopold I of Belgium. Maximilian agreed to assume the Mexican throne provided
the Mexican people would accept him as ruler and that England and
France would guarantee him their support. Achille Bazaine, French
commander-in-chief, secured pro-imperial plebiscites in those portions of Mexico where French troops were in control. A treaty
with Napoleon was arranged and on April 10, 1864, Maximilian accepted the throne.

In June the new emperor and his bride arrived in Mexico
City. They found themselves in trouble from the start. Maximilian
faced a republican-led insurrection. He declined to restore confiscated lands to the clergy. He antagonized the land owners by instigating an inquiry into the legality of land titles. He chose ex-
Confederates from the United States as colonists, thereby angering
both the Mexicans and the United States government. In February
the latter, which refused to recognize the new Mexican empire, demanded that the French withdraw their troops.

Napoleon realized that the Mexican venture was a failure and ordered the troops to return home. The United States gave unofficial aid to the Juárez government. Maximilian, alarmed at Napoleon's disregard of his pledge to support the Mexican empire, sent Carlota to France and to Pope Pius IX to ask for military aid. No such aid was forthcoming and Carlota, realizing that her husband's cause was hopeless, became insane.

In 1867 Juárez attacked. His forces besieged those of Maximilian who, betrayed by Miguel López, one of his officers, surrendered at Querétaro on the night of May 14. Maximilian was tried by court martial, convicted and executed by a firing squad on June 19, 1867. The Empress Carlota died in Belgium in 1927 without regaining her reason. Juárez was reelected President of Mexico for two terms between 1867 and 1872.

Suggested Readings

Baker, Nina Brown. Juárez, Hero of Mexico. New York: Vanguard Press, 1942.

Bancroft, Hubert Howe. The History of Mexico. San Rafael, Calif.: Bancroft Press, 1888.

Barnes, Nancy, pseud. Carlota, American Empress. New York: Messner, 1943.

Baz, Gustavo. Vida de Benito Juárez. Mexico: 1874.

Blancké, Wilton Wendell. Juárez of Mexico. New York: Frederick A. Praeger, 1971.

Cadenhead, Ivie Edward. Benito Juárez. New York: Twayne, 1973.

Case, Lynn M. French Opinion on War and Diplomacy During the Second Empire. Philadelphia: University of Pennsylvania Press, 1954.

Chase, Stuart. Mexico: A Study of Two Americas. New York: Macmillan, 1931.

Corley, Thomas A. B. Democratic Despot: A Life of Napoleon III. London: Barrie and Rockliff, 1961.

Corti, E. C. C. Maximilian and Charlotte in Mexico. New York: Knopf, 1928.

Coy, Harold. The Mexicans. Boston: Little, Brown, 1970.

Dabbs, Jack A. The French Army in Mexico, 1861-1867: A Study in Military Government. New York: Humanities Press, 1963.

Dawson, Daniel. The Mexican Adventure. London: George Bell & Sons, 1935.

Guedalla, Philip. The Second Empire. New York: Putnam's, 1922.

Hall, Frederick. Mexico and Maximilian. New York: Hurst & Co., 1867.

Harding, Bertita. Phantom Crown: The Story of Maximilian and Carlota. Indianapolis: Bobbs-Merrill, 1934.

Hyde, Harford Montgomery. Mexican Empire: The History of Maximilian and Carlota of Mexico. London: Macmillan, 1946.

Lally, Frank E. French Opposition to the Mexican Policy of the Second Empire. Baltimore: Johns Hopkins University Press, 1931.

Martin, Percy P. Maximilian in Mexico. London: 1914.
Rivera Cambas, Manuel. Historia de la Intervencion Europea y
  Norte Americano en Mexico del Imperio de Maximiliano de Haps-
  burgo. Mexico City: 1888.
Sencourt, Robert. Napoleon III: The Modern Emperor. New York:
  Appleton-Century, 1934.
Smith, Arthur D. Howden. Conqueror. Philadelphia: Lippincott,
  1933.
Strode, Hudson. Timeless Mexico. New York: Harcourt, Brace,
  1944.
Thompson, James M. Louis Napoleon and the Second Empire. New
  York: Noonday Press, 1955.
Vance, Marguerite. Ashes of Empire: Carlota and Maximilian of
  Mexico. New York: Dutton, 1959.
Williams, Roger. The World of Napoleon III, 1851-1870 (Gaslight
  and Shadow). New York: Collier Books, 1962.

THE MATTERHORN TRAGEDY (1865)

Edward Whymper (1840-1911) was a British artist, wood-en-
graver, illustrator, author and mountain climber. He is best known
for his successful attempt to climb the Matterhorn in July, 1865,
after seven previous failures.

Whymper was not a novice mountaineer. In 1861 he had
scaled Mont Pelvoux (12,970 feet) and in 1864 Barre des Écrins
(13,462 feet), the second highest and highest peaks, respectively,
in the French Dauphiné range. He regarded the Matterhorn as a
great challenge to mountain climbers. This Alpine peak, called by
the French Mont Cervin and by the Italians Monte Silvio, more than
14,000 feet high, is just southwest of Zermatt, between the Swiss
cantons of Velais and Piedmont. It was first scaled in July, 1865,
by a seven-man party of climbers led by Whymper. Four of the
party were lost.

Whymper's climbers consisted of himself, Lord Francis Douglas, guide Michel-Auguste Croz, Douglas Hadow, a minister named
Charles Hudson, known as "Old Peter," and the
latter's son, also named Peter and called "Young Peter." The sev-
en men camped overnight within 3,000 feet of the summit and next
day reached the topmost peak of the Matterhorn without incident.
There they raised a small flag and then, for an hour, enjoyed the
magnificent view. They were particularly elated because they had
beaten a rival party of climbers led by Jean-Antoine Carrel which
was also attempting to be first to reach the summit of the mountain.
Carrel, determined that the honor of the first ascent should go to
an Italian, had originally agreed to climb with the Whymper party
but had defected when an Italian team had appeared a few days before Whymper's departure and announced its plans to beat the Englishmen to the summit.

Whymper and his party then prepared to descend. While the leader completed a sketch of the summit the others arranged themselves in order, fastening themselves together in line with a mountaineer's rope, Croz in front. Then came Hadow, Hudson, Douglas and Old Peter. Whymper and Young Peter tied themselves together separately from the others and started after them. It was suggested that a rope be tied to the rocks to assist the party over a "difficult bit." Hudson, to whom Whymper made the suggestion, assented but the idea was not carried out.

At three in the afternoon Whymper and Young Peter tied on at the tail of the line, with Whymper bringing up the rear. Croz, leading the party, laid aside his ice axe and assisted Hadow with his descent, actually placing Hadow's feet in position on the slippery ice. Hadow stumbled and fell, knocking Croz over. The two men slid down the rocks to the cliff, dragging Hudson and Lord Douglas after them. Whymper and the Taugwalders braced themselves and seized the rope which broke halfway between Old Peter and Douglas. The four men in the lead--Croz, Hadow, Hudson and Douglas--disappeared over the edge of the cliff, to fall almost four thousand feet to their deaths on the Matterhorngletscher below.

The two Taugwalders panicked but Whymper was able to calm them. Under his direction they fastened the end of what was left of the rope to a rock. Whymper, examining the rope which had broken, found it to be the weakest of the three the party had brought with them.

Although the Taugwalders were completely unnerved Whymper managed to guide them to safety. Two hours later they "arrived at the snow upon the ridge descending toward Zermatt, and all peril was over."

Suggested Readings

Clark, Ronald W. The Day the Rope Broke: The Story of the First Ascent of the Matterhorn. New York: Harcourt, Brace, 1965.

Engel, Claire Éliane. "Edward Whymper" in her They Came to the Hills. London: Allen & Unwin, 1952.

Hindley, Geoffrey. "The Golden Age" in his The Roof of the World: Encyclopedia of Discovery and Exploration, Vol. 16. London: Aldus Books, 1971.

Kernahan, Coulson. In Good Company. Freeport, N.Y.: Books for Libraries, 1968.

Lunn, Sir Arnold Henry Moore. A Century of Mountaineering, 1857-1957. London: Allen & Unwin, 1957.

———. Matterhorn Centenary. Chicago: Rand McNally, 1965.

Rébuffat, Gaston. Men and the Matterhorn. Translated by Eleanor Brockett. New York: Oxford University Press, 1973.

———. On Ice and Snow and Rock. Translated by Patrick Evans. New York: Oxford University Press, 1971.

———. Starlight and Storm. Translated by Wilfrid Noyle and

Sir John Hunt; technique section translated by Roland LeGrand.
New York: Dutton, 1957.
_____, and Pierre Tairraz. Between Heaven and Earth. Trans-
lated by Eleanor Brockett. New York: Oxford University
Press, 1965.
Rey, Guido. The Matterhorn. Translated by J. E. C. Eaton. Ox-
ford: Basil Blackwell, 1949.
Whymper, Edward. "Adventure on the Matterhorn" in Thomas,
Lowell, ed. Great True Adventures. New York: Hawthorn
Books, 1955.
_____. Scrambles Amongst the Alps. Revised and edited by
Heg Tyndale. New York: Scribner's, 1937 (Originally pub-
lished 1871).

MENDEL'S LAW OF GENETICS (1865)

Gregor Johann Mendel was an Austrian botanist and Roman
Catholic priest. Following his graduation from the University of
Vienna he entered the Augustinian monastery at Brünn in 1843. Here,
using plants of the garden pea growing in the monastery garden as
his subjects, he began the experiments which extended over a period of eight years and culminated in his law of genetics.

Mendel began his experiments in hybridization prior to reading the works of Charles Darwin but eventually came to realize the
relationship of his own experiments to the theory of natural selection. His research, which involved the cross-breeding of tall and
dwarf varieties of pea, resulted in Mendel's law of hereditary transmission of physical characteristics. This law consists of three
principles: segregation, dominance and independent assortment.

The principle of segregation was evolved from Mendel's finding that entities of hereditary transmission (genes) occur in pairs
in the ordinary body cells but separate in the formation of sex cells,
with each member of the pair becoming part of a separate sex cell.

The inequality of effect of genes led to the principle of dominance. "Many genes can cause the expression of a characteristic
despite being paired with another gene which would otherwise express the characteristic differently." Here the stronger gene of
the pair is called "dominant" and the weaker is called "recessive."

The third principle of Mendel's law, that of independent assortment, was put forth when he discovered that "the expression of
a gene for any single characteristic, such as height, is usually not
influenced by the expression of another characteristic, such as the
color of the flower."

Mendel's experiments showed how natural selection could
work and also introduced a quantitative idea into biology, thus pro-

viding a scientific basis for further studies in heredity. He prepared a paper describing his findings and sent it to Karl Wilhelm
von Nägeli, a famous Swiss botanist. Nägeli was not particularly
impressed and returned the paper with derogatory comments concerning its merit. He refused to correspond further with Mendel
concerning the matter.

Having announced his findings in 1865 Mendel, in the following year, published a paper concerning his experiments and conclusions in the Brünn Natural History Society Transactions. This
was followed by another paper which appeared in 1870. Mendel had
been appointed abbot of the Brünn monastery and after 1868 made
no more experiments, devoting himself to administrative matters.
He died in 1884.

By the turn of the century three other botanists, working independently in the field of heredity, had accumulated sufficient data
to justify the publication of scientific papers concerning their findings. These botanists--Karl Erich Correns of Germany, Erich
Tschermak von Seysenegg of Austria and Hugo De Vries of the Neth-
erlands--while making literature searches on the subject discovered
Mendel's writings of a quarter of a century earlier. In 1900 these
three stated their own discoveries as confirmation of the earlier
work of the Catholic priest of the Brünn monastery.

Mendel's law of genetics is the basis of today's scientific
theory of heredity.

Suggested Readings

Auerbach, Charlotte. The Science of Genetics. New York: Harper,
    1961.
Carlson, Elof A. The Gene: A Critical History. Philadelphia:
    Saunders, 1966.
Caullery, Maurice. A History of Biology. New York: Walker,
    1966.
Dawes, Ben. A Hundred Years of Biology. London: Duckworth,
    1935.
Dunn, L. C. A Short History of Genetics. New York: McGraw-
    Hill, 1965.
Iltis, Hugo. Life of Mendel. New York: Norton, 1932.
Paterson, David. Applied Genetics: The Technology of Inheritance.
    New York: Doubleday, 1969.
Pomerantz, Charlotte. Why You Look Like You Whereas I Tend to
    Look Like Me. New York: Scott, 1969.
Sturtevant, Alfred Henry. A History of Genetics. New York: Har-
    per & Row, 1965.
Wallace, Bruce, and Adrian M. Srb. Adaptation. Englewood Cliffs,
    N. J. : Prentice-Hall, 1964.
Zirkle, Conway. Evolution, Marxian Biology, and Social Scene.
    Philadelphia: University of Pennsylvania Press, 1959.

THE DISCOVERY OF ANTISEPTIC SURGERY (1867)

Prior to the second half of the nineteenth century submitting to surgery was risky and dangerous. Until William T. G. Morton and Charles T. Jackson discovered in 1846 that sulphuric ether could be used as an anesthetizing agent, operations were accompanied by considerable pain to the patient. Surgical anesthesia eliminated the need for anyone to suffer excruciating agony while under the knife but it was found that following surgery many patients died or were left permanently debilitated or crippled. The medical profession did not know what caused such "hospital diseases" as tetanus, gangrene, erysipelas, septicemia and pyemia. Puerperal fever, also called "childbed fever," often contracted by women who gave birth to their children in hospitals, was generally fatal.

Joseph L. Lister, an English surgeon, is generally thought of as the discoverer of antiseptic surgery. Like so many others, however, he was preceded by earlier researchers in the same field. Dr. Ignaz Philipp Semmelweis, a Hungarian obstetrician, did pioneer research in puerperal fever and proved, in the 1840's, that it is contagious. He believed that the fever, coming from within the hospital rather than from the outside, was carried from one woman to another by the hands of the physicians and medical students making pre-natal examinations of female patients. By requiring that such examiners wash and disinfect their hands between examinations he was able to demonstrate, through his mortality records, that his theory was correct. His ideas, however, were not accepted by the medical profession.

Louis Pasteur, a French chemist, did basic research in bacteriology, putting his findings to practical use in the wine, beer and silk industries. He also proved that anthrax, chicken cholera and hydrophobia (rabies) are all caused by bacteria and in the 1880's developed a method of inoculating humans and animals with a mild form of disease, thus securing immunity.

In 1864 Lister, practicing in Glasgow, learned of Pasteur's work in putrefaction. Thomas Anderson, a professor of chemistry at the University of Glasgow, had called Lister's attention to Pasteur's research and suggested that some connection might exist between the French chemist's findings and the unanswered questions concerning the dreaded hospital diseases.

Lister duplicated several of Pasteur's experiments and concluded that the germ theory applied to gangrene, puerperal fever, pyemia and the others. He realized that some agent which would kill the bacteria was needed, and Anderson supplied a quantity of carbolic acid which, he thought, might be effective. This acid had been used to treat garbage in the city of Carlisle. It had been noted that cattle which had grazed in the fields near the garbage dumps had ceased to sicken when the acid had been used.

Lister used a carbolic acid solution on a patient in 1865, and also on subsequent patients. The first one died but the succeeding four survived and did not contract any of the hospital diseases. In 1867 he published a paper, "On a New Method of Treating Compound Fracture, Abscess, Etc. , " in Lancet, the journal of British medicine.

Years after Semmelweis had done his work with puerperal fever the results of his antiseptic methods came to Lister's attention. The latter found that he and the Hungarian obstetrician had independently reached essentially the same conclusions. Like Semmelweis, Lister found his concept of antiseptic surgery opposed by many practicing physicians, notably Dr. James Y. Simpson, a Scottish physician. However, hospital mortality statistics showed that Lister and his predecessor were correct and antiseptic surgery gained general acceptance in medical circles and today is practiced universally.

Joseph Lister was made First Baron Lister of Lyme Regis by Queen Victoria. He died in 1912.

Suggested Readings

Benz, Francis E. Pasteur: Knight of the Laboratory. New York: Dodd, Mead, 1938.

Burton, Mary June. Louis Pasteur: Founder of Microbiology. New York: Franklin Watts, 1963.

Cheyne, William Watson. Lister and His Achievement. London: Longmans, Green, 1925.

De Kruif, Paul. Microbe Hunters. Edited by Harry G. Grover. New York: Harcourt, Brace, 1932.

Eberle, Irmengarde. Modern Medical Discoveries. New York: Crowell, 1958.

Fulop-Miller, René. Triumph Over Pain. New York: Literary Guild of America, Inc. , 1938.

Gallagher, Richard. Diseases That Plague Modern Man. Dobbs Ferry, N. Y. : Oceana Publications, 1969.

Gaughran, Eugene R. L. "From Superstition to Science: The History of a Bacterium, " Transactions, New York Academy of Sciences, January, 1969.

Glaser, Hugo. The Road to Modern Surgery. New York: Dutton, 1962.

Glasscheib, Hermann S. The March of Medicine. New York: Putnam's, 1964.

Godlee, Rickman John. Lord Lister. Oxford: Clarendon Press, 1924.

Haggard, Howard W. Devils, Drugs and Doctors. New York: Harper, 1929.

Lewis, Sinclair. Arrowsmith (fiction). New York: Modern Library, 1925.

Major, Ralph H. A History of Medicine. Springfield, Ill. : Thomas, 1954.

Malkus, Alida Sims. The Story of Louis Pasteur. New York:
    Grosset & Dunlap, 1952.
Metchnikov, Ilia Ilich. The Founders of Modern Medicine. New
    York: Walden Publications, 1939.
Mettler, Cecilia C. History of Medicine. Philadelphia: Blakiston,
    1947.
Singer, Charles, and E. Ashworth Underwood. A Short History of
    Medicine. New York: Oxford University Press, 1962.
Truax, Rhoda. Joseph Lister, Father of Modern Surgery. New
    York: Bobbs-Merrill, 1944.
Winslow, Charles-Edward Amory. The Conquest of Epidemic Di-
    sease. Princeton, N. J. : Princeton University Press, 1943.
Witton's Microbiology. New York: McGraw-Hill, 1961.
Wood, Laura Newbold. Louis Pasteur. New York: Messner, 1948.
Young, Agatha. Scalpel: Men Who Made Surgery. New York:
    Random House, 1956.

THE EMS TELEGRAM (1870)

In 1868 Queen Isabella of Spain was deposed following the
Spanish Revolution and a new ruling family was sought. The throne
was offered to Prince Leopold of Hohenzollern, a distant relative
of William I, King of Prussia. France and Prussia were suspicious
of each other and France was unwilling to see a Hohenzollern king
on the throne of Spain, just beyond her border. Count Otto Eduard
Leopold von Bismarck, Chancellor of the North German Federation
and Minister-President of Prussia, secretly promoted Prince Leopold's candidacy, hoping to precipitate a crisis with France and thus
further German unity.

It became known that Bismarck favored Prince Leopold and
France threatened war. The Hohenzollern family backed down and
it appeared that France had scored a diplomatic victory.

Napoleon III of France, wishing to press the point that France
did not wish a Hohenzollern on the Spanish throne, instructed Count
Vincente Benedetti, the French ambassador to Berlin, to interview
King William and get him to pledge that the candidacy would never
again be renewed.

On the morning of July 13, 1870, Benedetti met the king who
was taking a stroll at the resort town of Ems, Germany. The former made his demand which was politely refused. That afternoon
the king ordered Heinrich Abeken, an official of the Prussian foreign office, to send a report of the day's events to Bismarck. Abeken sent a lengthy telegram, which was to become known as the
"Ems Telegram, " to Bismark. The latter was authorized to publish news of the king's meeting with Benedetti.

The telegram reached Bismarck in Berlin where he was dining with Prussian generals Albrecht von Roon and Helmuth von Moltke. The Chancellor promptly edited the message with his pencil and read the revised version to the two generals. His revision reduced the message to two statements: that Count Benedetti had made demands on the king which were to stand forever, and that the king refused to see the Count again. He eliminated all reference to the courteous manner in which the king had talked with the ambassador. The edited version of the telegram was released to the press.

The French considered the telegram a diplomatic slap in the face. They declared war. France was isolated diplomatically and the southern German states rallied to the cause of Prussia. The Franco-Prussian War which followed resulted in an overwhelming victory for Prussia and her allies.

Suggested Readings

Busch, Moritz. Bismarck in the Franco-Prussian War, 1870-1871. New York: Scribner's, 1879.

Eyck, Erich. Bismarck and the German Empire. London: George Allen & Unwin, 1958.

Hamerow, Theodore S., ed. Otto von Bismarck, an Historical Assessment. Boston: Heath, 1962.

Hollyday, Frederic B. M., ed. Bismarck. Englewood Cliffs, N. J.: Prentice-Hall, 1970.

Howard, Michael. The Franco-Prussian War. New York: Macmillan, 1962.

Lord, Robert Howard. The Origins of the War of 1870. Cambridge, Mass.: Harvard University Press, 1924.

Ludwig, Emil. "Bismarck" in his Genius and Character. Translated by Kenneth Burke. New York: Harcourt, Brace 1927.

Ollivier, Emile. The Franco-Prussian War and Its Hidden Causes. Boston: Little, Brown, 1912.

Pflanze, Otto. Bismarck and the Development of Germany. Princeton, N. J.: Princeton University Press, 1963.

Rich, Norman. Friedrich von Holstein: Politics and Diplomacy in the Era of Bismarck and Wilhelm II. Cambridge: The University Press, 1965.

Richter, Werner. Bismarck. Translated by Brian Battershaw. New York: Putnam's, 1965.

Steefel, Lawrence D. Bismarck, the Hohenzollern Candidacy and the Origins of the Franco-German War of 1870. Cambridge, Mass.: Harvard University Press, 1962.

White, Andrew Dickson. "Bismarck" in his Seven Great Statesmen in the Warfare of Humanity with Unreason. New York: Century, 1910.

HEINRICH SCHLIEMANN AND THE RESURRECTION
OF TROY (1870-1890)

For many years scholars held the belief that around 1000 or
1100 B. C. Greek minstrels composed songs and traveled from place
to place entertaining. Gradually the best-liked pieces came to be
those that were concerned with the fighting around an imaginary
city called Ilios or Troia (Troy).

Somewhere between 1200 and 800 B. C. Homer, a blind poet
(or perhaps several poets), arranged these Troy stories in order,
making one continuous account of a Trojan war, including the adventures of the leaders preparing for the war and returning home
after burning the city. Two great narrative poems, the Iliad and
the Odyssey, telling the central episodes of the story, survive.

The Trojan legend made a great impression on Heinrich
Schliemann, the son of an improvident German pastor. As a young
man Schliemann made a great deal of money in the indigo trade in
Russia and in other business ventures. He also acquired a knowledge of languages, including modern and ancient Greek.

In 1863 he retired from business a wealthy man and set about
proving his theory that a real Troy, as described by Homer, had
actually existed and that it had actually been besieged and destroyed
by the Greeks.

In 1870 Schliemann began his excavations on the hill or
mound of Hissarlik, $3\frac{1}{2}$ miles from the Aegean Sea and 3 3/4 miles
from the Dardanelles. Here his diggers found the remains of five
ancient cities, one on top of another.

Following Schliemann's death in 1890 his excavations were
continued by his former assistant, Wilhelm Dörpfeld. The latter's
work in 1893 and 1894 threw new light on Schliemann's discoveries,
and still later excavations, carried on in 1932 by the American
archaeologist Carl William Blegen under the sponsorship of the University of Cincinnati, brought forth additional information.

In all, nine separate cities were unearthed, five by Schliemann plus four others which he had overlooked. These ranged from
Troy I, a rude village with its foundations on the rock and dating
somewhere between 3000 and 2500 B. C. , through Troy II, III, IV, V,
VI, VIIA, VIIB, VIII, and IX. These were considered nine cities in
all, as Troy VIIA was a reconstruction of Troy VI which had been
destroyed by an earthquake.

Troy II was identified by Schliemann as the Homeric Troy.
This was a prehistoric fortress with strong ramparts and large
brick houses where the diggers found a valuable mass of gold treasure. It dated from 2500 to 2000 B. C. Dörpfeld's later discoveries, however, showed that the real Homeric city was Troy VIIA,

which was destroyed by fire in the early 12th century B. C. , the traditional date of the Trojan war.

Suggested Readings

Alexander, Marc. "Heinrich Schliemann and Troy" in his The Past. Worthington, Ohio: A. Lynn, 1965.

Blegen, Carl W. Troy and the Trojans. London: Thames & Hudson, 1963.

————, et al. Troy. Princeton, N. J. : Princeton University Press, 1950.

Braymer, Marjorie. The Walls of Windy Troy: A Biography of Heinrich Schliemann. New York: Harcourt, Brace, 1960.

Cohen, Daniel. "Heinrich Schliemann, Archaeologist Extraordinary, " Science Digest, March, 1963.

————. Secrets from Ancient Graves. New York: Dodd, Mead, 1968.

Colum, Padriac. The Golden Fleece and the Heroes Who Lived Before Achilles. New York: Macmillan, 1921.

Cottrell, Leonard. Digs and Diggers: A Book of World Archaeology. Cleveland: World, 1964.

Cross, E. A. "Schliemann" in his World Literature. New York: American Book Co. , 1935.

De Camp, L. Sprague, and Catherine C. De Camp. "Troy and the Nine Cities" in their Ancient Ruins and Archaeology. Garden City, N. Y. : Doubleday, 1964.

Falls, C. B. The First 3,000 Years: Ancient Civilizations of the Tigris, Euphrates, and Nile Rivers and the Mediterranean Sea. New York: Viking Press, 1960.

Geddes, William D. The Problem of the Homeric Poems. London: Macmillan, 1878.

Homer. The Iliad of Homer. London: Macmillan, 1921.

Johnson, Dorothy Marie. Farewell to Troy (fiction). Boston: Houghton Mifflin, 1964.

Leaf, Walter. Homer and History. London: Macmillan, 1915.

————. Troy: A Study in Homeric Geography. London: Macmillan, 1912.

Lorimer, H. L. Homer and the Monuments. London: Macmillan, 1950.

Mackay, L. A. The Wrath of Homer. Toronto: University of Toronto Press, 1948.

Myres, Sir John L. Homer and His Critics. London: Routledge & Kegan Paul, 1958.

Nylander, Carl. "The Fall of Troy, " Antiquity, Vol. XXXVIII, 1963.

Page, Denys L. History and the Homeric Iliad. Berkeley, Calif. : University of California Press, 1959.

Payne, Robert. The Gold of Troy. New York: Funk & Wagnalls, 1959.

Schliemann, Heinrich. Ilios: The City and Country of the Trojans. New York: Harper, 1881.

————. Troja. Results of the Latest Researches and Discover-

ies on the Site of Homer's Troy and in the Heroic Tumuli and
Other Sites, Made in the Year 1882. And a Narrative of a
Journey in the Troad in 1881. New York: Blom, 1967.

Schreiber, Hermann, and Georg Schreiber. Vanished Cities. New
York: Knopf, 1957.

Schuchardt, C. Schliemann's Excavations: An Archaeological and
Historical Study. London: Macmillan, 1891.

Silverberg, Robert. Lost Cities and Vanished Civilizations. Philadelphia: Chilton, 1962.

Smith, A. H. , M. A. , F. S. A. "Troy: The City Sung by Homer" in
Hamerton, J. A. , ed. Wonders of the Past: The Romance of
Antiquity and Its Splendours, Vol. IV. New York: William H.
Wise, 1933.

Tolman, Herbert Cushing, and Gilbert Campbell Scoggin. Mycenae-
an Troy. New York: American Book Co. , 1903.

Woolley, C. Leonard. Digging Up the Past. New York: Scribner's,
1931.

THE STANLEY-LIVINGSTONE MEETING (1871)

In 1840 David Livingstone, a Scottish physician, missionary
and explorer, went to Africa to spread the Word of God among the
African people. A year later he arrived at Kuruman, a South African settlement founded by the missionary Robert Moffat, whose
daughter he married in 1844.

Livingstone traveled extensively through Central Africa and
his explorations resulted in the first knowledge of the region. He
discovered Victoria Falls, Lake Nyasa, Chilwa, Mweru and Bang-
weulu as well as the Zambezi and Luapula Rivers. In all he made
three major journeys, combining exploration with his major activities as a missionary.

On March 19, 1866, he sailed from Zanzibar to the mainland with an entourage of 60 men and an assortment of pack animals. His mission was to discover the sources of the Nile River
and explore the watersheds of Central Africa. He traveled along
the Ruvuma River to Lake Tanganyika which he reached in 1867.

During this period little was heard of Livingstone and his
party and his welfare became a matter of international concern.
In 1869 James Gordon Bennett, Jr. , publisher of the New York
Herald, sent Henry M. Stanley to Africa to find Livingstone. In
contrast to the idealistic Livingstone, Stanley was a hard-headed,
practical journalist who had never been to Africa. An Anglo-American born John Rowlands, he had come to New Orleans as a cabin
boy and was adopted by Henry Morton Stanley, whose name he took.
Becoming a reporter following service in the American Civil War,
he worked for several newspapers before accepting a position with
the Herald.

He reached Zanzibar on January 6, 1871. On March 21 he left for the interior with about 200 men and an ample supply of provisions. On November 10 he met Livingstone at Ujiji on Lake Tanganyika. His famous greeting, "Dr. Livingstone, I presume?" is still remembered.

The Livingstone party had suffered great hardships. Some of his men had deserted and he suffered from ulcers, malaria and dysentery. The supplies sent him from Zanzibar had been plundered by members of the caravan transporting them and Livingstone was virtually destitute.

Stanley nursed the Scottish explorer and missionary back to health. Livingstone refused to return to Europe and Stanley gave him the supplies he needed to continue his explorations. The two men conducted a joint exploration of the northern end of Lake Tanganyika, following which Stanley returned home. In 1873 Bennett sent him to West Africa to cover the British campaign against the Ashantis. Livingstone died at Zambia in May of that year and Stanley decided to take up the former's work where he had left it but with emphasis on exploration rather than missionary activities. His expedition, financed by the New York Herald and the London Daily Telegraph, left Zanzibar on November 17, 1874, to make a boat survey of the coasts of certain African lakes. He continued his explorations for much the rest of his life. As a naturalized American citizen, he repatriated himself as a British subject in 1895 and was knighted four years later. He last visited Africa in 1897 and died in 1904.

Suggested Readings

Anstruther, Ian. Dr. Livingstone, I Presume? New York: Dutton, 1956.

Arnold, Richard. The True Story of David Livingstone. Chicago: Children's Press, 1964.

Benét, Laura. Stanley, Invincible Explorer. New York: Dodd, Mead, 1955.

Busoni, Rafaello. Stanley's Africa. New York: Viking Press, 1944.

Charles, Elizabeth. Three Martyrs of the Nineteenth Century: Studies from the Lives of Livingstone, Gordon and Patteson. New York: Negro Universities Press, 1969.

Golding, Vautier. The History of H. M. Stanley. London: T. C. and E. C. Jack, 1906.

Hall-Quest, Olga. With Stanley in Africa. New York: Dutton, 1961.

Hird, Frank. H. M. Stanley: The Authorized Life. London: S. Paul & Co., 1935.

Huxley, Elspeth. "The Challenge of Africa" in her Encyclopedia of Discovery and Exploration, Vol. 12. London: Aldus Books, 1971.

Ludwig, Emil. "Stanley" in his Genius and Character. Translated by Kenneth Burke. New York: Harcourt, Brace, 1927.

Newbolt, Sir Henry John. "David Livingstone" and "Sir Henry Mor-
    ton Stanley" in his Book of the Long Trail. New York: Long-
    mans, Green, 1919.
Seth, Ronald. Milestones in African History. Philadelphia: Chil-
    ton, 1969.
Stanley, Henry Morton. Autobiography. Edited by Dorothy Stanley.
    London: Sampson Low, 1909.
_____. How I Found Livingstone. London: Sampson Low, 1872.
_____. In Darkest Africa. London: Sampson Low, 1890.
_____. Through the Dark Continent. London: Sampson Low,
    1878.
Sterling, Thomas, and the editors of Horizon Magazine. The Ex-
    ploration of Africa. New York: American Heritage Publishing
    Co. , 1963.
Wasserman, Jacob. Bula Matari, Conqueror of a Continent. New
    York: Liveright, 1933.

THE TICHBORNE CLAIMANT (1871-1872)

The affair of the Tichborne Claimant involved a lawsuit based
on the spurious claim of Arthur Orton, alias Thomas Castro, that
he was Roger Charles Doughty Tichborne, supposedly lost at sea in
1854, but miraculously rescued.

Orton was an English butcher who had emigrated to Australia
in 1852. Tichborne was a wealthy young baronet and heir to the
family fortune. Orton, after various unsuccessful ventures, saw an
advertisement in an Australian newspaper offering a reward for information leading to the discovery of Roger Tichborne. This advertisement was one of several inserted in South American and Australian newspapers by Lady Tichborne, Roger's mother, who believed her son to still be alive.

Orton, having assumed the name Thomas Castro, arranged
to be "discovered" as the lost heir to the Tichborne baronetcy and
fortune. He returned to England at the invitation of Lady Tichborne
who unquestioningly accepted him as her son.

Other members of the Tichborne family were skeptical. Orton bore no physical resemblance to Roger and showed a remarkable ignorance of matters about which Roger would have been familiar.

In 1871 Orton brought action for the ejection of Sir Alfred
Tichborne, the 12th baronet. The trial lasted 102 days and the decision was against him. Further, the Lord Chief Justice indicated
that, in his opinion, Orton had been "guilty of wilful and corrupt
perjury. "

Orton was subsequently tried in a criminal case which lasted

188 days. Found guilty, he was sentenced to serve fourteen years
penal servitude. In 1895, following his release from prison, he
confessed his imposture. He died in poverty in 1898.

Suggested Readings

Atlay, James Beresford. The Tichborne Case. London: 1916.
"The Baronet and the Butcher" in Crimes and Punishment, Vol. 6.
    Editorial presentation: Jackson Morley. London: BPC, 1973.
Deeson, A. F. L. Great Swindlers. New York: Drake Publishers,
    1972.
Felstead, Sidney Theodore, and Lady Muir. Famous Criminals and
    Their Trials. London: Oxford University Press, 1926.
Finger, Charles J. "The Tichborne Claimant" in his Romantic Ras-
    cals. New York: McBride, 1927.
Griffiths, Arthur. Mysteries of Police and Crime. London: 1901.
Kenealy, Maurice Edward. The Tichborne Tragedy. London: 1913.
Klein, Alexander. Grand Deception: The World's Most Spectacular
    and Successful Hoaxes, Impostures, Ruses and Frauds. Phil-
    adelphia: Lippincott, 1955.
Maugham, Frederick H. The Tichborne Case. Westport, Conn.:
    Hyperion Press, 1975 (Originally published 1936).
Report of the Select Committee of the Parliament of New South
    Wales on the Case of William Creswell. Sydney, Australia:
    1906.
Smith, Edward H. "The Lost Heir of Tichborne" in his Mysteries
    of the Missing. New York: Lincoln MacVeagh-The Dial Press,
    1927.
Stoker, Bram. Famous Imposters. London: 1896.
Symons, Julian. "The Con Man of All Time?" in his A Pictorial
    History of Crime. New York: Crown Publishers, 1966.
Woodruff, Douglas. The Tichborne Claimant. New York: Farrar,
    Straus and Giroux, 1957.

THE BANK OF ENGLAND SWINDLE (1872-1873)

The Bank of England is considered as impregnable as any
financial institution in the world and has been so regarded for many
years. In 1872 four American sharpers challenged this impregna-
bility and very nearly succeeded in perpetrating one of the most gigantic and audacious swindles of the last century.

In August, 1872, Austin Bidwell and his brother George arrived in England from America, accompanied by George Macdonnell.
The brothers were small-time financial racketeers who had resolved
to defraud the Bank of England although they had not, at that time,
formulated any scheme by which this could be accomplished. Macdonnell was a master forger of financial documents.

The three took rooms in a modest section of London. Austin Bidwell, who had been appointed "front man" for the group, registered at the aristocratic Golden Cross Hotel, thus providing a
high-class and impressive accommodation address. He used the
name "Frederick Albert Warren."

It was then that the scheme for defrauding the bank was conceived. The instrument by which this was to be accomplished was
the bill of exchange, a written authorization or order to pay a specific sum of money to a designated person at a specified future
time. These had originated in the Middle Ages when a trader in
one country, purchasing a consignment of goods which took a long
time to deliver, gave his supplier a note promising payment at a
later date. These bills of exchange became negotiable, and a seller, wishing to collect the monies due him at once, could do this
by discounting the bill at a bank. The bank, in turn, held the bill
until the settlement date and then redeemed it from the purchaser
of the goods at full face value. Thus, it was only necessary for
the three conspirators to establish an account with the Bank of England and then present, for payment at a discount, forged bills of
exchange due sometime in the future. When the Bank presented
the bills for payment it would, of course, learn that they were
counterfeit, but by that time Macdonnell and the Bidwell brothers
would have disappeared.

Austin Bidwell, posing as a representative of the Pullman
Palace Car Company, visited the exclusive tailor shop of Edward
Hamilton Green, who had been found to have an account at the Western Branch of the Bank of England. Bidwell, using his "Warren"
alias, ordered five expensive suits and two frock coats. When
these were ready he paid for them in cash, explaining to the tailor
that, as an American commission agent, he was not a local resident and did not care to open an account. He asked the tailor to
keep a large sum of money for him in the office safe, he having
no bank account in England. Green, reluctant to accept the responsibility of holding a large amount of another's cash, offered
to introduce "Warren" to his bankers at the Western Branch. The
introduction being made, "Warren" made a large cash deposit and
thanked Green for his trouble.

The next step was to determine whether the Bank would accept bills of exchange without making an investigation prior to payment. Macdonnell presented an authentic bill to the London and
Westminster Bank where it was accepted without question and the
money was paid on the spot.

Greatly encouraged by this practice of English banks, quite
different from those in America which habitually asked questions before
paying currency, Macdonnell set about forging bills of exchange due
for payment three months in the future. "Warren" gave Colonel
Peregrine Madgwick Francis, manager of the Western Branch, a
genuine bill of exchange. Although the Branch did not ordinarily
accept such instruments, this being the prerogative of the Main

Bank, the Colonel arranged an exception in the case of "Warren."

A fourth American, Edwin Noyes Hills, was recruited. His function was to handle an account at the Continental Bank in London's Lombard Street. "Warren" was to deposit checks drawn on his Western Branch account in the Continental Bank, from which the proceeds would be siphoned off by Hills. "Warren" opened the new account and appointed Hills his "confidential clerk." Hills, under the name of "Charles Johnson Horton," drew the money from the Continental Bank in cash, to be ultimately divided by the four members of the swindling team.

The forged bills, prepared by Macdonnell, were sent to the Western Branch by registered mail and the proceeds were transferred by check to the Continental Bank, from which they were withdrawn, all according to plan. Then, on February 28, 1873, having realized almost 100,000 pounds, the quartet decided that it was time to disband. All evidence was burned, including check books, credit slips, correspondence and wooden engraving blocks.

Macdonnell hurriedly prepared three final bills which were sent to Colonel Francis. They arrived at his office on Friday, February 28. A bank clerk noticed that these bills were undated and the Colonel ordered them taken to B. W. Blydenstein & Co., the acceptor, for completion. Blydenstein declared the instruments to be forgeries.

The police were notified. "Horton" was arrested when he appeared at the Continental Bank to collect the last batch of cash. The other members of the gang, learning from the newspapers that the game was up, divided the booty and separated. Eventually the three were caught and returned to England. All four were tried at Old Bailey in August, 1873, convicted and sentenced to life imprisonment.

Suggested Readings

Bidwell, Austin Biron, Defendant. The Bank of England Forgery. Edited by George Dilnot. London: G. Bles, 1929.
Clapham, Sir John. The Bank of England: A History by Sir John Clapham. New York: Macmillan, 1945.
Deeson, A. F. L. Great Swindlers. New York: Drake Publishers, 1972.
Gibson, Walter Brown, ed. The Fine Art of Swindling. New York: Grosset & Dunlap, 1966.
Giuseppi, John. Bank of England: A History from Its Foundation in 1694. Chicago: Henry Regnery, 1966.
Hancock, Ralph, and Henry Chafetz. The Compleat Swindler. New York: Macmillan, 1968.
Hopkins, R. Thurston. Famous Bank Forgeries, Robberies and Swindles. London: S. Paul, 1936.
Klein, Alexander. The Double Dealers: Adventures in Grand Deception. Philadelphia: Lippincott, 1958.

_____. Grand Deception: The World's Most Spectacular and Suc-
    cessful Hoaxes, Impostures, Ruses and Frauds. Philadelphia:
    Lippincott, 1955.
Symons, Julian. "Robbing the Bank of England" in his A Pictorial
    History of Crime. New York: Crown Publishers, 1966.
"They Swindled the Bank of England" in Crimes and Punishment,
    Vol. 2. Editorial presentation: Jackson Morley. London:
    BPC, 1973.

THE BRITISH PURCHASE OF THE
SUEZ CANAL SHARES (1875)

        The Suez Canal, connecting the Mediterranean Sea with the
Gulf of Suez, an arm of the Red Sea, was completed in 1869. Its
construction was promoted by Vicomte Ferdinand Marie de Lesseps,
a retired French diplomat, who organized the Universal Company
of the Maritime Suez Canal. This concern was authorized to cut
a canal and operate it on lease for 99 years, following which its
ownership would revert to the Egyptian government. The Company
was originally a private Egyptian concern, incorporated under French
law.

        Great Britain did not participate in the building of the canal.
Henry John Temple, Viscount Palmerston, the British prime minis-
ter when its construction was first discussed, opposed the project.
He felt that such a canal would threaten his country's control of
India and further that it would, by weakening the Ottoman Empire,
encourage Russia's expansionist policy in the Near East.

        In spite of Great Britain's objections the canal was, in due
course, completed. Palmerston's successors did not take kindly to
the canal until Benjamin Disraeli, Earl of Beaconsfield, returned to
the office of prime minister in 1874. Disraeli felt that, while Palmerston's objections had some merit, the canal was of great commercial and strategic value to Great Britain in that it shortened the
time required to travel from England to India by several weeks.
He decided to "obtain a voice in the Universal Company to insure
British interests."

        Disraeli's attempts to purchase the canal shares held by de
Lesseps were unsuccessful. However, Ismail I, Khedive of Egypt,
was the holder of 176,602 shares and Egypt's financial affairs were
chaotic and the country was facing bankruptcy. The Khedive had
no choice but to hypothecate or sell his shares, which represented
a 44 percent interest in the Universal Company and which had been
issued to him as payment for the 99-year lease mentioned above.

        Ismail negotiated secretly with a group of French financiers.
On November 15, 1875, Edward Henry Smith Stanley, Earl of Derby and Great Britain's foreign secretary, was told of these negotia-

tions and took no action. Disraeli, a close friend of Baron Lionel Rothschild of the family of international bankers was, on the previous evening, dining with Rothschild at the latter's home in London. While they were at dinner the banker received a telegram from one of his Paris informants. Having read the message he told Disraeli that Egypt's debt-ridden Khedive had offered his shares to the French government but had become impatient with France's terms. Disraeli is said to have asked, "How much?" and Rothschild, after an exchange of telegrams with his Paris office, determined that the asking price was four million pounds sterling. Prime Minister Disraeli then said, "We will take them."

On November 17 Disraeli laid his proposal before the Cabinet and, after some objections, the purchase was authorized. The Rothschild bank underwrote the transaction, charging 3 percent interest, and the Khedive agreed, on November 23, to sell his shares to Great Britain.

Parliament's approval was needed. Despite the objections of the Liberal Party under William Ewart Gladstone, the purchase and loan were approved. The acquisition of the Khedive's shares did not give Great Britain the ownership or even a controlling interest in the Suez Canal and represented essentially insurance against any designs which France might have against either Egypt or the canal itself. The transaction was, however, quite profitable to Great Britain. In 1935 the holdings acquired from Ismail I figured in the national assets at more than 93 million pounds, and the dividends received almost from the start exceeded the 3 percent interest charged by the Rothschilds for the loan.

Suggested Readings

Beatty, Charles. De Lesseps of Suez. Buffalo, N. Y. : McClelland, 1956.
_____. Ferdinand De Lesseps. London: Eyre and Spottiswoode, 1956.
Blake, Robert. Disraeli. Garden City, N. Y. : Anchor Books, 1968.
Buckle, George E. The Life of Benjamin Disraeli, Earl of Beaconsfield. Vol. V: 1868-1876. London: John Murray, 1920.
Jones, Wilbur P. Lord Derby and Victorian Conservatism. Oxford: Basil Blackwell, 1956.
Marlowe, John. World Ditch: The Making of the Suez Canal. New York: Macmillan, 1964.
Maurios, André. Disraeli: A Picture of the Victorian Age. Translated by Hamish Miles. New York: Appleton, 1928.
Monypenny, William Flavelle, and George Earle Buckle. The Life of Benjamin Disraeli, Earl of Beaconsfield. New York: Macmillan, 1929.
Morley, John. The Life of William Ewart Gladstone. New York: Macmillan, 1903.
Morton, Frederick. The Rothschilds: A Family Portrait. New York: Atheneum, 1962.

Parker, Louis N. Disraeli (play). New York: French, 1911.
Pearson, Hesketh. Dizzy: The Life and Personality of Benjamin
    Disraeli, Earl of Beaconsfield. New York: Harper & Row,
    1951.
Seton-Watson, R. W. Britain in Europe, 1789-1914. Cambridge:
    The University Press, 1945.
Ward, A. W. , and George P. Gooch, eds. The Cambridge History
    of British Foreign Policy, Vol. III. New York: Macmillan,
    1923.

THE FIRST PRACTICAL INCANDESCENT LAMP (1879)

        Electric lighting is defined as "illumination by means of any
of a number of devices which convert electrical energy into light. "
Thomas Alva Edison, the American inventor, is generally thought
to be the man who conceived the means of creating artificial light
by using a conductor heated by an electric current as a light source.
However, his 1879 invention of a practical incandescent electric
light bulb was preceded by a number of other researchers who had
attempted, unsuccessfully, to solve the problem.

        In 1809 Sir Humphry Davy produced light from electric arcs,
using a large battery as a source of current.   He also made a fine
platinum wire incandescent by passing a current through it in air.
Davy's arc lights, after the materials used in the rods between
which the arc formed had been improved, were later used for il-
luminating streets and in lighthouses.   Warren de la Rue, an English astronomer, constructed an improved arc lamp in 1820.   This
used a battery as a source of current and was prohibitively expensive to operate.

        In 1831 Michael Faraday, Davy's assistant and associate,
produced a workable electric generator, making large-scale lighting
possible.   In 1840 William Robert Grove, a British jurist and physicist, invented a battery which produced twice the voltage of previous such devices.   This battery had a positive terminal which
was immersed in a diluted solution of sulfuric acid and a negative
terminal which was suspended in concentrated nitric acid.   With
this battery Grove was able to obtain almost two volts from a single cell and hydrogen polarization was prevented.   Using his improved
battery, he gave a demonstration of the lighting of an incandescent
lamp before the Royal Society of London.   This lamp employed a
coil of platinum wire as a filament.   Platinum does not oxidize
readily and so produced light for a time in the presence of air
without burning out.   However, its cost made the use of it far too
expensive for commercial applications.

        Other inventors sought a filament which could be kept hot
in a vacuum, thus avoiding oxidation and increasing the brilliance
of the light generated.   In 1860 Joseph Wilson Swan, an English

chemist and electrician, produced a carbon-filament incandescent
lamp. His vacuums, however, were poor and his lamps burned
out after being used only a short time. Edison, working independently of Swan, experimented with a number of substances from
which a practical filament might be made. "He tried paper, cloth,
thread, fishline, fibre, celluloid, boxwood, coconut shells, spruce,
hickory, maple shavings, rosewood, punk, cork, flax, bamboo, and
the hair out of a redheaded Scotchman's beard." The vacuum problem was overcome and Edison's lamps, using a carbon filament,
were shown to be commercially practical. Tungsten filaments were
substituted for carbon in 1907 and lamps filled with inert gas were
developed in 1913.

The incandescent electric lamp, considered by many to be
the most important of all Edison's inventions--over 1,000--was followed but not supplanted by various miscellaneous special purpose
lamps. These include the photo flash bulb, the fluorescent lamp,
the photo flood lamp, the mercury vapor arc lamp, the neon lamp
and the sodium-vapor lamp.

Suggested Readings

Bright, Arthur A. , Jr. The Electric-Lamp Industry: Technologi-
    cal Change and Economic Development, from 1800-1947. New
    York: Macmillan, 1949.
Burlingame, Roger. Inventors Behind the Inventor. New York:
    Harcourt, Brace, 1947.
Cressy, Edward. A Hundred Years of Mechanical Engineering.
    New York: Macmillan, 1937.
Dos Passos, John. "The Electrical Wizard" in his The 42nd Paral-
    lel. New York: Random House, 1930.
Finch, James K. Engineering and Western Civilization. New York:
    McGraw-Hill, 1951.
Josephson, Matthew. Edison. New York: McGraw-Hill, 1959.
Kirby, Richard S. , et al. Engineering in History. New York:
    McGraw-Hill, 1956.
Lewis, Floyd A. The Incandescent Light. New York: Shorewood
    Publishers, 1961.
Morgan, Alfred P. The Pageant of Electricity. New York: Ap-
    pleton-Century-Crofts, 1939.
O'Dea, William T. The Social History of Lighting. New York:
    Macmillan, 1958.
Sharlin, Harold I. The Making of the Electrical Age. New York:
    Abelard-Schuman, 1963.
Usher, Abbott P. A History of Mechanical Inventions. New York:
    McGraw-Hill, 1929.

THE DISCOVERY OF VACCINATION (1881)

Louis Pasteur, the French chemist, educator and researcher,

is generally thought of as the man who first conceived the idea of vaccinating animals and human beings against disease.   While he was successful in developing vaccines for the prevention of anthrax, fowl cholera and hydrophobia, he was preceded in this field by the ancient Chinese who practiced primitive artificial immunization against smallpox by placing scabs from smallpox patients in the nose.   Edward Jenner, the English physician, in 1796 inoculated subjects with the vaccine of cowpox which rendered them immune to smallpox.   His discovery, however, was not followed up until Pasteur developed a method of producing vaccines.

The French scientist who was to be called "the Father of Vaccination" was born in Dôle, Jura Department, in 1822, the son of an ex-soldier and tanner.   He was educated at Arbois College, the Royal College of Besançon and the École Normale in Paris. Following graduation he taught physics, geology and chemistry at various French universities.   In 1889 he became director of the Pasteur Institute, which position he retained until his death in 1895.

Pasteur's first important contribution to science was made in 1848.   While investigating the effects of tartaric acids on a ray of polarized light he discovered that one type of the acid has iso- meric constituents.   This scientific breakthrough was a milestone in sterochemistry.   Other research in this field led to discoveries concerning the processes of fermentation and putrefaction in wine, milk, alcohol and other liquids.   It had previously been thought that these processes were caused by spontaneous generation.   Pas- teur showed that this concept is false and that fermentation and putrefaction are caused by minute organisms, called variously "germs," "microbes," or "bacteria."   These, found in air to which the affected substances have been exposed, cause contamination. Pasteur's discoveries made possible the scientific processing of beer, milk and wine and led to important contributions to the germ theory of disease.

In 1865 Pasteur investigated a mysterious disease which, for twenty years, had attacked silkworms and which threatened to ruin the French silk industry.   He found that the trouble stemmed, not from one but from two separate silkworm diseases.   By devis- ing a method of destroying the diseased adult bacilli he saved his country's silk industry from extinction.

Robert Koch, the German physician and pioneer bacteriolo- gist, had done anthrax research in the 1870's and had isolated a pure culture of the anthrax bacillus in 1876.   In 1883 he published details of a method of preventive inoculation against this disease. Meanwhile, in 1881, Pasteur embarked on one of the most impor- tant research projects of his career: the curbing of anthrax, fowl cholera and hydrophobia.   His investigations convinced him that these diseases were all caused by specific bacteria and could be prevented and cured by inoculation with artificially grown cultures of the disease-producing organisms.   He conducted numerous ex- periments with animals and on July 6, 1885, inoculated a human

being with successful results.   The patient, a boy named Joseph
Meister, had been severely bitten by a rabid dog.

The only other known treatment for such wounds was cauter-
ization with a red-hot iron, thus hopefully burning away the infection.   Pasteur's vaccine was injected into the boy's body and, although he had been attacked by the dog two days earlier, the treatment was successful.   Young Meister failed to show the customary
symptoms of rabies: breathlessness, spasms, tormenting thirst
and the inability to swallow.

News of the success of this application of Pasteur's vaccine
spread rapidly and he soon had patients coming to his Paris laboratory from virtually all parts of Europe.   Three years later the
Pasteur Institute for the prevention and cure of hydrophobia was
established.

Pasteur's discovery that most diseases are caused by specific micro-organisms had a profound influence on his contemporaries and successors.   Joseph Lister, a British physician, instituted a technique of antiseptic surgery in which septic infections
are treated chemically and absolute cleanliness prevails in hospital
operating rooms.   Research in immunity reactions and kindred medical areas still continues, being conducted by such men as the American biochemist Louis Pillemer.

Suggested Readings

Benz, Francis E.   Pasteur: Knight of the Laboratory.   New York:
    · Dodd, Mead, 1938.
Burton, Mary June.   Louis Pasteur: Founder of Microbiology.   New
    York: Franklin Watts, 1963.
Cheyne, William Watson.   Lister and His Achievement.   London:
    Longmans, Green, 1925.
De Kruif, Paul.   Microbe Hunters.   Edited by Harry G. Grover.
    New York: Harcourt, Brace, 1932.
Duclaux, Émile.   Pasteur: The History of a Mind.   Translated by
    Erwin F. Smith and Florence Hedges.   Philadelphia: Saunders,
    1920.
Eberle, Irmengarde.   Modern Medical Discoveries.   New York:
    Crowell, 1958.
Gallagher, Richard.   Diseases That Plague Modern Man.   Dobbs
    Ferry, N. Y. : Oceana Publications, 1969.
Gaughran, Eugene R. L.   "From Superstition to Science: The History
    of a Bacterium, " Transactions, New York Academy of Scien-
    ces, January, 1969.
Glaser, Hugo.   The Road to Modern Surgery.   New York: Dutton,
    1962.
Glasscheib, Hermann S.   The March of Medicine.   New York: Put-
    nam's, 1964.
Godlee, Rickman John.   Lord Lister.   Oxford: Clarendon Press,
    1924.

Lewis, Sinclair. Arrowsmith (fiction). New York: Modern Li-
    brary, 1925.
Loir, Adrien. A l'ombre de Pasteur (Souvenirs, personels). Pa-
    ris: Le Mouvement Sanitaire, 1938.
Major, Ralph H. A History of Medicine. Springfield, Ill.: Thom-
    as, 1954.
Malkus, Alida Sims. The Story of Louis Pasteur. New York:
    Grosset & Dunlap, 1952.
Metchnikov, Ilia Ilich. The Founders of Modern Medicine. New
    York: Walden Publications, 1939.
Mettler, Cecilia C. History of Medicine. Philadelphia: Blakiston,
    1947.
Pasteur, Louis. Oeuvres de Pasteur, Réuins par Pasteur Vallery-
    Radot. Paris: Masson et Cie, 1922-1939.
Singer, Charles, and E. Ashworth Underwood. A Short History of
    Medicine. New York: Oxford University Press, 1962.
Truax, Rhoda. Joseph Lister, Father of Modern Surgery. New
    York: Bobbs-Merrill, 1944.
Vallery-Radot, René. The Life of Pasteur. Translated by Mrs.
    R. L. Devonshire. Garden City, N. Y.: Sun Dial Press, 1937.
Winslow, Charles-Edward Amory. The Conquest of Epidemic Di-
    sease. Princeton, N. J.: Princeton University Press, 1943.
Witton's Microbiology. New York: McGraw-Hill, 1961.
Wood, Laura Newbold. Louis Pasteur. New York: Messner,
    1948.

THE ERUPTION OF KRAKATOA (1883)

Krakatoa, a small island in Sunda Strait, between Sumatra
and Java, situated 100 miles west of Batavia, was the scene of the
most devastating volcanic eruption of modern times on the night of
August 26/27, 1883.

Prior to the eruption Krakatoa had an area of approximately
18 square miles. The explosion was of such violence that the island's area was reduced to six square miles.

This volcanic explosion produced what is said to be "the loud-
est noise ever heard by man." It was audible 3,000 miles away.
Tons of rock were discharged from the crater, much of it in the
form of fine dust. This was diffused through the upper atmosphere
by aerial currents and brilliant colorations of sunrise and sunset,
caused by refraction of the sun's rays on these particles, were reported by observers from all parts of the world.

The volcanic eruption was accompanied by a submarine earthquake which generated waves as much as 50 feet high and which
traveled more than 8,000 miles. More than 36,000 people were
killed along the coasts of Sumatra and Java. Property damage was
in the millions.

Following another, though much less severe, eruption in 1927, the then residents of the island were evacuated and presently Krakatoa is uninhabited.

Suggested Readings

Abbot, C. G., and E. E. Fowle. "Volcanoes and Climate," Smithsonian Miscellaneous Collections, Vol. 60, 1913.
Ashdown, E. "A Floating Lava Bed," Nature, Vol. XXIX, 1883; Vol. XXX, 1884.
Boutelle, C. "Watch Waves from Krakatoa," Science, Vol. III, 1884.
Bullard, Fred M. Volcanoes in History, in Theory, in Eruption. Austin, Tex.: University of Texas Press, 1962.
_____. Volcanoes of the Earth. Rev. edition. Austin, Tex.: University of Texas Press, 1976.
Cotteau, E. "A Week at Krakatoa," Proceedings of the Royal Society of Australia, Vol. II, 1885.
Dalby, R. J. "The Krakatoa Eruption of 1883," The Listener, March 17, 1937.
Decker, R. W., and D. Hadikusumo. "Results of 1960 Expedition to Krakatoa," Journal of Geophysical Research, Vol. 66, No. 10, 1961.
Furneaux, Rupert. Krakatoa. Englewood Cliffs, N. J.: Prentice-Hall, 1964.
Krüger, Christoph, ed. Volcanoes. New York: Putnam's, 1971.
Le Conte, J. "Atmospheric Waves from Krakatoa," Science, Vol. III, 1884.
Ollier, Cliff. Volcanoes. Cambridge, Mass.: M. I. T. Press, 1969.
Van Doorn, M. C. "The Eruption of Krakatoa," Nature, Vol. XXIX, 1883.
Verbeek, R. D. M. "The Krakatoa Eruption," Nature, Vol. XXX, 1884.
Vincent, E. A. Volcanoes and Their Activity. New York: Wiley, 1962.
Watson, Captain W. J. "The Java Disaster," Nature, Vol. XXIX, 1883.
Wexler, H. "Spread of the Krakatoa Dust Cloud," Bulletin of the American Meteorological Society, February, 1951.

THE DEVELOPMENT OF THE DAIMLER
INTERNAL COMBUSTION ENGINE (1883)

Following the invention of the steam engine in the late 17th century attempts were made to adapt it to self-propelled road vehicles. Such inventors as Nicolas Joseph Cugnot, William Murdock, William Symington, Richard Trevithick and Oliver Evans built working models of steam carriages in the 18th and early 19th centuries. These vehicles, however, were all basically impractical due to mech-

anical problems of bulk and weight.   Such problems were overcome
in the late 19th and early 20th centuries and steam propelled automobiles built by the White Motor Company, the Stanley Brothers,
Abner Doble and others operated successfully on roads and streets.
Large steam engines were found to be suited for power sources on
locomotives as demonstrated by George Stephenson in 1814, as well
as in boats and stationary installations of various sorts.   It was
not until Rudolf Diesel built the first successful diesel engine in
1897 that steam was replaced by this new type of power source in
many locomotives and ships.

The first internal combustion engine was designed by Christian Huygens, a Dutch scientist, in 1678.   It is thought that it was
intended to be operated by gunpowder but was never built.   Two
centuries later Jean Joseph Étienne Lenoir built a practical internal combustion engine using coal gas for fuel.   In 1866 Eugen Lang-
en and Nikolaus August Otto developed a more efficient gas engine,
and in 1876 Otto constructed a four-cycle engine similar to those
used in most automobiles and many aeroplanes and small boats today.   Other inventors also worked on the problem during the 19th
century.

During the 1870's Gottlieb Daimler, a German engineer and
inventor, worked with Otto as his assistant.   In 1883 he left to
build his own engines, which used gasoline for fuel.   The Daimler
engine was small, high speed, light in weight and efficient.   In
partnership with Wilhelm Maybach, who became technical director
of the Daimler Motor Company at Cannstatt, Germany, he built,
in 1890, a practical automobile called the Mercedes, after his daughter.   Maybach invented the spray-nozzle carburetor, the honeycomb
radiator and the change-speed gear, all of which were incorporated
in the cars manufactured by the Daimler concern.

Virtually all automobiles manufactured today use a four-cycle
engine employing the principles of the Daimler-built cars.   The internal combustion engine has been adapted to many purposes, such
as propelling aeroplanes, motor boats, motorcycles and lawn mow-
ers as well as road vehicles.   Since its inception it has been improved and modified.   The original one-cylinder engine has spawned
engines with four, six, eight, twelve and sixteen cylinders.   A two-
cycle engine is used in a few makes of automobile and the Wankel
rotary engine, also used in some makes of car, was developed in
the 1960's.

The Daimler internal combustion engine made the automobile
possible and during the late nineteenth and through the twentieth
century many makes of passenger cars and heavy trucks were put
on the market, both in Europe and the United States.

Suggested Readings

Bird, Anthony. Antique Automobiles. New York: Dutton, 1967.

_____. The Motor Car, 1765-1914. London: B. T. Batsford, 1960.
Burlingame, Roger. Inventors Behind the Inventor. New York: Harcourt, Brace, 1947.
Cardwell, D. S. L. Steam Power in the Eighteenth Century. London: Sheed and Ward, 1963.
Cohn, David L. Combustion on Wheels. Boston: Houghton Mifflin, 1944.
Cressy, Edward. A Hundred Years of Mechanical Engineering. New York: Macmillan, 1937.
Epstein, Ralph C. The Automobile Industry: Its Economic and Commercial Development. New York: Arno Press, 1972.
Evans, Arthur F. The History of the Oil Engine. London: S. Low, Marston & Co., 1932.
Finch, James K. Engineering and Western Civilization. New York: McGraw-Hill, 1951.
Glasscock, C. B. The Gasoline Age. Indianapolis: Bobbs-Merrill, 1937.
Hill, Frank Ernest. The Automobile. New York: Dodd, Mead, 1967.
Janeway, Elizabeth. The Early Days of Automobiles. New York: Random House, 1956.
Kirby, Richard S., et al. Engineering in History. New York: McGraw-Hill, 1956.
Marcus, Abraham, and Rebecca B. Marcus. Power Unlimited. Englewood Cliffs, N. J.: Prentice-Hall, 1959.
Nitske, W. Robert, and Charles Morrow Wilson. Rudolf Diesel: Pioneer of the Age of Power. Norman, Okla.: University of Oklahoma Press, 1965.
Rolt, L. T. C. The Mechanicals: Progress of a Profession. London: William Heinemann, Ltd. and Son, 1967.
Schieldrop, Edgar B. The Highway. London: Hutchinson Publishing Group, 1939.
Scott-Moncrief, David. The Veteran Motor Car. New York: Scribner's, 1956.
Usher, Abbott P. A History of Mechanical Inventions. New York: McGraw-Hill, 1929.

THE "SUPERMAN" PHILOSOPHY OF NIETZSCHE'S
THUS SPAKE ZARATHUSTRA (1883-1885)

Friedrich Wilhelm Nietzsche, the exponent of the "superman" philosophy, presented the basic tenets of his doctrine in his allegorical Thus Spake Zarathustra, the best known of his many writings. Zarathustra is the principal character in the tale. As Nietzsche's spokesman he proclaims a new dogma, replacing the one based on God. He holds, among other things, that the old doctrine is obsolete "because God is dead."

Using allegory to present his ideas on morality, man's will

to power, atheism and eternality, he appeals not only to the philosopher but also to the humanist and literary scholar.   This and
Nietzsche's other publications exerted a profound influence on the
official philosophy and propaganda of National Socialism in the German Third Reich and on the personal philosophy of Adolf Hitler.

Nietzsche was born in Röcken, near Leipzig, in 1844.   He
attended the University of Bonn where he studied philosophy under
Friedrich Wilhelm Ritschl, the German classical philologist.   About
1865 he discovered Arthur Schopenhauer's World as Will and Idea
and found in it "a mirror in which I espied the world, life, and
my own nature depicted with frightful grandeur. "   Schopenhauer's
essential pessimism colored the remainder of Nietzsche's life and
thinking and later, when he came to denounce pessimism as a form
of decadence, he remained basically an unhappy man.

In 1869 he became a professor of classical philosophy at the
University of Basel, and about 1870 he met the German composer
Richard Wagner.   For a while the two men were friends and agreed
in their aesthetic and artistic opinions.   However, as Nietzsche developed his own distinctive philosophy he drew away from the doctrines of both Wagner and Schopenhauer.   In 1874 he and Wagner
had a violent quarrel and became enemies.   In 1889 he suffered a
mental collapse and retired to Weimar where he lived with his mother and sister.   He died in 1900.

Nietzsche's "superman" philosophy, as put forth in Thus
Spake Zarathustra and his other writings, holds that in any generation only a few individuals possess the qualities which will permit
them to do what is impossible for the ordinary, or average, man.
The "will-power" of the superman involves a continuous and intense
effort to overcome the limitations of ordinary men.   It maintains
further that "the weak, the mediocre, the timorous and the sickly, "
who realize their shortcomings when compared to the superman,
"band together and set up a standard of life glorifying the traits of
humility, gentleness, patience, love and forgiveness which protect
their own weakness and makes for their common safety. "   These
traits, Nietzsche feels, are idealized as virtues and are the marks
of "a slave morality which expresses the will to power of the inferior. "   Slave morality, says Nietzsche, which glorifies mediocri-
ty, "is to be maintained and encouraged by the vast body of inferior men. "   The supermen, however, must not permit themselves
to be imposed upon by this morality and thus "forfeit their birth-
right of independence and absolute determination. "   As the superman does not propagate supermen, Nietzsche feels that the master
class must be constantly supplied by a program of selective breeding.

Thus Spake Zarathustra was well known in literary circles
by the end of the nineteenth century.   It has influenced the thinking
of many philosophers, both pro and con and, as mentioned above,
had a profound effect on Nazi Germany's political philosophy.

Suggested Readings

Altizer, Thomas J. , ed. Toward a New Christianity: Readings
in the Death of God Theology. New York: Harcourt, Brace,
1969.
Brinton, Crane. Nietzsche. New York: Harper & Row, 1965.
Chisholm, Roderick M. , et al. Philosophy. Englewood Cliffs,
N. J. : Prentice-Hall, 1964.
Collins, James. A History of Modern European Philosophy. Mil-
waukee, Wis. : Bruce Publishing Co. , 1954.
Copleston, Frederick, S. J. Friedrich Nietzsche, Philosopher of
Culture. London: Burns, Oates and Washbourne, 1942.
Durant, Will. "Friedrich Nietzsche" and "Schopenhauer" in his
The Story of Philosophy. Garden City, N. Y. : Doubleday,
1926.
_____. The Mansions of Philosophy. Garden City, N. Y. : Gar-
den City Publishing Co. , 1929.
Hollingdale, R. J. Nietzsche: The Man and His Philosophy. Ba-
ton Rouge, La. : Louisiana State University Press, 1965.
Jaspers, Karl. Nietzsche. Translated by C. Wallroff and F.
Schmitz. Tucson, Ariz. : University of Arizona Press, 1965.
Kaufman, Walter. Nietzsche: Philosopher, Psychologist, Anti-
Christ. New York: Meridian Books, 1956.
McDaniel, Stanley V. The Major Works of Nietzsche. New York:
Monarch, 1965.
Mencken, Henry L. The Gist of Nietzsche. Belfast, Me. : Bern
Porter, 1973 (Originally published 1910).
Morgan, George A. What Nietzsche Means. New York: Harper
Torch Books, 1965.
Nietzsche, Friedrich. Thus Spake Zarathustra. New York: Mac-
millan, 1906 (Originally published 1883-1885).
Santayana, George. Egotism in German Philosophy. Brooklyn,
N. Y. : Haskell House, 1971 (Originally published 1916).
Schopenhauer, Arthur. The Philosophy of Arthur Schopenhauer.
Translated by Belfort Bax and James Gibson Hume. New York:
Tudor, 1936.
_____. Studies in Pessimism. East Saint Clair Shores, Mich. :
Scholarly Press, 1903.
Shaw, Bernard. Man and Superman: A Comedy and a Philosophy
(play). New York: Brentano's, 1903.

THE SIEGE OF KHARTOUM (1884-1885)

Khartoum, the capital of the Republic of Sudan, is situated
on the Blue Nile and is 432 miles southwest of Port Sudan. It was
founded by the Egyptians in 1822 and in 1830 was made the capital
of their Sudanese possessions.

About 1880 Mohammed Ahmed, a Moslem agitator, proclaimed
himself Mahdi and, with his followers, overran Egyptian Sudan. His

forces defeated the Anglo-Egyptians in November, 1883, whereupon the British government ordered the Egyptians to abandon the Sudan.

General Charles George Gordon, known as "Chinese Gordon" and "Gordon Pasha," a British colonial soldier and administrator, was dispatched to the Sudan and given the responsibility of evacuating the beleaguered Egyptian garrisons. He arrived at Khartoum in February, 1884, and was able to evacuate approximately 2,500 persons, including women, children, sick and wounded, before the city was surrounded by the Mahdi's soldiers on March 12.

That month Gordon requested that troops under the command of Zobeir Rahama Pasha, an Egyptian slave trader and governor of the White Nile district, be sent against the Mahdi's forces. British and Egyptian authorities distrusted him and Gordon's request was refused by the British government. Several subsequent requests for assistance were refused. The British declined to open the road from Suakin to Berber. When the garrison at Berber surrendered Gordon found himself isolated. The fortifications at Khartoum were weak, his troops were small in number and food supplies were inadequate. In spite of this the general was able to withstand the siege for ten months. Following the murder of two British companions Gordon was the only Englishman remaining in Khartoum.

The city fell to the forces of the Mahdi on January 26, 1885, at which time Gordon was killed. Belatedly the British government had sent supporting troops under the command of General Garnet Joseph Wolseley. This force arrived at Khartoum after it had fallen and Gordon had died.

The city was destroyed by the Mahdists and was abandoned for Omdurman. In 1898 it was occupied by the Anglo-Egyptian army and again became the capital of Sudan.

Suggested Readings

Abdulla, Achmed, and T. C. Pakenham. "Charles George Gordon" in their Dreams of Empire. New York: Stokes, 1929.

Bermann, Richard A. The Mahdi of Allah: The Story of the Dervish, Mohammed Ahmed. New York: Macmillan, 1932.

Charles, Elizabeth. Three Martyrs of the Nineteenth Century: Studies from the Lives of Livingstone, Gordon and Patteson. New York: Negro Universities Press, 1969.

Crabites, Pierre. Gordon, the Sudan and Slavery. Westport, Conn.: Negro Universities Press, 1933.

Elton, Godfrey Elton. Gordon of Khartoum: The Life of General Charles George Gordon. New York: Knopf, 1954.

Gordon, Charles George. Khartoum Journal. Edited by Lord Elton. New York: Vanguard Press, 1961 (Originally written 1884-85).

Hagedorn, Hermann. "'Chinese' Gordon" in his The Book of Courage. Philadelphia: Winston, 1920.

Hake, A. E. The Story of Chinese Gordon. London: Remington, 1884.

Johnson, David. Gordon at Khartoum. New York: Grossman Pub-
    lications, 1974.
Nutting, Anthony. Gordon at Khartoum: Martyr or Misfit? New
    York: Potter, 1966.
Orrmont, Arthur. Chinese Gordon, Hero of Khartoum. New York:
    Putnam, 1966.
Strachey, Lytton. "General Gordon" in his Eminent Victorians.
    New York: Modern Library, 1918.
Turnbull, Patrick. Gordon of Khartoum. New York: International
    Publications Service, 1976.
Wortham, H. E. Chinese Gordon. Boston: Little, Brown, 1933.

THE BOULANGER EPISODE (1886-1889)

Georges Ernest Boulanger was a French general and political agitator who became Minister of War in 1886. A protégé of
Georges Clemenceau, leader of the Radical Republicans, he was
popular with the French masses because, to them, he seemed a
champion who would avenge France's defeat by a coalition of German states in the Franco-Prussian war. The fact that he appeared
ready to plunge his country into a conflict for which it was completely unprepared seemed unimportant, but it was this devil-may-
care attitude which eventually led to the downfall of the cabinet of
Charles de Freycinet in 1887.

Boulanger became an open menace to the government. He
was the rallying point for those who were dissatisfied with the
Third Republic, particularly the Bonapartists and the Royalists.
He was removed from the war ministry and from the army, upon
which he entered politics and was elected to the Chamber of Deputies. Here, in June, 1888, he demanded a drastic revision of
the constitution and favored a strong presidential system. He fought
a duel with Charles Floquet, the elderly Premier, and was severely
wounded. He was, in spite of this, elected again in January, 1889.
It was learned that he had been plotting with the Bonapartists and
Royalists and the government felt that, following his election, he
would move against it.

In March he fled the country and in August was tried in absentia for plotting against the Republic and was condemned to exile.
His flight rather than remaining in France and taking decisive action lost him many supporters and the entire Boulangist movement
collapsed. This triggered similar collapses of both the causes of
the Bonapartists and the Royalists.

On September 30, 1891, Boulanger committed suicide at Ix-
elles, Belgium. The incident--some historians consider it a crisis--
reinforced opposition in French republican and parliamentary circles
to all attempts to curb the powers of Parliament. The example of
Boulanger, lumped with those of Napoleon I and Napoleon III, were

considered instances of dictators or would-be dictators using popular plebiscites to overcome republican parliamentary government.

Suggested Readings

Barlatier, P. L'Adventure du général Boulanger. Paris: 1949.
Brogan, Denis W. France Under the Republic: The Development
    of Modern France, 1870-1939. Vol. IV: The Republic in Dan-
    ger. New York: Harper & Row, 1940.
Bury, J. P. T. France, 1814-1940. Philadelphia: University of
    Pennsylvania Press, 1949.
Buthman, William C. The Rise of Nationalism in France. New
    York: Columbia University Press, 1939.
Chapman, Guy. The Third Republic of France: The First Phase,
    1871-1894. London: St. Martin's Press, 1962.
Dansette, A. Le Boulangisme. Paris: 1938.
Gagnon, Paul A. France Since 1789. New York: Harper & Row, 1962.
Maurois, André. A History of France. New York: Farrar,
    Straus, 1956.
_____. An Illustrated History of France. New York: Viking
    Press, 1960.
Recouly, Raymond. The Third Republic. Edited by Funcke-Bre-
    tano. London: William Heinemann, 1928.
Seager, Frederic H. The Boulanger Affair: Political Crossroads
    of France, 1886-1887. Ithaca, N. Y. : Cornell University Press,
    1969.
Wright, Gordon. France in Modern Times: 1760 to the Present.
    Chicago: Rand McNally, 1960.

JACK THE RIPPER AND THE WHITECHAPEL MURDERS (1888)

Between August 31 and November 9, 1888, five women, all
prostitutes, were brutally murdered and mutilated in or near the
Whitechapel district of London's East End by an assailant known only as "Jack the Ripper. " His identity has never been established.

The first victim was Mary Ann Nicholls whose body was
found in Buck's Row, Whitechapel, on the morning of August 31.
Her throat had been cut and her body mutilated. Her remains were
discovered at 3:20 A. M. by George Cross, a market porter, who
was on his way to work.

On September 8 the mutilated body of Annie Chapman, a
widow turned prostitute, was found in Hanbury Street, Spitalfields.
Being without funds she had left her lodgings in Dorset Street in
search of a customer and sometime between 2:00 and 5:00 A. M.
was attacked and killed in the same manner as Mary Ann Nicholls.
Her body was discovered by John Davies, a market porter who, like
George Cross, was on his way to work.

The police made several arrests "on suspicion," including a man named William Henry Piggott and another named John Pizer. As the murder of Mary Ann Nicholls had occurred near a slaughter house it was surmised that the murderer may have worn a leather apron, such as abattoir workers use, to protect his clothes from blood stains. When such an apron, freshly washed, was found the newspapers nicknamed the murderer "Leather Apron."

On September 27 the Central News Agency received a letter written in red ink and signed "Jack the Ripper." This letter, post-marked "London East Central," bragged of past murders and promised others, stating that "the next job I do I shall clip the lady's ears off and send them to the police." The writer of this letter was never traced.

A double murder was committed on September 30. The victims were Elizabeth Stride, killed in a courtyard off Berner Street, Whitechapel, and Catherine Eddowes, who died in Mitre Square, Aldgate. Elizabeth Stride's body was found by Louis Diemschultz, a hawker of cheap jewelry, who was driving his pony cart to an open house entertainment at the International Workmen's Educational Club. The police fixed the time of the murder at shortly before one o'clock. Like the other victims, Elizabeth Stride's throat had been cut and her body mutilated.

Within an hour of the Stride murder the body of Catherine Eddowes was found in Mitre Square. It was discovered by Police Constable Edward Watkins. The throat was cut and the right ear was missing. The body had been horribly mutilated. The police fixed the time of the Eddowes killing at somewhere between 1:30 and 1:45 A.M.

On November 9, 1888, the last of Jack the Ripper's five victims was found in her room, No. 13 Miller's Court, Dorset Street, Spitalfields. The mutilated body of Mary Jane Kelly was discovered by Thomas Bowyer who had, on instructions from his employer John M'Carthy, who was Mary's landlord, gone to the girl's room to collect the rent.

The Whitechapel murders were not the only ones to be committed in London in the fall of 1888. However, the five described above had so much in common that the authorities felt that they had been committed by one person who was not involved in any of the others. All the victims were prostitutes. In each case the throat had been cut and the body mutilated, apparently by one who was familiar with anatomy, such as a surgeon or, perhaps, a man whose trade was slaughtering animals. Several letters received by the police had common characteristics and showed evidence of an intimate knowledge of the details of the killings. All had occurred in the same part of London's East End, the murderer obviously having to have a detailed knowledge of the area in order to avoid the police patrols.

The Whitechapel murders, which created great excitement, ceased as suddenly as they began. They inspired a number of novels and short stories. However, the identity of Jack the Ripper and his motives for his atrocious murders remain as much of a mystery today as when the grisly acts were perpetrated.

Suggested Readings

Abrahamsen, David, M. D. The Murdering Mind. New York: Harper & Row, 1973.

Anderson, Sir Robert. The Lighter Side of My Official Life. London: 1910.

Barker, Richard H. The Fatal Caress. New York: Random House, 1947.

Bromberg, Walter. Mold of Murder: A Psychiatric Study of Homicide. New York: Grune & Stratton, 1961.

Burke, Thomas. "Hands of Mr. Ottermole" (short story) in Queen, Ellery, pseud, ed. 101 Years Entertainment: The Great Detective Stories. Boston: Little, Brown, 1941.

Catton, Joseph. Behind the Scenes of Murder. New York: Norton, 1940.

Cullen, Tom A. When London Walked in Terror. Boston: Houghton Mifflin, 1965.

"East End Slaughters: Jack the Ripper" in Infamous Murders. London: Verdict Press/Phoebus Publishing Co., 1975.

Godwin, John. "Was It 'Jill the Ripper'?" in his Unsolved: The World of the Unknown. Garden City, N. Y.: Doubleday, 1976.

Griffiths, Arthur. Mysteries of Police and Crime. London: 1901.

Guttmacher, M. S. The Mind of the Murderer. Freeport, N. Y.: Books for Libraries, 1960.

Hynd, Alan. "The Case of the Compulsive Killer" in his Sleuths, Slayers and Swindlers: A Casebook of Crime. New York: Barnes, 1959.

Jesse, F. Tennyson. Murder and Its Motives. London: Harrap, 1952.

Lester, David, and Gene Lester. Crime of Passion: Murder and the Murderer. Chicago: Nelson Hall, 1975.

London, Jack. The People of the Abyss. New York: Macmillan, 1903.

McCormick, Donald. The Identity of Jack the Ripper. London: Harrap, 1959.

McDade, Thomas M., compiler. The Annals of Murder. Norman, Okla.: University of Oklahoma Press, 1961.

Reinhardt, James Melvin. The Psychology of Strange Killers. Springfield, Ill.: Thomas, 1962.

Scott, Sir Harold, with Philippa Pearce. From Inside Scotland Yard. New York: Macmillan, 1965.

Stevenson, Robert Louis. "The Strange Case of Dr. Jekyll and Mr. Hyde" (fiction) in his Merry Men and Other Tales and Fables. New York: Scribner's, 1905 (Originally published 1886).

Thompson, Laurence Victor. The Story of Scotland Yard. New York: Random House, 1954.

"Who Was Jack the Ripper?" in <u>Crimes and Punishment</u>, Vol. 20.
    Editorial presentation: Jackson Morley. London: BPC, 1973.
Wilson, Colin, and Patricia Pitman. <u>Encyclopedia of Murder</u>.
    New York: Putnam, 1962.
Winslow, L. Forbes. <u>Recollections of Forty Years</u>. London: 1910.
Wolfgang, Marvin E., compiler. <u>Studies in Homicide</u>. New York:
    Harper & Row, 1967.
Woodhall, Edwin T. <u>Jack the Ripper, or When London Walked in
    Terror</u>. London: Harrap, 1937.

THE BOTTOMLEY SWINDLES (c. 1890-1922)

The swindler and confidence man have always been and, no doubt, will always be with us. Some of the more notorious were Giuseppe Balsamo, better known as Cagliostro, Serge Alexandre Savisky, Ivar Kreuger, Charles Ponzi, Joseph R. "Yellow Kid" Weil, Ernest Terah Hooley, Jabez Balfour, Whittaker Wright and a gentleman who signed spurious checks "D. S. Windle," whose real name has never been determined.

One British swindler, called by newspaper reporters "The Man of Millions," was Horatio William Bottomley who succeeded in mulcting the public of thousands of pounds before being sentenced to a seven-year prison term for fraud in 1922.

Born in 1860, Bottomley was the son of a tailor and had been raised in an orphanage. He was, at various times, an orator, politician, lawyer and journalist. He promoted literally dozens of bogus companies, was a member of Parliament for South Hackney and founded and edited the weekly news magazine <u>John Bull</u>. This publication specialized in sensational disclosures and attacks on various political figures.

During World War I Bottomley, a spellbinding orator, addressed recruiting meetings with great effectiveness. His admirers did not know that he received more than 27,000 pounds for his services in a patriotic cause.

The British government proposed a Victory Loan, the minimum subscription to which was five pounds. This sum was more than the average British citizen could afford and Bottomley advertised in <u>John Bull</u> that anyone subscribing one pound to the Loan would be given a one-fifth share in a five-pound bond. The interest was to be accumulated and, according to Bottomley's advertisements, distributed later in the form of large money prizes.

Certain difficulties stood in the way of the scheme. One of the companies which Bottomley had promoted had gone bankrupt under suspicious circumstances and a pamphlet, <u>Horatio Bottomley Exposed</u>, was being circulated. He was accused of chicanery in con-

nection with certain business promotions, the charges being true,
as shown by public records. He sold stock in the London and
Southwestern Canal Company, a concern which supposedly was to
operate cargo boats on the canal. The shareholders brought suit
when it was discovered that there was no traffic on the canal for
the reason that there was no water in it. Bottomley was able to
cover the obligations of the Company and thus avoid court action.

John Bull conducted racing sweepstakes and prize contests
which, though illegal in Great Britain, were handled by a firm established by Bottomley in Switzerland. "The Man of Millions" sold
thousands of sweepstakes tickets but made a point of seeing to it
that tickets for the probable runners went to friends and associates
who agreed to accept nominal sums rather than large cash prizes
should their entries win.

Horatio Bottomley Exposed imperilled the Victory Loan project in that it deterred many potential investors from purchasing the
one pound shares. Bottomley persuaded Reuben Bigland, an associate and friend, to find a printer who, for a consideration of 100
pounds, would agree to reprint the pamphlet and stand suit for libel. The pamphlet was reprinted and published and Bottomley
brought suit as planned. He conducted his own case in court, judgment was found for him and he was awarded 500 pounds damages,
a sum he never collected from the printer or anyone else. He then
proceeded with his Victory Loan campaign, selling more than 650,000
pounds worth of bonds. Most of the proceeds disappeared into the
promoter's pockets. The swindle was exposed when his inadequate
accounting system proved incapable of dealing with the distribution
of the shares and prizes.

It was obvious that the Victory Loan bond promotion was a
wholesale fraud. Bigland, following a quarrel with Bottomley, accused him publicly of a long list of illegal business transactions.
Bottomley countered by charging Bigland with obtaining money by
threats. He brought suit but the charge was dismissed. Bottomley sued a second time and it was realized that it was he rather
than Bigland who should be on trial. Thousands of demands for re-
payment of subscriptions were sent to the John Bull office. The
bond project headed by Bottomley went into receivership and on May
19, 1922, "The Man of Millions" was formally charged. He was
convicted of fraud and imprisoned, as mentioned above. After being released from prison he returned to journalism, went bankrupt
once again and appeared briefly on the London stage. He died in
1933, having lost his friends, money, influence, health and reputation.

Suggested Readings

Deeson, A. F. L. Great Swindlers. New York: Drake Publishers,
    1972.
Gibson, Walter Brown, ed. The Fine Art of Swindling. New York:
    Grosset & Dunlap, 1966.

Hancock, Ralph, and Henry Chafetz. The Compleat Swindler. New
   York: Macmillan, 1968.
Klein, Alexander. Grand Deception: The World's Most Spectacular
   and Successful Hoaxes, Impostures, Ruses and Frauds. Phil-
   adelphia: Lippincott, 1955.
Leff, Arthur A. Swindling and Selling. New York: Free Press,
   1976.
MacDougall, Curtis D. Hoaxes. New York: Macmillan, 1940.
Mehling, Harold. The Scandalous Scamps. New York: Holt, 1956.
Raymond, E. T. , pseud. "Mr. Horatio Bottomley" in his Uncen-
   sored Celebrities. New York: Holt, 1919.
Symons, Julian. "Great British Swindlers" in his A Pictorial His-
   tory of Crime. New York: Crown Publishers, 1966.
Turner, Barry. "Horatio Bottomley, Man of Millions" in Taylor,
   A. J. P. , editor in chief. Purnell's History of the 20th Century,
   Vol. 4. New York: Purnell, 1971.

THE FRENCH PANAMA CANAL SCANDAL (1892-1893)

Ferdinand de Lesseps promoted the Suez Canal, which opened
in 1869.   In 1880 he organized the Interoceanic Canal Company
which was to build a similar canal across the Isthmus of Panama.
The Company was underfinanced from its inception as the promoters
did not appreciate the gigantic engineering problems which had to
be solved before the contemplated canal could be constructed.   Soon
they were in serious financial trouble.   The directors felt that the
only way out of their fiscal quagmire was to seek a lottery loan,
something requiring the permission of the French government.

Upon receiving the request to approve such a loan, the government made an investigation of the Panama situation.   A public
works expert, Armand Rousseau, submitted an adverse report and
as a consequence the request was denied.

Two years later, in 1888, the French Chamber of Deputies
finally voted its approval of the Panama canal lottery loan.   However, a tight money period combined with general public suspicion
of the project led to the loan being undersubscribed, and in 1889
the Interoceanic Canal Company went into receivership.

The shareholders demanded an investigation into the affairs
of the Company.   Édouard Drumont, editor of the anti-Semitic newspaper La Libre Parole, published a series of stories exposing corruption in political circles and supporting the shareholders' demands.
Other French journals made similar disclosures and the government,
though reluctant, eventually had no choice but to pursue the inquiry.

Leading members of the Canal Company's board of directors
were tried and subsequently certain members of the Chamber of
Deputies, suspected of taking bribes, were similarly tried.   In both

proceedings the question arose as to why the Chamber, after refusing to authorize the original lottery loan, had approved it in 1888.
It turned out that the Canal Company had bribed journalists, members of the Chamber and other government officials to obtain a
vote favorable to their request.

It was learned that Baron Jacques de Reinach, a banker and
speculator, and Dr. Cornelius Herz, a businessman with a shady
financial background, had acted as intermediaries between the Company and the Chamber of Deputies.   Both men were Jewish, "which
lent particular relish to the scandal. "

Most of the men accused of taking bribes were Republicans,
and it was hoped by their political opponents, the Right Wing Conservatives, that this would weaken Republican influence in the country.   Reinach died suddenly under mysterious circumstances and
Herz fled from France, which events strengthened the hopes of the
Conservative members of the Chamber.

Only one politician was sentenced for accepting a bribe and
the Republicans fared as well in the elections of 1893 as they had
previously.   De Lesseps and his son, Charles Aimée Marie, were
convicted of fraudulent bankruptcy in the same year.   The father,
by then senile, died on December 7, 1894, unaware of his disgrace.

Suggested Readings

Beatty, Charles.   De Lesseps of Suez.   Buffalo, N. Y. :   McClelland,
     1956.
     _____.   Ferdinand De Lesseps.   London: Eyre and Spottiswoode,
     1956.
Brogan, Denis W.   France Under the Republic: The Development
     of Modern France, 1870-1939.   New York: Harper & Row,
     1940.
Buthman, William C.   The Rise of Nationalism in France.   New
     York: Columbia University Press, 1939.
Byrnes, Robert F.   Antisemitism in Modern France.   New Bruns-
     wick, N. J. :   Rutgers University Press, 1950.
Chapman, Guy.   The Third Republic of France: The First Phase,
     1871-1894.   London: St. Martin's Press, 1962.
Chidsey, Donald Barr.   The Panama Canal, an Informal History.
     New York: Crown Publishers, 1970.
Long, Laura.   De Lesseps, Builder of Suez.   New York: Longmans,
     Green, 1958.
Mack, Gerstle.   The Land Divided: A History of the Panama Canal
     and Other Isthmian Canal Projects.   New York: Knopf, 1944.
Recouly, Raymond.   The Third Republic.   Translated by E. F. Buck-
     ley.   New York: Putnam's, 1928.
Shirer, William L.   The Collapse of the Third Republic.   New York:
     Simon & Schuster, 1969.
Simon, Maron J.   The Panama Affair.   New York: Scribner, 1971.

THE DREYFUS CASE (1894-1899)

The central figure of this famous court case was the French
Jewish artillery officer, Captain Alfred Dreyfus, an innocent victim
of a gross miscarriage of justice.

In 1894 Dreyfus, as a member of the general staff, was accused of having written an anonymous letter to the German military
attaché at Paris, disclosing French military information. Despite
inadequate evidence a secret court martial found Dreyfus guilty and
condemned him to public degradation and imprisonment at the French
penal colony on Devil's Island. Following this, anti-Jewish demonstrations broke out all over France.

Two years later Lieutenant-Colonel Georges Picquart, head
of the French War Office Intelligence Department, discovered evidence which apparently absolved Dreyfus and implicated Major Marie
Charles Ferdinand Walsin Esterhazy, a French infantry officer, as
the writer of the letter. Picquart's superiors, however, refused to
reopen the case and he was replaced by Lieutenant-Colonel Hubert
Joseph Henry.

Major Esterhazy was then accused of forging the incrimin-
ating document, this accusation being made in a letter written by
Matthiew Dreyfus, brother of Captain Dreyfus, and addressed to the
French Minister of War. Esterhazy was tried by court martial in
1898 as the result of pressure brought by Auguste Scheurer-Kestner,
Vice President of the French Senate, but was acquitted.

The Dreyfus case became an important political issue, and
such prominent persons as Georges Clemenceau, Anatole France
and Emile Zola agitated for a reversal of Dreyfus' 1894 conviction.

In 1898 Zola published an open letter in the newspaper L'Au-
rore. In this letter, titled J'Accuse ("I Accuse") Zola charged the
government and general staff with hiding the truth. He was tried
for libel and was found guilty but escaped to England. Public demand was such that eventually a new trial was held. Colonel Henry
had confessed that he had forged certain documentary evidence. He
was arrested but before he could be tried he committed suicide in
prison.

Esterhazy was dismissed from the service and left France
for England where he admitted writing the original letter which had
led to Dreyfus' trial and conviction.

Dreyfus was retried in 1899 and again found guilty. He was
sentenced to ten years imprisonment, but shortly after the trial the
government overruled the decision of the court and granted him a
full pardon. Subsequently the Court of Cassation, the French high
court of appeals, reviewed the second court martial and nullified
its findings on the grounds that false evidence had been accepted by

420   Footnotes to World History

the court and that the court had also refused to admit testimony
which would have proved Dreyfus innocent.

Dreyfus was reinstated in the French army with the rank of
Major and in World War I served as a Lieutenant-Colonel and was
appointed to the Legion of Honor.

Suggested Readings

Arendt, Hannah. Origins of Totalitarianism. New York: Meridian
   Books, 1958.
Aymar, Brandt, and Edward Sagarin. "Captain Alfred Dreyfus" in
   their A Pictorial History of the World's Great Trials. New
   York: Crown Publishers, 1967.
Byrnes, Robert F. Antisemitism in Modern France. Vol. I, The
   Prologue to the Dreyfus Affair. New Brunswick, N. J. : Rut-
   gers University Press, 1950.
Chapman, Guy. The Dreyfus Case: A Reassessment. New York:
   Reynal & Hitchcock, 1955.
Derfler, Leslie. The Dreyfus Affair: Tragedy of Errors? Boston:
   Heath, 1963.
"The Dreyfus Affair" in Crimes and Punishment, Vol. 11. Editor-
   ial presentation: Jackson Morley. London: BPC, 1973.
Halasz, Nicholas. Captain Dreyfus: The Story of a Mass Hysteria.
   New York: Grove Press, 1957.
"Justice in Slow Motion" in Crimes and Punishment, Vol. 3. Ed-
   itorial presentation: Jackson Morley. London: BPC, 1973.
Kayser, Jacques. The Dreyfus Affair. New York: Covici, Friede,
   1931.
Kedward, H. R. The Dreyfus Affair: Catalyst for Tensions in
   French Society. London: Longmans, Green, 1965.
Lewis, David L. Prisoners of Honor: The Dreyfus Affair. New
   York: Morrow, 1973.
McDay, Donald. The Dreyfus Case: By the Man--Alfred Dreyfus--
   and His Son--Pierre Dreyfus. New Haven, Conn. : Yale Uni-
   versity Press, 1937.
McKown, Robin. "The Dreyfus Affair" in his Seven Famous Trials
   in History. New York: Vanguard Press, 1963.
Paléologue, Maurice. An Intimate Journal of the Dreyfus Case.
   New York: Criterion Books, 1957.
Reinach, Joseph. Histoire de L'Affaire Dreyfus: Le Procès de
   1894. Paris: Editions de la Revue Blanche, 1901-1911.
Schecter, Betty. The Dreyfus Affair: A National Scandal. Boston:
   Houghton Mifflin, 1965.
Schwartzkoppen, Max von. The Truth About Dreyfus: From the
   Schwartzkoppen Papers. New York: Putnam's, 1931.
Symons, Julian. "The Scandals That Rocked France" in his A Pic-
   torial History of Crime. New York: Crown Publishers, 1966.
Thomas, Marcel. "The Dreyfus Affair" in Taylor, A. J. P. , editor-
   in-chief. Purnell's History of the 20th Century, Vol. 1. New
   York: Purnell, 1971.
Tuchman, Barbara W. The Proud Tower. New York: Macmillan,
   1965.

Werstein, Irving. <u>I Accuse: The Story of the Dreyfus Case.</u> New
    York: Messner, 1967.
Zola, Emile. <u>L'Affaire Dreyfus: La Vérité en Marche.</u> Paris:
    Bibliothèque-Charpentier, 1901.

THE OSCAR WILDE LAWSUITS (1895)

      John Sholto Douglas, the Eighth Marquis of Queensberry,
was a fiery-tempered former naval officer, champion amateur boxer and brawler who on one occasion had attacked the British prime
minister with a whip. His son, Alfred Bruce Douglas, known as
"Bosie," was the opposite of his father in every way, being given
to the writing of poetry and authoring such books as <u>The City of the
Soul</u> and <u>Sonnets and Lyrics.</u> He was a close friend of Oscar Wilde,
the Irish poet, playwright, novelist and wit. "Bosie" had met Wilde
in 1892 and from then on a homosexual relationship had existed between them. Queensberry most understandingly detested Wilde, particularly after he had forbidden his son to associate with him and
his ultimatum had been ignored.

      In 1895 Queensberry left his calling card at the Albemarle
Club in London. On this he had written "To Oscar Wilde posing
as a somdomite." Even though the word was misspelled the Marquis' meaning was clear and Wilde had no choice but to sue for libel. This he did, although against his better judgment. On March
2 Queensberry was arrested. A month later he pleaded not guilty
to the charge of criminal libel, stating that the libel was true and
should be publicized for the public benefit.

      Queensberry had spent the month between his arrest and the
start of the trial investigating Wilde's background and his detectives
had uncovered ample evidence of the playwright's unconventional conduct with members of his own sex. Wilde, separated from his wife
and family, had spent the time in Southern France, vacationing with
"Bosie."

      When Wilde returned to England he was urged by his friends
to leave the country rather than press his suit. This he declined
to do and the trial proceeded. Under cross examination Wilde displayed his mastery of epigrams and witty repartee but the case was
decided in favor of Queensberry who was found not guilty after Wilde,
on advice of counsel, withdrew the prosecution.

      The withdrawal meant legally that the Irish playwright was
admitting the truth of the charge of sodomy and was hoping to avoid
criminal proceedings against him "which would otherwise have been
inevitable."

      Queensberry then sent the information his detectives had gath-
ered to the Director of Public Prosecutions and Wilde was arrested.

Also taken into custody was Alfred Taylor, a procurer with whom
Wilde was associated.

At the first trial in which Wilde was the defendant various
male witnesses testified to having had sexual relations with him
for which he paid them various sums of money. It was shown that
these relations had been suggested by Wilde. He was found not
guilty on eight counts but the jury could not reach a decision concerning the others. This meant that the playwright must be tried
a second time. Taylor was found guilty of procuring.

On May 22, 1895, Oscar Wilde was charged, in a new indictment, with fifteen counts. Again the jury could not agree on
all of them. A third trial, lasting five days, followed. Wilde was
then found guilty. He was sentenced to serve two years in prison
at hard labor.

Queensberry then sued Wilde for the costs he had incurred
in the libel trial. The playwright was unable to pay and went bankrupt.

Having served his prison sentence, Wilde went to Paris where,
under the name of Sebastian Melmoth, he died on November 30, 1900,
at the age of 46. Queensberry died the same year, and "Bosie,"
who passed away in 1945, devoted his life to journalism and writing.

Suggested Readings

Bendz, Ernst. "The Real Oscar Wilde," Englische Studien, De-
    cember, 1916.
Birnbaum, Martin. "Oscar Wilde" in his Fragments and Memories.
    London: Mathews, 1920.
Braybrooke, Patrick. Oscar Wilde, a Study. London: Braithwaite,
    1930.
Cooper-Prichard, A. H. "Reminiscences of Oscar Wilde," Corn-
    hill Magazine, February, 1930.
Esdaile, A. "The New Hellenism," Fortnightly Review, October,
    1910.
Harris, Frank. Oscar Wilde: His Life and Confessions. New
    York: Covici, Friede, 1930.
"Oscar and Bosie" in Crimes and Punishment, Vol. 16. Editorial
    presentation: Jackson Morley. London: BPC, 1973.
Powys, J. C. "Oscar Wilde" in his Suspended Judgments. New
    York: Shaw, 1916.
Ransome, Arthur. Oscar Wilde: A Critical Study. London: Seck-
    er, 1912.
Renier, G. J. Oscar Wilde. New York: Appleton, 1933.
Shanks, Edward. "Oscar Wilde," London Mercury, July, 1924.
Sherard, R. H. The Life of Oscar Wilde. New York: Dodd, Mead,
    1928.
_____. Oscar Wilde Twice Defended. Chicago: Argus Press,
    1935.

Sherman, S. P. "Oscar Wilde" in his Critical Woodcuts. New York: Scribner, 1926.

Stokes, Leslie, and Sewell Stokes. Oscar Wilde (play). New York: Random House, 1938.

Symons, Arthur, A Study of Oscar Wilde. London: Sawyer, 1930.

Wilde, Oscar. Some Letters to Alfred Douglas. Edited by A. C. Dennison, Jr., and Harrison Post. San Francisco: Nash, 1924.

THE INVENTION OF THE DIESEL ENGINE (1897)

By the early nineteenth century the steam engine had been successfully used as a source of power in boats, locomotives and stationary applications, such as mine pumps. Nikolaus August Otto, Gottlieb Daimler and others designed and built practical internal combustion engines in the 1870's and 1880's, based on earlier inventions, and the electric motor, developed by a number of inventors, came into being about the same time. Another power source, the diesel engine, first saw the light of day in 1897. This internal combustion device was the invention of Rudolf Diesel, a German mechanical engineer, who applied a theory of the French physicist Nicolas Léonard Sadi Carnot to his engine.

In 1824 Carnot had published his Reflections on the Motive Power of Heat. Here he suggested that, at least in theory, it should be possible to construct an engine which would be self-igniting, being fired by the heat generated by the compression of air to one-fourteenth of its original volume. The Otto and Daimler engines differed from the steam engine in one important particular. In the former fuel, either a flammable gas or a liquid, was ignited in a closed-end cylinder, generating sufficient pressure to move a piston, whereas in the steam engine the fuel was burned outside the cylinder. Here steam pressure, generated in a boiler, was used to move the piston. In both cases the reciprocating motion of the piston was changed to rotary motion by means of a crank assembly.

Diesel's engine resembled the internal combustion engines of Otto and Daimler in that the fuel was burned in the cylinder but, unlike these engines, did not use an electric spark to ignite it. Instead, Carnot's theory of compression, mentioned above, was put to practical application.

Ackroyd Stuart, a British engineer, had built and patented a small oil-burning self-igniting engine in 1892, but his invention was inefficient and failed commercially. Diesel, who had been working on the problem in Augsburg, took out German patents in 1892 and 1893. He experimented with pulverized coal as a fuel and, finding this to be impractical, substituted kerosene. In 1897 he operated his first engine, which burned kerosene. It used the two-cycle principle but he found, after further research, that the four-cycle system was more efficient. Today most such engines run on four cycles.

The diesel engine operates somewhat differently from the
four-cycle Otto/Daimler engines. The first (suction) stroke draws
air, but no fuel, into the cylinder through an intake valve. The
air is then compressed as the piston returns to the head of the cylinder, the compression raising its temperature to about 800° (400° C.).
Vaporized fuel is then injected into the cylinder. The fuel burns
instantly, driving the piston away from the cylinder head. On the
fourth (exhaust) stroke the piston returns to the head of the cylinder and the burned fuel is expelled through a second valve.

The diesel engine is highly efficient. It is, in general, a
slow speed device with crankshaft speeds of 100 to 750 revolutions
per minute, as contrasted with Otto/Daimler engines which normally revolve at 2,500 to 5,000 R.P.M., although some types of die-
sels are designed to operate at a crankshaft speed of up to 2,000.
Because they use a high compression ratio of 14 to 1 or even higher they are more heavily built than Otto/Daimlers. This disadvantage is offset by their greater efficiency and by the fact that they
operate on fuel oils which are comparatively inexpensive.

Soon after World War I improved models of diesel engines
were being used in motor trucks, as marine engines and for power-
ing tractors. The diesel locomotive, inaugurated in 1934, has today replaced most steam locomotives. Smaller versions of the diesel engine have been perfected and may be found furnishing the motive power for certain passenger automobiles.

Rudolf Diesel died on the evening of September 29, 1913,
when he mysteriously disappeared from the deck of the steamer
Dresden while traveling on the English Channel between Antwerp
and Harwich. His invention has lived after him and is considered
one of the major contributions to twentieth century industrialization.

Suggested Readings

Burlingame, Roger. Inventors Behind the Inventor. New York:
    Harcourt, Brace, 1947.
Cardwell, D. S. L. Steam Power in the Eighteenth Century. Lon-
    don: Sheed and Ward, 1963.
Carnot, Nicolas Léonard Sadi. Reflections on the Motive Power of
    Heat. Paris: 1824.
Cohn, David L. Combustion on Wheels. Boston: Houghton Mifflin,
    1944.
Cressy, Edward. A Hundred Years of Mechanical Engineering.
    New York: Macmillan, 1937.
Cummins, Clessie L. My Days With the Diesel. Philadelphia:
    Chilton, 1967.
Epstein, Rudolph C. The Automobile Industry: Its Economic and
    Commercial Development. New York: Arno Press, 1972.
Evans, Arthur F. The History of the Oil Engine. London: S. Low,
    Marston & Co., 1932.
Finch, James K. Engineering and Western Civilization. New York:
    McGraw-Hill, 1951.

Glasscock, C. B. The Gasoline Age. Indianapolis: Bobbs-Merrill, 1937.

Kirby Richard S. , et al. Engineering in History. New York: Mc-Graw-Hill, 1956.

Marcus, Abraham, and Rebecca B. Marcus. Power Unlimited. En-glewood Cliffs, N. J. : Prentice-Hall, 1959.

Nitske, W. Robert, and Charles Morrow Wilson. Rudolf Diesel: Pioneer of the Age of Power. Norman, Okla. : University of Oklahoma Press, 1965.

Rolt, L. T. C. The Mechanicals: Progress of a Profession. Lon-don: William Heinemann, Ltd. , and Son, 1967.

Usher, Abbott P. A History of Mechanical Inventions. New York: McGraw-Hill, 1929.

THE DISCOVERY OF POLONIUM AND RADIUM (1898)

One of the most important scientific breakthroughs of the late nineteenth century was made by Pierre Curie and his wife Ma-rie, who discovered the radioactive elements polonium and radium in 1898.

Pierre Curie was a French chemist. He conducted research-es on piezoelectricity, the magnetic properties of bodies at various temperatures and kindred subjects. In 1895 he married Marie (Mar-ja) Sklodowska, a Polish-born physical chemist who had been edu-cated in Warsaw and at the Sorbonne in Paris. Together the hus-band and wife investigated radioactivity, basing their research on the groundwork performed by the German chemist Martin Heinrich Klaproth and the French physicist Antoine Henri Becquerel.

Uranium, a radioactive element, was discovered by Klaproth in 1789 in the metallic ore pitchblende. It was first isolated in the metallic state in 1842. In 1896 Becquerel demonstrated its radio-active qualities by producing an image on a photographic plate cov-ered with a light-absorbing substance. Investigations of radioactiv-ity made by the Curies shortly afterward led to the discovery of polonium and radium in 1898 and the isolation of the latter in 1902.

Pierre and Marie Curie discovered that pitchblende was four times more radioactive than its principal component, uranium. They separated the ore into many chemical fractions in order to isolate the unknown sources of radioactivity. Polonium, or Radium F, was discovered first, in July, 1898, and in December of that year a sec-ond new element, which was christened "radium, " was announced. Polonium was isolated by the use of bismuth sulfide and a highly radioactive barium chloride fraction was treated with barium to re-move the radioactive substance. This substance was discovered to be radium, a new element.

Polonium, though scientifically interesting, has few practical

applications, principally because of its extremely short half-life of
140 days. Radium, on the other hand, has a half-life of 1,620
years. Extracting it from pitchblende was an almost endless task,
as a ton of the ore contained little more than a trace of radium.

Other scientists took up the investigation of radioactivity.
Sir Joseph John Thomson, the British physicist and discoverer of
electrons, headed a group of men who worked on the project at Cavendish Laboratories in England. Ernest Rutherford, one of Thomson's disciples, investigated the radioactive element thorium and
found that it gave off a gas which was itself highly radioactive. In
1902 Rutherford and Frederick Soddy, after conducting experiments
at McGill University in Canada, published a new theory of radioactivity. The work of these and other researchers, such as Lord
Kelvin and Jean Perrin, laid the groundwork for today's practical
applications of atomic energy.

The Curies and Antoine Becquerel were awarded the Nobel
Prize for physics in 1903 and Marie was awarded it for chemistry
in 1911. In 1906 Pierre Curie was killed in a street accident. His
wife, who never remarried, carried on their work until her death
in 1934.

Radium had been found effective in the treatment of cancer.
Radium radiations have a harmful effect on normal cells, causing
"radium burns" to those cells which are over-exposed to them. However, cancerous cells are often more sensitive to radiation than normal cells and, under carefully controlled conditions, may be destroyed without harming the healthy cells. Commercial applications
of radium include the manufacture of luminous paint, the application
of which to such objects as clock faces, door knobs and the like,
causes them to glow in the dark.

Suggested Readings

Bigland, Eileen. Madame Curie. New York: Criterion Books,
    1957.
Bolton, Sarah K. "Marie Curie, Scientist (1867-1934)" in her Lives
    of Girls Who Became Famous. New York: Crowell, 1949.
Curie, Eve. Madame Curie, A Biography by Eve Curie. Translat-
    ed by Vincent Sheehan. Garden City, N.Y.: Doubleday, 1937.
Curie, Marie. Pierre Curie. Translated by C. and V. Kellogg.
    New York: Macmillan, 1923.
Einstein, Albert. Out of My Later Years. New York: Philosoph-
    ical Library, 1950.
Henriod, Lorraine. Marie Curie. New York: Putnam, 1970.
Jaffe, Bernard. "Curie: The Story of Marie and Pierre" in his
    Crucibles: The Great Chemists, Their Lives and Achievements.
    New York: Tudor Publishing Co., 1930.
McKown, Robin. Marie Curie. New York: Putnam's, 1959.
Rubin, Elizabeth. The Curies and Radium. New York: Watts,
    1961.

Rutherford, Ernest Rutherford. Radioactive Substances and Their Radiations. Cambridge: Cambridge University Press, 1913.

Sague, Mary Landon. "Marie Sklodowska Curie" in Mizwa, Stephen P., ed. Great Men and Women of Poland. New York: Macmillan, 1943.

Viol, J. "Commercial Production and Uses of Radium," Journal of Chemical Education, Vol. 3, 1926.

THE FASHODA INCIDENT (1898-1899)

In 1875 the finances of Egypt were in a state of chaos. Ismail Pasha, the Khedive had, through reckless and ill-advised investments in private and public projects, plunged his country into a hopeless morass of debt. In an effort to regain some measure of solvency he sold his shares in the Suez Canal Company to the British government. This focused British attention on the canal and the future of Egypt.

In the 1890's England and France both wished to extend their colonial possessions in Africa. England sought to establish a continuous strip of British-held territory extending north to south from Cairo to the Cape of Good Hope. France had similar ideas and envisioned an extension of its territory and sphere of influence across Africa east to west, from Senegal on the Atlantic coast to Somaliland on the Red Sea.

In the two decades following Ismail Pasha's sale of his Suez Canal Company stock England had--despite the protests of Tewfik Pasha, the new Khedive--exerted an increasingly great control over Egypt's internal affairs. Egypt had become a British protectorate and France was losing ground. It was this situation that caused the latter country to seek other areas in Africa to acquire and which led to her plans to establish the above-mentioned east-west strip. She decided to control the water supply of Egypt by taking over the headwaters of the Nile River. Sir Edward Grey, British Minister of War, stated in a speech in the House of Commons that such a move by the French "would be viewed as an unfriendly act," and took immediate steps to prevent France from carrying out her intentions. Horatio Herbert Kitchener, a prominent British general officer, headed an Anglo-Egyptian force which started up the Nile River. Simultaneously a French force of Sengalese soldiers commanded by Captain Jean Baptiste Marchand started eastward from Brazzaville in the French Congo. Both armies were proceeding to Fashoda, a fortress on the Upper Nile which was of extreme strategic importance for controlling the headwaters of that river.

Marchand and his men arrived at Fashoda on July 10, 1898. Two months later Kitchener's forces arrived by boat. The reinforcements Marchand expected failed to materialize and the French captain realized that his troops, though occupying the fortress, stood

no chance whatever against Kitchener's militarily superior forces.
The two commanders met and discussed the situation.   They
decided to engage in no hostilities until instructions were received
from their respective governments.

Théophile Delcassé, French Minister of Foreign Affairs,
realized that France's position at Fashoda was hopeless.   Kitchener
had numerical superiority at the fortress and Great Britain's naval
supremacy in the Mediterranean was unquestioned.   Further, it was
apparent that an eventual clash with Germany was inevitable; the
French wished to be able to count on the assistance of Great Britain
when the time came for a show of force.   Marchand and his men
retired from the Upper Nile on November 3, 1898, and a war between England and France was narrowly averted.

In March of the following year France renounced all territory along the Nile.   She received in exchange certain virtually
worthless lands in the Sahara Desert.

Suggested Readings

Buthman, William C.   The Rise of Integral Nationalism in France.
     New York: Columbia University Press, 1939.
Gooch, George P.   Before the War.   New York: Russell and Rus-
     sell, 1938.
Hayes, Carlton J. A.   A Generation of Materialism, 1871-1900.   New
     York: Harper & Row, 1941.
Hinsley, F. H.   "British Foreign Policy and Colonial Questions,
     1895-1904" in Benians, E. A. , et al. , eds.   The Cambridge His-
     tory of the British Empire, Vol. III.   Cambridge: The Univer-
     sity Press, 1959.
Langer, William L.   The Diplomacy of Imperialism, 1890-1892.
     New York: Knopf, 1935.
LeMay, G. H. L.   British Supremacy in South Africa, 1899-1907.
     Oxford: The University Press, 1965.
Magnus, Philip.   Kitchener: Portrait of an Imperialist.   New York:
     Dutton, 1959.
Mathews, J. J.   Egypt and the Formation of the Anglo-French En-
     tente of 1904.   Philadelphia: University of Pennsylvania Press,
     1939.
Moon, Parker T.   Imperialism and World Politics.   New York:
     Macmillan, 1962.
Nicolson, Harold.   Diplomacy.   3rd edition.   New York: Oxford
     University Press, 1963.
Seaman, L. C. B.   From Vienna to Versailles.   New York: Harper
     & Row, 1963.
Seth, Ronald.   Milestones in African History.   Philadelphia: Chil-
     ton, 1969.
Sterling, Thomas, and the editors of Horizon Magazine.   The Ex-
     ploration of Africa.   New York: American Heritage Publishing
     Co. , 1963.

Taylor, Alan John Percivale. The Struggle for Mastery in Europe, 1848-1918. Oxford: Clarendon Press, 1954.

Walker, Eric A. A History of Southern Africa. London: Longmans, Green, 1962.

Ward, A. W., and George P. Gooch, eds. The Cambridge History of British Foreign Policy. New York: Macmillan, 1923.

THE BAGHDAD RAILWAY CONCESSION (1899)

In the latter part of the nineteenth century the Turkish empire was in serious financial and political trouble. Sultan Abdul Hamid II favored the construction of a railroad through the region of Anatolia and connecting Constantinople with Mesopotamia. He felt that such a railroad would bring his country together by permitting the rapid movement of troops to suppress internal rebellions and protect the Ottoman Empire from enemies outside its borders. It was further thought that economic development of the Tigris and Euphrates River valleys would be stimulated by such a line and that this, in turn, would generate much-needed tax revenues.

The Turkish government realized that it lacked both the funds and the technical skills required for the construction of a rail line and that financial and technical assistance would have to come from outside the country. A concession to plan and build the line would have to be granted and whatever European country received the concession would realize substantial economic, commercial and political advantages.

Great Britain's interest in the project lessened following the opening of the Suez Canal in 1869. However, she realized that such a railroad, granting a potential access to India, in which she was vitally interested, could have dire consequences should it be controlled by a hostile foreign power. Russia, whose aggressive policy in the Ottoman Empire had resulted in her steady expansion, hoped ultimately to acquire Constantinople and control of the straits between the Mediterranean and the Black Sea. Consequently she had looked with disfavor on any plan which would assist the Turkish Empire.

The European Trunk Railway was completed to Constantinople, linking central and western Europe with the Ottoman Empire in 1888. It was then that Abdul Hamid became interested in the building of rail lines within his own empire. French and English entrepreneurs had constructed some lines in the area and the sultan tried unsuccessfully to get the English to agree to build a line to Baghdad. French financiers were willing to underwrite the project but the sultan, fearing that France was already over-influential in the Ottoman Empire, declined to deal with them. Germany, which had both financial and technical capabilities for constructing the proposed line, was anxious to participate in the exploitation of underdeveloped coun-

tries. Further, she had not interfered unduly in Turkey's internal
affairs. On October 4, 1888, Georg von Siemens, managing director of the Deutsche Bank, received a concession to extend an existing railroad from Constantinople through Anatolia to Angora. It
was understood that eventually this road would be extended further
to Baghdad. The Anatolian Railway Company was organized to perform the work which proceeded for the next ten years, despite Russia's disapproval.

France was not pleased with the arrangement but her displeasure was mollified to some degree when her financiers were
permitted to invest in the project. England's attitude was one of
satisfaction, her statesmen feeling that German participation would
offset Russia's territorial ambitions and France's influence on Turkish affairs.

Baron Adolf Hermann Marschall von Bieberstein, the German ambassador to Constantinople, sought further concessions for
the Anatolian Railway Company. He was supported in this by Sir
Nicholas O'Conor, the English ambassador, and on November 25,
1899, Sultan Abdul Hamid signed a preliminary concession authorizing the construction of the railway to Baghdad and from there to
Basra. The final agreement was settled on March 5, 1903. By
this time Great Britain's attitude toward Germany's participation
in Middle East activities had changed to some degree. She was
unhappy with Germany's pro-Boer sympathies during the Boer War
and viewed with alarm Germany's decision to build a large, powerful navy. Following the signing of the 1903 agreement England did
what she could to obstruct the building of the Baghdad Railway. In
this she was assisted by France and Russia, whose partner she became following the Triple Entente of 1907. When World War I broke
out in 1914 the Railway was still incomplete.

Suggested Readings

Chapman, Maybelle K. Great Britain and the Baghdad Railway, 1888-
    1914. Northampton, Mass.: Smith College Studies in History,
    1948.
Earle, Edward M. Turkey, the Great Powers, and the Baghdad
    Railway. New York: Macmillan, 1923.
Herschlag, Z. Y. Turkey: An Economy in Transition. The Hague:
    Brill, 1958.
Hoffman, Ross J. S. Great Britain and the German Trade Rivalry.
    New York: Russell and Russell, 1933.
Jastrow, Morris. The War and the Baghdad Railway. Philadelphia:
    Lippincott, 1917.
Langer, William L. The Diplomacy of Imperialism. New York:
    Knopf, 1935.
Lewis, Bernard. The Emergence of Modern Turkey. 2nd edition.
    London: Oxford University Press, 1961.
_____. The Middle East and the West. New York: Harper &
    Row, 1968.

Moon, Parker T. Imperialism and World Politics. New York:
    Macmillan, 1926.
Thornburg, Max W. Turkey: An Economic Appraisal. Westport,
    Conn. : Greenwood Press, 1949.
Wolf, John B. The Diplomatic History of the Baghdad Railway.
    Columbia, Mo. : University of Missouri Press, 1936.

THE BOER WAR (1899-1902)

The Boer War, also known as the South African War, was
fought in South Africa from October 12, 1899 to May 31, 1902.
The opposing nations were Great Britain and the Boer Republics of
the Transvaal (the "South African Republic") and Orange Free State.

The Dutch had colonized the area around the Cape of Good
Hope in 1652. The descendants of the original settlers, called Boers, not liking the infiltration of British subjects (Uitlanders) into
their area, migrated north during the "Great Trek" of 1836-1838.
They founded the Transvaal or South African Republic in 1852 and
the Orange Free State in 1854. Here the Uitlanders were taxed
heavily and denied citizenship as Stephanus Johannes Paulus Kruger,
President of the Transvaal, felt that they would attempt to take over control of the Boer government if granted citizenship. The British, not unnaturally, resented these measures.

The agricultural economy of the Boers was endangered when,
in 1867, a diamond strike was made at Kimberley in the Orange
Free State, attracting countless foreigners to the mines. In 1878
Sir Leander Starr Jameson, a British physician and statesman, had
gone to South Africa where he became associated with Cecil Rhodes,
a diamond tycoon and empire builder. The Uitlanders were planning
an uprising in Johannesburg against the Boer government, and on
December 29, 1895, Jameson, in an unauthorized attempt to assist
his fellow countrymen, led a force of 600 men in a raid into the
Transvaal. The raid was unsuccessful and, following a pitched battle lasting 36 hours, Jameson surrendered to the Boers. He was
turned over to the British who tried him, found him guilty and sentenced him to ten months confinement, of which he served eight.
The so-called Jameson Raid was one of the more important precipitating causes of the Boer War. It resulted in the Boers imposing
further restrictions on the Uitlanders and a military alliance between the Transvaal and the Orange Free State.

Great Britain felt that she was rightfully entitled to certain
commercial interests in Africa. Through Sir Arthur Milner, governor of Cape Colony, she attempted to negotiate with President
Kruger in an effort to resolve their differences. However, the situation became progressively worse. By May, 1899, no agreement
had been reached. In August Kruger offered certain concessions
to the British. These were refused as the latter had reached the

the point where they felt that British leadership in South Africa was
the only solution to the problem.

In September, 1899, many Uitlanders left the Transvaal and
the British started a military buildup.   On October 9 Kruger gave
the British an ultimatum and on October 11 war was declared.   The
Orange Free State, honoring her alliance with the Transvaal, associated herself with that nation.

Historians consider the Boer War in terms of three phases.
The first of these--lasting from October, 1899 to February, 1900--
was characterized by a strong Boer offensive.   The British were
besieged at Kimberley, Ladysmith and Mafeking.   Phase 2, from
February to September, 1900, saw British victories.   Field Marshal
Frederick Sleigh Roberts, commanding the British forces, annexed
the Transvaal and occupied all major cities.   The third phase, lasting from September, 1900, to May, 1902, was largely one of guerrilla warfare conducted by Boer generals Louis Botha and Christiaan
Rudolph DeWet.   Field Marshal Roberts had been replaced by General Horatio Herbert Kitchener who captured Boer women and children and confined them in unsanitary concentration camps.   The death
rate of the inmates was horrendous and lessened only after the military was forced to improve conditions within the camps.   Guerrilla
soldiers were hunted down systematically and by the middle of 1902
the British were victorious.   The war ended with the signing of the
Treaty of Vereeniging on May 31 of that year, with the Boers ac-
knowledging allegiance to Great Britain and becoming British subjects.   The Dutch language was to be preserved in the schools and
courts and representative government was to be introduced as soon
as practicable.

The Boer War laid the foundations for the forthcoming Union
of South Africa which was formed in 1910 by uniting the Transvaal,
the Orange Free State, Natal and the Cape Colony.

Suggested Readings

Abdullah, Achmed, and T. C. Pakenham.   "Cecil Rhodes" in their
    Dreamers of Empire. New York: Stokes, 1929.
Burt, Alfred L.   The Evolution of the British Empire and the Com-
    monwealth from the American Revolution. Boston: Heath, 1956.
Butler, Jeffrey.   The Liberal Party and the Jameson Raid.   Oxford:
    The University Press, 1961.
Doyle, Arthur Conan.   The Great Boer War.   18th enlarged edition.
    Mystic, Conn. : Verry, 1976 (Originally published 1900).
Emerson, Rupert, and Martin Kilson, eds.   The Political Awaken-
    ing of Africa. Englewood Cliffs, N. J. : Prentice-Hall, 1965.
Holt, Edgar.   The Boer War. London: Putnam's, 1958.
LeMay, G. H. L.   British Supremacy in South Africa, 1899-1907.
    Oxford: The University Press, 1965.
Lovell, R. I.   The Struggle for South Africa.   New York: Macmil-
    lan, 1934.

Ludwig, Emil. "Rhodes" in his Genius and Character. Translated
    by Kenneth Burke. New York: Harcourt, Brace, 1927.
McClellan, Grant S. South Africa. New York: H. W. Wilson, 1962.
Magnus, Philip. Kitchener: Portrait of an Imperialist. New York:
    Dutton, 1959.
Marais, L. S. The Fall of Kruger's Republic. Oxford: The Uni-
    versity Press, 1961.
Newton, A. P. , E. A. Benians, and Eric A. Walker, eds. The Cam-
    bridge History of the British Empire. Vol. III: South Africa,
    Rhodesia and the High Commission Territories. New York:
    Macmillan, 1936.
Ransford, Oliver. The Battle of Majuba Hill: The First Boer War.
    New York: Crowell, 1967.
Seth, Ronald. Milestones in African History. Philadelphia: Chil-
    ton, 1969.
Sterling, Thomas, and the editors of Horizon Magazine. The Ex-
    ploration of Africa. New York: American Heritage Publishing
    Co. , 1963.
Walker, Eric A. A History of Southern Africa. London: Long-
    mans, Green, 1962.

FREUD'S THE INTERPRETATION OF DREAMS (1900)

Sigmund Freud, called "The Copernicus of the Mind, " was
an Austrian neurologist who conceived the systematic structure of
theories concerning the relation of conscious and unconscious psy-
chological processes known as psychoanalysis. In his most significant book, The Interpretation of Dreams, published in 1900, he
analyzed many of his own dreams and expounded all of the fundamental concepts comprising the foundations of psychoanalytic doctrine and technique.

Freud was born of Jewish parents in Frieberg, Moravia, in
1856. As a child his parents took him to Leipzig and from there
to Vienna where he lived for most of his life. He entered the University of Vienna in 1873 where he studied medicine although he
had considered becoming a lawyer. His choice of medicine as a career
was made because of his desire to study natural science and pursue theoretical studies rather than engage in actual medical practice.

At the university he performed research on the central nervous system, studying under Ernst Wilhelm von Brücke, a German
physician. He received his M. D. in 1881 and continued his research
while working as a demonstrator in the physiological laboratory.

Freud next spent three years at the General Hospital of Vienna in order to gain practical medical experience. He concentrated on psychiatry, dermatology and nervous diseases. Subsequently
he studied in Paris under the French neurologist Jean Martin Charcot, director of the Salpetrière, the mental hospital. Charcot's

434 Footnotes to World History

work on hysteria influenced Freud to turn his attention to the field
of psychopathology. Despite opposition from Viennese physicians
he set up his own clinic in that city in 1886, where he specialized
in nervous diseases. His fellow men of medicine opposed the revolutionary ideas of Charcot and their resentment delayed acceptance
of Freud's later findings on the origin of neurosis.

Freud published On Aphasia in 1891 and an encyclopedia article, Infantile Cerebral Palsy, in 1897. His subsequent writings
had to do with explanations for mental disorders.

In Vienna Freud collaborated with Josef Breuer, an Austrian
physician. In 1895 these two published a paper titled Studies on
Hysteria in which the symptoms of hysteria were "ascribed to manifestations of undischarged emotional energy associated with forgotten psychic traumas. " Treatment involved placing the patient in a
hypnotic state in which he was led to recall and reenact the trau-
matic experience, "thus discharging by catharsis the emotions causing the symptoms. "

From 1895 to 1900 Freud developed and expanded many of
the concepts which were later incorporated into psychoanalytic practice. The use of hypnosis was abandoned, being replaced by an in-
terviewing technique in which the patient, lying relaxed on a couch,
talked spontaneously (called "free association"). He thus revealed
unconscious mental processes as the source of neurotic disturbance.
Dream analysis led to Freud's discoveries of infantile sexuality and
of the Oedipus Complex. During this period he developed the theory
of transference, and in 1900 The Interpretation of Dreams was published. The medical profession still regarded his work with antag-
onism and his subsequent writings, The Psychopathology of Everyday Life (1904) and Three Contributions to the Sexual Theory (1905),
increased this hostility. In 1906 the mood changed to some degree
and he attracted a number of pupils and followers, including Alfred
Adler, Wilhelm Stekel, Otto Rank, Abraham Brill, Ernest Jones,
Carl Gustav Jung, Eugen Bleuler and Sandor Ferenczi. Adler and
Jung withdrew from the group, each having developed a different
theoretical basis for disagreement with Freud's emphasis on the sexual origin of neurosis.

Sigmund Freud spent the remainder of his life conducting
further research, lecturing and publishing books and articles on
medicine as well as on cultural and philosophic problems. Following the Nazi invasion of Austria he escaped to England where he
died in 1939. He was "never accorded full recognition during his
lifetime but is generally acknowledged as one of the great creative
minds of modern times. "

Suggested Readings

Allers, Rudolf. The Successful Error: A Critical Study of Freud-
    ian Psychoanalysis. London: Sheed and Ward, 1941.

Bennett, E. A. C. G. Jung. New York: Dutton, 1962.
Choisy, Maryse. Sigmund Freud: A New Appraisal. New York:
    Citadel Press, 1963.
Costigan, Giovanni. Sigmund Freud: A Short Biography. New
    York: Macmillan, 1965.
Denker, Henry A. A Far Country (play). New York: Random
    House, 1961.
Dreiser, Theodore. "Dreiser on Freud, " Psychoanalytic Review
    July, 1931.
Dry, Avis M. The Psychology of Jung: A Critical Interpretation.
    New York: Wiley, 1961.
Esper, Erwin A. A History of Psychology. Philadelphia: Saund-
    ers, 1964.
Flugel, John C. , and Donald J. West. A Hundred Years of Psy-
    chology. New York: Basic Books, 1964.
Freud, Sigmund. The Basic Writings of Sigmund Freud. New York:
    Random House, 1945.
_____. The Interpretation of Dreams. New York: Macmillan,
    1936 (Originally published 1900).
Fromm, Erich. Beyond the Chains of Illusion: My Encounter with
    Marx and Freud. New York: Pocket Books, 1963.
Glover, Edward. Freud or Jung. New York: Norton, 1950.
Grinker, Roy. "Reminiscences of a Personal Contact with Freud, "
    American Journal of Orthopsychiatry, October, 1940.
Hughes, H. Stuart. Consciousness and Society. New York: Vin-
    tage Books, 1958.
Jones, Ernest. The Life and Works of Sigmund Freud. New York:
    Basic Books, 1957.
Mazlish, Bruce. The Riddle of History. New York: Harper &
    Row, 1966.
Murphy, Gardner. Historical Introduction to Modern Psychology.
    New York: Harcourt, Brace, 1949.
Neill, Thomas P. Makers of the Modern Mind. Milwaukee, Wis. :
    Bruce Publishing Co. , 1949.
Philip, Howard L. Jung and the Problem of Evil. New York: Mc-
    Bride, 1959.
Puner, Helen Walker. Freud, His Life and Mind. New York: Dell,
    1947.
Stern, Karl. The Third Revolution: A Study of Psychiatry and Re-
    ligion. Garden City, N. Y. : Image Books, 1961.
Wittels, Fritz. Freud and His Times. New York: Grosset & Dun-
    lap, n. d.
_____. Sigmund Freud. London: George Allen & Unwin, 1942.
Wortis, Joseph. "Fragments of a Freudian Analysis, " American
    Journal of Orthopsychiatry, October, 1940.

THE BOXER REBELLION (1900)

The "Boxer Rebellion" of 1900 was a Chinese nationalist uprising against Chinese Christians, foreigners and the representatives

of foreign powers. A reform movement had failed, the emperor
was discredited and Tzu Hsi, the dowager empress and regent of
China, had seized the throne for herself. She was vigorously opposed to Occidental methods and influences.

Chinese citizens interpreted the dowager empress's action
as presaging a return to the old order of China for the Chinese.
Economic insolvencies, bad crops, floods and a hatred of foreign
missionaries caused great resentment of the European partition of
the country to break out in a number of attacks on the aliens.

The Boxers were an old secret Chinese religious society,
called in Chinese the "Righteous Harmony Band." This society, in
1899, had instituted a campaign of terror against the foreign nationals. In June, 1900, the outbreaks culminated in and around Peking,
the capital of China. Railroad and telegraph communications were
cut off. Aliens were compelled to fortify themselves within the
city. On June 19, 1900, all foreigners were given 24 hours in
which to leave. The German minister was assassinated and the
Chinese army surrounded that part of the city where the foreign
legations were located, completely shutting them off.

The foreigners fled to the British legation where they built
bombproof cellars, raised barricades, installed artillery and prepared for a long siege.

On August 4 a relief column of Japanese, Russian, French,
American and British troops arrived from Taku. After heavy fighting the besieged legation, the occupants of which had been reduced
to eating horse meat, was relieved and Peking was occupied.

After the uprisings in Peking and elsewhere had been suppressed the Allies retained possession of the city until a peace treaty
was signed on September 7, 1901. By the terms of the treaty China was required to pay several million dollars in indemnities, of
which $24,000,000 was for the United States. Further conditions
stipulated punishment for the rioters, the conversion of ad valorem
into specific duties, severe penalties against any further anti-foreign
disturbances and the fortification and guarding of the foreign legation
district in Peking.

On January 5, 1908, the United States Senate passed a resolution remitting to China approximately $13,000,000 of the Boxer
indemnity, and all further payments were remitted by the Senate in
June, 1924. When the Chinese Republic entered World War I on
the side of the Allies on August 14, 1917, Great Britain, Russia,
Japan and France suspended indemnity payments after that date.

Suggested Readings

Backhouse, E. T. , and John O. Bland. Annals and Memoirs at the
    Court of Peking. New York: AMS Press, 1970 (Originally pub-
    lished 1914).

_____. China Under the Empress Dowager. Philadelphia: Lip-
pincott, 1910.
Bourne, Peter, pseud. Twilight of the Dragon (fiction). New York:
Putnam's, 1954.
Chang, Hsin-hai. Fabulous Concubine (fiction). New York: Simon
& Schuster, 1956.
Clements, Paul H. The Boxer Rebellion. New York: AMS Press,
1915.
Farmer, Lydia. "Tzu Hsi" in her A Book of Famous Queens. Re-
vised by Willard A. Heaps. New York: Crowell, 1964.
Fleming, Peter. The Siege at Peking. New York: Knopf, 1959.
Hirschfeld, Burt. Fifty-Five Days of Terror: The Story of the
Boxer Rebellion. New York: Messner, 1964.
Lingley, Charles Ramsdell, and Allen Richard Foley. Since the
Civil War. New York: Appleton, 1935.
Martin, Christopher. The Boxer Rebellion. New York: Abelard-
Schuman, 1968.
Martin, William A. Siege in Peking: China Against the World.
New York: Barnes & Noble, 1972 (Originally published 1900).
Mitchison, Lois. China. New York: Walker, 1966.
Pong, David. "The Boxer Rising" in Taylor, A. J. P., editor in
chief. Purnell's History of the 20th Century, Vol. I. New
York: Purnell, 1971.
Purcell, Victor W. The Boxer Uprising: A Background Study. Ham-
den, Conn.: Shoe String Press, 1963.
Steiger, George N. China and the Occident. New Haven, Conn.:
Yale University Press, 1927.
Tan, Chester C. The Boxer Catastrophe. New York: Octagon
Books, 1966.
Werstein, Irving. The Boxer Rebellion: Anti-Foreign Terror Seiz-
es China. New York: Watts, 1971.

THE TIBETAN INVASION (1903-1904)

Since the 17th century Tibet, located in South Asia between
India and China, was nominally a Chinese dependency. The Buddhist
lamas or monks of Lhasa, its capital city, who dominated the administration of the country, paid little attention to the tutelage, or
even the advice, of China.

Tibet is a country of mountains, snowbound wilderness, great
distances from place to place, squalor and poverty. It has no railroads and only one airfield able to accommodate cargo planes. In
the late 18th century British colonial officials, initially Warren Hastings, who had obtained a dominant position in neighboring India, attempted to secure a foothold in Tibet. This was unsuccessful, primarily because of Tibetan resentment over a British-supported Nepalese invasion in 1790. All during the 19th century the Tibetans did
what they could to exclude European travelers. In the early 20th
century Great Britain became alarmed over the Russian influence in

Tibet. By 1900 Chinese influence had sunk to a very low level, and both Great Britain and Russia each feared that the other would seek to replace China as Tibet's suzerain. Both countries had, for fifty years, penetrated into Asia to the borders of Afghanistan, Persia and Tibet and hoped to be able to eventually dominate these last remaining independent regions. Dorjieff, a Mongolian lama, was known to have made frequent trips from Lhasa to St. Petersburg and the English felt he might be a courier concerned with secret treaties and espionage in the interests of the Russian government.

Lord Curzon, then Viceroy and Governor-general of India, believed the rumors concerning Dorjieff. He became convinced that Russia was about to move into Tibet and ultimately attempt to dominate Asia. His concern was increased when, in 1902, Tibetan officials began to cause trouble on the Indian border, infringing grazing rights and preventing Indian traders from entering their country. Curzon saw English imperial authority being flouted and wrote two letters to the Dalai Lama at Lhasa. When these communications were ignored he contacted the Secretary of State for India in London. The Secretary indicated that the matter would be considered but Curzon, deciding to check a supposed Russian advance on Tibet, appointed Colonel Francis Younghusband to lead a British diplomatic mission to the frontier of that country.

The colonel and his staff arrived at the Tibetan city of Khamba Jong. They remained there for five months but, unable to persuade either the Tibetans or the Chinese to negotiate, returned to India. Curzon then insisted that the British government authorize a military expedition into Tibet. On October 1, 1903, such an expedition was approved. It was to proceed to Gyangtse, halfway between the Indian frontier and Lhasa. Approval was given in spite of the misgivings of Prime Minister Arthur James Balfour and the cabinet.

Curzon, highly pleased with the decision, assigned Colonel Younghusband to lead the invasion. The latter entered Tibet on December 11, 1903, with a force of 1,150 soldiers and 10,000 coolies. Also with him was a British general officer, 7,000 mules, 5,000 bullocks and over 4,000 yaks. The party was armed with rifles, Maxim guns and artillery.

Younghusband hoped to meet and confer with the Tibetan negotiators who had ignored him at Khamba Jong. Curzon wished to "teach the Tibetans and the Russians a lesson," but whether he planned to do this with bullets or talk has never been made clear. The British government hoped merely to avoid any international entanglements. The instructions given Colonel Younghusband were vague and contradictory.

The British force reached the outskirts of the village of Guru on January 13, 1904. Here the colonel conferred with a Tibetan general from Lhasa and three lamas. The discussion led nowhere. After waiting for over two months for a second conference which did

not materialize, Younghusband and his men, who had suffered greatly in the cold Himalayan winter weather, advanced from their camp
to Guru. Here they were met by the Tibetan general who demanded that they withdraw. This the British refused to do and they then
captured the general and his men. The general then shot and wounded a British sikh whereupon fighting broke out. Half the Tibetan
force was killed, including the general. None of Younghusband's
party was killed.

In spite of this "victory" Younghusband, unable to persuade
the Tibetans to negotiate, decided to advance to Lhasa. More fighting ensued and 2,700 Tibetans died, the British death toll being under 40. On August 3 the British entered Lhasa. Younghusband and
his men found no Russians. The Dalai Lama had fled the city, leaving a regent behind.

On September 7 a treaty was negotiated. Tibet agreed, a-
mong other things, to open markets for trade at Gyangtse and Gar-
tok, to respect the Indian frontier, to pay a 50,000 pound indemnity
and to have no dealings with other foreign powers without British
consent. It appeared that, like India, Tibet was to become a British satellite.

The British government was extremely dissatisfied with what
Colonel Younghusband had done. The indemnity was considered far
too large and it was felt that the treaty could lead to nothing but
political embarrassment. The treaty was permitted to "lapse into
obscurity, " particularly when it was realized that Russia was not interfering in Tibet's affairs. Three years later Russia and Great Britain
mutually agreed to conduct all negotiations with Tibet through China.

The Chinese paid the Tibetan indemnity to Great Britain. In
1910 the Chinese entered Tibet but were driven out in 1913. From
then until 1950 Tibet was independent. In that year the Chinese returned again and in 1951 the country became an autonomous province
of the People's Republic of China.

Colonel Younghusband was knighted and became the British
Resident in Kashmir. He died in 1942.

Suggested Readings

Dugdale, Blanche E. C. Arthur James Balfour, First Earl of Bal-
    four, K. G. , O. M. , F. R. S. , etc. London: Hutchinson, 1936.
Fleming, Peter. Bayonets to Lhasa: The First Full Account of the
    British Invasion of Tibet in 1904. New York: Harper, 1961.
Ford, Robert. Wind Between the Worlds. New York: McKay, 1957.
Gardiner, A. G. "Arthur James Balfour" and "Lord Curzon" in his
    Prophets, Priests and Kings. London: J. M. Dent, 1914.
Gilbert, Martin. "Tibetan Tragedy" in Taylor, A. J. P. , editor in
    chief. Purnell's History of the 20th Century. New York: Pur-
    nell, 1971.

Leslie, Sir Shane, Bart. Studies in Sublime Failure. Freeport,
    N. Y. : Books for Libraries, 1970.
Migot, André. Tibetan Marches. Translated by Peter Fleming.
    New York: Dutton, 1955.
Moon, Penderel. Warren Hastings and British India. London: Ox-
    ford University Press, 1947.
Mosley, Leonard Oswald. Curzon: The End of an Epoch. London:
    Longmans, Green, 1960.
Newbolt, Sir Henry John. "Francis Younghusband" in his Book of
    the Long Trail. New York: Longmans, Green, 1919.
Raymond, E. T. , pseud. "Earl Curzon of Kedleston" in his Un-
    censored Celebrities. New York: Holt, 1919.
Syme, Ronald. Invaders and Invasions. New York: Norton, 1964.
Thubten, Sigme Norbu, and Colin M. Turnbull. Tibet. New York:
    Simon & Schuster, 1968.
Younghusband, Sir Francis. The Light of Experience: A Review
    of Some Men and Events of My Time. London: Constable,
    1927.

THE ENTENTE CORDIALE (1904)

The term "entente cordiale, " used in international diplomacy,
signifies friendly relations or a community of interests between two
or more countries. "It suggests a relationship tantamount to an
alliance, although a formal alliance or treaty is not necessary to
cement an entente cordiale. "

For centuries France and England had fought intermittent
wars. William the Conqueror, Duke of Normandy, invaded England
in 1066 on the death of Edward the Confessor and defeated King
Harold Godwinson of England in the Battle of Hastings. Joan of
Arc, the French heroine, in the early 15th century led her country's armies to victories over the English at Orléans and elsewhere.
France and England engaged in warfare on both land and sea in the
Napoleonic Wars, with England finally emerging victorious when her
troops, commanded by Arthur Wellesley, Duke of Wellington, won
the Battle of Waterloo in 1815.

During the nineteenth century the international situation was
such that England and France could easily come into conflict over
several issues. In the Far East tension was growing between Japan and Russia, allies of Great Britain and France respectively.
When the Russo-Japanese War broke out in 1904 England and France
were faced with the choice of either cooperating or else finding
themselves involved against each other in the War, something neither country desired. A repetition of the Fashoda Incident of 1898-
1899 was not wanted by either party. Other problems, such as
those involving North Africa and the Newfoundland fisheries, marred
Anglo-French relations.

Between 1898 and 1901 England attempted repeatedly and unsuccessfully to enter into an alliance with Germany.   By 1904 France
came to realize that an entente with England might compensate for
her unsuccessful alliance with Russia.

Théophile Delcassé, France's Minister of Foreign Affairs,
had negotiated settlement of the Fashoda Incident and agreement
with Great Britain on their differences concerning the Nile Valley
and Central Africa.   In 1900 he worked with Sir Thomas Barclay,
a British official, lawyer and publicist, to cement better international understanding between his country and Great Britain.   On
October 14, 1903, both countries signed the Anglo-French Treaty
of Arbitration, promising to submit their major disputes to the Permanent Court of Arbitration at the Hague.

Delcassé also accompanied President Emile Loubet to England in 1903 when the latter and King Edward VII of England exchanged visits to each other's countries.   While in England Delcassé entered into negotiations with Henry Charles Keith Petty-Fitz-
maurice, Marquis of Lansdowne and Great Britain's Foreign Secretary, to settle the outstanding differences between the two countries.
These negotiations led to the signing of the Entente Cordiale by Lansdowne and Paul Pierre Cambon, the French ambassador at London,
on April 8, 1904.

The Entente Cordiale was not a military pact.   It did cement
good Anglo-French relations and enabled the two states to work together during World War I.   It settled a number of comparatively
trivial disputes, including those concerning the Newfoundland fisheries, West African boundaries, the New Hebrides Islands, Mada-
gascar and Siam.   The situation in Egypt and Morocco was also
clarified, with France allowing Great Britain a free hand in Egypt
and Great Britain in turn allowing France a free hand in Morocco.
The latter country was eventually to be partitioned between France
and Spain, with the Spanish controlling the coastal area opposite
Gibraltar and the French occupying the hinterland.

Delcassé's plan was to gain French ascendancy in Morocco.
Germany took insult at this as she, too, had interests in Morocco
and the French Minister of Foreign Affairs was ignoring them.   Germany's attempts to defend her position in 1905 and again in 1911
led to two serious Moroccan crises.   These, in turn, led to the
strengthening of the relationship between England and France and
helped unite them against Germany and her allies in World War I.

In 1907 the Anglo-French Alliance was expanded to include
Russia and the Entente Cordiale became the Triple Entente.

Suggested Readings

Albertini, Luigi.   The Origins of the War of 1914.   London: Oxford University Press, 1952-1957.

Churchill, Rogers P. The Anglo-Russian Convention of 1907. Ce-
    dar Rapids, Iowa: Torch Press, 1939.
Ensor, Robert C. "England, 1870-1914" in The Oxford History of
    England, Vol. XIV. Oxford: Clarendon Press, 1936.
Fay, Sidney B. The Origins of the World War. New York: Mac-
    millan, 1966.
Florinsky, Michael T. Russia: A History and Interpretation. New
    York: Macmillan, 1965.
Gooch, George P. "Continental Agreements" in Ward, A. W. , and
    George Peabody Gooch, eds. The Cambridge History of British
    Foreign Policy, 1783-1919, Vol. III. Cambridge: The Univer-
    sity Press, 1923.
Grey, Sir Edward. Twenty-Five Years, 1892-1916. New York:
    Frederick A. Stokes, 1925.
Halévy, Elie. Imperialism and the Rise of Labour, 1895-1905.
    New York: Barnes & Noble, 1961.
Hinsley, F. H. "Great Britain and the Powers, 1904-1914" in Ben-
    ians, E. A. , et al. , eds. The Cambridge History of the Brit-
    ish Empire, Vol. III. Cambridge: The University Press, 1959.
Mathews, J. J. Egypt and the Formation of the Anglo-French En-
    tente of 1904. Philadelphia: University of Pennsylvania Press,
    1939.
Moon, Parker T. Imperialism and World Politics. New York:
    Macmillan, 1926.
Nicolson, Harold. Diplomacy. 3rd edition. New York: Oxford
    University Press, 1963.
Pribram, Alfred F. England and the International Policy of the
    Great Powers, 1871-1914. Oxford: Clarendon Press, 1931.
Seaman, L. C. B. From Vienna to Versailles. New York: Harper
    & Row, 1963.
Sontag, Raymond J. European Diplomatic History, 1871-1932. New
    York: Appleton-Century-Crofts, 1933.
Taylor, A. J. P. The Struggle for Mastery in Europe. Oxford:
    Clarendon Press, 1954.

THE RUSSO-JAPANESE WAR (1904-1905)

The Russo-Japanese War of 1904-1905 was the outcome of
the conflicting imperial ambitions of Russia and Japan. Russian
expansion in Eastern Asia ran counter to the plans of Japan to gain
a foothold on the Asiatic mainland.

Russia had leased Port Arthur, a seaport on the Yellow Sea
in Northeast China in Kwantung Territory, Manchuria, from China
in 1898. Russia's intention was to make it the headquarters of Russian naval powers in the Pacific and an important naval port. In
1900 Russia occupied Amur Province and tried to secure China's
assent to the occupation. Because of the protests of Great Britain
and Japan, Russia promised to vacate Chinese territory within the
next eighteen months, which promise she failed to keep.

Japan then negotiated with Russia from 1901 to 1904, proposing that the two countries delimit their respective spheres of influence in Manchuria and Korea. Russian statesmen Count Sergei Witte, Count Vladimir Lamsdorff and General Aleksei Kuropatkin favored agreement with Japan but a militant group headed by Alexander Bezobrazov persuaded Tsar Nicholas II that only a "policy of strength" would settle the "Japanese danger to Russian interests."

Undaunted, the Japanese made an alliance with Great Britain in 1902, thereby bettering their chances of victory in the event of an armed conflict with Russia. Negotiations between Japan and Russia in 1903 resulted in a stalemate and on February 9, 1904, the Japanese made a surprise attack on the Russian fleet at Chemulpo and Port Arthur, completely decimating it.

The first important land engagement was the Battle of the Yalu, fought on April 30. The forces of General Kuropatkin, commander of the Russian army, were outnumbered four to one by the Japanese under General Kuroki. This encounter resulted in a complete rout of the Russians who lost 2,300 men, compared to 1,100 Japanese killed and wounded. Other battles were fought, with the Russian armies being defeated in Manchuria. Port Arthur was besieged by the Japanese and on January 2, 1905, General Stoessel, commanding a Russian force of approximately 41,000 men, surrendered. Mukden fell to the Japanese in March, which practically terminated land hostilities. On May 27 a naval battle was fought in the Straits of Tsushima, between Korea and Japan, in which Admiral Rozhdestevenski's Russian fleet was virtually annihilated. Although hostilities continued for a time the Russo-Japanese War was over for all practical purposes, with Japan the undisputed victor.

Tsar Nicholas, realizing his cause was lost, accepted the good offices of President Theodore Roosevelt and Emperor William II of Germany, to negotiate a peace settlement. Representatives of the powers concerned met at Portsmouth, New Hampshire. The treaty, signed on September 5, 1905, resulted in peace between the two warring nations. The various disputes which brought on the war were resolved, with Japan acquiring Port Arthur, which she retained until 1945. Japan felt that the peace terms were overly mild and out of frustration adopted an attitude of militant nationalism. In Russia the loss of the war and of Port Arthur and other territories led to a challenge of Tsar Nicholas' autocratic government and eventually to the Russian revolution and the overthrow of the Tsar.

Suggested Readings

Charques, Richard Denis. A Short History of Russia. New York: Dutton, 1956.

Clarkson, Jesse D. A History of Russia. New York: Random House, 1969.

Dallin, David. The Rise of Russia in Asia. New Haven, Conn.: Yale University Press, 1949.

Dilts, Marion May. The Pageant of Japanese History. New York:
    Longmans, Green, 1947.
Florinsky, Michael T. Russia: A History and Interpretation. New
    York: Macmillan, 1965.
Hingley, Ronald. Tsars, 1533-1917. New York: Macmillan, 1968.
Kluchevsky, Vasily O. A History of Russia. Translated by C. J.
    Hogarth. New York: Russell and Russell, 1960 (Originally
    published 1913).
Langer, Paul Fritz. Japan, Yesterday and Today. New York:
    Holt, 1966.
Langer, William L. The Diplomacy of Imperialism, 1890-1892.
    New York: Knopf, 1935.
Latané, John H. America as a World Power, 1897-1907. Saint
    Clair Shores, Mich. : Scholarly Press, 1971.
Malozemoff, Andrew. Russian Far Eastern Policy, 1881-1904, With
    Special Emphasis on the Causes of the Russo-Japanese War.
    Berkeley, Calif. : University of California Press, 1958.
Martin, Christopher, pseud. The Russo-Japanese War. New York:
    Abelard, 1967.
Meyer, Milton W. Japan, a Concise History. Boston: Allyn and
    Bacon, 1966.
Pares, Bernard. The Fall of Russian Monarchy. London: Jon-
    athan Cape, 1939.
_____. A History of Russia. New York: Knopf, 1960.
Pringle, Henry F. Theodore Roosevelt: A Biography. New York:
    Harcourt, Brace, 1956.
Riasanovsky, Nicholas Valentine. A History of Russia. New York:
    Oxford University Press, 1963.
Roosevelt, Theodore. Autobiography. Edited by Wayne Andrews.
    New York: Octagon Books, 1973.
Seth, Ronald. Milestones in Japanese History. Philadelphia: Chil-
    ton, 1969.
Vernadsky, George. A History of Russia. New Haven, Conn. :
    Yale University Press, 1954.
Walsh, Warren B. Russia and the Soviet Union. Ann Arbor, Mich. :
    University of Michigan Press, 1958.
White, John A. The Diplomacy of the Russo-Japanese War. Prince-
    ton, N. J. : Princeton University Press, 1964.
Wren, Melvin C. The Course of Russian History. New York: Mac-
    millan, 1968.

BLOODY SUNDAY (1905)

Tsar Nicholas II ascended the Russian throne in 1894. He
was a weak, though well-intentioned ruler. Easily dominated by
others, he was a firm believer in the autocratic principles of his
father, Tsar Alexander III.

The oppression and police control of the Russian minorities
which had characterized the country for centuries were increased

after Nicholas came to power. Jews especially were the victims
of tsarist policies, being forced to live in certain areas, forbidden
to engage in various professions and killed in great numbers in
pogroms fomented by the government. Factory workers, particularly in industrialized cities such as St. Petersburg and Moscow, suffered miserable living and working conditions. Wages were low,
hours were long and protests were met with violence on the part
of the employers and civil and military authorities.

This situation resulted in the development of an underground
revolutionary movement, its overt tactics taking the form of strikes
and the unionization of workers. Tsar Nicholas and such advisers
as Konstantin Detrovich Pobedonostsev, Procurator of the Holy Synod, opposed any change from the status quo. An economic depression between 1900 and 1905 intensified the bitter feelings of the working classes and resulted in their approving the aims and acts of
various revolutionary reformers. Peasants' revolts occurred, aided
by such organizations as the Social Revolutionary Party. In 1902
the Society for the Mutual Help of the Workers in the Engineering
Industry was founded in Moscow by Sergei Zubatov, head of that
city's security police. This society was supported by the imperial
government and had as its aim the prevention of the workers from
adopting a program of political reform. It failed to succeed in
Moscow but reappeared in St. Petersburg under the leadership of
Father Georgi Gapon, a Russian orthodox priest and revolutionary.
Its aims and objectives soon changed.

Father Gapon's organization was at first non-political in nature, but by 1904 its membership had grown to over 18,000 and included many militant believers in the "action, not words" tactics
of the Social Revolutionary Party. In January, 1905, a factory in
St. Petersburg dismissed a large number of workers and this led
to a general strike.

On Sunday, January 22, 1905, a popular demonstration, now
known as "Bloody Sunday," though intended to be peaceful, culminated in a massacre of workers. Thousands of persons, led by Father Gapon, marched on the Winter Palace in St. Petersburg to present a petition to the Tsar who, unbeknown to them, had left the
city several days before. The marchers intended no violence, as
mentioned above, but were prepared to use force if their demands
were not met. Police spies within Father Gapon's organization had
informed the government of the impending march and soldiers, loyal to the Tsar, were waiting at the Winter Palace. The marchers,
when commanded to disperse, refused to do so and the royal troops
fired on them, killing about 100 workers and wounding many others.

Father Gapon escaped to London. He published an open letter to the Tsar denouncing him for refusing to accept the petition
calling for social and economic reforms. In his letter Gapon said,
in part, "let all blood which has to be shed fall upon thee, hangman,
and thy kindred."

The march of the workers on "Bloody Sunday" was unsuccessful in itself but it did make the Russian common man realize "the
hollowness of Romanov autocracy. " It led eventually to the Revolution of 1917 and the reputed execution of Nicholas and his family
the following year.

Suggested Readings

Almedingen, Martha Edith von. The Romanovs: Three Centuries
    of an Ill-Fated Dynasty. New York: Holt, 1966.
Botkin, Gleb E. The Real Romanovs. New York: Fleming H.
    Revell, 1931.
Chamberlain, William Henry. The Russian Revolution, 1917-1921.
    New York: Macmillan, 1935.
Charques, Richard Denis. A Short History of Russia. New York:
    Dutton, 1956.
Clarkson, Jesse D. A History of Russia. New York: Random
    House, 1969.
Florinsky, Michael T. Russia: A History and Interpretation. New
    York: Macmillan, 1965.
Frankland, Noble. Imperial Tragedy: Nicholas II, Last of the
    Tsars. New York: Coward-McCann, 1961.
Hingley, Ronald. Tsars, 1533-1917. New York: Macmillan, 1968.
Kluchevsky, Vasily O. A History of Russia. Translated by C. J.
    Hogarth. New York: Russell and Russell, 1960 (Originally
    published 1913).
Massie, Robert K. Nicholas and Alexandra. New York: Atheneum,
    1967.
Miliukov, Paul. Russia and Its Crisis. Chicago: University of
    Chicago Press, 1906.
Moscow, Henry, and the editors of Horizon Magazine. Russia Un-
    der the Czars. New York: American Heritage Publishing Co. ,
    1962.
Pares, Bernard. A History of Russia. New York: Knopf, 1960.
Riasanovsky, Nicholas Valentine. A History of Russia. New York:
    Oxford University Press, 1963.
Schapiro, Leonard. The Communist Party of the Soviet Union. New
    York: Random House, 1960.
Vernadsky, George. A History of Russia. New Haven, Conn. :
    Yale University Press, 1954.
Von Laue, Theodore H. Why Lenin? Why Stalin? A Reappraisal
    of the Russian Revolution, 1900-1930. Philadelphia: Lippin-
    cott, 1964.
Wren, Melvin C. The Course of Russian History. New York: Mac-
    millan, 1968.

EINSTEIN'S THEORY OF RELATIVITY (1905 and 1916)

Albert Einstein, the German-American theoretical physicist,

has been called "the world's greatest scientist." He was educated in Switzerland and obtained his Ph. D. from the University of Zurich while tutoring mathematics and physics and working as a patent examiner with the Swiss patent office in Bern. He also held several teaching positions in European universities.

In 1905 he published three papers. One offered an explanation of the photoelectric effect which dealt with the quantum theory upon which the German physicist Max Planck had worked. Another analyzed mathematically the theory of the Brownian Movement. The third was his Special Theory of Relativity. In this he made his initial presentation of his theory which was concerned with the relativistic nature of uniform motion and the interdependence of space and time. Here he postulated the equivalence of mass and energy in the equation $E = mc^2$ (i. e. , energy equals mass times the velocity of light squared). This equation was shown to be valid some years later by the power released in atomic explosions, such as by the atomic bombs dropped on the Japanese cities of Hiroshima and Nagasaki in August, 1945.

Until Einstein's time the physical laws generally accepted by scientists (now called "classical laws") were those laid down by the British natural philosopher and mathematician Sir Isaac Newton in the late 17th century. Until 1887 the principles of classical physics were considered sound and well substantiated. In that year Albert Michelson and Edward Morley, American physicists, performed an experiment in which they sought to determine the rate of the motion of the earth through the ether. The result of this experiment was both surprising and inexplicable: the apparent velocity of the planet earth through space was zero at all times of the year.

In the 1890's Hendrik Antoon Lorentz, a Dutch physicist, and George Francis FitzGerald, his Irish associate, formulated, following the Michelson-Morley experiment, the Lorentz-FitzGerald contraction, a theory of the change of shape of a body due to its motion through the ether. This theory states that "no difference can be detected between the velocity of light in a system in motion and a system at rest because a system in motion contracts in the direction of the motion. "

Albert Einstein developed his special theory of relativity from those of his predecessors, extending and transforming classical concepts. He claimed that it is impossible to determine absolute motion employing either mechanical devices or an apparatus using light. He also held that as neither absolute motion nor absolute rest can be determined, the concepts "absolute space" and "absolute time" are meaningless.

In 1916 he published the General Theory of Relativity, a paper in which he developed a revolutionary theory of gravitation. This amplified and extended the scope of his 1905 Special Theory of Relativity, put forth the idea that the forces of gravity and inertia are equivalent, that absolute motion could not be detected and led to several astronomical predictions which were later verified.

Today physicists generally accept Einstein's theories concerning relativity. Until his death in 1955 he continued his research. Expelled from Germany by Adolf Hitler's Nazi government in the early 1930's, he came to the United States, became an American citizen and joined the faculty of Princeton University. In August, 1939, he wrote a letter to President Franklin D. Roosevelt urging the United States to inaugurate immediate nuclear research. The program which followed led to the construction of the atomic bombs used in World War II and ushered in the atomic age.

Suggested Readings

Barnett, Lincoln. The Universe and Doctor Einstein. New York: Mentor Books, 1952.

Bergson, Henri. Duration and Simultaneity, With Reference to Einstein's Theory. Translated by Leon Jacobson. New York: Bobbs-Merrill, 1965.

Bondi, Hermann. Relativity and Common Sense: A New Approach to Einstein. Garden City, N. Y.: Anchor Books, 1964.

Born, Max. Einstein's Theory of Relativity. New York: Dover Publications, 1962.

Einstein, Albert. Investigations on the Theory of the Brownian Movement. New York: Dover Publications, 1926 (Originally published 1905).

_____. The Meaning of Relativity. 5th edition. Princeton, N. J.: Princeton University Press, 1956.

_____. Relativity: The Special and General Theory. Translated by Robert W. Lawson. New York: Crown Publications, 1961 (Originally published 1905 and 1916).

Frank, Philipp. Einstein: His Life and Times. Translated by George Rosen. New York: Knopf, 1963.

Garbedian, H. Gordon. Albert Einstein, Maker of Universes. New York: Funk & Wagnalls, 1939.

Gardner, Martin. Relativity for the Millions. New York: Pocket Books, 1965.

Jeans, James. The New Background of Science. Ann Arbor, Mich.: University of Michigan Press, 1959.

Levi, Albert W. Philosophy and the Modern World. Bloomington, Ind.: Indiana University Press, 1959.

Russell, Bertrand. The ABC of Relativity. Revised edition, edited by Felix Pirani. New York: Mentor Books, 1959.

Sciama, Denis William. Physical Foundations of General Relativity. Garden City, N. Y.: Doubleday, 1969.

THE TRIPLE ENTENTE (1907)

The Triple Entente entered into by Great Britain, France and Russia on August 31, 1907, was the outgrowth of the military coalition known as the Triple Alliance, concluded by Germany, Austria-

Hungary and Italy in the latter part of the 19th century, and the Entente Cordiale of April 8, 1904, involving Great Britain and France.   The object of the Triple Entente was to counterbalance the Triple Alliance.

The negotiations leading to the Triple Entente were initiated by France, which approached Russia.   In the late 1880's it was realized that a diplomatic understanding existed between these two powers when France made substantial loans to Russia for the purpose of developing the latter country's industry and transportation facilities.   A Franco-Russian military pact was entered into in 1893.

The French government, represented by Théophile Delcassé, French Minister of Foreign Affairs, initiated negotiations for an alliance with Great Britain.   These two countries were both involved in expanding and consolidating their possessions in Africa and the Far East and, as such, were rivals.   However, they realized that the Triple Alliance made it advisable that they form a coalition for mutual protection, and this situation eventually led to the Entente Cordiale of 1904.   Great Britain, in April of that year, commenced negotiations for an entente with Russia.   King Edward VII of England and Aleksandr Petrovich Izvolski, Russian Minister of Foreign Affairs, held a series of conversations concerning the possibility of such an agreement.   Although Great Britain had been an ally of Japan since 1902 and Japan was, in 1904 and 1905, at war with Russia, the conditions of the agreement between Great Britain and Japan were such that the former was free to negotiate with Russia. British statesmen Sir Edward Grey and Sir Charles Hardinge both wished to settle their country's differences with Russia concerning Persia and India.   They feared that, unless these differences were resolved Russia would consummate an alliance with Germany, which was attempting to negotiate such an agreement.   The Russian foreign office opposed Germany's extending the terms of the Björkö Treaty of July, 1905, in which William II of Germany and Nicholas II of Russia had agreed to furnish mutual aid in case either country was attacked by a third European power.   Another consideration was the enlargement of the German naval forces.

Grey, Hardinge and, later, Sir Arthur Nicolson, British Ambassador to Russia who had succeeded Hardinge in that capacity in 1906, devoted their efforts to developing an agreement acceptable to the Russians.   The latter country was represented in these negotiations by Izvolski who favored rapprochement with Great Britain and believed that an Anglo-Russian entente would strengthen Russia's alliance with France and complement the 1904 Entente Cordiale. He believed further that a pact with Great Britain would help settle differences in Asia and would eliminate any need for a Russo-German alliance.   By allying herself with Great Britain and France, Russia, as Izvolski saw the situation, could frustrate Austria in the Balkans and Germany in Turkey.

The negotiations, which took over a year to complete, lasted until August, 1907.   The two countries were mutually suspicious and the talks moved slowly. One of the conditions insisted upon by the British was that Russia sign a treaty with Japan by which both powers agreed to respect each other's rights in the Far East. On July 30, 1907, Russia and Japan signed such a pact and a month later, on August 31, 1907, Nicolson and Izvolski signed the convention establishing the Anglo-Russian Entente. This completed a web of treaties bringing Great Britain, Russia and France together in what came to be called the "Triple Entente." In the next few years these three countries became increasingly cooperative and the tension between them and the nations of the Triple Alliance became more and more severe, eventually culminating in 1914 with the outbreak of World War I.

Suggested Readings

Albertini, Luigi. The Origins of the War of 1914. London: Oxford University Press, 1952-1957.

Churchill, Rogers P. The Anglo-Russian Convention of 1907. Cedar Rapids, Iowa: Torch Press, 1939.

Ensor, Robert C. "England, 1870-1914" in The Oxford History of England, Vol. XIV. Oxford: Clarendon Press, 1936.

Fay, Sidney B. The Origins of the World War. New York: Macmillan, 1966.

Florinsky, Michael T. Russia: A History and Interpretation. New York: Macmillan, 1965.

Gooch, George P. "Continental Agreements" in Ward, A. W., and George Peabody Gooch, eds. The Cambridge History of British Foreign Policy, 1783-1919, Vol. III. Cambridge: The University Press, 1923.

Grey, Sir Edward. Twenty-Five Years, 1892-1916. New York: Frederick A. Stokes, 1925.

Hinsley, F. H. "British Foreign Policy and Colonial Questions, 1895-1904" and "Great Britain and the Powers, 1904-1914" in Benians, E. A., et al., eds. The Cambridge History of the British Empire, Vol. III. Cambridge: The University Press, 1959.

Mathews, J. J. Egypt and the Formation of the Anglo-French Entente of 1904. Philadelphia: University of Pennsylvania Press, 1939.

Moon, Parker T. Imperialism and World Politics. New York: Macmillan, 1926.

Nicolson, Harold. Diplomacy. 3rd edition. New York: Oxford University Press, 1963.

_____. Portrait of a Diplomatist: Sir Arthur Nicolson, Bart., First Lord Carnock: A Study in the Old Diplomacy. New York: Harcourt, Brace, 1930.

Pribram, Alfred F. England and the International Policy of the Great Powers, 1871-1914. Oxford: Clarendon Press, 1931.

Seaman, L. C. B. From Vienna to Versailles. New York: Harper & Row, 1963.

Sontag, Raymond J. European Diplomatic History, 1871-1932. New York: Appleton-Century-Crofts, 1933.

Taylor, A. J. P.   The Struggle for Mastery in Europe, 1848-1918.
Oxford: Clarendon Press, 1954.

THE DAILY TELEGRAPH EPISODE (1908-1909)

Near the end of the first decade of the twentieth century diplomatic relations between Germany and England became strained.
Germany's foreign policy on the continent was extremely aggressive
and England's friendly relations with France and Russia generated
economic and naval Anglo-German rivalry.   Some citizens of the
two countries wished to establish more friendly inter-relations.
One such was Colonel Edward James Montague Stuart-Wortley, a
staff officer in the British War Office and personal friend of William II, Emperor of Germany.

In the autumn of 1908 William, while visiting in England,
had discussed world affairs with Colonel Stuart-Wortley.   The colonel suggested that the emperor's pro-British sentiments be written
up in the form of an interview and published in a British newspaper.
William agreed and in due course the typescript of the proposed
article was delivered to him.   He sent it on to Prince Bernhard
von Bülow, Chancellor of the German Empire, for evaluation prior
to publication.   Bülow glanced at it and forwarded it to the German
foreign office where it came to the attention of Wilhelm von Stem-
rich, undersecretary of state.   The latter, unwilling to criticize
the emperor's statements, passed the manuscript on to Reinhold
Klehmet, a counselor in the German foreign office.   Klehmet, unaware that he was to evaluate the article, approved it sans assessment and gave it to Baron Wilhelm von Schoen, who also approved
it.

The article appeared in the Daily Telegraph, a British newspaper, on October 28, 1908.   It stated, among other things, that
Emperor William, while wishing for nothing better than to live on
good terms with England, was getting tired of being misrepresented,
considering the doubting of his word as a personal insult.   He referred to the Boer War, when he had taken England's side, refusing
Prussian and French suggestions for joint intervention.   On that occasion, he said, he prepared a plan of campaign against the Boers
which he turned over to the British officials, by whom it was used
successfully.   This success he considered "a matter of curious co-
incidence."

In his Daily Telegraph article the emperor stated that the
enlargement of the German navy was designed, not as a threat
against Great Britain, but merely to defend Germany's merchant
shipping and colonies and for potential use in the Far East.   He
felt, he said, that in view of Japanese development and China's national awakening, Great Britain would be only too glad of the German fleet.

The article caused immediate repercussions throughout the
world. France and Russia were angry that Emperor William should
disclose secret matters discussed at high political levels concerning the Boer War. Japan did not appreciate his remarks concerning the Far East. The British press did not take William's remarks seriously, the Times merely observing that the chance of a
war in the Pacific was an unusual reason for accumulating naval
vessels in the North Sea, particularly when many of them did not
carry sufficient coal to make long cruises.

Bülow admitted that he had not read the article carefully and
offered to resign his post. The emperor declined to accept his
resignation. In November the political parties meeting at the German Reichstag demanded guarantees that the emperor's blunder
would not be repeated. Bülow accepted responsibility for the article
but criticized it, calling it "provocative" and warning William that
he must not discuss political questions publicly in the future. Should
he do so, said the chancellor, he would have no choice but to submit his resignation.

Emperor William was shocked and disappointed at Bülow's
discussion of the matter before the Reichstag. The chancellor persuaded William to sign a document accepting the statements made
to the Reichstag. This precipitated a severe, though temporary,
emotional breakdown, and William talked of abdicating. In January, 1909, upon appearing in public he was greeted with applause.
This restored his self-confidence and he sought means by which he
could rid himself of Bülow. In June, 1909, the chancellor declared
that unless certain legislation he favored was passed by the Reichstag he would resign. The Reichstag did not comply with his wishes and Emperor William accepted his resignation on June 24, 1909.

Suggested Readings

Albertini, Luigi. The Origins of the War of 1914. London: Ox-
    ford University Press, 1952-1957.
Balfour, Michael. The Kaiser and His Times. Boston: Houghton
    Mifflin, 1964.
Bloch, Camille. The Causes of the World War: An Historical Sum-
    mary. Translated by Jane Soames. London: George Allen and
    Unwin, 1935.
Carroll, E. Malcolm. Germany and the Great Powers, 1866-1914:
    A Study in Public Opinion and Foreign Policy. Hamden, Conn. :
    Archon Books, 1966 (Originally published 1938).
Cowles, Virginia. The Kaiser. New York: Harper & Row, 1963.
Dawson, William H. The German Empire, 1867-1914 and the Unity
    Movement. Hamden, Conn. : Archon Books, 1966 (Originally
    published 1919).
Fay, Sidney B. The Origins of the World War. New York: Mac-
    millan, 1966.
Fischer, Fritz. Germany's Aims in the First World War. London:
    Chatto and Windus, 1967.

Hale, Oron J. Publicity and Diplomacy: With Special Reference to
    England and Germany, 1890-1914. New York: Appleton, 1940.
Manserg, Nicolas. The Coming of the First World War. Toronto:
    Longmans, Green, 1949.
Moon, Parker T. Imperialism and World Politics. New York:
    Macmillan, 1926.
Pribram, Alfred F. England and the International Policy of the
    Great Powers, 1871-1914. Oxford: Clarendon Press, 1931.
Renouvin, Pierre. The Immediate Origins of the War. Translated
    by Theodore Carswell Hume. New York: Howard Fertig, 1969.
Rich, Norman. Friedrich von Holstein: Politics and Diplomacy in
    the Era of Bismarck and Wilhelm II. Cambridge: The Univer-
    sity Press, 1965.
Schmitt, Bernadotte E. The Coming of the War, 1914. New York:
    Scribner's, 1930.
_____. England and Germany, 1740-1914. New York: Howard
    Fertig, 1967.
Taylor, Alan John Percivale. The Struggle for Mastery in Europe,
    1848-1918. Oxford: Clarendon Press, 1954.
Woodward, E. L. Great Britain and the German Navy. Oxford:
    Clarendon Press, 1935.

THE ARCHER-SHEE POSTAL ORDER CASE (1908-1910)

George Archer-Shee was the thirteen-year-old son of Martin
Archer-Shee, an official of the Bank of England. In October, 1908,
young George, a naval cadet at the Royal Naval College at Osborne
on the Isle of Wight, was accused of stealing and cashing a five-
shilling postal order belonging to Terence Back, a fellow-cadet.

The officials at the College, convinced of the boy's guilt,
recommended to the Admiralty that he be dismissed. The Admiralty, after a perfunctory investigation, concurred in the College's
recommendation and wrote to the boy's father, asking him to withdraw his son from the College.

Martin Archer-Shee did not believe that the boy was a thief.
He and Major Martin, George's thirty-six-year-old stepbrother,
traveled to Osborne. George, when questioned by his father, denied taking the postal order. His father and stepbrother believed
him. An interview with Captain Christian, administrator of the
College, got them nowhere. The Captain stated: "The matter has
been decided by the Admiralty. I am not at liberty to discuss it
any further. "

The boy's father enlisted the legal assistance of Sir Edward
Carson, one of the outstanding barristers of the day. Carson, after a long talk with the boy and his father, was convinced that George
was innocent. Bringing a court action against the Crown presented
legal difficulties and Carson found it necessary to present a Petition

of Right. This, two years after the alleged theft, was approved
and handed to the Admiralty, much to that body's embarrassment.

In July, 1910, Sir Rufus Isaacs, solicitor-general for the
United Kingdom, was assigned to handle the Admiralty's case. His
instructions were to have the proceedings dismissed. He and Carson met in court on July 10.

Isaacs' counter to Carson's Petition of Right was an obscure
legal move known as the demurrer. He contended that Martin Archer-Shee had no legal right to present the case. Carson protested
vigorously, realizing that if the suit was dismissed on a legal technicality, the facts of the case could not be brought out and young
George would be deprived of a fair hearing. Justice Ridley found
for Isaacs.

Carson immediately appealed and a second hearing was arranged. Again Isaacs presented a demurrer. The Appeals Court,
impatient at the long-drawn-out arguments concerning obscure legal
points, demanded that the facts be made known.

The primary objective of the second hearing was to determine
whether or not George Archer-Shee had stolen and converted the
five-shilling postal order. Isaacs had called in a handwriting expert named Thomas Gurrin who stated that the signature "Terence
Back" on the postal order had been forged by young George. Carson proceeded to nullify Gurrin's contention, showing that he had
been proved wrong in a previous case where he had testified concerning the handwriting of one Adolf Beck.

Carson reviewed the circumstances surrounding the case to
the judges and jury. He then called Martin Archer-Shee to the witness stand. The father testified to the arbitrary actions of Captain
Christian and the endless delays of the Admiralty and said, under
oath, that the handwriting on the postal order was not that of his
son. George followed his father to the witness stand and, in spite
of two days of rigorous cross-examination on the part of Isaacs,
failed to contradict himself. Other witnesses testified to George's
good character. Clara Tucker, the postmistress who had cashed
the postal order, was unable to identify the cadet who had tendered
it.

Captain Christian then testified for the Admiralty. Carson
would have normally subjected him to cross-examination, but instead, after a short whispered conference with Isaacs, told the
Court he had no questions to ask.

Isaacs then announced, "I say now, on behalf of the Admiralty, that I accept the statements of George Archer-Shee that he did
not write the name on the postal order, and did not cash it, and
consequently that he is innocent. "

The Admiralty awarded Martin Archer-Shee "costs and com-

pensation" in the amount of 7,120 pounds.   Young George did not
seek readmission at Osborne.   He was killed at the battle of Yprès
in World War I at the age of nineteen.   The old saying, "you can't
fight city hall," was definitely disproved in the Archer-Shee postal
order case.

Suggested Readings

Archer-Shee, George.   Archer-Shee Case: The Case on Which Ter-
    ence Rattigan Based "The Winslow Boy." Edited by Ewen Mon-
    tagu.   North Pomfret, Vt.: David and Charles, 1974.
Bennett, Rodney M.   Archer-Shee Against the Admiralty: The Story
    Behind "The Winslow Boy." Chippewa Falls, Wis.: Hale, 1973.
Brown, J. M.   "Let Right Be Done," Saturday Review of Literature,
    November 29, 1947.
"The Case of the Winslow Boy," Life, November 24, 1947.
Gribble, Leonard.   Justice? Stories of Famous Modern Trials.
    New York: Abelard-Schuman, 1971.
Rattigan, Terence.   The Winslow Boy (play).   London: H. Hamil-
    ton, 1946.
_____.   "The Winslow Boy" (play condensation) in Mantle, Burns,
    ed.   The Best Plays of 1947-1948.   New York: Dodd, Mead,
    1948.
"The Winslow Boy" in Crimes and Punishment, Vol. 3.   Editorial
    presentation: Jackson Morley.   London: BPC, 1973.
Woollcott, Alexander.   "The Archer-Shee Case," Atlantic Monthly,
    February, 1939.
_____.   "The Archer-Shee Case" (condensation), Reader's Digest,
    April, 1939.

THE PEARY-COOK CONTROVERSY (1909-1930)

The first European known to have visited the Arctic regions
was Pytheas, a Greek mathematician and explorer who, about 325
B.C., sailed around the Iberian Peninsula north to the British Isles
and from there to the Arctic Ocean.   During the succeeding centuries other explorers investigated the Arctic.   Eventually it was
realized that the earth is round, not flat as had previously been
supposed, and in due course attempts were made to reach the Pole
at the top of the world.

In 1893 Fridtjof Nansen and Hjalmar Johansen tried to reach
the North Pole with kyaks and sledges.   They came within 272 miles
of their goal.   Ten years later President Theodore Roosevelt asked Nansen to recommend an American explorer to lead an expedition to the
Pole.   Nansen suggested Robert E. Peary, a young naval officer, for
the assignment.   Peary had already made several expeditions to Greenland and regions adjacent.   He had headed an Arctic expedition in 1891-
1892, on which Dr. Frederick A. Cook served as surgeon.   He had also participated in attempts to reach the Pole in 1898-1902.

456 Footnotes to World History

On July 17, 1908, he left on a voyage in the Roosevelt, navigated by Captain Bob Bartlett, and announced on September 6, 1909, that he and five companions had reached the Pole on April 6 of that year.

When Peary reached Indian Harbor, Newfoundland, on September 6 he learned that the discovery of the Pole had been claimed five days earlier by Dr. Cook, the physician who had acted as surgeon on his 1891-1892 expedition. Cook claimed to have climbed Mount McKinley in Alaska successfully in 1906 and to have reached the North Pole on April 21, 1908, approximately a year earlier than Peary.

Cook's claims were widely credited. The University of Copenhagen awarded him an honorary degree and he lectured extensively concerning his alleged achievement. Peary, however, challenged Cook's claim and the latter was examined by the geographical societies of the United States and Great Britain. Peary's records were also examined and in November, 1909, a sub-committee of the National Geographic Society reported that, having considered the data furnished by Peary, it was "unanimously of the opinion that Commander Peary had reached the North Pole on April 6, 1909." Cook's claims of climbing Mount McKinley and reaching the Pole were declared fraudulent.

The controversy raged for the next twenty years, with each explorer accusing the other of making false claims. Peary was awarded honors by a number of geographical societies, honorary doctorates from several universities and was promoted to the naval rank of rear admiral. In 1923 Cook was imprisoned for a violation of the United States postal laws in connection with a fraudulent oil transaction. He was released in 1930 and pardoned by President Franklin D. Roosevelt in 1940. Although Cook always maintained that his claims as an explorer were authentic he became known as the man who made up a story about his conquest and Peary remained the declared conqueror of the North Pole.

Suggested Readings

Clark, Electa. Robert Peary, Boy of the North Pole. Indianapolis: Bobbs-Merrill, 1962.
Cook, Frederick A. My Attainment of the Pole. New York: The Polar Publishing Co., 1911.
Hobbs, William H. Exploring About the North Pole of the Winds. Westport, Conn.: Greenwood Press, 1930.
_____. Peary. Westport, Conn.: Greenwood Press, 1936.
Peary, Robert E. Nearest the Pole: A Narrative of the Polar Expedition of the Peary Arctic Club in the S. S. "Roosevelt," 1905-1906. New York: AMS Press, 1907.
_____. The North Pole: Its Discovery in 1909 Under the Auspices of the Peary Arctic Club. Introduction by Theodore Roosevelt and foreword by Gilbert H. Grosvenor. Westport, Conn.: Greenwood Press, 1968 (Originally published 1910).

_____. Northward Over the "Great Ice" ... in the Years 1886
and 1896-1897. New York: 1898.
_____. Secrets of Polar Travel. New York: 1917.
"Robert E. Peary, After 23 Years Siege, Reaches North Pole; Adds
  'The Big Nail' to New York Yacht Club's Trophies; Dr. Cook
  to Submit Records to University of Denmark, " New York Herald,
  September 7, 1909, p. 1.
Stafford, Marie Peary. Discoverer of the North Pole, the Story
  of Robert E. Peary. New York: Morrow, 1959.
Weems, J. E. The Race for the Pole. New York: Holt, 1960.
Willis, Thayer. "The Cook-Peary Controversy" in his The Frozen
  World: Encyclopedia of Discovery and Exploration, Vol. 14.
  London: Aldus Books, 1971.

THE CRIPPEN-ROBINSON MURDER (1910)

   The first time in history that a murderer was trapped through
the use of radio was in 1910 when Dr. Hawley Harvey Crippen and
his mistress, Ethel Le Neve, traveling from Antwerp to Quebec on
the passenger liner Montrose, were spotted by Captain Kendall, commander of the vessel, who notified Scotland Yard.

   Dr. Crippen's wife Cora, who used "Belle Elmore" as a
stage name, was a second-rate singer and actress, termagant and
profligate who bullied and humiliated her husband. They had lived
in London since the turn of the century. Crippen practiced as a
physician and doubled as man-of-all-work in the rooming house operated by his wife. She had a series of lovers, notably an American entertainer named Bruce Miller.

   Ethel Le Neve, who had been hired by Crippen as bookkeep-
er and secretary, became his mistress. She was 24, unmarried
and the exact opposite of Cora Crippen. She became genuinely fond
of her employer.

   In 1910 Crippen's wife disappeared and Ethel Le Neve moved
into his house. On March 26 Crippen inserted a death notice in the
Era, a magazine, stating that Cora had died of pneumonia in California. Ethel was seen in public wearing clothes and jewels which
belonged to Cora, and reports of this "tastelessness" reached the
ears of Chief Inspector Walter Dew of Scotland Yard. Dew visited
Crippen who told him that Cora was not dead but that she had run
away with Bruce Miller and was living in America. Crippen said
that his publishing the death notice had been a matter of pride; he
did not wish to admit publicly that his wife had deserted him. Inspector Dew insisted on searching the house but found nothing incriminating. Satisfied with Crippen's explanation, he left.

   Crippen was not sure that Dew believed his story. Feeling
that he might be arrested, he and Ethel Le Neve fled to Rotterdam,

she wearing boys' clothing and posing as the doctor's son. He assumed the name "John Philip Robinson."

On July 11 Inspector Dew returned to the Crippen home to
check some details of the story he had been told. Finding the house
deserted, he instituted a second search. Clothing and some remains of a human body were found buried in the cellar. These
were identified with Cora Crippen and a warrant was issued for the
arrest of the doctor and his mistress.

On July 20 "John Philip Robinson" and his "son" embarked
on the Montrose at Antwerp. Captain Kendall, who had learned
from the newspapers that the Daily Mail was offering a hundred
pound reward for information concerning the suspected wife-killer,
became suspicious. "Robinson" was more demonstratively attentive
to his "son" than is customary in a father-and-son relationship.

Kendall sent a radio message to Scotland Yard, saying he
believed that Dr. Crippen and Ethel Le Neve were aboard his vessel. Inspector Dew and two police matrons took passage on the
Laurentic, a faster steamer than the Montrose, and scheduled to
arrive at Quebec ahead of her.

When the Montrose arrived at her destination Dew was waiting. He arrested the runaways and returned them to London. There
the two were tried separately, Crippen first. He was found guilty
of murder and sentenced to hang. Ethel Le Neve was acquitted and
promptly dropped from sight. Dr. Crippen/"John Philip Robinson"
was hanged on November 23, 1910.

Suggested Readings

Abrahamsen, David, M. D. The Murdering Mind. New York: Har-
    per & Row, 1973.
"Arrest by Radio: Dr. Crippen" in Infamous Murders. London:
    Verdict Press/Phoebus Publishing Co. , 1975.
Birkenhead, Frederick Edwin Smith. "Ethel Le Neve: Crippen's
    Mistress" in his Famous Trials of History. Garden City, N.Y.:
    Garden City Publishing Co. , 1928.
Bromberg, Walter. Mold of Murder: A Psychiatric Study of Homi-
    cide. New York: Grune & Stratton, 1961.
Catton, Joseph. Behind the Scenes of Murder. New York: Nor-
    ton, 1940.
"Doctor Crippen" in Crimes and Punishment, Vol. 3. Editorial
    presentation: Jackson Morley. London: BPC, 1973.
Guttmacher, M. S. The Mind of the Murderer. Freeport, N.Y.:
    Books for Libraries, 1960.
Hynd, Alan. "The Case of the Lady Who Lost Her Head" in his
    Sleuths, Slayers and Swindlers: A Casebook of Crime. New
    York: Barnes, 1959.
Jesse, F. Tennyson. Murder and Its Motives. London: Harrap,
    1952.

Lawes, Warden Lewis E. Meet the Murderer! New York: Harper, 1940.

Lester, David, and Gene Lester. Crime of Passion: Murder and the Murderer. Chicago: Nelson Hall, 1975.

McDade, Thomas L., compiler. The Annals of Murder. Norman, Okla.: University of Oklahoma Press, 1961.

Reinhardt, James Melvin. The Psychology of Strange Killers. Springfield, Ill.: Thomas, 1962.

Roberts, Carl E. B. The New World of Crime. London: Noble, 1933.

Scott, Sir Harold Richard, with Philippa Pearce. From Inside Scotland Yard. New York: Macmillan, 1965.

Sparrow, Gerald. Women Who Murder. New York: Abelard, 1970.

Symons, Julian. "The Gentle Poisoner: Crippen and Others" in his A Pictorial History of Crime. New York: Crown Publishers, 1966.

Thompson, Laurence Victor. The Story of Scotland Yard. New York: Random House, 1954.

Wilson, Colin, and Patricia Pitman. Encyclopedia of Murder. New York: Putnam, 1962.

Wolfgang, Marvin E., compiler. Studies in Homicide. New York: Harper & Row, 1967.

THE RACE TO THE SOUTH POLE (1910-1912)

The South Pole, sometimes called "The Bottom of the World," is located on a flat, snow-covered plateau on the Antarctic continent. In 1909 Ernest Shackleton, an Irish explorer, led a British expedition to within 97 miles of the Pole before being forced to turn back because of a shortage of food and the approach of the Antarctic winter. A few months later Roald Amundsen of Norway and Robert Falcon Scott of England engaged in a dramatic race to be the first men to reach the South Pole.

Amundsen had succeeded in making his way through the Northwest Passage in the 45-foot sloop Gjöa some time before, the first man to do so. He then inaugurated an expedition to the North Pole but when, in 1909, Robert E. Peary of America reached that objective, Amundsen turned his attention to Antarctica and the South Pole.

Scott had been a member of the 1901-1904 expedition which had reached the South Polar Plateau. On June 1, 1910, he and his crew sailed from London to New Zealand in the Terra Nova. In August Amundsen also headed South in the Fram, apparently intending to round Cape Horn and proceed to the Arctic Ocean. However, he secretly changed his plans and headed instead for the Madeira Islands, from which he intended to try for the South Pole. When, in October, Scott reached New Zealand he received a cable from Amundsen reading "Beg leave to inform you proceeding to Antarctica." The race for the South Pole was under way.

Amundsen reached the Bay of Whales, 60 miles closer to the Pole than Scott's camp in McMurdo Sound. On November 3 Amundsen and four companions reached their southernmost supply depot. He had brought Siberian huskies to pull his sledges. Scott who, with his party, had left McMurdo Sound on November 1, had brought ponies to pull his equipment. These animals proved unable to stand the freezing weather and drifting snow and eventually had to be destroyed.

Both parties suffered extreme hardship. On December 7, 1911, Amundsen reached 88° 23' which was the farthest point south Shackleton's party had reached in 1909. On December 14 the Amundsen party arrived at the South Pole and on December 17 it started back to the base.

Scott, together with four companions, Edgar Evans, Captain Oates, Lieutenant Bowers and Edward Wilson, arrived at the Pole on January 18, 1912, to find the Norwegian flag left there by Amundsen and his men. This caused Scott bitter disappointment as he had long dreamed of being the first man to set foot on the South Pole. The following day the five started the trek back to the home depot. The party was plagued by blizzards, scurvy, frostbite and fatigue. By January 25 it had reached a point 89 miles from the depot. Amundsen, in the meantime, had arrived at his base camp on the Bay of Whales. His round trip to the Pole and back had taken just 99 days.

Scott and his party reached Beardmore Glacier on February 7. They became lost and the food supply ran dangerously low. Evans died of frostbite and exposure. Captain Oates, the next to die, wandered away into a blizzard and was never seen again.

On March 21, 1912, when only eleven miles from the food depot, Scott, Bowers and Wilson, caught in a blizzard, died in their tent. Their bodies were discovered by a searching party the following November. Scott had kept a diary during the race to the Pole and it is from this, which was recovered, that we know the tragic story of his last expedition.

Roald Amundsen continued his activities as an explorer. In 1920 he sailed through the Northeast Passage to the east. In May, 1926, he flew over the North Pole in the dirigible Norge, accompanied by Lincoln Ellsworth and Umberto Nobile. In June, 1928, he disappeared while on a flight to rescue Nobile who was lost while returning from the North Pole following the wreck of the dirigible Italia which had been engaged in an exploring expedition.

Suggested Readings

Amundsen, Roald. The South Pole: An Account of the Norwegian Antarctic Expedition in the "Fram" 1910-1912. Translated by A.G. Chater. New York: Barnes & Noble, 1976 (Originally published 1912).

Berger, Melvin. South Pole Station. New York: Day, 1971.
Bixby, William. The Impossible Journey of Sir Ernest Shackleton.
    Boston: Little, Brown, 1960.
_____. Robert Scott, Antarctic Pioneer. Philadelphia: Lippin-
    cott, 1970.
Brown, Michael. Shackleton's Epic Voyage. New York: Coward-
    McCann, 1969.
Dukert, Joseph M. This Is Antarctica. New York: Coward-Mc-
    Cann, 1972 (Originally published 1965).
Holwood, Will, pseud. The True Story of Captain Scott at the South
    Pole. Chicago: Children's Press, 1964.
Kugelmass, J. Alvin. Roald Amundsen: A Saga of the Polar Seas.
    New York: Messner, 1955.
Lansing, Alfred. Endurance: Shackleton's Incredible Voyage. Lon-
    don: Hodder, 1961.
_____. Shackleton's Valiant Voyage. New York: Whittlesey
    House, 1960. (Abridged portion of Endurance: Shackleton's In-
    credible Voyage).
Newbolt, Sir Henry John. "Robert Falcon Scott" in his Book of the
    Long Trail. New York: Longmans, Green, 1919.
Scott, Robert F. Scott's Last Expedition. Edited by Leonard Hux-
    ley. London: 1913 (Originally written in diary form, 1910-
    1912).
_____. The Voyage of the "Discovery." Westport, Conn. :
    Greenwood Press, 1969 (Originally published 1905).
Strong, Charles S. South Pole Husky. New York: Longmans,
    Green, 1950.
Willis, Thayer. "Duel for the South Pole" and "Shackleton into
    Antarctica" in his The Frozen World: Encyclopedia of Discov-
    ery and Exploration, Vol. 14. London: Aldus Books, 1971.

THE THEFT AND RECOVERY OF THE
"MONA LISA" (1911-1913)

One of the most audacious art thefts of all time was the stealing of Leonardo da Vinci's masterpiece, the "Mona Lisa" ("La Gioconda"), from the Salon Carrê Gallery of the Louvre Museum, Paris, on August 21, 1911.

This famous picture is an oil portrait of Lisa di Anton Maria,
wife of Francesco del Giocondo of Florence and was painted in that
city sometime between 1500 and 1504, although some authorities
put the date between 1503 and 1506. It was acquired by Francis I
of France in the sixteenth century, he paying 4,000 gold florins for
it. The "Mona Lisa" hung in his palace until Louis XIV had it
moved to Versailles. After the French Revolution it became the
property of the state and was eventually placed in the Louvre.

Leonardo's world-famous painting was stolen from its place
on the Louvre wall sometime before 8:30 on the morning of August

21. The theft, however, was not discovered until nearly 9:00 on
the following day, it being generally supposed by museum attendants
that the "Mona Lisa" had been taken away to be photographed. The
loss was not reported to the deputy director of museums until nearly noon, after visitors began asking where they might view the picture.

The attendants at the photographic studio had no knowledge
of the missing masterpiece. The police were summoned and an
investigation was launched. The building was searched from top
to bottom but without result. The heavy gold frame which had surrounded the painting was found but it was empty.

The Paris Journal offered a reward of 50,000 francs for the
recovery of the picture, "with no questions asked." Many theories
were advanced concerning the theft. A wealthy American, someone suggested, had offered a million dollars for it. Someone had
become infatuated with the "Mona Lisa's" enigmatic smile and,
somehow, had taken the painting from the museum. An art forger
planned to make a dozen copies and sell them secretly, as the genuine painting, to millionaire art lovers.

A number of persons were arrested on suspicion and released
for lack of evidence. These included a young art student who was
carrying a wrapped framed painting, the poet Guillaume Apollinaire
and his friend Pablo Picasso, the world-famous sculptor and post-
impressionist and cubist painter.

Someone informed the authorities that he had seen a man
running from the Louvre on the morning of the theft. The man
had thrown something into a "patch of waste." The police searched
the area and found a brass doorknob which was later found to have
been removed from the door of the Salon Carré.

Henri Droux, leading the investigation, reasoned that the
thief had hidden in the Louvre overnight and had, next morning, removed the picture from its frame and made off with it. However,
no trace of the thief or the painting was found.

On November 30, 1913, art dealer Alfredo Geri received a
letter in his Florence office. This letter, bearing a Paris post-
mark and signed "Leonard," stated: "I have stolen the 'Mona Lisa.' " The writer explained that his act was prompted by a desire
to return the masterpiece to Italy, where it was created and where
it belonged. He said further that the picture was in his possession
and that, though a poor man, he would not ask money for it.

Geri and Giovanni Poggi, director of the Uffizi Gallery, arranged to meet "Leonard" at Geri's office on Wednesday, December
10. "Leonard" kept the appointment but did not bring the picture
with him. He asked $100,000 for its return. On December 11
"Leonard" took the two men to his Florence hotel and produced the
long-lost masterpiece from the false botton of his trunk. The picture was unharmed.

Under police questioning, "Leonard" indicated that his real name was Vincenzo Perugia, that he was a workman from Dumenza, Italy, who had been employed at the Louvre as a picture framer and that he had stolen the painting "for the glory of Italy and vengeance for the depradations of Napoleon, who plundered my beloved country. "

The "Mona Lisa" was exhibited in Florence, Rome and Milan before being returned to France under heavy guard. On June 14,. 1914, Perugia was tried in a Florence court. He told how he had engineered the theft, wearing a workman's blouse. Mingling with a group of similarly clad workers, he stole quietly away, took the picture from the wall, removed it from its frame, placed it beneath his blouse and walked boldly out.

The Italian populace approved Perugia's action. The man maintained that he had not tried to sell the painting in London, as alleged, nor to Geri, the Florentine dealer. He stated that Geri had offered him money for the painting, a statement Geri denied under oath, saying that it was Perugia who had demanded money.

Found guilty, Perugia was sentenced to serve one year and fifteen days in jail. On appeal his sentence was reduced to seven months. As he had already spent more time than this in confinement he was immediately freed. He insisted, forever afterwards, that his sole concern in taking the priceless painting from the Louvre was to bring it back to Florence. "Little else, " he said, "interests me. "

Suggested Readings

"La Gioconda Is Stolen in Paris, " New York Times, August 23, 1911, p. 1.

McMullen, Roy. Mona Lisa: The Picture and the Myth. Boston: Houghton Mifflin, 1975.

"Mona Lisa Thief, " Newsweek, September 10, 1947.

"Mona Lisa's Return, " Literary Digest, January 3, 1914.

"The Most Popular Man in Italy" in Crimes and Punishment, Vol. 18. Editorial presentation: Jackson Morley. London: BPC, 1973.

"Police Have Clues to Lost Mona Lisa, " New York Times, August 25, 1911, p. 4.

"Recovery of the Mona Lisa, " Independent and Weekly Review, December 25, 1913.

"Romantic Solution of the Mona Lisa Mystery, " Current Literature, October, 1911.

"60 Detectives Seek Stolen Mona Lisa, " New York Times, August 24, 1911, p. 4.

"Startling Theft of a Priceless Painting, " Harper's Weekly, September 9, 1911.

Teall, G. "The Mona Lisa and Its Theft, " World Today, October, 1911.

"Vanishing of Mona Lisa, " Outlook, September 2, 1911.

"Will the Theft of the Mona Lisa Help the Louvre?" Review of Reviews, October, 1911.

THE PILTDOWN MAN HOAX (1911-1953)

In 1911 Charles Dawson, an English lawyer and amateur anthropologist, claimed to have found a fossil fragment of a human skull at Piltdown, a parish near Uckfield, East Sussex. Dawson brought his find to the British Museum. Subsequent diggings on Piltdown Common unearthed more than twenty fragments of brown bones and teeth, including a portion of a lower jaw and other cranial fossils. These diggings were conducted by Dr. Arthur Smith Woodward, paleontologist of the Museum.

The jaw was definitely that of an ape, with one significant exception: two molar teeth were intact and the surfaces of these were flat. Only a human jaw, with its free-swinging motion, could have worn them down to that flat-top shape. This caused the scientists to consider the owner of the jaw a "missing link" in human evolution.

Other fossils, found nearby, including portions of a prehistoric human skull, seemingly identified Dawson's find as originally belonging to a primitive man, the earliest known human presumed to have lived in the early ice age, some 500,000 years ago. Dr. Woodward gave the "Piltdown man" the scientific name Eoanthropus dawsoni or "Dawson's Dawn Man."

A skull was reconstructed, patterned after the Piltdown fragments. This skull, with its unusually high forehead and simian jaw, caused a great deal of scientific controversy. This raged until 1950 when Dr. Kenneth Oakley, a geologist on the staff of the British Museum, applied a chemical dating test to the Piltdown fragments. Dr. Oakley measured the fluorine content of the fragments and determined that the bones were not half a million years old, but only 50,000. Oakley's estimate was correct, so far as the cranial fragments were concerned, but his assumption that the jaw was equally old was wrong.

The discussion continued until 1953, when a Dr. Weiner discussed the Piltdown riddle with Oakley. It occurred to him that a hoax may have been perpetrated, and that the fossil teeth may have been deliberately filed flat. Weiner and Professor Wilfred Le Gros Clark obtained a chimpanzee's molar tooth, filed and stained it and compared it with the teeth produced by Dawson. Scientific instruments, such as the Geiger counter and the X-ray spectrograph, were used.

The results were conclusive. Someone had obtained an ape's teeth and fossilized and stained them. The scratches on the Piltdown

teeth, detected under magnification, showed that they had been artificially filed.

In 1953 Oakley, Weiner and Clark declared that the Piltdown
jaw and teeth were counterfeit. Weiner conducted an intensive investigation which showed that the other Piltdown relics were all
forgeries. Further investigation by Weiner made it clear that
Charles Dawson, the original "finder" of the fossils, was guilty on
circumstantial evidence at least of perpetrating a hoax. Dawson
"found" relics of a second Piltdown man in 1915, near the site of
his first "discovery." The second relics, like the first, were determined to be bogus, having been artificially stained with iron and
bichromate. No further Piltdown discoveries were made following
Dawson's death in 1916.

Suggested Readings

Andrews, Roy Chapman. Meet Your Ancestors. New York: Vi-
    king Press, 1963.
Armagnac, Alden P. "Dawson's Dawn Man" in Klein, Alexander,
    ed. The Double Dealers. Philadelphia: Lippincott, 1958.
Borer, Mary Cathcart. Mankind in the Making. London: Fred-
    erick Warne, 1962.
Day, Michael H. Fossil Man. New York: Grosset & Dunlap, 1970.
Klein, Alexander. Grand Deception: The World's Most Spectacular
    and Successful Hoaxes, Impostures, Ruses and Frauds. Phil-
    adelphia: Lippincott, 1955.
MacDougall, Curtis D. Hoaxes. New York: Macmillan, 1940.
Oakley, Kenneth P. "The Fluorine-Dating Method," Yearbook of
    Physical Anthropology, 1949.
_____. Frameworks for Dating Fossil Man. Revised edition.
    Chicago: Aldine Publishing Co., 1968.
_____. Man the Tool-Maker. Chicago: University of Chicago
    Press, 1976.
_____. The Problem of Man's Antiquity. New York: Johnson
    Reprint Corp., 1964.
_____. "Swanscombe Man," Yearbook of Physical Anthropology,
    1952.
_____, et al. "The Solution of the Piltdown Problem," Bulletin
    of the British Museum (Natural History), Vol. 2, 1953.
"Piltdown Man" in Crimes and Punishment, Vol. 13. Editorial pre-
    sentation: Jackson Morley. London: BPC, 1973.
Smith, H. Allen. The Compleat Practical Joker. Garden City,
    N.Y.: Doubleday, 1959.
Vlahos, Olivia. Human Beginnings. New York: Viking Press, 1966.

THE "BRIDES-IN-THE-BATH" MURDERS (1912-1914)

One of the more notorious murderers of the 20th century was

George Joseph Smith, and Englishman and polygamist who married several women for their money and then drowned them in their baths.

Smith had a checkered career. As an incorrigible youth he had attempted a number of occupations, including a hitch in the army, songwriter, baker, junk shop owner and antique dealer. In 1898 he married Caroline Beatrice Thornhill under the assumed name of George Oliver Love. After a few months of marriage she left him and in 1908 he married bigamously Edith Pegler, using his own name. In 1910, calling himself Henry Williams, he married Beatrice "Bessie" Mundy. She had some savings and income from a trust left to her by her father. Smith, by chicanery, obtained possession of her assets and promptly deserted her. In March, 1912, she met her "husband" by chance and returned to him. On July 7 each made a will in favor of the other, and four days later Bessie was "found" by Smith, dead by drowning in her bath. At the coroner's inquest it was decided that the woman had had an epileptic seizure during which she drowned by accident. Smith inherited 2,571 pounds from Bessie's estate.

In 1913 Smith married Alice Burnham, a nurse, again using his own name. He was able to acquire possession of her assets-- 104 pounds--and also induced her to take out a life insurance policy for 500 pounds, naming him as beneficiary. She also, at his request, made a will in his favor. The two then visited Blackpool and shortly afterwards Alice Burnham was found drowned in her bath. The coroner's jury found that the death was accidental. Smith spent the Christmas holidays with Edith Pegler.

A year later he "married" Margaret Lofty, using the name John Lloyd. Like his other "wives," she made a will in his favor and that evening was found dead in her bath. The "husband" was exonerated by the coroner's jury.

An account of Margaret Lofty's death appeared in the newspapers and was seen by the late Alice Burnham's father. His suspicions aroused, he contacted the police who placed Smith under observation. On February 1, 1915, Smith was arrested when he went to a solicitor's office in connection with Margaret's will. He was indicted, first for bigamy and then for murder. While charged with the killing of three women, the indictment covered only the murder of Bessie Mundy.

George Smith's trial opened on June 22, 1915, in London's Central Criminal Court. The case was prosecuted by Archibald Bodkin, with Sir Edward Marshall Hall acting as defense counsel and Mr. Justice Scrutton as presiding judge. Smith pleaded not guilty. In spite of the energetic defense of Hall during the nine-day-trial, Smith was found guilty, the jury being out only twenty minutes. Scrutton sentenced him to death by hanging. An appeal was made to the Court of Criminal Appeal, which concurred in the findings of the lower court. The Home Secretary refused a reprieve and the sentence was carried out at Maidstone Prison.

Suggested Readings

Abrahamsen, David, M. D. The Murdering Mind. New York: Harper & Row, 1973.

"The Brides in the Bath" in Crimes and Punishment, Vol. 4. Editorial presentation: Jackson Morley. London: BPC, 1973.

"The Brides in the Bath: George Smith" in Infamous Murders. London: Verdict Press/Phoebus Publishing Co., 1975.

Bromberg, Walter. Mold of Murder: A Psychiatric Study of Homicide. New York: Grune & Stratton, 1961.

Catton, Joseph. Behind the Scenes of Murder. New York: Norton, 1940.

Guttmacher, M. S. The Mind of the Murderer. Freeport, N. Y.: Books for Libraries, 1960.

Hynd, Alan. "The Case of the Amorous Antique Dealer" in his Sleuths, Slayers and Swindlers: A Casebook of Crime. New York: Barnes, 1959.

Jesse, F. Tennyson. Murder and Its Motives. London: Harrap, 1952.

Lawes, Warden Lewis E. Meet the Murderer! New York: Harper, 1940.

Lester, David, and Gene Lester. Crime of Passion: Murder and the Murderer. Chicago: Nelson Hall, 1975.

McDade, Thomas M., compiler. The Annals of Murder. Norman, Okla.: University of Oklahoma Press, 1961.

Reinhardt, James Melvin. The Psychology of Strange Killers. Springfield, Ill.: Thomas, 1962.

Roberts, Carl E. B. The New World of Crime. London: Noble, 1933.

Scott, Sir Harold, with Philippa Pearce. From Inside Scotland Yard. New York: Macmillan, 1965.

Symons, Julian. "My Mother Was a Buss Horse" in his A Pictorial History of Crime. New York: Crown Publishers, 1966.

Thompson, Laurence Victor. The Story of Scotland Yard. New York: Random House, 1954.

Wilson, Colin, and Patricia Pitman. Encyclopedia of Murder. New York: Putnam, 1962.

Wolfgang, Marvin E., compiler. Studies in Homicide. New York: Harper & Row, 1967.

THE RISE AND FALL OF MATA HARI (1912-1917)

Gertrud Margarete Zelle, better remembered by her assumed name, "Mata Hari" (Javanese for "Eye of the Morning"), was a Dutch-born German spy. In 1912 Traugott von Jagow, a German "spymaster," recruited her into his country's secret service. She was then appearing in a Berlin theater as a chorus girl and had something of a reputation as a "courtesan, hypnotist, mystic and sexual blackmailer. "

Von Jagow arranged her enrollment at a spy school in Lor-
rach. Following her graduation she was, as the result of the spymaster's maneuvering, invited to diplomatic parties and receptions
at German embassies in Amsterdam, Cairo, Madrid, Paris and
other large cities. Meeting high-ranking diplomatic and military
figures was not difficult for her and she was able, in the course of
casual affairs she had with them, to obtain information concerning
the movements of troops and supplies and attack and defense plans.
For her services the Germans paid her 200,000 francs a month.

Until 1914 her espionage produced little of practical use to
the Germans. Then a Dutch importer-exporter, one of her trans-
ient lovers, disclosed details of a shipment of food which was to
be transported from England to France. She relayed the information to von Jagow by secret code and, as a consequence, seventeen
Allied freighters were met by German submarines, torpedoed and
sunk.

Mata Hari's next assignment was at a French army hospital
at Vittel where, as a Red Cross nurse, she obtained vital military
information from Captain Marov, a wounded Russian army officer.
The proposed Allied counteroffensive, the details of which he disclosed to her, resulted in a surprise attack on Vittel by German
troops. A quarter of a million Allied soldiers died.

It was then that the seductive German spy decided to betray
her employers and engage in counterespionage work for France.
She contacted Captain Ladoux, head of the French Intelligence Service. Ladoux was not deceived. For a time she was permitted to
play both ends against the middle and then, on Ladoux's orders,
was arrested at her Paris hotel by an Intelligence agent named Troi-
let.

Charged with spying, Mata Hari's courtmartial began on July
24, 1917, six months after her arrest. She was tried before a
seven-judge court, found guilty and condemned to die before a firing squad.

While in prison awaiting her execution she made an unsuccessful attempt to escape. On October 15 she was taken to a military rifle range at Vincennes Barracks outside Paris and executed
by a squad of Zouaves. She was 41 years old.

Suggested Readings

Barton, George. "The Romantic Life of the Dutch Javanese Dancer
    Who Was Shot as a Spy" in his Celebrated Spies and Famous
    Mysteries of the Great War. Boston: Page, 1919.
Coulson, Major Thomas. Mata Hari, Courtesan and Spy. New
    York: Harper, 1930.
_____. "Mata Hari, Seductress of the Allies," Forum, February,
    1930.

_____. "Mata Hari: The Dance of Death," Forum, April, 1930.
_____. "Mata Hari: The Red Dancer," Forum, January, 1930.
_____. "Mata Hari: Trapped," Forum, March, 1930.
Heymans, C. S. "Mata Hari, the Spy," Review of Reviews, January, 1930.
"Mata Hari" in Crimes and Punishment, Vol. 6. Editorial presentation: Jackson Morley. London: BPC, 1973.
Rogers, Cameron. "Mata Hari" in his Gallant Ladies. New York: Harcourt, Brace, 1928.
"Vampire of a Real Tank," Literary Digest, October 13, 1917.
Waagenaar, Sam. Mata Hari. New York: Appleton-Century, 1965.

THE RISE AND FALL OF IVAR KREUGER (1913-1932)

A financial empire crashed on March 12, 1932, when the Swedish financier and forger, Ivar Kreuger, known as the "Match King," committed suicide in Paris. His death caused a financial panic as the shares of the companies which he owned or controlled plummeted to rock bottom.

Ivar Kreuger was born in Kalmar, Sweden, in 1880. As a young man he worked in his father's match factory. He then studied mechanical engineering and worked briefly in the United States and Mexico, holding a variety of jobs in both countries.

In 1908 he returned to Sweden where he established the construction company of Kreuger & Toll. In 1913 he realized that, with the new popularity of smoking cigars and pipes, the manufacture and sale of matches offered a profitable business opportunity to anyone who could monopolize the industry. Matches were cheap to produce and the selling price could be easily increased. He saw also that it would be possible to pack 46 matches in each box rather than the usual 50, and few persons would be aware of it. "Who ever counts the number of matches in a box?" he asked.

Kreuger & Toll acquired interests in the Swedish match industry and expanded them steadily. Within two years the "Match King" had gained control of seven factories. In 1917 he organized the Swedish Match Company as a holding company for the factories he had acquired and for other enterprises under his control.

His next step was to establish an international match monopoly of the manufacture and sale of matches in a number of countries, including Estonia, Greece, Germany, Latvia and Ecuador. This he accomplished by making large loans to governments.

Ivar Kreuger began to live extravagantly, maintaining town houses, apartments and country mansions in a dozen different countries. He had a number of mistresses, the most permanent of which was Ingaborg Hassler, who left him to marry but returned after six months.

By 1924 Kreuger controlled 70 percent of the world's match production. However, by this time he was greatly overexpanded and in need of funds or, at least, credit. He stated, in 1925, that he had loaned 25 million dollars to Spain at 16 percent interest annually. He also spoke of a similar arrangement with Poland. While he had, in the past, made loans to foreign governments in order to secure match monopolies, these 1925 loans were fictitious, but on the strength of them he was able to borrow money from both American and French banks. The bankers making the loans were pledged to secrecy, as to disclose such information, Kreuger said, "would probably bring about war."

In October, 1929, the famous Wall Street Crash occurred. This was followed by the economic depression that lasted for a decade. The financial empire founded by Kreuger & Toll found itself in financial difficulties. In the winter of 1931 Kreuger sailed to America where he attempted to negotiate a $13,000,000 loan from J. P. Morgan & Co., needing the money to pay interest on several outstanding obligations. Morgan personally refused to grant the loan. Kreuger returned to Europe on the luxury liner Ile de France, and Morgan dispatched a detective to travel with him to see that he did not commit suicide.

On March 11, 1932, he met in Paris with several bankers and businessmen to ask for additional loans and further credit. He asserted that he had some $60,000,000 in Italian treasury bills which he could put up as collateral. "I got them from Benito Mussolini," he said. "He gave them to me in payment for a secret loan." Krister Littorin, an associate of Kreuger, showed that the Italian dictator had never made such an arrangement, and if Italian bills were in Kreuger's possession they must be forged. Shortly afterwards the meeting adjourned. The "Match King" did not get the loan he desired from the bankers.

Kreuger went to a gun shop and purchased a revolver and ammunition. When he did not appear at the meeting scheduled for the following day, Littorin went to his apartment. There he found that, sometime during the night, Ivar Kreuger had shot himself.

The death of the "Match King" precipitated a financial panic from which it took weeks to recover. In his suicide note, addressed to Littorin, he said, in part, "I have made such a mess of things that I believe this to be the most satisfactory solution for all concerned."

Suggested Readings

Barman, T. G. "Ivar Kreuger, His Life and Work," Atlantic Monthly, August, 1932.
Churchill, Allen. The Incredible Ivar Kreuger. New York: Rinehart, 1957.
Deeson, F. L. Great Swindlers. New York: Drake Publishers, 1972.

"Four Masters of Fraud--They Won and Lost ... the Millions They
Milked from the Unwary," Newsweek, April 1, 1957.

Gibson, Walter Brown, ed. The Fine Art of Swindling. New York:
Grosset & Dunlap, 1966.

Hancock, Ralph, and Henry Chafetz. The Compleat Swindler. New
York: Macmillan, 1968.

Hertzberg, S. "The Aftermath of the Kreuger Crash," Current History, November, 1933.

————. "Ivar Kreuger's Liabilities," Current History, November, 1932.

"The Man Who Cheated the World" in Crimes and Punishment, Vol.
2. Editorial presentation: Jackson Morley. London: BPC,
1973.

Shaplen, Robert. Kreuger, Genius and Swindler. New York: Knopf,
1960.

Symons, Julian. "Stavisky and Kreuger" in his A Pictorial History
of Crime. New York: Crown Publishers, 1966.

"Why the House of Kreuger Fell," Literary Digest, February 4,
1933.

Whyte, F. "Interpretation of Ivar Kreuger," Contemporary Review,
April, 1933.

THE BLACK HAND PLOT (1914)

Since the early nineteenth century trouble had been brewing
between the various European nations. The idea of political democracy, with people of like ethnic origin, similar political ideas and
speaking a common language, had gained general acceptance. However, this was largely ignored by those who negotiated peace settlements, particularly the Congress of Vienna of 1814-1815, following
the downfall of Napoleon I. Revolutions and strong nationalistic
movements did result in nullifying some of the reactionary and anti-
nationalistic work of the Congress, but by the end of the nineteenth
century a number of areas remained in Europe where the problem
of nationalization was still unresolved. This situation generated tensions, not only within the regions involved but also between the various European nations. Because of this war was inevitable.

World War I was triggered when, on June 28, 1914, Archduke Francis Ferdinand, heir-apparent of Austria-Hungary, was shot
to death, along with his morganatic wife Sophie, by Gavrilo Princip,
a Bosnian terrorist and student who lived in Serbia. The assassination took place at Sarajevo, Bosnia, where Ferdinand was making a
state visit to attend some army maneuvers.

Shortly before noon, while crowds gathered to see the royal
pair, Princip jumped on the running board of the touring car in
which Ferdinand and his wife were riding, and fired a pistol. Two
shots struck the Archduke and a third hit Sophie, who was attempting to shield him. Both died almost immediately.

The events which led up to the double assassination were essentially as follows: Seven young Serbian nationalists formed the group which was to kill the Archduke. They were armed with pistols and hand bombs. They also carried capsules of poison, to be used in case it became necessary to commit suicide. On the morning of June 28 they took up separate positions on the Appel Quay where they waited for the four-vehicle motorcade carrying Ferdinand and his wife to pass. When the vehicles arrived at the Cumuria Bridge where Mohammed Mehmed Basić (one of the conspirators) was stationed he did nothing though armed, explaining later that a policeman was standing nearby. When Archduke Ferdinand's car came abreast of Nedjelko Cabrinović, another member of the gang who was standing a few paces away from Basić, Cabrinović threw a bomb at the Archduke's head. His aim was poor and the bomb missed its mark, exploding in the street. No one was killed but a few people were hurt by flying fragments and were removed to the hospital. Cabrinović was instantly seized and taken into custody.

The first two cars of the motorcade raced towards city hall. On the way they passed Vasco Cubrilović, Danilo Ilić and Cvijetko Popović, three other members of the gang. These did nothing.

Arriving at the city hall, the Archduke and his wife were given a formal speech of welcome by Fehim Effendi Curcić, Burgomeister of Sarajevo, who was not aware of the bombing. Although General Oskar Potiorek, the military governor, advocated a continuance of the day's program, the Archduke overruled him, saying that he should go to the hospital to see how those who had been injured by the bomb were faring. The royal couple entered their touring car, the second in line, and the procession started. When it reached the Imperial Bridge it passed by Trifko Grabez, assassin No. 6, who did nothing.

The lead car made a wrong turn into Francis Joseph Street. The procession stopped prior to turning in the right direction, along Appel Quay. Gavrilo Princip, standing not five feet away, leaped forward and killed the royal couple with his pistol, as described above.

Princip then attempted to shoot himself. His pistol was knocked down by a spectator. He was able to swallow a poison capsule but promptly vomited. He was arrested immediately.

Under police questioning Princip and Nedjelko Cabrinović at first refused to talk. Then Ilić, arrested only as a suspected subversive, volunteered to "tell all" in exchange for his life. Mohammed Basić escaped but the other three conspirators were arrested on July 5.

The investigation, handled by an inept police judge named Leo Pfeffer, was badly bungled. Much later it was learned that the assassination plot had been engineered by the Black Hand, a Greater Serbia terror society, originally linked to the War Ministry in Belgrade. The pistols, bombs and poison had come from Serbia and were furnished by Milan Ciganović, a secondary figure in the organization, who was working under the orders of Colonel Dragutin Dimitrievic, chief of intelligence of the Serbian army and a high-ranking Black Hand official.

It was also learned long after the fact that Serbian Prime Minister Nikola Pasić had learned of the assassination plot and had ordered that Princip, Grabez and Cabrinović be intercepted. This was not accomplished and he suggested, through Finance Officer Bilinski, that Archduke Ferdinand cancel the trip. Bilinski, however, said only, "let us hope nothing happens," and on June 28 the royal couple died in their automobile at Sarajevo.

The assassins were tried in due course. Though convicted of the actual shooting, Princip was spared the death penalty because he was only nineteen. In 1918 he died in prison of tuberculosis.

On July 23, 1914, Austria presented a series of harsh demands to Serbia as a follow-up to the assassination. Serbia rejected the ultimatum a day later.

Suggested Readings

Albertini, Luigi. The Origins of the War of 1914. London: Oxford University Press, 1952-1957.

Baldwin, Hanson. World War I. New York: Harper & Row, 1962.

Barnes, Harry Elmer. The Genesis of the World War: An Introduction to the Problems of War Guilt. New York: Knopf, 1926.

Benns, F. Lee. Europe Since 1914 in Its World Setting. New York: Appleton-Century-Crofts, 1945.

Bloch, Camille. The Causes of the World War: An Historical Summary. Translated by Jane Soames. London: George Allen and Unwin, 1935.

Dedijer, Vladimir. "Sarajevo" in A. J. P. Taylor, editor-in-chief. Purnell's History of the 20th Century. New York: Purnell, 1971.

Falls, Cyril. The Great War, 1914-1918. Toronto: Longmans, Green, 1953.

Fay, Sidney B. "The Black Hand Plot," Current History, November, 1925.

_____. The Origins of the World War. New York: Macmillan, 1966.

Fischer, Fritz. Germany's Aims in the First World War. London: Chatto and Windus, 1967.

"Heir to Austria's Throne Is Slain with His Wife by a Bosnian Youth to Avenge Seizure of His Country," New York Times, June 28, 1914, p. 1.

Liddell Hart, B. H. The Decisive Wars of History: A Study in Strategy. Part II. Boston: Little, Brown, 1929.

Lingley, Charles Ramsdell, and Allen Richard Foley. Since the Civil War. New York: Appleton, 1935.

Manserg, Nicolas. The Coming of the First World War. Toronto:
    Longmans, Green, 1949.
Millis, Walter. Road to War: America, 1914-1917. Boston:
    Houghton Mifflin, 1935.
Moon, Parker T. Imperialism and World Politics. New York:
    Macmillan, 1926.
Myers, Philip Van Ness. Medieval and Modern History. 2nd rev.
    ed., including the World War, 1914-1918. Boston: Ginn, 1920.
Pribram, Alfred F. England and the International Policy of the
    Great Powers, 1871-1914. Oxford: Clarendon Press, 1931.
Reeder, Red. The Story of the First World War. New York:
    Duell, Sloan, 1962.
Remak, Joachim. Sarajevo: The Story of a Political Murder. New
    York: Criterion Books, 1959.
Renouvin, Pierre. The Immediate Origins of the War. Translated
    by Theodore Carswell Hume. New York: Howard Fertig, 1969.
Schmitt, Bernadotte E. The Coming of the War, 1914. New York:
    Scribner's, 1930.
            . England and Germany, 1740-1914. New York: Howard
    Fertig, 1967.
Seaman, L. C. B. From Vienna to Versailles. New York: Harper
    & Row, 1963.
Sellman, R. R. The First World War. New York: Criterion Books,
    1962.
Smith, Daniel M. The Great Departure: The United States and
    World War I, 1914-1920. New York: Wiley, 1965.
Symons, Julian. "The End of a World" in his A Pictorial History
    of Crime. New York: Crown Publishers, 1966.
Taylor, Alan John Percivale. The Struggle for Mastery in Europe.
    Oxford: Clarendon Press, 1954.
Tuchman, Barbara W. The Guns of August. New York: Macmillan,
    1962.
Von Montgelas, Max Graf. The Case for the Central Powers. Trans-
    lated by Constance Vesey. New York: Knopf, 1925.

THE INAUGURATION OF SUBMARINE WARFARE (1914)

Since earliest times man has conducted warfare on the surface of the sea. The oar-propelled galleys of the Battle of Actium
(31 B. C.) and the sailing ships used in the American Civil War
(1861-1865) were alike in that they were unable to descend below
the surface, maneuver and reemerge. The idea of undersea warfare, however, had been considered for centuries. The diving bell
was known as early as 300 B. C. The Dutch inventor Cornelis Dreb-
bel built a leather-encased wooden rowboat in the 1620's. This,
propelled by oars, reputedly used air tubes supported on the surface of the water by floats to replenish the oxygen supply when the
boat was submerged. It was used successfully on the Thames River.

David Bushnell, an American inventor, designed and built the

Turtle, the first undersea water craft to be used for military purposes.   This primitive vessel made an unsuccessful attempt to sink
the British flagship Eagle in New York Harbor on September 6, 1776.
In 1779 Robert Fulton, inventor of the first practical steamboat, constructed an improved submarine, the Nautilus.   Simon Lake, an
American mechanical engineer and naval architect, did pioneer work
in undersea craft and in 1897 built the Argonaut, the first submarine to operate successfully in the open sea.

The era of sailing ships for military combat came to an end
following the Civil War battle between the ironclad steam-propelled
Merrimac and Monitor at Hampton Roads, Virginia, in March, 1862.
During the next hundred years the nations of the world built battleships, such as the Maine, the Dreadnaught, and the Arizona.   These
were large and expensive and made necessary the construction of
deep water docking and other facilities.

In 1906 the Germans adapted the diesel engine to the submarine.   With the invention of the self-propelled torpedo and the
periscope the submarine became a formidable weapon of naval warfare.

On September 5, 1914, the British light cruiser Pathfinder
was sunk by the German submarine U-21 off the Firth of Forth, and
on September 13 the British retaliated by sinking the German cruiser Helga off Heligoland.   The Helga was sunk by the British submarine E-9.

Extensive submarine warfare came to full fruition on Septem-
22, 1914, in the North Sea when the German submarine U-9, commanded by Lieutenant Otto Weddigen, sank three British cruisers,
the Aboukir, the Hogue, and the Cressy.   Up to this time the possibility of British shipping being attacked by German U-boats was
not taken seriously, although at the beginning of World War I the
British Admiralty had assigned surface ships to patrol the southern
North Sea and protect the English Channel from enemy mine layers
and destroyers.   With the sinking of the three British cruisers it
became obvious that undersea warfare was not something to be taken
lightly.   One 493-ton submarine, manned by 29 men had, in the
space of one hour, destroyed three British vessels and caused the
loss of 1,400 men.

The German navy turned its attention to the sinking of British merchant vessels.   The British Glitra went to the bottom on
October 20, 1914, the victim of a torpedo fired from a German submarine.   The British passenger liner Lusitania was torpedoed and
sunk by a German U-boat on May 7, 1915, ten miles off Kinsdale
Head, Ireland.   Some 1,152 persons were lost.   The Lusitania was
unarmed but the Germans declared that she was carrying contraband
of war.

In the first four months of 1917 German submarines sank
1,147 ships, totaling 2,224,000 tons.   During World Wars I and II

476   Footnotes to World History

the submarines of all navies in these wars destroyed over 13,000
merchant ships, for a grand total of 36 million tons.

Suggested Readings

Abbott, Henry L. The Beginning of Modern Submarine Warfare.
    Edited by Frank Anderson. Hamden, Conn.: Shoe String Press,
    1966.
Bishop, Farnham. The Story of the Submarine. New York: Ap-
    pleton, 1943.
Cable, Frank T. The Birth and Development of the American Sub-
    marine. New York: Harper, 1924.
Churchill, Winston S. The World Crisis, 1916-1918. Condensed
    edition. New York: Scribner's, 1931.
Commager, Henry Steele, ed. "The First 'Lusitania' Note" (Doc.
    No. 405) in his Documents of American History, 8th edition.
    New York: Appleton, 1968.
Corbett, Edmund V., ed. "Torpedoing of the 'Lusitania'" in his
    Great True Stories of Tragedy and Disaster. New York: Arch-
    er House, 1963.
Dönitz, Karl. Memoirs: Ten Years and Twenty Days. Translated
    by R. H. Stevens, in collaboration with David Woodward. Cleve-
    land: World, 1959.
Jane, Fred T. Fighting Ships. London: Sampson, Low, Marston,
    1897-1914.
Macintyre, Captain Donald. The Battle of the Atlantic. London:
    B. T. Batsford, 1961.
_____. Fighting Under the Sea. New York: Norton, 1965.
_____. U-Boat Killer. New York: Norton, 1957.
Marder, Arthur J. From the Dreadnaught to Scapa Flow. London:
    Oxford University Press, 1961.
Newbolt, Henry. Naval Operations, Vol. V. London: Longmans,
    Green, 1931.
Parkes, Oscar. British Battleships. London: Seeley Service,
    1957.
Parsons, W. Barclay. Robert Fulton and the Submarine. New
    York: Columbia University Press, 1922.
Sharp, Harold S. "The Battle of the Ironclads (1862)," "The Sink-
    ing of the 'Lusitania' (1915)," and "The Voyage of the 'Turtle'
    (1778)" in his Footnotes to American History: A Bibliographic
    Source Book. Metuchen, N. J.: Scarecrow Press, 1977.
Steinberg, Jonathan. Yesterday's Deterrent. London: Macdonald
    & Co., 1965.
Stephens, Edward. Submarines: The Story of Underwater Craft
    from the Diving Bell of 300 B. C. to Nuclear-Powered Ships.
    New York: Golden Press, 1962.
Verne, Jules. 20,000 Leagues Under the Sea (science fiction). New
    York: Macmillan, 1962 (Originally published 1870).
Von Tirpitz, Alfred P. My Memoirs. New York: Dodd, Mead,
    1919.
Wallechinsky, David, and Irving Wallace. "The 'Lusitania'" in their
    The People's Almanac. Garden City, N. Y.: Doubleday, 1975.

Woodward, E. L. Great Britain and the German Navy. Oxford:
    Clarendon Press, 1935.
Zim, Herbert Spencer. Submarines: The Story of Undersea Boats.
    New York: Harcourt, Brace, 1942.

THE EXECUTION OF EDITH CAVELL (1915)

Edith Cavell, born at Swardeston, Norfolk, about 1872, was
an English nurse who was executed by a German firing squad on
October 12, 1915, for assisting English, French and Belgian prisoners of war to escape from Belgium. The daughter of a vicar, she
was educated at Brussels and, at the age of 21, decided to become
a trained nurse. She went to London where she trained at London
Hospital, also nursing at the Shoreditch Infirmary at Hoxton and the
St. Pancras Infirmary.

In 1906 she left England and returned to Brussels where she
was appointed matron of the Berkendael Medical Institute. At the
outbreak of World War I this became a Red Cross hospital. Brussels was then a part of the German Empire, with Baron Moritz
Ferdinand von Bissing acting as Governor-General. Von Bissing
gave Edith Cavell permission to continue her hospital work but kept
her under close surveillance.

The Englishwoman was a dedicated nurse. She ministered
to German, French, Belgian and English patients alike, without regard for nationality or military rank. The German authorities were
suspicious of an "enemy alien who performed acts of mercy," and
on August 5, 1915, she was arrested, taken to prison and placed
in solitary confinement.

Although the arrest was made in secrecy an English traveler
learned of it and informed the British authorities of the plight of
one of their subjects. The British government requested Walter
Hines Page, American ambassador to Great Britain, to obtain what
information he could from Brand Whitlock, the American minister
to Belgium. Whitlock wrote to Baron von der Lancken, head of the
political department of the German military government in Brussels,
asking for particulars. The Baron did not reply. Then, in answer
to Whitlock's second letter, written several days later, he stated
that Edith Cavell was charged with giving Belgian and British soldiers money and furnishing guides to help them to the Dutch border
from which they could make their way to England or France. "She
is in solitary confinement," he wrote, "and no one may see her."

A month later Edith Cavell was tried in the Chamber of
Deputies by a military court. Whitlock arranged for an American
lawyer to act as her legal counsel but the lawyer was not permitted
to talk with her or see any of the documents pertaining to the case
until the trial began.

After two months confinement Edith Cavell and several other persons appeared in court. The nurse wore her Red Cross uniform and denied nothing. She spoke of helping more than 200 French, Belgian and English soldiers to flee from Brussels. Originally charged only with helping men to reach a neutral country, her admission that she had helped them to reach England put a different light on the matter. She was, in her two-day trial, convicted of spying and sentenced to die by the firing squad. Brand Whitlock was kept in ignorance of the court's sentence until the last minute. When he was advised of the sentence by two nurses he sent his aide to confer with von der Lancken. The Baron maintained that no such sentence would be imposed on such short notice but found, when he telephoned the prison, that the death sentence had indeed been meted out and that Edith Cavell was to die the following morning. In spite of Whitlock's urgent requests von Bissing refused to intervene.

Early on the morning of October 12 Edith Cavell was blindfolded and conducted to the place of execution. There the death sentence was carried out. Executed with her was Philippe Baucq, a Belgian who had furnished guides for the escaping men.

The death of the English nurse aroused widespread indignation. Sir Edward Grey, British Secretary of State for Foreign Affairs, denounced the act bitterly. Edith Cavell's memorial service was conducted at Westminster Abbey and a commemorative statue to her was erected at St. Martin's Place, London. At the London Hospital where she took her training the Edith Cavell Home was established and by some she is considered an English martyr equivalent to France's Joan of Arc.

Suggested Readings

Barton, George. "Miss Edith Cavell: First Martyr of the Great War" in his Celebrated Spies and Famous Mysteries of the Great War. Boston: Page, 1919.

"Brutal Deed and a Lasting Memory," Independent and Weekly Review, November 1, 1915.

De Leeuw, Adele Louise. Edith Cavell: Nurse, Spy, Heroine. New York: Putnam, 1968.

"Edith Cavell's Last Letter," Literary Digest, June 23, 1917.

Edwards, Clayton. "Edith Cavell" in his A Treasury of Heroes and Heroines. New York: Hampton Publishing Co., 1920.

Elkon, Juliette. Edith Cavell, Heroic Nurse. New York: Messner, 1956.

Gibson, H. "The Last Hours of Edith Cavell," World's Work, October, 1917.

Hagedorn, Hermann. "Edith Cavell" in his The Book of Courage. Philadelphia: Winston, 1920.

Hoehling, Adolph A. A Whisper of Eternity: The Mystery of Edith Cavell. New York: T. Yoseloff, 1957.

"Inspiration in Edith Cavell's Death," Outlook, November 24, 1915.

Judson, Helen. Edith Cavell. New York: Macmillan, 1941.
McKown, Robin. Heroic Nurses. New York: Putnam, 1966.
"Martyr Memorialized," Literary Digest, June 1, 1918.
"Mercy and War," Living Age, December 4, 1915.
"Miss Cavell's Execution," Review of Reviews, December, 1915.
Ryder, Rowland. Edith Cavell. New York: Stein & Day, 1975.
Whitlock, Brand. "The Execution of Edith Cavell," Everybody's
  Magazine, October, 1918.

THE "BLUEBEARD" LANDRU MURDERS (1915-1919)

Between 1915 and 1919 Henri Désiré Landru, popularly known as "Bluebeard," had "intimate relations" with no fewer than 283 women and murdered at least ten of them for their property.

Landru's technique was that of inserting matrimonial advertisements in Paris newspapers and following up replies, seducing the respondents and persuading them to turn their assets over to him. He used a variety of aliases and maintained homes and apartments in various parts of France.

In 1915 a widow named Anna Columb answered one of Landru's advertisements, in which he used the name Cuchet. She came to live with him in his Paris flat, turning her furniture over to him to sell. She learned that he had a villa at Gambais where he was known as Monsieur Fremyet. Landru's use of two names did not seem to disturb her.

At this time "Bluebeard" Landru was having affairs of a similar nature with other women, using a different assumed name with each, in spite of the fact that he had a legal wife and four children who lived at Clichy, where he operated a garage.

On Christmas Eve, 1916, Anna Columb invited Madame Pelat, her sister, to visit her and meet her lover. Shortly afterwards Anna disappeared and the sister, surprised that her letters to Anna remained unanswered, wrote to the local mayor. The mayor had recently received a similar letter from a Mademoiselle Lacoste whose sister, Celestine Buisson, had vanished after visiting the villa at Gambais. Following an investigation, which disclosed that the villa was occupied by a "Monsieur Dupont" who seemed to have disappeared, the mayor referred Mademoiselle Lacoste to Madame Pelat. The two ladies got together, compared notes and found that Cuchet-Fremyet and Dupont were remarkably similar. The police were at this time investigating the disappearance of still another woman, "a genuine Madame Cuchet who had, with her son, gone to live with a Monsieur Diard and who had not been seen since." The police determined that these various names all applied to one individual person and a warrant was issued for the arrest of the man who was using them.

Mademoiselle Lacoste recognized the man she knew as Monsieur Dupont walking on a Paris street in the company of a young woman. She followed them into a shop where the man made a purchase of china, ordering it to be delivered. Losing the couple in a crowd, she informed the police who traced the purchaser of the china to a Monsieur Lucien Guillet at a Paris apartment.

The next day Landru--for it was he--was arrested in his apartment. A black notebook, which he attempted to destroy, contained the names and addresses of his various conquests and much other incriminating evidence. A search of the villa at Gambais was made and a stove, in which Landru allegedly burned the bodies of his victims, was discovered, as were bone fragments of a number of human bodies. Also found were women's clothing and personal possessions.

The names of seven women other than those mentioned above were found in Landru's notebook. It was determined that these women had mysteriously disappeared without trace after meeting him and giving him their money and other assets.

On December 7, 1921, Landru was brought to trial in the Court of Assize at Versailles. It was shown that, prior to his campaign of wholesale seduction and murder for profit, "Bluebeard" Landru had had a checkered criminal career, had been sentenced to prison for fraud seven times and had had "no definite stable occupation. " He was considered "an imposter and an adventurer. " The jury, out for an hour and a half, found him guilty of virtually all charges. He was condemned to die by the guillotine. The sentence was carried out early one morning in March, 1922.

Suggested Readings

Abrahamsen, David, M. D. The Murdering Mind. New York: Harper & Row, 1973.
"Bluebeard" in Crimes and Punishment, Vol. 1. Editorial presentation: Jackson Morley. London: BPC, 1973.
"Bluebeard: Henri Landru" in Infamous Murders. London: Verdict Press/Phoebus Publishing Co. , 1975.
Bromberg, Walter. Mold of Murder: A Psychiatric Study of Homicide. New York: Grune & Stratton, 1961.
Catton, Joseph. Behind the Scenes of Murder. New York: Norton, 1940.
Guttmacher, M. S. The Mind of the Murderer. Freeport, N. Y. : Books for Libraries, 1960.
Hynd, Alan. "The Case of the Busy Bluebeard" in his Sleuths, Slayers and Swindlers: A Casebook of Crime. New York: Barnes, 1959.
Jesse, F. Tennyson. Murder and Its Motives. London: Harrap, 1952.
Lawes, Warden Lewis E. Meet the Murderer! New York: Harper, 1940.

Lester, David, and Gene Lester. Crime of Passion: Murder and the Murderer. Chicago: Nelson Hall, 1975.

Lustgarden, Edgar Marcus. "Henri Désiré Landru" in his Business of Murder. New York: Scribner, 1968.

McDade, Thomas M. , compiler. The Annals of Murder. Norman, Okla. : University of Oklahoma Press, 1961.

Reinhardt, James Melvin. The Psychology of Strange Killers. Springfield, Ill. : Thomas, 1962.

Roberts, Carl E. B. The New World of Crime. London: Noble, 1933.

Symons, Julian. "The Motor Bandits and the French Bluebeard" in his A Pictorial History of Crime. New York: Crown Publishers, 1966.

Wilson, Colin, and Patricia Pitman. Encyclopedia of Murder. New York: Putnam, 1962.

Wolfgang, Marvin E. , compiler. Studies in Homicide. New York: Harper & Row, 1967.

THE DEATH OF RASPUTIN (1916)

Grigori Efimovich Rasputin was a Siberian-born monk who attained such a baleful influence over Tsar Nicholas II and Tsarina Alexandra of Russia that late in December, 1916, he was assassinated by a group of aristocrats who hoped that his elimination would persuade the tsar to grant reforms which would avert the impending revolution. In spite of their efforts Nicholas' policies culminated in the 1917 revolution and he and his family were allegedly executed by the Bolsheviks in July, 1918.

Rasputin was notorious for his ignorance, his indulgence in wild orgies and his philosophy that one must sin in order that he might obtain forgiveness. He lived in his native village of Pokrovskoe until he was 35, marrying a wealthy girl and fathering three children. In 1904 he deserted his family and became a member of the Khlysty, a religious sect. He acquired a reputation as a holy man and in 1907 came to the attention of Father Feofan, the tsarina's confessor, who presented him at court. There he made a profound impression on the royal couple following a miraculous cure he performed on their fifteen-month-old son Alexis, who was suffering from haemophilia.

From then on Rasputin could do no wrong in the eyes of Nicholas and Alexandra, particularly the latter. He became the most influential individual in her entourage, dominating the Holy Synod of the Russian Orthodox Church. He exerted great influence on governmental policy and indulged in orgies which scandalized the citizens of Russia and other countries, becoming an object of universal hatred.

Prince Felix Yussopov, V. M. Purishkevich and two relatives

of the tsar, feeling that "if Rasputin were not to die soon the country would become dominated by a madman," determined to do away with him. He was invited to the prince's palace in St. Petersburg for cakes and wine and accepted the invitation, hoping to meet and later seduce the Grand Duchess Irina, Yussopov's beautiful wife.

Rasputin arrived at the palace around midnight. He was escorted to a basement room where he helped himself to wine and chocolate cake, both of which contained poison. Although he ate and drank freely, the poison had no effect on him. Prince Yussopov, annoyed at the failure of the poison to accomplish its objective, shot the monk in the back. Rasputin fell to the floor and was left for dead. Two hours later, when Purishkevich and the prince examined him, he proved to be still alive. He attempted to crawl up the stairs. Yussopov shot him twice more and he was battered with a heavy piece of steel, yet still survived. The assassins then took him by automobile to the Neva River and pushed him beneath the ice. The body was found 48 hours later and the tsarina had it buried in the royal chapel.

Suggested Readings

Alexander, Grand Duke of Russia. Always a Grand Duke. Garden City, N. Y.: Garden City Publishing Co., 1933.
_____. Once a Grand Duke. New York: Cosmopolitan Book Corp., 1932.
_____. Twilight of Royalty. New York: R. Long & R. R. Smith, 1932.
Alexandrov, Victor. The End of the Romanovs. Boston: Little, Brown, 1967.
Almedingen, E. M. Tomorrow Will Come. New York: Holt, Rhinehart and Winston, 1968.
Anastasia, Grand Duchess of Russia (Anna Anderson). I Am Anastasia: The Autobiography of the Grand Duchess of Russia. New York: Harcourt, Brace, 1958.
Anastasia, Grand Duchess of Russia (Eugenia Smith). Anastasia: The Autobiography of H. I. H. The Grand Duchess Anastasia Nicholaevna of Russia. New York: Robert Speller & Sons, 1963.
Cash, Anthony. The Russian Revolution. Garden City, N. Y.: Doubleday, 1967.
Fülöp-Miller, René. Rasputin, the Holy Devil. New York: Garden City Publishing Co., 1928.
Gillard, Pierre. Thirteen Years at the Russian Court. Translated by Appleby Holt. London: Hutchinson & Co., 1921.
Goldston, Robert C. The Russian Revolution. Indianapolis: Bobbs-Merrill, 1966.
Hingley, Ronald. Tsars, 1533-1917. New York: Macmillan, 1968.
Hosking, Geoffrey A. "Rasputin and the 'Dark Forces'" in Taylor, A. J. P., editor-in-chief. Purnell's History of the 20th Century, Vol. 3. New York: Purnell, 1971.
Marie, Grand Duchess of Russia. Education of a Princess. New York: Viking Press, 1931.

_____. A Princess in Exile. New York: Viking Press, 1932.
Massie, Robert K. Nicholas and Alexandra. New York: Atheneum, 1967.
Moorehead, Alan. The Russian Revolution. New York: Harper, 1958.
Moscow, Henry, and the editors of Horizon Magazine. Russia Under the Czars. New York: American Heritage Publishing Co., 1962.
Null, Gary. The Conspirator Who Saved the Romanovs. Englewood Cliffs, N.J.: Prentice-Hall, 1971.
Obolensky, Prince Serge. One Man in His Time. New York: McDowell, Obolensky, 1958.
Purishkevich, Vladimir. Comme J'ai Tué Raspoutine. Paris: Povolozky, 1923.
"Rasputin" in Crimes and Punishment, Vol. 14. Editorial presentation: Jackson Morley. London: BPC, 1973.
Rasputina, Maria. My Father. London: Cassell, 1934.
Riasanovsky, Nicholas Valentine. A History of Russia. New York: Oxford University Press, 1963.
Richards, Guy. The Hunt for the Czar. Garden City, N.Y.: Doubleday, 1970.
_____. Imperial Agent: The Goleniewski-Romanov Case. New York: Devin-Adair, 1966.
Rodzianko, Michael. The Reign of Rasputin. London: Philpot, 1927.
Smythe, James P., pseud. Rescuing the Czar, Two Authentic Diaries Arranged and Translated by James P. Smythe, A.M., Ph.D. San Francisco: California Printing Co., 1920.
Vorres, Ian. The Last Grand Duchess: Her Imperial Highness Grand Duchess Olga Alexandrovna. New York: Scribner's, 1965.
Vyrubova, Anna. Memories of the Russian Court. New York: Macmillan, 1923.
Wilson, Colin. Rasputin and the Fall of the Romanovs. New York: Farrar, Strauss, 1964.
Yusopov, Prince Felix. La fin de Raspoutine. Paris: Libraire Plon, 1927.
_____. Lost Splendor. Translated by Ann Green and Nicholas Katkov. New York: Putnam, 1954.
_____. Rasputin. New York: Dial Press, 1927.

THE CRUISE OF THE SEEADLER (1916-1917)

The Seeadler, a German raider disguised as a Norwegian merchant vessel and captained by Count Felix von Luckner, captured and sank a number of English and French ships during World War I before being wrecked on a reef in the Society Islands.

Von Luckner was born in 1881. His parents urged him to follow the family tradition and become a cavalry officer but he wished to be an officer in the German navy. At the age of thirteen

he ran away to sea, shipping on the Russian tramp steamer <u>Niobe</u>
bound around Cape Horn to Australia.   There he worked at an assortment of land jobs before signing on the <u>Golden Shore,</u> bound for
Seattle.   From there he made other voyages, alternating with stints
as a member of the Mexican army, a ranch worker and a barroom
proprietor, living an aimless life of adventure.

When he was twenty he studied for and passed the examinations for the German navy, becoming an officer on a warship.   In
1916 he was placed in command of the raider <u>Seeadler.</u>

The ship's logbook and papers were faked.   The crew members, though German, all spoke fluent Norwegian, smoked Norwegian
tobacco and could, if mecessary, describe their "homes in Norway"
which they actually had never seen.

The <u>Seeadler</u> carried a deckload of lumber which her man-
ifest indicated was being transported from Christiana to Australia.
Although a sailing vessel, she had been modified by the installation
of two diesel engines for driving propellers.   There were quarters
for a detachment of marines and for the crews of the vessels which
von Luckner expected to capture and sink.   Other modifications included the positioning of a hidden cannon, secret doors and hatches
and a dining room which, actually an elevator, could be used to
lower "unwelcome guests," such as members of an overly-persist-
ent search party, to a lower deck where they would be dealt with
by the marines.   Fuel oil and provisions for a two-year cruise were
taken aboard.

On December 23, 1916, the disguised raider set sail from
Wilhelmshaven for the Skagerrack and the British blockade.   An intense storm was raging but von Luckner, sailing north, managed to
evade the English ships and the mines which had been planted.   Then,
veering south, he encountered a British cruiser.   The <u>Seeadler</u> was
stopped and a search party came aboard.   Von Luckner and his men,
playing the part of Norwegian sailors, were cleared and permitted
to continue their voyage.

That night, having run the blockade, the deck cargo of lumber was jettisoned.   Off Gibraltar von Luckner encountered the British steamer <u>Gladys Royal,</u> carrying coal.   The German flag was
hoisted and a section of the <u>Seeadler's</u> rail was lowered, revealing
the previously hidden cannon.   A shot was fired across the bow of
the British steamer and the steamer struck her colors.   The captain and crew of the captured vessel were brought aboard the <u>See-</u>
<u>adler</u> and the former was sunk by means of a time bomb placed in
the hold.

Von Luckner's next victim was the <u>Lundy Island,</u> another
British vessel.   The crew of this ship was taken aboard the German
raider and the ship, like the <u>Gladys Royal,</u> was sunk.

Other victims followed.   The French bark, <u>Charles Gounod,</u>

was captured and sent to the bottom. Another British ship and then two French ships followed, then another Britisher and another French vessel.

Eventually the Seeadler had no more room for additional passengers. Her skipper had anticipated this and, after taking the French bark Cambronne, he loaded his "guests" aboard, cut off the topmasts to reduce speed and sent her on her way to Rio de Janeiro. He then headed south, going around Cape Horn. In the Pacific his raider was spotted by a British cruiser but escaped in the fog.

Von Luckner encountered and destroyed a few enemy schooners and then, needing fresh water and provisions, set sail for Mopelia in the Society Islands. There the Seeadler was wrecked, having been driven ashore by a tidal wave.

Having lost his raider, von Luckner took five men and a lifeboat and set off to find a sailing vessel. After a short stop at one of the Cook Islands they went on to the Fiji Islands, 2,000 miles away. After a grueling trip in their open boat they arrived at their destination. At Suva the six men were arrested by British officials and sent to an internment camp off New Zealand. They escaped, captured the schooner Moa and sailed for Mopelia where they intended to rescue the members of the crew of the Seeadler who had remained there. Before they could reach Mopelia they were captured by a British ship off Curtis Island. Von Luckner was imprisoned once more but was liberated when the Armistice terminated the hostilities.

Following his cruise in the Seeadler, von Luckner married and turned to lecturing and writing. In 1937-1939 he made a world cruise in his yacht, the Sea Devil. His men, with the exception of the ship's doctor who died of heart failure, eventually all returned home safely. During the cruise of the Seeadler not one life was lost, either German or an enemy's.

Suggested Readings

Alexander, Roy. The Cruise of the Raider "Wolf." Garden City, N.Y.: Garden City Publishing Co., 1941.
Bacon, Admiral Sir Reginald, and Francis E. McMurtrie. Modern Naval Strategy. Brooklyn, N.Y.: Chemical, 1941.
"The Career and Fate of the Raider 'Seeadler': A German Adventure in the Pacific," Current History, June, 1918.
Hagedorn, Hermann. "Felix von Luckner" in his The Book of Courage. Philadelphia: Winston, 1920.
Hoehling, Adolph A. Great War at Sea: A History of Naval Action, 1914-1918. New York: Crowell, 1965.
Hoyt, Edwin Palmer. Phantom Raider. New York: Crowell, 1969.
Middlemas, R.K. "The Raiders" in Taylor, A.J.P., editor in chief. Purnell's History of the 20th Century, Vol. 3. New York: Purnell, 1971.

Thomas, Lowell. Count Luckner, the Sea Devil. Garden City,
    N. Y. : Doubleday, 1927.
    _____. The Sea Devil's Fo'c'sle. Garden City, N. Y. : Double-
    day, 1929.
    _____, ed. "Adventure at Sea" in his Great True Adventures.
    New York: Dell, 1955.

THE RICHTHOFEN FLYING CIRCUS (1917-1918)

        The Wright Brothers--Orville and Wilbur--made the first
successful aeroplane flight at Kitty Hawk, North Carolina, on December 13, 1903. By 1913 the aeroplane, though greatly improved
over the original Wright biplane, was still little more than a sophisticated toy. By 1917 it had come to be a potent weapon of war and
the men who flew such craft were daring heroes.

        Following the outbreak of World War I in 1914, the warring
nations at first used aircraft for observation and bombing purposes.
Then pilots took to shooting at enemy flyers, first with shotguns,
pistols and rifles and later with machine guns mounted on their
planes. Before the 1918 Armistice ended hostilities the war in the
air became largely a matter of individual pilots fighting duels with
enemy pilots. A number of great air fighters were developed. These
included the Americans Captain Eddie Rickenbacker, with 26 victories, Lieutenant Frank Luke with nineteen, Major Raoul Lufbery with
seventeen, Major George Vaughn with thirteen, and Captains Field
E. Kindley and Elliott White Springs with twelve apiece.

        These American records were impressive but were overshad-
owed by the British Major Edward Mannock who scored 73 victories
and Major William Bishop of Canada who downed 72 enemy aircraft. Twenty-eight other United Kingdom flyers bettered Rickenbacker's record. Captain René Fonck of France defeated 73 enemy
pilots, Captain Georges Guynemer, also a Frenchman, scored 52
times. In all, eight French pilots had 27 or more victories, beating Rickenbacker's 26. Italian and Belgian aces also scored heavily. The all-time record, however, was set by Rittmeister Baron
Manfred von Richthofen who, prior to his death in action on April
21, 1918, was credited with shooting down no fewer than eighty Allied planes. Forty-one other German fighters bettered Rickenbacker's record but no flyer came near equaling that of Richthofen. The
German runner-up was Oberlieutenant Ernst Udet with a score of 62.

        Richthofen was a Prussian nobleman. In 1912 he became
a lieutenant in the First Uhlan Regiment, a cavalry unit. He was
ordered to transfer to a supply unit but rather than complying he
requested an assignment in the Flying Service. His request was
granted and he was sent to Cologne for training. He qualified as
an observer and was given further flying instruction by Franz Zeu-
mer, his pilot. His first solo flight ended with a wrecked plane,
but on December 25, 1915, he qualified as a pilot.

He met Lieutenant Oswald Boelcke, a famous German combat flyer, who was later assigned the task of forming a fighter squadron of his own in August, 1916. He recruited young Richthofen, who reported to his new command and further training followed, with emphasis on formation flying. On September 17, 1916, a squadron of twelve Fokkers, led by Boelcke, encountered a group of British planes and Richthofen downed one of them. His career was under way.

In October Boelcke was killed when his machine collided with another plane. His fighter squadron was given to another German officer and on November 20 Richthofen defeated two enemy aircraft. He had started a collection of inscribed silver cups, made to his order by a Berlin jeweler. A new cup was added each time he scored another kill.

On November 23, 1916, he bested the British ace, Major Lanoe George Hawker. This was his eleventh victory. In 1917 he was credited with shooting down a total of 47 British planes and became Germany's ace of aces. His red Albatross and his Fokker Triplane were well known to his Allied enemies on the Western Front. Commanding the Jagdstaffel II which came to be known as the "Flying Circus," he flew in tight formations with his fellow-aviators and together they scored an impressive record of victories.

In 1918 Richthofen continued to shoot down Allied aircraft. He was beginning to tire, having received a serious head wound in August of the previous year. On April 21 he met his end. No one knows for sure who was responsible for his death. That he was shot down and crashed in the village of Sailly-le-Sec in the Amiens area of the Somme has been established but the name of the man who got him is a matter of conjecture.

Richthofen had left his main formation to chase the Canadian flyer, Lieutenant W. R. May. He was, in turn, attacked by Captain Roy Brown, another Canadian. Brown fired at a red Fokker triplane which crashed. It turned out to be piloted by Richthofen. Brown did not see the Fokker hit the ground but two of his flight claimed to have done so.

Another version is that Richthofen was brought down by two Australian machine gunners who were guarding an artillery battery. These ground troops were awarded the Distinguished Conduct Medal for their act.

Richthofen's flying career lasted nineteen months, during which time he earned every decoration his country could bestow. He died at the age of 26.

Suggested Readings

Adamson, Hans Christian. Eddie Rickenbacker. New York: Macmillan, 1946.

Anonymous. Death in the Air. London: William Heniemann, Ltd.,
     1933.
Archibald, Norman. Heaven High, Hell Deep, 1917-1918. New
     York: Boni, 1935.
Arnold, Major General H. H., and Colonel Ira C. Eaker. Winged
     Warfare. New York: Harper, 1941.
Ashmore, Major General E. H. Air Defense. London: Longmans,
     Green, 1929.
Bacon, W. Stevenson, ed. Sky Fighters of World War I. New
     York: Fawcett, 1961.
Barnett, Lieutenant Gilbert, R. A. F. V. C.'s of the Air. London:
     Burrow, 1919.
Barrett, William E. The First War Planes. New York: Fawcett,
     1960.
Biddle, Major Charles J. The Way of the Eagle. New York: Scrib-
     ner's, 1919.
Bishop, Major William A. Winged Warfare. New York: Doran,
     1918.
Black, Archibald. The Story of Flying. New York: Whittlesey
     House, 1940.
Burrows, William E. Richthofen: A True History of the Red Bar-
     on. New York: Harcourt, Brace, 1969.
Cheesman, E. F., ed. Fighter Aircraft of the 1914-1918 War.
     Letchworth, Herts: Harleyford Publications, 1960.
_____. Reconnaissance and Bomber Aircraft of the 1914-1918
     War. Los Angeles: Aero Publishers, 1962.
Codman, Charles. Contact. Boston: Little, Brown, 1937.
Cooke, David Coxe. Sky Battle, 1914-1918: The Story of Aviation
     in World War I. New York: Norton, 1970.
Cross, Toy. The Fighter Aircraft Pocketbook. New York: Sports
     Car Press, 1962.
Cuneo, John R. The Air Weapon, 1914-1916. Harrisburg, Pa.:
     Military Service Publishing Co., 1947.
Drake, Vivian. Above the Battle. New York: Appleton, 1918.
Fokker, Anthony H. G., and Bruce Gould. Flying Dutchman: The
     Life of Anthony Fokker. New York: Holt, 1931.
Gibbons, Floyd. The Red Knight of Germany: The Story of Baron
     von Richthofen, Germany's Great War Bird. Garden City,
     N. Y.: Garden City Publishing Co., 1927.
Goldberg, Alfred, ed. A History of the United States Air Force.
     Princeton, N. J.: Van Nostrand, 1957.
Gray, Peter, and Owen Thetford. German Aircraft of the First
     World War. London: Putnam's, 1962.
Green, William, and John Fricker. The Air Forces of the World.
     New York: Hanover House, 1958.
Gribble, Leonard R. Heroes of the Fighting R. A. F. London: Har-
     rap, 1941.
Grinnell-Milne, Duncan William. Wind in the Wires. Edited by
     Stanley M. Ulanoff. Garden City, N. Y.: Doubleday, 1968.
Gurney, Gene. Five Down and Glory. New York: Putnam's, 1958.
_____. Flying Aces of World War I. New York: Random House,
     1965.
Hall, James Norman. High Adventure. Boston: Houghton Mifflin,
     1918.

_____, and Charles Nordhoff, eds. The Lafayette Flying Corps. Boston: Houghton Mifflin, 1920.

Hall, Lieutenant Bert. In the Air. New York: New Library, 1918. _____, and Lieutenant John J. Miles. One Man's War. New York: Holt, 1929.

Hartney, Lt. Col. Harold E. Up and At 'Em. Harrisburg, Pa. : Stackpole, 1940.

Jones, H. A. The War in the Air. Oxford: Oxford University Press, 1931.

Jones, Wing Commander Ira ("Taffy"). King of Air Fighters. New York: Ivor Nicholson & Watson, 1935.

Knight, Clayton, and K. S. Knight. We Were There with the Lafayette Escadrille. New York: Grosset & Dunlap, 1961.

Lawson, Don, compiler. Great Air Battles: World Wars I and II. New York: Lothrop, 1968.

McCudden, James Thomas Byford. Five Years in the Royal Flying Corps. London: The "Aeroplane"·& General Publishing Co. , 1925.

Macmillan, Norman. Great Airmen. London: Bell, 1935.

Maitland, Lieutenant Lester J. Knights of the Air. Garden City, N. Y. : Doubleday, 1929.

Mason, Herbert Molloy, Jr. The Lafayette Escadrille. New York: Random House, 1964.

Michaelis, Ralph. From Bird Cage to Battle Plane. New York: Crowell, 1943.

Middleton, Edgar. Glorious Exploits of the Air. New York: Appleton, 1918.

Nordhoff, Charles, and James Norman Hall. Falcons of France. Boston: Little, Brown, 1930.

Paine, Ralph D. The First Yale Unit. Cambridge, Mass. : Riverside Press, 1925.

Parsons, Edwin C. I Flew with the Lafayette Escadrille. Indianapolis: E. C. Seale, 1963.

Reynolds, Quentin. They Fought for the Sky. New York: Rinehart, 1957.

Richthofen, Captain Manfred Freiherr von. Autobiography. Translated by T. Ellis Barker. New York: McBride, 1918.

Rickenbacker, Captain Edward V. Fighting the Flying Circus. New York: Stokes, 1919.

_____. Rickenbacker. Englewood Cliffs, N. J. : Prentice-Hall, 1967.

Roberts, Lieutenant E. M. , R. F. C. A Flying Fighter. New York: Harper, 1918.

Robertson, Bruce, ed. Von Richthofen and the Flying Circus. Letchworth, Herts: Harleyford Publications, 1958.

Springs, Elliott White, ed. War Birds: The Diary of an Unknown Aviator. New York: Doran, 1926.

Strange, Lt. Col. L. A. Recollections of an Airman. London: Hamilton, 1933.

Thetford, O. G. , and E. J. Riding. Aircraft of the 1914-1918 War. Bucks, England: Harleyford Publications, 1954.

Throm, Edward L. , and James S. Crenshaw. Popular Mechanics Aviation Album. New York: Popular Mechanics Co. , 1953.

Toulmin, H. A., Jr. Air Service A. E. F., 1918. New York: Van
     Nostrand, 1927.
Veil, Charles, as told to Howard Marsh. Adventure's a Wench.
     New York: Morrow, 1944.
Vigilant, pseud. German War Birds. London: Hamilton, 1951.
_____. Richthofen--The Red Knight of the Air. London: Ham-
     ilton, 1951.
Whitehouse, Arch. The Years of the Sky Kings. Garden City, N. Y.:
     Doubleday, 1959.
Wynne, H. Hugh. "Escadrille Lafayette," Cross and Cockade Jour-
     nal, Vol. 2, No. 1, 1961.

THE ROMANOV ASSASSINATION CONTROVERSY (1918)

One of the legends which has recurred throughout history is
the one which maintains that a person or persons who supposedly
died at a particular time did not die but, rather, escaped and lived
incognito.   Joan of Arc is thought by some to have escaped the
stake in 1431.   Christopher Marlowe, the British poet and dramatist, supposedly killed by Ingram Frisar in a tavern brawl in 1593,
is said by some historians to have been spirited away and held in
seclusion on a nobleman's estate where he wrote plays attributed to
William Shakespeare.   Jesse James may not have been killed by
Bob Ford in 1882.   Richard Sorge, the spy, was reported to have
been seen alive two years after his supposed execution in 1944.
Adolf Hitler is thought by some to have faked his 1945 suicide in
a Berlin bunker and may still be alive today.

Until recently it was thought that Tsar Nicholas II of Russia,
together with Tsarina Alexandra, his four daughters and his son
Alexis were assassinated by Bolshevist revolutionaries on the night
of July 16/17, 1918.   Evidence has since come to light which indicates that the royal family may have been saved and their mass
execution never consummated.   This is said to have been accomplished by Charles James Fox, an American adventurer, with the
possible assistance of Aaron Simanovitsch, a Kiev jeweler and secretary to Grigori Rasputin, the Siberian monk who exercised great
influence over the imperial family.

The Romanov family had ruled Russia since 1613 when Michael Romanov, an untitled boyar, was elected tsar.   Over the next
three centuries the royal families of Russia, Germany and England
had intermarried until the rulers of these countries could all trace
a family relationship to the others.

Nicholas II came to the Russian throne in 1894.   He believed
in the autocratic principles taught him by his father, Alexander III,
and opression and police control increased during his reign, which
was characterized by popular discontent.   General dissatisfaction with
his foreign and domestic policies culminated in the Russian revolution
of 1917.

Once started the tide of revolution could not be halted. Soldiers ordered to fire on rioting mobs mutinied and joined the rioters. On March 15, 1917, Nicholas was forced to abdicate. He surrendered his throne, requesting that it go directly to his brother, the Grand Duke Michael, rather than to his young son Alexis. Michael refused to become tsar, leaving the administration to a provisional government organized by the fourth Duma.

Following his abdication Tsar Nicholas and his family were sent to Tsarskoye Selo and placed under house arrest. It then appeared that the revolutionaries planned to bring charges of treason against the royal family. Such a trial could result only in conviction and the death sentence. An attempt to escape failed and the family was then sent to the village of Ekaterinburg, Siberia. There Simanovitsch and Fox, with the connivance of the bribed local officials and soldiers, supposedly arranged an elaborate escape plan. The royal family was to be apparently massacred in the cellar of the Ipatiev House in which they were being held. Blood, obtained from a local coroner, was to be liberally scattered about and bullets were to be shot into the cellar walls. Seven corpses, also obtained from the coroner, were to be thrown into the shaft of the abandoned "Four Brothers" mine, together with personal items which could be identified with the Romanovs. The corpses were to be burned and doused with sulfuric acid, which would make identification impossible. The ex-tsar and his family, in disguise, were to be smuggled out of the country, using forged passports and other documents which had been prepared for them. This elaborate escape plan was said to have had the approval of Kaiser William of Germany and to have been financed by King George V of England.

The seven members of the family, a doctor and a maid supposedly left by truck, going to Odessa and on to Poland, their final destination. After the trucks departed the scene was set, the blood spilled, the bullets fired and the effects of the imperial family and seven corpses placed in the mine shaft, burned with gasoline and soaked with acid.

According to historians Gary Null, Guy Richards and others, the plan succeeded. Alexis is said to have assumed the name Colonel Michal Goleniewski and to have stated that his father, the former tsar, died in the Polish village of Ciosaniec in 1952 and was buried under an assumed name.

Two women, each claiming to be the Grand Duchess Anastasia, have appeared. They are Anna Anderson, now residing in Virginia and Eugenia Smith, living in Illinois. Other women have made similar claims. A man, using the name of Eugene Ivanov, stated he was the tsar's son Alexis. Other claimants have turned up from time to time. As of this writing none of these persons have been accepted as members of the Romanov family and the millions of dollars the tsar is known to have deposited in banks around the world other than in Russia are still undistributed. That money which was in the Imperial Bank at Moscow was appropriated by the Bolsheviks in 1917 "in the name of the people."

Suggested Readings

Alexander, Grand Duke of Russia. Always a Grand Duke. Garden
  City, N. Y.: Garden City Publishing Co., 1933.
_____. Once a Grand Duke. New York: Cosmopolitan Book
  Corp., 1932.
_____. Twilight of Royalty. New York: R. Long and R. R.
  Smith, 1932.
Alexandrov, Victor. The End of the Romanovs. Boston: Little,
  Brown, 1967.
Almedingen, E. M. The Romanovs: Three Centuries of an Ill-Fated
  Dynasty. New York: Holt, Rinehart and Winston, 1966.
_____. Tomorrow Will Come. New York: Holt, Rinehart and
  Winston, 1968.
Anastasia, Grand Duchess of Russia (Anna Anderson). I Am Ana-
  stasia: The Autobiography of the Grand Duchess of Russia.
  New York: Harcourt, Brace, 1958.
Anastasia, Grand Duchess of Russia (Eugenia Smith). Anastasia:
  The Autobiography of H. I. H. The Grand Duchess Anastasia
  Nicholaevna of Russia. New York: Robert Speller & Sons,
  1963.
Auclères, Dominique. Anastasie, qui êtes vous? Paris: Hachette,
  1962.
Benns, F. Lee. Europe Since 1914 in Its World Setting. New
  York: Appleton-Century-Crofts, 1945.
Botkin, Gleb E. The Real Romanovs. New York: Fleming H.
  Revell Co., 1931.
_____. The Woman Who Rose Again. New York: Fleming H.
  Revell Co., 1937.
Bulygin, Captain Paul P., and Alexander F. Kerensky. "The Sor-
  rowful Quest" in their The Murder of the Romanovs. New York:
  McBride, 1935.
Cash, Anthony. The Russian Revolution. Garden City, N. Y.: Dou-
  bleday, 1967.
Daniels, Robert V., ed. "The Abdication of Nicholas II" in his
  The Russian Revolution. Englewood Cliffs, N. J.: Prentice-
  Hall, 1972.
Dehn, Lili. The Real Tsaritsa. London: Thornton Butterworth,
  1922.
Dieterichs, General Michael D. The Murder of the Imperial Family
  and Members of the House of Romanov in the Urals. Vladiv-
  ostok: Vladivostok Military Academy, 1922.
Floyd, David. "Overthrow of the Tsar" in Taylor, A. J. P., editor-
  in-chief. Purnell's History of the 20th Century, Vol. 3. New
  York: Purnell, 1971.
Frankland, Noble. Imperial Tragedy: Nicholas II, Last of the Tsars.
  New York: Coward-McCann, 1961.
Gilliard, Pierre. Thirteen Years at the Russian Court. Translated
  by Appleby Holt. London: Hutchinson & Co., 1921.
Goldston, Robert C. The Russian Revolution. Indianapolis: Bobbs-
  Merrill, 1966.
Hingley, Ronald. Tsars, 1533-1917. New York: Macmillan, 1968.
Marie, Grand Duchess of Russia. Education of a Princess. New
  York: Viking Press, 1931.

_____. A Princess in Exile. New York: Viking Press, 1932.

Markov, Serge V. How We Tried to Save the Tsaritsa. New York: Putnam, 1929.

Massie, Robert K. Nicholas and Alexandra. New York: Atheneum, 1967.

Moorehead, Alan. The Russian Revolution. New York: Harper, 1958.

Moscow, Henry, and the editors of Horizon Magazine. Russia Under the Czars. New York: American Heritage Publishing Co., 1962.

Null, Gary. The Conspirator Who Saved the Romanovs. Englewood Cliffs, N. J.: Prentice-Hall, 1971.

Obolensky, Prince Serge. One Man in His Time. New York: McDowell, Obolensky, 1958.

O'Conor, John F. Nicholas A. Sokolov's Investigation of the Alleged Murder of the Russian Imperial Family. New York: Robert Speller & Sons, 1970.

Preston, Sir Thomas H. "Last Days of the Tsar," Sunday Telegraph (London), July 14, 1968.

Pridham, Vice-Admiral Sir Francis, K. B. E., C. B. Close of a Destiny. London: Alan Wingate, 1956.

Rathlef-Keilmann, Harriet von. Anastasia, the Survivor of Ekaterinburg. Translated by Stewart Flint. London: Putnam's, 1928.

Riasanovsky, Nicholas Valentine. A History of Russia. New York: Oxford University Press, 1963.

Richards, Guy. The Hunt for the Czar. Garden City, N. Y.: Doubleday, 1970.

_____. Imperial Agent: The Goleniewski-Romanov Case. New York: Devin-Adair, 1966.

Smythe, James P., pseud. Rescuing the Czar, Two Authentic Diaries Arranged and Translated by James P. Smythe, A. M., Ph. D. San Francisco: California Printing Co., 1920.

Summers, Anthony, and Tom Mangold. The File on the Tsar. New York: Harper & Row, 1976.

Vorres, Ian. The Last Grand Duchess: Her Imperial Highness Grand Duchess Olga Alexandrovna. New York: Scribner's, 1965.

Vyrubova, Anna. Memories of the Russian Court. New York: Macmillan, 1923.

Wilton, Robert. The Last Days of the Romanovs. New York: Doran, 1920.

Yusupov, Prince Felix. Lost Splendor. Translated by Ann Green and Nicholas Katkov. New York: Putnam, 1954.

THE GREAT INFLUENZA PANDEMIC (1918-1919)

Influenza, also known by the abbreviation "flu" and sometimes called "grippe," is an acute, infectious and contagious respiratory disease. "It is characterized by a sudden onset of extreme weakness, and generally by catarrh of the nasal and respiratory passages. It may occur pandemically, epidemically, or sporadically."

Pandemics of influenza have been recognized for many centuries. The first such occurred in 1510, spreading over the whole of Europe. Recent pandemics occurred in 1889, in 1918-1919 and in 1957-1958. The 1918-1919 pandemic appeared in three distinct waves and one theory is that it originated at Fort Leavenworth, Kansas, on or about March 11, 1918. On that date 107 patients, members of the armed services, were admitted to the post hospital suffering from influenza.

The disease shortly reached epidemic proportions at the Fort. Those soldiers who did not contract it or who recovered rapidly from its effects were sent to Europe. Only later was it realized that many of these troops who fought alongside others acted as carriers for the virus.

Another theory is that the influenza pandemic originated in the rat-infested trenches of France. The medical services provided the military in World War I were notoriously sub-standard, particularly in the French army. Isolated cases of influenza occurring in Europe may well have been incorrectly diagnosed even before the outbreaks of the disease which occurred simultaneously with the arrival of American troops at Brest and St. Nazaire.

Before the disease had run its course in the spring of 1919 it had spread to virtually every country in the world. More than 27 million people died, largely in India, China and Africa. In the United States many deaths were reported and it is estimated that at least 20 million Americans contracted influenza but recovered from it. In France over 70,000 cases were treated and a death rate of 32 percent was reported. In June, 1918, Berlin had 160,000 cases. In Manchester over half the residents contracted the disease and the death rate there was 7.9 percent. The city of London was hard hit, with over 15,000 inhabitants dying. Asia and Africa were severely affected, as were China and India, where it was impossible to collect statistics concerning the ravages of the disease.

Doctors throughout the world sought a cure but, despite their efforts, no effective vaccine was found. Without a remedy the physicians could only order their patients quarantined that the disease might not be transmitted to others. Nostrums and quack remedies proliferated. One such was the taking of snuff. Others were compresses of hot towels soaked in vinegar and whiskey, and ginger, soda and sugar taken in a glass of hot milk. People were urged to wear gauze masks over the mouth and nose whenever out in public, and to avoid shaking hands or borrowing library books.

In November, 1918, the epidemic abated to some degree but broke out again, particularly in Europe, early in 1919, reaching a peak in March of that year. Then, for some unknown reason, it subsided and then disappeared.

In 1933 the National Institute for Medical Research in London identified the virus responsible for influenza. It was then possible to seek out a vaccine by the use of which the disease could be prevented and controlled. In 1976 in the United States a nationwide program of vaccination to prevent what was commonly called "swine flu" was inaugurated. Inoculations were given without charge to all who wished them.

Other diseases for which no cure is presently known are being investigated. These are the so-called "green monkey fever" and a mysterious "bleeding fever" which killed over 300 persons in Central Africa in 1976. This last, according to some scientists, "poses the gravest danger due to a virus disease encountered in public health care in more than 25 years."

Suggested Readings

Allen, Frederick Lewis. Only Yesterday. New York: Harper, 1931.

Cravens, Gwyneth, and John S. Marr. The Black Death (fiction). New York: Dutton, 1977.

Crawfurd, Raymond. Plague and Pestilence in Literature and Art. Oxford: Clarendon Press, 1914.

De Kruif, Paul. Microbe Hunters. Edited by Harry G. Grover. New York: Harcourt, Brace, 1932.

Dorolle, P. "Old Plagues in the Jet Age," World Health Organization Chronicle, March, 1969.

Eberle, Irmengarde. Modern Medical Discoveries. New York: Crowell, 1958.

Gallagher, Richard. Diseases That Plague Modern Man. Dobbs Ferry, N. Y. : Oceana Publications, 1969.

Gaughran, Eugene R. L. "From Superstition to Science: The Story of a Bacterium," Transactions, New York Academy of Sciences, January, 1969.

Haggard, Howard W. Devils, Drugs and Doctors. New York: Harper, 1929.

Hirst, Leonard B. The Conquest of Plague. Oxford: Clarendon Press, 1953.

"Influenza" in The Merck Manual of Diagnosis and Therapy, 8th edition. Rahway, N. J. : Merck & Co. , Inc. , 1950.

McNeill, William H. Plagues and Peoples. New York: Anchor Press, 1976.

Major, Ralph H. A History of Medicine. Springfield, Ill. : Thomas, 1954.

Mettler, Cecilia C. History of Medicine. Philadelphia: Blakiston, 1947.

Pollitzer, R. Plague. Geneva: World Health Organization, 1954.

Sullivan, Mark. Our Times, the United States, 1900-1925. New York: Scribner's, 1928-1935.

Turner, Barry. "The Influenza Pandemic" in Taylor, A. J. P. , editor-in-chief. Purnell's History of the 20th Century. New York: Purnell, 1971.

Winslow, Charles-Edward Amory. The Conquest of Epidemic Disease. Princeton, N. J. : Princeton University Press, 1943.

Witton's Microbiology. New York: McGraw-Hill, 1961.

THE FOUNDING OF THE LEAGUE OF NATIONS (1919)

The League of Nations, an alliance for the preservation of peace among nations, was suggested by President Woodrow Wilson and formulated in June, 1919, at the Versailles Peace Conference.

For a century before 1914 no general war had occurred in Europe. It was erroneously presumed that none of the major European countries would condone such a general conflict "because they were too advanced. " Over the years a maze of alliances had been entered into by various European nations and these ultimately helped lead to World War I which broke out in 1914 and lasted four years. As the war went on many statesmen and high-ranking government officials reasoned that a world forum of some sort was needed to prevent a recurrence of such a universal conflict. On January 8, 1918, Wilson, in an address to the American Congress, proposed his Fourteen Points as a basis for world peace. These he considered the "only possible" program and were subsequently taken as the basis for peace negotiations. They covered such areas as "open covenants of peace openly arrived at, " "freedom of navigation upon the seas, " "reduction of national armaments, " "evacuation and restoration of Belgium" and "the formulation of a permanent association of states to preserve peace. " By November, 1918, when the War ended, most of the belligerents had expressed their consent to the idea of establishing a League of Nations.

The Covenant of the League, as finally approved, contained 26 articles, these being the first 26 articles of the Treaty of Versailles. Article X pledged the signers "to respect and preserve as against external aggression the territorial integrity and existing political independence of all members of the League. " The United States was never a member of the League, as the Senate objected to the provisions of Article X and refused to ratify membership. Forty-four other nations, however, became members. Communist Russia was excluded until 1934 because of her declared intention to promote world-wide revolution. She was ousted in 1939.

The organization of the League consisted of the Assembly, the Council and the Secretariat. Permanent headquarters were located at Geneva. The Assembly, composed of three representatives of each state, with each state having one vote, met regularly. The Council met three times each year to discuss such matters as political disputes, supervision of mandates and plans for world disarmament. The Secretariat, with its secretary-general and his staff, remained permanently in Geneva.

After 1920 the League attempted to put through a program of disarmament and of the peaceful settlement of disputes between various powers. In these aims it was anything but successful. It had taken no action concerning the Japanese invasion of Manchuria in 1931, despite the urgings of Victor Alexander Lytton who, as chairman of the League's commission to investigate the situation, recom-

mended peaceful means of forcing Japan to withdraw her forces.
Again, in 1935, the League found itself unable to prevent Fascist
Italy's invasion of Ethiopia.

Although the League had had some successful results, such
as its supervision of the financial rehabilitation of Austria between
1922 and 1926, the Italian-Ethiopian fiasco spelled its doom.   In
1936 it virtually collapsed. Italy withdrew her membership and
joined Japan and Nazi Germany, who had withdrawn earlier.   It met
for the last time on April 8, 1946, when the remaining members
met to transfer the League's records and functions to the United
Nations which had been formed at San Francisco the year before.

Suggested Readings

Bailey, Thomas A.   Woodrow Wilson and the Lost Peace.   New
York: Quadrangle/The New York Times Co. , 1963.

Baker, Ray Stannard.   Woodrow Wilson and the World Settlement:
Written from His Unpublished and Personal Material.   New York:
Doubleday, 1923.

_____. Woodrow Wilson, Life and Letters.   Westport, Conn. :
Greenwood Press, 1939.

_____, and W. E. Dodds, eds.   The Public Papers of Woodrow
Wilson. New York: Kraus Reprint, 1927.

Benns, F. Lee.   Europe Since 1914 in Its World Setting.   New York:
Appleton-Century-Crofts, 1945.

Braeman, John, ed.   Wilson.   Englewood Cliffs, N. J. :   Prentice-
Hall, 1972.

Commager, Henry Steele, ed.   "The Defeat of the League of Nations" (Doc. No. 436) in his Documents of American History,
8th edition.   New York: Appleton, 1968.

_____. "The Fourteen Points" (Doc. No. 423) in his Documents
of American History, 8th edition.   New York: Appleton, 1968.

_____. "President Wilson's Exposition of the League of Nations
to the Senate Committee on Foreign Relations" (Doc. No. 435)
in his Documents of American History, 8th edition.   New York:
Appleton, 1968.

Dos Passos, John.   "Meester Veelson" in his Nineteen-Nineteen.
New York: Random House, 1931.

Garraty, John A.   Henry Cabot Lodge: A Biography.   New York:
Knopf, 1953.

Hansen, Harry.   "The Forgotten Men of Versailles" in Leighton,
Isabel, ed.   The Aspirin Age, 1919-1941   New York: Simon
& Schuster, 1949.

House, Edward M.   The Intimate Papers of Colonel House.   Edited
by Charles Seymour.   Saint Clair Shores, Mich. : Scholarly
Press, 1971.

Knudson, John I.   A History of the League of Nations.   Atlanta,
Ga. : Turner E. Smith & Co. , 1938.

Lingley, Charles Ramsdell, and Allen Richard Foley.   Since the
Civil War. New York: Appleton, 1935.

Miller, D. H.   The Drafting of the Covenant.   New York: Putnam's,
1928.

Seaman, L. C. B.   From Vienna to Versailles.   New York: Harper
& Row, 1963.
Seymour, Charles.   American Diplomacy During the World War.
Hamden, Conn. :   Shoe String Press, 1973.
Sharp, Harold S.   "The Fourteen Points (1918)" in his Footnotes to
American History: A Bibliographic Source Book.   Metuchen,
N. J. :   Scarecrow Press, 1977.
Smith, Gene.   When the Cheering Stopped: The Last Years of Wood-
row Wilson.   New York: Morrow, 1964.
Walters, P. F.   A History of the League of Nations.   London: Ox-
ford University Press, 1960.
Wilson, Woodrow.   The Case for the League of Nations.   Edited by
H. Foley.   Port Washington, N. Y. :   Kennikat Press, 1967.
Zimmern, Alfred.   The League of Nations and the Rule of Law,
1918-1935.   London: Macmillan, 1936.

THE CONQUEST OF MOUNT EVEREST (1922-1976)

Ever since the Himalayan Mount Everest in South Central
Asia on the frontier of Nepal and Tibet was discovered in the year
1852 to be the highest in the world (29, 028 feet) it has constituted
a challenge to men to climb to its peak.   Winds of over 100 miles
per hour, temperatures below 20° below zero Farenheit and an extremely rarefied atmosphere make the climb exceedingly difficult.

The first expedition, in 1922, following a reconnaissance
made in 1921, was headed by Brigadier General C. G. Bruce, a
British army officer.   On this expedition three members of the
group reached a height of 26, 985 feet.   A few days later two other
climbers succeeded in reaching a height of 27, 300 feet.   A third
attempt by this party resulted in the death of seven climbers.

In 1924 two climbers on a second expedition, also headed by
General Bruce, reached a height of 28, 200 feet, and British moun-
taineers George H. Leigh-Mallory and Andrew Irvine were lost on
the mountain close to the summit.   They were last seen at 12:50
P. M. on June 8 by N. E. Odell, a geologist and mountaineer, who
watched them ascend to the 28, 000-foot level, a little over a thousand feet below the summit.   They were "going strong" on their
upward climb.   Then the mist closed in and they were never seen
again.   It is thought that they were blown over a precipice or that
they froze to death.   Some evidence was found at one of the lower
camps indicating that they may have had trouble with their oxygen
apparatus.

Four members of a 1933 British expedition climbed to within
a thousand feet of the summit.   Other British expeditions, in 1936
and 1938, were unsuccessful, as was an American attempt to reach
the peak in 1950.   In 1952 two Swiss attempts were also unsuccessful.

Mount Everest was finally conquered on May 29, 1953 when, on a British expedition led by Colonel Henry C. J. Hunt, Edmund P. Hillary of New Zealand and Tenzing Bhutia (Tenzing Norgay), a Nepalese guide and climber, succeeded in reaching the summit. For his feat Hillary was knighted by Queen Elizabeth II.

Other climbing parties attempted to scale the world's highest mountain. By 1976 Everest had been successfully climbed thirteen times. In that year Dr. Chris Chandler and Robert Cormak, members of the American Bicentennial Everest Expedition, reached the top on October 8. A second group from the same party planned another attempt but on October 10 expedition leader Phil Trimble decided to abandon it. Climbers Gerry Roach, Rick Ridgeway and Hans Bruyntjes were to have constituted the second team. Trimble reported, "It's very windy and cold and the weather seems to be getting worse. A second summit attempt is not worth the risks it would entail." The second team climbed to 24,500 feet before the assault on Mount Everest was called off.

Suggested Readings

Bruce, The Hon. C. G. , and Other Members of the Expedition. The Assault on Mount Everest. New York: Longmans, Green, 1923.
Douglas, William O. Exploring the Himalaya. New York: Random House, 1958.
Hillary, Sir Edmund P. Nothing Venture, Nothing Win. New York: Coward, McCann, 1975.
_____, ed. Challenge of the Unknown. New York: Dutton, 1958.
Hindley, Geoffrey. "Exploring the Himalaya" in his The Roof of the World: Encyclopedia of Discovery and Exploration, Vol. 16. London: Aldus Books, 1971.
Howard-Bury, Lt. Col. C. K. , D. S. O. , and Other Members of the Expedition. Mount Everest: The Reconnaissance, 1921. New York: Longmans, Green, 1922.
Life Magazine. Issue of June 29, 1953.
Lunn, Sir Arnold Henry Moore. A Century of Mountaineering, 1857-1957. London: Allen and Unwin, 1957.
McCallum, John Dennis. Everest Diary; Based on the Personal Diary of Lute Jerstad, One of the First Five Americans to Conquer Mount Everest. Chicago: Follett, 1966.
Murray, William H. The Story of Everest. New York: Dutton, 1953.
Noel, Captain John. The Story of Everest. Boston: Little, Brown, 1927.
Norton, Lt. Col. E. F. , D. S. O. The Fight for Everest: 1924. New York: Longmans, Green, 1925.
Ruttledge, Hugh. Attack on Everest. New York: McBride, 1935.
_____. Everest, the Unfinished Adventure. London: Hodder & Stoughton, 1937.
Shipton, Eric, and the Himalaya Committee of the Royal Geographical Society, London. The Mount Everest Reconnaissance Expedition, 1951. London: Hodder & Stoughton, 1952.

Smythe, F. S. The Mountain Vision. London: Hodder & Stoughton,
     1941.
Tenzing Norgay, in collaboration with J. R. Ullman. Tiger of the
     Snows: The Autobiography of Tenzing of Everest. New York:
     Putnam, 1955.
Tilman, Harold W. Mount Everest, 1938. Cambridge: Cambridge
     University Press, 1948.
Times (London). "Mount Everest Supplement," July, 1953.
Wibberley, Leonard. The Epics of Everest. New York: Dell,
     1966.
Younghusband, Sir Francis. The Epic of Mount Everest. New
     York: Longmans, Green, 1926.
_____. Everest: The Challenge. New York: Nelson, 1936.

THE DISCOVERY OF TUTANKHAMEN'S TOMB (1922)

The ancient Egyptians believed that the ka, a duplicate of
the body, or soul, accompanied the body throughout life and, after
death, departed from the body to take its place in the kingdom of
the dead.   As the ka could not exist without the body, every effort
was made to preserve the corpse, including burial in exceedingly
elaborate tombs.   As it was thought that the ka would need divers
objects in the hereafter, such things as furniture, reading material,
chariots and musical instruments were placed in the tomb with the
mummified corpse.

Originally the tombs of the ancient Egyptian pharaohs were
pyramids, and about eighty of these were constructed.   Because of
the gold ornaments and other valuable objects that were placed in
the pyramids they attracted tomb robbers who broke in and stole
what they could.

The pharaohs had firmly established themselves at Thebes
on the east bank of the Nile River, some 450 miles upstream from
Memphis, near modern Cairo.   About 1500 B. C. the concept of the
burial of illustrious Egyptians in conspicuous pyramids was abandoned, these being replaced by burial vaults, the locations of which
were secret.   A number of such vaults were built in the Valley of
the Tombs of the Kings, a desolate ravine near Thebes.

The first Egyptian ruler to be buried in a secret tomb was
Thutmose I, the third pharaoh of the Eighteenth Dynasty, who died
in 1501 B. C.   The burial place was cut in the living rock by workmen who were sworn to secrecy concerning its location.   The mouth
of the sepulcher was concealed with stones and a mortuary temple
where services could be held was constructed several miles away.

Other similar hidden tombs were built over the next five centuries.   The last pharaoh, so far as is known, to be buried in the
royal Valley was Ramses XII (1118-1090 B. C.).   In spite of the ef-

forts made to keep their locations secret, robbers found and plundered many of them.   In Greek and Roman times some of the tombs
were open to the public as tourist attractions.

In the early nineteenth century Giovanni Belzoni, an Italian
explorer and archaeologist, discovered the tomb of Seti I and also
opened the second pyramid of Giza.   Other Egyptologists did similar research.   In 1902 Howard Carter, an Englishman, excavated
the tomb of Thutmose IV.   In this and other tombs which he and
his fellow excavators opened the antiquities found were few in number or badly damaged.

It was hoped that some day a tomb might be discovered which
had not been despoiled by grave robbers.   Carter and George Herbert, Lord Carnarvon, another British Egyptologist, made such a
discovery on November 29, 1922, when the tomb of King Tutankhamen, an obscure pharaoh of the Eighteenth Dynasty, was found.
This tomb, though not overlooked by robbers, was virtually intact,
the thieves having failed to penetrate the inner chamber.

Carter made the actual discovery.   In spite of statements by
such prominent Egyptologists as Theodore Davis that all Egyptian
tombs had been discovered, Carter and Lord Carnarvon continued to
seek further burial places.   Finding the tomb of Tutankhamen below that of Ramses VI (1157 B.C.) proved them correct.   It is
thought that Ramses was not aware of the earlier tomb's existence
(1358 B.C.) as its entrance was hidden under tons of chippings
dumped there from the excavations of nearby tombs.

Tutankhamen's tomb was not nearly so elaborate as that of
the other pharaohs, such as Ramses II or Seti I, but the priceless
antiquities it contained, having been missed by tomb robbers, constituted the greatest find of its type in the records of Egyptology.
The tomb contains four chambers approached by a rough downward
passage.   The ante-chamber is 25 feet long and twelve feet wide.
The sepulchral hall is approximately the same size and there are
two annexes.

Only the outer chambers were explored in 1922-1923, Carter
and Lord Carnarvon devoting their efforts first to studying and class-
ifying the objects already retrieved.   Many of these were fragile
and had to be handled with great care.

In 1923 the sepulcher containing the pharaoh's body was opened
and further treasures were found.   These added tremendously to the
historical details of an obscure ancient age.

Tutankhamen was a little-known pharaoh who died a comparatively young man.   He succeeded Akhnaton, the "Heretic Pharaoh,"
who attempted to replace the worship of the god Amen with that of
Aton, the "Disc of the Sun."   The Egyptian people refused to accept the new religion and Akhnaton found it necessary to move to
Tell-el-Amarna.   When Tutankhamen ascended the throne he restored
the old religion.

Today the Valley of the Tombs of the Kings is easily accessible by automobile. Visitors may enter some of the tombs which have been the resting places of Egyptian rulers and nobles for over 3,000 years.

Suggested Readings

Aldred, Cyril. Egypt to the End of the Old Kingdom. New York: McGraw-Hill, 1965.
_____. The Egyptians. London: Thames and Hudson, 1961.
Alexander, Marc. "Howard Carter and Tutankhamen" in his The Past. Worthington, Ohio: A. Lynn, 1965.
Asimov, Isaac. The Egyptians. Boston: Houghton Mifflin, 1967.
Barker, Felix, in collaboration with Anthea Barker. "Into the Unknown" in their The First Explorers: Encyclopedia of Discovery and Exploration, Vol. I. London: Aldus Books, 1971.
Baumann, Hans. The World of the Pharaohs. New York: Pantheon Books, 1960.
Brendon, J. A., B. A., F. R. Hist. S. "Tutankhamen and His Treasures: How the Tomb Was Found and Opened" in Hamerton, J. A., ed. Wonders of the Past: The Romance of Antiquity and Its Splendours, Vol. I. New York: William H. Wise, 1933.
Bruckner, Karl. Golden Pharaoh. Translated by Frances Lobb. New York: Pantheon Books, 1959.
Carter, Howard, and A. C. Mace. The Tomb of Tut-ank-Amen. New York: Cooper Square, 1954.
Casson, Lionel, and the editors of Time-Life Books. Ancient Egypt. New York: Time, Inc., 1965.
Cohen, Daniel. Secrets from Ancient Graves: Rulers and Heroes of the Past Whose Lives Have Been Revealed Through Archaeology. New York: Dodd, Mead, 1968.
Cottrell, Leonard. Digs and Diggers: A Book of World Archaeology. Cleveland: World, 1964.
_____. Land of the Pharaohs. Cleveland: World, 1960.
Desroches-Noblecourt, Christiane. Tutankhamen. New York: New York Graphic Society, 1963.
Edwards, Amelia B. Egypt and Its Monuments. New York: Harper, 1891.
Falls, C. B. The First 3,000 Years: Ancient Civilizations of the Tigris, Euphrates, and Nile River Valleys and the Mediterranean Sea. New York: Viking Press, 1960.
Farmer, Lydia. "Nefertiti" in her A Book of Famous Queens. Revised by Willard A. Heaps. New York: Crowell, 1964.
Glubok, Shirley. Discovering Tut-ankh-Amen's Tomb. New York: Macmillan, 1968.
Grant, Michael. The Ancient Mediterranean. New York: Scribner's, 1969.
Hall, H. R., D. Litt., F. S. A. "Tutankhamen and His Treasures: First Fruits of a Great Discovery" in Hamerton, J. A., ed. Wonders of the Past: The Romance of Antiquity and Its Splendours, Vol. I. New York: William H. Wise, 1933.
Hawkes, Jacquetta, and the editors of Horizon Magazine. Pharaohs

of Egypt. New York: American Heritage Publishing Co. , 1965.
Hayter, A. G. K. , M. A. , F. S. A. "Tell-el-Amarna: City of Akhna-
ton and Tutankhamen" in Hamerton, J. A. , ed. Wonders of the
Past: The Romance of Antiquity and Its Splendours, Vol. IV.
New York: William H. Wise, 1933.
Mackenzie, Donald A. "500 Years Before Tutankhamen: Models
Made in This World to Work in the Next" in Hamerton, J. A. ,
ed. Wonders of the Past: The Romance of Antiquity and Its
Splendours, Vol. I. New York: William H. Wise, 1933.
Mertz, Barbara. Temples, Tombs and Hieroglyphs: The Story of
Egyptology. New York: Coward-McCann, 1964.
Petrie, Sir W. M. Flinders. Seventy Years in Archaeology. Lon-
don: Sampson, Low, Marston & Co. , 1931.
Sewell, Barbara. Egypt Under the Pharaohs. New York: Putnam,
1968.
Vandenberg, Philipp, pseud. The Curse of the Pharaohs. Trans-
lated by Thomas Weyr. Philadelphia: Lippincott, 1975.
Van Dine, S. S. , pseud. The Scarab Murder Case (fiction). New
York: Scribner's, 1927.
Warren, Ruth. The Nile: The Story of Pharaohs, Farmers and
Explorers. New York: McGraw-Hill, 1968.
Weigall, Arthur. "Thebes in Its Splendour" and "The Valley of the
Tombs of the Kings" in Hamerton, J. A. , ed. Wonders of the
Past: The Romance of Antiquity and Its Splendours, Vol. I.
New York: William H. Wise, 1933.
Woolley, C. Leonard. Digging Up the Past. New York: Scribner's,
1931.

THE MUNICH BEER HALL PUTSCH (1923)

Following World War I Germany, by the Treaty of Versailles
of June 28, 1919, was saddled with full responsibility for the war.
She lost her navy, her merchant marine, her colonial empire and
many natural resources. Her army was reduced to impotence. For
the next five years unexampled economic and political chaos resulted,
the German mark becoming virtually worthless as inflation ran ram-
pant. Many German businessmen were bankrupted and people saw
their life's savings vanish. This situation caused a bitter anti-Allies
feeling on the part of the German people and formed the setting in
which Adolf Hitler rose to power.

Hitler was a fervid German nationalist. Following service
as a corporal in the German army, he joined an obscure political
organization, the German Workers' Party, later renamed the National Socialist German Workers or, popularly, the Nazi Party.
Brown-shirted storm troopers were recruited and the augmented
Party achieved a measure of prominence in Bavaria.

On November 8, 1923, Hitler, with the aid of World War I
hero General Erich Ludendorff, staged his ill-fated Munich Beer Hall

Putsch, an attempt to force officials of the Bavarian state, army
and police to swear loyalty to him and to a proposed Nazi revolution.   It had been announced in the press that on that evening Gustav von Kahr, State Commissioner, would address a meeting at the
Buergerbräukeller, a large beer hall on the outskirts of Munich.
He was to speak on the program of the Bavarian government, and
among the notables present would be General Otto von Lossow and
Colonel Hans von Seisser.   These were the men the future Führer
wished to enlist in his cause.

        Hitler alerted his storm troopers for duty at the beer hall.
At a quarter of nine they surrounded the place and Hitler, pistol in
hand, strode inside.   He was accompanied by Rudolf Hess, Hermann
Goering and other Nazi Party members.   Jumping on a table he
fired his pistol into the air and announced that the National Revolution had begun.

        While Goering spoke to the assembly Hitler herded Kahr,
Lossow and Seisser into an adjoining room.   There he urged them
to join the new government which he and Ludendorff were forming.
Despite the fact that their captor was armed, the three men declined
to cooperate.   Hitler then returned to the hall and announced that
those in the next room had joined him in the formation of the new
National Government, and that "the Bavarian ministry was removed."
He stated that he would direct government policy and that Ludendorff
would be commander-in-chief of the army.

        The Munich beer hall putsch had been conceived without Lu-
dendorff's knowledge.   He had been sent for and when he arrived
he stated that he would cooperate although he resented the fact that
a former corporal rather than he was to be the dictator of Germany.
He advised Kahr, Lossow and Seisser to join with him and Hitler
and they appeared to do so.   However, once free of the threat of
Hitler's pistol they repudiated their agreement.   Lossow rushed to
army headquarters and requested reinforcements from outlying garrisons.   By dawn regular army troops had appeared and broken up
the meeting at the beer hall.

        The following day Ludendorff and Hitler decided to test the
intent of the German government toward the Nazi Party.   The two
men led a march on the war ministry.   They were accompanied by
Goering, Hess, Alfred Rosenberg, Max Erwin von Scheubner-Rich-
ter, Hitler's bodyguard Ulrich Graf and other Nazi officials, all of
whom marched at the head of the procession.   Following them were
3,000 brown-shirted storm troopers and a truck containing machine
guns and machine gunners.   The marchers reached the ministry
shortly after noon, where they encountered a detachment of police.
A shot was fired, followed by volleys from both sides.   Scheubner-
Richter was killed and Goering was wounded.   Sixteen Nazis were
killed, as were three policemen.   Others were wounded.

        Hitler fled but was soon captured and arrested.   He was
tried, along with Ludendorff and eight other prisoners.   Found guil-

ty of treason, he was sentenced to serve five years at Landsberg Fortress. After nine months he was released. During his imprisonment he dictated the work Mein Kampf ("My Struggle") to Rudolf Hess. In this he set forth his program for the restoration of Germany to a dominant position in Europe.

Suggested Readings

Abosch, Heinz. The Menace of the Miracle: Germany from Hitler to Adenauer. Translated by Douglas Garman. New York: Monthly Review Press, 1963.

Appel, Benjamin. Hitler, from Power to Ruin. New York: Grosset & Dunlap, 1964.

Archer, Jules. The Dictators. New York: Hawthorn Books, 1967.

Bradley, General Omar N. A Soldier's Story. New York: Holt, Rinehart, 1951.

Bullock, Alan. Hitler: A Study in Tyranny. New York: Harper & Row, 1962.

Carr, Albert H. Zolotoff. Men of Power: A Book of Dictators. New York: Viking Press, 1956.

Churchill, Winston S. The Second World War. Vol. I: "The Gathering Storm." Boston: Houghton Mifflin, 1948.

Elliott, Brendan John. Hitler and Germany. New York: McGraw-Hill, 1968.

Falls, Cyril Bentham. The Great War. New York: Putnam, 1959.

Fuller, John F. C. A Military History of the Western World. New York: Funk & Wagnalls, 1954.

Goldston, Robert. The Life and Death of Nazi Germany. Indianapolis: Bobbs-Merrill, 1967.

Grunberger, Richard. Germany, 1918-1945. New York: Harper & Row, 1966.

Haines, C. Grover, and J. Ross Hoffman. The Origins and Background of the Second World War. New York: Oxford University Press, 1943.

Heiden, Konrad. Der Fuehrer: Hitler's Rise to Power. Boston: Houghton Mifflin, 1944.

Hitler, Adolf. Mein Kampf. Boston: Houghton Mifflin, 1943.

Höhne, Heinz. Order of the Death's Head: The Story of Hitler's S. S. Translated by Richard Barry. New York: Coward McCann, 1969.

Holborn, Hajo. A History of Modern Germany. Vol. III: 1840-1945. New York: Knopf, 1969.

Hutton, J. Bernhard. Hess: The Man and His Mission. New York: Macmillan, 1970.

Jarman, T. L. The Rise and Fall of Nazi Germany. New York: New York University Press, 1956.

Marshall, S. L. A. World War I. New York: American Heritage Press, 1964.

Nazi Conspiracy and Aggression. Washington, D. C. : Office of the United States Chief of Counsel for Prosecution of Axis Criminality, 1946-1948.

Nicholls, A. J. "The Munich Putsch" in Taylor, A. J. P. , editor-in-

chief.   Purnell's History of the 20th Century, Vol. 5.   New
    York: Purnell, 1971.
Prittie, Terence, and the editors of Life.   Germany.   New York:
    Time, Inc. , 1961.
Reeder, Red.   The Story of the First World War.   New York: Du-
    ell, Sloan and Pearce, 1962.
Sapinsley, Barbara.   From Kaiser to Hitler: The Life and Death
    of a Democracy, 1919-1933.   New York: Grosset & Dunlap,
    1968.
Schoenbaum, David.   Hitler's Social Revolution.   Garden City, N. Y. :
    Doubleday, 1966.
Shirer, William L.   The Rise and Fall of Adolf Hitler.   New York:
    Random House, 1961.
_____ .   The Rise and Fall of the Third Reich: A History of
    Nazi Germany.   New York: Simon & Schuster, 1960.
Smith, Bradley F.   Adolf Hitler: His Family, Childhood and Youth.
    Stanford, Calif. :   Stanford University Press, 1967.
Speer, Albert.   Inside the Third Reich.   New York: Macmillan,
    1970.
Stein, George H. , ed.   Hitler.   Englewood Cliffs, N. J. :   Prentice-
    Hall, 1968.
Strasser, Otto.   Hitler and I.   Boston: Houghton Mifflin, 1940.
Taylor, Alan John Percivale.   The Origins of the Second World War.
    New York: Atheneum, 1961.
Toland, John.   Adolf Hitler.   Garden City, N. Y. :   Doubleday, 1977.
Wheeler-Bennett, John W.   Munich: Prologue to Tragedy.   New
    York: Duell, Sloan and Pearce, 1948.
_____ .   The Nemesis of Power: The German Army in Politics,
    1918-1945.   New York: Viking Press, 1952.
Wilmot, Chester.   The Struggle for Europe.   New York: Harper &
    Row, 1952.

THE BRITISH GENERAL STRIKE (1926)

The only general strike in English history started on the
morning of May 3, 1926.   It lasted nine days.

The idea of a general strike in Great Britain was not new.
The roots of such a strike went back as far as the Welsh Socialist
Robert Owen's Grand National Consolidated Trade Union of the 1830's
and the Chartism of the 1840's.   The 1926 strike was triggered when,
the year before, Great Britain returned to the gold standard at the
pre-World War I exchange rate of $4. 86 to the pound.   This move,
from the viewpoint of British industry, was ill-advised.   In the case
of coal mining the operators found that selling prices in export markets were raised by 10 percent, to a level where they could not
compete with non-British coal producers.   They attempted to regain
their original position in the world coal market by reducing the wages paid to the miners.

Notice of the wage cut was given to the miners a month after
England returned to the gold standard. Wage scales previously
agreed upon were terminated and working hours were increased.
The Trades Union Congress General Council promptly acted in defense of the mine workers. The government approved a subsidy to
keep wages at their former level while a commission under Sir Herbert Samuel studied the situation to determine what could be done
to reorganize the coal mining industry. These steps were taken
after other unions threatened to strike in sympathy with the coal
miners. This led to a general belief that the industrial unions were
sufficiently strong to win in any dispute they might have with the
employers. Actually, while the commission studied the matter the
government set about mobilizing volunteers to keep vital services
operating in the event of a strike.

Nine months later Samuel's commission recommended changes
in the coal industry. These changes, however, were to be made
some time in the future and no relief for the present was suggested.
The owners then declared a national lock-out and on April 30, 1926,
the miners retaliated by striking. Again the latter appealed to the
Trades Union Council for backing. Leaders of the T. U. C., however, were not seriously preparing for a general strike. Its members thought that a threat of such a strike would be sufficient to
force the government to negotiate. It was not until Ernest Bevin,
general secretary of the Transport and General Workers' Union, insisted that the miners could achieve their ends only if all unions
joined forces that coordinated strike action was agreed to.

On May 1, 1926, delegates representing 3,650,000 organized
workers pledged to strike. It was agreed that house and hospital
building should not be interfered with and that supplies of such necessities as food and milk should be maintained.

Negotiations with the government were inaugurated by the
T. U. C. Winston S. Churchill and Neville Chamberlain demanded a
show-down. Lord Birkenhead, a member of Prime Minister Stanley
Baldwin's cabinet, favored industrial peace. Birkenhead made sug-
gestions which embodied some of the recommendations proposed by
Sir Herbert Samuel's commission.

The T. U. C. representatives then conferred with the miners
and the Cabinet waited at No. 10 Downing Street for their answer.
Then Thomas Marlowe, editor of the Daily Mail, telephoned the Cabinet to report that his printers had refused to set type for an editorial titled "For King and Country" which he had written. This
editorial denounced the T. U. C. 's plans for a sympathetic strike,
calling it "a revolutionary act aimed at destroying the government. "
It urged "all law-abiding men and women" to resist it.

Lord Birkenhead felt that the printers had done "a bloody
good job. " Other cabinet members disagreed and a letter, signed
by Prime Minister Baldwin, was sent to the T. U. C. This letter
stated that the "overt action" of the printers "was a gross interfer-

ence with the freedom of the press" and that further negotiations
were out of the question "until the action was repudiated and the
strike notices withdrawn. "

This was the first information the T. U. C. delegates had of
the Daily Mail incident. The action of the printers constituted a
wildcat strike and had not been approved by the officials of the
printers' union. Arthur Pugh, T. U. C. chairman and Walter Cit-
rine, general secretary, immediately went to No. 10 Downing Street
with a letter declaring that the printers' strike had not been authorized and that they felt that an amicable agreement could be reached.
Baldwin had gone home to bed and could not be reached.

Negotiations were at an end and on the following day a general strike was called. The workers ceased work and thousands of
British citizens, in response to a government call for volunteers,
replaced them. Students drove buses and taxicabs. Canteens,
manned by society matrons and debutantes, were set up. Hobbyists
used their special skills in industrial and commercial areas. The
strike was without violence and in at least one instance policemen
and striking union members engaged in playing football.

Neither the union leaders nor the government officials favored the strike. It was realized that it could, unless terminated,
result in outright revolution, something to be avoided at all costs.
After nine days it was ended despite the protests of the miners who
felt that they had been sold out. These carried on for an additional
six months but eventually returned to work on the mine owners'
terms.

The short-lived British General Strike resulted in the passage of a new Trade Disputes Act. This legislation restricted the
powers of the unions and caused a good deal of bitterness. However, it is generally agreed that the strike, while almost a farce,
convinced both capital and labor that it was an unsatisfactory method
of settling their differences.

Suggested Readings

Cole, G. H. D. , and Raymond Postgate. The British Common People,
    1746-1946. New York: Barnes & Noble, 1961.
Crook, Wilfrid H. Communism and the General Strike. Hamden,
    Conn. : Shoe String Press, 1960.
Due, John F. Intermediate Economic Analysis. Homewood, Ill. :
    Richard D. Irwin, 1953.
Flanders, Allan, and H. A. Clegg, eds. The System of Industrial
    Relations in Great Britain. London: Oxford University Press,
    1960.
Francis-Williams, Lord. "The General Strike" in Taylor, A. J. P. ,
    editor in chief. Purnell's History of the 20th Century, Vol. 4.
    New York: Purnell, 1971.
Middlemas, Keith, and John Barnes. Baldwin: A Biography. Lon-
    don: Weidenfeld & Nicolson, 1969.

Mowat, Charles Loch. Britain Between the Wars, 1918-1940. London: Methuen, 1956.
Pelling, Henry. A History of British Trade Unionism. London: Oxford University Press, 1963.
_____. A Short History of the Labour Party. New York: St. Martin's Press, 1972.
Phelps Brown, Ernest H. The Economics of Labor. New Haven, Conn. : Yale University Press, 1962.
_____. The Growth of British Industrial Relations. London: Oxford University Press, 1959.
Symons, Julian. The General Strike. London: Cresset Press, 1957.
Taylor, A. J. P. English History, 1914-1945. New York: Oxford University Press, 1965.
United Kingdom Ministry of Labour. Industrial Relations Handbook. London: Her Majesty's Stationery Office, 1961.
Wibberley, Leonard. The Life of Winston Churchill. New York: Ariel Books, 1956.

THE DISCOVERY OF PENICILLIN (1928)

Antibiotics are substances produced by one microbial culture which are harmful, in dilute solution, to another microbe. Louis Pasteur, the French chemist discovered, in the late 19th century, that certain saprophytic bacteria can kill germs of anthrax and chicken cholera and developed a method of inoculation which prevented severe attacks of these diseases. This was the first application of what is called the "antibiotic effect. "

Other scientists, including the German bacteriologist Rudolf von Emmerich, made similar discoveries. Sir Alexander Fleming-- the British bacteriologist who had, in 1922, found an antiseptic called lysozyme which has strong antimicrobial power--discovered penicillin, the archetype of antibiotics, in 1928.

Fleming observed a culture of staphylococcus germs which had been left uncovered for several days. Some particles of mold had accidentally fallen into the culture and Fleming noticed that around each such particle the bacteria in the culture had died and no new growth had replaced them. He isolated the mold which, he reasoned, had released a chemical having antibacterial qualities. This mold was later identified by an American mycologist as penicillium notatum, similar to the mold which grows on stale bread. This was named "penicillin. "

Further research disclosed that the mold affected some, but not all, bacteria. As it was not poisonous to the corpuscles found in the blood stream it could apparently be used as an antibacterial agent. In 1929 Fleming published his findings but little attention was paid to them by the medical world, and for the next decade pen-

icillin was used primarily in research laboratories for isolating
strains of bacteria. Additional experiments were conducted by Harold Raistrick, an English biochemist.

In 1939 Sir Howard Walter Florey, an Australian pathologist
and Ernst Boris Chain, a German-English biochemist, doing research sponsored by Oxford University, isolated a yellow powder
which was penicillin. After its effectiveness as a bacteriostatic
was demonstrated on laboratory animals and on human beings, Florey succeeded in interesting several American pharmaceutical firms
in the wholesale manufacture of the product, to be used to combat
infections resulting from wounds received in World War II. It was
first used in 1943 and found to be highly effective.

Penicillin has proved useful in the treatment of syphilis, gon-
orrhea, scarlet fever, gas gangrene, osteomyelitis and other ailments. It has also been successfully used to treat patients who are
allergic to sulfa drugs or who are infected by bacteria which have
developed immunity to such drugs.

Fleming was knighted in 1944. In the following year he,
Florey and Chain were awarded the Nobel Prize for physiology and
medicine.

Suggested Readings

Benz, Francis E. Pasteur: Knight of the Laboratory. New York:
    Dodd, Mead, 1938.
Burton, Mary June. Louis Pasteur: Founder of Microbiology. New
    York: Franklin Watts, 1963.
Cheyne, William Watson. Lister and His Achievement. London:
    Longmans, Green, 1925.
De Kruif, Paul. Microbe Hunters. Edited by Harry R. Grover.
    New York: Harcourt, Brace, 1932.
Eberle, Irmengarde. Modern Medical Discoveries. New York:
    Crowell, 1958.
Epstein, Samuel, and Beryl Williams. Miracles from Microbes.
    New Brunswick, N. J. : Rutgers University Press, 1946.
Gallagher, Richard. Diseases That Plague Modern Man. Dobbs
    Ferry, N. Y. : Oceana Publications, 1969.
Gaughran, Eugene R. L. "From Superstition to Science: The History
    of a Bacterium, " Transactions, New York Academy of Science,
    January, 1969.
Glasscheib, Hermann S. The March of Medicine. New York: Put-
    nam's, 1964.
Lewis, Sinclair. Arrowsmith (fiction). New York: Modern Library,
    1925.
Ludovici, L. J. Fleming: Discoverer of Penicillin. London: An-
    drew Dakers, 1952.
Major, Ralph H. A History of Medicine. Springfield, Ill. : Thomas,
    1954.
Malkus, Alida Sims. The Story of Louis Pasteur. New York: Gros-
    set & Dunlap, 1952.

Marti-Ibanez, Felix. Men, Molds, and History. New York: MD
    Publications, 1958.
Maurios, André. The Life of Sir Alexander Fleming. New York:
    Dutton, 1959.
The Merck Manual of Diagnosis and Therapy. 8th edition. Rahway,
    N. J.: Merck & Co., Inc., 1950.
Metchnikov, Ilia Ilich. The Founders of Modern Medicine. New
    York: Walden Publications, 1939.
Mettler, Cecilia C. History of Medicine. Philadelphia: Blakis-
    ton, 1947.
Ratcliff, J. D. Yellow Magic: The Story of Penicillin. New York:
    Random House, 1945.
Reinfeld, Fred. Miracle Drugs and the New Age of Medicine. New
    York: Sterling Publishing Co., 1962.
Singer, Charles, and E. Ashworth Underwood. A Short History of
    Medicine. New York: Oxford University Press, 1962.
Sokolf, Boris. The Story of Penicillin. Chicago: Ziff-Davis, 1945.
Truax, Rhoda. Joseph Lister, Father of Modern Surgery. New
    York: Bobbs-Merrill, 1944.
Vallery-Radot, René. The Life of Pasteur. Translated by Mrs.
    R. L. Devonshire. Garden City, N. Y.: Sun Dial Press, 1937.
Winslow, Charles-Edward Amory. The Conquest of Epidemic Di-
    sease. Princeton, N. J.: Princeton University Press, 1943.
Witton's Microbiology. New York: McGraw-Hill, 1961.
Wood, Laura Newbold. Louis Pasteur. New York: Messner, 1948.

THE RUSSIAN FIVE-YEAR PLANS (1928-1971)

By the year 1928 the Russian economy had been largely destroyed by World War I, the 1917 revolution and the civil war of
1918-1921. Joseph Stalin, the Russian dictator from 1928 until his
death in 1953, instituted a series of plans for the economic improve-
ment of his country. He forced the peasantry into collective farms,
transformed the labor camps into slave-labor enterprises and sought
to develop Russian industry.

The first of the Five-Year Plans, set up in 1928, was declared completed before the scheduled date in 1933. Its objectives
were to be financed by confiscation of the surplus stocks of the peasants and the profits realized from collective agriculture. Despite
their protests some 55 percent of the Russian peasantry were forced
into collectivism. They retaliated by destroying great quantities of
grain, livestock and poultry. Thousands of resisting peasants were
shot and others were deported to serve terms of hard labor in Siberia. The production of agricultural products became badly disorganized and in 1930 an artificially induced famine occurred in
which several million persons died of malnutrition and disease. Industrialization, according to the Plan, was to be inaugurated on a
gigantic scale; the labor force was to be disciplined and employed
in the construction and operation of dams, hydroelectric plants, mines,
canals and factories of various sorts.

The first Five-Year Plan posed a number of serious problems for the Stalin government. The resistance of the peasants delayed gains in agricultural productivity until the period of the second
Five-Year Plan (1934-1938). Industrialization also provided immense problems. Skilled laborers were hard to find and the ex-
farmer, recruited into the ranks of industry proved, in many cases,
incompetent and unwilling to learn the new skills required to operate modern machinery. The "Black Book" was introduced. In this
records of each individual worker were kept and punishment, including deportation to Siberia, was meted out to the non-conformists.

Other problems arose. Adequate housing in industrial areas
had been extremely difficult to obtain before the inauguration of the
Plans, and the influx of additional workers served to make this
shortage even more acute. Nevertheless industrialization recorded
significant gains.

The aims of the second Five-Year Plan were essentially a
continuation of the first, with the added objective of mechanizing
agriculture. The third Plan (1938-1943) sought to complete "the
establishment of a classless ... society." This was to be accomplished by further industrialization "which would overtake and sur-
pass the leading capitalist countries in technical perfection, productivity and volume of output." World War II interrupted this program and, with the fourth Five-Year Plan, instituted in 1946, the
Russian Communists hoped to restore the economy to its pre-war
level. The fifth Plan (1951) sought to build heavy industry and the
sixth (1956) aimed to achieve massive increases in agriculture and
industrial output. This was discontinued in 1958 and a Seven-Year
Plan was substituted for it the following year. In 1966 still another Five-Year Plan was announced.

These Plans, particularly the first five, resulted in great
changes in Soviet society. The original (primarily agricultural)
economy was superseded by a high degree of industrialization. Ur-
banization increased and the individual peasant farms were largely
replaced by collectivized operations run on scientific principles. Today Russia is one of the most powerful nations in the world.

Suggested Readings

Abramovich, Raphael R. The Soviet Revolution, 1917-1939. New
     York: International Universities Press, 1962.
Benns, F. Lee. Europe Since 1914 in Its World Setting. New
     York: Appleton-Century-Crofts, 1945.
Daniels, Robert V. The Conscience of the Revolution: Communist
     Opposition in Soviet Russia. Cambridge, Mass. : Harvard Uni-
     versity Press, 1960.
Deutscher, Isaac. Stalin: A Political Biography. 2nd rev. ed.
     New York: Oxford University Press, 1967.
Duranty, Walter. Duranty Reports Russia. New York: Viking
     Press, 1934.

Ehrlich, A. The Soviet Industrialization Debate. Cambridge,
    Mass.: Harvard University Press, 1950.
Embree, George Daniel. The Soviet Union Between the 19th and
    20th Party Congresses, 1952-1956. The Hague: Martinus Ny-
    hoff, 1959.
Laqueur, Walter. The Fate of the Revolution: Interpretations of
    Soviet History. London: Weidenfeld and Nicolson, 1967.
Leonhard, Wolfgang. The Kremlin Since Stalin. Translated by
    Elizabeth Wiskemann and Marion Jackson. New York: Fred-
    erick A. Praeger, 1962.
Nove, Alec. Economic Rationality and Soviet Politics. New York:
    Frederick A. Praeger, 1964.
Payne, Robert. The Rise and Fall of Stalin. New York: Simon
    & Schuster, 1965.
Ponomaryov, Boris N., et al. History of the Communist Party of
    the Soviet Union. Moscow: Foreign Languages Publishing House,
    1960.
Randall, F. Stalin's Russia. New York: Free Press, 1965.
Schapiro, Leonard. The Communist Party of the Soviet Union. New
    York: Random House, 1960.
Souvarine, B. Stalin: A Critical Survey of Bolshevism. New York:
    Longmans, Green, 1939.
Tucker, Robert C. The Soviet Political Mind: Studies in Stalinism
    and Post-Stalin Change. New York: Frederick A. Praeger,
    1963.
Warth, Robert. Joseph Stalin. New York: Twayne Publishers,
    1969.

THE DÜSSELDORF VAMPIRE (1929-1930)

In a career of murder and sex crimes lasting a quarter of
a century Peter Kürten, called the "Düsseldorf Vampire" and the
"Monster of Düsseldorf," stands unique. For a period of over a
year he terrorized the inhabitants of the German city of Düsseldorf
in a manner not unlike America's "Boston Strangler" and London's
"Jack the Ripper." Students of criminology regard such perverted
sex murderers as Albert Fish, Lucien Léger, Neville Heath and
John Reginald Halliday Christie as comparatively minor figures beside Kürten.

The Düsseldorf Vampire" was born in 1883, one of thirteen
children of a mentally deranged alcoholic. As a boy he witnessed
scenes of violence in his home. At the age of nine he was introduced to the sadistic sport of abusing animals by a degenerate dog
catcher who boarded in his parents' home. About this time he
drowned a young boy in the Rhine River.

As a young man he practiced various perversions with animals, committed arson and served a two-year prison sentence. Released from confinement, he attacked a young girl with whom he was

having sexual intercourse, leaving her unconscious.   He served additional prison sentences for theft and assault.   A paranoid, he blamed the world for what he considered injustices heaped upon him and resolved to avenge himself.

So far as is known, Kürten's career as a sex murderer began on May 25, 1913, when he strangled and stabbed a 13-year-old girl named Christine Klein.   The Klein girl died.   From that date until May 24, 1930, when he was arrested by the Düsseldorf police, he committed at least 68 crimes, mostly murders and not including theft and assault, for which he had spent twenty years in prison.

By 1929 the citizens of Düsseldorf realized that a mass murderer was at large.   Forty-six violent crimes, displaying every kind of perversion, had been committed.   On August 23 five-year-old Gertrude Hamacher and her 14-year-old foster sister Louise Lenzen were attacked by the then-unknown assailant who strangled both and cut their throats.   Later that night Gertrude Schulte, a 26-year-old servant girl, was accosted by a strange man, later found to be Kürten, who attempted to rape her, stabbed her with a knife and left her for dead.   Fortunately she survived the multiple stab wounds inflicted by her assailant.

The attacks continued.   Within the space of a half-hour he assaulted and wounded two women and a man.   He killed three more women, either with a bludgeon or a razor-sharp Bavarian dagger. A few weeks later a man accosted Maria Budlick, an out-of-work domestic, at the Düsseldorf railroad station.   He offered to show her the way to a hotel.   She accepted his offer but became suspicious.   A second man appeared, asked, "Is everything all right?," and the first man left hurriedly.   The Budlick girl then agreed to go with her rescuer to his apartment in the Mettmannerstrasse. There he gave her a glass of milk and a sandwich.   He then promised to escort her to a hotel but took her instead into the Grafenburg Woods.   There he attempted to rape her and then, for some inexplicable reason, changed his mind.   He asked her if she remembered where his apartment was located, and she answered, "No."   However, she recalled seeing the word "Mettmannerstrasse" on a signboard.   This, in due course, led to the apprehension and arrest of Peter Kürten by the Düsseldorf authorities.

The trial of the Düsseldorf Vampire began in April, 1931. He was charged with nine murders and seven attempted murders. To prevent his escape he was placed in a wooden cage in the courtroom.   For a man who had terrorized his fellow-citizens for over a year he was remarkably unlike the stereotypic sex fiend.   Neatly and quietly dressed, he appeared to be a junior executive or businessman.

Speaking in a quiet, well modulated voice, Kürten gave a dispassionate account of the horrible crimes of which he was guilty, denying nothing.   The prosecution did not bother to present any evidence to speak of: Kürten's detailed, almost fussy, confession was to be the most damning evidence of all. The psychiatrists who examined him had declared him legally sane. After a short deliberation the jury found him guilty on all counts. Dr. Rose, the presiding judge, sentenced him to death nine times. He was executed by the guillotine on the morning of July 2, 1932.

Suggested Readings.

Abrahamsen, David, M. D. The Murdering Mind. New York: Harper & Row, 1973.

Bromberg, Walter. Mold of Murder: A Psychiatric Study of Homicide. New York: Grune & Stratton, 1961.

Catton, Joseph. Beyond the Scenes of Murder. New York: Norton, 1940.

Guttmacher, M. S. The Mind of the Murderer. Freeport, N. Y. : Books for Libraries, 1960.

Jesse, F. Tennyson. Murder and Its Motives. London: Harrap, 1952.

Lawes, Warden Lewis E. Meet the Murderer! New York: Harper, 1940.

Lester, David, and Gene Lester. Crime of Passion: Murder and the Murderer. Chicago: Nelson Hall, 1975.

McDade, Thomas M. , compiler. The Annals of Murder. Norman, Okla. : University of Oklahoma Press, 1961.

Reinhardt, James Melvin. The Psychology of Strange Killers. Springfield, Ill. : Thomas, 1962.

Roberts, Carl E. B. The New World of Crime. London: Noble, 1933.

Symonds, Julian. "Sex Murderers, England and France, " in his A Pictorial History of Crime. New York: Crown Publishers, 1966.

"The Vampire of Düsseldorf: Peter Kürten" in Infamous Murders. London: Verdict Press/Phoebus Publishing Co. , 1975.

Wilson, Colin, and Patricia Pitman. Encyclopedia of Murder. New York: Putnam, 1962.

Wolfgang, Marvin E. , compiler. Studies in Homicide. New York: Harper & Row, 1967.

THE MAGINOT LINE (1929-1940)

The Maginot Line, a series of fortifications along the east frontier of France, built by the French between 1929 and 1940, was designed to furnish a defense against a resurgent Germany. It was, in a sense, a modern Great Wall of China.

Following World War I France sought means of protecting herself against Germany should this ever be necessary. She took three steps to achieve this protection. One was the seeking of a defensive alliance with Great Britain, whereby the British would be obligated to assist France against Germany in case of war. Great

Britain, however, refused to enter into such a pact. Another was
the signing of defensive alliances with Czechoslovakia, Poland, Romania, Yugoslavia and, later, with Soviet Russia. A third was negotiating and signing an alliance with Belgium and the construction
of a 196 mile series of fortifications between the Belgian border to
a spot near the Swiss border. This came to be called the "Maginot Line," after André Maginot, French Minister of War.

The decision to build the Line was based on the tactics of
World War I, which was fought largely in the trenches. The French
had, over a three-year period, found that offensive tactics gained
them little territory and involved a high casualty rate. Consequently Marshals Joseph Joffre and Henri Pétain, French commanders,
concluded that any future war should be fought with the French maintaining a defensive position against Germany's offensive. The two
commanders suggested the construction of an impregnable line of
fortifications along the Franco-German border. André Maginot and,
later, Paul Painlevé, who subsequently became Minister of War,
accepted the suggestion.

Maginot persuaded the French legislature to authorize funds
to finance the Line's construction, and following his death in 1932
the work was continued by successive Ministers of War. When completed in 1940 the Line consisted of several groups of underground
forts, interconnected within each group by a system of tunnels.
Mined areas and tank traps were installed before each fort. The
forts were protected from aeroplane and artillery attack by cover-
ings of steel reinforced with concrete. Facilities for troop quarters, storage of supplies, hospitalization of wounded and communication services were provided.

The strongest fortification lines were built one behind the
other between the cities of Metz and Mulhouse, and further strongholds were made available by modernizing forts at critical points
behind the two lines.

A smaller Line, called the Little Maginot Line, was built
along the Belgian border. This, an extension of the major Line,
was to be reinforced by mobile French forces which would move
into Belgium and help that country defend itself against any German
attack.

World War II erupted in 1939 and Belgium, unwilling to pro-
voke Germany, broke her pact with France. The Maginot Line held
against the Germans, who did not subject it to a major frontal attack. Instead, in 1946, they flanked it, driving through the low
countries to the north and attacking from the rear.

Suggested Readings

Benns, F. Lee. Europe Since 1914 in Its World Setting. New York:
       Appleton-Century-Crofts, 1945.

Benoist-Méchin, Jacques. Sixty Days That Shook the West: The
    Fall of France, 1940. Translated by Peter Wiles. New York:
    Putnam's, 1963.
Chapman, Guy. Why France Fell: The Defeat of the French Army
    in 1940. New York: Holt, 1968.
Churchill, Winston S. The Second World War. Vol I: "The Gath-
    ering Storm. " Boston: Houghton Mifflin, 1948.
Collier, Basil. The Second World War: A Military History. New
    York: Morrow, 1967.
Draper, Theodore. The Six Weeks War. New York: Viking Press,
    1944.
Ellis, Major L. F. The War in France and Flanders. London: Her
    Majesty's Stationery Office, 1953.
Fuller, John F. C. Armament and History. New York: Scribner's,
    1945.
_____. The Second World War, 1939-1945. London: Eyre &
    Spottiswoode, 1948.
Rowe, Vivian. The Great Wall of France. New York: Putnam's,
    1961.
Shirer, William L. The Collapse of the Third Republic. New York:
    Simon & Schuster, 1969.
_____. The Rise and Fall of the Third Reich: A History of Na-
    zi Germany. New York: Simon & Schuster, 1960.
Simon, Yves. The Road to Vichy, 1918-1938. Translated by James
    A. Corbett and George J. McMorrow. New York: Sheed and
    Ward, 1942.
Snyder, Louis L. The War: A Concise History, 1939-1945. New
    York: Dell Publishing Co. , 1964.
Spears, General Sir Edward L. Assignment to Catastrophe. Vol.
    II: "The Fall of France. " New York: A. A. Wyn, 1955.
Taylor, A. J. P. The Origins of the Second World War. London:
    Hamish Hamilton, 1961.
Taylor, Telford. The March of Conquest. New York: Simon &
    Schuster, 1958.
Werth, Alexander. The Twilight of France, 1933-1940. New York:
    Harper & Row, 1942.
Weygand, Maxime. Recalled to Service. London: William Heine-
    mann, Ltd. , 1952.
Wilhelm, Maria. For the Glory of France: The Story of the French
    Resistance. New York: Messner, 1968.
Wilmot, Chester. The Struggle for Europe. New York: Harper &
    Row, 1952.
Wolfers, Arnold. Britain and France Between Two Wars. New
    York: Harcourt, Brace, 1940.
Young, Peter. World War: 1939-1945. New York: Crowell, 1966.

THE SORGE AND ABEL SPY RINGS
(1929-1944 and 1948-1955)

Two of the all-time great Russian spies were Dr. Richard

Sorge and Colonel Rudolph Abel. Sorge did his best work in Japan during World War II and Abel operated in New York City after the hostilities ended.

Sorge was born in Russia in 1895 and grew up in Germany where, as a student, he absorbed and advocated the left wing doctrine. He joined the Communist Party and became the Party's chief of intelligence in Germany. Following espionage training in Russia he established spy rings in England and Scandinavia. In the late 1920's he was assigned to Tokyo where he was instructed to learn Japan's military intentions as they pertained to Russia.

In Japan Sorge proceeded to organize his spy ring. He recruited as agents Agnes Smedley, a writer of books on China, a Japanese correspondent named Ozaki Hotsumi, a Yugoslav newspaperman named Branko de Voukelitch, a Japanese named Miyagi Yotoku and several others. In 1933 he was given the additional assignment of spying on the Germans in Japan. This necessitated his becoming a member of the Nazi Party, which he accomplished without difficulty, the Party's intelligence system then being anything but efficient.

Sorge was outwardly a correspondent for the Frankfurt Times. This gave him entre to the German embassy in Tokyo where he soon made friends who were to prove valuable contacts for his spying mission. Ozaki, who had become a member of a club of Japanese intellectuals, gathered information which he passed on to Sorge who, in turn, relayed it to the Kremlin. Through his contacts at the German embassy, made possible by his newspaper correspondent cover, Sorge obtained valuable information about Germany's proposed plans.

Colonel Osaki, head of the Japanese Intelligence Office, was aware that a spy ring was operating within his country. In due course he came to suspect Sorge as the leader of such a ring. He arranged to introduce him to a beautiful Japanese girl who was one of Osaki's own operatives. Sorge, extremely susceptible to feminine charms, became an habitué of the nightclub where the girl was employed as a dancer. One night as he was driving her home he inadvertently dropped a small piece of paper. This he retrieved and tore into bits, throwing the pieces out the car window. The girl informed Japanese Intelligence of the incident, the torn paper was recovered and when the bits were pieced together they were found to contain an incriminating message. The following day Sorge was arrested. He was subsequently tried, found guilty and, on September 29, 1943, sentenced to be executed as a spy.

Sorge's ultimate fate is not known for certain. According to one account he was executed in November, 1944, as were Ozaki Hotsumi and other members of his ring. An English diplomat claimed to have seen him in Shanghai three years later. In 1947 the girl who betrayed him to the Japanese Intelligence Office was murdered.

Colonel Rudolf Abel was another outstanding Russian spy.   In 1948, following World War II, Igor Gouzenko, a Russian cipher clerk, defected and turned over to the authorities a list of Russian spies and their contacts.   The Kremlin realized that the Russian spy ring in the United States had to be rebuilt.   The project was assigned to Abel, who had been a member of the Russian secret service since its inception in 1917.

Abel was in New York City at the time of Gouzenko's defection.   He set himself up as a photographer in a Fulton Street studio, which he also used for portrait paintings and as a radio repair shop and amateur radio station.   He gave parties in his studio and was generally regarded by his artist friends as a semi-Bohemian.

Under the cover of a photographer-artist-radio repairman Abel contacted the undetected members of the old Russian spy ring and reorganized them.   He also recruited certain American embassy members who had at one time been stationed in Russia and, while there, had cooperated with Soviet Intelligence.   Within five years Abel was directing the activities of a reconstructed espionage organization and transmitting data in code to Moscow by means of his radio transmitter.

In 1955 Abel hired Reino Hayhanen, a Finn, as an assistant spy.   Hayhanen, a heavy drinker, proved unreliable and irresponsible.   Disgusted, Abel indicated that the Finn "would enjoy a vacation in Russia."   Hayhanen traveled as far as Paris and then, feeling that the Russian authorities would "liquidate" him, reported to the American embassy where he disclosed the details of the Abel spy ring.

The ring was destroyed.   Colonel Abel was arrested, tried and sentenced to thirty years in prison.   In 1962 he was released, to be exchanged for Gary Powers, the American U-2 pilot who was being held prisoner by the Soviet authorities.

Suggested Readings

Dallin, David.   Soviet Espionage.   New Haven, Conn. :   Yale University Press, 1955.

Dirksen, Herbert von.   Tokio, London.   Stuttgart: W. Kohlhammer Verlag, 1949.

Erickson, John.   The Soviet High Command, A Military-Political History, 1918-1941.   London: St. Martin's Press, 1962.

Farago, Ladislas.   The Game of the Foxes: The Untold Story of German Espionage in the United States and Great Britain During World War II.   New York: David McKay, 1971.

Franklin, Charles.   The Great Spies.   New York: Hart, 1967.

Johnson, Chalmers.   An Instance of Treason: Ozaki Hotsumi and the Sorge Spy Ring.   Stanford, Calif. :   Stanford University Press, 1964.

Lyushkoff, General G. S. "The Far Eastern Red Army," Contem-
    porary Japan, October, 1939.
Maruyama, Masao. Thought and Behavior in Modern Japanese Pol-
    itics. Edited by I. Morris. London: Oxford University Press,
    1963.
Massing, Hede. This Deception. New York: Duell, Sloan, 1951.
Meissner, Hans Otto. The Man with Three Faces. New York:
    Rinehart, 1955.
Presseisen, Ernst L. Germany and Japan: A Study in Totalitarian
    Diplomacy. The Hague: Nijhoff, 1958.
Schellenberg, Walter. "The Case of Richard Sorge" in his The
    Schellenberg Memoirs. Edited and translated by Louis Hagen.
    London: André Deutsch, 1956.
Smedley, Agnes. Daughter of Earth. New York: Coward-McCann,
    1935.
_____. "The Tokyo Martyrs," Far East Spotlight, March, 1949.
"The Spy Masters" in Crimes and Punishment, Vol. 5. Editorial
    presentation: Jackson Morley. London: BPC, 1973.
Tolischus, Otto D. Tokyo Record. New York: Reynal & Hitch-
    cock, 1943.
U. S. Army, Far East Command, Military Intelligence Section. A
    Partial Documentation of the Sorge Espionage Case. Tokyo:
    Toppan Printing Co. , 1950.
_____. "The Sorge Spy Ring--A Case Study in International Es-
    pionage in the Far East. " U. S. 81st Congress, First Session.
    Congressional Record, Vol. 95, Part 12 (February 9, 1949),
    Appendix, pp. A705-A723.
U. S. House of Representatives, 82nd Congress, First Session, Com-
    mittee on Un-American Activities. Hearings on the American
    Aspects of the Richard Sorge Spy Case. Washington, D. C. :
    Government Printing Office, 1951.
U. S. Senate, 82nd Congress, First Session, Committee on the Judi-
    ciary. Institute of Pacific Relations Hearings, Part 2. Wash-
    ington, D. C. : Government Printing Office, 1951.
Willoughby, Charles A. Shanghai Conspiracy: The Sorge Spy Ring.
    New York: Dutton, 1952.
_____. Sorge: Soviet Master Spy. London: William Kimber,
    1952.

THE JULIA WALLACE MURDER (1931)

The murder of 50-year-old Julia Wallace in January, 1931,
remains one of the most baffling unsolved crimes in British criminal history. Her husband, William Herbert Wallace, a 52-year-
old insurance salesman and amateur chess enthusiast, was accused
of the murder. He was tried at the Liverpool Spring Assizes in
April, 1931, was found guilty by the jury and was condemned to die.
However, the Court of Criminal Appeal quashed the verdict in May
of that year and Wallace was freed.

The affair began on the evening of January 19, 1931, when Samuel Beattie, steward of the City Café in North John Street, Liverpool, received a telephone call from a man who identified himself as "Qualtrough." The caller indicated that he wished to purchase some insurance from Wallace who was expected to arrive later that evening to participate in a chess tournament scheduled to be held at the café. Beattie stated that Wallace had not yet arrived and suggested that "Qualtrough" call back later. "Qualtrough" then asked that Wallace visit him at 7:30 the following evening at his home, 25 Menlove Gardens East, Mossley Hill.

When Wallace arrived at the café Beattie relayed the telephone message to him. Wallace denied knowing anyone by the name of "Qualtrough." He played in the chess tournament and then left for his home at 29 Wolverton Street, Anfield.

On the following evening Wallace set out for the "Qualtrough." residence. Although he was familiar with Liverpool he was unable to find either Menlove Gardens East or anyone by the name of Qualtrough. After searching in vain for over two hours and asking directions from several people, none of whom was able to help him, he returned home, arriving at approximately nine o'clock. The front door of his house was stuck closed and he was unable to open it. He walked to the rear and tried the back door, which also refused to open. He banged on the rear door, attracting the attention of his neighbors, John and Florence Johnson. They suggested that Wallace try the door again, which he did. To his apparent amazement it opened at once. He entered the house and then rushed back outside, shouting that his wife had been killed. The Johnsons followed him back in. They found the body of Julia Wallace, fully clothed, on the floor of the sitting room. She was lying on a raincoat belonging to her husband. Her skull was split partially open, apparently from being beaten with a heavy weapon. It was later learned that an iron bar, customarily used as a poker, was missing. The room was spattered with blood.

The police were summoned. They searched the premises, finding no evidence which would incriminate the husband of the dead woman. An examination of the body by Professor John MacFall, an expert in forensic medicine, disclosed that death had come about six in the evening, an hour before Wallace stated he had left the house to keep his appointment with "Qualtrough."

Following a police investigation Wallace was arrested and charged with murder. His trial began on April 22, 1931. Samuel Beattie testified to having received the telephone call at the City Café on January 19 and people of whom Wallace had asked directions to Menlove Gardens East the following evening gave evidence on his behalf. The prosecution maintained that Wallace could have made the telephone call to the café, pretending to be a non-existent "Qualtrough," disguising his voice so that it would not be recognized by the steward. He could have worn the raincoat with nothing under it, bludgeoned his wife to death, removed the raincoat and placed

it beneath her body and then bathed carefully to remove all traces
of blood from himself.

As stated above, Wallace was found guilty and sentenced to
die, but the verdict was overturned and the man went free. Following his release he returned to his home on Wolverton Street
where he lived until, for reasons of health, he moved to the country where he died of natural causes in February, 1933.

Other than Wallace, no one has ever been charged with the
death of the unfortunate woman. The iron bar with which the murder may have been committed was never found and, to the end of
his life, William Herbert Wallace maintained his innocence. If
he did kill Julia Wallace, no motive for the crime was ever
established.

Suggested Readings

Abrahamsen, David, M. D. The Murdering Mind. New York: Har-
     per & Row, 1973.
Bromberg, Walter. Mold of Murder: A Psychiatric Study of Hom-
     icide. New York: Grune & Stratton, 1961.
Catton, Joseph. Behind the Scenes of Murder. New York: Nor-
     ton, 1940.
Guttmacher, M. S. The Mind of the Murderer. Freeport, N. Y. :
     Books for Libraries, 1960.
Jesse, F. Tennyson. Murder and Its Motives. London: Harrap,
     1952.
Lawes, Warden Lewis E. Meet the Murderer! New York: Har-
     per, 1940.
Lester, David, and Gene Lester. Crime of Passion: Murder and
     the Murderer. Chicago: Nelson Hall, 1975.
McDade, Thomas M. , compiler. The Annals of Murder. Norman,
     Okla. : University of Oklahoma Press, 1961.
"A Mysterious Telephone Call: William Wallace" in Infamous Mur-
     ders. London: Verdict Press / Phoebus Publishing Company,
     1975.
Reinhardt, James Melvin. The Psychology of Strange Killers.
     Springfield, Ill. : Thomas, 1962.
Roberts, Carl E. B. The New World of Crime. London: Noble,
     1933.
Scott, Sir Harold, with Philippa Pearce. From Inside Scotland
     Yard. New York: Macmillan, 1965.
Thompson, Laurence Victor. The Story of Scotland Yard. New
     York: Random House, 1954.
Wilson, Colin, and Patricia Pitman. Encyclopedia of Murder. New
     York: Putnam, 1962.
Wolfgang, Marvin E. , compiler. Studies in Homicide. New York:
     Harper & Row, 1967.

THE CHACO WAR (1932-1935)

The Chaco is a region of 100,000 to 115,000 square miles in Central South America lying between the Pilcomayo and the Paraguay Rivers. It embraces parts of Southeastern Bolivia and Northern Paraguay and is contiguous to the Chaco central region of Formosa Territory in Northern Argentina. The area is waterless and desolate and is inhabited chiefly by Indians. A few cattle are pastured in the Chaco and quebracho wood, used in the tanning of leather, grows there.

Argentina, Paraguay and Bolivia all could make legitimate claims to the area when the Spanish empire in South America broke up and these nations were formed. This was because the land was poorly mapped and the Spanish boundary lines were overlapping. From 1870 on the exact position of the Bolivia-Paraguay boundary was disputed by these two countries, both claiming the entire Chaco territory. Bolivia wished to secure an outlet on the navigable Paraguay River and had pushed her frontier towards the Southeast, eventually occupying more than half the disputed area. Paraguay countered by building a chain of block houses on a North-South line along the 60th meridian and Bolivia then built a similar line of fortifications. War between the two nations broke out in May, 1932, although no formal declaration of war was ever made by either belligerent.

Daniel Salamanca, an elderly lawyer, had been President of Bolivia since March, 1931. He was committed to a "hard and arrogant line" on the Chaco question. He knew little of geography and less of war. He flatly refused to consider an offer of mediation made by the Paraguayans shortly after the war began. The League of Nations Council urged the two warring nations to consider their obligations under the Covenant and also supported the Commission of Conciliation formed by the neutral Pan-American members in 1931 to negotiate a settlement. These overtures were unsuccessful. Bolivia accepted provisionally a proposal to arbitrate, made by the Commission in December, 1932, but Paraguay rejected it.

The Bolivian forces were commanded by General Hans Kundt, a German mercenary. Kundt, who had served in World War I, used the tactics of trench warfare, totally unsuited to the waterless terrain of the Chaco. General José Félix Estigarribia, commander-in-chief of the Paraguayan forces, being familiar with General Kundt's philosophy of military tactics, was able eventually to lead his command to victory, despite the fact that the Bolivians had mobilized 250,000 men while Paraguay's forces numbered only 140,000. Kundt was hampered by the interference of the militarily incompetent President Salamanca while Estigarribia was fully supported by Eusebio Ayala, President of Paraguay. Under Estigarribia's leadership the Paraguayan resources were put to much more efficient use than were those of Bolivia.

Bolivia fought alone. Paraguay was given clandestine assistance by the Argentine government which provided gasoline, mortar shells, trucks, military intelligence and money. For this Carlos Saavedra Lamas, Argentine Foreign Minister, was awarded the Nobel Peace Prize in 1936. Some historians consider this award highly absurd.

The Chaco War was a struggle for territory of economic importance to both sides and to which both warring nations could lay serious claims. President Salamanca was forced to resign in 1934. Paraguay resigned from the League of Nations and her army threatened the oil fields around Camiri in the Bolivian foothills. In June, 1935, Bolivia, having lost a number of encounters with the Paraguayan forces, agreed to an armistice.

Bolivia's losses were 57,000 men; Paraguay's were 36,000. A peace treaty was signed in July, 1938, and in October of that year an arbitration commission delimited the frontier, giving Paraguay a major part of the Chaco region.

Following the Chaco War Paraguay moved towards an authoritarian militarism. Bolivia "embarked on a confused and wounded process of integration that was to culminate nearly 20 years later in the social revolution of the 1950's. "

Suggested Readings

"Battle of 100 Hours Ends, " Literary Digest, April 28, 1934.
"Bolivia and Paraguay Lock Horns Again, " Literary Digest, August 13, 1932.
"Chaco War Climax, " Literary Digest, March 2, 1935.
Deas, Malcolm. "The Chaco War" in Taylor, A. J. P. , editor in chief. Purnell's History of the 20th Century, Vol. 6. New York: Purnell, 1971.
De Ronde, Philip. Paraguay, a Gallant Little Nation: The Story of Paraguay's War with Bolivia. New York: Putnam's, 1935.
Doyle, H. G. "Chaco War, " Current History, July, 1933.
———. "War Clouds in South America, " Current History, September, 1932.
"Economics of the Chaco War, " New Republic, February 22, 1933.
Fifer, J. V. Bolivia Land, Location and Politics Since 1825. Cambridge: The University Press, 1972.
"Gran Chaco: Paraguay Declares War on Bolivia, " News Week, May 20, 1933.
Herring, H. "Paraguay Victorious in the Chaco, " Current History, January, 1935.
Inman, S. G. "South America Goes to War, " Christian Century, March 1, 1933.
"Open War in the Gran Chaco, " Literary Digest, May 20, 1933.
Osborne, Harold. Bolivia: A Land Divided. London: Royal Institute of International Affairs, 1954.
"Paraguay Crushes the Bolivian Army, " News Week, December 23, 1933.

Raine, Philip. Paraguay. New Brunswick, N. J. : Scarecrow
    Press, 1956.
Warren, Harris Gaylord. Paraguay: An Informal History. Nor-
    man, Okla. : University of Oklahoma Press, 1949.
White, J. W. "Warfare in the Chaco Jungle, " Current History, Ap-
    ril, 1933.
Zook, David, Jr. The Conduct of the Chaco War. New York: Hip-
    porene Books, 1950.

THE STAVISKY AFFAIR (1932-1934)

Serge Alexandre Stavisky, born in the Ukraine in 1886 the
son of a Jewish dentist, precipitated a gigantic financial swindle
which caused a general strike, resulted in the downfall of two French
ministries, created a sensation in French politics and generally discredited the Third Republic.

Stavisky and his family emigrated to France in the 1890's
and settled in Paris. Prior to 1926 he had engaged in petty frauds,
worked as a gigolo in Paris night clubs and sold cocaine and other
drugs. In that year he defrauded a Paris stockbroker of $7\frac{1}{2}$ million
francs. He was apprehended, questioned by the police and released
pending trial.

While out on bail he perpetrated a series of increasingly
large frauds. He liquidated the debts of each swindle with the proceeds of the following one and therefore was technically guilty of
fraud only in the case of the last swindle in the chain. These
reached a climax with his Bayonne bonds scheme, perpetrated in
1932. He floated a gigantic loan on the municipal pawnshop of
Bayonne in Southwestern France, first arranging to have the fake
jewelry in pawn appraised at the value of genuine stones and gems.
Dalimier, the French minister of labor, recommended the purchase
of the bonds and Stavisky was able to sell 200 million francs worth
to the investing public. He found himself financially overextended
and was not able to pay the interest on the bonds when it became
due. In November, 1933, an official complaint was made against
the Bayonne pawnshop and on December 29 a warrant was issued
for Stavisky's arrest. Stavisky, however, had disappeared, having
fled to Chamonix.

In January, 1933, the facts of the case became public and
it appeared that Stavisky had perpetrated his fraudulent activities
with the knowledge, consent and assistance of various highly placed
officials. Action Française, an intellectual group of right wing nationalist anti-Republican leagues, led the attack. For years this
organization had criticized the policies of the French Third Republic, declaring its leaders corrupt and incompetent.

On January 8, 1934, it was announced that Stavisky was dead.

Some considered him a suicide; others contended that the police had traced him to a villa at Chamonix, broken into his bedroom and shot him in the head. Action Française contended that he had been murdered to conceal the involvement of high ranking officials in his illegal activities. Camille Chautemps, then French minister of the interior, refused to appoint a committee to investigate the affair and nightly rioting occurred in the Paris streets. On January 27 Chautemps submitted his resignation.

President Albert Lebrun invited Edouard Daladier, a French statesman, to form a government and on January 29 the invitation was accepted. Daladier, in order to win Socialist support for his administration, discharged Prefect of Police Jean Chiappe who had right wing sentiments and was suspected by the Left of being involved in the Stavisky affair. This generated a new crisis, as the Right saw in it a deal between Daladier and the Socialists.

On February 5, 1934, the Croix de Feu, one of the Leagues, organized a large demonstration in Paris. Other components joined in and on the following evening a violent riot occurred in which fifteen persons, including one policeman, were killed.

Further riots seemed inevitable. Daladier resigned the next day, after only eleven days in office. Gaston Doumergue, another Radical but an enemy of the Socialists, formed a new government which restored confidence and the demonstrations by the Leagues subsided.

On February 24 an inquiry into the Stavisky affair was started. Three days before it opened the dismembered body of Albert Prince, a magistrate who had been in charge of the prosecution of Stavisky for fraud in 1926, was found on a railroad track near Dijon. The Left called it suicide and the Right called it murder. The inquiry revealed a great deal of information on Stavisky's dealings with public figures and seventeen deputies were directly implicated. However, neither Stavisky's death nor that of Albert Prince has ever been explained satisfactorily.

Suggested Readings

"Aftermath--Hunger, " Newsweek, November 21, 1960.

Boulanger, Roger. "The Stavisky Affair" in Taylor, A. J. P. , editor in chief. Purnell's History of the 20th Century, Vol. 6. New York: Purnell, 1971.

Deeson, A. F. L. Great Swindlers. New York: Drake Publishers, 1972.

"Four Masters of Fraud--They Won and Lost ... the Millions They Milked from the Unwary, " Newsweek, April 1, 1957.

Gibson, Walter Brown, ed. The Fine Art of Swindling. New York: Grosset & Dunlap, 1966.

Hancock, Ralph, and Henry Chafetz. The Compleat Swindler. New York: Macmillan, 1968.

Klein, Alexander. The Double Dealers: Adventures in Grand De-
  ception. Philadelphia: Lippincott, 1958.
_____. Grand Deception: The World's Most Spectacular and Suc-
  cessful Hoaxes, Impostures, Ruses and Frauds. Philadelphia:
  Lippincott, 1955.
Morgan, T. "Stavisky and the Fall of France," Horizon, Summer,
  1976.
Seaver, R. "Facts into Fiction," Film Comment, July, 1975.
Shirer, William L. The Collapse of the Third Republic. New York:
  Simon & Schuster, 1969.
Symons, Julian. "Stavisky and Kreuger" in his A Pictorial History
  of Crime. New York: Crown Publishers, 1966.
Warner, G. "The Stavisky Affair and the Riots of February 6,
  1934," History Today, June, 1958.

THE LE MANS MURDERS (1933)

While most murders are committed by individuals, cases of
homicide involving two or more persons working together are not
unknown. The killing of Bobby Franks in Chicago in 1924 was done
by Richard Loeb and his friend Nathan Leopold, Jr. Bonnie Parker and her lover, Clyde Barrow, bank robbers and killers, preyed
on the American Southwest in the early 1930's. Raymond Fernan-
dez and his mistress, Martha Beck, known as the "Lonely Hearts
Killers," did away with their victims jointly. Ian Brady and Myra
Hindley, his mistress, committed their multiple murders together
in 1965 and 1966. The Papin Sisters, Christine, 28, and Lea, 21,
were also killers in common, and their trial at Le Mans, France,
made headlines.

The Papin Sisters were domestics, employed by René Lancelin, an attorney of Le Mans. On February 2, 1933, he had been
away from home on business during the day. He was to meet his
wife and his 27-year-old daughter Geneviève at the home of a friend
where they were to be dinner guests. When the two women did not
appear at the friend's house he telephoned home. As no one answered the phone he returned to his residence to find the door
locked. All the lights were out except the one in the upstairs room
which was occupied by Christine and Lea Papin. Attorney Lancelin,
unable to enter the house, notified the police.

A police inspector arrived and forced his way in. There,
on the first floor landing, he found the battered bodies of Madame
and Geneviève Lancelin. Their eyes had been gouged from their
heads which had been savagely beaten with a hammer and a pewter
pot, both of which were found near the lifeless bodies. Both women
had been stabbed repeatedly with a knife, which was also found near
the bodies. The walls were streaked with blood.

The Papin sisters were found huddled together naked in a bed in their upstairs bedroom. Christine immediately confessed to the crime. She said that some time before she had broken an electric iron while using it and that Madame Lancelin had had it repaired and deducted five francs, the cost of the repairs, from her wages. When the girls were ironing on February 2 the iron malfunctioned, blowing the house fuses. When the mistress and her daughter returned the latter proceeded to scold the sisters about the broken iron. The sisters then attacked Madame and Geneviève Lancelin, gouging out their eyes and then battering and stabbing them.

Lea Papin confirmed her sister's story. The girls were arrested and charged with murder. Their trial began on September 20, 1933, in the Palais de Justice at Le Mans. Both girls confessed freely to the murders and expressed no regrets for having committed them. The courtroom was filled to capacity with eager spectators fascinated by the "bizarre story of a monstrous murder." The judge, almost unable to believe the sisters' unemotional, self-incriminating testimony, questioned them carefully. They showed no signs of emotion or regret for what they had done. When interrogated concerning their family background they stated that their father was an habitual drunkard and that, after an unhappy childhood they had worked together as household servants, changing jobs frequently until they were employed by the Lancelins. Their previous employers regarded them as "willing, hard-working and honest."

It was disclosed that the two girls had no social life or friends and seemed interested only in their work and in each other. The matter of lesbianism was considered and it was shown only that the sisters were extremely fond of each other but not in a homosexual way. No depravity or mental illness was proven and the doctors who examined the Papin Sisters declared them completely normal with "no burden of a defective heredity." The doctors said further that their examinations disclosed "no question of an attachment of a sexual nature."

Although the two sisters pleaded "not guilty" they were both convicted of murder. Christine, the elder, was sentenced to death and her younger sister Lea, for whom the jury found extenuating circumstances, feeling that she was dominated by Christine, was given ten years at hard labor. Christine's sentence was later reduced to confinement in prison for life. Neither girl appealed.

Christine Papin served four years during which she showed signs of insanity. She was transferred to a hospital where she died in 1939. Lea served her sentence, was released from prison and disappeared from view.

Suggested Readings

Abrahamsen, David, M. D. The Murdering Mind. New York: Harper & Row, 1973.
Bromberg, Walter. Mold of Murder: A Psychiatric Study of Homicide. New York: Grune & Stratton, 1961.

Catton, Joseph. Behind the Scenes of Murder. New York: Norton, 1940.

Guttmacher, M. S. The Mind of the Murderer. Freeport, N. Y. : Books for Libraries, 1960.

Jesse, F. Tennyson. Murder and Its Motives. London: Harrap, 1952.

Lawes, Warden Lewis E. Meet the Murderer! New York: Harper, 1940.

Lester, David, and Gene Lester. Crime of Passion: Murder and the Murderer. Chicago: Nelson Hall, 1975.

McDade, Thomas M. , compiler. The Annals of Murder. Norman, Okla. : University of Oklahoma Press, 1961.

"The Maids of Le Mans: The Papin Sisters" in Infamous Murders. London: Verdict Press/Phoebus Publishing Co. , 1975.

Reinhardt, James Melvin. The Psychology of Strange Killers. Springfield, Ill. : Thomas, 1962.

Roberts, Carl E. B. The New World of Crime. London: Noble, 1933.

Sparrow, Gerald. Women Who Murder. New York: Abelard, 1970.

Wilson, Colin, and Patricia Pitman. Encyclopedia of Murder. New York: Putnam, 1962.

Wolfgang, Marvin E. , compiler. Studies in Homicide. New York: Harper & Row, 1967.

THE REICHSTAG FIRE (1933)

On the evening of February 27, 1933, not quite a week before the party elections, the Reichstag, Berlin capital of the Papen-Hitler government, burst into flames. Adolf Hitler, then Chancellor, was dining at the home of Dr. Joseph Goebbels and Vice-Chancellor Franz von Papen was entertaining President Paul von Hindenburg at the Herrenklub in the Vosstrasse. Dr. Ernest Hanfstaengl telephoned Goebbels to report the fire and an attendant at the Herrenklub told Papen and Hindenburg of it.

Goebbels confirmed the truth of the report and relayed the information to Hitler. Hanfstaengl took Hindenburg home and then drove to the Reichstag which was burning in a dozen places. Goebbels and Hitler raced to the scene in an automobile where they met Papen.

The Communists were immediately charged with arson. However, according to available evidence, it has been established "beyond a reasonable doubt that it was the Nazis who planned the fire and carried it out for their own political ends. " Hermann Goering is said to have boasted of being responsible for the Reichstag fire, although he denied any complicity both when interrogated and in his trial at Nuremberg following the war.

A few days before the fire Marinus van der Lubbe, a feeble-

minded Dutch Communist arsonist, had been arrested in a Berlin
bar when he was heard to brag that he had attempted to set fire
to several public buildings and was intending to burn the Reichstag.
This happenstance furnished the Nazis a golden opportunity to blame
the forthcoming conflagration on the Communists.

On the evening of February 27 Karl Ernst, a Brown Shirt
storm trooper, led a small group of fellow troopers through an underground tunnel to the Reichstag.   There they deposited incendiary
chemicals and scattered gasoline liberally through the building.
Shortly thereafter the self-igniting chemicals did their work and the
Reichstag was soon burning furiously.

Although the idea of the fire was undoubtedly conceived by
Goebbels and Goering, the Communists were blamed for it and the
Nazis promptly retaliated.   Van der Lubbe was urged to attempt to
set the Reichstag afire but he was obviously nothing more than a
dupe of the Nazis.   He was tried in Leipzig and at the trial it was
shown that he could not, in the short time available to him, have
carried in sufficient incendiary materials to have set such a blaze.
He was not aware of the participation of Ernst and his fellow Nazi
pyromaniacs.

Ernst Torgler, a Communist leader, surrendered to the police when he learned that Goering had implicated his party in the
setting of the fire.   Shortly afterwards several other Communists
were arrested.   All were tried and Torgler and some others were
acquitted or taken into "protective custody. "   In a rigged trial van
der Lubbe was found guilty, sentenced to die and executed.

On February 29 Hitler persuaded President Hindenburg to
sign a decree which suspended constitutional provisions guaranteeing
individual and civil liberties and vastly increased the powers of the
Reich government.   With this document and financial support from
German "big business, " the Nazis then launched a gigantic propaganda campaign, using all media including radio, street parades and
billboard and newspaper advertisements.   The Russian government
announced that it had discovered Communist documents proving that
"the burning of the Reichstag by the Communists was to be the signal for a bloody insurrection and civil war. "   These "documents"
were never published, or even produced.

The election was held on March 5, 1933.   In spite of terrorist tactics and the propaganda campaign, Hitler's Nazi Party received only 44 percent of the votes cast.   However, the 52 Reichstag seats held by the Nationalist Party plus the 288 Nazi seats
gave a majority of sixteen.   While short of the 213 majority needed to
establish a dictatorship by consent of Parliament, this was sufficient
to carry on the day-to-day government business in line with Hitler's
objectives.

Suggested Readings

Abosch, Heinz. The Menace of the Miracle: Germany from Hitler to Adenauer. Translated by Douglas Garman. New York: Monthly Review Press, 1963.

Appel, Benjamin. Hitler, from Power to Ruin. New York: Grosset & Dunlap, 1964.

Archer, Jules. The Dictators. New York: Hawthorn Books, 1967.

Beloff, Max. The Foreign Policy of Soviet Russia, 1929-1941. London: Oxford University Press, 1949.

Bullock, Alan. Hitler: A Study in Tyranny. New York: Harper & Row, 1962.

Carr, E. H. German-Soviet Relations Between the Two World Wars. 1919-1939. Baltimore: Johns Hopkins University Press, 1951.

Churchill, Winston S. The Second World War. Vol. I: "The Gathering Storm." Boston: Houghton Mifflin, 1948.

Elliott, Brendan John. Hitler and Germany. New York: McGraw-Hill, 1968.

Goldston, Robert. The Life and Death of Nazi Germany. Indianapolis: Bobbs-Merrill, 1967.

Grunberger, Richard. Germany, 1918-1945. New York: Harper & Row, 1966.

Haines, C. Grover, and J. Ross Hoffman. The Origins and Background of the Second World War. New York: Oxford University Press, 1943.

Heiden, Konrad. Der Fuehrer: Hitler's Rise to Power. Boston: Houghton Mifflin, 1944.

Hitler, Adolf. Mein Kampf. Boston: Houghton Mifflin, 1943.

Höhne, Heinz. Order of the Death's Head: The Story of Hitler's S. S. Translated by Richard Barry. New York: Coward McCann, 1969.

Holborn, Hajo. A History of Modern Germany. Vol. III: 1840-1945. New York: Knopf, 1969.

Jarman, T. L. The Rise and Fall of Nazi Germany. New York: New York University Press, 1956.

Nazi Conspiracy and Aggression. Washington, D. C. : Office of the United States Chief of Counsel for the Prosecution of Axis Criminality, 1946-1948.

Prittie, Terence, and the editors of Life. Germany. New York: Time, Inc. , 1961.

Sapinsley, Barbara. From Kaiser to Hitler: The Life and Death of a Democracy, 1919-1933. New York: Grosset & Dunlap, 1968.

Schlesinger, Arthur M. , Jr. The Age of Roosevelt. Boston: Houghton Mifflin, 1957.

Schoenbaum, David. Hitler's Social Revolution. Garden City, N. Y. : Doubleday, 1966.

Shirer, William L. The Rise and Fall of Adolf Hitler. New York: Random House, 1961.

_____. The Rise and Fall of the Third Reich: A History of Nazi Germany. New York: Simon & Schuster, 1960.

Smith, Bradley F. Adolf Hitler: His Family, Childhood and Youth. Stanford, Calif. : Stanford University Press, 1967.

Snell, John L. The Outbreak of the Second World War: Design or
    Blunder? Boston: Heath, 1962.
          , ed. The Nazi Revolution: Germany's Guilt or Germany's
    Fate? Boston: Heath, 1939.
Speer, Albert. Inside the Third Reich. New York: Macmillan,
    1970.
Stein, George H., ed. Hitler. Englewood Cliffs, N.J.: Prentice-
    Hall, 1968.
Strasser, Otto. Hitler and I. Boston: Houghton Mifflin, 1940.
Taylor, Alan John Percivale. The Origins of the Second World
    War. New York: Atheneum, 1962.
Tobias, Fritz. The Reichstag Fire: Legend and Truth. London:
    Secker and Warburg, 1963.
Toland, John. Adolf Hitler. Garden City, N.Y.: Doubleday, 1977.
Wheeler-Bennett, John W. The Nemesis of Power: The German
    Army in Politics, 1918-1945. New York: Viking Press, 1952.
Wilmot, Chester. The Struggle for Europe. New York: Harper &
    Row, 1952.

THE GREAT BLOOD PURGE (1934)

Adolf Hitler was appointed Chancellor of Germany by the
aged President Paul von Hindenburg on January 30, 1933. This
was arranged by former Chancellor Franz von Papen and a conservative group of politicians. These conservatives wrongly imagined
that they could use Hitler to promote their own interests. Within
the next four months he assumed full control, destroyed the Communist and Socialist parties and the labor unions, eliminated the
federal structure of the republic and forced both the bourgeois and
the right wing parties to dissolve. On March 23, 1933, the Reichstag enacted legislation granting him dictatorial powers.

In the spring of 1934 Hitler was faced with trouble within
the Nazi Party. His ambition to become actual dictator was hampered by the S.A. (Sturmabteilungen) his armed storm troopers or
"Brown Shirts," led by Ernst Röhm and numbering between two and
three million men, a force larger than the regular army.

Röhm, who favored a second revolution, wished the SA to be
made the nucleus of a new force, the other components of which
would be the army and Heinrich Himmler's Schuetzstaffeln ("Black
Shirts"), the combined force to be under Röhm's leadership. This
proposal was opposed by the army high command and appeal was
made to President von Hindenburg. This led to bad feeling between
Röhm and General Werner von Blomberg, Minister of War. The
situation came to a head when, in April, it was realized that von
Hindenburg had not much longer to live and the matter of the presidential succession had to be settled.

Hitler was aware that the conservative elements in Germany

wished to restore the Hohenzollern monarchy following von Hindenburg's death and that this constituted a serious threat to his ambitions. He survived the crisis by the use of radical, cold-blooded methods. While on naval maneuvers aboard the battleship Deutschland he, General Blomberg, Colonel Freiherr von Fritsche and Admiral Erich Raeder agreed to suppress Röhm and the SA, support the army and make Hitler president in name and dictator in fact.

On June 4, 1934, Hitler met with Röhm and attempted to persuade him to abandon his idea of a second revolution. Unsuccessful in this, Hitler then ordered the SA to go on leave and forbade its members to wear their brown uniforms during the month of July.

On June 30 Hitler met with Röhm again, this time at Wiesse, near Munich. There, with the help of Hermann Goering, President of the Reichstag, Himmler and members of the SS, he had the leaders of the SA murdered. Shot were Röhm, Edmund Heines, SA leader in Silesia, Karl Ernst, SA leader in Berlin, Gustav von Kahr, General Kurt von Schleicher and his wife, General von Bredow and Gregor Strasser, the last being the leader of the German left wing.

Just how many of Hitler's political opponents died in the Great Blood Purge is not known. On July 15 Hitler, in a speech at the Reichstag, asserted that 77 "enemies of the state" had been done away with. Other sources put the figure at anywhere between 401 and more than a thousand.

President Paul von Hindenburg died on August 2, 1934. Hitler assumed complete command of Germany and, abandoning the title of "President," was called "Führer and Reich Chancellor."

Suggested Readings

Archer, Jules. The Dictators. New York: Hawthorn Books, 1967.
Bullock, Alan. Hitler: A Study in Tyranny. New York: Harper
    & Row, 1962.
Elliott, Brendan John. Hitler and Germany. New York: McGraw-
    Hill, 1968.
Heiden, Konrad. Der Fuehrer: Hitler's Rise to Power. Boston:
    Houghton Mifflin, 1944.
Hitler, Adolf. Mein Kampf. Boston: Houghton Mifflin, 1943.
Holborn, Hajo. A History of Modern Germany. Vol. III: 1840-
    1945. New York: Knopf, 1969.
Jarman, T. L. The Rise and Fall of Nazi Germany. New York:
    New York University Press, 1956.
Ravenscroft, Trevor. Spear of Destiny. New York: Putnam, 1973.
Sapinsley, Barbara. From Kaiser to Hitler: The Life and Death
    of a Democracy, 1919-1933. New York: Grosset & Dunlap, 1968.
Schoenbaum, David. Hitler's Social Revolution. Garden City, N.Y.:
    Doubleday, 1966.
Shirer, William L. The Rise and Fall of Adolf Hitler. New York:
    Random House, 1961.

_____ . The Rise and Fall of the Third Reich: A History of Na-
    zi Germany. New York: Simon & Schuster, 1960.
Smith, Bradley F. Adolf Hitler: His Family, Childhood and Youth.
    Stanford, Calif. : Stanford University Press, 1967.
Speer, Albert. Inside the Third Reich. New York: Macmillan,
    1970.
Stein, George H. , ed. Hitler. Englewood Cliffs, N. J. : Prentice-
    Hall, 1968.
Strasser, Otto. Hitler and I. Boston: Houghton Mifflin, 1940.
Sulzberger, C. L. The American Heritage Picture History of World
    War II. New York: American Heritage Publishing Co. , 1966.
Taylor, Alan John Percivale. The Origins of the Second World
    War. New York: Atheneum, 1961.
Wheeler-Bennett, John W. The Nemesis of Power: The German
    Army in Politics, 1918-1945. New York: Viking Press, 1952.

THE DOLLFUSS ASSASSINATION (1934)

In the early chapters of his book, Mein Kampf, Adolf Hitler
wrote that the reunion of Austria and Germany was "a task to be
furthered, with every means our lives long. " His effort to take
over the former country was not immediately successful, even though
he resorted to assassination in his attempt to do so.

The victim was Chancellor Engelbert Dollfuss who, at noon
on July 25, 1934, was murdered by members of the Nazi Black
Shirts wearing Austrian army uniforms. Led by Otto Planetta, a
Nazi storm trooper, the Guards broke into the Federal Chancellery
at Vienna. Planetta fired two shots at the Chancellor, one entering his neck and the other wounding him in the armpit. The shooting was done at a range of two feet.

Dollfuss, after a brilliant career as an Austrian statesman,
which included positions as president of the federal railways and
minister of agriculture and forestry, was appointed Chancellor in
1932. As Chancellor and as a leading member of the Christian
Socialist Party, he resisted Germany's efforts to incorporate with
Austria. To achieve this resistance he made an alliance with the
Heimwehr (Home Guard) which was reputedly backed by Benito Mussolini, dictator of Italy.

Hitler came into power in Germany and President Wilhelm
Miklas of Austria, in March, 1933, invested Chancellor Dollfuss
with extraordinary powers. Dollfuss promptly dissolved parliament,
the Communist Party and the Schutzbund and abolished freedom of
assembly, press and speech and in June outlawed the Nazi Party,
including the wearing of the Nazi uniform.

Fourteen months later Dollfuss was assassinated. Hitler was
attending the opera at Beyrouth when news of the Austrian chancel-

lor's death was relayed to him. He was, according to witnesses, pleased and excited, although he denied having any connection with the murder. Dollfuss' death was announced on the Vienna radio as a "resignation."

Kurt von Schuschnigg, the new Austrian chancellor, tried to preserve Austrian independence by treaties with Italy and other neighboring countries. When, in 1936, the Rome-Berlin Axis was formed, Italy's position became doubtful. In 1938 Schuschnigg reached an agreement with Hitler concerning Austro-German relations. The Austrian Nazi leader, Artur von Seyss-Inquart, was placed in charge of the Austrian police, paving the way for the Nazis to gain control of the country. Hitler, on March 12, 1938, declared Austria to be a part of Germany and the country was immediately occupied by Nazi troops.

Suggested Readings

Archer, Jules. The Dictators. New York: Hawthorn Books, 1967.

Ball, Margaret M. Post-War German-Austrian Relations: The Anschluss Movement, 1918-1936. Stanford, Calif.: Stanford University Press, 1937.

Braunthal, Julius. The Tragedy of Austria. London: Victor Gollancz, 1948.

Brook-Shepherd, Gordon. Anschluss: The Rape of Austria. London: Macmillan, 1963.

_____. Dollfuss. New York: St. Martin's Press, 1961.

_____. Prelude to Infamy: The Story of Chancellor Dollfuss of Austria. Stamford, Conn.: Astor-Honor, Inc., 1962.

Bullock, Alan. Hitler: A Study in Tyranny. New York: Harper & Row, 1962.

Elliott, Brendan John. Hitler and Germany. New York: McGraw-Hill, 1968.

Gehl, Jurgen. Austria, Germany, and the Anschluss, 1931-1938. New York: Oxford University Press, 1963.

Goldston, Robert. The Life and Death of Nazi Germany. Indianapolis: Bobbs-Merrill, 1967.

Grunberger, Richard. Germany, 1918-1945. New York: Harper & Row, 1966.

Gulick, Charles A., Jr. Austria: From Habsburg to Hitler. Berkeley, Calif.: University of California Press, 1948.

Haines, C. Grover, and J. Ross Hoffman. The Origins and Background of the Second World War. New York: Oxford University Press, 1943.

Heiden, Konrad. Der Fuehrer: Hitler's Rise to Power. Boston: Houghton Mifflin, 1944.

Hitler, Adolf. Mein Kampf. Boston: Houghton Mifflin, 1943.

Höhne, Heinz. Order of the Death's Head: The Story of Hitler's S.S. Translated by Richard Barry. New York: Coward McCann, 1969.

Holborn, Hajo. A History of Modern Germany. Vol. III: 1840-1945. New York: Knopf, 1969.

Jarman, T. L.   The Rise and Fall of Nazi Germany.   New York:
    New York University Press, 1956.
MacDonald, Mary.   The Republic of Austria, 1918-1934:   A Study
    in the Failure of Democratic Government.   London: Oxford
    University Press, 1946.
Namier, Lewis B.   Europe in Decay: A Study in Disintegration,
    1936-1940.   London: Macmillan, 1949.
Prittie, Terence, and the editors of Life.   Germany.   New York:
    Time, Inc., 1961.
Schlesinger, Arthur M., Jr.   The Age of Roosevelt.   Boston:
    Houghton Mifflin, 1957.
Schuschnigg, Kurt von.   Austrian Requiem.   Translated by Franz
    von Hildebrand.   New York: Putnam's, 1964.
                . My Austria.   New York: Knopf, 1938.
Shirer, William L.   The Rise and Fall of Adolf Hitler.   New York:
    Random House, 1961.
                . The Rise and Fall of the Third Reich: A History of Na-
    zi Germany.   New York: Simon & Schuster, 1960.
Speer, Albert.   Inside the Third Reich.   New York: Macmillan,
    1970.
Stein, George H., ed.   Hitler.   Englewood Cliffs, N. J. :   Prentice-
    Hall, 1968.
Taylor, Alan John Percivale.   The Origins of the Second World
    War.   New York: Atheneum, 1961.
Toland, John.   Adolf Hitler.   Garden City, N. Y. :   Doubleday, 1977.
Wilmot, Chester.   The Struggle for Europe.   New York: Harper
    & Row, 1952.
Wiskemann, Elizabeth.   "Dollfuss: The Road to Anschluss" in Tay-
    lor, A. J. P. , editor-in-chief.   Purnell's History of the 20th
    Century, Vol. 6.   New York: Purnell, 1971.
                . The Rome-Berlin Axis: A History of the Relations Be-
    tween Hitler and Mussolini.   London: Oxford University Press,
    1949.

THE ASSASSINATION OF ALEXANDER I
OF YUGOSLAVIA (1934)

On October 9, 1934, King Alexander I of Yugoslavia arrived
at Marseille, France, on the light cruiser Dubrovnik. He had
traveled to France for the purpose of making a state visit and was
met by Jacques Piétri, the French Minister of Marine, and other
members of an official welcoming party.

At 4 P. M. a launch brought the king and his entourage ashore
at the Quai des Belges, where a guard of honor had been assembled.
The troops comprising the guard were solely for display and were
in no manner concerned with the security of the king.   At the wharf
the king was welcomed by Louis Barthou, the French Foreign Minister.   Bands played the national anthems of Yugoslavia and France
and the Mayor of Marseille led the two to a waiting automobile in

which they were to ride in a procession.   The car which had been assigned to the king was an old landaulet, the rear half of which had been lowered.

King Alexander took his seat on the right hand side of the car and Barthou sat on his left.   General Alphonse Georges, assigned to accompany the king during the visit, sat in a collapsible side seat. He was unarmed.   Lieutenant-Colonel Poillet and Captain Vigoreaux, mounted army escorts, were waiting.   The king's car was chauffeured by a French soldier named Froessac.

A second car was occupied by Bogoljub Jevtić, the Yugoslav Foreign Minister, Jacques Piétri and the Mayor of Marseille.   A third car carried General Dimitrijević, the king's personal attaché and the local chief of police.

The motorcade got under way.   As it proceeded up the Canebière, the main thoroughfare of the port, spectators cheered.   General Georges noticed that Poillet and Vigoreaux, the cavalry escort, were riding in advance of the king's car and not to the left and right where they were supposed to be.

Suddenly a man, later found to be using the alias "Petrus Kelemen," jumped from the crowd, sprang onto the running board of the royal automobile and began firing at its occupants with a Mauser pistol.   Captain Vigoreaux subsequently testified that he thought the sound of the pistol shots was that of distant machine guns.   Froessac, the chauffeur, looked around, saw the assassin and attempted to push him from the running board with one hand while steering the car with the other.   Failing in this, he stopped the car and, from his seat, attempted to throw the man off the car. The crowd, not realizing that the king had been shot, continued to cheer.

General Georges sprang at the assassin who shot the general four times, wounding him in the chest, the side and both arms. King Alexander was slumped in the right hand corner of the car and Barthou was on his knees, moaning in agony.

Celestin Galy, a police officer, saw the assassin on the running board of the car but thought him to be an overly-aggressive photographer, and so merely ordered him away.   The assassin promptly shot him in the stomach.   He died a few months later.

Louis Barthou, who had been shot in the right arm above the elbow, staggered from the car and wandered away.   He was later found and taken to the hospital, dying from loss of blood.   The regicide fell from the running board and rolled on the ground.   A policeman shot him in the head, rendering him unconscious but not killing him.

Froessac, on instructions from the chief of police, started the car and drove to the Prefecture.   There Dr. Assali, who had been

summoned, pronounced the king dead. When the body was examined
it was found to have been hit by two bullets, one each through the
heart and liver. General Georges, who had been seriously wounded, ultimately recovered. Two bystanders, both women, were fatally shot. In all, ten persons were wounded, six mortally, including "Kelemen," who died that evening in the hospital to which he
had been taken. He had spoken not one word after shooting the king.

An official investigation of the assassination disclosed that
security arrangements had been surprisingly lax. Responsibility
for the insufficient protection provided King Alexander has never
been definitely placed. It has been alleged that the key to the regicide lay in the complex international Yugoslavian political situation
and that certain foreign powers were attempting to exploit it for
their own ends. "Petrus Kelemen" has never been identified. A
Macedonian terrorist, he was a member of IMRO (the Internal Macedonian Revolutionary Organization) who had already perpetrated a
number of political murders in various countries. It is possible
that he was loaned by IMRO to the Ustasi, a Croat terrorist organization which had embarked on a program of intimidation in Yugoslavia in protest against the Serbian policies and rule of King Alexander.

"Petrus Keleman" had at least three accomplices in the assassination of the king. One was Mio Kralj, whose assignment was
to throw bombs into the crowd, but who lost his nerve and fled.
The other two were Zvonim Pospicil and Ivan Ragic, who were to
make a second attempt on King Alexander's life should the first one
fail. In February, 1936, these three were apprehended, arrested
and tried, along with certain other Ustasi leaders who were judged
in absentia. Kralj, Pospicil and Ragic were sentenced to life imprisonment, the others to death.

Suggested Readings

"After the Assassination," New Republic, October 24, 1934.
"Alexander and Barthou: Outstanding Political Figures," Literary
    Digest, October 20, 1934.
Armstrong, H. F. "After the Assassination of King Alexander,"
    Foreign Affairs, January, 1935.
"Assassination of Jugo-Slav King," Catholic World, November, 1934.
Gordon-Smith, G. "Peace and Union in Balkans," National Repub-
    lic, March, 1934.
Graham, Stephen. Alexander of Yugoslavia: The Story of the King
    Who Was Murdered at Marseille. New Haven, Conn.: Yale
    University Press, 1939.
Hurwood, Bernhardt Jackson. Society and the Assassin: A Back-
    ground Book on Political Murder. New York: Parents' Maga-
    zine Press, 1970.
Leab, Daniel J. "Murder in Marseille" in Taylor, A. J. P., editor
    in chief. Purnell's History of the 20th Century, Vol. 6. New
    York: Purnell, 1971.

McConnell, Brian. History of Assassination. Nashville, Tenn. :
    Aurora, 1970.
Melville, C. F. "Alexander of Yugoslavia, " Nineteenth Century and
    After, November, 1934.
Roberts, Allen. Turning Point: The Assassination of Louis Bar-
    thou and King Alexander I of Yugoslavia. New York: St. Mar-
    tin's Press, 1970.
"Secret Societies, A Balkan Institution, " Literary Digest, October
    27, 1934.
Symons, Julian. "The End of a World" in his A Pictorial History
    of Crime. New York: Crown Publishers, 1966.
"Three Will Hang for Plot Against Alexander, " News Week, April
    7, 1934.
Vukdjevich, Stephen. Alexander I, Creator of the State and Unifier.
    Belgrade, 1937 (in Serbian).
"Yugoslavian King, Barthou Killed in France by Assassin, " News
    Week, October 13, 1934.

THE ITALIAN CONQUEST OF ETHIOPIA (1935-1936)

On October 3, 1935, the kingdom of Ethiopia in Eastern Africa declared war on Italy. This war, which was to result in an
overwhelming victory for the Italian forces, was occasioned by Italy's invasion of the African kingdom after a year of mounting tension and intensive preparation.

In the 19th century Italy had attempted, along with other
European nations, to "colonize" various areas on the African continent. Her colonies of Eritrea and Somaliland were poor, compared to those of other European countries and she attempted to add
Ethiopia, the last African country free of European domination, to
her others. In 1896 her armies were decisively defeated by Ethiopian forces at Aduwa and, by means of a treaty, Italy recognized
Ethiopia's complete independence.

Italy, however, continued to covet the Ethiopian territory.
In 1906 she signed an agreement with Great Britain and France by
which all three nations would maintain the status quo of the African
country. In 1928 she signed a treaty of friendship and non-aggression with Haile Selassie, at that time the Ethiopian emperor.

Italy was dissatisfied with the division of spoils resulting
from the Versailles Treaty of 1919 following World War I, the conditions of which were not met. This increased her desire to take
over the Ethiopian kingdom, regardless of whatever agreements may
have been made with other European countries or with Haile Selassie.

In December, 1934, Italian and Ethiopian military units clashed
at Wal Wal, a nomadic water source claimed by Italy. The Italians

were the aggressors and the incident was followed by an Italian
claim for compensation and an apology. Ethiopia requested arbitration under the terms of the 1928 treaty of friendship and non-
aggression.

The Ethiopian request was promptly rejected by Benito Mussolini, the Italian dictator, who had decided on a policy of colonial
aggrandizement. Under pressure from Great Britain and France,
Mussolini agreed to arbitrate the Wal Wal incident, but this was
lip service only and came to nothing. The League of Nations postponed taking any action in the matter and Mussolini used the time
to assemble troops, armaments and equipment in preparation for an
invasion of the African kingdom.

On September 3, 1935, a settlement of the Wal Wal affair
was announced but Italy had no intention of honoring it. The following day she presented the League Council a memorandum stating
that Ethiopia "was a barbarous and uncivilized state who, by her
conduct, openly placed herself outside the Covenant of the League. "
On October 3 the world was informed that "Ethiopia's warlike, aggressive spirit had imposed war on Italy. "

By using intensive propaganda methods, Mussolini succeeded
in arousing an emotional feeling of patriotism in the Italian people.
The brainwashed soldiers who embarked at Naples were enthusiastic
at the prospect of "winning riches and glory in defense of their country. " They were well equipped with modern weapons and, by contrast, the Ethiopian forces with their outmoded Etienne rifles and
spears stood little chance of repelling them. The Italian invaders
used motorized columns, mustard gas and tanks. Their ground
troops were reinforced with combat and observation aircraft.

Italy's first commander in chief in Ethiopia was General Em-
ilio de Bono. Mussolini, dissatisfied with what he considered the
general's lack of aggression, replaced him with General Pietro Badoglio in November. Badoglio had, as chief of staff, advised against
the Ethiopian aggression but, as a professional soldier, believed
that "wars are won only by smashing the enemy. " He embarked on
a program of meeting the Ethiopian forces head on and, using his
modern arms and equipment, overwhelming them. A battle at Mount
Aradam was won by the Italians and from then on "a series of blows
never gave the Ethiopians time to recover. " Haile Selassie urged
that his troops use guerrilla tactics but was overruled by his feudal
chiefs who remembered the 1896 victory at Aduwa and reasoned that
history would repeat itself 40 years later. This was not to be.

On May 5, 1936, General Badoglio, moving south from Eritrea, entered and took Addis Ababa, the Ethiopian capital. On May
9 he linked up with General Rodolfo Graziani in Diredawa, advancing from Italian Somaliland.

Four days later Mussolini proclaimed King Victor Emmanuel
of Italy emperor of Ethiopia. Haile Selassie fled through Palestine

to England where he took refuge.   He appealed to the League of
Nations, addressing the Assembly in person on June 29.

In 1940 Italy declared war on Great Britain.   British forces,
assisted by Ethiopian patriot elements, invaded Ethiopia and by November, 1941, the Italians had been driven out and Haile Selassie
resumed his throne.

Historians consider the Italo-Ethiopian war directly responsible for the failure of the League of Nations.   The League was
doomed as it had demonstrated that it was unable to halt the war
and enforce the sanctity of peace "which the democracies regarded
as an article of faith. "

Suggested Readings

Archer, Jules.   The Dictators.   New York: Hawthorn Books, 1967.
Badoglio, Pietro.   The War in Abyssinia.   London: Methuein, 1937.
Baer, George W.   The Coming of the Italian-Ethiopian War.   Cam-
    bridge, Mass. :   Harvard University Press, 1967.
Baker, Ray Stannard.   Woodrow Wilson and the World Settlement.
    Gloucester, Mass. :   Peter Smith, 1948.
Barker, Lieut. -Colonel A. J.   "The Rape of Ethiopia" in Taylor,
    A. J. P. , editor-in-chief.   Purnell's History of the 20th Century,
    Vol. 6.   New York: Purnell, 1971.
Benns, F. Lee.   Europe Since 1914 in Its World Setting. New York:
    Appleton-Century-Crofts, 1945.
Binchey, Daniel.   Church and State in Fascist Italy.   London: Ox-
    ford University Press, 1941.
Dos Passos, John.   "Meester Veelson" in his Nineteen-Nineteen.
    New York: Random House, 1931.
Haines, C. Grover, and J. Ross Hoffman.   The Origins and Back-
    ground of the Second World War.   New York: Oxford Univer-
    sity Press, 1943.
Hansen, Harry.   "The Forgotten Men of Versailles" in Leighton,
    Isabel, ed.   The Aspirin Age, 1919-1941.   New York: Simon
    & Schuster, 1949.
Macartney, M. H. H. , and P. Cremona.   Italy's Foreign and Colon-
    ial Policy, 1914-1937.   London: Oxford University Press, 1938.
Mosley, Leonard.   Haile Selassie: The Conquering Lion.   London:
    Weidenfeld and Nicolson, 1964.
Salvemini, Gaetano.   Prelude to World War II.   London: Victor
    Gallancz, Ltd. , 1953.
Seton-Watson, R. W.   Britain and the Dictators.   London: Methuen,
    1939.
Snell, John L.   The Outbreak of the Second World War: Design or
    Blunder?   Boston: Heath, 1962.
Syme, Ronald.   Invaders and Invasions.   New York: Norton, 1964.
Taylor, Alan John Percivale.   The Origins of the Second World War.
    New York: Atheneum, 1961.
Walters, F. P.   A History of the League of Nations.   London: Ox-
    ford University Press, 1960.

Ward, A. W. , and George P. Gooch, eds. The Cambridge History
  of British Foreign Policy. New York: Macmillan, 1923.
Wiskemann, Elizabeth. The Rome-Berlin Axis: A History of the
  Relations Between Hitler and Mussolini. London: Oxford University Press, 1949.
Zimmern, Alfred. The League of Nations and the Rule of Law,
  1918-1935. London: Macmillan, 1936.

JOHN MAYNARD KEYNES' THE GENERAL THEORY OF EMPLOYMENT, INTEREST, AND MONEY (1936)

        Economics, the science treating of the production, distribu-
tion and consumption of goods and services, is one which is characterized by many differing schools of thought. One of the outstanding economists of the twentieth century was the British John Maynard Keynes (1883-1946) who, in 1936, published his significant
theory of economics in his book The General Theory of Employment,
Interest, and Money. Keynes did not agree with the classical economists who argued that alternate periods of depression and prosperity are caused by the law of supply and demand. He contended that
it is possible for man to control and alter economic conditions by
the use of judicious policy.

        Keynes, the son of an economist, attended Cambridge Uni-
versity, became a civil servant, was a Cambridge professor and,
in 1919, went to the Versailles Peace Talks as a member of the
British delegation. He was dissatisfied with the "vindictive character of the settlement" and in his book The Economic Consequences
of the Peace (1919) criticized it severely. He became wealthy from
speculation in international currency, continued to teach at Cambridge, edited the Economic Journal, acted as an economic consult-
ant, and continued writing and publishing books. These included a
tract on monetary reform (1923) and A Treatise on Money (1930).

        The stock market crash of October, 1929, ushered in the
worldwide economic depression which was to last for almost a
decade. The classical economists, holding to their theory of supply and demand, believed that these forces would shortly restore
the pre-crash prosperity. They reasoned that investment in economic facilities, such as factories, was necessary, inasmuch as expansion would create a demand for goods and services. Increased
prices must necessarily follow such expansion as firms and individuals competed for the available services and commodities. This,
in turn, would discourage additional investment after prices reached
unreasonable highs, whereupon stagnation and depression would set
in and prices would decline.

        The Great Depression, however, did not show any signs of
disappearing. Keynes' 1936 book, The General Theory of Employment, Interest, and Money, offered an explanation of the Depression.

It is considered his major work and one of the most influential publications of the twentieth century.

Keynes proposes that the economy is not governed by supply and demand which were thought to correct imbalances. He argues that the savings which supposedly would be invested when prices sank sufficiently to make such investment attractive would not necessarily exist, having been dissipated as the depression deepened. By the same token, he states, savings tend to increase in boom times, "thus threatening the possibility of excess savings which would not be adequately used for investment purposes. " This would cause the economy to recede. He contends further that investment as such is not a reliable stimulus to the economy as knowledgeable businessmen are well aware that overexpansion can be uneconomical and financially disastrous.

Franklin Delano Roosevelt in 1933, during his first term as President, had inaugurated a series of government-sponsored work projects such as the Civilian Conservation Corps and the Federal Emergency Relief Administration. These were designed to relieve unemployment. Keynes visited the President in 1934 and was favorably impressed with the idea of the government spending money to compensate for unemployment in private industry. In his 1936 book he proposes government aid as a solution to the unemployment situation, feeling that such aid would stimulate the economy and hasten the return of prosperity.

Keynesian economic theory was accepted in some circles and rejected in others. One detractor was D. H. Robertson, a British economist who differed with Keynes intellectually. Other critics have accused him of socialist and even communist leanings, claiming that his theories favor total state control of the economy. Still others feel that he over-generalizes and gives insufficient consideration to specific problems.

Suggested Readings

Bakke, E. Wright. Citizens Without Work. New Haven, Conn. :
    Yale University Press, 1940.
_____. The Unemployed Worker. New Haven, Conn. : Yale
    University Press, 1940.
Brown, Douglas V. , et al. The Economics of the Recovery Program. New York: Da Capo Press, 1971.
Buchanan, James M. , and Richard E. Wagner. The Political Legacy of Lord Keynes. New York: Academic Press, 1977.
Dillard, Dudley E. The Economics of John Maynard Keynes. New
    York: Prentice-Hall, 1948.
Due, John F. Intermediate Economic Analysis. Homewood, Ill. :
    Richard D. Irwin, 1953.
Fellner, W. "Employment Theory and Business Cycles" in Ellis,
    H. S. , ed. A Survey of Contemporary Economics. Philadelphia: Blakiston, 1948.

Goldston, Robert C. The Great Depression: The United States in
  the Thirties. Indianapolis: Bobbs-Merrill, 1968.
Hansen, Alvin H. A Guide to Keynes. New York: McGraw-Hill,
  1953.
————. Monetary Theory and Fiscal Policy. New York: Mc-
  Graw-Hill, 1949.
Harris, Seymour E. John Maynard Keynes, Economist and Policy
  Maker. New York: Scribner's, 1955.
————, ed. The New Economics. New York: Knopf, 1948.
Harrod, R. F. The Life of John Maynard Keynes. New York: Har-
  court, Brace, 1951.
Hatch, Alden. Franklin D. Roosevelt: An Informal Biography. New
  York: Holt, 1947.
Hayek, Friedrich A. The Road to Serfdom. Chicago: University
  of Chicago Press, 1944.
Holland, Kenneth, and Frank Ernest Hill. Youth in the CCC. Wash-
  ington, D. C. : Brookings Institution, 1942.
Hopkins, Harry L. Spending to Save: The Complete Story of Re-
  lief. New York: Norton, 1936.
Hutt, William H. Keynesianism. Chicago: Henry Regnery Co. ,
  1963.
Keynes, John Maynard. The Economic Consequences of the Peace.
  New York: Harper & Row, 1971 (Originally published 1919).
————. The General Theory of Employment, Interest, and Money.
  New York: Harcourt, Brace, 1936.
————. A Treatise on Money. New York: Harcourt Brace,
  1930.
Kimmel, Lewis. Federal Budget and Fiscal Policy, 1789-1958.
  Washington, D. C. : Brookings Institution, 1959.
Leijonkufvud, Axel. On Keynesian Economics and the Economics
  of Keynes. New York: Oxford University Press, 1968.
Lekachman, Robert. The Age of Keynes. New York: Random
  House, 1966.
Leuchtenburg, William E. Franklin D. Roosevelt and the New Deal,
  1932-1940. New York: Harper, 1963.
Moley, Raymond, with the assistance of Elliot A. Rosen. The First
  New Deal. New York: Harcourt, Brace, 1966.
Morgan, Theodore. Income and Employment. New York: Prentice-
  Hall, 1947.
Robinson, Joan. Introduction to the Theory of Employment. Lon-
  don: Macmillan, 1937.
Ruggles, Richard. An Introduction to National Income and Income
  Analysis. New York: McGraw-Hill, 1949.
Schnittkind, Henry Thomas. Franklin Delano Roosevelt. New York:
  Putnam, 1962.
Searle, Charles. Harry L. Hopkins, New Deal Administrator, 1933-
  38 (Unpublished Ph. D. dissertation, University of Illinois, 1953).
Seldes, Gilbert. The Years of the Locust: America, 1929-1932.
  New York: Da Capo Press, 1973.
Shannon, David A. The Great Depression. Englewood Cliffs, N. J. :
  Prentice-Hall, 1960.
Sherwood, Robert E. Roosevelt and Hopkins: An Intimate History.
  New York: Harper & Row, 1950.

Spero, Sterling D. Government Jobs. Philadelphia: Lippincott, 1945.

Wecter, Dixon. The Age of the Great Depression, 1929-1941. New York: Macmillan, 1948.

THE ABDICATION OF EDWARD VIII (1936)

On June 10, 1931, Mrs. Ernest Simpson (Wallis Warfield), the American previously-divorced wife of a London stockbroker, was presented at the English court. There she met Eward, Prince of Wales, the bachelor future King of England.

Following the death of his father, George V, Edward ascended the throne on January 20, 1936. In November of that year he told Prime Minister Stanley Baldwin that he wished to marry Mrs. Simpson who, in the meantime, had divorced her stockbroker husband. Baldwin and the cabinet opposed the marriage which would transgress the views of the Church of England on divorce and re-marriage. The situation was particularly acute as Edward, as King, was Supreme Governor of the Church. Cosmo Gordon Lang, Archbishop of Canterbury, upheld the Church's view.

Edward was legally entitled to marry any woman he chose, but constitutionally he was obliged to accept the views of the cabinet. It was feared that many English citizens would oppose the marriage of their monarch to a twice-divorced American commoner and that the unity of the British people and solidarity of the Commonwealth would be irreparably damaged should the nuptials take place.

The English press had not publicized the situation prior to December 3, on which date the story broke and made headlines the world over. On December 5 Edward notified Prime Minister Baldwin that he intended to abdicate. Parliament was informed of the King's decision on December 10 and the following day an Abdication Bill was introduced. It passed both houses and received the royal assent. This made the former king a private citizen. He was succeeded on the throne by his brother, the Duke of York, who became King George VI. Edward was made Duke of Windsor.

That evening Edward made a worldwide radio broadcast in which he announced his decision. He said, "I have found it impossible to carry the heavy burden of responsibility and to discharge my duties as King as I should wish to do, without the help and support of the woman I love.... And now we all have a new king. I wish him and you, his people, happiness and prosperity with all my heart. God bless you all! God save the King!"

Edward and the former Mrs. Simpson were married on June 3, 1937, following which they lived briefly in France. Edward was governor of the Bahama Islands from 1940 to 1945 and died in Paris on May 28, 1972. His wife, known as the Duchess of Windsor, was not accorded the title of Royal Highness nor did the royal family receive or acknowledge her.

Suggested Readings

Annual Register. London: St. Martin's Press, 1936.

Beaverbrook, Lord. The Abdication of King Edward VIII. Edited by A. J. P. Taylor. New York: Atheneum, 1966.

Bocca, Geoffrey. The Woman Who Would Be Queen. New York: Rinehart, 1934.

Bolitho, Hector. King Edward VIII. Philadelphia: Lippincott, 1937.

Brody, Iles. Gone with the Windsors. Philadelphia: Winston, 1953.

Hibbert, Christopher. Edward: The Uncrowned King. London: St. Martin's Press, 1972.

Inglis, Brian. Abdication. New York: Macmillan, 1966.

Mackenzie, Compton. The Windsor Tragedy. New York: Stokes, 1938.

Martin, Ralph G. The Woman He Loved. New York: Simon & Schuster, 1973.

Middlemas, Keith, and John Barnes. Baldwin: A Biography. London: Weidenfeld & Nicolson, 1969.

Mowat, Charles Loch. Britain Between Two Wars. London: Methuen, 1956.

Raymond, John, ed. The Baldwin Age. London: Eyre & Spottiswoode, 1961.

Taylor, A. J. P. English History, 1914-1945. New York: Oxford University Press, 1965.

Times (London). "The History of the Times: The 150th Anniversary and Beyond, 1912-1948." Vol. IV, Part II, 1921-1948. New York: Macmillan, 1952.

Wilson, Edwina. Her Name Was Wallis Warfield. New York: Dutton, 1936.

Windsor, The Duchess of. The Heart Has Its Reasons. New York: McKay, 1956.

Windsor, The Duke of. The Crown and the People. New York: Funk & Wagnalls, 1954.

_____. A King's Story: The Memoirs of the Duke of Windsor. New York: Putnam, 1951.

_____. Windsor Revisited. Boston: Houghton Mifflin, 1960.

Young, G. M. Stanley Baldwin. London: Rupert Hart-Davis, 1952.

THE SPANISH CIVIL WAR (1936-1939)

The Spanish Civil War, originally designed as a short-lived military take-over from the Republicans by the Nationalists, became a long-drawn-out affair lasting from 1936 to 1939.

In the spring of 1936 Spain found herself in a state of chaos.

She had remained neutral in World War I and during this period her industries and shipyards prospered. This prosperity, the result of war manufactures, led the working classes to demand higher wages and better working conditions. Simultaneously military juntas began to spread, despite the efforts of the government to prevent them, for fear that the army officers would exert excessive influence on governmental affairs. Other disturbing factors contributed to the general unrest and within a five-year period no fewer than twelve cabinets fell.

On September 13, 1923, General Miguel Primo de Rivera took over the civil administration of Catalonia and two days later extended his military coup d'etat to Madrid. King Alfonso XIII, rather than act against the revolt, asked the general to form a government. The latter established a military dictatorship, proclaimed military law, dissolved the cortes (national legislative body), imposed strict press censorship and did away with trial by jury.

In 1925 the military dictatorship was replaced by a civil government, with Primo de Rivera as prime minister and virtual dictator. He had created the Union Patriótica, a semifascist party, to which all members of the new government belonged. Martial law was dispensed with in 1927 and the dictator established a program of financial reforms but neglected to institute the social reforms so badly needed in a situation where the peasants were extremely poor and at odds with both the aristocracy and the military.

The policies of the Union Patriótica government generated much resentment and on January 28, 1930, Primo de Rivera resigned, dying suddenly in Paris the same year. The monarchy was in a state of ruin, a situation not helped by the series of cabinets which attempted unsuccessfully to restore order. Outbreaks led by the Republicans occurred frequently. Republican candidates were voted into office and in April, 1931, King Alfonso left Spain but did not abdicate. The Second Spanish Republic was proclaimed immediately and the cortes found the king guilty of high treason. His property was confiscated and he was forbidden to return to Spain. He died in exile in 1941.

For the next five years the Republican government remained in control. Many changes were made. A new constitution was promulgated, calling for universal suffrage, a cortes and a ministry responsible to it. Education was secularized rather than church-dominated, the Jesuit order was dissolved and church property was confiscated. Many large estates were broken up and the land was redistributed.

Political strife continued. The Socialists, Syndicalists and Communists, all supporters of the Republican government, did not agree among themselves, nor could they act together to curb the disorders caused by the Anarchists and the Falange (Spanish Fascist party). This last, organized by José Antonio Primo de Rivera, the son of General de Rivera, responded violently to the actions of the

Anarchists, thereby demonstrating that the Republicans were unable
to cope with the problem.

Military officers planned a revolt to take over the Spanish
government and restore order. They had the support of the Falange
and the Monarchists who hoped to restore the king to the throne.
José Calvo Sotelo, Monarchist parliamentary leader, complained of
the civil disorder but Manuel Azaña, president of the Spanish Republic, was unable to take decisive action because of his apprehension concerning the Leftist extremists.

On July 13, 1936, Calvo Sotelo was arrested and killed in
retaliation for the Falangist assassination of a Liberal party member. This triggered the Spanish Civil War. On July 17 a military
revolt against the Republican government broke out. President
Azaña arranged for weapons to be distributed to the trade unions
and proletarian organizations. As a result of Azaña's action what
had been intended as a quick military take-over became, as mentioned above, a civil war lasting almost three years.

The Nationalists, supported by the church, landed aristocrats
and many moderates, were also able to obtain military assistance
from Benito Mussolini, dictator of Italy, and from Adolf Hitler, the
German Führer. General Francisco Franco had, by October, 1936,
emerged as the Nationalist leader and he proclaimed himself Caudillo (military leader) of Spain. Germany and Italy withdrew their
recognition of the legitimate Spanish government and shortly afterward recognized Franco.

The Republicans (Loyalists) were extremely disorganized.
The Anarchists inaugurated a reign of terror and precipitated a
proletarian revolution. Joseph Stalin, Russian dictator, furnished
the Republicans with troops, munitions, aeroplanes and military advisers and obtained control of the direction of the war. President
Azaña and Francisco Largo Caballero, leader of the Socialist party,
were unable to stop the revolution. The Western Powers avoided
taking part in the situation, not wishing to see it expand into a
wholesale European war.

Early in the conflict the rebel army reached the capital,
Madrid, and the government was removed to Valencia. At Madrid
the battle became a stalemate which continued until the end of the
hostilities. In other sectors Franco's forces were more successful and by the middle of 1937 Spain was completely occupied by the
insurgents. By 1939 the Nationalists, with their superior military
forces, prevailed and in April Franco seized Madrid and the war
was over.

Spain was reorganized as a totalitarian state. Political opposition to the party in power was prohibited by law and thousands
of Franco's opponents were sent to prison. Strikes and lockouts became illegal and trade unions were abolished. General Francisco
Franco was recognized as Caudillo of Spain, with absolute authority.

Suggested Readings

Brenan, Gerald. The Spanish Labyrinth: An Account of the Social
    and Political Background of the Civil War. Cambridge: The
    University Press, 1950.
Cattell, David C. Communism and the Spanish Civil War. Berke-
    ley, Calif. : University of California Press, 1955.
Goldston, Robert C. Civil War in Spain. Indianapolis: Bobbs-
    Merrill, 1966.
Guttmann, Allen, ed. American Neutrality and the Spanish Civil
    War. Boston: Heath, 1963.
Hemingway, Ernest. For Whom the Bell Tolls (fiction). New York:
    Scribner's, 1940.
Jackson, Gabriel. The Spanish Republic and the Civil War, 1931-
    1939. Princeton, N. J. : Princeton University Press, 1965.
Payne, Stanley G. Falange: A History of Spanish Fascism. Stan-
    ford, Calif. : Stanford University Press, 1961.
————. Franco's Spain. New York: Crowell, 1967.
————. Politics and the Military in Modern Spain. Stanford,
    Calif. : Stanford University Press, 1967.
Puzzo, Dante E. Spain and the Great Powers, 1936-1941. New
    York: New York University Press, 1962.
Ramos Oliveira, Antonio. Politics, Economics and Men of Modern
    Spain, 1808-1946. Translated by Teener Hall. London: Vic-
    tor Gollancz, 1946.
Snellgrove, Laurence Ernest. Franco and the Spanish Civil War.
    New York: McGraw-Hill, 1965.
Thomas, Hugh. The Spanish Civil War. New York: Harper &
    Row, 1961.
Werstein, Irving. Cruel Years: The Story of the Spanish Civil
    War. New York: Messner, 1969.

THE ANSCHLUSS (1938)

    Following World War I the Federal Republic of Austria,
formed after the disintegration of Austria-Hungary in 1918, was
handicapped by a number of circumstances. The war had left it
financially impoverished. The dismemberment of the Austro-Hun-
garian Empire deprived Austria of Bohemia and Moravia, both industrial areas, thus destroying the prewar balance between industry
and agriculture. The principle of dynastic nationalism which had
prevailed under the Hapsburgs no longer applied and "no other approach to nationalism seemed adequate to sustain an independent
Austria. "

    Because of these various factors a majority of the Austrians
began to favor Anschluss (union with Germany) despite the fact that
this was contrary to the provisions of the Treaty of Versailles and
the Treaty of St. Germain. Throughout the 1920's many Austrians
and Germans agitated for the Anschluss, although this was opposed

by France, Italy, Czechoslovakia, Yugoslavia and Romania. In
March, 1931, Austria and Germany announced a mutual agreement
on plans for a customs union but this idea was abandoned because
of the opposition of the countries mentioned above.

When Adolf Hitler became chancellor of Germany in 1933
the Anschluss movement lost favor with most Austrians, who did
not wish to ally themselves with National Socialism (Nazism). The
idea, however, was favored by the Austrian Nazi party which hoped
to seize control of that country.

In the Putsch of July 25, 1934, Austrian Nazis assassinated
Englebert Dollfuss, the Austrian chancellor, and took control of the
radio station at Vienna. Dollfuss was replaced as chancellor by Kurt
von Schuschnigg, founder and head of Ostmärkische Sturmscharen,
a patriotic organization the aim of which was to defend Austria's
independence. The Putsch failed when the Austrian government
stepped in and when Benito Mussolini, the Italian Fascist dictator,
sent four army divisions to the Austrian frontier. Hitler reconsidered his original intention of assisting the rebels and bided his
time.

Financial and political problems faced the Schuschnigg regime
and when the Italo-Ethiopian War of 1935 brought about an establishment of harmonic relations between Italy and Germany, the Austrian
government was forced to seek accommodation with Adolf Hitler.
Negotiations between the two countries resulted in the Austro-German Agreement of July, 1936. It was agreed that Hitler would respect Austrian independence. However, Schuschnigg was required
to admit two crypto-Nazis into the Austrian government and to agree
that his country s foreign policy would reflect the premise that Austria considered herself a German state.

When, in 1938, Hitler believed himself sufficiently strong
militarily and politically to force his demands on Austria successfully he met with Schuschnigg at Berchtesgaden on February 12.
Here he made a number of new demands of the Austrian chancellor,
including the appointment of Austrian Nazis to high governmental
positions. Artur von Seyss-Inquart, a German politician, was to
be made Austrian Minister of the Interior and Security. Schuschnigg
agreed to Hitler's demands but, upon returning to Austria, he attempted to nullify Germany's gains by announcing a plebiscite concerning Austrian independence. Hitler demanded that Schuschnigg
be replaced by Seyss-Inquart as chancellor. Seyss-Inquart was to
ask the German army to occupy Austria "to restore order. "

On March 12, 1938, German forces invaded Austria and on
April 10 a Nazi-controlled plebiscite in that country recorded a vote
of 99.73 percent in favor of the Anschluss. Schuschnigg was arrested and held in prison and at a concentration camp, from which
he was liberated in 1945. Seyss-Inquart, appointed by Hitler as
governor of the Austrian territory, later held several high level
positions in the Nazi party. He was hanged as a war criminal in
1946.

Suggested Readings

Archer, Jules. The Dictators. New York: Hawthorn Books, 1967.

Ball, Margaret M. Post-War German-Austrian Relations: The Anschluss Movement, 1918-1936. Stanford, Calif.: Stanford University Press, 1937.

Braunthal, Julius. The Tragedy of Austria. London: Victor Gollancz, 1948.

Brook-Shepherd, Gordon. Anschluss: The Rape of Austria. London: Macmillan, 1963.

_____. Dollfuss. New York: St. Martin's Press, 1961.

_____. Prelude to Infamy: The Story of Chancellor Dollfuss of Austria. Stamford, Conn.: Astor-Honor, Inc., 1962.

Bullock, Alan. Hitler: A Study in Tyranny. New York: Harper & Row, 1962.

Elliott, Brendan John. Hitler and Germany. New York: McGraw-Hill, 1968.

Gehl, Jürgen. Austria, Germany and the Anschluss, 1931-1938. New York: Oxford University Press, 1963.

Goldston, Robert. The Life and Death of Nazi Germany. Indianapolis: Bobbs-Merrill, 1967.

Grunberger, Richard. Germany, 1918-1945. New York: Harper & Row, 1966.

Gulick, Charles A., Jr. Austria: From Habsburg to Hitler. Berkeley, Calif.: University of California Press, 1948.

Haines, C. Grover, and J. Ross Hoffman. The Origins and Background of the Second World War. New York: Oxford University Press, 1943.

Heiden, Konrad. Der Fuehrer: Hitler's Rise to Power. Boston: Houghton Mifflin, 1944.

Hitler, Adolf. Mein Kampf. Boston: Houghton Mifflin, 1943.

Holborn, Hajo. A History of Modern Germany. Vol. III: 1840-1945. New York: Knopf, 1969.

Jarman, T. L. The Rise and Fall of Nazi Germany. New York: New York University Press, 1956.

MacDonald, Mary. The Republic of Austria, 1918-1934: A Study in the Failure of Democratic Government. London: Oxford University Press, 1946.

Namier, Lewis B. Europe in Decay: A Study in Disintegration, 1936-1940. London: Macmillan, 1949.

Prittie, Terence, and the editors of Life. Germany. New York: Time, Inc., 1961.

Schlesinger, Arthur M., Jr. The Age of Roosevelt. Boston: Houghton Mifflin, 1957.

Schuschnigg, Kurt von. Austrian Requiem. Translated by Franz von Hildebrand. New York: Putnam's, 1964.

_____. My Austria. New York: Knopf, 1938.

Shirer, William L. The Rise and Fall of Adolf Hitler. New York: Random House, 1961.

_____. The Rise and Fall of the Third Reich: A History of Nazi Germany. New York: Simon & Schuster, 1960.

Speer, Albert. Inside the Third Reich. New York: Macmillan, 1970

Stein, George H. , ed.   Hitler.   Englewood Cliffs, N. J. :   Prentice-
    Hall, 1968.
Taylor, Alan John Percivale.   The Origins of the Second World
    War.   New York: Atheneum, 1961.
Toland, John.   Adolf Hitler.   Garden City, N. Y. :   Doubleday, 1977.
Weingast, David Elliott.   Franklin D. Roosevelt, Man of Destiny.
    New York: Messner, 1952.
Wilmot, Chester.   The Struggle for Europe.   New York: Harper
    & Row, 1952.
Wiskemann, Elizabeth.   "Dollfuss: The Road to Anschluss" in Tay-
    lor, A. J. P. , editor-in-chief.   Purnell's History of the 20th
    Century, Vol. 6.   New York: Purnell, 1971.
_____. The Rome-Berlin Axis: A History of the Relations Be-
    tween Hitler and Mussolini.   London: Oxford University Press,
    1949.

THE NAZI INVASION OF POLAND (1939)

        After the German occupation of Prague and the annexation of
Czechoslovakia on March 15, 1939, Adolf Hitler, the German Führer, went about the taking over of Poland.   Ten days later Colonel
Jozef Beck, Prime Minister of Poland, was "requested" to report
to Berlin by Joachim von Ribbentrop, Prime Minister of Germany.
Beck was advised of Germany's demands.   One had to do with the
Free City of Danzig, in which Poland had certain economic inter-
ests.   The Germans stipulated that Danzig was to come under their
control.   A second demand stipulated that Germany was to receive
an extraterritorial road and railway across the Polish Corridor.
Third, Poland was to join with Germany in an anti-Russian policy.
Beck refused these demands.

        England and France, deeply concerned by the Nazi occupation
of Prague, had agreed that, should Germany invade Poland, they
would give the latter country full support.   This decision was announced by Neville Chamberlain, Prime Minister of Great Britain,
on March 31.   However, because of Germany's geographic position,
the two allies could not give effective direct assistance to Poland
and it was realized that greater help could come from Russia.   Because of this European diplomacy centered on Moscow.   Here Joseph Stalin, the Russian dictator, determined to learn the feelings
of both the Germans and the Allies, he being apprehensive concerning the increasingly great power manifested by Adolf Hitler.

        On Stalin's instructions Maksim Litvinov, Russian Commissar
for Foreign Affairs, on April 16 suggested a mutual assistance pact
between his country and the Allies.   On the 19th the Russian ambassador in Berlin sought to learn from the German Foreign Ministry how relations between his country and the Reich might be improved.   The Allies, after a three-week delay, rejected the Russian
proposal.   The German Ministry's answers to the Russian ambassador were noncommital.

Vyacheslav Mikhailovich Molotov replaced Litvinov as Russian Commissar for Foreign Affairs. On May 22 Hitler concluded a pact with Benito Mussolini, the Fascist dictator of Italy. This, known as the "Pact of Steel," pledged Germany and Italy to fight as allies in the event that either of them should go to war. On May 23 Hitler informed his generals that war with Poland was inevitable. German diplomats, hoping to keep Russia out of the impending conflict, negotiated with that country. The Allies also sent representatives to Moscow but were unable to come to any immediate agreement, particularly as Colonel Beck opposed Communistic Russia.

In August, 1939, Stalin decided to side with Hitler as he felt he could gain more by dealing with him than from Chamberlain and the French Premier, Edouard Daladier. The Russo-German Non-Aggression Pact was signed on August 24. This, a secret protocol, specified the manner in which Poland would be divided by the two aggressors.

Hitler then felt that because of his pacts with Italy and Russia his position was secure and that any help which Great Britain and France might give Poland would be unavailing. He ordered an attack on August 26, 1939. The British, however had, on August 25, signed a formal treaty with Poland and Mussolini gave Hitler to understand that, in the event of war, Italy would remain neutral. Consequently, Hitler ordered the invasion of Poland to be postponed.

Adolf Hitler then tried to separate the Poles from their French and English allies. When it became obvious that this attempt would be unsuccessful he ordered his forces to attack. At 4:45 on the morning of Friday, September 1, 1939, six panzer divisions, supported by the Nazi Luftwaffe, assailed Poland, with fantastic success. Within two weeks the defending armies were completely routed.

The Russians entered Poland from the east on September 17, seeking to secure their share of the conquered territory, and by October 2 all Polish resistance was at an end. England and France declared war against Germany on September 3. World War II was under way and was to continue until 1945.

Suggested Readings

Archer, Jules. The Dictators. New York: Hawthorn Books, 1967.
Armstrong, Hamilton Fish. When There Is No Peace. New York: Macmillan, 1940.
Beloff, Max. The Foreign Policy of Soviet Russia, 1929-1941. London: Oxford University Press, 1949.
Bullock, Alan. Hitler: A Study in Tyranny. New York: Harper & Row, 1962.
Carr, E. H. German-Soviet Relations Between the Two World Wars, 1919-1939. Baltimore: Johns Hopkins University Press, 1951.

Churchill, Winston S.   The Second World War.   Vol. I: "The Gathering Storm. "   Boston: Houghton Mifflin, 1948.
Ciano, Count Galeazzo.   The Ciano Diaries, 1939-1943.   Edited by H. Gibson.   Garden City, N. Y. :   Doubleday, 1946.
Colvin, Ian.   Vansittart in Office.   London: Victor Gollancz, 1965.
Dahlerus, J. Birger.   The Last Attempt.   Translated by A. Dick.   London: Hutchinson & Co. , 1948.
Dean, Vera Michelis.   Europe in Retreat.   New York: Knopf, 1939.
Elliott, Brendan John.   Hitler and Germany.   New York: McGraw-Hill, 1968.
Eubank, Keith.   Munich.   Norman, Okla. :   University of Oklahoma Press, 1963.
Goldston, Robert.   The Life and Death of Nazi Germany.   Indianapolis: Bobbs-Merrill, 1967.
Haines, C. Grover, and J. Ross Hoffman.   The Origins and Background of the Second World War.   New York: Oxford University Press, 1943.
Heiden, Konrad.   Der Fuehrer: Hitler's Rise to Power.   Boston: Houghton Mifflin, 1944.
Henderson, Sir Neville.   Failure of a Mission.   New York: Putnam's, 1940.
Hindus, Maurice.   We Shall Live Again.   Garden City, N. Y. :   Doubleday, 1939.
Hitler, Adolf.   Mein Kampf.   Boston: Houghton Mifflin, 1943.
Holborn, Hajo.   A History of Modern Germany.   Vol. III: 1840-1945.   New York: Knopf, 1969.
Jarman, T. L.   The Rise and Fall of Nazi Germany.   New York: New York University Press, 1956.
Langer, William L. , and S. Everett Gleason.   The Challenge to Isolation, 1937-1940.   New York: Harper & Row, 1952.
Namier, Lewis B.   Diplomatic Prelude, 1938-1939.   New York: Macmillan, 1948.
_____ .   Europe in Decay: A Study in Disintegration, 1936-1940.   London: Macmillan, 1949.
Ravenscroft, Trevor.   Spear of Destiny.   New York: Putnam, 1973.
Reynaud, Paul.   In the Thick of the Fight.   Translated by James P. Lambert.   New York: Simon & Schuster, 1955.
Rossi, A.   The Russo-German Alliance, August, 1939--June, 1941.   Boston: Beacon Press, 1951.
Sapinsley, Barbara.   From Kaiser to Hitler: The Life and Death of a Democracy, 1919-1933.   New York: Grosset & Dunlap, 1968.
Schoenbaum, David.   Hitler's Social Revolution.   Garden City, N. Y. :   Doubleday, 1966.
Seton-Watson, R. W.   Britain and the Dictators.   London: Methuen & Co. , 1939.
Shirer, William L.   The Rise and Fall of Adolf Hitler.   New York: Random House, 1961.
_____ .   The Rise and Fall of the Third Reich: A History of Nazi Germany.   New York: Simon & Schuster, 1960.
Smith, Bradley F.   Adolf Hitler: His Family, Childhood and Youth.   Stanford, Calif. :   Stanford University Press, 1967.
Snell, John L.   The Outbreak of the Second World War: Design or Blunder?   Boston: Heath, 1962.

Sontag, Raymond J. , and James S. Biddle, eds. Nazi-Soviet Relations, 1939-1941: Documents from the Archives of the German Foreign Office. Washington, D. C. : Department of State, 1948.

Speer, Albert. Inside the Third Reich. New York: Macmillan, 1970.

Stein, George H. , ed. Hitler. Englewood Cliffs, N. J. : Prentice-Hall, 1968.

Strasser, Otto. Hitler and I. Boston: Houghton Mifflin, 1940.

Sulsberger, G. L. The American Heritage Picture History of World War II. New York: American Heritage Publishing Co. , 1966.

Syme, Ronald. Invaders and Invasions. New York: Norton, 1964.

Taylor, Alan John Percivale. The Origins of the Second World War. New York: Atheneum, 1962.

Toynbee, Arnold, and Veronica M. Toynbee, eds. Survey of International Affairs, 1939-1946. The Eve of War, 1939. London: Oxford University Press, 1959.

Ulam, Adam B. Expansion and Coexistence: The History of Soviet Foreign Policy, 1917-67. New York: Frederick A. Praeger, 1968.

Werstein, Irving. Betrayal: The Munich Pact of 1938. Garden City, N. Y. : Doubleday, 1969.

Wheeler-Bennett, John W. Munich: Prologue to Tragedy. New York: Duell, Sloan & Pearce, 1948.

————. The Nemesis of Power: The German Army in Politics, 1918-1945. New York: Viking Press, 1952.

THE SCUTTLING OF THE ADMIRAL GRAF SPEE (1939)

World War II began with the invasion of Poland by Nazi Germany on September 1, 1939. France and the United Kingdom declared war on Germany on September 3, and ultimately most but not all of the nations of the world were engaged in the conflict, although some of them remained neutral during the early stages of the war.

In 1939 Germany had three pocket battleships, the Deutschland, the Admiral Scheer and the Admiral Graf Spee. On August 21 the Graf Spee, as she was generally called, left Wilhelmshaven--before war was actually declared--and took up a position in the South Atlantic. She was on a raiding expedition, similar to the one conducted by Felix von Luckner in his Seeadler in World War I, except that she was not disguised as a Norwegian cargo vessel as was the Seeadler.

The Graf Spee, commanded by Captain Hans Langsdorff of the German navy, attacked no enemy shipping until September 30, when she sank the British cargo ship Clement off Pernambuco, Brazil. She then left for the mid-Atlantic where, between October 5 and 10 she sank three more British ships: The Ashlea, Newton Beach and Huntsman. Subsequently she destroyed five other English

vessels: the Trevanion, Africa Shell, Doric Star, Streonshaln and
Tairoa, representing 50,000 tons of shipping in all. In every case
the officers and crews of the sunken vessels were taken aboard the
Graf Spee.

     The British Admiralty soon learned of the raiding activities
of the pocket battleship and Commodore, later Rear Admiral, Henry Harwood was ordered to apprehend the raider. He conducted a
three-vessel squadron consisting of the cruisers Ajax, Achilles and
Exeter to Montevideo, capital of Uruguay, in the South Atlantic
Ocean at the mouth of the River Plate. On December 13, 1939,
the three British cruisers met in battle with the Graf Spee. All
four ships suffered severe damage but none went to the bottom.
The Graf Spee sought refuge in the territorial waters of Montevideo
Harbor and the Exeter, which had suffered the greatest damage,
withdrew to Port Stanley in the Falkland Islands for repairs. The
Achilles and the Ajax guarded the harbor, standing ready to attack
the Graf Spee should Captain Langsdorff attempt to escape from the
port to the open sea. Shortly afterwards Harwood's two remaining
vessels were joined by the British cruiser Cumberland.

     At the time of the Battle of the River Plate Uruguay was
neutral. Under international law a vessel belonging to a belligerent
country seeking refuge in a neutral port may remain there no longer than 24 hours. Failure to leave prior to the 24-hour deadline
results in the internment of the vessel and its officers and crew.
Commodore Harwood realized that reinforcements would be needed
if the Graf Spee was to be defeated in battle. Such reinforcements,
in the form of other English as well as French ships were available but at such a distance away that it would be necessary to length-
en the time that the Graf Spee would remain in Montevideo Harbor.
By dispatching British ships from the harbor, thus invoking the
Emergency Clause of the International Agreement, the time allotted
the Graf Spee to remain at Montevideo for repairs was increased to
72 hours, to expire at 8 P.M. on Sunday, December 17.

     The crew of the Graf Spee was transferred to the German
merchantman Tacoma. At 7:30 the German battleship got under
way and started to move from the inner harbor. Just outside the
three-mile limit she stopped. Two launches loaded with men left
the battleship and headed for the Tacoma. At 7:55 a tremendous
explosion was heard and a column of fire and smoke rose into the
air. In a few minutes the Graf Spee was blazing from stem to
stern. She had been deliberately scuttled by means of time bombs
placed in her hold, her captain not wishing to risk further battle
with his crippled ship. She settled into the mud and burned for
three days.

     Captain Langsdorff and his men were sent to Buenos Aires.
The men were interned in Argentina. In the early morning of December 20 Langsdorff, at the Naval Arsenal in Buenos Aires, wrapped
himself in the flag of the Imperial German Navy and shot himself.

     On December 14 the German High Command of the Navy had

falsely announced that the Graf Spee had engaged three British cruisers and put them out of action. On December 17 another announcement stated that the Graf Spee had scuttled herself and on December 21 it was further stated that Captain Langsdorff had "followed
his ship" and thus "fulfilled like a fighter and hero the expectations
of his Führer, the German people and the navy. "

Although it was later learned that the scuttling had been done
at the personal order of Adolf Hitler, General Alfred Jodl noted in
his diary on December 18 that the Führer was "very angry about
the scuttling of the Graf Spee without a fight" and had sent for Admiral Erich Raeder to whom he gave a merciless tongue-lashing.

Suggested Readings

Dove, Captain Patrick. I Was "Graf Spee's" Prisoner! London:
    Withy/Grove Press, 1940.
Gilpatrick, Guy. "The Glencannon Collection" (short story) in his
    The Last Glencannon Omnibus. New York: Dodd, Mead, 1953.
"Graf Spee Echo, " Newsweek, April 8, 1940.
"Graf Spee Saga Touches Off Spurt of High Drama in War: Scuttling
    at Montevideo Matched by Sub and Air Feats in North Sea Fight-
    ing, " Newsweek, December 25, 1939.
Haines, C. Grover, and J. Ross Hoffman. The Origins and Back-
    ground of the Second World War. New York: Oxford Univer-
    sity Press, 1943.
Marder, Arthur J. From the Dreadnaught to Scapa Flow. London:
    Oxford University Press, 1961.
Murphy, M. "DSC: Battle of the Plate and the Graf Spee. Inter-
    view with Lieut. A. Cameron, " New Yorker: April 18, 1942.
Newbolt, Henry. Naval Operations. London: Longmans, Green,
    1931.
"Pocket into Pocket: Battle Off Uruguay, December 13, " Time,
    December 25, 1939.
Powell, Michael. Death in the South Atlantic: The Last Voyage of
    the "Graf Spee" (historical fiction). New York: Rinehart, 1956.
Roskill, S. W. The War at Sea. London: Her Majesty's Stationery
    Office, 1955-1961.
"The Scuttling of the 'Spee', " New Republic, December 27, 1939.
Shirer, William L. The Rise and Fall of Adolf Hitler. New York:
    Random House, 1961.
_____. The Rise and Fall of the Third Reich: A History of
    Nazi Germany. New York: Simon & Schuster, 1960.
Taylor, Alan John Percivale. The Origins of the Second World War.
    New York: Atheneum, 1961.
Woodward, E. L. Great Britain and the German Navy. Oxford:
    Clarendon Press, 1935.
Young, Peter. World War: 1939-1945. New York: Crowell, 1966.

THE EVACUATION FROM DUNKIRK (1940)

When, in 1939, Germany invaded Poland, great numbers of British soldiers were sent to France. Germany had planned a gigantic offensive against Belgium, France and Holland and on May 10, 1940, launched a powerful air and ground force offensive. The Nazi armies broke through the French and British in Belgium on May 13 and headed toward the English Channel. On May 20 General Karl Rudolf Gerd von Rundstedt's heavy tanks reached the Channel at Abbéville.

General John Gort, commander-in-chief of the British Expeditionary Force, alarmed at the progress of the German panzers, informed headquarters that he contemplated the withdrawal of nine divisions to the Channel for evacuation by sea. Preparations for such an evacuation were made, the maneuver being given the code-word "Operation Dynamo."

The German forces advanced north from Abbéville and the Allies slowed them down at Boulogne and Calais. It became apparent that Dunkirk, on the French coast, was the only port from which an evacuation to Dover could be made. On May 6 von Rundstedt ordered his troops to rest and regroup at Gravelines, he being concerned with the large number of German tanks which had been disabled in combat.

Field Marshal Hermann Goering advised Adolf Hitler that, should the Allies attempt a sea evacuation, his Luftwaffe could stop it by bombing from the air. Hitler agreed and ordered von Rundstedt to hold what servicable tanks he had remaining for future use.

On May 26 Winston Churchill, England's prime minister, Sir Anthony Eden, Secretary of State for War and the War Cabinet ordered Operation Dynamo to be activated. Admiral Sir Bertram Ramsay, British flag officer at Dover, had anticipated this and dispatched the first contingent of ships from that port. The Germans renewed their aggression at Gravelines but were hampered by Allied troops.

On the night of May 26 the evacuation from Dunkirk, which was to be the greatest in military history, began. The French navy, under Admiral Jean Abrial, cooperated with Admiral Ramsay, embarking soldiers on the dunes of Dunkirk and carrying them, in small boats, to the larger ships in deep water farther from shore. At first there were unsufficient naval launches, and the British asked for and received help from civilian yachtsmen, fishermen and others who had small craft at their disposal.

In spite of the air bombings by Goering's Luftwaffe, countered by the resistance of the Royal Air Force, the evacuation from Dunkirk was successful. Early on the morning of June 4, 1940, the last British ship left the port. About 338,000 men were rescued. Of the 760 ships used by the British, 228 were sunk by bombing attacks. About sixty of the French ships were lost. While the British were forced to leave their heavy armaments and equipment behind, their technically qualified men were rescued. These, furnished with new materiel, were able to continue the war which eventually resulted in an Allied victory and the defeat of Nazi Germany.

Suggested Readings

Archer, Jules. The Dictators. New York: Hawthorn Books, 1967.

Benoit-Mèchin, Jacques. Sixty Days That Shook the West: The Fall of France, 1940. Translated by Peter Wiles. New York: Putnam's, 1963.

Bullock, Alan. Hitler: A Study in Tyranny. New York: Harper & Row, 1962.

Carse, Robert. Dunkirk, 1940: A History. Englewood Cliffs, N.J.: Prentice-Hall, 1970.

Chalfont, Alan. Montgomery of Alamein. New York: Atheneum, 1976.

Chalmers, Rear Admiral W.S. Full Cycle. London: Hodder & Stoughton, 1959.

Churchill, Winston S. The Second World War. Vol. II: "Their Finest Hour." Boston: Houghton Mifflin, 1949.

Collier, Richard. The Sands of Dunkirk. New York: Dutton, 1961.

Eden, Sir Anthony. Full Circle: The Memoirs of Anthony Eden. Boston: Houghton Mifflin, 1960.

Elliott, Brendan John. Hitler and Germany. New York: McGraw-Hill, 1968.

Ellis, Major L. F. The War in France and Flanders. London: Her Majesty's Stationery Office, 1953.

Fuller, John F.C. A Military History of the Western World. New York: Funk & Wagnalls, 1954.

_____. The Second World War, 1939-1945. London: Eyre & Spottiswoode, 1948.

Goldston, Robert. The Life and Death of Nazi Germany. Indianapolis: Bobbs-Merrill, 1967.

Harris, John. Ride Out the Storm (historical fiction). New York: Mason/Charter, 1976.

Heiden, Konrad. Der Fuehrer: Hitler's Rise to Power. Boston: Houghton Mifflin, 1944.

Hitler, Adolf. Mein Kampf. Boston: Houghton Mifflin, 1943.

Holborn, Hajo. A History of Modern Germany. Vol. III: 1840-1945. New York: Knopf, 1969.

Jacobsen, H.A. and J. Rohwer, eds. "Dunkirk 1940" in their Decisive Battles of World War II: The German View. Translated by Edward Fitzgerald. New York: Putnam, 1965.

Jarman, T.L. The Rise and Fall of Nazi Germany. New York: New York University Press, 1956.

Kesselring, Field Marshal Alfred. A Soldier's Story. New York: Morrow, 1954.

Namier, Lewis B. Europe in Decay: A Study in Disintegration, 1936-1940. London: Macmillan, 1949.

Richards, Denis. "Collapse in the West" in Royal Air Force, 1939-1945. London: Her Majesty's Stationery Office, 1953.

Roskill, S. W. The War at Sea. London: Her Majesty's Stationery
    Office, 1955-1961.
Schoenbaum, David. Hitler's Social Revolution. Garden City, N. Y.:
    Doubleday, 1966.
Sears, Stephen W. and the editors of American Heritage. Air War
    Against Hitler's Germany. New York: American Heritage Pub-
    lishing Co., 1964.
Seton-Watson, R. W. Britain and the Dictators. London: Methuen
    & Co., 1939.
Shirer, William L. The Collapse of the Third Republic. New York:
    Simon & Schuster, 1969.
_____. The Rise and Fall of Adolf Hitler. New York: Random
    House, 1961.
_____. The Rise and Fall of the Third Reich: A History of
    Nazi Germany. New York: Simon & Schuster, 1960.
Spears, General Sir Edward L. Assignment to Catastrophe. Vol.
    II: "The Fall of France." New York: A. A. Wyn, 1955.
Speer, Albert. Inside the Third Reich. New York: Macmillan,
    1970.
Stein, George H., ed. Hitler. Englewood Cliffs, N. J.: Prentice-
    Hall, 1968.
Strasser, Otto. Hitler and I. Boston: Houghton Mifflin, 1940.
Sulzberger, C. L., ed. The American Heritage Picture History of
    World War II. New York: American Heritage Publishing Co.,
    1966.
Taylor, Telford. The March of Conquest. New York: Simon &
    Schuster, 1958.
Toynbee, Arnold, and Veronica M. Toynbee, eds. Survey of Inter-
    national Affairs, 1939-1946. The Eve of War, 1939. London:
    Oxford University Press, 1959.
Trevor-Roper, H. R., ed. Hitler's War Directives, 1939-1945.
    London: Sidgwick, 1964.
Webbe, Stephen. "Deliverance at Dunkirk" in Taylor, A. J. P., ed-
    itor-in-chief. Purnell's History of the 20th Century, Vol. 7.
    New York: Purnell, 1971.
Werth, Alexander. The Twilight of France, 1933-1940. New York:
    Harper & Row, 1942.
Weyr, Thomas. World War II. New York: Messner, 1969.
Wheeler-Bennett, John W. The Nemesis of Power: The German
    Army in Politics, 1918-1945. New York: Viking Press, 1952.
Young, Peter. World War: 1939-1945. New York: Crowell, 1966.

THE SURRENDER OF FRANCE (1940)

        Following World War I France looked for means of protecting
herself from a resurgent Germany. She sought alliances with Great
Britain and nations on Germany's eastern border and between 1929
and 1940 constructed the Maginot Line. This was a system of fortifications which was built along the Franco-German border. The
French considered the Maginot Line impregnable. However, when

Germany attacked France in 1940 her armies outflanked the Line
and the French army by moving through the Ardennes Forest, a
maneuver the French had considered impossible.

World War II had started in 1939 with the German invasion
of Poland. In April, 1940, Norway fell to the Nazis and Adolf Hitler, the German Führer, continued his aggressive tactics by invading France, which was weak and demoralized.

The French people were disappointed with the Third French
Republic. French leaders realized that their country's armies were
no match for Germany's panzer divisions and, like Great Britain,
had attempted to appease the German Reich. The French forces
remained behind the Maginot Line and did not go to the aid of Poland
when Germany crossed her borders.

General Karl Rudolf Gerd von Rundstedt was appointed commander of the German army Group A, which was originally scheduled to cross through Belgium and attack northern France. France
anticipated such an attack and countered by moving her mobile troops
north along the Franco-Belgian border. General Erich von Manstein,
Rundstedt's chief of staff, suggested an attack through the Ardennes
Forest, as mentioned above. The Führer approved Manstein's suggestion and made his preparations. The German forces invaded
Belgium on May 10, 1940, and Group A made the successful advance
through the Ardennes.

General Maurice Gustave Gamelin, inspector general of the
French army, was relieved from his post by the order of Premier
Paul Reynaud and replaced by General Maxime Weygand. Reynaud
assumed the administration of the Ministry of War and recalled
Marshal Henri Pétain, the World War I hero, as his deputy.

General Weygand's troops were unable to overcome the German forces which advanced on Paris, surrounding the defending army
and trapping it at the rear of the Maginot Line. Reynaud's appeal
to Great Britain for support in the way of troops and fighter planes
was refused by Prime Minister Winston S. Churchill who realized
that he would need every available military resource to defend his
own country.

The German panzer divisions approached Paris and on June
11, 1940, the French cabinet withdrew to Tours. Benito Mussolini,
the Italian dictator, declared war on France and Great Britain and
sent troops into southern France. Churchill urged the French to
refuse to surrender, to retreat to North Africa, and to continue
fighting from there. Reynaud agreed but the French military officials refused to continue the conflict. Consequently, Reynaud resigned, being replaced by Marshal Pétain. On June 22, at Compiègne, France surrendered to Germany and representatives of the
Pétain ministry signed armistice agreements with both Germany and
Italy. These agreements included German military occupation of the
northern half of France and the entire French Atlantic seaboard,

French responsibility for the costs of the occupations, and internment of the French fleet in its home ports for the duration of the
war. Italy was to retain control of the areas captured by her troops
and various zones in the French colonial territories in Africa were
to be demilitarized, as was a broad zone along the Franco-Italian
frontier.

Pétain formally abolished the Third French Republic in July
and established himself as a virtual dictator. France was liberated
following the Allied invasion of Normandy on June 6, 1944.

Suggested Readings

Benoist-Méchin, Jacques. Sixty Days That Shook the West: The
    Fall of France, 1940. Translated by Peter Wiles. New York:
    Putnam's, 1963.
Chapman, Guy. Why France Fell: The Defeat of the French Army
    in 1940. New York: Holt, 1968.
Churchill, Winston S. The Second World War. Vol. II: "Their
    Finest Hour." New York: Houghton Mifflin, 1949.
Collier, Basil. The Second World War: A Military History. New
    York: Morrow, 1967.
Draper, Theodore. The Six Weeks War. New York: Viking Press,
    1944.
Ellis, Major L. F. The War in France and Flanders. London: Her
    Majesty's Stationery Office, 1953.
Fuller, John F. C. Armament and History. New York: Scribner's,
    1945.
_____. The Second World War, 1939-1945. London: Eyre &
    Spottiswoode, 1948.
Reynaud, Paul. In the Thick of the Fight. Translated by James P.
    Lambert. New York: Simon & Schuster, 1955.
Rowe, Vivian. The Great Wall of France. New York: Putnam's,
    1961.
Shirer, William L. The Collapse of the Third Republic. New York:
    Simon & Schuster, 1969.
_____. The Rise and Fall of the Third Reich: A History of Nazi
    Germany. New York: Simon & Schuster, 1960.
Simon, Yves. The Road to Vichy, 1918-1938. Translated by James
    A. Corbett and George J. McMorrow. New York: Sheed and
    Ward, 1942.
Snyder, Louis L. The War: A Concise History, 1939-1945. New
    York: Dell Publishing Co., 1964.
Spears, General Sir Edward L. Assignment to Catastrophe. Vol.
    II: "The Fall of France." New York: A. A. Wyn, 1955.
Taylor, Telford. The March of Conquest. New York: Simon &
    Schuster, 1958.
Werth, Alexander. The Twilight of France, 1933-1940. New York:
    Harper & Row, 1942.
Weygand, Maxime. Recalled to Service. London: William Heine-
    mann, Ltd., 1952.
Wilhelm, Maria. For the Glory of France: The Story of the French
    Resistance. New York: Messner, 1968.

Wilmot, Chester. The Struggle for Europe. New York: Harper &
    Row, 1952.
Wolfers, Arnold. Britain and France Between Two Wars. New
    York: Harcourt, Brace, 1940.
Young, Peter. World War: 1939-1945. New York: Crowell, 1966.

THE ASSASSINATION OF LEON TROTSKY (1940)

Three influential Russian Communist leaders were Nikolai
Lenin, Joseph Stalin and Leon Trotsky. Lenin, creator of the Bolshevist Party and the Third (Communist) International, died of
arteriosclerosis in January, 1924, and a struggle broke out between
Trotsky, Soviet foreign minister and commander of the Red Army
and Stalin, general secretary of the Bolshevists. Both men wished
to control the Party and the government.

From about 1918 on Trotsky and Stalin had differed over
matters of both strategy and policy. Trotsky advocated world Communist revolution and Stalin favored building "socialism in one country." The struggle between the two men was finally won by Stalin
and in 1927 Trotsky was expelled from the Party and exiled to Alma-
Ata in Asia. In 1929 he was accused of counter-revolutionary activities and deported to Constantinople. Later, in France, from
which he was also expelled, in Norway, and ultimately in Mexico
City, where he settled upon the invitation of President Lázaro Cár-
denas who granted him political asylum, he continued to agitate for
a world-wide Communist revolution. He repeatedly denounced Stalin
as a betrayer of the true objectives of the Bolshevist Party created
by Lenin. Stalin made counter-charges and remained Trotsky's bitter enemy.

On August 20, 1940, a friend whom Trotsky knew as "Frank
Jacson, a young Canadian," visited him at his Mexico City villa.
Jacson was the lover of Sylvia Agelof, one of Trotsky's disciples.
Although the day was warm and sunny, the visitor wore a hat and
carried a raincoat over his arm. "It might rain," he said. Although feeling ill, Jacson had come to show Trotsky the manuscript
of a political article he had written. At Trotsky's suggestion the
two men went into the house as did Natalya, Trotsky's wife, who
had joined them outside.

Jacson and Trotsky went to the latter's study and Natalya
proceeded to the kitchen. Hearing a scream and the sound of breaking furniture, she rushed into the study. There she found her husband, blood streaming from his face. He had been struck with an
ice axe which Jacson had concealed under his raincoat.

The assailant was captured in the study by two of Trotsky's
bodyguards, the ice axe still in his possession. The Russian, suffering great brain injury but still alive, was taken to the hospital.

He was conscious and able to talk and accused Jacson, as a political enemy, of assaulting him.   An operation was performed but
within 24 hours Leon Trotsky was dead.

Jacson and Sylvia Agelof were arrested.   The girl was exonerated but Jacson was brought to trial and in 1943 was given a
twenty-year prison term.   It was learned that he had been involved
in a previous attempt to assassinate the Russian politician with machine guns.

The investigation made into Jacson's past revealed that this
was not his true name, nor was the name "Jacques Mornard," which
he was found to have used.   His fingerprints matched those of one
Ramón Mercador who, in 1935, had been arrested in Barcelona.

Over the next several years the story was pieced together.
The assassin had been born in Cuba and had acquired a firm belief in Communism from his mother.   He had fought on the Republican side in the Spanish Civil War and had then attended an espionage school in Moscow.   He had been hand-picked by Stalin for
the mission of killing Leon Trotsky and had deliberately sought out
and cultivated Sylvia Agelof, Trotsky's trusted ally, in order to
worm his way into the latter's confidence.

In 1953 he was eligible for parole.   It was denied and he
served almost all of his twenty-year sentence, being released on
May 6, 1960.   Using still another name, Jesus Hernandez, he left
for Cuba and from there went to Russia.   He was made welcome
there and learned that he had been awarded the Order of a Hero of
the Soviet Union.   He retired to Prague where he worked as a radio
and television repairman.

Suggested Readings

Archer, Jules.   Trotsky, World Revolutionary.   New York: Mess-
    ner, 1973.
Carmichael, Joel.   Trotsky: An Appreciation of His Life.   New
    York: St. Martin's Press, 1975.
Deutscher, Isaac.   The Prophet Outcast: Trotsky, 1929-1940.   Lon-
    don: Oxford University Press, 1963.
    _____.   Stalin: A Political Biography.   2nd rev. edition.   New
    York: Oxford University Press, 1967.
Eastman, Max.   "Great in Time of Storm: The Character and Fate
    of Leon Trotsky" in his Heroes I Have Known.   New York: Si-
    mon and Schuster, 1942.
Goldman, Albert.   The Assassination of Leon Trotsky: The Proofs
    of Stalin's Guilt.   New York: Pioneer, 1940.
Hernandez, Jesus.   I Was a Minister of Stalin.   Mexico City: 1953.
Levine, Isaac Don.   The Mind of an Assassin.   New York: Farrar,
    Straus and Cudahy, 1959.
Payne, Robert.   The Rise and Fall of Stalin.   New York: Simon
    and Schuster, 1965.

Sánchez Salazar, Leandro A., with the collaboration of Julian Gor-
    kin. Murder in Mexico: The Assassination of Leon Trotsky.
    Translated by Phyllis Hawley. London: Secker & Warburg,
    1950.
Schneider, Isidor. The Judas Time. New York: Knopf, 1946.
Serge, Victor, and Natalya Sedova Trotsky. The Life and Death of
    Leon Trotsky. Translated by Arnold J. Pomerans. New York:
    Basic Books, 1975.
Smith, Irving H., ed. Trotsky. Englewood Cliffs, N. J.: Prentice-
    Hall, 1973.
"Trotsky" in Crimes and Punishment, Vol. 2. Editorial presenta-
    tion: Jackson Morley. London: BPC, 1973.
Warth, Robert. Joseph Stalin. New York: Twayne, 1969.
Wolfe, Bernard. The Great Prince Died (fiction). New York:
    Scribner's, 1959.
Wolfenstein, E. Victor. The Revolutionary Personality: Lenin,
    Trotsky, Gandhi. Princeton, N. J.: Princeton University Press,
    1967.
Wyndham, Francis, and David King. Trotsky: A Documentary.
    New York: Frederick A. Praeger, 1972.

THE "LORD HAW-HAW" BROADCASTS (1940-1945)

The phrase "Jairmany calling, Jairmany calling" was the
opening signal on radio broadcasts originating in Berlin and beamed
through Western Europe. These broadcasts, intended to break down
the morale of Allied troops in their fight against the Axis powers,
were made by William Joyce, an American Nazi sympathizer, who
was known to his listeners as "Lord Haw-Haw."

Joyce was born in New York in 1906. His Irish father was
a naturalized American citizen who, after living in the United States,
returned to his native country, taking his son and his English wife
with him. Being opposed to Home Rule, he moved to England, where
young William grew up. The boy attended London University where
he had a brilliant scholastic career, particularly in the field of political science. His extreme right wing views led him to become a
member of the British Union of Fascists and he adopted the philosophy of its leader, Sir Oswald Mosley, an admirer of the Nazi Führer, Adolf Hitler.

In 1933 Joyce and his wife Margaret, traveling on British
passports, made a vacation trip to Germany. His political views
were such that he had come to the notice of Scotland Yard, which
kept a dossier on him. He was advised by a friend that he might
be arrested under the Emergency Powers Act as Mosley had been.
The two returned to England without incident.

In August, 1939, he renewed his passport and he and his wife
left for Germany a second time, arriving in September. There they

learned that, should war be declared, they would be interned.   They
decided to return to England but found that this was not possible as
Joyce had converted his English currency into German marks which
could not be used to purchase tickets to foreign countries.   The two
had no choice but to remain in Germany.

The expatriate worked as a translator, then as a newscaster.
His voice, a parody of that of the upper-class British gentleman,
was ideal for the propaganda broadcasts which he delivered.   His
technique was not unlike that of "Tokyo Rose" who beamed radio
messages to the Allied troops in the Pacific during World War II.
He dispensed much trivia which attempted to give the impression
that German spies "were everywhere and knew everything, " even to
the fact that the town clock in a British village was ten minutes
slow.

When Berlin fell in 1945, Dr. Joseph Goebbels, the Nazi
Propaganda Minister who committed suicide that same year, attempted to keep Joyce out of British hands.   Goebbels had been greatly
impressed with Joyce's performance and he assisted him and his
wife to reach the Danish border.   There they were apprehended by
Captain Perry, a British officer who recognized Joyce's voice when
he spoke to him in English.   Joyce was carrying forged papers iden-
tifying him as "Fritz Hansen. "   Perry, thinking he was reaching for
a weapon, shot and wounded him in the leg.

Joyce was taken to London where he was tried for high treason "by adhering to the King's enemies outside the King's reach. "
His case was tried in September, 1945, being prosecuted by Sir
Hartley Shawcross.   The defense, handled by G. O. Slade, was unable to overcome the prosecution's contention that Joyce, though
born in the United States, had applied for, been granted and traveled
on a British passport, "which clothed him with the status of a British subject and required from him the duty of faithfulness and allegiance to the British Crown. "

William Joyce was found guilty as charged and hanged at
Wandsworth Prison, London, on January 3, 1946.

Suggested Readings

Abosch, Heinz.   The Menace of the Miracle: Germany from Hitler
    to Adenauer.   Translated by Douglas Garman.   New York:
    Monthly Review Press, 1963.
Appel, Benjamin.   Hitler, from Power to Ruin.   New York: Gros-
    set & Dunlap, 1964.
Archer, Jules.   The Dictators.   New York: Hawthorn Books, 1967.
Bullock, Alan.   Hitler: A Study in Tyranny.   New York: Harper
    & Row, 1962.
Collier, Basil.   The Second World War: A Military History.   New
    York: Morrow, 1967.
Eisenhower, General Dwight D.   Crusade in Europe.   New York:
    Doubleday, 1948.

Elliott, Brendan John. Hitler and Germany. New York: McGraw-
   Hill, 1968.
Fuller, John F. C.   The Second World War, 1939-1945   London:
   Eyre & Spottiswoode, 1948.
Goldston, Robert.   The Life and Death of Nazi Germany.   Indian-
   apolis: Bobbs-Merrill, 1967.
Grunberger, Richard. Germany, 1918-1945. New York: Harper
   & Row, 1966.
Heiden, Konrad. Der Fuehrer: Hitler's Rise to Power.   Boston:
   Houghton Mifflin, 1944.
Holborn, Hajo. A History of Modern Germany. Vol. III: 1840-
   1945. New York: Knopf, 1969.
Prittie, Terence, and the editors of Life. Germany. New York:
   Time, Inc., 1961.
Shirer, William L.   The Rise and Fall of Adolf Hitler.   New York:
   Random House, 1961.
_____. The Rise and Fall of the Third Reich: A History of
   Nazi Germany. New York: Simon & Schuster, 1960.
Stein, George H., ed. Hitler. Englewood Cliffs, N. J.: Prentice-
   Hall, 1968.
Sutton, Felix.   The How and Why Wonder Book of World War II.
   New York: Grosset & Dunlap, 1962.
Thompson, Laurence Victor. The Story of Scotland Yard. New
   York: Random House, 1954.
Toland, John. Adolf Hitler. Garden City, N. Y.: Doubleday, 1977.
"William Joyce" in Crimes and Punishment, Vol. 8.   Editorial pre-
   sentation: Jackson Morley. London: BPC, 1973.
Wilmot, Chester.   The Struggle for Europe. New York: Harper &
   Row, 1952.

THE QUISLING DEFECTION (1940-1945)

When World War II began in 1939 Norway maintained its traditional neutrality. The fact that German ships were sinking Norwegian vessels and engaging in maritime warfare along the Norwegian coast made neutrality exceedingly difficult to maintain. On
April 8, 1940, both France and Great Britain announced that they
had mined Norwegian territorial waters in order to prevent the
shipment of iron ore to Germany, and on the same day Norway was
invaded by the latter country.

Shortly after the invasion Vidkun Quisling, head of the Norwegian Nazi Party, conferred in Berlin with Adolf Hitler, whom he
held in high esteem. Quisling promised to do everything in his
power to "re-cement relationships" and convince the Norwegian people that they were fortunate "to be taken under the wing of the Nazi
eagle. "

In July he wrote Hitler, stating that for years he had advocated "a great Germanic community with Norway's voluntary affilia-

tion, " and was proclaiming himself head of the Norwegian government. King Haakon of Norway, after a vain attempt to direct resistance to the German army and its Norwegian collaborators, withdrew to London where, until 1945 when the war was over, he and his cabinet maintained a Norwegian government-in-exile.

Josef Terboven was appointed German Commissioner for Norway. The Norwegian political leaders refused to cooperate with him whereupon he dissolved all political parties in Norway except the Nazi Party, set up the National Union and announced the abolition of King Haakon's monarchy. Quisling, as government head, then proceeded to emulate the methods of his idol Hitler, employing Nazi terrorism in the form of concentration camps, secret police, censorship, persecutions of Jews and mass arrests and executions. The Norwegian people, under the leadership of Foreign Minister Trygve Lie in London, resisted as best they could.

In September, 1941, Quisling proclaimed martial law, on orders from Berlin. In spite of this the loyal Norwegian underground continued its resistance to the invaders by espionage, sabotage and other similar techniques.

The Allied advance on the European continent commenced early in 1945. The Nazi troops in Norway held out until May 8, when they were forced to surrender. King Haakon returned from London on June 7, one of his first official acts being to reestablish the death penalty, abolished in 1876, that traitors might be punished as they deserved. Several Nazi officials, including Terboven, committed suicide, and over 15,000 Norwegian collaborationists were arrested, tried and punished.

Vidkun Quisling was tried in Oslo, the trial lasting from August 22 to September 10, 1945. He gave an eight-hour speech in his own defense, calling himself the "saviour of Norway." Despite his oratory he was found guilty of high treason and sentenced to die before the firing squad. The sentence was carried out on October 24. Today, as then, the name "Quisling" has come to be synonymous with "traitor."

Suggested Readings

Appel, Benjamin. Hitler, from Power to Ruin. New York: Grosset & Dunlap, 1964.
Archer, Jules. The Dictators. New York: Hawthorn Books, 1967.
Ash, Bernard. Norway, 1940. London: Cassell & Co., 1964.
Bullock, Alan. Hitler: A Study in Tyranny. New York: Harper & Row, 1962.
Churchill, Winston S. The Second World War. Vol. I: "The Gathering Storm." Boston: Houghton Mifflin, 1948.
Dean, Vera Michelis. Europe in Retreat. New York: Knopf, 1939.
Derry, T. K. The Campaign in Norway. London: Her Majesty's Stationery Office, 1952.

Fuller, John F. C. A Military History of the Western World. New
York: Funk & Wagnalls, 1954.
_____. The Second World War, 1939-1945. London: Eyre &
Spottiswoode, 1948.
Goldston, Robert. The Life and Death of Nazi Germany. Indian-
apolis: Bobbs-Merrill, 1967.
Haines, G. Grover, and J. Ross Hoffman. The Origins and Back-
ground of the Second World War. New York: Oxford Univer-
sity Press, 1943.
Hansson, Per. The Greatest Gamble. Translated by Maurice Mi-
chael. New York: Norton, 1967.
Heiden, Konrad. Der Fuehrer: Hitler's Rise to Power. Boston:
Houghton Mifflin, 1944.
Hitler, Adolf. Mein Kampf. Boston: Houghton Mifflin, 1943.
Holborn, Hajo. A History of Modern Germany. Vol. III: 1840-
1945. New York: Knopf, 1969.
Jarman, T. L. The Rise and Fall of Nazi Germany. New York:
New York University Press, 1956.
Macintyre, Captain Donald. Narvik. New York: Norton, 1960.
Macleod, R. , ed. Time Unguarded: The Ironside Diaries, 1937-
1940. New York: David MacKay, 1962.
Moulton, J. L. The Norwegian Campaign of 1940. London: Eyre
and Spottiswoode, 1966.
Namier, Lewis B. Europe in Decay: A Study in Disintegration,
1936-1940. London: Macmillan, 1949.
Outze, Borge, ed. Denmark During the Occupation. Copenhagen,
1946.
"Quisling" in Crimes and Punishment, Vol. 14. Editorial presenta-
tion: Jackson Morley. London: BPC, 1973.
Richards, Denis. "Collapse in the West" in Royal Air Force, 1939-
1945. London: Her Majesty's Stationery Office, 1953.
_____. "Scandinavian Misadventure" in Royal Air Force, 1939-
1945. London: Her Majesty's Stationery Office, 1953.
Schoenbaum, David. Hitler's Social Revolution. Garden City, N. Y. :
Doubleday, 1966.
Shirer, William L. The Challenge of Scandinavia. Boston: Hough-
ton Mifflin, 1955.
_____. The Rise and Fall of Adolf Hitler. New York: Random
House, 1961.
_____. The Rise and Fall of the Third Reich: A History of
Nazi Germany. New York: Simon & Schuster, 1960.
Snell, John L. The Outbreak of the Second World War: Design or
Blunder? Boston: Heath, 1962.
Speer, Albert. Inside the Third Reich. New York: Macmillan,
1970.
Stein, George H. , ed. Hitler. Englewood Cliffs, N. J. : Prentice-
Hall, 1968.
Strasser, Otto. Hitler and I. Boston: Houghton Mifflin, 1940.
Sulzberger, G. L. The American Heritage Picture History of World
War II. New York: American Heritage Publishing Co. , 1966.
Trevor-Roper, H. R. The Last Days of Hitler. New York: Collier
Books, 1962.
_____, ed. Hitler's War Directives, 1930-1945. London: Sidg-
wick, 1964.

Weyr, Thomas. World War II. New York: Messner, 1969.
Young, Peter. World War: 1939-1945. New York: Crowell, 1966.

THE HESS FLIGHT (1941)

On the evening of Saturday, May 10, 1941, a lone German airman calling himself Hauptmann Alfred Horn flew a two-engine Messerschmitt ME 110 from a small private airfield outside Munich to a farm near Dumbarton, Scotland. His mission was to meet the Duke of Hamilton, a British flyer and statesman and, through him, confer with high British officials with the object of persuading England to cease hostilities with Germany and join her in an assault on the Soviet Union.

"Horn" was later found to be Rudolf Hess, ranked only by Adolf Hitler and Hermann Goering in the Nazi hierarchy. As a young man Hess had served in World War I and, after a career as an infantryman, had been transferred to the Imperial Flying Corps. There he qualified as a military pilot but the Armistice of 1918 was declared before he could be assigned to active flying combat duty.

After the war Hess attended Munich University and became a member of the National Socialist, or Nazi Party. Here he met Adolf Hitler, to whom he became fanatically loyal.

At the university Hess studied under Dr. Karl Haushofer, a professor of geo-politics and a man who was unable to relate his intellectual theorizing to the reality of practical situations. Haushofer made a great impression on his pupil.

In 1940 London was being subjected to heavy aerial bombing by the German Luftwaffe. Dr. Haushofer felt that Germany should effect a peace treaty with Great Britain and that the two countries should unite against Russia. He discussed his ideas with Hitler, who rejected them, and he then talked with Hess, urging him to intercede with the Fuehrer. Goering pointed out to Hitler that, should Germany continue its war with England and at the same time attack Russia, the United States could become embroiled in the conflict on the side of Russia. Hitler reluctantly agreed that unofficial feelers should be put out concerning the possibility of a peace treaty with Great Britain. When the matter came to the attention of the British Prime Minister Winston Churchill he flatly refused to negotiate with Germany under any circumstances.

Dr. Haushofer conferred further with Hess, urging that a high-ranking Nazi official go to England and talk with the Duke of Hamilton. An attempt was made to arrange a conference in neutral Portugal but the letters written in Germany proposing this went unanswered.

Hess, Goering and Alfred Rosenberg convinced Hitler that a

Nazi official should fly to England. Hess volunteered for the mission. The Fuehrer, however, was somewhat skeptical. He agreed to the idea but with the proviso that, should the plan fail, the German Reich would disavow all knowledge of it and claim that Hess, suffering from hallucinations, had acted on his own volition.

Although he had not piloted an aircraft since World War I, Hess proceeded to brush up on his flying. Willi Messerschmitt, a prominent government aircraft designer and manufacturer, made a plane available to him and furnished instructions in flying and navigation. The plane was fitted with extra fuel tanks and a high-powered radio.

Hess made two unsuccessful attempts to fly to Scotland. Each time he was forced back by mechanical failures or inclement weather. Then, on May 10, 1941, at 1,800 hours, he took off, flying north from Munich across Germany, over Holland and across the North Sea. He was spotted by a British fighter pilot but escaped into a fog bank.

At Renfrewshire, Scotland, he parachuted from his plane, injuring his ankle. The plane burst into flames in a nearby field. Hess was captured by David McLean, a Scottish farmer, who turned him over to the Home Guard.

The German flyer was identified as Rudolf Hess by Ivone Kirkpatrick, former first secretary at the British embassy in Berlin. The Duke of Hamilton was summoned and he and Kirkpatrick talked with the prisoner at Buchanan Castle at Turnhouse where the latter had been taken. Although, for political reasons, the British authorities wished to keep the story of the flight out of the newspapers, Eric Schofield, a journalist, was able to ferret out the facts and publish them in the Glasgow Daily Record.

When it became obvious that the Hess peace mission had failed to achieve its purpose the German Reich denounced him as a traitor and he was formally expelled from the Nazi Party. Scapegoats, including Karlheinz Pintsch, his adjutant, were arrested, tried as accomplices and punished. On May 15 Hitler publicly expressed surprise at the flight and declared Hess to be mentally unbalanced. Within days Germany attacked Russia without the aid of Great Britain.

Hess was placed in captivity. A token attempt to rescue him made by German troops was unsuccessful. He remained a prisoner until the end of World War II, and was tried as a war criminal, along with 21 other Nazi leaders, at the Nuremberg war-crimes trials of 1945-46. He was found guilty on two of the four charges and sentenced to imprisonment at Spandau Prison, Berlin, together with six others. These six have since been freed, either because they had served out their sentences or for other reasons. At this writing Hess, who had been sentenced to confinement for life, is the sole inmate of Spandau.

Suggested Readings

Appel, Benjamin. Hitler, from Power to Ruin. New York: Gros-
   set & Dunlap, 1964.
Archer, Jules. The Dictators. New York: Hawthorn Books, 1967.
Bradley, General Omar N. A Soldier's Story. New York: Holt,
   Rinehart, 1951.
Bullock, Alan. Hitler: A Study in Tyranny. New York: Harper
   & Row, 1962.
Carr, Albert H. Zolotoff. Men of Power: A Book of Dictators.
   New York: Viking Press, 1956.
Collier, Basil. The Second World War: A Military History. New
   York: Morrow, 1967.
Eisenhower, General Dwight D. Crusade in Europe. New York:
   Doubleday, 1948.
Elliott, Brendan John. Hitler and Germany. New York: McGraw-
   Hill, 1968.
Fuller, John F. C. The Second World War, 1939-1945. London:
   Eyre & Spottiswoode, 1948.
Goldston, Robert. The Rise and Fall of Nazi Germany. Indian-
   apolis: Bobbs-Merrill, 1967.
Grunberger, Richard. Germany, 1918-1945. New York: Harper
   & Row, 1966.
Heiden, Konrad. Der Fuehrer: Hitler's Rise to Power. Boston:
   Houghton Mifflin, 1944.
Hitler, Adolf. Mein Kampf. Boston: Houghton Mifflin, 1943.
Holborn, Hajo. A History of Modern Germany. Vol. III: 1840-
   1945. New York: Knopf, 1969.
Hutton, J. Bernhard. Hess: The Man and His Mission. New York:
   Macmillan, 1970.
Jarman, T. L. The Rise and Fall of Nazi Germany. New York:
   New York University Press, 1956.
Prittie, Terence, and the editors of Life. Germany. New York:
   Time, Inc., 1961.
Shirer, William L. The Rise and Fall of Adolf Hitler. New York:
   Random House, 1961.
   _____. The Rise and Fall of the Third Reich: A History of
   Nazi Germany. New York: Simon & Schuster, 1960.
Speer, Albert. Inside the Third Reich. New York: Macmillan,
   1970.
Stein, George H., ed. Hitler. Englewood Cliffs, N. J.: Prentice-
   Hall, 1968.
Toland, John. Adolf Hitler. Garden City, N. Y.: Doubleday, 1977.
Trevor-Roper, H. R., ed. Hitler's War Directives, 1939-1945.
   London: Sidgwick, 1964.
Weyr, Thomas. World War II. New York: Messner, 1969.
Young, Peter. World War, 1939-1945. New York: Crowell, 1966.

THE SINKING OF THE BISMARCK (1941)

The greatest sea hunt of World War II involved the six-day

search for the German battleship Bismarck by vessels of the British navy. The Bismarck, commanded by Admiral Lutjens and with Captain Lindemann second in command, was the pride of the German navy. Displacing 42,000 tons, she was "the world's largest, most dangerous, most modern ship of war yet launched."

In May, 1941, the Bismarck was in harbor at Gdynia, the North Poland seaport on the Bay of Danzig, preparing for a voyage. Her mission was to seek and destroy British convoys in the Atlantic. She was to be accompanied by the Prinz Eugen, a German cruiser.

On May 21 a British secret agent in Malmo advised the British Operational Intelligence Center in London by code telegram that the German battleship had departed Gdynia and was proceeding north through the Kattegat, a waterway separating Denmark from Sweden. With her were the Prinz Eugen and eleven merchant ships. Later that day the ships were spotted by air reconnaissance in Grimstad Fiord, south of Bergen, Norway. Before British bombers could be dispatched to make an attack, mist and rain closed in and, with zero visibility, the idea of an immediate air attack was abandoned.

The Bismarck proceeded north and west around Iceland toward the Atlantic by way of Denmark Strait. The Hood, twenty years older than the Bismarck and England's largest battleship, was ordered to proceed from Scapa Flow in the Orkney Islands north of Scotland. She was accompanied by the Prince of Wales, a British fighting ship only recently commissioned. The two vessels headed west and south in order to intercept the Bismarck in the Atlantic below Denmark Strait.

A storm was raging and all vessels were pitching and tossing. Visibility was bad. British cruisers were dispatched to determine, if possible, the location of the German warships. One of these, the Suffolk, spotted them in Denmark Strait. The Hood, advised of the location of the Bismark, steamed to intercept her. With her was the Prince of Wales.

The three ships met and commenced firing. A shell from the Bismarck penetrated the Hood's ammunition magazine detonating the explosives stored there and she was literally blown to pieces. The Prince of Wales, badly damaged, withdrew into the safety of a smoke screen. The Bismarck, other than a ruptured oil tank, suffered virtually no damage.

The British admiralty instructed the Home Fleet to go into action, with orders to search for and intercept the Bismarck. Destroyers were removed from convoy duty to join in the search. Prime Minister Winston Churchill gave personal orders that the Bismarck was to be sunk. In the meantime that vessel encountered the Suffolk but did not sink her. The Prinz Eugen and the Bismarck parted company and the former returned to her home port.

The British Force H, consisting of the aircraft carrier Ark

Royal, two cruisers, the Renown and the Sheffield, plus six destroyers, left Gibraltar, heading west out of the Mediterranean.
The Ark Royal carried Swordfish bombing planes. The Bismarck
was sighted by the British Suffolk and attacked by a group of planes,
one torpedo scoring a hit which did little damage. While the planes
returned to their ship to refuel and rearm the Bismarck changed
her course and eluded them. The weather remained bad, dense
clouds rendered visibility near zero and the wind was nearly of
gale force.

American PBY Catalina amphibious planes took off from
bases in Northern Ireland to join in the search. Leonard Smith,
an American navy ensign, acting on a spotting tip from the U.S.
coast guard cutter Modoc which had caught sight of the Bismarck,
put out in a Catalina from Londonderry. Six hours later he sent a
message to the British Operational Intelligence Center in London
which led to the sinking of the German battleship.

The ships of the British fleet were running low on fuel oil.
The Bismarck was steaming towards the French coast and within a
matter of hours could reach a position where she could be protected
from the air by the German Luftwaffe.

Fifteen Swordfish bomber planes left the Ark Royal and headed towards the Bismarck. The British Sheffield, traveling alone,
narrowly missed being sunk by Swordfish bombs. This tragedy was
averted by an emergency radio message from the Ark Royal.

The Swordfish returned to their ship for additional fuel and
armament. Once again they took off and, sighting the Bismarck,
dropped their bombs in a steady stream. The German battleship's
rudder and steering mechanism were put out of commission and she
proceeded ahead in a tight circle. Another bomb hit her starboard
bow.

Five destroyers under the unified command of Captain Vian
came out of the darkness and encircled the Bismarck. They were
joined shortly thereafter by the Rodney, King George V and the Norfolk. The British ships opened fire on the Bismarck and Captain
Lindemann and Admiral Lutjens were killed. Planes from the Ark
Royal arrived at the scene but were not needed; the German battleship was done for. German submarines had been dispatched to take
part in the battle but arrived too late. The planes of the Luftwaffe
were not able to defend the Bismarck from the air as the battle took
place beyond their maximum flying range.

The Bismarck's fate was sealed when torpedoes fired from
the Dorsetshire completed the work done by the British planes and
ships. The Bismarck rolled over and sank. Adolf Hitler's proud-
est, most deadly battleship was gone forever. Historians have
opined that, had she survived and later returned to action, the
course of world history may well have been changed.

Suggested Readings

"British Fleet Sinks Nazi Battleship 'Bismarck' After 1, 750 Mile Chase to Avenge H. M. S. 'Hood', " Life, June 9, 1941.

"End of the 'Bismarck, ' " Life, August 11, 1941.

Forester, C. S.   The Last Nine Days of the "Bismarck. "   Boston: Little, Brown, 1959.

Grenfell, Russell.   The "Bismarck" Episode.   New York: Macmillan, 1949.

Haines, C. Grover, and J. Ross Hoffman.   The Origins and Background of the Second World War.   New York: Oxford University Press, 1943.

Hale, W. H.   "The Lesson of the Bismarck, "   New Republic, June 9, 1941.

Kennedy, Ludovic Henry Coverley.   Pursuit: The Chase and Sinking of the "Bismarck. "   New York: Viking Press, 1974.

"Lessons From the Bismarck: Controversy of Sea Power v. Air Power Settled by Hood-Bismarck Affair and Battle for Crete, " Time, June 9, 1941.

Muller, E.   "The Last Days of the Bismarck, "   Reader's Digest, February, 1942.

_____ .   "On Board the Bismarck, "   Harper's Magazine, February, 1942.

Parkes, Oscar.   British Battleships.   London: Seeley Service, 1957.

Roskill, S. W.   The War at Sea.   London: Her Majesty's Stationery Office, 1955-61.

Schofield, Brian Betham.   The Loss of the "Bismarck. "   Annapolis, Md. :   U. S.   Naval Institute, 1972.

Shirer, William L.   The Sinking of the "Bismarck. "   New York: Random House, 1962.

Taylor, Alan John Percivale.   The Origins of the Second World War.   New York: Atheneum, 1961.

Toland, John.   Adolf Hitler.   Garden City, N. Y. :   Doubleday, 1977.

Wibberley, Leonard.   The Life of Winston Churchill.   New York: Ariel Books, 1956.

Woodward, E. L.   Great Britain and the German Navy.   Oxford: Clarendon Press, 1935.

Young, Peter.   World War: 1939-1945.   New York: Crowell, 1966.

THE NAZI SABOTEURS (1942)

On the night of June 13, 1942, a group of four German saboteurs landed on Amagansett Beach, Long Island. The men came ashore in a rubber dinghy dropped from a submarine. Tne group was headed by George John Dasch and included Peter Burger, Heinrich Harmheinck and Richard Quirin. Four nights later another similar group consisting of Herbert Hans Haupt, Hermann Otto Neubauer, Edward Kerling and Werner Thiel landed at Ponte Vedra Beach, Florida, 25 miles south of Jacksonville.

The saboteurs were dressed in German navy fatigues and
brought with them boxes of explosives, detonators, timing devices
and similar equipment. These boxes, along with the fatigues, were
buried on the beach.

John C. Cullen, a member of the coast guard, while on patrol found Dasch and his three fellow-Nazis burying their explosives
and uniforms. He challenged the men, one of whom explained that
they were fishermen who had come from Southampton and run aground.
This man, who later was identified by Cullen as Dasch, offered the
coastguardsman money. "Forget about this, " he said, "and I'll
give you some money and you can have a good time. " Cullen accepted the money, which turned out to be $260, and returned to his
station where he reported the matter to his superior, Warren Barnes,
chief of the Amagansett Coast Guard Station, and handed over the
supposed bribe. He then took Barnes and a patrol party to the area
of the beach where he had encountered the "fishermen. " In the
morning coastguardsmen dug up the items the Nazis had buried.

Five days after landing at Amagansett Beach, Dasch took a
train to Washington, registered at the Mayflower Hotel and telephoned the Federal Bureau of Investigation. He was interrogated
and signed a confession, implicating himself and the other seven
saboteurs. As a result of the information he gave, all his fellow-
Nazis were rounded up and in custody by June 27.

The eight would-be saboteurs were tried by a military court
at Washington, of which retired Major General Frank D. McCoy
was president. The prosecution was handled by Attorney General
Francis Biddle and F. B. I. director J. Edgar Hoover attended the
sessions. Dasch was defended by Colonel Carl Ristine and the
others by Colonels Cassius Dowell and Kenneth Royall. The proceedings were secret, the press being admitted on only one occasion
when the court was not in session.

The formal charge was violating and conspiring to violate
the law of war, in that the accused, "as enemies of the United
States, acting for and on behalf of the German Reich ... passed
through American military lines for the purpose of committing sabotage.... " The eight were also accused of spying. They all pleaded "not guilty. "

Coastguardsman Cullen was the first prosecution witness to
be called. He testified as to what had occurred at Amagansett
Beach on the night of June 13, and identified Dasch as the man with
whom he had spoken and who had given him money. Cullen's testimony was confirmed by Barnes, who identified the objects which
had been dug from the sand.

Dasch and Burger testified that they were not in sympathy
with the Nazi Party's objectives and had never intended to use the
explosives to destroy American railroads, industrial plants or water
systems. Burger had at one time been confined in a German con-

centration camp. Dasch's defense was based on the fact that he
had informed the F. B. I. of the sabotage plot and identified the men
involved in it.

All eight defendants were found guilty and sentenced to die
in the electric chair, the court recommending that Dasch and Burger's sentences be commuted to life imprisonment. President Franklin D. Roosevelt reduced Burger's sentence to life imprisonment and
that of Dasch to thirty years. The other six were electrocuted on
August 8, 1942, and buried in nameless graves in the District of
Columbia.

In 1948 President Harry S Truman commuted the unserved
portions of Burger and Dasch's sentences and both men were deported to Germany. Burger disappeared from the scene. Dasch
was still living in 1959 when he published a book describing the
affair.

Suggested Readings

Archer, Jules. The Dictators. New York: Hawthorn Books, 1967.
"Army Sticks to No Admission as Nazi Saboteurs Are Tried, "
    Newsweek, July 20, 1942.
Cousins, Norman. "Saboteurs, " Saturday Review, August 8, 1942.
Cushman, R. E. "The Case of the Nazi Saboteurs, " American Po-
    litical Science Review, December, 1942.
Dasch, George John. Eight Spies Against America. London: Har-
    rap, 1959.
"Death for the Saboteurs!" Newsweek, July 6, 1942.
"Eight Against America" in Crimes and Punishment, Vol. 4. Ed-
    itorial presentation: Jackson Morley. London: BPC, 1973.
"Espionage: Seven Generals v. Eight Saboteurs, " Time, July 20,
    1942.
Farago, Ladislas. The Game of the Foxes: The Untold Story of
    German Espionage in the United States and Great Britain During
    World War II. New York: McKay, 1971.
"Saboteur Finale, " Newsweek, August 10, 1942.
"Saboteurs and the Court, " New Republic, August 10, 1942.
Sayers, M. , and A. E. Kahn. "Sabotage: The Secret War Against
    America, " Reader's Digest, October, 1942.
Shirer, William L. The Rise and Fall of Adolf Hitler. New York:
    Random House, 1961.
_____. The Rise and Fall of the Third Reich: A History of
    Nazi Germany. New York: Simon & Schuster, 1960.
Waite, Robert G. , ed. Hitler and Nazi Germany. New York: Holt,
    Rinehart, 1965.

OPERATION BERNHARD (1942-1945)

In 1942 Heinrich Himmler, the Nazi Gestapo chief, conceived

the scheme known as "Operation Bernhard" by which he believed
that the economy of Great Britain could be destroyed and, he hoped,
World War II would be shortened.   His idea was to engrave large
quantities of counterfeit English five, ten and twenty pound notes
and circulate them in Allied countries.

Major Bernhard Kruger, a German army officer, was put
in charge of the operation and his given name was assigned to it.
Expert printers and engravers were recruited, by Himmler's order,
from various concentration camps.   They were sent to Berlin where
they were imprisoned at Sachsenhausen.   Printing presses, ink, engraving tools, paper and similar supplies were delivered and the
prisoners, who had not been informed what their fate was to be,
realized that they were expected to exercise their technical skills
for the benefit of the Nazis.

Almost 150 men were set to installing and readying the presses and engraving plates from which the spurious banknotes would be
printed.   It was Himmler's intention to produce two hundred million bogus English pounds at the rate of 40,000 individual notes
monthly.   The notes, if the plan was to be successful, would have
to be virtually undetectable as the forgeries they were.

Technical difficulties arose, particularly as to the linen
threads embedded in the paper on which genuine currency is engraved.   Major Kruger, using imported linen, was eventually able
to produce a paper which was sufficiently like the genuine article
to fulfill his purpose.   Genuine notes were photographed and plates
to be used to produce the counterfeits were prepared by the prisoner-technicians.

After a sufficient number of forged English notes had been
made, Kruger had them circulated in neutral countries, particularly
Spain, Turkey and Switzerland.   This "test run" showed that the
spurious currency was accepted without question as the genuine Bank
of England issue.   Encouraged by this, Kruger than arranged for
distribution of his product all through Europe.   Spies, secret agents
and saboteurs were furnished with counterfeit notes which they used
for bribes, buying information and exchanging for genuine currency.
Bills with slight imperfections were sent to occupied countries.
Other bills were dropped over England by air, in the hope that people finding them would put them in circulation.   Some of these did
enter the supply of circulating money, but in many cases the find-
ers turned the notes in to police stations.

Many of the counterfeits were identified as spurious.   The
Bank of England retaliated by issuing notes of a new design.   Kruger
than turned his attention to counterfeiting American currency, including 50 and 100 dollar bills.   Himmler arranged to move the
plant and printing technicians to a new location, an underground
complex in the Austrian Alps.   Here the work went on.

Operation Bernhard finally terminated when Berlin fell to the

Allies in 1945. Himmler, captured by the British, committed suicide on May 23, as Adolf Hitler did in April. Kruger, taking
great quantities of counterfeit money with him, attempted to flee.
Orders had been given that the counterfeiting plant be destroyed
and the prisoner-technicians "liquidated." This, however, was not
accomplished. The printing presses and other equipment were left
intact and the prisoners were liberated by Allied troops.

It is estimated that Operation Bernhard produced several
million pounds in spurious currency. Of this, 22 million was found
at the printing plant awaiting shipment and another 37 million was
found floating in the Enns River in Austria.

Suggested Readings

Abosch, Heinz. The Menace of the Miracle: Germany from Hitler
to Adenauer. Translated by Douglas Garman. New York:
Monthly Review Press, 1963.
Appel, Benjamin. Hitler, from Power to Ruin. New York: Gros-
set & Dunlap, 1964.
Archer, Jules. The Dictators. New York: Hawthorn Books, 1967.
Bullock, Alan. Hitler: A Study in Tyranny. New York: Harper
& Row, 1962.
Collier, Basil. The Second World War: A Military History. New
York: Morrow, 1967.
Eisenhower, General Dwight D. Crusade in Europe. New York:
Doubleday, 1948.
Elliott, Brendan John. Hitler and Germany. New York: McGraw-
Hill, 1968.
Fuller, John F. C. The Second World War, 1939-1945. London:
Eyre & Spottiswoode, 1948.
Goldston, Robert. The Life and Death of Nazi Germany. Indian-
apolis: Bobbs-Merrill, 1967.
Grunberger, Richard. Germany, 1918-1945. New York: Harper
& Row, 1966.
Heiden, Konrad. Der Fuehrer: Hitler's Rise to Power. Boston:
Houghton Mifflin, 1944.
Holborn, Hajo. A History of Modern Germany. Vol. III: 1840-
1945. New York: Knopf, 1969.
"Operation Bernhard" in Crimes and Punishment, Vol. 12. Ed-
itorial presentation: Jackson Morley. London: BPC, 1973.
Prittie, Terence, and the editors of Life. Germany. New York:
Time, Inc., 1961.
Shirer, William L. The Rise and Fall of Adolf Hitler. New York:
Random House, 1961.
_____. The Rise and Fall of the Third Reich: A History of
Nazi Germany. New York: Simon & Schuster, 1960.
Stein, George H., ed. Hitler. Englewood Cliffs, N.J.: Prentice-
Hall, 1968.
Sutton, Felix. The How and Why Wonder Book of World War II.
New York: Grosset & Dunlap, 1962.
Toland, John. Adolf Hitler. Garden City, N.Y.: Doubleday, 1977.

Wilmot, Chester. The Struggle for Europe. New York: Harper
& Row, 1952.

THE CASABLANCA CONFERENCE (1943)

        Casablanca, the chief seaport of the kingdom of Morocco on
the North African Atlantic coast, was the scene of one of the most
important top level conferences of World War II.   President Franklin D. Roosevelt of the United States and Winston S. Churchill,
Prime Minister of Great Britain met, at Roosevelt's suggestion,
from January 14 to January 24, 1943, to plan strategy.   Joseph
Stalin, the Soviet dictator, though invited, was unable to attend because the Battle of Stalingrad was in progress and he found it impossible to leave Russia.

        Roosevelt was accompanied by General George C. Marshall,
American Army Chief of Staff, Fleet Admiral Ernest King, Chief
of Naval Operations, and Harry L. Hopkins, his chief civilian adviser.   Churchill's party included General Sir Alan Brooke, Chief
of the Imperial General Staff.

        The Axis forces had been defeated at the Battle of El Ala-
mein and Northwest Africa had been invaded by the Anglo-American
forces.   The various decisions which had to be made concerning
further conduct of the war fell into two classes: first, the decision
to continue limited war in the Mediterranean and, second, the open
declaration of a policy of requiring nothing less than unconditional
surrender of the enemy.

        The conferees came to an amicable agreement on a number
of matters, such as continuing the bombardment of Germany and the
priorities given to the transport of supplies across the Atlantic.   The
problem of selecting a leader of the French in liberated French Africa was solved by appointing General Henri Giraud as commander.
General Charles de Gaulle, head of the French Committee of National Liberation, was not happy with the selection.   He was ap-
peased by being named commander with Giraud.

        The problem of deciding on future strategy in the Mediter-
ranean posed some difficulties.   Churchill wished to continue the
war in that area until a sufficient number of troops could be assembled for a cross-channel invasion of France.   This, plus an
invasion of Italy would, he felt, make feasible an attack on Germany through "the soft underbelly of Europe."   These tactics were
opposed by General Marshall and Admiral King who felt that Germany could be defeated only by a massive invasion across the channel.   King believed further that more emphasis should be placed on
the war being fought in the Pacific against the Japanese.   President
Roosevelt overruled King and referred to an agreement made by the
American Chiefs of Staff in 1940 that, in the event of a two-front

war, the one in Europe should take precedence. He agreed to a limited continuation of the Mediterranean conflict and General Dwight D. Eisenhower was appointed Allied Supreme Commander in North Africa and the Western Mediterranean. Eisenhower's deputy was to be the British General Sir Henry Alexander, commander of the Middle East forces. These two were to plan an invasion of Sicily after the Axis forces were defeated in North Africa.

The promulgation of the "unconditional surrender" doctrine was the most controversial decision made at the Casablanca Conference. On the last day Roosevelt announced to the press that "elimination of German, Japanese and Italian war power means the unconditional surrender by Germany, Italy and Japan. " He added that he did not have in mind the destruction of German, Italian and Japanese citizens but only "the destruction of the philosophies which are based on conquest and the subjugation of other people. " Churchill, according to some historians, had previously discussed the matter with his staff and had agreed to such a course of action. Others believe that the British Prime Minister was surprised at what he considered an impromptu announcement but indicated his agreement.

It has been contended that the "unconditional surrender" policy enunciated by Roosevelt did the Allied cause more harm than good as it served notice on the Axis that nothing less than complete defeat was acceptable, and thus prolonged the war.

Suggested Readings

Baldwin, Hanson. Great Mistakes of the War. New York: Harper & Row, 1949.

Churchill, Winston S. The Second World War. Boston: Houghton Mifflin, 1950.

Collier, Basil. The Second World War: A Military History. New York: Morrow, 1967.

Divine, Robert A. Roosevelt and World War II. Baltimore: Johns Hopkins University Press, 1969.

Feis, Herbert. Churchill, Roosevelt, Stalin. Princeton, N. J. : Princeton University Press, 1957.

Fuller, John F. C. The Second World War, 1939-1945. London: Eyre & Spottiswoode, 1948.

Greer, Thomas. What Roosevelt Thought. East Lansing, Mich. : Michigan State College Press, 1958.

Hatch, Alden. Franklin D. Roosevelt: An Informal Biography. New York: Holt, 1947.

Kecskemeti, Paul. Strategic Surrender. Stanford, Calif. : Stanford University Press, 1958.

Peare, Catherine O. The FDR Story. New York: Crowell, 1962.

Roosevelt, James, and Stanley Shalett. Affectionately, F. D. R. : A Son's Story of a Lonely Man. London: Harrap, 1960.

Schlesinger, Arthur M. , Jr. The Age of Roosevelt. Boston: Houghton Mifflin, 1957.

Schnittkind, Henry Thomas.   Franklin Delano Roosevelt.   New York:
     Putnam, 1962.
Sherwood, Robert E.   Roosevelt and Hopkins: An Intimate History.
     New York: Harper & Row, 1950.
Smith, Gaddis.   American Diplomacy During the Second World War.
     New York: Harper & Row, 1962.
Toland, John.   Adolf Hitler.   Garden City, N.Y.:   Doubleday, 1977.
Weingast, David Elliott.   Franklin D. Roosevelt, Man of Destiny.
     New York: Messner, 1952.
Wheeler-Bennett, John W.   The Nemesis of Power: The German
     Army in Politics, 1918-1945.   New York: Viking Press, 1952.
Wilmot, Chester.   The Struggle for Europe.   New York: Harper
     & Row, 1952.
Young, Peter.   World War: 1939-1945.   New York: Crowell, 1966.

THE MURDER OF SIR HARRY OAKES (1943)

On the morning of July 8, 1943, the body of Sir Harry Oakes,
a naturalized British citizen and self-made millionaire, was found
in his bed at Nassau.   He had been battered to death and his body
had been sprinkled with gasoline and set afire.   In October of that
year his son-in-law, Count Alfred de Marigny, was tried for the murder.
The jury found him not guilty.

The events leading up to Oakes' death were complicated.
His daughter Nancy, eldest of his five children, had married Marigny
after an extremely short courtship without her father's knowledge or
consent.   Oakes, a man with a violent temper, felt that the count,
who had been previously married and divorced twice, was a fortune
hunter.   Marigny, however, was a successful businessman and a
champion yachtsman.

At first Oakes seemed to like his new son-in-law, offering
him a position with one of his mining enterprises.   The count refused and the relationship between the two men deteriorated, with
Oakes making a new will early in 1943.   By this will his daughter's
husband would inherit no part of Oakes' money.

One evening Oakes took exception to a remark Marigny made
concerning the Duke of Windsor, governor of the Bahamas and former King of England.   The incident, which led to a "blazing row"
at a dinner party given by Nancy and her husband, ended with Oakes
stamping out in a fury and taking his fifteen-year-old son Sydney
with him.   A few nights later Sydney was spending the night at the
home of his sister.   Oakes appeared, pounded on the door and--when
Marigny opened it--entered, ordered his son to get up and dress,
and took him away.   Marigny stated that he never saw Oakes alive
again.

On the afternoon of July 7 Oakes called for Harold Christie,

a real estate developer and a friend of both Marigny and Sir Harry
Oakes. The two men drove to Westbourne, Oakes' home, where
they played a set of tennis and then had cocktails with several other guests. Some of the party left and the others stayed at Westbourne for dinner. A storm came up and the dinner guests, with
the exception of Christie, drove home. Christie spent the night in
the Oakes home and next morning, on going to his host's room to
waken him, found him murdered.

The Duke of Windsor, when informed of the death of Sir Harry Oakes, summoned two Miami detectives, Captains Edward Mel-
chin and James Barker, to conduct an investigation. In due course
Marigny was accused of murdering his father-in-law.

The trial commenced on October 18, 1943. Sir Oscar Daly
was the presiding judge. The prosecution was handled by the at-
torney-general, Eric Hallinan, who was assisted by Alfred Adderley,
an eminent Negro attorney. Godfrey Higgs and Ernest Callender
served as defense counsel.

An examination of Marigny's person showed that hairs on
his arms and beard had been singed and, as mentioned above, Sir
Harry Oakes' body had been burned after he was beaten. Marigny
explained, on the witness stand, that he had lit some hurricane
lamps at a dinner party he was giving in his home when the storm
broke, and that he had involuntarily singed himself. Several of his
dinner guests, including Betty Roberts, confirmed his statement.

By a nine to three verdict the jury found Marigny not guilty
of the murder of Sir Harry Oakes. The following day he, at his
own request, took a lie detector test in front of his wife, counsel
and a number of friends and reporters. He passed it with flying
colors.

Subsequently two attempts, unexplained to this day, were made
on Marigny's life. In 1949 his marriage to Nancy Oakes was annulled. He married for a fourth time and went to live in South
America.

The person who killed Oakes has never been identified. The
consensus is that, as a loud-mouthed bully who struck it rich by
accident and spent the rest of his life abusing people and pushing
them around, Oakes "had it coming. "

Suggested Readings

Abrahamsen, David, M. D. The Murdering Mind. New York: Harper & Row, 1973.
Bolitho, Hector. King Edward VIII. Philadelphia: Lippincott, 1937.
Bromberg, Walter. Mold of Murder: A Psychiatric Study of Homicide. New York: Grune & Stratton, 1961.
Catton, Joseph. Behind the Scenes of Murder. New York: Norton, 1940.

Guttmacher, M. S. The Mind of the Murderer. Freeport, N. Y.:
    Books for Libraries, 1960.
Jesse, F. Tennyson. Murder and Its Motives. London: Harrap,
    1952.
Lawes, Warden Lewis E. Meet the Murderer! New York: Har-
    per, 1940.
Lester, David, and Gene Lester. Crime of Passion: Murder and
    the Murderer. Chicago: Nelson Hall, 1975.
McDade, Thomas M., compiler. The Annals of Murder. Norman,
    Okla.: University of Oklahoma Press, 1961.
Reinhardt, James Melvin. The Psychology of Strange Killers.
    Springfield, Ill.: Thomas, 1962.
Roberts, Carl E. B. The New World of Crime. London: Noble,
    1933.
"Who Killed Sir Harry?" in Crimes and Punishment, Vol. 6. Ed-
    itorial presentation: Jackson Morley. London: BPC, 1973.
Wilson, Colin, and Patricia Pitman. Encyclopedia of Murder. New
    York: Putnam, 1962.
Windsor, The Duke of. A King's Story: The Memoirs of the Duke
    of Windsor. New York: Putnam, 1951.
Wolfgang, Marvin E., compiler. Studies in Homicide. New York:
    Harper & Row, 1967.

THE HITLER ASSASSINATION PLOTS (1943-1944)

The assassination of statesmen by cranks and political opponents has been practiced for hundreds of years. Julius Caesar
was stabbed by a group of Roman nobles, including Brutus and Cassius, in 44 B. C. Four American presidents--Lincoln, Garfield,
McKinley and Kennedy--were shot to death and attempts were made
on the lives of at least three others--both Roosevelts and Gerald Ford. An unsuccessful plot to murder Lincoln, then president-
elect, was foiled by Allan Pinkerton, the Anglo-American detective,
in 1859. Benito Mussolini met a violent death at the hands of Italian partisans in 1945 and Mahatma Gandhi was killed by a Hindu
fanatic three years later. Many similar examples could be cited.

One of the most spectacular men of modern times was Adolf
Hitler, the German Chancellor and Fuehrer. Between 1933 and
1939 he brought on World War II and exercised virtually unlimited
power within his sphere before his suicide in 1945. Such a man
would, in the course of his political maneuverings, inspire both
fanatical followers and implacable enemies. Certain of Hitler's enemies opposed his actions, political and military goals and methods
for achieving his ends to the extent that at least six attempts to assassinate him were made. His enemies also tried to arrest him.
None of these were successful.

On August 4, 1941, at Borisov, U. S. S. R., certain officers
of an army group commanded by Field Marshal Fedor von Bock de-

termined to arrest Hitler and put him on trial. Bock, approached by Major General von Treschkow and Lieutenant von Schlabrendorff, refused to have anything to do with the proposal until Hitler had been arrested. This plot failed because Hitler appeared surrounded by a number of personal guards and the conspiritors were unable to get near him and take him into custody.

At Smolensk, on March 13, 1943, an attempt was made to kill the Fuehrer by means of time bombs disguised as bottles of brandy. Field Marshal Gunther von Kluge, like Bock, declined to support the plot, so Treschkow and Schlabrendorff, trying a second time to do away with the German dictator, proceeded without him. The two prepared the bombs and Colonel Brandt, a member of Hitler's staff, was asked to take them aboard the aircraft on which the latter and his entourage would be traveling. On this occasion the bombs failed to explode and Schlabrendorff was able to retrieve them before they could be discovered for what they were.

General von Treschkow was not a man who was easily discouraged. Hitler was scheduled to be present at a Heroes Memorial Day celebration at the Armory in Unter den Linden, Berlin, on March 21, 1943. Colonel von Gersdorff was in the building with two bombs containing ten-minute fuses. Hitler's visit was to have lasted thirty minutes but he stayed for only eight, leaving the colonel insufficient time to set the fuses.

A new type of military overcoat for use by the troops in Russia had been designed and Hitler was scheduled to inspect it in Berlin sometime in November, 1943. Axel von dem Bussche, a young officer with a deep hatred for the dictator and all that he represented, had agreed to model the coat at the inspection. He planned to put a bomb in each of two pockets and blow himself and the Fuehrer to pieces while the inspection was progressing. Hitler postponed the inspection on several occasions and, late in November, the warehouse in which the coats were stored was completely destroyed in an air raid. There being no coats to be shown to the Fuehrer, the inspection was canceled.

Another attempt on Hitler's life was abandoned on July 11, 1944. On this occasion Colonel Claus von Stauffenberg and another officer went to Obersalsberg for a conference with Hitler. A bomb had been hidden in the colonel's briefcase. It had been hoped that other Nazi officials, such as Hermann Goering or Heinrich Himmler, would be present and could also be done away with. This, however, was not the case and it was decided to postpone the assassination until additional prospective victims were present.

Three days later Colonel Stauffenberg attempted to plant a bomb at Hitler's headquarters at Rastenburg, East Prussia. Both Goering and Himmler were present, as was the Fuehrer. As the colonel began preparing the fuse Hitler was called from the room and did not return. This attempt was consequently abandoned.

On July 20, 1944, the so-called "July Plot" was activated.

Adolf Hitler was holding daily conferences at his headquarters at
Rastenburg. Colonel Stauffenberg entered the room, accompanied
by Field Marshal Wilhelm Keitel. General Heusinger was making
an oral report to the Fuehrer, and Stauffenberg, excusing himself
"to make an urgent telephone call to Berlin," placed his briefcase,
which contained a live bomb, next to a heavy wooden support beneath a table at which Hitler was sitting. Colonel Brandt, who
was present, thinking that the briefcase might be in Hitler's way,
moved it to the other side of the support. Ten minutes later the
bomb went off. Brandt, two officers and a stenographer died in
the blast and two other officers were severely wounded. Hitler and
the others in the room received only slight injuries.

Stauffenberg, hearing the explosion, concluded that the German dictator was dead. He flew back to Berlin. When it was
learned that Hitler had survived the bombing the entire anti-Nazi
conspiracy collapsed. Bock and certain principals in the plot committed suicide. Stauffenberg was executed by a firing squad and
other members of the group were executed in ways less humane
than shooting.

Suggested Readings

Appel, Benjamin. Hitler, from Power to Ruin. New York: Grosset & Dunlap, 1964.

Archer, Jules. The Dictators. New York: Hawthorn Books, 1967.

Bullock, Alan. Hitler: A Study in Tyranny. New York: Harper
& Row, 1962.

Carr, Albert H. Zolotoff. Men of Power: A Book of Dictators.
New York: Viking Press, 1956.

Elliott, Brendan John. Hitler and Germany. New York: McGraw-
Hill, 1968.

Goldston, Robert. The Life and Death of Nazi Germany. Indianapolis: Bobbs-Merrill, 1967.

Heiden, Konrad. Der Fuehrer: Hitler's Rise to Power. Boston:
Houghton Mifflin, 1944.

Hitler, Adolf. Mein Kampf. Boston: Houghton Mifflin, 1943.

Jarman, T. L. The Rise and Fall of Nazi Germany. New York:
New York University Press, 1956.

Kurtz, Harold. "The July Plot" in Taylor, A. J. P. , editor-in-chief.
Purnell's History of the 20th Century, Vol. 7. New York: Purnell, 1971.

Prittie, Terence, and the editors of Life. Germany. New York:
Time, Inc. , 1961.

Shirer, William L. The Rise and Fall of Adolf Hitler. New York:
Random House, 1961.

_____. The Rise and Fall of the Third Reich: A History of
Nazi Germany. New York: Simon & Schuster, 1960.

Speer, Albert. Inside the Third Reich. New York: Macmillan,
1970.

Stein, George H. , ed. Hitler. Englewood Cliffs, N. J. : Prentice-
Hall, 1968.

Strasser, Otto. Hitler and I. Boston: Houghton Mifflin, 1940.
Toland, John. Adolf Hitler. Garden City, N. Y. : Doubleday, 1977.
Trevor-Roper, H. R. The Last Days of Hitler. New York: Collier
    Books, 1962.
Wheeler-Bennett, John W. The Nemesis of Power: The German
    Army in Politics, 1918-1945. New York: Viking Press, 1952.

THE FOUNDING OF THE WORLD BANK (1944)

Representatives from 44 nations met at the United Nations
Monetary and Financial Conference, better known as the Bretton
Woods Conference, from July 1 to July 22, 1944. The principal
result of the conference, held at Bretton Woods, a New Hampshire
vacation resort, was the creation of the International Monetary Fund
and the International Bank for Reconstruction and Development, commonly known as the World Bank.

As stated in the Articles of Agreement, the chief objectives
of the Bank are "to assist in the reconstruction and development of
territories of members by facilitating the investment of capital for
productive purposes ... "; "to promote private foreign investment
by means of guarantees or participation in loans"; and "to supplement private investment by providing, on suitable conditions, finance
for productive purposes out of its own capital. ... "

Loans are granted only to member nations wishing to finance
specific projects. Before a loan application is approved the Bank's
advisers must be satisfied that the borrower can meet the conditions
imposed by the Bank. These conditions are intended to insure that
the loan will be repaid and that it will be used profitably. The
borrower must be unable to negotiate a loan for its specific pro-
ject(s) elsewhere on reasonable terms. The project must be technically feasible and economically sound.

After the loan has been made the borrower is required to
render periodic reports concerning the progress of the project for
which the loan was granted. Similar reports are tendered by the
Bank's own experts. These reports are made to the Bank's headquarters in Washington, D. C.

The Bank's early loans were made primarily to European
countries for the purpose of restoring industries which had been
damaged or destroyed in World War II. More recently, loans have
been made to underdeveloped countries in Africa, Latin America,
the Far East and elsewhere. These later loans were made to finance the construction of power plants, railway lines and agricultural facilities. By September, 1973, the Bank's membership included
117 countries. During fiscal 1973 it approved loans totaling 3. 56
billion dollars. Over a five year period loans to Africa increased
214 percent and loans to Latin America grew by 128 percent.

The Bank's funds come primarily from member nations' subscriptions to, or purchase of, the Bank's capital shares, priced at
$100,000 each.   Twenty percent of each $100,000 is paid into the
Bank and the remaining 80 percent is deposited only when the Bank
calls for it in order to pay its own financial obligations.

Additional funds are raised from the sale of securities deposited by borrowers as collateral for their loans.

The World Bank has a staff of about 2,700 persons.   "All
powers of the Bank are vested in a Board of Governors consisting
of one governor appointed by each member nation. " Meetings are
held at least annually.   Seventeen executive directors, who meet
each month at the Washington headquarters, exercise the powers
delegated to them by the member nation governors.   The five member nations holding the largest number of the Bank's capital shares
appoint five of the executive directors.   The other twelve are elected by the Board of Governors, not including the governors representing the five nations holding the largest number of shares.   The
chief officer or president is elected by the executive directors.   He
may be neither a governor nor a director.

The Articles of Agreement require that all members of the
World Bank must also be members of the International Monetary
Fund.   This is a specialized agency of the United Nations designed
to promote international monetary cooperation and stabilization of
currencies, to facilitate expansion of international trade and to help
members meet temporary difficulties in foreign payments.   The Fund
was established in December, 1945, and, like the World Bank, was
an outgrowth of the Bretton Woods Conference.   Its administrative
apparatus is nearly identical to that of the World Bank.

Suggested Readings

Allardice, Corbin, ed.   Atomic Power.   New York: Pergamon
       Press, 1957.
"Bankers Reject World Fund Plan as Easy Dollars for Other Na-
       tions, " Newsweek, February 12, 1945.
"Banks and Bretton Woods, " Time, October 9, 1944.
"Bretton Woods and the A. B. A. , " Business Week, February 10,
       1945.
International Bank for Reconstruction and Development.   Population
       Policies and Economic Development: A World Bank Staff Report.
       Baltimore, Md. : Johns Hopkins University Press, 1974.
Lindley, E. K.   "Wall Street vs. Main Street?, " Newsweek, March
       26, 1945.
McNamara, Robert S.   One Hundred Countries, Two Billion People.
       New York: Frederick A. Praeger, 1973.
Mason, Edward Sagendorph.   The World Bank Since Bretton Woods.
       Washington, D. C. : Brookings Institution, 1973.
Morris, James.   The Road to Huddersfield: A Journey to Five Con-
       tinents. New York: Pantheon Books, 1963.

"New Storm Hits World Bank, " Business Week, September 26, 1970.
Oliver, Robert W. International Economic Co-operation and the
    World Bank. London: Macmillan, 1975.
Smithies, A. "International Bank for Reconstruction and Develop-
    ment, " American Economic Review, December, 1944.
Stone, I. F. "What Bretton Woods Did, " Nation, August 5, 1944.
Trewhitt, Henry L. McNamara. New York: Harper, 1971.
Williams, J. H. "International Monetary Plans: After Bretton
    Woods, " Foreign Affairs, October, 1944.
"World Bank: Considerably Revised Plan Finally Released by Trea-
    sury, " Newsweek, October 8, 1943.

THE BATTLE OF THE BULGE (1944-1945)

The Battle of the Bulge, fought by German forces against a combined American and British army between December 16, 1944, and January 28, 1945, was the last German offensive of World War II. It resulted in a decisive Allied victory and made the total defeat of the German war machine a matter of months.

In September, 1944, Adolf Hitler, Chancellor and Führer of Germany, realized that his troops were being pushed back on all fronts. The German navy was largely confined to its ports and the Luftwaffe had few aircraft which were still serviceable. The Allied army, in the west, was ready to invade Germany.

The Führer resolved to launch a gigantic counter-offensive against the Anglo-American armies. His plan was to marshal his forces, overcome the Allies and then strike against the Russian troops. He felt that this maneuver would be successful as the Allies had fewer troops than did the Soviets and were forced to rely on long supply lines stretching to the Normandy ports.

On December 16, 1944, the German forces struck in the weakly held Ardennes sector in Belgium, hoping to split the Allied armies, destroy those of the north and drive through to Antwerp. The Allies were caught off guard and the Germans scored a breakthrough, with the American First Army, commanded by General Courtney H. Hodges, being hardest hit.

The German operation was commanded by Field Marshal Karl von Rundstedt. The Sixth Panzer Army, under General Sepp Dietrich and the Fifth Panzer Army, commanded by General Hasso von Manteuffel, formed the arms of a pincer movement, with Antwerp as the objective.

General Dwight D. Eisenhower, Supreme Commander of the Allied Expeditionary Force, countered by dividing command of the Allied forces around the bulge created by the German offensive, with the northern armies directed by General Bernard Law Montgomery

and the southern armies by General Omar N. Bradley. Their instructions were to "permit the defensive line to give but not to
split. " Reinforcements were to be brought up and General George
S. Patton's Third Army was to come in from the south and relieve
the troops defending the bulge.

     The fighting centered around Bastogne. Brigadier General
Anthony McAuliffe, acting commander, received a communique from
the German General Heinrich von Luetwitz demanding immediate surrender. McAuliffe's one-word reply, "Nuts!" literally translated
to the German courier by Colonel Joseph Harper, commander of
the 327th Glider Infantry Regiment, as "Go to Hell!" made headlines.

     By late December the Hitler forces found it necessary to
abandon their siege of Bastogne after reinforcements arrived from
the 101st Airborne Division. Late in December, 1944, the Nazis
started a tactical withdrawal. The Führer continued to reinforce
his soldiers at the bulge, but to no avail. By the end of January,
1945, his troops were in full retreat. He lacked the manpower to
continue the contest with either the Allies or the Russians and in
April he committed suicide. The Russians had entered Berlin and
the Allied troops had reached the Elbe River. World War II ended
in Europe with the surrender of Germany on May 7, 1945, to be
followed by the occupation of the country and the trials of war criminals at Nuremberg.

Suggested Readings

Abosch, Heinz. The Menace of the Miracle: Germany from Hitler
    to Adenauer. Translated by Douglas Garman. New York:
    Monthly Review Press, 1963.
Archer, Jules. The Dictators. New York: Hawthorn Books, 1967.
Baldwin, Hanson. Great Mistakes of the War. New York: Harper
    & Row, 1949.
Bradley, General Omar N. A Soldier's Story. New York: Holt,
    Rinehart, 1951.
Bullock, Alan. Hitler: A Study in Tyranny. New York: Harper
    & Row, 1962.
Carr, Albert H. Zolotoff. Men of Power: A Book of Dictators.
    New York: Viking Press, 1956.
Chalfont, Alun. Montgomery of Alamein. New York: Atheneum,
    1976.
Churchill, Winston S. The Second World War. Vol. VI: "Triumph
    and Tragedy. " Boston: Houghton Mifflin, 1953.
Collier, Basil. The Second World War: A Military History. New
    York: Morrow, 1967.
Dahlerus, J. Birger. The Last Attempt. Translated by A. Dick.
    London: Hutchinson & Co. , 1948.
Divine, Robert A. Roosevelt and World War II. Baltimore: Johns
    Hopkins University Press, 1969.
Eisenhower, General Dwight D. Crusade in Europe. New York:
    Doubleday, 1948.

Elliott, Brendan John. Hitler and Germany. New York: McGraw-Hill, 1968.

Ellis, Major L. F. The War in France and Flanders. London: Her Majesty's Stationery Office, 1953.

Fuller, John F. C. A Military History of the Western World. New York: Funk & Wagnalls, 1954.

_____. The Second World War, 1939-1945. London: Eyre & Spottiswoode, 1948.

Gardner, Brian. The Year That Changed the World: 1945. New York: Coward-McCann, 1963.

Goldston, Robert. The Life and Death of Nazi Germany. Indianapolis: Bobbs-Merrill, 1967.

Grunberger, Richard. Germany, 1918-1945. New York: Harper & Row, 1966.

Heiden, Konrad. Der Fuehrer: Hitler's Rise to Power. Boston: Houghton Mifflin, 1944.

Hitler, Adolf. Mein Kampf. Boston, Houghton Mifflin, 1943.

Holborn, Hajo. A History of Modern Germany. Vol. III: 1840-1945. New York: Knopf, 1969.

Jacobsen, H. A., and J. Rohwer, eds. Decisive Battles of World War II: The German View. Translated by Edward Fitzgerald. New York: Putnam, 1965.

Jarman, T. L. The Rise and Fall of Nazi Germany. New York: New York University Press, 1956.

Kilpatrick, Lyman B., Jr. "The Bulge in the Ardennes: Hitler's Last Threat" in his Captains Without Eyes: Intelligence Failures in World War II. Toronto: Collier-Macmillan, 1969.

Montgomery of Alamein, Field Marshal. Memoirs. Cleveland: World, 1958.

Peare, Catherine O. The FDR Story. New York: Crowell, 1962.

Prittie, Terence, and the editors of Life. Germany. New York: Time, Inc., 1961.

Schlesinger, Arthur M., Jr. The Age of Roosevelt. Boston: Houghton Mifflin, 1957.

Sears, Stephen W. and the editors of American Heritage. Air War Against Hitler's Germany. New York: American Heritage Publishing Co., 1964.

_____. The Battle of the Bulge. New York: American Heritage Publishing Co., 1969.

Shepherd, David. We Were There at the Battle of the Bulge. New York: Grosset & Dunlap, 1961.

Shirer, William L. The Rise and Fall of Adolf Hitler. New York: Random House, 1961.

_____. The Rise and Fall of the Third Reich: A History of Nazi Germany. New York: Simon & Schuster, 1960.

Speer, Albert. Inside the Third Reich. New York: Macmillan, 1970.

Stein, George H., ed. Hitler. Englewood Cliffs, N. J.: Prentice-Hall, 1968.

Steinberg, Alfred. The Man from Missouri: The Life and Times of Harry S Truman. New York: Putnam, 1962.

Sulzberger, C. L. The American Heritage Picture History of World War II. New York: American Heritage Publishing Co., 1966.

Sutton, Felix. The How and Why Wonder Book of World War II.
 New York: Grosset & Dunlap, 1962.
Toland, John. Adolf Hitler. Garden City, N.Y.: Doubleday, 1977.
 _____. The Battle of the Bulge. New York: Random House,
  1966.
Trevor-Roper, H.R. The Last Days of Hitler. New York: Collier
 Books, 1962.
 _____, ed. Hitler's War Directives, 1939-1945. London: Sidg-
 wick, 1964.
Von Luttichau, Charles V.P. "The German Counteroffensive in the
 Ardennes" in Greenfield, Kent Roberts, ed. Command Deci-
 sions. Washington, D.C.: Government Printing Office, 1960.
Weingast, David Elliott. Franklin D. Roosevelt, Man of Destiny.
 New York: Messner, 1952.
Weyr, Thomas. World War II. New York: Messner, 1969.
Wilmot, Chester. The Struggle for Europe. New York: Harper
 & Row, 1952.
Young, Peter. World War: 1939-1945. New York: Crowell, 1966.

THE ACID-BATH MURDERER (1944-1949)

In the case of sex murders it is often difficult to tell whether
frustration or monetary gain is the primary motive. A case in
point is that of John George Haigh who, between 1944 and 1949, murdered six persons. Haigh, known as the "Acid-Bath Murderer" and
the "Vampire Murderer," shot his victims, drank of their blood
and disposed of their bodies by dissolving them in drums of sulfuric
acid. He also profited financially by their deaths.

In 1944 Haigh, a 39-year-old self-employed research engineer, killed William Donald McSwann, an amusement park arcade
operator. Shortly afterward he murdered McSwann's parents and in
February, 1948, Dr. Archibald Henderson and his wife Rosalie suffered the same fate. In each instance Haigh drank some of the
blood of his victim and dissolved the body in acid. He was able,
by forgery, to divert part of each of these murdered person's assets into his own pockets.

It was not until February, 1949, that Haigh was apprehended.
His sixth and last victim was Mrs. Helen Durand-Deacon, a wealthy
69-year-old widow, a resident of the Onslow Court Hotel, a London
retirement home where Haigh also lived. Mrs. Durand-Deacon had
devised some artificial fingernails which she hoped might be manufactured from plastic. She discussed her idea with Haigh who declared it practical and suggested that they travel to "his factory"
at Crawley, Sussex, to "choose the materials." She consented to
go with him and of Friday, February 18, 1949, Haigh drove her to
Crawley in his automobile. After having tea at the George Hotel
the two went to a small factory in Leopold Road. This factory did
not belong to Haigh as he had stated, but was rented by him for use
in his "engineering research."

Having entered the deserted building, Haigh produced a .38 Webley revolver from his pocket and shot Mrs. Durand-Deacon in the neck, killing her instantly. He then made an incision in an artery, collected blood in a glass and drank it. He then stripped the body, put what money and articles of value she had to one side and placed his victim's remains in a 45-gallon drum. He then pumped a solution of sulfuric acid into the drum, using a small hand pump. The drum had been specially lined to hold corrosive materials.

Haigh then went to a restaurant in Crawley where he ate a light meal. He next returned to the Onslow Court Hotel, leaving the body in its bath of acid. The factory, he knew, would be closed over the weekend and he reasoned that by the following Monday the body would have been completely dissolved, thus destroying all evidence of his crime.

Back at the hotel he learned, to his horror, that Mrs. Durand-Deacon had told a friend, Mrs. Constance Lane, of her proposed visit to Crawley. He had expected her to keep her artificial fingernail venture a "company secret." When her absence was noticed on the following day Haigh hastily disposed of his victim's jewelry in South London, Surrey and Sussex. Mrs. Lane, alarmed at her friend's protracted absence, insisted that Haigh contact the police and report a missing person. Unable to refuse, he proceeded to the station where he said that he "knew nothing of the matter; that Mrs. Durand-Deacon had failed to keep her appointment with him and that he, assuming that she had changed her plans, drove down to Crawley alone."

The police constable to whom he reported believed his story but Police Sergeant Alexandria Maude Lambourne became suspicious. She had been sent to the Onslow Court Hotel to question the guests there and failed to appreciate Haigh's "glib tongue and superficial charm." She reported her feelings to her superior who, in turn, communicated with Scotland Yard. It was soon learned that Haigh had served three prison sentences: one for theft and two for fraud.

John George Haigh was summoned to the police station for further questioning. After interrogation he stated that he had destroyed Mrs. Durand-Deacon's body in a vat of acid and that, as he saw it, he could not be convicted of murder in a situation where the body had ceased to exist. He also confessed to shooting the woman and drinking her blood.

The Scotland Yard authorities examined the factory at Crawley and found that the body of the murdered woman had not been completely dissolved by the acid. The dental plates were still intact and were later shown to have been made for Mrs. Durand-Deacon.

The "Acid-Bath Murderer" was brought to trial on July 18, 1949. Although the defense entered a plea of insanity, Haigh was found guilty and sentenced to die.

Suggested Readings

Abrahamsen, David, M. D. The Murdering Mind. New York: Harper & Row, 1973.
"The Acid-Bath Blood Drinker: George Haigh" in Infamous Murders. London: Verdict Press/Phoebus Publishing Co., 1975.
Bromberg, Walter. Mold of Murder: A Psychiatric Study of Homicide. New York: Grune & Stratton, 1961.
Catton, Joseph. Behind the Scenes of Murder. New York: Norton, 1940.
Guttmacher, M. S. The Mind of the Murderer. Freeport, N. Y. : Books for Libraries, 1960.
Jesse, F. Tennyson. Murder and Its Motives. London: Harrap, 1952.
Lawes, Warden Lewis E. Meet the Murderer! New York: Harper, 1940.
Lester, David, and Gene Lester. Crime of Passion: Murder and the Murderer. Chicago: Nelson Hall, 1975.
McDade, Thomas M. , compiler. The Annals of Murder. Norman, Okla. : University of Oklahoma Press, 1961.
Reinhardt, James Melvin. The Psychology of Strange Killers. Springfield, Ill. : Thomas, 1962.
Roberts, Carl E. B. The New World of Crime. London: Noble, 1933.
Scott, Sir Harold, with Philippa Pearce. From Inside Scotland Yard. New York: Macmillan, 1965.
Symonds, Julian. "Sex Murderers: England and France" in his A Pictorial History of Crime. New York: Crown Publishers, 1966.
Thompson, Laurence Victor. The Story of Scotland Yard. New York: Random House, 1954.
Wilson, Colin, and Patricia Pitman. Encyclopedia of Murder. New York: Putnam, 1962.
Wolfgang, Marvin E. , compiler. Studies in Homicide. New York: Harper & Row, 1967.

THE YALTA CONFERENCE (1945)

Early in 1945 it became obvious that Germany would be defeated by the Allied Powers in World War II. Leaders of the Allied nations met in Yalta in the Crimea, U. S. S. R. , from February 4 to February 11 to plan policies and discuss problems which would arise following Germany's surrender.

The United States was represented by President Franklin D. Roosevelt. With him were special assistant Harry L. Hopkins and Secretary of State Edward R. Stettinius, Jr. Prime Minister Winston S. Churchill and Foreign Secretary Sir Anthony Eden represented England and Joseph Stalin, Soviet dictator and Vyacheslav Molotov, Soviet Commissar of Foreign Affairs, were there to negotiate for Russia.

Roosevelt, Churchill and Stalin had met previously at Teheran but had put off the making of a number of decisions until a later date. Many of the agreements made at Yalta were ratifications of earlier accords worked out by foreign ministers. Among other things it was decided that, following the Allied victory, Germany would be divided into four zones of occupation--American, British, French and Soviet--and would be governed by an Allied Control Commission in Berlin. Germany would be required to pay war damages, which reparations would be collected by the confiscation of German assets and the dismantling of industrial plants. Following the war, Nazi war criminals were to be tried by an international court of justice.

The Soviets agreed to declare war on Japan and were, in turn, to acquire the Kuril Islands and Northern Sakhalin from that country. Further, the Manchurian railroad was to be placed under the Sino-Soviet administration and Port Arthur was to be restored to its pre-1904 status as a Russian naval base.

Poland was to form a representative government to organize elections for a constituent assembly. Russia's acquisition of Polish territories north of the Curzon Line, an ethnic boundary, was compensated for by awarding certain former German lands east of the Oder and Neisse Rivers to Poland. The Communist government and the London Polish government were to form a united Polish government with free elections to be held immediately.

The United Nations, soon to be formed, was to invite China and France to become members and an agreement was reached on veto power and permanent membership in the Security Council for the "Big Five."

The signatories of the final Yalta Declaration agreed that the democratic principles of the Atlantic Charter should be universally applied and that the Declaration gave the world an assurance of lasting peace.

Most of the agreements arrived at at Yalta were considered temporary, but when the fighting ceased and the Cold War began these agreements quickly became permanent. As some of these agreements infringed on the sovereignty of several nations its protocols were not fully published until 1947.

Suggested Readings

Baldwin, Hanson. Great Mistakes of the War. New York: Harper & Row, 1949.

Churchill, Winston S. The Second World War. Vol. VI: "Triumph and Tragedy." Boston: Houghton Mifflin, 1953.

Collier, Basil. The Second World War: A Military History. New York: Morrow, 1967.

Deane, John R. The Strange Alliance. New York: Viking Press, 1947.

Deutscher, Isaac. Stalin: A Political Biography. 2nd revised edition. New York: Oxford University Press, 1967.

Divine, Robert A. Roosevelt and World War II. Baltimore: Johns Hopkins University Press, 1969.

Eden, Sir Anthony. Full Circle: The Memoirs of Anthony Eden. Boston: Houghton Mifflin, 1960.

Feis, Herbert. Churchill, Roosevelt, Stalin. Princeton, N. J. : Princeton University Press, 1957.

Fuller, John F. C. The Second World War, 1939-1945. London: Eyre & Spottiswoode, 1948.

Gardner, Brian. The Year That Changed the World: 1945. New York: Coward-McCann, 1963.

Goulden, Joseph C. "Reconsidering the Russians" in his The Best Years: 1945-1950. New York: Atheneum, 1976.

Greer, Thomas. What Roosevelt Thought. East Lansing, Mich. : Michigan State College Press, 1958.

Hatch, Alden. Franklin D. Roosevelt: An Informal Biography. New York: Holt, 1947.

McNeill, William H. America, Britain and Russia: Their Cooperation and Conflict, 1941-1946. London: Royal Institute of International Affairs, 1953.

Payne, Robert. The Rise and Fall of Stalin. New York: Simon & Schuster, 1965.

Peare, Catherine O. The FDR Story. New York: Crowell, 1962.

Schlesinger, Arthur M. , Jr. The Age of Roosevelt. Boston: Houghton Mifflin, 1957.

Schnittkind, Henry Thomas. Franklin Delano Roosevelt. New York: Putnam, 1962.

Sherwood, Robert E. Roosevelt and Hopkins: An Intimate History. New York: Harper & Row, 1950.

Smith, Gaddis. American Diplomacy During the Second World War. New York: Harper & Row, 1962.

Snell, John L. Illusion and Necessity. Boston: Houghton Mifflin, 1963.

_____, ed. The Meaning of Yalta: Big Three Diplomacy and the New Balance of Power. Baton Rouge, La. : Louisiana State University Press, 1956.

_____. The Nazi Revolution: Germany's Guilt or Germany's Fate? Boston: Heath, 1939.

Stettinius, Edward R. , Jr. Roosevelt and the Russians: The Yalta Conference. Edited by Walter Johnson. Garden City, N. Y. : Doubleday, 1949.

Toynbee, Arnold, and Veronica M. Toynbee, eds. Survey of International Affairs, 1939-1946. The Eve of War, 1939. London: Oxford University Press, 1959.

U. S. Department of State. The Conferences at Malta and Yalta. Washington, D. C. : Government Printing Office, 1955.

Warth, Robert. Joseph Stalin. New York: Twayne Publishers, 1969.

Weingast, David Elliott. Franklin D. Roosevelt, Man of Destiny. New York: Messner, 1952.

Wibberley, Leonard. The Life of Winston Churchill. New York: Ariel Books, 1956.

Wilmot, Chester. The Struggle for Europe. New York: Harper
  & Row, 1952.
Young, Peter. World War: 1939-1945. New York: Crowell, 1966.

THE DEATHS OF BENITO MUSSOLINI AND
CLARETTA PETACCI (1945)

Benito Mussolini, the Italian Premier and dictator, started
life as a newspaper editor and publisher. A Marxian Socialist, he
was, in 1904, expelled from Switzerland where he had been educated at the University of Lausanne. He was also later expelled from
Austria. He established and edited newspapers at Forli and Milan
and, in 1914, having urged that Italy enter World War I against the
Central Powers, was driven from the Socialist party.

In 1919 he founded the first "Fascio di Combattimento" (the
Fascist) at Milan. The object of this organization was to suppress
Bolshevism and by 1922 it had a membership of over four million.
On October 28, 1922, he led a march on Rome and became Premier. In this capacity he made a number of significant changes in
Italian national policies, including the amending of the electoral
laws to assure Fascist control of government. Opposition parties
and newspapers were suppressed and for the next two decades Mussolini was the virtual dictator of Italy.

When France fell to the German Nazi forces in May, 1940,
Mussolini led Italy into World War II on the German side. In July,
1943, after his country was invaded by the Allies, he was deposed
and imprisoned by his successor, General Pietro Badoglio. In
September he was rescued by German paratroopers under the direction of Otto Skorenzy. He conferred with Adolf Hitler who told
him that "secret weapons were about to change the course of the
war" which had been going against the Axis powers. However, the
Allies landed in Normandy on June 6, 1944, and Russia was scoring tremendous victories. Field Marshal Albert Kesselring's troops
were retreating and it was obvious that it was only a matter of
time before the German-Italian combination would go down in defeat.

On April 17, 1945, Mussolini, who had abandoned his wife
Rachele and had been joined at Salò on Lake Garda by his mistress
Claretta Petacci, decided to attempt to escape to Milan. He had
learned that the Fascist government no longer existed except in
theory and that the Committee of National Liberation had ordered
Fascist officials to be executed without trial. He requested the
German government to supply an aeroplane in which he could escape
to Spain, but such a plane was not forthcoming.

On April 25 Mussolini met with Cardinal Schuster, Archbishop of Milan, Gian-Riccardo Cella, an industrialist, and other
members of the Committee of National Liberation. They proposed

to him that he and his Fascist associates surrender and consider
themselves prisoners of war. Mussolini agreed to accept the conditions laid down by the Committee and then departed to confer with
the Germans, saying he would return shortly. However, he did not
come back, having been convinced by the Milan prefect of police
that he would be turned over to a people's tribunal rather than to
the Allies. This would, of course, mean immediate execution.

At 8 P.M. Mussolini, his mistress and an entourage of Fascist officials left Milan by motorcade. They stopped at Como, remaining there for a few hours. He called his wife by telephone and
urged her to start a new life, realizing that, for him, the end was
in sight.

Next day the trip was resumed and that night the party
stopped at Menaggio. On the following day, April 27, the motorcade
proceeded northward, towards the Swiss frontier. At the village
of Dongo the column was halted at a road block by a group of partisans. Mussolini was recognized and he and Claretta Petacci were
taken into custody. That evening they were moved to the barracks
at Germasino.

A Communist partisan named Walter Audisio, calling himself "Colonel Valerio," conferred with General Cadorna, telling
him that he had instructions "to go find Mussolini and execute him."
The general offered no objections. Il Duce and his mistress were
taken to the home of a peasant at Bolzanigo, above Azzano, where
they spent their last hours together. In the morning "Colonel Valerio" appeared, told the two that he had come to release them,
and escorted them to an automobile in which they started for Lake
Como.

The car was stopped before the gate of the Villa Belmonte.
"Colonel Valerio" ordered Mussolini and his mistress to get out of
the car and they did so. "Valerio" shot at Mussolini with a pistol
which missed fire. He then killed the two with a submachinegun,
followed by a coup de grâce through the heart with a revolver. A
little later fifteen Fascist army officers were executed at Dongo,
with "Colonel Valerio" officiating. All seventeen bodies were loaded on a truck. On the following day they were taken to a yard in
front of a garage in the Piazza Loreto in Milan. There a noose
was placed around Mussolini's ankles and his body was hoisted to
the roof of the garage porch where it hung head down six feet above
the sidewalk. The body of Claretta Petacci was similarly hung beside that of her lover.

Suggested Readings

Archer, Jules. The Dictators. New York: Hawthorn Books, 1967.
Benns, F. Lee. Europe Since 1914 in Its World Setting. New
    York: Appleton-Century-Crofts, 1945.
Bradley, General Omar M. A Soldier's Story. New York: Holt,
    Rinehart, 1951.

Carr, Albert H. Zolotoff. Men of Power: A Book of Dictators.
    New York: Viking Press, 1956.
Churchill, Winston S. The Second World War. Vol. VI: "Tri-
    umph and Tragedy. " Boston: Houghton Mifflin, 1953.
Décaux, Alain. "The End of the Dictators" in Taylor, A. J. P. ,
    editor-in-chief. Purnell's History of the 20th Century, Vol. 8.
    New York: Purnell, 1971.
Eisenhower, General Dwight D. Crusade in Europe. New York:
    Doubleday, 1948.
Fuller, John F. C. The Second World War, 1939-1945. London:
    Eyre & Spottiswoode, 1948.
Gardner, Brian. The Year That Changed the World: 1945. New
    York: Coward-McCann, 1963.
Kesselring, Field Marshal Albert. A Soldier's Story. New York:
    Morrow, 1954.
Sulsberger, C. L. The American Heritage History of World War II.
    New York: American Heritage Publishing Co. , 1966.
Weyr, Thomas. World War II. New York: Messner, 1969.
Wiskemann, Elizabeth. The Rome-Berlin Axis: A History of the
    Relations Between Hitler and Mussolini. London: Oxford Uni-
    versity Press, 1949.
Young, Peter. World War: 1939-1945. New York: Crowell, 1966.

THE DEATHS OF ADOLF HITLER AND
EVA BRAUN (1945)

Eva Braun, the daughter of lower middle-class Bavarian peasants, was Adolf Hitler's mistress for twelve years prior to their marriage in 1945 which took place a few hours before their simultaneous suicides. She had never been taken into the Führer's confidence so far as his political and military schemes were concerned, and spent much of her time in the background, waiting to be sent for.

On April 15, 1945, she joined her lover in Berlin, during the last days of the Third German Reich. The city was virtually surrounded by Russian troops and its fall was imminent. Hitler and some members of his staff, together with their families, had taken refuge in a bunker within the city. Among those present were Hermann Goering, Dr. Joseph Goebbels, Heinrich Himmler, Joachim von Ribbentrop, Martin Bormann, Admiral Karl Doenitz, Field Marshal Wilhelm Keitel, General Alfred Jodl and General Hans Krebs.

It became increasingly apparent that Berlin was doomed. Some of Hitler's followers urged him to leave the city and seek refuge in Czechoslovakia, which he declined to do. He flew into a rage and accused Goering of disloyalty and expelled him from the Nazi Party, also expelling certain other Party leaders at the same time.

On April 29 Hitler and Eva Braun were married. Walter
Wagner, a municipal councilor, performed the ceremony. The
marriage certificate was witnessed by Goebbels and Bormann and
a macabre wedding breakfast followed.

Hitler retired to his quarters where he dictated two documents. The first of these, characteristically, was an hysterical,
scathing attack on the Jews and also contained a statement of his
reasons for desiring to remain in Berlin to perish rather than attempt an escape. He also formally expelled Goering, Himmler and
the leader of the S.S. from the Nazi Party and appointed Admiral
Karl Doenitz to succeed him. He then dictated his will, leaving
his possessions to the Nazi Party, "or, if this no longer exists, to
the State." He left his collection of paintings as the nucleus of a
picture gallery to be established in Linz. His relatives were to
receive "everything that is of value as a personal memento or is
necessary for maintaining a petit-bourgeois standard of living."
His body, as well as that of his wife, was to be burned immediately.
Bormann was named as executor.

The Führer then went to bed. He had, in his testament,
ordered Bormann and Goebbels to leave Berlin and join the new
government. After Hitler's death Bormann obeyed and was reported killed trying to get through the Russian lines. Goebbels and his
wife preferred to die in the bunker. They had their six children
killed by injections of poison and then, at their request, were shot
by storm troopers.

On April 28 Benito Mussolini, dictator of Italy, and his mistress, Claretta Petacci, were assassinated by Italian partisans, the
news of their deaths reaching Hitler on the afternoon of the following day. The Führer then began preparations for his own death.
He had his dogs done away with and gave his female secretaries
capsules of poison which they were to use if and when they considered death advisable. He directed that his papers be destroyed.
Early on the morning of April 30 he emerged from his private
quarters and shook hands with the members of his entourage. After lunch that day he ordered Erich Kempka, his chauffeur, to deliver 200 liters of gasoline to the bunker garden. Kempka was able
to obtain 180 liters which were taken to the garden as directed.

Hitler and his wife then said goodbye to the group and retired to their rooms. Shortly afterwards the sound of a single revolver shot was heard. After waiting a decent interval Goebbels,
Bormann and some others entered Hitler's quarters to find that the
Führer had shot himself in the mouth. His wife, whose body lay
beside his on the sofa, had taken poison.

Heinz Linge, Hitler's valet, and an orderly carried the two
bodies, each wrapped in a blanket, to a shell hole in the garden.
Gasoline was poured over them and ignited. As the bodies burned
Bormann and Goebbels raised their right hands in a Nazi salute of
farewell. Like its leader, the German Third Reich was finished.

Suggested Readings

Abosch, Heinz. The Menace of the Miracle: Germany from Hitler to Adenauer. Translated by Douglas Garman. New York: Monthly Review Press, 1963.

Appel, Benjamin. Hitler, from Power to Ruin. New York: Grosset & Dunlap, 1964.

Archer, Jules. The Dictators. New York: Hawthorn Books, 1967.

Bradley, General Omar N. A Soldier's Story. New York: Holt, Rinehart, 1951.

Bullock, Alan. Hitler: A Study in Tyranny. New York: Harper & Row, 1962.

Carr, Albert Zolotoff. Men of Power: A Book of Dictators. New York: Viking Press, 1956.

Churchill, Winston S. The Second World War. Vol. VI: "Triumph and Tragedy." Boston: Houghton Mifflin, 1953.

Décaux, Alain. "The End of the Dictators" in Taylor, A. J. P., editor-in-chief. Purnell's History of the 20th Century, Vol. 8. New York: Purnell, 1971.

Eisenhower, General Dwight D. Crusade in Europe. New York: Doubleday, 1948.

Elliott, Brendan John. Hitler and Germany. New York: McGraw-Hill, 1968.

Fuller, John F. C. The Second World War, 1939-1945. London: Eyre & Spottiswoode, 1948.

Gardner, Brian. The Year That Changed the World: 1945. New York: Coward-McCann, 1963.

Goldston, Robert. The Life and Death of Nazi Germany. Indianapolis: Bobbs-Merrill, 1967.

Grunberger, Richard. Germany, 1918-1945. New York: Harper & Row, 1966.

Gun, Nerin E. Eva Braun: Hitler's Mistress. New York: Meredith Press, 1968.

Holborn, Hajo. A History of Modern Germany. Vol. III: 1840-1945. New York: Knopf, 1969.

Jarman, T. L. The Rise and Fall of Nazi Germany. New York: New York University Press, 1956.

Prittie, Terence, and the editors of Life. Germany. New York: Time, Inc., 1961.

Shirer, William L. The Rise and Fall of Adolf Hitler. New York: Random House, 1961.

_____. The Rise and Fall of the Third Reich: A History of Nazi Germany. New York: Simon & Schuster, 1960.

Speer, Albert. Inside the Third Reich. New York: Macmillan, 1970.

Stein, George H., ed. Hitler. Englewood Cliffs, N. J.: Prentice-Hall, 1968.

Toland, John. Adolf Hitler. Garden City. N. Y.: Doubleday, 1977.

Trevor-Roper, H. R. The Last Days of Hitler. New York: Collier Books, 1962.

_____, ed. Hitler's War Directives, 1939-1945. London: Sidgwick, 1964.

THE FOUNDING OF THE UNITED NATIONS (1945)

On January 8, 1918, President Woodrow Wilson suggested an alliance for the preservation of peace among nations. This was formulated at the 1919 Versailles Peace Conference following World War I. The first meeting of what came to be the League of Nations was held at Geneva on November 15, 1920, with 42 nations represented. The last meeting occurred on April 8, 1946, when its records and functions were transferred to the United Nations which had been organized in San Francisco between April 26 and June 26, 1945. The United States was never a member of the League.

In many ways the League of Nations had failed to achieve its objectives. While it can be credited with averting several wars, putting Austria, Hungary and Greece on sound financial bases and curbing drug traffic, it was unable to settle disputes concerning Japan's aggression against China and Italy's invasion of Ethiopia. However, many parts of the Charter of the United Nations were based on the Covenant of the League of Nations.

Like its predecessor, the United Nations was dedicated to the maintenance of international peace and security. It also was to develop friendly relations between nations, cooperate in solving international problems and act as a center for coordinating the actions of nations in achieving these goals.

Cordell Hull, American Secretary of State from 1933 to 1944, was an active proponent of the United Nations. He was forced to resign in 1944 because of ill health and was succeeded by Edward R. Stettinius, Jr., formerly Undersecretary of State.

In August, 1941, Winston S. Churchill, Prime Minister of Great Britain, and President of the United States Franklin D. Roosevelt met aboard ships in mid-Atlantic to consider the problems of international conduct after hostilities in Europe should cease. At this time Roosevelt, remembering that Congress had declined to approve Woodrow Wilson's proposal that the United States join the League of Nations, refused to commit his country to join any postwar political organization of an international nature. The Joint Atlantic Charter of August 14, 1941, signed by the representatives of 26 nations in January, 1942, covered only a military pact against Germany, Italy and Japan and dealt with general principles of international peacetime deportment. The four principal signatories were the United States, China, Great Britain and Russia and the document was called "Declaration by United Nations."

Cordell Hull devoted much time and effort to urging the acceptance of a postwar international organization. The 1942 Moscow Conference of the foreign ministers from Great Britain, Russia, China and the United States resulted in the issuance of the Moscow Declaration on General Security. Hull considered the United Nations

to have been born as the result of this Conference. The signatories
to the Declaration expressed their belief that their nations "recognize the necessity of establishing at the earliest practicable date a
general international organization ... for the maintenance of international peace and security. "

Further talk at Dumbarton Oaks, near Washington, D. C. ,
followed in 1944. These were expansions of the basic principles
laid down at the Moscow Conference, with a few major and minor
revisions and became the basis of the Charter of the United Nations. The Dumbarton Oaks proposals provided for a Security Council. Other meetings were held at Bretton Woods and Hot Springs.
These laid the foundations for the International Labor Organization,
The Food and Agriculture Organization, the International Bank for
Reconstruction and Development and the International Monetary Fund.

Problems dealing with membership and voting strength of the
major powers in the General Assembly and Security Council were
worked out, both at the Yalta Conference in February, 1945, and
at the succeeding San Francisco Conference. Other problems, eventually solved, concerned Russia's demand that its 16 republics each be
given one vote in the General Assembly to offset the votes of the
British Commonwealth bloc and the Latin American bloc, and the
question of veto power.

In June, 1945, the Charter of the United Nations was signed
by representatives of 51 nations and since that time an additional
75 have joined the organization. The United Nations is considered
a compromise and "its organization has to be viewed against a background of a complex system of wartime alliances. "

Since its establishment, with headquarters in New York City,
it has dealt with problems concerning Indonesia, South Africa, Palestine, Kashmir, China, Korea, Algeria, Hungary, Egypt, the Congo and Cyprus, among others.

Suggested Readings

Bailey, Thomas A. Woodrow Wilson and the Lost Peace. New
    York: Macmillan, 1944.
Baker, Ray Stannard. Woodrow Wilson and the World Settlement:
    Written from His Unpublished and Personal Material. New
    York: Doubleday, 1923.
Byrnes, James F. Speaking Frankly. New York: Harper & Row,
    1947.
Claude, Innis L. , Jr. Swords into Ploughshares. 2nd edition.
    New York: Random House, 1959.
Commager, Henry Steele, ed. "The Defeat of the League of Na-
    tions" (Doc. No. 436) in his Documents of American History,
    8th edition. New York: Appleton, 1968.
Divine, Robert A. Roosevelt and World War II. Baltimore: Johns
    Hopkins University Press, 1969.

Donovan, Frank. Mr. Roosevelt's Four Freedoms: The Story Be-
    hind the United Nations Charter. New York: Dodd, Mead,
    1966.
Feis, Herbert. Churchill, Roosevelt, Stalin. Princeton, N. J. :
    Princeton University Press, 1957.
Gardner, Brian. The Year That Changed the World: 1945. New
    York: Coward-McCann, 1963.
Goodspeed, Stephen. The Nature and Functions of International Or-
    ganizations. 2nd edition. New York: Oxford University Press,
    1967.
Greer, Thomas. What Roosevelt Thought. East Lansing, Mich. :
    Michigan State College Press, 1958.
Hatch, Alden. Franklin D. Roosevelt: An Informal Biography.
    New York: Holt, 1947.
Hull, Cordell. The Memoirs of Cordell Hull. New York: Mac-
    millan, 1948.
Meigs, Cornelia. The Great Design. Boston: Little, Brown, 1964.
Russell, Ruth B. A History of the United Nations Charter: The
    Role of the United States, 1940-1945. Washington, D. C. :
    Brookings Institution, 1958.
Schnittkind, Henry Thomas. Franklin Delano Roosevelt. New York:
    Putnam, 1962.
Smith, Gaddis. American Diplomacy During the Second World War,
    1941-1945. New York: Wiley, 1965.
Stettinius, Edward R. , Jr. Roosevelt and the Russians: The Yalta
    Conference. Edited by Walter Johnson. Garden City, N. Y. :
    Doubleday, 1949.
Vandenberg, Arthur H. , Jr. , ed. The Private Papers of Senator
    Vandenberg. Boston: Houghton Mifflin, 1952.
Walters, F. P. A History of the League of Nations. London: Ox-
    ford University Press, 1960.
Wibberley, Leonard. The Life of Winston Churchill. New York:
    Ariel Books, 1956.

THE NUREMBERG WAR-CRIMES TRIALS (1945-1946)

Following World War II, which resulted in victory for the
Allies, certain German and Japanese leaders were tried by the International Military Tribunal for crimes against peace, crimes
against humanity and war crimes.

The most important of these trials were held in Nuremberg,
Germany, under the authority of the London Agreement and Control
Council Law No. 10. The former was signed on August 8, 1945,
and the latter was promulgated by the Allied Control Commission in
Berlin on December 20 of the same year.

The London Agreement provided for the establishment of the
above-mentioned International Military Tribunal, a court composed
of one judge and one alternate judge from each of the signatory na-

tions: the United States, France, Great Britain and the Soviet Union. The American judges, appointed by President Harry S Truman, were Francis Biddle and John Johnston Parker, respectively judge and alternate.

In addition to the establishment of the court and judges, the London Agreement also provided for the appointment of four chief prosecutors. The American prosecutor was U. S. Supreme Court Justice Robert H. Jackson.

The Nuremberg Trials commenced on November 20, 1945. The defendants were charged on four counts: 1) Conspiracy to seize power, establish a totalitarian regime and prepare and wage a war of aggression. 2) Crimes against peace: the actual waging of aggressive wars. 3) Violations of the laws of war: of international conventions, internal penal laws and of general principles of criminal law. 4) Crimes against humanity, including imprisonment in concentration camps, use of torture and deliberate extermination of noncombatants.

Adolf Hitler, the German Führer and head of the Nazi Party, was not tried, he having committed suicide on April 30, 1945. The defendants were Karl Doenitz, Hans Frank, Wilhelm Frick, Hans Fritsche, Walter Funk, Hermann Goering, Rudolf Hess, Alfred Jodl, Ernst Kaltenbrunner, Wilhelm Keitel, Erich Raeder, Alfred Rosenberg, Fritz Sauckel, Albert Speer, Julius Streicher, Constantin von Neurath, Franz von Papen, Joachim von Ribbentrop, Hjalmar von Schacht, Baldur von Schirach and Artur von Seyss-Inquart. Robert Ley and Martin Bormann were also charged. Ley committed suicide in his prison cell and Bormann was tried in absentia. The latter was thought to have been killed by the Russians in the last days of the war but this has not been definitely established. At the trial he was found guilty and sentenced to die by hanging.

In addition to the individuals tried, seven Nazi organizations were also charged as criminal. These included the Gestapo (Geheime Stattspolizei or Secret State Police), the S. S. (Schutzstaffeln) or Defense Corps), the S. A. (Sturmabteilungen or Storm Troops) and the High Command and General Staff of the German Armed Forces.

The Court held more than 400 public sessions. Proceedings were conducted in English, French, German and Russian, with multiple simultaneous translations being used. Evidence included secret military documents impounded by the victorious Allies, some covering meetings held by Hitler and his immediate associates. Motion pictures of Nazi atrocities were shown.

The Court handed down its judgment on September 30 and October 1, 1946. It found that, for the most part, the leaders of the Nazi government had indeed committed crimes against peace by initiating and waging wars of aggression against the Allies and had violated the Kellogg-Briand Pact of 1928. It also found the German government guilty of crimes against humanity and of war crimes. Its findings for the individual defendants were as follows:

Defendant	Verdict	Sentence
Doenitz	Guilty on counts 2, 3	10 years imprisonment
Frank	Guilty on counts 3, 4	Death by hanging
Frick	Guilty on counts 2, 3, 4	Death by hanging
Fritsche	Not guilty	
Funk	Guilty on counts 2, 3, 4	Life imprisonment
Goering	Guilty on counts 1, 2, 3, 4	Death by hanging
Hess	Guilty on counts 1, 2	Life imprisonment
Jodl	Guilty on counts 1, 2, 3, 4	Death by hanging
Kaltenbrunner	Guilty on counts 3, 4	Death by hanging
Keitel	Guilty on counts 1, 2, 3, 4	Death by hanging
Raeder	Guilty on counts 1, 2, 3	Life imprisonment
Rosenberg	Guilty on counts 1, 2, 3, 4	Death by hanging
Sauckel	Guilty on counts 3, 4	Death by hanging
Speer	Guilty on counts 3, 4	20 years imprisonment
Streicher	Guilty on count 4	Death by hanging
von Neurath	Guilty on counts 1, 2, 3, 4	15 years imprisonment
von Papen	Not guilty	
von Ribbentrop	Guilty on counts 1, 2, 3, 4	Death by hanging
von Schacht	Not guilty	
von Schirach	Guilty on count 4	20 years imprisonment
von Seyss-Inquart	Guilty on counts 2, 3, 4	Death by hanging

Goering committed suicide in his cell by taking poison before
his sentence could be carried out.   Twelve other trials followed, at
which about 185 individuals were indicted.   These persons were lesser criminals than those first tried, but who had been instrumental
in carrying out the Nazi government's official policies.   Of these,
35 were acquitted, 120 were given prison sentences, and the others
were hanged.

Suggested Readings

Abosch, Heinz.   The Menace of the Miracle: Germany from Hitler
    to Adenauer.   Translated by Douglas Garman.   New York:
    Monthly Review Press, 1963.
Appel, Benjamin.   Hitler, from Power to Ruin.   New York: Gros-
    set & Dunlap, 1964.
Archer, Jules.   The Dictators.   New York: Hawthorn Books, 1967.
Aymar, Brandt, and Edward Sagarin.   "Nuremberg" in their A Pic-
    torial History of the World's Great Trials.   New York: Crown
    Publishers, 1967.

Benton, Wilburn E., and George Grimm, eds. Nuremberg: Ger-
    man Views of the War Trials. Dallas: Southern Methodist
    University Press, 1955.
Bernstein, Victor H. Final Judgment: The Story of Nuremberg.
    New York: Boni & Gaer, 1947.
Bullock, Alan. Hitler: A Study in Tyranny. New York: Harper
    & Row, 1962.
Churchill, Winston S. The Second World War. Vol. VI: "Triumph
    and Tragedy." Boston: Houghton Mifflin, 1953.
Collier, Basil. The Second World War: A Military History. New
    York: Morrow, 1967.
Davidson, Eugene. The Trial of the Germans: An Account of the
    Twenty-two Defendants Before the International Military Tri-
    bunal at Nuremberg. New York: Macmillan, 1966.
Dean, Vera Michelis. Europe in Retreat. New York: Knopf, 1939.
Fuller, John F. C. The Second World War, 1939-1945. London:
    Eyre & Spottiswoode, 1948.
Gardner, Brian. The Year That Changed the World: 1945. New
    York: Coward-McCann, 1963.
Gilbert, G. M. Nuremberg Diary. New York: Farrar, Straus,
    1947.
Glueck, Sheldon. The Nuremberg Trial and Aggressive War. New
    York: Knopf, 1946.
Goldston, Robert. The Life and Death of Nazi Germany. Indian-
    apolis: Bobbs-Merrill, 1967.
Hankey, Lord. Politics and Errors. Chicago: Henry Regnery,
    1950.
Harris, Whitney R. Tyranny on Trial: The Evidence at Nurem-
    berg. Dallas: Southern Methodist University Press, 1954.
Hitler, Adolf. Mein Kampf. Boston: Houghton Mifflin, 1943.
Holborn, Hajo. A History of Modern Germany. Vol. III: 1840-
    1945. New York: Knopf, 1969.
Höne, Heinz. Order of the Death's Head: The Story of Hitler's
    S. S. Translated by Richard Barry. New York: Coward-Mc-
    Cann, 1969.
Hutton, J. Bernhard. Hess: The Man and His Mission. New York:
    Macmillan, 1970.
International Military Tribunal. The Trial of German Major War
    Criminals: Opening Speeches of the Chief Prosecutors. Lon-
    don: His Majesty's Stationery Office, 1946.
_____. The Trial of Major War Criminals Before the Interna-
    tional Military Tribunal: Nuremberg, 14 November, 1945--1 Oc-
    tober, 1946. Official Record of the Proceedings. Nuremberg,
    1947.
Jackson, Robert H. The Case Against the Nazi War Criminals:
    Opening Statements for the United States of America. New
    York: Knopf, 1946.
_____. The Nürnberg Case. New York: Knopf, 1947.
Jarman, T. L. The Rise and Fall of Nazi Germany. New York:
    New York University Press, 1956.
"Justice at Nuremberg" in Crimes and Punishment, Vol. 10. Ed-
    itorial presentation: Jackson Morley. London: BPC, 1973.
Kelley, Douglas M. 22 Cells in Nuremberg: A Psychiatrist Ex-
    amines the Nazi Criminals. New York: Greenberg, 1947.

608   Footnotes to World History

McKown, Robin. "The Nuremberg Trial" in his Seven Famous
    Trials in History. New York: Vanguard Press, 1963.
Man, John. "Nuremberg: Nazism on Trial" in Taylor, A. J. P.,
    editor-in-chief. Purnell's History of the 20th Century, Vol. 8.
    New York: Purnell, 1971.
Musmanno, Michael A. The Eichmann Kommandos. Philadelphia:
    Macrae Smith, 1961.
Nazi Conspiracy and Aggression. Washington, D. C. : Office of the
    United States Chief of Counsel for Prosecution of Axis Crimin-
    ality, 1946-1948.
Prittie, Terence, and the editors of Life. Germany. New York:
    Time, Inc. , 1961.
Sapinsley, Barbara. From Kaiser to Hitler: The Rise and Death
    of a Democracy, 1919-1933. New York: Grosset & Dunlap,
    1968.
Shapiro, William E. , project editor, and the staff of CBS News.
    Trial at Nuremberg. New York: Watts, 1967.
Shirer, William L. The Rise and Fall of Adolf Hitler. New York:
    Random House, 1961.
_____. The Rise and Fall of the Third Reich: A History of
    Nazi Germany. New York: Simon & Schuster, 1960.
Speer, Albert. Inside the Third Reich. New York: Macmillan, 1970.
Stein, George H. , ed. Hitler. Englewood Cliffs, N. J. : Prentice-
    Hall, 1968.
Steinberg, Alfred. The Man from Missouri: The Life and Times
    of Harry S Truman. New York: Putnam, 1962.
Toland, John. Adolf Hitler. Garden City, N. Y. : Doubleday, 1977.
Trevor-Roper, H. R. The Last Days of Hitler. 3rd edition. New
    York: Collier Books, 1962.
Wechsler, Herbert. Principles, Politics and Fundamental Law.
    Cambridge, Mass. : Harvard University Press, 1961.
Woerzel, Robert K. The Nuremberg Trials in International Law.
    New York: Frederick A. Praeger, 1960.
Young, Peter. World War: 1939-1945. New York: Crowell, 1966.

THE NUCLEAR ARMS RACE (1945-1978)

    World War II came to a dramatic end when, on August 4
and 5, 1945, atomic bombs were dropped on the Japanese cities of
Hiroshima and Nagasaki.

    In August, 1939, Dr. Albert Einstein wrote President Frank-
lin Delano Roosevelt advising him that German scientists were seeking a method of manufacturing bombs using the power generated by
nuclear fission. He urged the President to institute a similar research program in the United States. Such a program, called the
"Manhattan Project, " was started. This culminated in the bombings
mentioned above.

    While the United States enjoyed a brief monopoly on atomic

weapons, other nations were also working on the problem. Research in Russia had been inaugurated as early as 1932 and Sergei Vavilov, a Russian nuclear scientist, made discoveries in 1934 which led to Nobel prizes being awarded to Russian scientists in 1958. About 1946 the Soviet government assigned General Boris Lvovich Vanikov to head a program to develop an atomic bomb.

Atomic spying was also the order of the day. On March 4, 1946, Dr. Allan Nunn May, a British physicist and espionage agent, was arrested, tried and convicted of turning classified information over to the Soviets. He was sentenced to ten years imprisonment. Other spying episodes involved Dr. Klaus Fuchs, a German-born naturalized British physicist and Julius and Ethel Rosenberg, together with their accomplices Harry Gold, David Greenglass and Martin Sobel.

Following the war an ideological and political conflict, called the "cold war," manifested itself. This conflict, involving the Western powers headed by the United States and the Communist bloc led by the Soviet Union, resulted in a situation involving tensions on an international scale. It seemed obvious that the control of atomic weapons was both vitally important and at the same time extremely difficult to achieve.

In October, 1945, President Harry S Truman delivered a message in which he advocated immediate measures to insure international atomic control. In the following months the United States, Canada and Great Britain issued a joint resolution proposing that an atomic control commission be established under the United Nations. This resulted in the setting up of the United Nations Atomic Energy Commission in January, 1946, by a unanimous vote of the General Assembly. At its first meeting Bernard Baruch, the United States representative, proposed the inauguration of limited international inspection of atomic energy installations. However, as late as February, 1949, neither the United States nor the Soviet Union, the former supported by a majority of the Commission members, was willing to alter its proposals and the meetings of the Commission were suspended in July of that year. The Russians detonated their first nuclear bomb on August 29, 1949, in Soviet Central Asia and President Truman informed the American people of it on September 23. This ended America's monopoly of nuclear weapons and occasioned much surprise as it had been generally thought that Russian technology was not sufficiently advanced to permit the construction of such devices.

In January, 1952, a new organization, the United Nations Disarmament Commission, in which were combined the functions of the Atomic Energy Commission and the Conventional Armaments Commission, found itself facing the same problems which had confronted its predecessors. The Western powers advocated a plan of gradual arms limitations, combined with inspection systems and atomic weapons controls. The Soviets, on the other hand, insisted on the destruction and prohibition of atomic weapons prior to the discussion of arms limitations.

In 1954 the Soviet Union indicated its willingness to arbitrate British and French proposals for the reduction of conventional armaments prior to the forbidding of nuclear weapons. In 1955 the Soviets agreed in principle to the establishment of control systems prior to the reduction of armaments, but no accord was reached. Further, the Russians declined to permit inspection of their facilities or to exchange other information concerning military or atomic installations.

In 1956 the Western powers rejected a Soviet proposal concerning an unsupervised ban on tests of nuclear weapons. In 1957 another Soviet plan was similarly rejected.

In October, 1958, an informal moratorium on nuclear weapons tests began. The French detonated several nuclear devices and the Russians, on September 1, 1961, broke the moratorium and set off over fifty similar devices. On March 2, 1962, President John F. Kennedy stated that the United States would resume the testing of atomic weapons unless the Soviets agreed to a test-ban treaty, including international inspection. The Russians refused and American tests were begun on April 25.

In August, 1963, all of the major nuclear powers except France signed a treaty banning nuclear weapons tests and by January, 1964, over 100 other nations had joined the pact. Then, in October, 1964, the Soviet-Chinese dispute which began with the Russian Twentieth Party Congress the preceding February, led to China's successful detonation of an atomic bomb.

The Atomic Energy Commission, a civilian agency of the United States government, is administering the national atomic energy program.

Suggested Readings

Aron, Raymond. On War. Translated by Terence Kilmartin. Garden City, N. Y.: Doubleday, 1959.
Aymar, Brandt, and Edward Sagarin. "Julius and Ethel Rosenberg and Martin Sobel" in their A Pictorial History of the World's Great Trials. New York: Crown Publishers, 1970.
Clark, Ronald William. The Birth of the Bomb. London: Phoenix House, 1961.
Dinerstein, Herbert S. War and the Soviet Union. New York: Frederick A. Praeger, 1962.
Fineberg, Andhil S. The Rosenberg Case: Fact and Fiction. New York: Oceana Publications, 1953.
Fleming, D. F. The Cold War and Its Origins. Garden City, N. Y.: Doubleday, 1961.
Gardner, Brian. The Year That Changed the World: 1945. New York: Coward-McCann, 1963.
Groueff, Stephane. Manhattan Project: The Untold Story of the Making of the Atomic Bomb. Boston: Little, Brown, 1967.

Groves, Richard Leslie. Now It Can Be Told: The Story of the Manhattan Project. New York: Harper, 1962.

Halle, Louis J. The Cold War as History. New York: Harper & Row, 1967.

Hersey, John R. Hiroshima. New York: Knopf, 1946.

Herz, John H. International Politics in the Atomic Age. New York: Columbia University Press, 1960.

Isenberg, Irwin, ed. The Russian-Chinese Rift: Its Impact on World Affairs. New York: H. W. Wilson, 1966.

Kardelj, Edvard. Socialism and War. Translated by Alec Brown. New York: McGraw-Hill, 1960.

Kennan, George F. Russia: The Atom and the West. New York: Harper & Row, 1958.

Kramish, Arnold. Atomic Energy in the Soviet Union. Stanford, Calif.: Stanford University Press, 1959.

Kugelmass, J. Alvin. J. Robert Oppenheimer and the Atomic Story. New York: Messner, 1953.

McLellan, David S. The Cold War in Transition. New York: Macmillan, 1966.

Marshall, Charles Burton. The Cold War: A Concise History. New York: Watts, 1965.

Meeropol, Robert, and Michael Meeropol. We Are Your Sons: The Legacy of Ethel and Julius Rosenberg. Boston: Houghton Mifflin, 1975.

Mehnert, Klaus. Peking and Moscow. New York: American Library of World Literature, 1964.

Moorehead, Alan. The Traitors. New York: Scribner's, 1952.

Purcell, John Francis. The Best-Kept Secret: The Story of the Atomic Bomb. New York: Vanguard Press, 1963.

Rees, David. The Age of Containment: The Cold War, 1945-1965. New York: St. Martin's Press, 1967.

Sherwin, Martin Jay. World Destroyed: The Atomic Bomb and the Grand Alliance. New York: Knopf, 1975.

Shute, Nevil, pseud. On the Beach (fiction). New York: Perennial Library, 1957.

Stimson, Henry L. "The Decision to Use the Atomic Bomb," Harper's Magazine, February, 1947. Reprinted in Knowles, Horace, ed. Gentlemen, Scholars and Scoundrels. New York: Harper, 1959.

Symons, Julian. "Great Modern Cases: The Rosenbergs" in his A Pictorial History of Crime. New York: Crown Publishers, 1966.

THE NEVILLE HEATH MURDERS (1946)

Neville George Clevely Heath, a depraved 29-year-old cashiered British Air Force officer and suave sex maniac with a penchant for beating women with a whip, abused and murdered two female friends before he was caught. He was tried, convicted of murder and hanged on October 26, 1946. Before his infamous ca-

reer was ended by the hangman he had been commissioned and discharged from military service three times. He was placed on probation for swindling a hotel, sent to prison for three years for burg-
lary and fined for the unauthorized wearing of military decorations.

On June 21, 1946, the body of 32-year-old actress Margery
Gardner was found in Room No. 4 of the Pembridge Court Hotel,
London. The girl had been mutilated, whipped and killed by suf-
focation, probably with a pillow.

The police investigation disclosed that Room No. 4 had been
rented to a man and woman on the previous Sunday, June 16. The
woman was not Margery Gardner and the man who accompanied her
signed the register "Mr. and Mrs. N. G. C. Heath " Superintendent
Thomas Barratt, the officer in charge of the case, determined the
identities of Heath and the murdered actress. Harry Harter, a taxi
driver, stated that he had picked the couple up at the Panama Club
in South Kensington the night before the killing and had driven them
to the Pembridge Court Hotel.

The police decided to send Heath's name and description to
the newspapers but did not see fit to publish his picture, reasoning
that if his likeness appeared in the papers it might prejudice the
chances of securing a conviction at his trial.

Heath had gone to the Ocean Hotel at Worthington, Sussex,
where he registered under his own name. There he looked up a
young woman named Yvonne Symonds whom he had met only the
previous Saturday. In a whirlwind courtship he had proposed marriage which she accepted, and they had spent the night of Sunday,
June 16, together in Room No. 4 of the Pembridge Court Hotel.

Heath later spoke of the Margery Gardner murder, saying
that it had taken place in the room where he and his fiancée had
spent the night. He said he had known the murdered girl and that
he had let her and one of her "gentleman friends" use it the night
she was killed.

Yvonne Symonds spoke to Heath only once again when she,
having seen "an appeal in the papers for him to come forward, "
called him on the telephone to tell him her parents were worried
about the situation. He indicated that he was going to London to
"sort things out. " Instead, he went to Bournemouth where he registered at the Tollard Royal Hotel, using the alias "Group-Captain
Rupert Brooke. "

Neville Heath was in serious trouble. He had told Yvonne
Symonds that Superintendent Barratt had taken him to the scene of
the murder, which statement was untrue and would not stand up if
Miss Symonds talked. He wrote Barratt, saying that he had registered at the Pembridge Court Hotel with a woman, not Margery
Gardner, that the latter had asked him if she might use his room
for a tryst with a male companion until two o'clock, and that he

had given her a key to the room. He identified the Gardner woman's male companion only as "Jack" and gave a description of him.
He said further that he had returned to the hotel at 3:00 A. M. to
find Margery Gardner murdered, that he was using an assumed
name, could be contacted by an advertisement placed in the personal column of the Daily Telegraph and that he had in his possession
the whip with which the actress had been beaten. This was, he
wrote, being forwarded to the police, but it never arrived.

Heath remained at the Tollard Royal until Saturday, July 6.
One of the other guests at Bournemouth was 21-year-old Doreen
Marshall, an ex-Wren who was staying at the Norfolk Hotel. She
met Heath and on Wednesday, July 3, had tea and then dinner with
him at the Tollard Royal. They sat and talked in the lounge until
midnight. According to witnesses, they quarreled. Shortly after
midnight the two left the hotel on foot. This was the last time that
anyone saw Doreen Marshall alive. Heath returned to the hotel,
entering his third story room by way of a fire escape and a ladder.
Later he explained that he wished to play a joke on his friend, the
night porter.

On Friday, July 12, the manager of the Norfolk Hotel called
Ivor Relf, manager of the Tollard Royal, to report that Doreen
Marshall "seemed to be missing, " and he believed that she had
dined at Relf's hotel on Wednesday.

On Saturday Relf mentioned the matter to Heath, or "Group
Captain Rupert Brooke, " who seemed unconcerned. Heath then
telephoned the police and, after ascertaining that they had a photograph of the missing girl, offered to come to the station to "see
if he could be of help. " On arriving at the station he was recognized as the man wanted in connection with the Margery Gardner
murder. He was arrested and identified as Heath, although he
claimed that he was Group-Captain Brooke. An artificial pearl,
later identified as belonging to the Marshall girl, was found in his
possession, as were other items connecting him with her. His hotel
room was searched and a blood-stained handkerchief was found in a
dresser drawer. It was also established that he had recently pawned
a watch and ring belonging to Miss Marshall.

On Monday the nude body of Doreen Marshall was found in
a clump of bushes near the road. Her throat had been cut and her
body, bearing a number of stab wounds, had been mutilated.

Neville George Clevely Heath was charged with both murders
but his trial dealt only with the death of the actress, Margery Gardner. The proceedings took only three days. On September 26, 1946,
Heath was condemned to hand and was executed on October 26.

Suggested Readings

Abrahamsen, David, M. D. The Murdering Mind. New York: Harper
    & Row, 1973.

Bromberg, Walter. Mold of Murder: A Psychiatric Study of Homicide. New York: Grune & Stratton, 1961.

Catton, Joseph. Behind the Scenes of Murder. New York: Norton, 1940.

Guttmacher, M. S The Mind of the Murderer. Freeport, N. Y. : Books for Libraries, 1960.

Jesse, F. Tennyson. Murder and Its Motives. London: Harrap, 1952.

Lawes, Warden Lewis E. Meet the Murderer! New York: Harper, 1940.

Lester, David, and Gene Lester. Crime of Passion: Murder and the Murderer. Chicago: Nelson Hall, 1975.

Lustgarden, Edgar Marcus. "Neville George Clevely Heath" in his Business of Murder. New York: Scribner, 1968.

McDade, Thomas M. , compiler. The Annals of Murder. Norman, Okla. : University of Oklahoma Press, 1961.

"An Officer and a Gentleman: Neville Heath" in Infamous Murders. London: Verdict Press/Phoebus Publishing Co. , 1975.

Reinhardt, James Melvin. The Psychology of Strange Killers. Springfield, Ill. : Thomas, 1962.

Roberts, Carl E. B The New World of Crime. London: Noble, 1933.

Scott, Sir Harold, with Philippa Pearce. From Inside Scotland Yard. New York: Macmillan, 1965.

Symons, Julian. "Sex Murderers, England and France, " in his A Pictorial History of Crime. New York: Crown Publishers, 1966.

Thompson, Laurence Victor. The Story of Scotland Yard. New York: Random House, 1954.

Wilson, Colin, and Patricia Pitman. Encyclopedia of Murder. New York: Putnam, 1962.

Wolfgang, Marvin E. , compiler. Studies in Homicide. New York: Harper & Row, 1967.

THE PACIFIC RAFT EXPEDITION (1947)

In the summer of 1947 Norwegian scientist Thor Heyerdahl and five companions made a successful voyage by balsa wood sailing raft from Callao, Peru, to the South Sea Islands. The trip was made to test Heyerdahl's theory that the ancient Peruvians could have made the 4, 300 mile voyage on similar craft and thus peopled Polynesia.

Heyerdahl had made extensive studies of the cultures of the Polynesians, comparing them to those of the pre-Inca Peruvians. He had found a number of anthropological similarities between the two. Obtaining financial backing from members of the Explorers Club, he also was aided by American and British military supply units which assisted him by authorizing the use of new-type survival equipment which he was to test during his voyage. He recruited five fellow-voyagers. These, accompanied by a green parrot, were Knut Haugland, Bengt Danielsson, Erik Hesselberg, Torstein Raaby and Herman Watzinger.

Balsa wood logs were obtained from the jungle in Ecuador and floated down the Palenque River to the coast. The raft, constructed at Callao, consisted of a platform of nine large logs lashed together with ordinary hemp ropes and partly covered with a bamboo deck. No nails, screws, or other metal fasteners were used in her construction. It was Heyerdahl's idea to emulate the rafts used by Kon-Tiki, the legendary Peruvian ruler who, about 500 A.D., reputedly made the voyage which the six men were to repeat some 1400 years later. However, a radio transmitter/receiver, navigation equipment, a primus stove, a rubber dinghy and military ten-in-one rations were included, as were some scientific instruments, two cameras and film. Also taken were fresh fruit, coconuts and edible roots.

On April 28, 1947, the Kon-Tiki, as the raft had been christened, was towed out of Callao harbor by the tug Guardian Rios and set adrift in the Humboldt current, fifty miles from land. The sail was raised, to take advantage of the trade winds, and the voyage began.

The six adventurers met rough weather almost at once. The Kon-Tiki however, rode out the storm and the men aboard realized that a raft was superior to a hollow hull which could fill with water or a vessel "so long it would not take the waves one by one."

Fish were found in abundance and soon became a staple food item. Flying fish often landed on the deck and were either eaten or else used as bait for other marine creatures.

More storms were encountered as the voyage continued but the balsa wood raft weathered them. The six mariners came through safely but the parrot was washed overboard.

On July 17 the sailors spotted two large boobies and knew that they were approaching land. On July 30 they sighted the island of Puka Puka in the Tuamotu group. Other islands were sighted and 97 days after leaving Callao the Kon-Tiki, assisted by a group of Polynesians which had paddled out to meet it, attempted to land on the island of Angateau. The raft was unable to cross the coral reef and the six voyagers continued their journey.

On August 7 the Kon-Tiki was drifting towards the Raroia reef. It was realized that the raft would be wrecked there and Raaby reported the situation by radio to an amateur operator at Rarotonga in the Cook Islands.

The raft was driven over the reef by the pounding waves. It was badly smashed but still afloat. All six navigators were safe and were able to salvage many of the supplies and provisions aboard. The island on which they landed was small and uninhabited.

Natives from a nearby island rescued the six men and took them to their village. Radio contact was established with Rarotonga and the French authorities dispatched the government steamer Tamara to the island to transport the voyagers and tow the wreck of the Kon-Tiki to Papeete. A trading vessel, the Maoae, which had run aground off the reef, was pulled free by the French vessel. The Tamara, carrying Heyerdahl and his companions and towing the raft behind, proceeded to Papeete. There the Kon-Tiki was hoisted aboard the Norwegian steamer Thor I, to be taken to America. The six voyagers went with her.

Suggested Readings

Alexander, Marc. "Thor Heyerdahl and Easter Island" in his The Past. Worthington, Ohio: A. Lynn, 1965.
Bushnell, Geoffrey. Peru. New York: Frederick A. Praeger, 1956.
"The Cruise of the 'Kon-Tiki'," Life, October 20, 1947.
"From Raft to Reef," Newsweek, August 25, 1947.
Gilbert, John. "The Polynesian Mystery" in his Charting the Vast Pacific: Encyclopedia of Voyage and Exploration, Vol. 7. London: Aldus Books, 1971.
Hesselberg, Erik. "Kon-Tiki" and I. London: Allen & Unwin, 1949.
Heyerdahl, Thor. "Adventure in the South Seas" in Thomas, Lowell, ed. Great True Adventures. New York: Dell, 1955.
_____. Aku-aku, The Secret of Easter Island. London: Allen & Unwin, 1958.
_____. "Kon-Tiki": Across the Pacific by Raft. Translated by F. H. Lyon. Chicago: Rand McNally, 1950.
_____. The "Kon-Tiki" Expedition: By Raft Across the South Seas. Leicester, England: Ulverscroft, 1950.
_____. "Our Four Months on an Ocean Raft," Reader's Digest, November, 1947.
_____. "The Voyage of the Raft 'Kon-Tiki'," Natural History, June, 1948.
_____. "The Voyage of the Raft 'Kon-Tiki'," (abridgment), Science Digest, October, 1948.
"Peru to Polynesia," Science Digest, November, 1947.
Rabling, Harold. The Story of the Pacific: Explorers of the Earth's Mightiest Ocean. New York: Norton, 1965.
"Six Against the Sea," Science Illustrated, July, 1947.
"Westward Voyage," Time, April 21, 1947.
"Word from a Raft," Time, July 7, 1947.

THE GAY GIBSON "PORTHOLE DEATH" (1947)

Did James Camb, promenade deck steward on the British passenger ship Durban Castle, murder the actress Gay Gibson on

the night of October 17/18, 1947, or did she die as the result of
a fit? This question has never been satisfactorily answered. There
is no doubt, however, that the girl passed away and that Camb disposed of the body by pushing it through a porthole into the shark-
infested ocean some 90 miles off the African coast.

Eileen Isabella Ronnie Gibson, who used the stage name
"Gay Gibson, " was a 21-year-old actress who had been performing
in Johannesburg, South Africa. She decided to return to England
to continue her career on London's West End stage. She embarked
on the Durban Castle on October 10, 1947, occupying outside first
class cabin 126 on B deck on the port side of the ship.

Steward James Camb, afterwards shown to be an aggressive
ladies' man, became interested in the girl shortly after the Durban
Castle left Cape Town. Although he was prohibited by the rules of
the ship from entering any of the passengers' cabins he visited Gay
Gibson in room 126 sometime after midnight on October 18. James
Murray, senior nightwatchman, had observed Camb and the girl
talking together earlier in the evening and at Camb's trial stated
that he had heard the steward tell her that "he had a bone to pick
with her. " About one o'clock boatswain's mate Conway, who was
in charge of a deck-washing detail, saw the young actress leaning
against the promenade deck rail and warned her that if she stayed
there she might get wet. She thanked him and departed. He, except for Camb, was the last person to see her alive.

At a few minutes before three the same morning Murray and
his assistant, Frederick Steer, heard a signal bell from one of the
cabins. Steer investigated and found that the bell had been rung in
cabin 126. Proceeding there he saw that two lights, green and red,
were showing outside, indicating that both the steward and the stewardess had been rung for. The light was on inside the cabin, being
visible through the grille door. Steer knocked and then opened the
door, which was unlocked. It was immediately slammed shut from
inside, but not before Steer saw James Camb standing there. Camb
said, "It's all right!"

Steer reported the incident to Murray and the two men returned to cabin 126. The lights were still on. Neither man entered the cabin and Murray referred the matter to the officer of
the watch who dismissed it, saying that the passengers' morals
were no concern of his. Not wishing to get a shipmate in trouble,
Murray did not at this time identify Camb as the man Steer had
seen inside the cabin.

At 7:30 the following morning the stewardess found the Gibson cabin empty. Captain Patey, when told that the girl was missing, ordered the ship to be searched. When Gay Gibson was not
found he ordered the ship to retrace its course in case she might
have fallen overboard and, somehow, escaped death by drowning or
from the sharks. The search was fruitless and the Durban Castle
resumed her voyage to Southampton.

Frederick Steer told the captain of having seen Camb in the Gibson cabin. Interrogated by the captain, Camb denied Steer's story. He was examined by Dr. Griffiths, the ship's doctor, who found scratches on his shoulders and wrists. Camb accounted for these by stating that he had suffered from heat rash and had scratched himself to ease the irritation.

The Southampton police had been notified of the situation by radio. When the vessel docked Camb was apprehended and questioned. He first denied but later admitted that he had been in Gay Gibson's cabin on the morning of October 18. He said further that he and the girl had had sexual relations with her consent, that she had clutched him, thereby inflicting scratches on his shoulders and wrists, and that she had suddenly foamed at the mouth, after which she became still. He was, he stated, unable to detect any pulse or hear her heart beating. Artificial respiration elicited no results and he had then pushed her body through the porthole into the ocean.

Camb was charged with murder. His trial commenced on the morning of March 18, 1948. According to the prosecution, he had entered Gay Gibson's cabin, tried to make love to her by force, was repulsed, strangled her and disposed of the body by way of the porthole. The defense claimed that intercourse was engaged in with the girl's consent, that she "died in a fit," and that Camb, panicking and demoralized, disposed of the dead girl's body by the porthole route. The prosecution contended that Gay Gibson had rung both pushbuttons in her cabin to summon help. It pointed out that an unused contraceptive had been found among the girl's possessions in her cabin and argued that, if intercourse had been with consent, the device would, in all probability, have been used. The defense countered with the argument that there could well have been at least one other similar device present, possibly brought into the cabin by Camb. It also pointed out that heat rash was a common malady in the tropics and that several passengers and crewmen on the <u>Durban Castle</u> had contracted it and had relieved the attendant itching by scratching the affected parts.

It was shown that some bloodstains were on the sheets of the bed in the missing girl's room. The defense held that these bolstered Camb's story of Gay Gibson dying "in a fit" rather than by strangulation.

James Camb's trial lasted four days. He was found guilty of murder and sentenced to die by hanging. He escaped the gallows because a clause for the abolition of capital punishment was then under discussion in Parliament and the death penalty was suspended for five years, being replaced by sentences of life imprisonment and the Camb sentence was included in this instance. It was later shown that Camb had assaulted other women passengers on at least three occasions. For technical reasons this could not be brought out at his trial.

Camb was released from prison in September, 1959. He

changed his name to Clarke and obtained employment as a waiter.
In 1967 he was placed on two years' probation for assaulting a female minor, and subsequently was returned to prison for sexual
misbehavior with three young girls.   Gay Gibson's body was never
recovered.

Suggested Readings

Abrahamsen, David, M. D.   The Murdering Mind.   New York: Har-
    per & Row, 1973.
Bromberg, Walter.   Mold of Murder: A Psychiatric Study of Hom-
    icide.   New York: Grune & Stratton, 1961.
Catton, Joseph.   Behind the Scenes of Murder.   New York: Norton,
    1940.
"Death Through the Porthole: Gay Gibson" in Infamous Murders.
    London: Verdict Press/Phoebus Publishing Co. , 1975.
Guttmacher, M. S.   The Mind of the Murderer.   Freeport, N. Y. :
    Books for Libraries, 1960.
Jesse, F. Tennyson.   Murder and Its Motives.   London: Harrap,
    1952.
Lawes, Warden Lewis E.   Meet the Murderer!   New York: Harper,
    1940.
Lester, David, and Gene Lester.   Crime of Passion: Murder and
    the Murderer.   Chicago: Nelson Hall, 1975.
McDade, Thomas M. , compiler.   The Annals of Murder.   Norman,
    Okla. : University of Oklahoma Press, 1961.
Reinhardt, James Melvin.   The Psychology of Strange Killers.
    Springfield, Ill. : Thomas, 1962.
Roberts, Carl E. B.   The New World of Crime.   London: Noble,
    1933.
Scott, Sir Harold, with Philippa Pearce.   From Inside Scotland
    Yard.   New York: Macmillan, 1965.
Symons, Julian.   "Question Marks" in his A Pictorial History of
    Crime.   New York: Crown Publishers, 1966.
Thompson, Laurence Victor.   The Story of Scotland Yard.   New
    York: Random House, 1941.
Wilson, Colin, and Patricia Pitman.   Encyclopedia of Murder.   New
    York: Putnam, 1962.
Wolfgang, Marvin E. , compiler.   Studies in Homicide.   New York:
    Harper & Row, 1967.

THE ASSASSINATION OF MAHATMA GANDHI (1948)

Mohandas Karamchand Gandhi, known as Mahatma Gandhi,
an Indian lawyer and nationalist leader, was born at Porbandar,
Western India, in 1869.   He was assassinated on the evening of
January 30, 1948, at New Delhi.

Gandhi studied law at University College, London.   In 1891

he returned to India and established a successful law practice in
Bombay.   In 1893 he was retained by an Indian resident of Durban,
Union of South Africa, to act as counsel in a lawsuit.   While in
South Africa Gandhi found himself treated as a member of an inferior race and was appalled at the manner in which Indian immigrants were discriminated against and denied their civil and political rights.

For twenty years he remained in South Africa where he
joined the struggle of the Indian residents for their basic rights
and became their leader.   In 1896 he began to teach a policy of
passive resistance and non-cooperation with the South African government.   His efforts met with some success and in 1914 the government made a few concessions.

Gandhi then returned to India where he assumed an active
role in the Indian campaign for home rule.   In 1919 the English
Parliament passed the Rowlatt Act which gave the Indian colonial
authorities powers to deal with so-called revolutionary activities.
The authorities were overly-enthusiastic in enforcing the provisions
of the Act.   This culminated in a massacre of Indians at Amritsar,
upon which Gandhi launched a program of passive resistance to the
British similar to the one employed in South Africa.   He was arrested but his influence was so great that the British were forced
to release him, although he was later arrested and imprisoned on
various occasions.

Between 1920 and 1948 Gandhi continued his activities, advocating ahimsa (non-injury) and hoping that eventually Great Britain
would realize the uselessness of violence and leave India.

In 1947 the passage of the British Independence of India Bill
provided for the partitioning of India by setting up two separate
dominions, India and Pakistan.   It was understood that the two contending nationalist groups, the Moslem League and the Congress
Party, would resolve their differences.   Gandhi opposed any partition of his country but ultimately was forced to agree, in the hope
that internal peace would be achieved after the Moslem demand for
separation had been satisfied.   However, riots occurred in Calcutta
and elsewhere.   In New Delhi Gandhi undertook a fast on January
13, 1948, to bring about communal peace.

On the evening of January 30, 1948, twelve days after the
termination of this fast, Gandhi emerged from his quarters at Birla
House, New Delhi, to conduct a prayer meeting.   He was supported
by his grand-nieces, Abha and Manu.   A crowd of approximately
500 people had assembled to attend the services.   Gandhi mounted
a wooden platform and greeted his followers in the traditional manner by placing his palms together.

It was a little past five o'clock.   A young Hindu, later identified as Nathuram Godse, a journalist and fanatic, pulled a pistol from
his pocket and fired at Gandhi three times.   Thirty minutes later the
latter was dead, having been shot in the chest, groin and stomach.

At his trial Godse stated, "I thought it my duty to put an
end to the life of the so-called father of a nation who had played
a very prominent part in bringing about the vivisection of the country." Although Gandhi opposed the partitioning of India his fasts
and appeals for Hindu-Moslem cooperation had made him unpopular
with many Hindu extremists. These people hoped that the end of
British rule in India would be followed by Hindu supremacy and
were extremely bitter when the partition became a reality.

Godse and an accomplice were hanged.

Suggested Readings

Ashe, Geoffrey. Gandhi. New York: Stein, 1968.
Bondurant, Joan V. Conquest of Violence: The Gandhian Philos-
    ophy of Conflict. Berkeley, Calif. : University of California
    Press, 1965.
Bose, Nirmal Kumar. My Days with Gandhi. Columbia, Mo. :
    South Asia Books, 1974 (Originally published 1953).
Coolidge, Olivia E. Gandhi. Boston: Houghton Mifflin, 1971.
Diwaker, R. R. , et al. Mohandas Karamchand Gandhi: A Bibli-
    ography. Columbia, Mo. : South Asia Books, 1974.
Eaton, Jeanette. Gandhi: Fighter Without a Sword. New York:
    Morrow, 1950.
Fischer, Louis. The Life of Mahatma Gandhi. New York: Mac-
    millan, 1962.
Gregg, Richard B. The Power of Nonviolence. New York: Schock-
    en Books, 1960 (Originally published 1938).
Midgley, Ruth. "The Death of Gandhi" in Taylor, A. J. P. , editor
    in chief. Purnell's History of the 20th Century, Vol. 8. New
    York: Purnell, 1971.
Mohan, Anand. Indira Gandhi: A Personal and Political Biography.
    New York: Meredith Press, 1967.
Polak, H. S. , et al. Mahatma Gandhi. Thompson, Conn. : Inter-
    Culture Associates, 1966.
Power, Paul F. , ed. The Meanings of Gandhi. Honolulu, Hawaii:
    East-West Center University Press, 1971.
Sheehan, Vincent. Mahatma Gandhi: A Great Life in Brief. New
    York: Knopf, 1955.
Wolfenstein, E. Victor. The Revolutionary Personality: Lenin,
    Trotsky, Gandhi. Princeton, N. J. : Princeton University Press,
    1967.
Woodcock, George. Mohandas Gandhi. Edited by Frank Kermode.
    New York: Viking Press, 1971.

THE MARSHALL PLAN (1948)

On June 5, 1947, General George Catlett Marshall, Secretary of State, presented the principles of his proposal to aid Euro-

pean post-war reconstruction, known as the "Marshall Plan," to
the graduating class of Harvard University where he gave the com-
mencement address. It was realized that, following World War II,
European manufacturing, agriculture and transportation were far
below pre-war levels and that if the European economy was to recover American aid was needed.

Marshall's ideas were reviewed by the Policy Planning Staff
of the United States State Department headed by George Kennan and
the plan was adopted.   The Economic Cooperative Administration
was established in 1948 to administer it.

France and Great Britain, represented by French Foreign
Minister Georges Bidault and British Foreign Secretary Ernest Bevin, met with the Soviet Commissar for Foreign Affairs, V. M. Molotov, on June 23, 1947.   Bidault and Bevin proposed the establishment of a coordinating committee to devise a general plan for recovery and to perform certain other administrative functions.   Molotov rejected the proposal on the grounds that such a committee
would concern itself with the internal affairs of the participating
nations.   He proposed an alternative plan which was a complete
reversal of Marshall's idea of European cooperation.   Molotov left
the conference on July 2, and on the following day 22 other European nations were invited to a meeting at Paris.   Czechoslovakia
was the only Eastern European state to accept and she, because of
Russian pressure, later withdrew her acceptance.   The Russians
called the Marshall Plan an example of American imperialism and
proposed the Molotov Plan, a series of barter agreements between
satellite nations.

On July 22, 1947, the Committee of European Economic Cooperation met in Paris.   Attending were delegates from Austria,
Belgium, Denmark, France, Greece, Iceland, Ireland, Italy, Luxembourg, the Netherlands, Norway, Portugal, Sweden, Switzerland,
Turkey and the United Kingdom.   A report outlining a four-year
recovery plan for the sixteen nations and West Germany was issued.

The participating nations agreed to cooperate in their efforts
to achieve economic recovery.   The various currencies were to be
stabilized if possible.   Balance of payments deficits were to be reduced, exports were to be maximized and imports minimized.   Power plants to exploit the natural resources of Germany and Italy were
to be constructed.

The Foreign Aid Act of 1947, an interim aid program, was
passed by the United States Congress in December, 1947, and on
April 3, 1948, the Marshall Plan became law, formally called the
Foreign Aid Assistance Act of 1948.   This Act created the Economic
Cooperative Administration (ECA) which was to engage in bilateral
agreements with the countries participating and coordinate the first
year's appropriations.

On January 1, 1952, the Marshall Plan was superseded by

the Mutual Security Agency. During its existence the Administration had extended about twelve and a half billion dollars to the sixteen European nations. Historians, economists and humanitarians view the Marshall Plan not only as a relief and recovery project but also as a tremendous step in reform.

Suggested Readings

Adams, W. , and L. E. Traywick. Readings in Economics. New York: Macmillan, 1948.

Fleming, D. F. The Cold War and Its Origins. Garden City, N. Y. : Doubleday, 1961.

Halle, Louis J. The Cold War as History. New York: Harper & Row, 1967.

Keynes, John Maynard. The Scope and Method of Political Economy. 4th edition. New York: London, 1930.

Knapp, Wilfred. A History of World Peace, 1939-1965. New York: Oxford University Press, 1967.

Price, Harry Bayard. The Marshall Plan and Its Meaning. Ithaca, N. Y. : Cornell University Press, 1955.

Rees, David. The Age of Containment: The Cold War, 1945-1965. New York: St. Martin's Press, 1967.

Robbins, Lionel. The Nature and Significance of Economic Science. New York: Macmillan, 1935.

Smith, Howard K. The State of Europe. New York: Knopf, 1949.

Steinberg, Alfred. The Man from Missouri: The Life and Times of Harry S Truman. New York: Putnam, 1962.

Urwin, Derek W. Western Europe Since 1945: A Short Political History. London: Longmans, Green, 1968.

Walker, E. Ronald. From Economic Theory to Policy. Chicago: University of Chicago Press, 1943.

Ward, Barbara. The West at Bay. New York: Norton, 1948.

THE DEATH OF JAN MASARYK (1948)

Czechoslovakia, comprising the Czech and Slovak provinces formerly ruled by the Austrian Hapsburgs, came into existence in 1918. On October 28 the National Committee, a Czech revolutionary body in Prague, assumed the government of Czech lands. The Slovak National Council united with the Czechs to form a single state, and on November 14 Tomáš Garrigue Masaryk was elected the first president of Czechoslovakia. He was reelected in 1920 and again in 1927, resigning from office in 1935. He was succeeded by Eduard Beneš.

Following World War II Russian Communist elements gained increasing control of the Czechoslovak government. This culminated in the spring of 1948 with a Communist seizure of complete power. Klement Gottwald, head of the Czechoslovak Communist Party since 1929, became premier.

The United States was not pleased with the Communist take-over of Czechoslovakia.   This dissatisfaction was increased by the results of the political crisis which occurred on February 20, 1948, when twelve Democratic ministers resigned from Gottwald's National Front cabinet.   It was then that the premier swore in a new cabinet dominated by Communists.

The new Gottwald government inaugurated a system of purges, which included the courts, parliament, the army, the legal profession, the educational system and opposition political parties, particularly the Social Democrats.

The only prominent non-Communist in the Gottwald regime was Jan Masaryk, Czechoslovakia's Foreign Minister, the son of Tomáš Garrigue Masaryk.   He was in violent opposition to the Communist policies of Premier Gottwald and, as the son of Czechoslovakia's almost legendary hero, exercised great influence as a leader of the Social Democrats.

On March 10, 1948, the pajama-clad body of Jan Masaryk was found in the courtyard of the Czernin Palace at Prague.   He had jumped--or been thrown--from the bathroom window of his third-floor quarters in the Palace.

Government officials pronounced his death a suicide.   A month later the leadership in control of the Social Democrat Party announced plans to merge with the Communist Party.   A new constitution, patterned after that of the U. S. S. R. , was approved without opposition on May 9.   President Beneš submitted his resignation on June 7, two days before he was to sign the new constitution. Gottwald became acting president, signing the constitution on June 8.   He was elected president by the National Assembly on June 14, with Antonin Zápotocky succeeding him as premier.   Beneš died of natural causes in September.

Whether Jan Masaryk committed suicide or was murdered has never been determined.   The investigation of his death was conducted by unscrupulous political opponents.   Persons who were in a position to discuss the matter knowingly were purged, fled the country, died under suspicious circumstances or remained discreetly silent, even twenty years later.   Conflicting stories were told by physicians, secretaries, servants, politicians, police officials and others.   As recently as 1969 an attempt was made to assassinate a still-surviving witness.

Suggested Readings

Bartosek, Karel.   The Prague Uprising.   Prague: Artia Press, 1965.
Betts, Reginald R. , ed.   Central and Southeast Europe, 1945-1948. London: Royal Institute of International Affairs, 1950.
Bolton, Glorney.   Czech Tragedy.   London: Watts, 1955.

Borsody, Stephen. The Triumph of Tyranny. New York: Macmillan, 1965.
Brown, J. F. The New Eastern Europe. New York: Praeger, 1966.
Brown, John, pseud. Who's Next? The Lesson of Czechslovakia. London: Hutchinson, 1951.
Brzezinski, Zbigniew. The Soviet Bloc: Unity and Conflict. Cambridge, Mass.: Harvard University Press, 1960.
Burks, R. V. The Dynamics of Communism in Eastern Europe. Princeton, N. J.: Princeton University Press, 1961.
Busek, Vratislav, and Nicolas Spulber. Czechoslovakia. London: Stevens, 1956.
Calvocoressi, Peter. Survey of International Affairs, 1947-1948. New York: Oxford University Press, 1949.
Communist Party of Czechoslovakia, Action Program, April, 1948.
Dallin, David. The New Soviet Empire. London: Hollis & Carter, 1951.
Davenport, Marcia. Too Strong for Fantasy. New York: Scribner's, 1967.
Friedman, Otto. The Break-up of Czech Democracy. London: Gollancz, 1950.
Gunther, John. Behind the Curtain. New York: Harper & Row, 1949.
Hasek, Jaroslav. The Good Soldier Schweik. New York: Doubleday, 1930.
Healey, Denis, ed. The Curtain Falls. New York: Praeger, 1951.
Kenman, George F. From Prague After Munich. Princeton, N. J.: Princeton University Press, 1968.
Kertesz, Stephen D. The Fate of East Central Europe. Notre Dame, Ind.: University of Notre Dame Press, 1956.
Kolarz, Walter. Books on Communism. Princeton, N. J.: Ampersand Press, 1963.
Korbel, Josef. The Communist Subversion of Czechoslovakia, 1938-1948. Princeton, N. J.: Princeton University Press, 1959.
Kozak, Jan. How Parliament Can Play a Revolutionary Part in Transition to Socialism. London: Independent Information Centre, 1961.
Lettrich, Jozef. History of Modern Slovakia. London: Thames & Hudson, 1955.
Lockhart, Sir Robert Bruce. Jan Masaryk: A Personal Memoir. New York: Putnam, 1956.
London, Artur. L'Aveu: Dans L'Engrenage du Proces de Prague. Paris: Gallimard, 1968.
Macartney, Carlile A., and A. W. Palmer. Independent Eastern Europe: A History. New York: St. Martin's Press, 1962.
Masaryk, Jan. Speaking to My Country. London: Lincolns-Prager, 1944.
———. Speeches in America. New York: Czechoslovak Information Service, 1942.
Masaryk, Tomáš G. The Spirit of Russia. New York: Barnes & Noble, 1961.
Mousset, Albert. The World of the Slavs. London: Stevens, 1950.
Neumann, William L. After Victory: Churchill, Roosevelt, Stalin. New York: Harper & Row, 1967.

Paloczi-Horvath, George. The Undefeated. London: Secker &
    Warburg, 1959.
Perrault, Gilles. L'Orchestre Rouge. Paris: Libraire Artheme
    Fayard, 1967.
Reisky de Dubnic, Vladimir. Communist Propaganda Methods.
    New York: Praeger, 1961.
Ripka, Hubert. Czechoslovakia Enslaved. London: Gollancz, 1950.
Schmidt, Dana Adams. Anatomy of a Satellite. Boston: Little,
    Brown, 1952.
Selver, Paul. Masaryk: A Biography. London: Michael Joseph,
    1940.
Seth, Ronald. The Executioners. New York: Hawthorn Press,
    1967.
Seton-Watson, Hugh. Eastern Europe Between the Wars. Hamden,
    Conn. : Shoe String Press, 1963.
_____. The Eastern European Revolution. New York: Praeger,
    1956.
Shepherd, Gordon. Russia's Danubian Empire. London: Heine-
    mann, 1954.
Starr, Richard F. The Communist Regimes in Eastern Europe:
    An Introduction. Stanford, Calif. : Stanford University Press,
    1967.
Sterling, Claire. The Masaryk Case. New York: Harper & Row,
    1968.
A Student of Affairs, pseud. How Did the Satellites Happen? Lon-
    don: Batchworth Press, 1952.
Sulzberger, Cyrus. A Long Row of Candles. New York: Mac-
    millan, 1969.
Taborsky, Edward. Communism in Czechoslovakia, 1948-1960.
    Princeton, N. J. : Princeton University Press, 1961.
Thomson, S. Harrison. Czechoslovakia in European History. Prince-
    ton, N. J. : Princeton University Press, 1943.
Tigrid, Pavel. Le Printemps de Prague. Paris: Seuil, 1968.
Western, J. R. The End of European Primacy, 1871-1945. New
    York: Harper & Row, 1965.
Zinner, Paul E. Communist Strategy and Tactics in Czechoslova-
    kia, 1919-1948. New York: Praeger, 1963.

THE BERLIN AIRLIFT (1948-1949)

        The city of Berlin, former capital of Germany, now com-
prises East Berlin, the capital of the German Democratic Republic and West Berlin, an exclave of the Federal Republic of Germany
(West Germany).   At the conclusion of World War II the city was
under the control of the United States, France, Great Britain and
the Soviet Union (the "Big Four" powers), each of which occupied a
separate sector.

        Inflation was running rampant and the black market was flour-
ishing.   Early in 1948 a meeting was held to discuss the problem

of currency reform. General Lucius D. Clay, military governor
of Germany, instituted a plan which was adopted by all except the
Russians who established their own currency and attempted to foist
it on the other nations.

Russian soldiers demanded the right to inspect western military trains coming into Berlin through the Soviet zone. Permission was refused, whereupon the Russians stopped all railway and
water traffic and set up road blocks. The Allies countered by closing their zones to the Russians. On June 22, 1948, the transport
of food into Berlin by ground and water ceased, the Russians ultimately admitting that their object was to force the Allies to capitulate.

Berlin was completely isolated from the western zones of
Germany. The only way in which the necessary supplies of food
and fuel could be brought into the beleaguered city was by air.
Access to Berlin by this method had been agreed to when the occupation accords had been made following the war, but this was
not the case with access by land. The Allies determined to establish the necessary airlift.

General Clay ordered the aircraft necessary to transport
supplies to Berlin. General Curtis LeMay, commander of the U. S.
Air Force in Europe, directed his forces to act. Eighty tons of
food and medicine were flown into Berlin the first day. American
and British airmen flew the planes, mostly C-47's. The French,
having no planes suitable for the lift, furnished logistic support.
The task seemed impossible to accomplish as the airlift could deliver not more than 700 tons daily in the planes available, and the
people of Berlin required nearly 4, 000 tons. President Harry S
Truman was urged to remove American troops from the area for
fear of otherwise antagonizing Russia. His reply was typical: "The
United States is going to stay. Period. "

The Berlin Airlift Task Force was established on June 29,
1948, its planes and flyers being augmented from the newly organized Military Air Transport Service. Under the command of Lieutenant General William H. Tunner the combined American and British flyers were soon delivering over 2, 200 tons of supplies daily.
Planes took off every three minutes from four airfields. Landings
were made by instrument and navigation was difficult. In spite of
this operations became more efficient and in August 120, 672 tons
of supplies were delivered by "Operation Vittles, " as it came to
be called. By September 5, 000 tons per day were landing in Berlin.

The Russians resorted to harassing tactics but no war-pro-
ducing incidents occurred as the Soviets felt that the airlift was
doomed to eventual failure. Instead, the operation became still
more viable and the Allies showed that the lift could be maintained
indefinitely.

The Kremlin called off the siege on May 12, 1949, but the

airlift continued until September 30, that a stockpile of emergency
supplies could be assembled.

"Operation Vittles" delivered almost $2\frac{1}{2}$ million tons of food,
coal and medicine. During its existence 276,926 flights were made,
at a cost to the Allies of over 200 million dollars. Thirty-five
aircraft were lost and 75 persons died.

Suggested Readings

Abosch, Heinz. The Menace of the Miracle: Germany from Hitler
    to Adenauer. Translated by Douglas Garman. New York:
    Monthly Review Press, 1963.
Clay, Lucius D. Decision in Germany. Garden City, N. Y. : Dou-
    bleday, 1950.
_____. Germany and the Fight for Freedom. Cambridge, Mass. :
    Harvard University Press, 1950.
Davidson, Walter Phillips. The Berlin Blockade: A Study in Cold
    War Politics. Princeton, N. J. : Princeton University Press,
    1958.
Fleming, D. F. The Cold War and Its Origins. Garden City, N. Y. :
    Doubleday, 1961.
Halle, Louis J. The Cold War as History. New York: Harper &
    Row, 1967.
Hangen, Welles. The Muted Revolution: East Germany's Challenge
    to Russia and the West. New York: Knopf, 1966.
Hartmann, Frederick H. Germany Between East and West: The Re-
    unification Problem. Englewood Cliffs, N. J. : Prentice-Hall,
    1965.
Hiscocks, Richard. The Adenauer Era. Philadelphia: Lippincott,
    1966.
Holborn, Hajo. A History of Modern Germany. Vol. III: 1840-
    1945. New York: Knopf, 1969.
Howley, Frank. Berlin Command. New York: Putnam's, 1950.
McLellan, David S. The Cold War in Transition. New York: Mac-
    millan, 1966.
Marshall, Charles Burton. The Cold War: A Concise History.
    New York: Watts, 1965.
Merkl, Peter H. The Origin of the West German Republic. New
    York: Oxford University Press, 1963.
Rees, David. The Age of Containment: The Cold War, 1945-1965.
    New York: St. Martin's Press, 1967.
Reiss, Curt. Berlin Story. New York: Dial Press, 1953.
Smith, Jean Eduard. The Defense of Berlin. Baltimore: Johns
    Hopkins University Press, 1963.
Steinberg, Alfred. The Man from Missouri: The Life and Times
    of Harry S Truman. New York: Putnam, 1962.
Ulam, Adam B. Expansion and Coexistence: The History of Soviet
    Foreign Policy, 1917-67. New York: Frederick A. Praeger,
    1968.
Windsor, Philip. "The Blockade of Berlin" in Taylor, A. J. P. , ed-
    itor-in-chief. Purnell's History of the 20th Century, Vol. 8.
    New York: Purnell, 1971.

THE NORTH ATLANTIC TREATY (1949)

Following World War II the relationship between the United States and Russia changed from one of wartime allied cooperation to postwar competition. In both Occupied Germany and Eastern Europe Russian foreign policy became increasingly militant. It was realized that in 1949 the nations of Western Europe were weak and unable to defend themselves against organized attack. It was also realized that Russia's seizure of power in Czechoslovakia in February, 1948, and her blockade of Berlin in June of that year might well be followed by an attempt to gain control of Western Europe by armed force.

The United States abandoned its traditional policy of isolationism from Old World, substituting one of interventionism, labeled "containment," in terms of the so-called Truman Doctrine. The Marshall Plan, an economic aid to European postwar construction which became law on April 3, 1948, was rejected by Russia which forbade its satellites to participate in it. This and other acts of the Kremlin resulted in the establishment of the North Atlantic Treaty Organization (NATO) which provides for unified military leadership for the common defense of fifteen Western nations.

Twelve nations signed the Treaty at Washington, D. C. , on April 4, 1949. These were Belgium, Canada, Denmark, France, Great Britain, Iceland, Italy, Luxembourg, the Netherlands, Norway, Portugal and the United States. Greece and Turkey signed in October, 1951 and West Germany added her signature in October, 1954.

The purpose of the Treaty, as stated in the Preamble, is that the signers "reaffirm their faith in the purposes and principles of the Charter of the United Nations and their desire to live in peace with all peoples and all governments. " Accordingly, "they are resolved to unite their efforts for collective defense and for the preservation of peace and security. "

Article 5 of the Treaty specifies that ". . . an armed attack against one or more of [the signers] in Europe or North America shall be considered an attack against them all" and provides that in the event of such an attack each signer will take "such action as it deems necessary, including the use of armed force, to restore and maintain international peace and security. "

In the 1960's NATO members became less worried about the possibility of an attack by Russia. The latter country had improved her nuclear technology, exploding a nuclear bomb late in 1949, and because of this some NATO members doubted that the United States would start a nuclear war in defense of Western Europe. They also resented the fact that NATO had no control over the Strategic Air Command, the main instrument of European defense. Further, the fact that NATO could not influence American foreign policy in other parts of the world, even though this could perhaps lead to war in Europe, was cause for uneasiness. Americans felt that the European countries should furnish more ground forces rather than spend money on nuclear weapons research as did France and Great Britain.

In March, 1966, France withdrew her troops from NATO. Today no NATO soldiers are permitted in that country, and in 1967 Supreme Headquarters Allied Powers Europe (SHAPE) transferred from Paris to Brussels.

Suggested Readings

Amme, Carl H. , Jr.   NATO Without France: A Strategic Appraisal. Stanford, Calif. : Stanford University Press, 1967.

Buchanan, Alastaire. Crisis Management: The New Diplomacy. Boulogne-sue-Seine, France, 1966.

Carmoy, Guy De. The Foreign Policies of France. Chicago: University of Chicago Press, 1969.

Cerney, Karl H. , and Henry W. Briefs, eds. NATO in Quest of Cohesion. New York: Frederick A. Praeger, 1965.

Cottrell, Alvin J. , and James E. Dougherty. The Politics of the Atlantic Alliance. New York: Frederick A. Praeger, 1964.

Fleming, D. F. The Cold War and Its Origins. Garden City, N. Y. : Doubleday, 1961.

Fox, William T. R. , and Annette B. Fox. NATO and the Range of American Choice. New York: Columbia University Press, 1967.

Grosser, Alfred. French Foreign Policy Under DeGaulle. Boston: Little, Brown, 1967.

Halle, Louis J. The Cold War as History. New York: Harper & Row, 1967.

Hess, John L. The Case for DeGaulle: An American Viewpoint. New York: Morrow, 1968.

Kennan, George F. Memoirs: 1925-1950. Boston: Little, Brown, 1967.

Kissinger, Henry A. The Troubled Partnership: A Re-Appraisal of the Atlantic Alliance. New York: McGraw-Hill, 1965.

Knorr, Klaus. NATO and American Security. Princeton, N. J. : Princeton University Press, 1959.

Kulski, Wladyslaw W. DeGaulle and the World: The Foreign Policy of the Fifth French Republic. Syracuse, N. Y. : Syracuse University Press, 1966.

MacCloskey, Monro. North Atlantic Treaty Organization: Guardian of Peace and Security. New York: Richards-Rosen Press, 1966.

NATO Information Service. NATO: Facts About the North Atlantic Treaty Organization. Paris, 1967.

Salvadori, Massimo. NATO: A Twentieth Century Community of Nations. Gloucester, Mass. : Peter Smith, 1967.

Serfaty, Simon. France, DeGaulle and Europe: The Policy of the Fourth and Fifth Republics Toward the Continent. Baltimore: Johns Hopkins University Press, 1968.

Vandenberg, Arthur H. , Jr. , ed. The Private Papers of Senator
    Vandenberg. Boston: Houghton Mifflin, 1952.
Wilcox, Francis O. , and W. Field Haviland, eds. The Atlantic
    Community: Progress and Prospects. New York: Frederick
    A. Praeger, 1963
Willis, F. Roy. France, Germany and the New Europe, 1945-1967.
    Stanford, Calif. : Stanford University Press, 1968.
    _____, ed. DeGaulle: Anachronism, Realist or Prophet? Glou-
    cester, Mass. : Peter Smith, 1967.

THE DEATH OF JOSEPH STALIN (1953)

       On March 6, 1953, Radio Moscow reported that Joseph Stalin
(real name Iosif Vissarionovich Dzhugashvili), the Russian political
leader, revolutionist and Soviet dictator, had died on the previous
day at 9:30 P. M. He was said to have suffered a stroke on March
4, which had led to partial paralysis complicated by heart and breath-
ing difficulties and from which he did not recover. Some historians,
including George Daniel Embree, "Monitor" (a pseudonym) and Robert Payne, contend that Stalin may have been murdered by party
officials. Others, including Robert Warth, feel that his death was
the result of natural causes.

       Stalin was born in the Georgian village of Gori, then in
Transcaucasia, in 1879, the son of a shoemaker. He attended a
theological seminary near Tiflis from which he was expelled, probably for activities in connection with Marxist propaganda. In 1896
he joined the Social Democratic Party and when it split in 1903 he
sided with the Bolsheviks. On several occasions he was exiled to
Siberia for political activities, but always managed to escape. He
also spent some time in prison, being freed after the February,
1917, Revolution.

       He became a close associate of Nikolai Lenin and rose to
power in the Communist Party. Lenin died in 1924 and Stalin eliminated the opposition of Leon Trotsky and other rival politicians,
establishing himself as virtual dictator.

       A number of important events occurred in Russia while it
was under Stalin's leadership. These include the development of
agriculture and industry under the Five-Year Plans, the exile of
Trotsky in 1929, non-aggression pacts with Poland, France, Italy
and Outer Mongolia between 1932 and 1934, and acceptance by Russia of membership in the League of Nations in 1934. Other events
include purges of the Communist Party and the army in 1936 and
1937, a 1939 non-aggression pact with Germany, the annexation of
Western Poland in 1939, war with Finland (1939-1940), and the annexation of Latvia, Estonia, Lithuania and Bessarabia in 1940. During World War II Stalin took over the direction of military operations
and attended the Yalta and Potsdam Conferences.

During his climb to power and quarter-of-a-century reign
Stalin had ruled as ruthlessly as any dictator in history.   Terror,
bloodshed, purges and suffering characterized his policies.   His
persecution of the Jews rivaled that of Hitler in Nazi Germany.
Many Russians, both low and high, feared him but also respected
him for the results he was able to achieve.

In 1952 Stalin was planning further purges of Jews, Communist officials and others, fearing that they were attempting to undermine his authority.   Particularly vulnerable were V. M. Molotov,
Lavrenti Beria, Nikita Khrushchev, Georgi Malenkov, Lazar Kag-
anovich and Anastas Mikoyan, all high-ranking Communist Party
members.   On January 13, 1953, the alleged "Doctor's Plot" was
announced.   It was charged that nine prominent physicians, six of
whom were Jews, had conceived a secret plan to murder, by im-
proper medical treatment, Communist Party leaders and high ranking Russian military officers.   Other charges of sabotage, assassination plots and economic crimes were contained in a dossier which
Stalin had prepared against his intended victims.   Historians are
generally agreed that his death was the only thing that saved Russia
from another round of persecutions, political murders, bloodshed
and horror.

Following Stalin's passing, Malenkov (the new premier) attempted to establish himself in the former's old dictatorial position.
This was thwarted by the other Party officials who were careful to
avoid any suggestion that another could rise to the heights of power
that Stalin had achieved.   Party leaders appealed to the people to
"remain calm. "   They also began to replace the hated secret police
with army units which were far more popular among the people.   A
campaign to downgrade Stalin was launched.   This reached a climax
at the 20th Congress of the Communist Party of the Soviet Union,
held in Moscow in February, 1956.   Khrushchev, in a lengthy speech,
charged that Joseph Stalin had fostered a "cult of the individual, "
centered upon himself, which led to a one-man rule.

Khrushchev charged further that Stalin had "bungled the Soviet war effort in World War II, was sickly suspicious of his colleagues and evidently had plans to finish off the old members of the
Political Bureau. "   The contents of this speech were made known to
the non-Soviet world by the United States Department of State the
following June.   With Stalin's death, either from natural or unnatural causes, a new era in Russian history was launched.

Suggested Readings

Daniels, Robert V.   The Conscience of the Revolution: Communist
        Opposition in Soviet Russia.   Cambridge, Mass. : Harvard Uni-
        versity Press, 1960.
Deutscher, Isaac.   Stalin: A Political Biography.   2nd rev. ed.
        New York: Oxford University Press, 1967.
Ehrlich, A.   The Soviet Industrialization Debate.   Cambridge, Mass. :
        Harvard University Press, 1950.

Embree, George Daniel. The Soviet Union Between the 19th and
    20th Party Congresses, 1952-1956. The Hague: Martinus
    Nyhoff, 1959.
Laqueur, Walter. The Fate of the Revolution: Interpretations of
    Soviet History. London: Weidenfeld and Nicolson, 1967.
Leonhard, Wolfgang. The Kremlin Since Stalin. Translated by
    Elizabeth Wiskemann and Marion Jackson. New York: Fred-
    erick A. Praeger, 1962.
"Monitor", pseud. The Death of Stalin: An Investigation. London:
    Allen Wingate, 1958.
Nove, Alec. Economic Rationality and Soviet Politics. New York:
    Frederick A. Praeger, 1964.
Payne, Robert. The Rise and Fall of Stalin. New York: Simon
    & Schuster, 1965.
Ponomaryov, Boris N., et al. History of the Communist Party of
    the Soviet Union. Moscow: Foreign Languages Publishing
    House, 1960.
Randall, F. Stalin's Russia. New York: Free Press, 1965.
Schapiro, Leonard. The Communist Party of the Soviet Union.
    New York: Random House, 1960.
Tucker, Robert C. The Soviet Political Mind: Studies in Stalinism
    and Post-Stalin Change. New York: Frederick A. Praeger,
    1963.
Warth, Robert. Joseph Stalin. New York: Twayne Publishers,
    1969.

THE ANDREA DORIA-STOCKHOLM COLLISION (1956)

Shortly before midnight on July 25, 1956, the luxury liners
Andrea Doria and Stockholm collided 45 miles off Nantucket, Mas-
sachusetts. The Andrea Doria sank; the Stockholm, though badly
damaged, was repaired and returned to service. The tragedy,
though costly in terms of money, was relatively minor as regards
loss of life when compared to such marine disasters as those involving the General Slocum in 1904, the Titanic in 1912, or the
Lusitania in 1915. The death toll on the Andrea Doria stood at
about fifty persons out of the 1,709 aboard at the time of the collision.

The reason for the disaster is shrouded in mystery. Both
ships were traveling at high rates of speed but the sea was calm,
though foggy. Each ship had spotted the other on its radar screen
well before the collision. Apparently the officers on each vessel
thought that the other was approaching from the opposite side. The
Andrea Doria suddenly emerged from a dense fog bank and only then
was it realized that she and the Stockholm were on a collision course.

In spite of the efforts made on both ships to avoid coming
together, the bow of the Stockholm rammed the Andrea Doria on the
starboard side, opening a huge rupture both above and below the

waterline.   The Stockholm's bow was crushed and she was in imminent danger of sinking.   The newer Andrea Doria, which had suffered far more severe damage, immediately sent out an S. O. S.

Fortunately a number of ships were in the immediate vicinity and, receiving the radio call for help, started to the rescue.
These included the navy transport Private William H. Thomas, the
freighter Cape Ann, coast guard and other ships and, most important, the ancient luxury liner Ile de France, the last commanded by
Raoul de Beaudean.

Captain de Beaudean ordered his liner to alter her course
and steer for the Andrea Doria.   For some reason he could not
make radio contact with the stricken vessel, although he had received her S. O. S.   From messages received from other ships he
learned that lifeboats were needed at the scene of the accident.   The
Ile de France was well equipped with such boats, which was not the
case with the other rescuing vessels.

Following the collision the Andrea Doria developed a 25°
list to starboard, making it impossible to launch the lifeboats on
the port side.   What boats were available could hold only a fraction
of the passengers and crew, and some had already been lowered,
virtually empty.   The Private William H. Thomas and the Stockholm
could spare few boats, having their own passengers to protect, and
the freighter Cape Ann carried only two lifeboats.

Captain de Beaudean ordered preparations made to take on
the passengers and crew of the sinking Andrea Doria.   In spite of
the thick fog he made good time to the scene of the collision.   He
brought his ship to a stop within 400 yards of the stricken vessel,
whose list had increased to 30°.   The fog began to lift and the sea
turned choppy.   The space between the two ships, however, remained relatively calm and lifeboat crews from the Ile de France
were able to operate a shuttle service, bringing passengers and
crewmen to safety.   Within ninety minutes of her arrival at the
scene, nearly 1,700 persons had been carried to the Ile de France
and to other vessels.

The estimated fifty persons killed on the Andrea Doria died,
for the most part, at the time of the collision.   Twelve hours after
the Stockholm had stove in her side, the Andrea Doria sank to the
bottom of the Atlantic, where she rests in 225 feet of water.   The
Stockholm, refitted with a new bow, is still in service.   The Ile de
France was scrapped in 1959.

Suggested Readings

"Against the Sea: Andrea Doria," Time, August 6, 1956.
"Andrea Doria Settlement," Time, February 4, 1957.
"As a Ship Lay Dying in the Night: Andrea Doria," Newsweek,
    August 6, 1956.

"For Doria, Bell Tolls a $40 Million Tune, " Business Week, August
    4, 1956.
"Just Who Was Wrong? Andrea Doria-Stockholm Collision, " News-
    week, August 20, 1956.
Lord, W. "Hours of Fear as People Lived Them: Andrea Doria, "
    Life, August 6, 1956.
"Man Failure: Andrea Doria, " Newsweek, August 6, 1956.
Moscow, Alvin. Collision Course: The "Andrea Doria" and the
    "Stockholm. " New York: Putnam, 1959.
_____ "The Mystery of the Andrea Doria, " TV Guide, March
    20, 1976.
Sutton, H. "One by Sea, One by Land: Doria-Stockholm Debacle, "
    Saturday Review, September 1, 1956.
"Third Mate's Story: Stockholm and Andrea Doria, " Time, October
    8, 1956.

THE SUEZ CANAL CRISIS (1956)

The Suez Canal is an artificial waterway stretching across
the Isthmus of Suez and connecting the Mediterranean Sea with the
Gulf of Suez, an arm of the Red Sea. Thus it is in the northeastern
section of the United Arab Republic and provides a short cut between American and European ports and ports in Oceania, Southern
Asia and Eastern Africa. In the early 1960's more than 18,000
ships passed through the canal each year.

Although several attempts were made to construct such a
canal as long ago as the thirteenth century B. C. , it was not until
the middle of the nineteenth century that Ferdinand de Lesseps, a
French engineer and diplomat, with the cooperation of Said Pasha,
the Egyptian viceroy, formed the Universal Company of the Maritime Suez Canal. This organization was authorized to build a canal
and operate it for 99 years, after which it would revert to the
Egyptian government. The Company was originally a private Egyptian concern incorporated under French law in 1858. The Canal
was opened to navigation in 1869 and in 1875 a substantial interest
was purchased by the British government.

The Suez Canal is supposedly open to vessels of all nations,
under the terms of an international convention agreed to in 1888.
In 1936 Great Britain acquired the right to maintain defense forces
in the Canal Zone.

War broke out between the nations of the Arab League and
Israel and the Egyptian government violated the 1888 convention by
denying use of the Canal to vessels bound for Israel. It also ignored a resolution of the United Nations Security Council (1951) requesting an end to this discrimination.

Egypt demanded that the British troops withdraw, abrogated

the 1936 treaty in 1951, and in 1955 the British troops left, following the signing of a new seven-year agreement which replaced the
original one.

On July 26, 1956, the Egyptian government took possession
of the Canal, the result of a decree of nationalization issued by
President Gamal Abdel Nasser, it being explained that the proceeds
from Canal operations were to be used to finance the construction
of the Aswân dam, financial support of which had been withdrawn by
Great Britain and the United States.

In October, 1956, Israeli invaded the Sinai Peninsula and
Egypt rejected an Anglo-French ultimatum to cease fire.   English
and French military units then invaded Egypt for the purpose of
keeping the Canal open, by force if necessary.   Egypt retaliated
by causing some forty ships to be sunk in the Canal, thus blocking
passage.

The United Nations intervened and a truce was negotiated,
with British, French and Israeli troops being withdrawn by the end
of the year.   A United Nations salvage team removed the sunken
vessels and the Canal was reopened in March, 1957.   In the following year a financial settlement was reached by the Universal Company and the United Arab Republic.

Suggested Readings

Beatty, Charles.   De Lesseps of Suez.   Buffalo, N. Y. :   McClel-
land, 1956.
———.   Ferdinand De Lesseps.   London: Eyre and Spottiswoode,
1956.
Beaufre, André.   The Suez Expedition, 1956.   Translated by Rich-
ard Barry.   New York: Frederick A. Praeger, 1969.
Burns, E. L. M.   Between Arab and Israeli.   New York: Ivan Obol-
ensky, 1963.
Dayan, Moshe.   Diary of the Sinai Campaign.   New York: Harper
& Row, 1965.
Eden, Sir Anthony.   Full Circle: The Memoirs of Anthony Eden.
Boston: Houghton Mifflin, 1960.
Henriques, Robert.   One Hundred Hours to Suez: An Account of
Israel's Campaign in the Sinai Peninsula.   New York: Viking
Press, 1957.
Khouri, Fred J.   The Arab-Israeli Dilemma.   Syracuse, N. Y. :
Syracuse University Press, 1968.
Marlowe, John.   World Ditch: The Making of the Suez Canal.   New
York: Macmillan, 1964.
Nutting, Anthony.   No End of a Lesson: The Story of Suez.   New
York: Clarkson N. Potter, 1967.
Robertson, Terence.   Crisis: The Inside Story of the Suez Con-
spiracy.   New York: Atheneum, 1965.
Thomas, Hugh.   Suez.   New York: Harper & Row, 1966.
Warner, Geoffrey.   "The Suez Crisis" in Taylor, A. J. P. , editor

in chief. Purnell's History of the 20th Century, Vol. 9. New
York: Purnell, 1971.

THE FORMATION OF THE COMMON MARKET (1957)

The European Common Market, the first step in establishing
an economically united Europe, was created by the Treaty of Rome
on March 25, 1957. It is officially known as the European Economic Community and was established to facilitate trade among its
members and otherwise promote their economic growth.

Following World War II Europe was both weak and destitute
and the European nations felt that they were being relegated to minor roles by the United States and the Soviet Union. They were
aware that, "in order to develop a political awareness a unified
economy would be necessary. " Konrad Adenauer, Chancellor of
West Germany, Alcide de Gasperi, Prime Minister of Italy and
Jean Monnet, French Minister of Economics, all favored an economically strong Europe.

From 1948 until 1957 there were a number of attempts at
unity. In 1948 the Marshall Plan, which provided an outright gift
to Europe, was overseen by the Economic Cooperative Administration, with sixteen nations participating. Later, such organizations
as Benelux, created by Belgium, the Netherlands, and Luxembourg,
abolished all frontier duties. In 1951 the European Coal and Steel
Community (ECSC) was formed, its objectives being to do away with
trade barriers, control the production of arms and restrict trusts.
The European Defense Community, which died in the French Assembly in 1954, was another attempt by European nations to achieve
economic cooperation.

The foreign ministers of the ECSC nations met at Messina
in 1955 to discuss the problem. The British, feeling that the meeting was pointless, walked out. However, under the leadership of
Paul Henri Spaak, Premier of Belgium, the talks continued near
Brussels and in May of 1956 the foundations of the European Common Market were laid. The 1957 Treaty of Rome, mentioned above,
was signed by the foreign ministers of Belgium, France, Germany,
Italy, Luxembourg, and the Netherlands. At the same time this
body created the European Atomic Energy Community.

The Treaty of Rome, containing 248 articles, had as its objective the gradual elimination of customs barriers within the next
twelve to fifteen years, thus creating an integrated mass market of
some 160 million people.

Steps were taken to implement the Treaty. Headquarters
were established in Brussels. Major issues are decided by the
Council of Ministers, formed for that purpose. The nine-member

European Commission is an executive body whose decisions are subject to Council veto. Cases involving violations of the Treaty are heard by a seven-judge Court of Justice.

The European Common Market became effective in January, 1958. Three years later tariffs had been cut on both industrial goods and agricultural products. Certain former African territories had been given associate status on a provisional basis, permitting them to share in the benefits of Market membership.

Great Britain had not taken the earlier organization seriously and in 1961 her possible membership was given consideration. After two years of study Charles de Gaulle, President of France, vetoed Great Britain's admission, considering that island empire not a part of the European continent and being suspicious of her economic ties with the United States. Following de Gaulle's death in 1970 President Georges Pompidou of France and Prime Minister Edward Heath of Great Britain discussed the matter in Paris. On January 1, 1973, Great Britain, along with Denmark and Ireland, became a member of the European Common Market.

Suggested Readings

Andrews, Stanley. Agriculture and the Common Market. Iowa City, Ia. : Iowa State University Press, 1973.

Bouvard, Marguerite. Labor Movements in the Common Market Countries: The Growth of a European Pressure Group. New York: Frederick A. Praeger, 1972.

Broad, Roger, and Robert Jarrett. Community Europe: A Short Guide to the Common Market. London: Oswald Wolff, 1967.

Davis, Ralph. The Rise of the Atlantic Economies. Ithaca, N. Y. : Cornell University Press, 1973.

Deniau, Jean François. The Common Market. Translated by Graham Heath. New York: Frederick A. Praeger, 1960.

Diebold, William, Jr. The United States and the Industrial World: American Foreign Economic Policy in the 1970's. New York: Frederick A. Praeger, 1972.

Einzig, Paul. The Case Against Joining the Common Market. New York: St. Martin's Press, 1971.

Farnsworth, C. H. Out of This Nettle: A History of Postwar Europe. New York: John Day, 1973.

Geiger, Theodore. The Fortunes of the West: The Future of the Atlantic Nations. Bloomington, Ind. : Indiana University Press, 1973.

Hallstein, Walter. Europe in the Making. Translated by Charles Roetter. New York: Norton, 1973.

Hoepli, Nancy L. , ed. The Common Market. New York: H. W. Wilson, 1975.

Ionescu, Ghita, ed. The New Politics of European Integration. New York: St. Martin's Press, 1972.

Isenberg, Irwin, ed. The Outlook for Western Europe. New York: H. W. Wilson, 1970.

Kissinger, Henry A. 1973: The Year of Europe. Washington, D. C.: Government Printing Office, 1973.

Kitzinger, Uwe. Diplomacy and Persuasion: How Britain Joined the Common Market. London: Thames and Hudson, 1973.

Knox, Francis. The Common Market and World Agriculture: Trade Patterns in Temperate-Zone Foodstuffs. London: Pall Mall, 1972.

Kohnstamm, Max, and Wolfgang Hager, eds. A Nation Writ Large? Foreign Policy Problems Before the European Community. New York: Wiley, 1973.

Korbel, Josef. Détente in Europe: Real or Imaginary? Princeton, N. J.: Princeton University Press, 1972.

Krause, Lawrence B. European Economy: Integration and the United States. Washington, D. C.: Brookings Institution, 1968.
_____, and W. S. Salant. European Monetary Unification and Its Meaning for the United States. Washington, D. C.: Brookings Institution, 1973.

Lindberg, L. N., and S. A. Scheingold. Europe's Would-Be Policy. Englewood Cliffs, N. J.: Prentice-Hall, 1970.
_____. Regional Integration, Theory and Research. Cambridge, Mass.: Harvard University Press, 1971.

Lippman, Walter. Western Unity and the Common Market. London: Hamish Hamilton, 1962.

Magnifico, Giovanni. European Monetary Unification. New York: Wiley, 1973.

Mally, Gerhard. The European Community in Perspective: The New Europe, the United States and the World. Boston: Heath, 1973.

Mowatt, R. C. Creating the European Community. New York: Harper, 1973.

Nystrom, J. Warren, and Peter Malof. The Common Market: The European Community in Action. Princeton, N. J.: Van Nostrand, 1962.

Walsh, A. E., and John Paxton. The Structure and Development of the Common Market. London: Hutchinson & Co., 1968.

Warnecke, S. J., ed. The European Community in the 1970's. New York: Frederick A. Praeger, 1972.

Weil, Gordon L., ed. A Handbook of the European Economic Community. New York: Frederick A. Praeger, 1965.

THE INTERNATIONAL GEOPHYSICAL YEAR (IGY)
(1957-1958)

The International Geophysical Year (IGY) opened on July 1, 1957, and closed eighteen months later. It involved cooperative scientific investigations by 67 participating nations which conducted research in such areas as meteorology, geomagnetism, ionosphere, solar activity, glaciology, seismology, oceanography, gravimetry and nuclear radiation. It was "conceived as the greatest attempt men have yet made to band together to examine, without passion or undue rivalry, their environment, their home and ultimate resource, the earth. "

The IGY of 1957-58 was not the first such effort.   It was preceded by the First and Second International Polar Years of 1882-83 (IPY$_1$) and 1932-33 (IPY$_2$), of which it was the "direct descendant. "

A number of scientific unions, formally organized in 1919, each dealing with one branch of science, provided quorums at which plans for the IGY were discussed.   Then, on April 5, 1950, a group of scientists met with Dr. J. A. Van Allen at his home in a Washington suburb to meet Sydney Chapman, a famous English geophysicist.   At this meeting it was proposed that a third Polar Year be held in 1957-58.   The attendees enthusiastically agreed and by October, 1951, the Comité Spécial de l'Année Géophysique Internationale (CSAGI) had been established and plans for the project, rechristened the International Geophysical Year, were under way.

Because it was realized that the entire world could not be covered with equal intensity, it was decided that research efforts would be concentrated in the polar regions, in the equatorial zone, and along several belts joining pole to pole.   Certain days were designated for special efforts which could not be carried on at all times.   Standardized instructions were prepared and distributed that uniformity of methodology might be achieved.   It was agreed that the data collected during the IGY would be freely circulated.   World data centers were established in Washington, D. C. , Moscow and a number of European cities.

The primary objective of the IGY was to add to man's knowledge of the earth and its more rapid changes.   Consequently, it was necessary to improve our knowledge of the sun.   Thus the IGY was a combined study of the earth and the sun, with emphasis on atmospheric changes.

With the exception of Antarctica the exploration of the earth's surface is essentially complete.   During the IGY new geographical features of the Antarctic were discovered: new mountain ranges, and information concerning the land covered by ice and ice-free areas. Earthquake waves were studied and progress was made in the as yet unperfected science of earthquake prediction.   Glaciers throughout the world were examined.   The oceans came under study.   Temperature measurements were made and water samples were taken from the surface down to 23,000 feet.   These, when analyzed, furnished information concerning ocean currents and the "age" of the deep Caribbean water.

Wind observations and studies of the upper atmosphere were made from various points throughout the world and the data obtained were coordinated and compared.   Such sophisticated devices as radar transmitters, satellites, weather balloons and rockets were used in this research.

The ionospheric program had as its aim the determining of
the worldwide pattern of the electron distribution, in both height
and geographical position by day and by night at different seasons.
Much information concerning this was gathered. Cosmic rays, nuclear radiation and the sun all came under study.

The IGY was highly successful. It generated a mountain of
data which is still being analyzed and evaluated. It led to a great
increase in international cooperation in science and is considered
"an example of how international relations can be amiably and fruit-
fully conducted." It led to a great number of scientific technical
advances and similar world-wide projects are contemplated for the
future.

Suggested Readings

Bates, D. R. The Planet Earth. London: Pergamon Press, 1957.
Berkner, L. V., and Hugh Odishaw, eds. Science in Space. New
     York: McGraw-Hill, 1961.
Carson, Rachel L. The Sea Around Us. New York: Oxford Uni-
     versity Press, 1951.
Chapman, Sydney. The Earth's Magnetism. London: Methuen,
     1951.
_____. IGY: Year of Discovery. The Story of the International
     Geophysical Year. Ann Arbor, Mich.: University of Michigan
     Press, 1959.
Dufek, G. J. Operation Deepfreeze. New York: Harcourt, Brace,
     1957.
Fraser, Ronald. Once Around the Sun: The Story of the Internation-
     al Geophysical Year 1957-8. London: Hodder & Stoughton, 1957.
Heiskanen, W. A., and F. A. Vening Meinesz. The Earth and Its
     Gravity Field. New York: McGraw-Hill, 1958.
Howell, B. F., Jr. Introduction to Geophysics. New York: Mc-
     Graw-Hill, 1959.
Jacobs, J. A., et al. Physics and Geology. New York: McGraw-
     Hill, 1959.
Jeffreys, Harold. The Earth. Cambridge: Cambridge University
     Press, 1959.
Löbsack, Theo. The Earth's Envelope. London: Collins, 1959.
Marshack, Alexander. The World in Space: The Story of the In-
     ternational Geophysical Year. New York: Nelson, 1958.
Massey, H. S. W. The New Age in Physics. New York: Harper,
     1960.
_____, and R. L. F. Boyd. The Upper Atmosphere. London:
     Hutchinson, 1958.
Moore, Ruth. The Earth We Live On: The Story of Geological
     Discovery. New York: Knopf, 1956.
"New Portrait of Our Planet: What IGY Taught Us," Life, Novem-
     ber 7, 14, 21, 28, 1960.
Newton, H. W. The Face of the Sun. London: Penguin Books, 1958.
Peters, B. "Progress in Cosmic Research Since 1947," Journal of
     Geophysical Research, February, 1959.

Pirie, A. Fallout. London: MacGibbon and Kee, 1958.
Richter, C. F. Elementary Seismology. San Francisco: Freeman,
    1958.
Ross, Frank Xavier. Partners in Science: The Story of the In-
    ternational Geophysical Year. New York: Lothrop, 1961.
Sharp, Robert. Glaciers. Seattle: University of Washington Press,
    1960.
Störmer, C. The Polar Aurora. Oxford: Clarendon Press, 1955.
Sullivan, Walter. Assault on the Unknown: The International Geo-
    physical Year. New York: McGraw-Hill, 1961.
Sutton, O. Graham. Understanding the Weather. London: Penguin
    Books, 1960.
Wilson, J. Tuzo. IGY: The Year of the New Moon. New York:
    Knopf, 1961.

THE CAPTURE OF KARL ADOLF EICHMANN (1960)

One of the most ruthless members of the Nazi party was
Karl Adolf Eichmann who, as administrator of the Office for Jewish
Emigration, was directly responsible for the deaths of more than
four million persons, mostly Jews. With the suicide of Adolf Hitler in a Berlin bunker on April 30, 1945 and the defeat of his forces
by the Allies, most of the leaders of the Nazi party were captured
and tried at Nuremberg by the International Military Tribunal in
1945-1946.

Such German military and civilian leaders as Hermann Goering, Rudolf Hess, Joachim von Ribbentrop, Alfred Rosenberg, Hjalmar von Schacht and Hans Fritsche--22 in all--were acquitted or
convicted and sentenced to death or imprisonment. Eichmann, however, dropped from sight and so could not be brought to trial with
the others.

Eichmann was gone but not forgotten. For fifteen years the
police of the world sought him, that he might be brought to justice,
but without success. Then, in 1959, "Operation Eichmann" was set
in motion by David Ben-Gurion, Prime Minister of Israel. A team
of top flight intelligence agents traced Eichmann from Europe to
South America and to the city of Buenos Aires. He had married,
changed his name to Ricardo Klement, fathered two boys and obtained a position as clerical supervisor at the Mercedes-Benz automobile factory.

On the afternoon of May 11, 1960, "Klement" left the factory
to take the bus to his home. He got off the conveyance at Liniares
Avenue and waited on the corner for the San Fernando bus which
would carry him to his suburban residence on Calle Garibaldi. Stepping into a nearby store, he purchased some cigarettes and then returned to the bus stop. A large sedan pulled up to the curb. Four
men sprang out and seized him. He asked, in Spanish, "What do

you want? " One man replied in German, referring to him as "Herr Obersturmbannführer. " He was hustled into the car and rendered unconscious by a blow on the head.

Eichmann's abductors took him to a house in the Buenos Aires suburbs. There he recovered consciousness and was told to strip to the waist. Examination showed a scar under his left arm where a tattoo, the mark of the S. S. commander, had been removed.

A photograph of Eichmann as a Nazi official was produced. The prisoner was found to resemble the man in the picture. A doctor located old fractures on the prisoner's skull and collarbone which matched X-ray plates depicting similar breaks known to have been suffered by Eichmann in the past.

The ex-Nazi was informed that he was being arrested and charged with committing crimes against the Jewish people. He was given a choice: either to be killed immediately or to sign a confession and be taken to Israel, there to be tried by a court of law. He agreed to the latter alternative.

Eichmann was held prisoner in the suburban house for the next several days, and news of the capture and confession was sent to Tel Aviv. On the night of May 20 he was taken to the Buenos Aires airport and put on a jet plane bound for Israel.

Operation Eichmann had succeeded. The former Nazi was tried for war crimes in the Israeli capital. During the proceedings he was kept under heavy guard. In the courtroom he was shielded by a bullet-proof glass box in order to prevent some overly enthusiastic Israeli from assassinating him before the law could take its course.

Eichmann's defense was that he was merely following the orders of his superiors as all military persons must. The court, however, found him guilty as charged and on May 31, 1962, he was hanged at Ramle Prison. His body was cremated and the ashes thrown into the sea.

Suggested Readings

Arendt, Hannah. Eichmann in Jerusalem: A Report on the Banality of Evil. New York: Viking Press, 1964.
"Eichmann" in Crimes and Punishment, Vol. 4. Editorial presentation: Jackson Morley. London: BPC, 1973.
Friedman, Tuviah. The Hunter. Edited and translated by David C. Gross. Garden City, N.Y.: Doubleday, 1961.
Glock, Charles Y., et al. The Apathetic Majority: A Study Based on Public Responses to the Eichmann Trial. New York: Harper & Row, 1966.
Harel, Isser. The House on Garibaldi Street: The First Full Ac-

count of the Capture of Adolf Eichmann, Told by the Former
Head of Israel's Secret Service. New York: Viking Press,
1975.
Hausner, Gideon. Justice in Jerusalem. New York: Harper, 1966.
Hone, Heinz. Order of the Death's Head: The Story of Hitler's
S. S. Translated by Richard Barry. New York: Coward-Mc-
Cann, 1969.
Hull, William Lovell. The Struggle for a Soul. Garden City, N. Y.:
Doubleday, 1963.
McKown, Robin. "The Nuremberg Trial" in his Seven Famous
Trials in History. New York: Vanguard Press, 1963.
Musmanno, Michael Angelo. The Eichmann Kommandos. Philadel-
phia: Macrae, 1961.
Pearlman, Maurice. The Capture and Trial of Adolf Eichmann.
New York: Simon and Schuster, 1963.
Reynolds, Quentin. Minister of Death: The Adolf Eichmann Story.
New York: Viking Press, 1960.
Robinson, Jacob. And the Crooked Shall Be Made Straight: The
Eichmann Trial, The Jewish Catastrophe, and Hannah Arendt's
Narrative. New York: Macmillan, 1965.
Russell, Lord, of Liverpool. The Record: The Trial of Adolf
Eichmann for His Crimes Against the Jewish People and Against
Humanity. New York: Knopf, 1963.

THE BERLIN WALL (1961)

After World War II Berlin was an island city in the Russian
zone of occupied Germany. According to the agreements of the
Yalta and Potsdam conferences, it was to be jointly occupied by
Russia, France, Great Britain and the United States, with access
from the west guaranteed by Russia. The city was to be governed
by the four-power Central Commission and unanimous consent was
needed for all decisions.

On June 22, 1948 Russia, wishing to incorporate Berlin into
its zone and force out western powers, blockaded all surface traffic
to the western sectors, including roads, rails and waterways. Four
days later the United States inaugurated an airlift of food, coal,
medicine and other vital supplies into West Berlin from Wiesbaden
and Frankfort, and later from other points. After nine months the
Russians lifted the blockade.

By tacit agreement the eastern and western sections of Berlin were ruled separately. These were, respectively, the German
Democratic Republic, governed by Chairman Walter Ulbricht, and
the Federal Republic of Germany, under the leadership of Chancellor Konrad Adenauer. Both sides maintained troops in their respective sectors.

The Russians attempted to incorporate Berlin into East Germany in the 1950's, arguing that the Potsdam Agreement had been voided by the creation of the West German government, a contention in which the western powers did not concur.

Nikita Khrushchev, the Russian Premier, attempted to force the West to accept his solution to the problem of Berlin. In November, 1958, he delivered an ultimatum stating that he would turn the city over to the East Germans if the problem was not solved within the next six months. In September, 1959, he visited the United States and conferred with President Dwight D. Eisenhower. It was mutually agreed to solve the Berlin problem but without any time limit being imposed.

For several years living conditions in West Germany had been superior to those in the East, and residents of the latter often moved across the border. From 1949 to 1959 over two million refugees came through Berlin, many of these being skilled workers.

President John F. Kennedy conferred with Khrushchev in Vienna in June, 1961, and at that time refused the Russian Premier's demands for a settlement. On August 13, 1961, the East German government commenced construction of a barrier wall between the two parts of the partitioned city to prevent further departures. The wall, constructed of concrete, sometimes referred to as the "Wall of Infamy," became a symbol of repression, emphasizing the fact that East Germany found it necessary to imprison its citizens to prevent them from leaving, although on certain holidays residents of the West were permitted to visit friends and relatives in the East.

A few East Berlin citizens managed to surmount the wall and escape to the western part of the city. Some of these escapes were highly dramatic, and in some cases the would-be escapee was captured or shot by the East German police.

Suggested Readings

Abosch, Heinz. The Menace of the Miracle: Germany from Hitler to Adenauer. Translated by Douglas Garman. New York: Monthly Review Press, 1963.

Fleming, D. F. The Cold War and Its Origins. Garden City, N. Y.: Doubleday, 1961.

Grosser, Alfred. The Federal Republic of Germany. New York: Frederick A. Praeger, 1963.

Halle, Louis J. The Cold War as History. New York: Harper & Row, 1967.

Hangan, Welles. The Muted Revolution: East Germany's Challenge to Russia and the West. New York: Knopf, 1966.

Hartmann, Frederick H. Germany Between East and West: The Reunification Problem. Englewood Cliffs, N. J.: Prentice-Hall, 1965.

Hiscocks, Richard. The Adenauer Era. Philadelphia: Lippincott, 1966.

Holborn, Hajo. A History of Modern Germany. Vol. III: 1840-
    1945. New York: Knopf, 1969.
MacCloskey, Monro. The Infamous Wall of Berlin. New York:
    Richards Rosen Press, 1967.
McLellan, David S. The Cold War in Transition. New York: Mac-
    millan, 1966.
Marshall, Charles Burton. The Cold War: A Concise History.
    New York: Watts, 1965.
Merkl, Peter H. The Origin of the West Berlin Republic. New
    York: Oxford University Press, 1963.
Rees, David. The Age of Containment: The Cold War, 1945-1965.
    New York: St. Martin's Press, 1967.
Smith, Jean Eduard. The Defense of Berlin. Baltimore: Johns
    Hopkins University Press, 1963.
Ulam, Adam B. Expansion and Coexistence: The History of Soviet
    Foreign Policy, 1917-67. New York: Frederick A. Praeger,
    1968.

THE PROFUMO-KEELER-WARD SCANDAL (1961-1963)

        The Profumo-Keeler-Ward scandal started on July 8, 1961,
when John Profumo, War Minister in the cabinet of British Prime
Minister Harold Macmillan, met and was temporarily attracted to
Christine Keeler, following a swimming pool party at Cliveden, the
home of Lord "Bill" Astor of Hever. Christine was a dancer turned
prostitute and was then living with Dr. Stephen Ward, an osteopath,
Soviet sympathizer and procurer. She was also having an affair
with Captain Eugene Ivanov, naval attaché at the Soviet Embassy
in London. Profumo briefly became her lover as well.

        Ward was under surveillance by the British Secret Service
because of his political views and it was known that a connection
between him, Ivanov and Profumo existed. The Secret Service was
then unaware of the part Christine Keeler played in the relationship;
this was to be learned later. Profumo was at that time married to
Valerie Hobson, the actress, and his infidelity plus the fact that he
was sharing a mistress, though temporarily, with a Soviet official
made him, as War Minister, susceptible to blackmail.

        In December, 1962, John Edgecombe, a West Indian Negro
with whom Christine had lived, appeared at Ward's flat and fired
a pistol several times. He was arrested and the incident was reported in the newspapers, the girl's name being mentioned. In dis-
cussing the story with her friends Christine spoke of Ward, Ivanov
and Profumo and stated that Ward had asked her to obtain information concerning nuclear warheads from the Russian. News of this
reached the ears of Colonel George Wiggs, a member of Parliament.
Wiggs began to put together a dossier on the case and also spoke to
Harold Wilson, leader of the Labor Party, concerning the security
implications involved.

Rumors concerning Profumo's relationship with a "call-girl ring" began to circulate. Christine did not appear in court when John Edgecombe was tried for the pistol-shooting incident. This was sufficient to cause Colonel Wiggs, in a speech to the House of Commons on March 21, 1963, to demand that the Home Secretary, speaking for the British government, deny categorically the truth of the rumors concerning Profumo's indiscretion. The following day Profumo, in a speech before the same body, denied any clandestine relationship with Christine Keeler.

John Edgecombe, convicted of carrying a pistol with intent to endanger human life, was sentenced to prison for a term of seven years. The girl returned to London from Spain where she had been vacationing. She was fined for failing to obey a summons to appear in court as a witness and was released.

The police began to investigate Ward's background and activities. Christine told the police that Ward had asked her to obtain information concerning nuclear warheads. The matter was reported to Prime Minister Macmillan.

On April 18 Aloysius "Lucky" Gordon, another West Indian Negro and former lover of Christine Keeler, attacked her physically, for which he was later arrested. Ward told Timothy Bligh, private secretary to Macmillan, that unless the police investigation of his activities was called off, he would make public the fact that Profumo lied to the House of Commons. Macmillan directed that Profumo be investigated. The latter, returning from a vacation in Venice, wrote Macmillan a letter admitting that he had lied. He excused his actions by stating that he had wished only to protect his wife and family.

John Profumo retired from public life. Gordon was tried for assault and sentenced to three years imprisonment but the sentence was later voided. At the trial, at which Christine testified, Ward's name came up. He was arrested and tried on charges of "living on immoral earnings" and of "procuring under-age girls for immoral purposes. " A parade of prostitutes and call-girls testified, one of whom was eighteen-year-old Mandy Rice-Davies, a friend of Christine. Ward was found guilty of two of the five charges against him. Before sentence could be pronounced he committed suicide by taking an overdose of drugs.

At this writing Christine Keeler, after two marriages and divorces, is living quietly in Chelsea.

Suggested Readings

Behr, E. "Crisis Over Christine, " Saturday Evening Post, July 13, 1963.
Bergquist, L. "Personal Report on Britain's Biggest Scandal, " Look, July 30, 1963.

"Britain's Spy Scandals: How They Grew," U.S. News and World Report, June 24, 1963.

Brogan, C. "The Profumo Affair," National Review, July 2, 1963.

"The Case of the Sensitive Osteopath," Time, March 29, 1963.

"Embarrassed Establishment," Nation, June 29, 1963.

"Ineffectual But Innocent: Lord Denning's Report," Time, October 4, 1963.

Irving, Clive, et al. Anatomy of a Scandal: A Study of the Profumo Affair. New York: M.S. Mill Co., 1963.

"Mac the Slack," Newsweek, July 1, 1963.

Northcott, C. "Pall on Profumory: The Ward-Keeler-Profumo Scandal," The Christian Century, August 21, 1963.

Panter-Downes, M. "Letter from London: Profumo Case," New Yorker, June 29, 1963.

Playfair, B. "Concerning the Denning Report," New Republic, December 21, 1963.

"The Price of Christine," Time, June 14, 1963.

"The Profumo Affair" in Crimes and Punishment, Vol. 9. Editorial presentation: Jackson Morley. London: BPC, 1973.

"The Scandal That's Rocking Britain: Profumo Case," U.S. News and World Report, June 17, 1963.

Symons, Julian. "Matters of Scandal and Concern" in his A Pictorial History of Crime. New York: Crown Publishers, 1966.

Tebbel, J. "Thunder on the Thames: The British Press and the Profumo Case," Saturday Review, July 13, 1963.

"The Time of the Trollop," Time, June 21, 1963.

West, R. "Dr. Stephen Ward Returns," Esquire, September, 1964.

"What the Hell ...," Newsweek, June 17, 1963.

THE BRITISH MAIL TRAIN ROBBERY (1963)

On August 8, 1963, a gang of masked men halted and robbed a Glasgow to London mail train of the equivalent of $7,368,095. The robbery occurred at Bridego Bridge near Cheddington Station and the police called it "the largest armed robbery ever carried out." It bettered the 1950 record set by the holdup of the Brinks armed car service in Boston when $2,750,000 was taken by six armed bandits.

The mail train consisted of a diesel locomotive and twelve coaches concerned exclusively with the transporting and sorting of mail. The coach second from the locomotive was known as the "high value package coach." This was carrying 128 mail bags containing currency which was being sent by Scottish banks to their London affiliates. Frank Dewhurst, a post office official, was in charge of the high value package coach and there were a number of postal employees sorting mail as the train sped through the night towards London.

At 2:00 A.M. the train passed through Leighton Buzzard in

Bedfordshire and was due to pull into the London station by 3:00.
Engineer Jack Mills was at the throttle and in the engine cab with
him was David Whitby, his fireman. Mills saw that the signal
light, known as the "distant signal," was displaying an amber warning light. This meant that the next light, called the "home signal,"
located at Sears Crossing some 1,300 yards ahead, was showing
red, indicating the presence of another train in the block and requiring the approaching train to stop until the track was clear. Had
the distant signal showed green the engineer would have known that
the track ahead was unobstructed and that he could proceed safely
without diminishing speed.

Seeing the red home signal, Mills brought the train to a
stop at Sears Crossing. He instructed Whitby to go to a trackside
telephone and find out from the dispatcher how long a delay they
could anticipate. Whitby discovered that the telephone wires had
been cut. As he made his way back to the diesel cab he saw the
shadowy figure of a man at the rear of the high value package coach.
Thinking that the man was one of the postal employees, Whitby addressed him. The man pushed him down the embankment where he
was grabbed by two other men and threatened with death if he gave
the alarm. Terrified, Whitby agreed to remain silent.

The men took the fireman back to the cab. This contained
several masked men. Engineer Mills had been beaten on the head
and was bleeding profusely. The engine and first two coaches had
been uncoupled from the rest of the train. Mills was instructed to
move these forward to Bridego Bridge, half a mile away, where the
track crossed over a road. The windows of the high value package
coach were smashed and the gang overpowered Dewhurst and his
assistants and proceeded to remove all but eight of the mail bags.
These were loaded into a truck and taken away. It was later learned
that the booty had been removed to Leatherslade Farm, some twenty
miles distant.

Mills and Whitby were handcuffed together and placed in the
coach with Dewhurst and his men. After the robbers departed Dewhurst sent two of his assistants to give the alarm, which they did
by telephone from Linslade, a nearby village.

Detectives from Scotland Yard were promptly called in. It
was soon determined that the signal lights had been tampered with
and that both the distant and home signals should have displayed
green rather than the amber and red seen by Mills and Whitby. The
farm to which the robbers had fled was located and various clues,
including a large number of fingerprints, were obtained. Neighbors,
when questioned, were able to furnish additional valuable information.

In Bournemouth two men rented a garage from Mrs. Ethel
Clark, a widow. When they paid her from a large roll of bills she
became suspicious and contacted the police. The men were arrested
and identified as Roger Cordrey and Gerald Boal, two members of
the holdup gang. Their truck, when searched, was found to contain

over £141,000 in bank notes, and an additional £300 was located in Boal's home.

A couple strolling through Redlands Wood in Surrey discovered two suitcases and a briefcase all containing large sums of money. These they turned over to the authorities who found an additional suitcase filled with notes near the scene.

Further arrests followed. In April, 1964, twelve of the gang were tried and convicted. One was discharged; the others received prison sentences ranging from three to thirty years. Bruce Reynolds, thought to be the mastermind of the plot, remained at liberty for a while but was eventually caught and given a 25-year sentence. Ronald Edwards and James White, two of the robbers, were not tried with the others but were later apprehended and sentenced to fifteen and eighteen years respectively. Some of the sentences were reduced on appeal. Defendant Ronald Biggs was discharged on a legal technicality but was tried separately at a later date and was convicted.

Biggs and Charles Wilson, another member of the gang, subsequently escaped from prison. Wilson was recaptured in Montreal. Biggs, who made a spectacular escape from confinement by climbing a prison wall and jumping to the roof of a parked truck is, at this writing, still at large. He is reported as having been seen in both Australia and South America. More than two million pounds of the stolen money have never been recovered.

Suggested Readings

"Bigger Than Brinks: Royal Mail Robbery," Newsweek, August 19, 1963.
"Britain's Great Train Robbery: Mystery Unravelled," U.S. News and World Report, January 6, 1964.
"Cheddington Caper: Royal Mail Robbery," Time, August 16, 1963.
"Greatest Train Robbery: Glasgow to London Mail Train," U.S. News and World Report, August 19, 1963.
Hamill, P. "Britain's Great Train Robbery," Reader's Digest, December, 1964.
————. "Great British Train Robbery: Seven Million in Cash," Saturday Evening Post, September 19, 1964.
"Stop! For the Greatest Train Robbery," with comment by E. Chapman. Life, August 23, 1963.
Symons, Julian. "The Great Train Robbery," Parts 1 and 2, in his A Pictorial History of Crime. New York: Crown Publishers, 1966.
"Train Robbery's Sequel: Covering the Loss, $7 Million Holdup," Business Week, August 17, 1963.
"Treasure Hunt: Theft of $7 Million from the Glasgow-London Royal Mail Train," Newsweek, August 26, 1963.
"Twelve Men in Dock, the Man Who Helped Police ... and the One Who Got Away" in Crimes and Punishment, Vol. 2. Editorial presentation: Jackson Morley. London: BPC, 1973.

THE SEIZURE OF THE PUEBLO (1968)

The U. S. S. Pueblo, captained by Lieutenant Commander Lloyd M. Bucher, a former submarine officer, was assigned to an electronics and radio intelligence-gathering mission known as "Operation Clickbeetle" in December, 1966. Bucher was ordered to Puget Sound Naval Shipyard where the vessel, which had been "mothballed, " was to be reactivated. He reported as ordered and installation of special electronic equipment, much of it classified as "secret, " was started.

The mission, according to Bucher, was mishandled from the start. His suggestions were frequently disregarded or disapproved. The steering engine was faulty but was not replaced. The electronic monitoring equipment, once installed, had to be rearranged although it had been positioned as indicated by the appropriate blueprints. Two interpreters assigned to the operation were woefully ignorant of the Korean language but their protests that the six-week language course they had been given did not qualify them for their assignment were overruled. Personnel difficulties were encountered when the specialists who were to operate the electronic equipment saw no reason why they should perform shipboard chores. Bucher felt that his executive officer was incompetent.

In January, 1968, the Pueblo, with her crew of six officers and 73 enlisted men plus two civilian oceanographers, left for the Sea of Japan. There, posing as a research vessel investigating ocean currents, salinity of sea water and similar matters, she was also to gather military intelligence. Commander Bucher had been ordered to remain in international waters, outside the twelve-mile limit at all times and under no circumstances to enter the coastal waters of North Korea. So long as he observed the twelve-mile limit the information-gathering activities of Operation Clickbeetle were perfectly legal and in full compliance with international law.

On January 23, 1968, the Pueblo was apprehended by a North Korean submarine chaser, four torpedo boats and two Mig aircraft. Although she was well outside the twelve-mile limit the Pueblo was ordered to heave to and was then fired upon. Fireman Duane Hodges was killed.

The American vessel's armament consisted of two 20-mm automatic cannon, both of which were covered with canvas and could not be fired. Inadequate provision had been made for equipment to destroy classified documents but the crew of the Pueblo burned what it could. Many such documents, however, fell into the hands of the North Koreans. The electronic equipment was rendered inoperative by being smashed with hammers.

The Pueblo was escorted into the port of Wosan. Bucher and his men were taken by train to a military prison. There they were interrogated, beaten and forced to sign "confessions" that they

had participated in an illegal spying mission on orders of the United
States.   The food served them was poor in quality and inadequate in
quantity.   Sanitation was minimal.

In December, 1968, Bucher, his crew, the two civilians and
the body of Duane Hodges were taken by train to Panmunjon.   There
they crossed the bridge separating North from South Korea, to be
greeted by Dick Friedland, an American State Department official,
Admiral Edward Rosenberg of the United States Navy and General
Charles H. Bonesteel, commanding general of the American ground
forces in Korea, among others.

The Pueblo's crew was flown to San Diego, California.   A
five-man court of inquiry was convened on January 20, 1969, its
mission being to investigate the circumstances surrounding the loss
of the vessel and the conduct of Bucher and his men.   After the hearing the court recommended that Bucher be tried by general court
martial and charged on five counts.   He was accused of

> (1) permitting his ship to be searched while he had the
> power to resist.   (2) Failing to take immediate and ag-
> gressive protective measures when his ship was attacked
> by North Korean forces.   (3) Complying with the orders
> of the North Korean forces to follow them into port.   (4)
> Negligently failing to completely destroy all classified ma-
> terial aboard the U. S. S. Pueblo and permitting such ma-
> terial to go into the hands of the North Koreans, and (5)
> negligently failing to insure before departure for sea that
> his officers and crew were properly organized, stationed
> and trained for emergency destruction of classified ma-
> terial.

The court added that the Commander in Chief of Pacific
Fleets concurred in the findings but ordered that the court martial
be reduced to a Letter of Reprimand.

John H. Chaffee, Secretary of the Navy, directed that all
charges be dropped against all parties.   "They have suffered enough, "
he said.

Bucher was assigned to the Naval Postgraduate School at
Monterey, California.   He has since left the navy, having completed twenty years of service.

Suggested Readings

Ambrister, Trevor.   Matter of Accountability: The True Story of
    the "Pueblo" Affair.   New York: Coward-McCann, 1970.
Brandt, Ed.   The Last Voyage of the U. S. S. "Pueblo".   New York:
    Norton, 1969.
Bucher, Commander Lloyd M.   "Pueblo Captain Tells His Story of
    Capture and Captivity; Excerpts from News Conference Decem-
    ber 23, 1968, " U. S. News and World Report, January 6, 1969.

_____, with Mark Rascovich. Bucher: My Story. Garden City,
    N. Y. : Doubleday, 1970.
Cousins, Norman. "In the Wake of the Pueblo, " Saturday Review,
    February 17, 1968.
"Crisis in Korea, " National Review, February 13, 1968.
Gallery, Daniel V. The "Pueblo" Incident. Garden City, N. Y. :
    Doubleday, 1970.
Getler, M. "Ship of Fools, " Aerospace Technology, February 12,
    1968.
"Heroes or Survivors?, " Time, January 10, 1969.
Murphy, Edward R. , Jr. , with Curt Gentry. Second in Command:
    The Uncensored Account of the Capture of the Spy Ship "Pueblo. "
    New York: Holt, 1971.
"Out of Hell Into Heaven: Release of Pueblo Crew, " Newsweek,
    January 6, 1969.
"Pueblo Case: What Should Captured Americans Do?, " U. S. News
    and World Report, January 20, 1969.
"Return of the Pueblo's Crew, " Time, January 3, 1969.
Schumacher, F. C. , and George C. Wilson. Bridge of No Return:
    The Ordeal of the U. S. S. "Pueblo. " New York: Harcourt,
    Brace, 1970.
"Territorial Waters: Where Do We Draw the Line?, " Senior Scho-
    lastic, March 7, 1968.
"What U. S. Confessed: Crew's Statements and Government's Apol-
    ogy, " U. S. News and World Report, January 6, 1969.

THE ENCYCLICAL HUMANAE VITAE
(OF HUMAN LIFE) (1968)

For almost 2,000 years the Roman Catholic Church has prohibited the use of artificial means of preventing human conception.
This edict was based originally on the Church's reaction to the virtually unlimited sexual license countenanced during the days of the
later Roman Empire.

Early in the 20th century some of the more liberal Christian churches began to modify this prohibition. In 1929 bishops of
the Anglican Communion, at the Lambeth Conference, gave "limited approval" to contraception. Pope Pius XI issued the encyclical
Casti Connubii (Chaste Marriage) on December 3, 1930. This
stated the Church's position on the matter and forbade the use of
contraceptives. The Pope's argument was that sexual intercourse
has as its primary purpose the procreation of children and that contraception, in thwarting this purpose, leads to "lustful indulgence. "
The question of the legitimacy of the "rhythm method, " by which
couples indulge in intercourse only at times when conception is
biologically improbable, was left unsettled. On October 29, 1951,
Pope Pius XII modified the original prohibition by stating in a
speech that the Catholic Church sanctioned the rhythm method under certain medical, social, or economic conditions.

Contraceptive pills became available in the 1950's, the use
of which set off new discussions among the theologians. Dr. John
C. Rock, a Catholic professor at the Harvard Medical School, writing in his 1963 book The Time Has Come, challenged the Church's
traditional teaching and argued that use of "the pill" to prevent un-
wanted pregnancies was justified. Churchmen advocated the use of
the pill and stated that the Church had left many aspects of the
birth control question still unresolved.

On June 23, 1964, Pope Paul VI announced that the matter
was under discussion but, until further notice, the Church's traditional position was unchanged. He also revealed that a commission
established by his predecessor, Pope John XXIII and consisting of
bishops, laymen and theologians, had studied the matter intensively.
A majority of the members of the commission recommended to the
Pope that new approaches to the subject be considered as should
the possibility of liberalizing the Church's traditional stand. In
July, 1968, Pope Paul VI issued the encyclical Humanae Vitae (Of
Human Life). This reaffirmed the Church's original position of forbidding artificial means of preventing human conception without compromise.

In his encyclical the Pope considered the new aspects of the
question, such as predictions of overpopulation. He stated that "the
sexual act is both an act of union and an act of procreation, and
man cannot choose to separate these two aspects. " He condemned
abortion, sterilization and "every action which ... proposes ... to
render procreation impossible. " He did, however, indicate that the
Catholic Church sanctions essential surgery, even though the result
of which might make conception impossible, and reaffirmed the legitimacy of the rhythm method under certain conditions.

Pope Paul argued that contraception tends to promote marital
infidelity and immorality, and that "man cannot assume absolute responsibility for regulating his own bodily functions. " He concluded
his encyclical with an appeal to the Church members and officials
to follow the principles it taught.

For the most part high ranking churchmen and many laymen
in Belgium and Canada supported the Pope's view. Some, however,
held that it was not an infallible papal pronouncement "as defined by
the First Vatican Council of 1869-1870. "

In the United States the encyclical received reasonably strong
endorsement. However, some theologians associated with the Catholic University of America at Washington, D. C. , in a published
statement branded the document as "narrow, reactionary and not
well thought out. " Patrick O'Boyle, Cardinal of Washington, suspended over thirty priests for signing this or a similar statement
of dissent. Most of the signers declined to recant and their suspensions were not lifted.

The matter of the Catholic Church's prohibition of using various means of contraception is, at this writing, unresolved. Some traditionalists feel that the old doctrine still applies. Many progressives, on the other hand, hold that no sin is committed when the message of Pope Paul's Humanae Vitae is ignored.

Suggested Readings

Birmingham, William, ed. What Modern Catholics Think of Birth Control. New York: New American Library, 1964.

Callahan, Daniel, ed. The Catholic Case for Contraception. New York: Macmillan, 1969.

Curran, Charles E. , ed. Contraception: Authority and Dissent. New York: Herder and Herder, 1959.

Egner, G. Contraception vs. Tradition. New York: Herder and Herder, 1967.

Guttmacher, Alan Frank. Babies by Choice or by Chance. Garden City, N. Y. : Doubleday, 1959.

Hoyt, Robert G. , ed. The Birth Control Debate. Kansas City, Mo. : The National Catholic Reporter, 1968.

Kelly, George A. Birth Control and Catholics. Garden City, N. Y. : Doubleday, 1963.

Kistner, Robert W. The Pill: Facts and Fallacies About Today's Oral Contraceptives. New York: Delacorte, 1969.

Noonan, John T. , Jr. Contraception: A History of Its Treatment by the Catholic Theologians and Canonists. Cambridge, Mass. : Harvard University Press, 1965.

Rock, John C. The Time Has Come: A Catholic Doctor's Proposals to End the Battle Over Birth Control. New York: Knopf, 1963.

Society of American Friends Service Committee. Who Shall Live? Man's Control Over Birth and Death: A Report. New York: Hill and Wang, 1970.

Vaughan, Paul. The Pill on Trial. New York: Coward-McCann, 1970.

Weinberg, Roy David. Laws Governing Family Planning. Dobbs Ferry, N. Y. : Oceana Publishers, 1968.

THE SEARCH FOR THE LOCH NESS MONSTER
(1972 and 1976)

As early as the year 565 A. D. Saint Columba, an Irish missionary called "The Apostle of Caledonia," is reported to have observed a large monster in Loch Ness, a 24-mile-long lake in north central Scotland. Since then other similar sightings have been reported in the 700-foot deep lake but to date none have been definitely confirmed.

In 1933 a British couple reported seeing "a creature with a long neck and body" in the lake and since then various expeditions have attempted to find such a "creature." In 1972 Robert Rines, president of the Academy of Applied Sciences, led an expedition to seek out "Nessie," as the monster came to be called. He used modern scientific devices, including underwater cameras, sonar equipment and other electronic apparatus with which he obtained photographs which aroused scientific interest. One picture, made clearer by the use of a computer, showed a diamond shaped object. Rines and Sir Peter Scott, a British artist and naturalist, considered this a picture of the flipper of an animal anywhere between 45 and 60 feet in length. Sonar readings furnished some corroborative evidence and the monster was provisionally named Nessiteras rhombopteryx--Ness mammal with a diamond shaped fin.

In 1975 the photographs taken by the members of the Rines party were made public, that "Nessie" might be included in the British list of protected species. It is cautiously estimated that if a Loch Ness monster population does exist, it does not number more than 15 or 20.

Some scientists doubt the existence of such a creature as the Loch Ness monster. Rines's use of a computer to enhance his photographs has been criticized and the lack of proven facts in connection with the monster has been deplored. It has been suggested that the photographs show the remains of a sunken Viking ship or that they resemble a plesiosaur, a reptile now generally believed to be extinct.

In June, 1976, another expedition to seek the Loch Ness monster was initiated. This, jointly sponsored by the Academy of Applied Sciences and the New York Times, was headed by Rines. Like the 1972 expedition, modern scientific equipment was used. Divers carrying underwater television cameras were sent into the lake. One photograph showed an object which resembled a long-necked sea serpent but which some scientists declared to be merely the remains of a sunken ship.

Whether "Nessie" is a myth or a reality is still open to dispute.

The Loch Ness monster is not the only such creature which many people believe to exist. In 1977 a 32-foot animal-reptile was caught in the nets of a Japanese fishing trawler 800 feet down in the waters off the coast of New Zealand. Photographs were taken but, unfortunately, most of the carcass was thrown back into the sea. Professor Yoshinori Imaizumi, director-general of animal research at the National Science Museum, suggests that the photographs could well be those of a plesiosaur. Similar creatures have been reported in Lake Champlain, in Lake Pohenegamook, Quebec, and Lake Okanogan, British Columbia.

The Abominable Snowman, a giant man-like creature has, according to some accounts, been seen in the Himalayas. Bigfoot, a legendary yeti or ape-man, is said to exist in the Pacific North-

west, in Southern Iowa and Southern Florida. Organizations such
as Bigfoot Research (Des Moines, Iowa) and the Bigfoot Research
Center (Hood River, Oregon) have been set up to investigate these
creatures. However, at this writing, no conclusive proof has been
submitted that they do, in fact, exist.

Suggested Readings

Baumann, Elwood D. Bigfoot: America's Abominable Snowman.
    New York: Watts, 1975.
_____. The Loch Ness Monster. New York: Watts, 1972.
Benedick, Jeanne. The Mystery of the Loch Ness Monster. New
    York: McGraw-Hill, 1976.
Costello, Peter. In Search of Lake Monsters. New York: Coward-
    McCann, 1974.
Dinsdale, Tim. Loch Ness Monster. Philadelphia: Chilton, 1961.
_____. Monster Hunt. Washington, D. C. : Acropolis Books,
    1972.
_____. Project Water Horse: The True Story of the Monster
    Quest at Loch Ness. Boston: Routledge, 1975.
Gould, Lieut.-Commander R. T. The Case for the Sea-Serpent.
    London: P. Allan, 1930.
_____. The Loch Ness Monster and Others. Secaucus, N. J. :
    Citadel Press, 1969.
Mackal, Roy P. Monsters of Loch Ness. Chicago: Swallow Press,
    1976.
Meredith, Dennis L. Search at Loch Ness: The Expedition of the
    New York Times and the Academy of Applied Sciences. New
    York: Quadrangle, 1977.
Napier, John Russell. Bigfoot: The Yeti and Sasquatch in Myth
    and Reality. New York: Dutton, 1972.
Sanderson, Ivan Terence. Abominable Snowman: Legend Come to
    Life. Philadelphia: Chilton, 1961.
Tchernine, Odette. In Pursuit of the Abominable Snowman. New
    York: Taplinger, 1971.
Thomas, Nick. "'Something' (Maybe) Lurks in the Depths of a Que-
    bec Lake, " Wall Street Journal, November 17, 1977, p. 1.
Witchell, Nicholas. The Loch Ness Story. Baltimore, Md. : Pen-
    guin Books, 1975.

THE ARAB OIL EMBARGO (1973-1974)

The United States has a vital need for energy. This need,
which is steadily increasing, has transformed the country from an
exporting to an importing one, with approximately 15 percent of her
energy being imported at an annual cost of more than 25 billion dollars. This badly needed energy is largely in the form of petroleum,
much of it produced in the Middle East where proven reserves amount
to billions of barrels. In the winter of 1972-1973 a shortage of nat-

ural gas greatly augmented the American demand for oil, particularly refined distillate fuel oils.

The increased demand for oil enhanced its importance in the Middle East. Some countries located there were reluctant to sell oil for export, either because they wished to force prices up or because they wished to conserve their supplies. Late in 1973 their reasons also became political. The Arab-Israeli war brought matters to a climax. The worldwide demand for oil combined with the lack of coordinated oil policy among the western oil-consuming nations put the Arab oil-producing countries in an excellent bargaining position.

Some time before the outbreak of the war in October pressures for raising oil prices and for either buying and/or nationalizing western oil installations had become intense in Iran, Lybia and the Persian Gulf. The oil producing countries' policies, already dictated by self-interest, were influenced both emotionally and patriotically. Outputs of petroleum were reduced and a unilateral price increase of 70 percent for crude oil was declared. On September 1 the Lybian government announced that it was nationalizing 51 percent of the holdings of eight major international oil companies in Lybia. Under the terms of the nationalistic decree Lybia would compensate the affected firms only on the basis of net book value (initial investment less accrued profits). No compensation was to be made for oil still in the ground and the oil companies were permitted to repurchase 51 percent of their own production. An initial price of $4.90 per barrel was announced. This was later raised to $8.925, including a $1.336 premium for low sulfur content.

After the Arab-Israeli war began the Arabs sought to use their dominant position as oil producers for political purposes. On October 17 eleven oil-producing states called the Organization of Arab Petroleum Exporting Countries (OPEC) announced a 5 percent a month cut in oil output, with only those countries supporting Israel to be affected. During the next few days a series of spokesmen declared that all oil shipments to the United States would be halted. Further, the initial cutback would be 10 percent.

On November 4, OPEC decided on an immediate 25 percent reduction of their September production levels. In addition, an embargo on shipments to the Netherlands went into effect.

Because of the anticipated shortage of fuel during the 1973-74 winter the White House, under the authority of the Economic Stabilization Act, ordered suppliers of middle distillates used for home heating to begin mandatory allocation to wholesale purchasers, starting November 1, 1973. Following the embargo congress approved the Emergency Petroleum Allocation Act of 1973. This legislation directed President Richard M. Nixon to "allocate crude oil and all refined products within thirty days and to establish price controls." In December the President appointed William E. Simon

administrator of the newly-formed Federal Energy Office (FEO),
replacing the White House Energy Policy Office which had been
headed by John Love. The FEO issued mandatory oil allocation
regulations on December 27, 1973, which were implemented on
January 15, 1974.

On March 18 representatives of OPEC, meeting in Vienna,
announced the lifting of the oil embargo against the United States.
Production of Arabian oil was increased by more than a million
barrels a day back up to September, 1973, levels. The FEO authorized increased fuel allocations by allowing refiners to draw
down their inventories and the fuel crisis in the United States appeared to be over. The rationing of gasoline, controlled by the
use of coupons, did not materialize, although Simon had ordered
such coupons printed as a precautionary measure. Authorities feel
that the ending of the oil embargo prevented a fuel crisis but that
long-range energy problems remain and some new ones have been
added.

Suggested Readings

Barrows, Gordon N. The International Petroleum Industry. New
    York: International Petroleum Institute, 1965.
Boveri, Margret. Minaret and Pipeline: Yesterday and Today in
    the Near East. Translated by Louisa Marie Sieveking. Lon-
    don: Oxford University Press, 1939.
Continuity and Change in the World Oil Industry. Beirut: Middle
    East Research and Publishing Center, 1970.
Crowther, James Gerald. About Petroleum. London: Oxford Uni-
    versity Press, 1938.
Frankel, Paul H. The Essentials of Petroleum: A Key to Oil Econ-
    omics. London: Chapman and Hall, 1946.
_____. Oil: The Facts of Life. London: Weidenfeld & Nicol-
    son, 1962.
Getty, J. Paul. My Life and Fortunes. New York: Meredith,
    1963.
Gulbenkian, Nubar. Portrait in Oil: The Autobiography of Nubar
    Gulbenkian. New York: Simon & Schuster, 1965.
Hartshorn, Jack Ernest. Oil Companies and Governments: An Ac-
    count of the International Oil Industry in Its Political Environ-
    ment. London: Faber & Faber, 1962.
Hopwood, Derek. The Arabian Peninsula. London: Allen & Un-
    win, 1972.
Howarth, David A. The Desert King: Ibn Saud and His Arabia.
    New York: McGraw-Hill, 1964.
Kirk, George E. Contemporary Arab Politics. New York: Fred-
    erick A. Praeger, 1961.
Longrigg, Stephen Hensley. Oil in the Middle East: Its Discovery
    and Development. New York: OUP, 1967.
Lufti, Ashraf. OPEC Oil. Beirut: Middle East Research and Pub-
    lishing Center, 1968.
Mikdashi, Zuhayr. A Financial Analysis of Middle East Oil Con-
    cessions, 1901-1965. New York: Frederick A. Praeger, 1966.

Mosley, Leonard. Power Play: Oil in the Middle East. New York:
    Random House, 1973.
Mughraby, Muamad A. Permanent Sovereignty Over Oil Resources.
    Beirut: Middle East Research and Publishing Center, 1966.
Pachachi, Nadim. The Role of OPEC in the Emergence of New
    Patterns in Government-Company Relationships. London: Royal
    Institute of International Affairs, 1972.
Stocking, George W. Middle East Oil. Nashville, Tenn.: Vander-
    bilt University Press, 1970.
Yamani, Ahmed Zaki. Economics of the Petroleum Industry. Bei-
    rut: Middle East Research and Publishing Center, 1970.